Conflict in
the Modern Middle East

Conflict in the Modern Middle East

An Encyclopedia of Civil War, Revolutions, and Regime Change

Jonathan K. Zartman, Editor

BLOOMSBURY ACADEMIC
NEW YORK • LONDON • OXFORD • NEW DELHI • SYDNEY

BLOOMSBURY ACADEMIC
Bloomsbury Publishing Inc
1385 Broadway, New York, NY 10018, USA
50 Bedford Square, London, WC1B 3DP, UK
29 Earlsfort Terrace, Dublin 2, Ireland

BLOOMSBURY, BLOOMSBURY ACADEMIC and the Diana logo
are trademarks of Bloomsbury Publishing Plc

First published in the United States of America by ABC-CLIO 2020
Paperback edition published by Bloomsbury Academic 2024

Copyright © Bloomsbury Publishing Inc, 2024

Cover photo: Houthi followers demonstrate against Saudi-led air strikes, September 11, 2015.
(Reuters/Khaled Abdullah)

All rights reserved. No part of this publication may be reproduced or
transmitted in any form or by any means, electronic or mechanical,
including photocopying, recording, or any information storage or retrieval
system, without prior permission in writing from the publishers.

Bloomsbury Publishing Inc does not have any control over, or responsibility for,
any third-party websites referred to or in this book. All internet addresses given
in this book were correct at the time of going to press. The author and publisher
regret any inconvenience caused if addresses have changed or sites have
ceased to exist, but can accept no responsibility for any such changes.

Library of Congress Cataloging-in-Publication Data
Names: Zartman, Jonathan K., editor.
Title: Conflict in the Modern Middle East : An Encyclopedia of Civil War,
Revolutions, and Regime Change / Jonathan K. Zartman, editor
Description: Santa Barbara, California : ABC-CLIO, An Imprint of ABC-CLIO, LLC, [2020] |
Includes bibliographical references and index.
Identifiers: LCCN 2019040891 (print) | LCCN 2019040892 (ebook) |
ISBN 9781440865022 (cloth) | ISBN 9781440865039 (ebook)
Subjects: LCSH: Civil war—Middle East—History—21st century—Encyclopedias. |
Civil war—Africa, North—History—21st century—Encyclopedias. |
Middle East—History—21st century—Encyclopedias. |
Middle East—Politics and government—21st century—Encyclopedias. |
Africa, North—History—21st century—Encyclopedias. |
Africa, North—Politics and government—21st century—Encyclopedias. | LCGFT: Encyclopedias.
Classification: LCC DS43 .C66 2020 (print) | LCC DS43 (ebook) | DDC 956.05/403—dc23
LC record available at https://lccn.loc.gov/2019040891
LC ebook record available at https://lccn.loc.gov/2019040892

ISBN: HB: 978-1-4408-6502-2
PB: 979-8-7651-2494-9
ePDF: 978-1-4408-6503-9
eBook: 979-8-2160-6477-0

To find out more about our authors and books visit www.bloomsbury.com
and sign up for our newsletters.

Contents

Alphabetical List of Entries   vii

Geographical List of Entries   xi

List of Primary Documents   xv

Preface   xvii

Introduction   xix

A-Z Entries

Primary Documents   321

Chronology   359

Bibliography   369

About the Editor   375

Contributors   377

Index   385

Alphabetical List of Entries

Abbas, Mahmoud

Abdullah II, King of Jordan

Academics for Peace in Turkey

Against Compulsory Hijab

Ahmadinejad, Mahmoud

Ahrar al-Sham Brigades

AKP-PKK Peace Talks (2005–2015)

Al-Abadi, Haider

Al-Ahmar, Ali Muhsin

Al-Assad, Bashar

Alawites (Nusayris)

Al-Awlaki, Anwar

Alevis

Algeria, The People's Democratic
Republic of

Algerian Protests (2011)

Al-Islah (Reform Party)

Al Jazeera

Al-Maliki, Nouri

Al Manar Television

Al-Qaeda Central

Al-Qaeda in the Arabian Peninsula
(AQAP)

Al-Qaeda in the Islamic Maghreb
(AQIM)

Al-Sadr, Muqtada

Al-Sharif, Manal

Ammar, Rachid

Ansar al-Sharia in Libya

Ansar Beit al Maqdis

April 6 Youth

Arab Nationalism

Arab Spring Movements (2011)

Armed Islamic Group (GIA)

Armenians

Army of Islamic Salvation (AIS)

Ashrawi, Hanan

Authoritarianism

Ba'athism

Badawi, Raif

Bahrain, Kingdom of

Barzani, Masoud

Basij

Battle of Sirte in 2011

Battle of Sirte in 2016

Belhaj, Abdul Hakim

Belmokhtar, Mokhtar

Ben Ali, Zine al-Abidine

Benghazi Attack

Benkirane, Abdelilah

Berbers (Imazighen)

Black October Riots (1988)

Black September

Bouazizi, Tarek el-Tayeb Mohamed

Bouteflika, Abdelaziz

Alphabetical List of Entries

Cedar Revolution (2005)
Civil Wars
Clientelism (Patrimonialism)
Constitutional Drafting Assembly
Coptic Orthodox Church
Corruption
Coup of 2016

Dahiya Doctrine
Demirtaş, Selahattin
Democracy Deficit
Demographics (Youth Bulge)
Development
Druze

Economic Protests (2017–2018)
Egypt, Arab Republic of
El-Sisi, Abdel Fattah Saeed Hussein Khalil
Ennahda Movement
Erdogan, Recep Tayyip
Ergenekon Scandal

Fatah Party
Fayyad, Salam
February 17th Revolution
February 20 Movement
Fikri, Mouhcine
Foreign Fighters
Framing Model
Free Syrian Army

General National Congress
General People's Congress
Gezi Park Protests (2013)
Ghannouchi, Rachid
Ghonim, Wael
Ghouta Chemical Weapons Attack of 2013
Ghouta Chemical Weapons Attack of 2018

Greed Model
Green Movement (2009)
Grievance Model
Gulf Cooperation Council (GCC)

Hadi, Abdu Rabbu Mansour
Haftar, Khalifa Belqasim
Hamas
Hamas-Fatah Conflict
Hariri, Saad
Hayat Tahrir al-Sham (HTS)
Hezbollah
Hizmet (Gülen) Movement
Houla Massacre (2012)
Houthis (Ansar Allah)

Ibadi Doctrine
Intifadas (I, II, and Knife)
Iran, Islamic Republic of
Iranian Azerbaijanis
Iraq, Republic of
Islamic Revolutionary Guard Corps (IRGC)
Islamic Salvation Front (FIS)
Islamic State (Daesh)
Islamism
Israel
Israeli Invasion of Lebanon (2006)

Jasmine Revolution
Jihad
Jordan, Hashemite Kingdom of
Jordanian Protests (2011)
Jumblatt, Walid
Justice and Development Party (Morocco)
Justice and Development Party (Turkey)

Khamenei, Ayatollah Sayyid Ali
Khatami, Mohammad

Alphabetical List of Entries

Khomeini, Ayatollah Sayyid Ruhollah Mūsavi

Kurdistan Regional Government (KRG)

Kurdistan Workers' Party (PKK)

Kurds

Kuwait, State of

Labor Migration: Receiving Countries

Labor Migration: Sending Countries

Lebanese Republic

Libya, State of

Libya Dawn Coalition

Libyan Civil War

Local Coordination Committees

Maronites

Middle East Road Map (2003)

Military Coups

Minorities

Modernization

Mohammed VI, King of Morocco

Morocco, Kingdom of

Morsi, Mohamed

Mubarak, Muhammad Hosni Sayyid

Mujahedin-e Khalq (MEK)

Muslim Brotherhood

Muslim Brotherhood in Jordan

Nakhla, Rami

Nasrallah, Hassan Abdel Karim

National Action Charter

National Liberation Front (FLN)

National Transition Council

Nezzar, Khaled

Ocalan, Abdullah

Oman, Sultanate of

Oman Protests (2011)

Operation Cast Lead

Operation Decisive Storm

Palestine

Palestine Liberation Organization

Palestinian Islamic Jihad

Party of Authenticity and Modernity

Patriotic Union of Kurdistan (PUK)

Pearl Roundabout Protests

Political Decision-Making in Iran

Popular Mobilization Forces (PMF)

Qaboos bin Said bin Taimur Al Said

Qaddafi, Muammar

Qatar

Quds Force

Rabi'a al-Adawiya Massacre

Rafsanjani, Ali Akbar Hashemi

Rajab, Nabeel

Rally for Culture and Democracy (RCD)

Refugees

Regime Change Cascades

Rentier State Politics

Rouhani, Hassan Feridun

Sahwa (Sunni Tribal Awakening)

Salafism

Salah, Ahmed Gaid

Saleh, Ali Abdullah

Salman, Mohammad bin

Saudi Arabia, Kingdom of

Saudi Arabian Protests (2011)

Saudi Sahwa (Islamic Awakening)

Sectarianism

Shabiha Militias

Shi'a

Social Media

Syrian Arab Republic

Syrian Civil War

Tahrir Square Protests (2011)

Takfiri Doctrine

Alphabetical List of Entries

Takrizards

Tamarod Movement (2013)

Tunisia, Republic of

Tunisian General Labor Union

Tunisian National Dialogue Quartet

Turkey, Republic of

United Arab Emirates (UAE)

Washington Consensus

Wasta

Women's Leadership in Protests

Yazidi

Yemen, Republic of

Yemen Civil War (2015)

Yemeni Socialist Party (YSP)

Yemen Uprising (2011)

Zaydi Doctrine

Geographical List of Entries

ALGERIA

Algeria, The People's Democratic Republic of

Algerian Protests (2011)

Armed Islamic Group (GIA)

Army of Islamic Salvation (AIS)

Belmokhtar, Mokhtar

Black October Riots (1988)

Bouteflika, Abdelaziz

Islamic Salvation Front (FIS)

National Liberation Front (FLN)

Nezzar, Khaled

Rally for Culture and Democracy (RCD)

Salah, Ahmed Gaid

BAHRAIN

Bahrain, Kingdom of

National Action Charter

Pearl Roundabout Protests

Rajab, Nabeel

EGYPT

Ansar Beit al Maqdis

April 6 Youth

Coptic Orthodox Church

Egypt, Arab Republic of

El-Sisi, Abdel Fattah Saeed Hussein Khalil

Ghonim, Wael

Morsi, Mohamed

Mubarak, Muhammad Hosni Sayyid

Muslim Brotherhood

Rabi'a al-Adawiya Massacre

Tahrir Square Protests (2011)

Tamarod Movement (2013)

IRAN

Against Compulsory Hijab

Ahmadinejad, Mahmoud

Basij

Economic Protests (2017–2018)

Green Movement (2009)

Iran, Islamic Republic of

Iranian Azerbaijanis

Islamic Revolutionary Guard Corps (IRGC)

Khamenei, Ayatollah Sayyid Ali

Khatami, Mohammad

Khomeini, Ayatollah Sayyid Ruhollah Mūsavi

Mujahedin-e Khalq (MEK)

Political Decision-Making in Iran

xii   **Geographical List of Entries**

Quds Force
Rafsanjani, Ali Akbar Hashemi
Rouhani, Hassan Feridun

IRAQ

Al-Abadi, Haider
Al-Maliki, Nouri
Al-Sadr, Muqtada
Barzani, Masoud
Iraq, Republic of
Kurdistan Regional Government
   (KRG)
Kurds
Patriotic Union of Kurdistan
   (PUK)
Popular Mobilization Forces (PMF)
Sahwa (Sunni Tribal Awakening)

ISRAEL

Dahiya Doctrine
Intifadas (I, II, and Knife)
Israel
Israeli Invasion of Lebanon
   (2006)
Operation Cast Lead

JORDAN

Abdullah II, King of Jordan
Black September
Jordan, Hashemite Kingdom of
Jordanian Protests (2011)
Muslim Brotherhood in Jordan

KUWAIT

Kuwait, State of

LEBANON

Al Manar Television
Cedar Revolution (2005)
Dahiya Doctrine
Hariri, Saad
Hezbollah
Jumblatt, Walid
Lebanese Republic
Maronites
Nasrallah, Hassan Abdel Karim

LIBYA

Ansar al-Sharia in Libya
Battle of Sirte in 2011
Battle of Sirte in 2016
Belhaj, Abdul Hakim
Benghazi Attack
Constitutional Drafting
   Assembly
February 17th Revolution
General National Congress
Haftar, Khalifa Belqasim
Libya, State of
Libya Dawn Coalition
Libyan Civil War
National Transition Council
Qaddafi, Muammar

MOROCCO

Benkirane, Abdelilah
February 20 Movement
Fikri, Mouhcine
Justice and Development Party
   (Morocco)
Mohammed VI, King of
   Morocco

Geographical List of Entries

Morocco, Kingdom of
Party of Authenticity and Modernity

OMAN

Ibadi Doctrine
Oman, Sultanate of
Oman Protests (2011)
Qaboos bin Said bin Taimur Al Said

PALESTINE

Abbas, Mahmoud
Ashrawi, Hanan
Fatah Party
Fayyad, Salam
Hamas
Hamas-Fatah Conflict
Palestine
Palestine Liberation Organization
Palestinian Islamic Jihad

QATAR

Qatar

SAUDI ARABIA

Al-Sharif, Manal
Badawi, Raif
Salman, Mohammad bin
Saudi Arabia, Kingdom of
Saudi Arabian Protests (2011)
Saudi Sahwa (Islamic Awakening)

SYRIA

Ahrar al-Sham Brigades
Al-Assad, Bashar

Alawites (Nusayris)
Free Syrian Army
Ghouta Chemical Weapons Attack of 2013
Ghouta Chemical Weapons Attack of 2018
Hayat Tahrir al-Sham (HTS)
Houla Massacre (2012)
Local Coordination Committees
Nakhla, Rami
Shabiha Militias
Syrian Arab Republic
Syrian Civil War

TUNISIA

Ammar, Rachid
Ben Ali, Zine al-Abidine
Bouazizi, Tarek el-Tayeb Mohamed
Ennahda Movement
Ghannouchi, Rachid
Jasmine Revolution
Takrizards
Tunisia, Republic of
Tunisian General Labor Union
Tunisian National Dialogue Quartet

TURKEY

Academics for Peace in Turkey
AKP-PKK Peace Talks (2005–2015)
Alevis
Coup of 2016
Demirtas, Selahattin
Erdogan, Recep Tayyip
Ergenekon Scandal
Gezi Park Protests (2013)
Hizmet (Gülen) Movement

xiv **Geographical List of Entries**

Justice and Development Party (Turkey)
Kurdistan Workers' Party (PKK)
Ocalan, Abdullah
Turkey, Republic of

UNITED ARAB EMIRATES

United Arab Emirates (UAE)

YEMEN

Al-Ahmar, Ali Muhsin
Al-Awlaki, Anwar
Al-Islah (Reform Party)
Al-Qaeda in the Arabian Peninsula (AQAP)
General People's Congress
Hadi, Abdu Rabbu Mansour
Houthis (Ansar Allah)
Operation Decisive Storm
Saleh, Ali Abdullah
Yemen, Republic of
Yemen Civil War (2015)
Yemeni Socialist Party (YSP)
Yemen Uprising (2011)
Zaydi

INTERNATIONAL

Al Jazeera
Al-Qaeda Central
Al-Qaeda in the Islamic Maghreb (AQIM)
Arab Nationalism
Arab Spring Movements (2011)
Armenians

Authoritarianism
Ba'athism
Berbers (Imazighen)
Civil Wars
Clientelism (Patrimonialism)
Corruption
Democracy Deficit
Demographics (Youth Bulge)
Development
Druze
Foreign Fighters
Framing Model
Greed Model
Grievance Model
Gulf Cooperation Council (GCC)
Islamic State (Daesh)
Islamism
Jihad
Labor Migration: Receiving Countries
Labor Migration: Sending Countries
Middle East Road Map (2003)
Military Coups
Minorities
Modernization
Refugees
Regime Change Cascades
Rentier State Politics
Salafism
Sectarianism
Shi'a
Social Media
Takfiri Doctrine
Washington Consensus
Wasta
Women's Leadership in Protests
Yazidi

List of Primary Documents

1. Excerpts from *The Taif Agreement,* Ta'if, Saudi Arabia (October 22, 1989)
2. *The Arab Peace Initiative,* Beirut Arab League Summit (March 28, 2002)
3. *The Amman Message* (July 26, 2005)
4. *The Damascus Declaration for Democratic National Change,* Damascus, Syria (October 16, 2005)
5. Excerpts from the *United Nations Security Council Resolution 1973* (March 17, 2011)
6. *The Al-Azhar Declaration in Support for the Arab Revolutions,* Nasr City, Cairo, Arab Republic of Egypt (October 31, 2011)
7. *United Nations Security Council Resolution 2118* (September 27, 2013)
8. Excerpts from *The Peace and National Partnership Agreement* (September 21, 2014)
9. *Marrakesh Declaration on the Rights of Religious Minorities in Predominantly Muslim Majority Communities,* Marrakesh, Morocco (January 27, 2016)

Preface

Understanding the purpose, utility, and scope of this book can help the reader gain the most benefit from it. This preface will also offer some notes regarding language and spelling and conclude with suggestions for further exploration. This book offers a starting point for research. It defines a few essential terms and crucial theoretical perspectives, or models, used to explain conflict. These apply broadly to the 22 states and territories commonly included in the term "Middle East and North Africa" (MENA). This broad region includes three major civilizations based on languages—Arabic, Turkish, and Persian—and several very large minority groups. The book title uses the term "modern" to focus on the protest movements that swept the region in 2011, and the evolving consequences from those events. It also discusses revolutions in two countries that came earlier and constitute major historical movements: the 2005 Cedar Revolution in Lebanon and the 2009 Green Revolution in Iran.

The book deals with people and events in multiple languages, based on analysis in English. It features contributions from 73 scholars in 17 countries. Although the source materials use a variety of spellings for the same person, group, or idea, this book has adopted the most common spelling in American English, striving for consistency. In the case of the group calling itself *al-Dawla al-Islamiya fi al-Iraq wa al-Sham* (The Islamic State in Iraq and Greater Syria), finding the most common short-hand expression proves elusive. Western journalists generally use an acronym based on a misleading translation of that phrase to say ISIS or ISIL. This book uses "The Islamic State" plus the acronym that local Arabs use: *Daesh*.

The size of this volume did not allow biographies of every significant personality, but this book seeks to note the heroic people who struggled against authoritarian leaders and constraining ideologies. The concluding section of original documents captures three issues: 1) UN Security Council Resolutions that represent intervention to promote human welfare in the midst of great suffering; 2) agreements between contending parties that seek a solution to their dispute; and 3) declarations of principle and aspirations for peace.

To get the most benefit from this book, each topic of interest ends with associated "see also" entries and a Further Reading section that provides sources for research on that topic. The focus of this book—on the most recent events—did not allow consideration of the historical figures that shaped the history of the region. The reader can gain profitable perspective from researching men like Mustapha xviii **Preface**

Kamal Ataturk, who created the modern Republic of Turkey; Reza Shah Pahlavi, who molded modern Iran; and Gamal Abdel Nasser, the charismatic advocate of Arab Nationalism and socialism, and leader of Egypt. Investigating the development of the ideas that drive current conflict, and the men who developed those ideas, such as Ibn Taymiyya, Sayid Qutb, Said Nursi, or Ali Shariati, will also add depth to your understanding.

The responsibility for any errors or omissions rests solely on the editor.

Introduction

When hundreds of thousands of people poured into the central public squares and traffic roundabouts of capital cities in the Middle East and North Africa, demanding political change, regional analysts admitted surprise, while people around the world paid attention. The wave of protest movements in 2011, which overthrew the governments of Tunisia and Egypt, initially inspired hope that people in this region might gain greater political freedom. These dreams died in the civil wars that developed in Yemen and Syria. When the government of Mohamed Morsi in Egypt turned dictatorial, and the military replaced him, it also reinforced the value of gaining a deeper understanding of the regional dynamics of conflict. This book offers a strong foundation and starting point for research in these issues.

The story of conflict in the Middle East and North Africa (MENA) offers inspiration from the lives of heroic personalities striving for liberty, and also warning from the monstrous behavior of leaders who terrorize their people and destroy their own countries to hold on to power. This chronicle gained global attention due to technological advancements enabling vast numbers of people not only to access information, but also to produce and broadcast video to the world. Their narrative, portraying the pain of everyday life, the suffering of the people, and their grievances against their governments, fueled the spread of protests, and drew the attention of the world. Tarek al-Tayeb Mohamed Bouazizi in Tunisia and Khaled Said in Egypt became internationally renowned as martyrs for the cause of freedom. However, the meaning that outsiders impute to the deaths of the thousands of people killed in these conflicts, and the hundreds of thousands displaced and driven into exile, reflects in part the history of the region, its demographic composition, the character of the people and their values, the nature of their political systems, and the involvement of other states. The following introduction provides that background.

CHANGING FORMS OF CONFLICT

When European states grew in power after the Industrial Revolution, they began seeking resources, extracted from colonies all over the world. Their military and commercial activities gradually encroached on the Ottoman Empire (1301–1922), which had controlled major portions of the Middle East. British help for the Arab Revolt in 1916–1918 substantially reduced the Ottoman domains. Over the next 30 years, many societies engaged in nationalist, anti-colonial struggles, creating new states in which the military dominated. In the initial stages of independent statehood, several states—Syria, Iraq, Egypt—suffered a series of military coups. Military coups generally result in a more authoritarian government, less responsive to the needs of the people, creating long-term grievances that could fuel a future revolution.

After World War II, the region became an arena of competition during the Cold War, with some states aligning with the West, and some becoming Soviet client states. More importantly, American plans to support the rebuilding of Europe and Japan, and the restoration of economic vitality in both regions to prevent the growth of communist movements, required stable access to oil at world market prices. The United States aligned with Saudi Arabia and Iran for this purpose. The United States intervened against Israel, Britain, and France, and in favor of Egypt, in the Suez Crisis of 1956. Egypt's victory in this conflict strengthened Egyptian President Gamal Abdel Nasser, who promoted an ideology of socialist, secular Arab nationalism. His ideological struggle with the conservative monarchies such as Saudi Arabia, called the Arab Cold War, included open warfare in Yemen.

In 1967, the Arab-Israeli War brought the United States into alignment with Israel versus the Soviet client states of Syria, Iraq, and Egypt. The Arab defeat in that war discredited Arab nationalism and strengthened the argument of the Islamists. The 1973 Ramadan or Yom Kippur War drew active intervention by both the Soviet Union and the United States in supplying ammunition to their clients. In response, Arab oil producers imposed an oil embargo on the United States, which caused oil prices to rise sharply. This in turn caused global economic stagnation and inflation, as well as massive flows of dollars to the oil producers.

In 1979, everything changed. The Islamic Revolution in Iran reduced American influence in the region and forced the United States into closer alignment with Saudi Arabia. The Soviet invasion of Afghanistan attracted large numbers of zealous young Muslim men to defend their Afghan brothers against the infidel Soviets. They received military training, experience, and ideological indoctrination. When they returned to their home countries, they became a powerful force for conflict against their own governments. All of these events combined to create a popular Western image of the region as dominated by the Israeli-Palestinian conflict and oil.

The 1980–1988 Iran-Iraq War initially did not enter the casual consciousness of everyday people in the West until both sides started attacking oil tankers in the Persian Gulf, which drew an American response, and ultimately a U.S. ship accidentally shot down an Iranian civilian airliner. This led Iran to accept a UN ceasefire. When Saddam Hussein invaded Kuwait on August 2, 1990, the massive coalition that formed to defend Saudi Arabia and expel Iraq raised hopes that the superpowers could cooperate to create a more peaceful world—a dream that quickly withered. The coalition that conducted the war decided to leave Saddam Hussein in power. The uprising by the Shi'as and the Kurds, the massive Iraqi

Introduction

government persecution that followed, and the weak international response, created a new image of the Middle East as a region of vulnerable people ruled by monstrous dictators.

The terrorist attacks on the United States on September 11, 2001, made global audiences aware of the power of militant Islamism as a motivating ideology of rebellion. The American reaction—the invasions of Afghanistan and then Iraq—and the enduring struggles, thoroughly disabused many people of their previous naïve hopes that people would govern themselves in peace, if only they could get rid of their rulers. The resulting pessimism, and the quagmire narrative, caused a great aversion to any future outside involvement in the region. The persistence of fighting made outsiders more aware of the power of sectarian appeals, as well as the diversity of communities in many states of the region. This fueled a growth in the literature on authoritarian resilience and the barriers to democratization. It reduced expectations that a popular movement could overcome the fear of repression to achieve any political opening.

In sum, the progression of different forms of conflict in the MENA region created a diverse array of images of the region in the minds of outside audiences. The massive protest movements of 2011 surpassed any of the expectations that even regional scholars held. These protests had nothing to do with the Israeli-Palestinian conflict. They did not reflect superpower rivalry, outside intervention, Islamist mobilization, or ethnic minority grievances. Instead, they began as protests motivated by economic grievances, political exclusion, corruption, and injustice. Many began in peripheral areas and moved to the cities. Although more-educated, liberal segments of the population provided an initial spark, they ultimately drew in huge numbers of unemployed young men in the cities. Each society reacted differently to reports of the Jasmine Revolution in Tunisia.

THE SCOPE OF THIS BOOK

This historical background leads to events covered here. This book defines "modern" in terms of the aftermath of the protest movements of 2011, commonly called the Arab Spring. This book describes the role of conflict in 22 countries, especially as people reacted to news of the Jasmine Revolution. In some cases the most significant popular revolt came before 2011. The 2005 Cedar Revolution in Lebanon provided some degree of guidance to later activists in other countries. Similarly, the 2009 Green Movement in Iran represents a precursor, foreshadowing events of the Arab Spring. For each country, this book provides vignettes of some of the most significant personalities in each country and those who gained prominence as a result of these protests. In addition to country-specific topics, this book also offers explanations of 32 topics that apply more broadly across the region, plus introductions to six minorities.

Because the protests in Tunisia sparked similar demonstrations in other autocratic, Arabic-speaking, predominantly Muslim states, the inclusion of North African states reflects the recognition that they share important qualities with the states of the Gulf and the Levant, commonly considered the Middle East. Although scholars dislike the term "Middle East," due to its origin in British colonial thinking, it has become ingrained in the media and public perception. Historians and politicians have described conflict in the region in material terms as the pursuit of power, expressed in a struggle to control resources and trade routes between regions. Land routes for trade between Europe, Asia, and Africa cross in the center of this region.

The involvement of Turkey and Iran in the Arab states, and the role of their competition in driving conflict, mandates their inclusion in this book. Turkey, as the heir to the Ottoman Empire, which controlled most of the Middle East for centuries, remains greatly involved in the politics of the region. Iran, as the heir to three great empires, which controlled territory as far west as Egypt, also exerts influence in many neighboring countries. In addition to material factors, the linguistic or cultural factors reinforce the competition that drives conflict in the region. The extent to which people appeal to these linguistic and cultural distinctions varies over time, as a result of other conditions, but Iranians and Turks proudly assert their non-Arab character, as well as difference from each other. The Persian, Turkish, and Arab cultural differences constitute the subtext for regional conflict. In addition, millions of Berbers and Kurds seek recognition and protection for their languages, adding another source of internal conflict.

Although Islam provides a grand unifying cultural environment that can bridge linguistic and national differences, in practice, politicians often appeal to different forms of Islamic doctrine to claim the loyalty of some parts of their population at the expense of others. Their political tactics (sectarianism) deepen the differences between religious communities. In addition to the role played by the difference between Sunnis and Shi'as in Iraq, Bahrain, Iran, and Saudi Arabia, two other forms of religious conflict shape politics in the region. First, militant activists seeking to justify their attacks on their neighbors and their own governments have exploited religious texts to form a narrative of struggle (*jihad*) and have created a strong ideological battle within Islam. Muslim teachers and politicians have confronted the errors of these movements with conventions and documents, as well as books by famous scholars. Second, the failures of the Mohamed Morsi government in Egypt, and his overthrow in the Tamarod (Rebellion), has led to a new regional polarization, with Turkey, Qatar, and the Muslim Brotherhood on one side, versus Saudi Arabia, Egypt and the United Arab Emirates on the other.

HOW TO USE THIS BOOK

As an encyclopedia with topics arranged alphabetically, this book is approachable in two ways. A top-down approach would begin with the central presentation of competing theoretical perspectives, called "civil wars," and the three subsidiary topics—Greed Model, Grievance Model, and Framing Model—and then move to either a specific country or to a concept such as "Regime Change Cascades." A bottom-up approach might start with a topic of interest such as the Kurds, and then follow all of the associated topics listed as "see also."

Introduction   xxiii

Conflict in the Modern Middle East draws on the national interests of many outside powers, engages the liberal sensitivities of people around the world, and reflects the competition of powerful ideological forces. This encyclopedia offers readers a thorough introduction to the concepts of conflict. It provides nine important documents recording a variety of efforts to respond to and stop conflict. The chronology of important events facilitates a big-picture appreciation of the progression of conflict. The bibliography provides a very select set of the most valuable resources for further study.

Jonathan K. Zartman

A

Abbas, Mahmoud

The president of the State of Palestine and the Palestinian National Authority (PA) since 2005, and the chairman of the Palestine Liberation Organization (PLO) since the demise of the historical Palestinian leader, Yasser Arafat in 2004. Mahmoud Abbas, also known as Abu Mazen, born in Safed, Mandatory Palestine, on November 15, 1935, fled with his family to Syria, becoming a refugee. He worked as a schoolteacher and gained a law degree from Damascus University. In the 1950s, he worked for the government of Qatar and joined Fatah in 1961. He lived in exile with other PLO leaders in Jordan, then Lebanon, and then Tunisia. In the late 1970s, he served as the head of the international department and developed contacts with leftist Israeli peace groups. In 1982 he received a doctorate from the Institute of Oriental Studies in Moscow. In 1980 he was elected a member of the PLO Executive Committee.

In 1984, he took office as the director of the Department of National and International Affairs, in which he coordinated the diplomatic conversations that led to the historic Conference of Madrid in 1991, which started the peace process in the Middle East. He is known also as the architect of the Oslo Accords, signed by Israel and the PLO in 1993. He participated in the Camp David peace talks in 2000. After these accords, he was appointed chief of the PLO's Department of Foreign Affairs. He held several public positions until he became president of the State of Palestine in 2005.

After the split with Hamas, he ruled the West Bank by executive decree, and in 2009 refused to give up office after the expiration of his term. After the failure of peace talks from 2008 to 2010, he has worked hard to gain international recognition for a Palestinian state. He engages in a power struggle and rivalry with the former leader of Fatah in the Gaza Strip. In April 2016, he established a Palestinian Authority constitutional court packed with his supporters, which claims the authority to overrule other PA branches of government. In November 2016, the Fatah General Congress reelected him to a five-year term. Despite pressure due to his age and poor health, he has refused to give up any of his three titles and continues to engage in active political struggle.

Carolina Bracco

See also: Fatah Party; Israel; Palestine; Palestine Liberation Organization

Further Reading

Abbas, Mahmoud. *Through Secret Channels: The Road to Oslo.* London: Garnet Publishing, 1995.

Parsons, Nigel Craig. *The Politics of the Palestinian Authority: From Oslo to Al-Aqsa.* London: Routledge, 2012.

Abdullah II, King of Jordan

The king of Jordan and eldest son of the former King Hussein Bin Talal and Princess Muna Al Hussein, born in Amman on January 30, 1962. Abdullah II holds social respect as a 41st-generation descendant of the Prophet Mohammad. His family gained the throne of Jordan as a result of the revolt started by his father's grandfather, the emir of Hejaz, Arabia, who rebelled—with British help—against the Ottoman Empire in 1916. He attended the Royal Military Academy Sandhurst in the United Kingdom in 1980. He was appointed as commander of a scouting company in the 13/18 battalion of the British Royal Hussars. He enlisted in the Jordan Armed Forces-Arab Army with the rank of first lieutenant, and then served as a platoon commander, and assistant commander of a company in the 40th Armored Brigade. In 1993, Abdullah II married Queen Rania Al Abdullah, and they have four children. On February 7, 1999, after his father's death, King Abdullah II ascended to the throne of the Kingdom of Jordan. Since then, King Abdullah II has prioritized strengthening his country's ties with the West: the United States, the European Union, and international economic institutions. For instance, Jordan became a member of the World Trade Organization in 2000, and a year later signed a free-trade agreement with the United States. He has worked to promote a broad and inclusive view of Islam, as seen in the July 26, 2005, Amman Message. In the aftermath of the Arab popular revolts of 2011, he engaged in rigorous political struggles to consolidate his rule.

Nur Köprülü

See also: Islamic State (Daesh); Israel; Jordan, Hashemite Kingdom of; Palestine Liberation Organization; Syrian Arab Republic; Primary Document: *The Amman Message*

Further Reading

Abdullah II, King of Jordan. *Our Last Best Chance: The Pursuit of Peace in Time of Peril*. New York: Penguin Books, 2012.

Ryan, Curtis R. *Jordan in Transition: From Hussein to Abdullah*. Boulder, CO: Lynne Reinner Publishers, 2002.

Academics for Peace in Turkey

A petition initiative by a group of academics in Turkey that began in 2012, urging political leaders to consider the sources of Turkey's conflict with the Kurds, and to take advantage of the knowledge already gained in studies of conflict resolution, peace processes, and the gender dimension of peace-building. This first petition, signed by around 300 academics in 50 different universities, came during a relatively open political atmosphere for peace negotiations and hope for ending the long civil war waged by the Kurdistan Workers' Party (PKK).

Three years later, the negotiations had collapsed, and the conflict was growing more intense. On January 16, 2016, more than 1,000 academicians at 90 Turkish universities responded to the UN-documented violence against Kurdish civilians by security forces. They signed and circulated a petition entitled "We will not be a party to this crime," and called on the government to terminate military operations against Kurds in the southeast. Immediately after the press release of the statement, the number of signatories, soon known as Academics for Peace, exceeded 2,000, supported by several hundred international scholars. The government responded with harsh measures of repression, removing by decree more than 500 of those who signed the petition from their teaching posts in public and private universities, under the charge of "making propaganda for a terrorist organization." The government subjected another 500 of them to disciplinary investigations. Academics for Peace also suffered detention and police custody, and 365 of them have been put on trial; many have fled the country. The sentencing process was still underway as of December 2018. Under this pressure, one of the signatories, a young recent PhD, committed suicide.

The growing international solidarity for the academics who signed the petition for peace caused Recep Tayyip Erdogan to call their demands for a negotiated political solution to the armed conflict between the PKK and Turkish security forces a "mandate-seeking" act. The government attitude of calling the signatories "traitors" caught them by surprise, due to its incompatibility with democracy, the rule of law, and a rational evaluation of evidence. Government persecution did not merely thwart the academic careers of the signatories, but also extended to public and social persecution: death threats drove some signatories to leave their neighborhoods. The government confiscated the passports of many, to hinder their flight to exile.

Seen in the context of the much more widespread purges of government and universities following the July 15, 2016, abortive coup, the persecution of the Academics for Peace provided an advance warning of a more general oppression of society. The signatories represented a diversity of ethnicity, religion, political party, gender, and professional status. No political party came to their defense. The two purges combined have seriously damaged Turkey's international reputation, and its educational and academic capabilities for many years in the future.

Kumru F. Toktamis

See also: AKP-PKK Peace Talks; Authoritarianism; Coup of 2016; Kurdistan Workers' Party (PKK); Kurds; Turkey, Republic of

Further Reading

Baser, Bahar, Samim Akgonul, and Ahmet Erdi Ozturk. "'Academics for Peace' in Turkey: A Case of Criminalising Dissent and Critical Thought via Counterterrorism Policy." *Critical Studies on Terrorism* 10, no. 2 (2017): 274–96.

Tekdemir, Omer, Mari Toivanen, and Bahar Baser. "Peace Profile: Academics for Peace in Turkey." *Peace Review* 30, no. 1 (2018): 103–11.

Against Compulsory Hijab

Two recent protests against Iran's enforcement of regulations mandating that women dress conservatively in the name of Islamic morality. The word *hijab* refers to various styles of traditional modest dress for women, though Iran imposes some restrictions on men as well. After the Islamic revolution in 1979, the religious teachers now running the government required women to wear loose-fitting clothing and a headscarf in public. It completely reversed the law issued by Reza Shah on January 8, 1936, banning all head-coverings, which also excluded many types of traditional male clothing. The revolutionary government finally made hijab mandatory for all women in 1983. These restrictions provoked some demonstrations and disorganized reactions. The advocates for *hijab ijbari* (the compulsory covering) argue in the name of national independence, religious law, rejection of corrupt royalists, and avoiding distractions when men and women must share a public space.

Recent protests against mandatory hijab have taken two forms: In 2014, an Iranian journalist and activist based in the United Kingdom and the United States began an online movement based on a Facebook page called "My Stealthy Freedom." She solicited photos from women in Iran without scarfs, to show their protest against compulsory covering. The initiative received wide international and national coverage, with many praises and some criticisms. Then, on December 27, 2017, Vida Movavid made a public display on *Enghelab* (Revolution) Street in Tehran, standing on a utility box while waving her white scarf on the end of a stick. Multiple people have imitated her action, removing their hijabs and waving them in the air, thus forming the movement known as the "Girls of Enghelab Street." The government morality police have punished this behavior severely.

Sayed Hassan Akhlaq Hussaini

See also: Iran, Islamic Republic of; Social Media; Women's Leadership in Protests

Further Reading

Alinejad, Masih. *The Wind in My Hair: My Fight for Freedom in Modern Iran.* New York: Little, Brown and Company, 2018.

Roja, Fazaeli. *Islamic Feminisms: Rights and Interpretations across Generations in Iran.* New York: Routledge, 2018.

Sadeghi, Hamideh. *Women and Politics in Iran: Veiling, Unveiling, and Reveiling.* Cambridge, UK: Cambridge University Press, 2007.

Ahmadinejad, Mahmoud

An Iranian politician, born on October 28, 1956, known for his staunchly conservative, energetic nationalism, opposition to liberal reforms, and antagonism to the United States and Israel. His very religious, lower-middle-class family moved to Tehran when he was one. He joined the revolution and supported the April 22, 1980, violent closure of all of the universities for two and a half years to purge the faculty. As a hardline supporter of Ayatollah Khomeini, in 1980 he was appointed district governor of two towns in succession, with a mixed Kurdish and Azerbaijani population. The Kurdish rebellion had been mostly suppressed by the time Ahmadinejad was sent to Sanandaj in 1984. He was able to resume his studies, and in 1986 received his bachelor's degree in civil engineering from the University of Science and Technology. He served his two years of military service with

Ahmadinejad, Mahmoud

the Islamic Revolutionary Guard Corps in Kermanshah, where he made friends with high-ranking officials, including the future commander of the Basij (voluntary, informal militia). He also worked with and befriended the leaders of the Badr Brigade, and Jalal Talebani, the leader of the Patriotic Union of Kurdistan.

In 1993, he was appointed governor general of the newly established province of Ardabil, but the new Khatami administration replaced him in 1997. By then he had completed his dissertation and received his doctorate in traffic engineering and planning, so he returned to his university to teach. In May 2003, opponents of President Khatami's reforms appointed Ahmadinejad mayor of Tehran, where he quickly introduced religious restrictions and requirements, and programs to help the poor. In 2005, while relatively unknown across the country, he ran for president against the very well-known, very wealthy, traditional conservative Ali Akbar Hashemi Rafsanjani. He campaigned actively in all the rural areas of the country, using populist themes and promising to solve the problems of unemployment, marriage, and housing. Ayatollah Ali Khamenei's oldest son, Mujtaba, served as his campaign manager, and he received strong support from the Basij.

His blend of uncompromising cultural and religious policies with sympathetic concern for the poor brought him victory in the election. He spent Iran's oil money freely on programs to support the poor, with purposeful disregard for rational economic planning. He provoked international criticism as an enthusiastic supporter of Iran's nuclear program, as an opponent of negotiations, and as a sponsor of a conference of Holocaust deniers. Critics complained of his strange behavior, with pompous claims to spiritual experiences, and an obsession with the return of the Hidden Imam—a future righteous ruler and deliverer in Shi'a doctrine. Repression continually strengthened while economic problems grew, partly due to increasing international sanctions on Iranian nuclear programs.

His reelection in the 2009 election resulted in the massive Green Movement protests against the readily apparent manipulation of the results. The regular police forces and Basij suppressed the demonstrations with considerable force. Ayatollah Khamenei very quickly intervened to authenticate the election results, which damaged the regime's legitimacy by demonstrating its autocratic character, at the expense of any republican pretentions.

In his second term, Ahmadinejad had conflicts with Supreme Leader Khamenei, and the government prosecuted his closest supporters for fraud. After his term ended in 2013, he initially kept quiet. On July 30, 2017, the Supreme Audit Court announced that Ahmadinejad faced sentencing for misusing two billion dollars, but no sentence has been pronounced. In November 2017, he began traveling around the country, holding events, agitating against the government, and the judiciary in particular. He has tried to exploit the protests that began in December 2017 over the declining economy, after U.S. president Donald Trump blocked the nuclear deal and renewed the imposition of sanctions. He remains cut off from the political elite and dismissed by them.

Tom Dowling

See also: Basij; Green Movement; Iran, Islamic Republic of; Islamic Revolutionary Guard Corps (IRGC); Khamenei, Ayatollah Sayyid Ali; Khatami, Mohammad; Kurds; Patriotic Union of Kurdistan (PUK); Rafsanjani, Ali Akbar Hashemi

Further Reading

Ansari, Ali. "Iran under Ahmadinejad: Populism and Its Malcontents." *International Affairs* 84, no. 4 (July 2008): 683–700.

Habibi, Nader. "Economic Legacy of Mahmud Ahmadinejad." *Middle East Brief* No. 74. Waltham, MA: Crown Center for Middle East Studies, June 2013.

Naji, Kasra. *Ahmadinejad: The Secret History of Iran's Radical Leader.* Berkeley: University of California Press, 2008.

Warnaar, Maaike. *Iranian Foreign Policy during Ahmadinejad: Ideology and Actions.* New York: Palgrave Macmillan, 2013.

Ahrar al-Sham Brigades

An alliance of several Salafist groups in Syria that have fought against the Bashar Assad government, as well as the Islamic State (Daesh). Hassan Abboud formed the *Harakat Ahrar al-Sham al-Islamiyya,* colloquially called the Ahrar al-Sham, after Assad released him, with other prisoners, from the Sednaya prison on March 26, 2011. Abboud reportedly had ties to al-Qaeda and Ayman al-Zawahiri. Ahrar al-Sham took part in various operations alongside Jabhat al-Nusra, including the takeover of Raqqa in March 2013. By early 2013, Ahrar al-Sham became an integral part of military operations in northern Syria, primarily the Idlib Governorate. From March 2013 to the end of the year, Ahrar and al-Nusra fought a number of battles to defend Syria against Daesh. A targeted bomb attack killed Hassan Abboud in September 2014, along with 27 senior military commanders of the group. After that, the leadership changed frequently, culminating in the appointment of Jaber Ali Basha as general commander.

Estimates of the size of the group vary from 10,000 to 20,000 fighters over the course of several years, which gave it a reputation as one of the most powerful rebel factions in northern Syria. Ahrar al-Sham conducted military operations with various groups in Syria, as the largest group in the Syrian Islamic Front in 2012. Despite working with Jabhat al-Nusra in its formative years, the two groups came into conflict in early 2017, marking a slow shift away from the extreme Sunni radicalism that made the group well known. It allegedly received funding from Saudi Arabia and Qatar.

Samanvya Singh Hooda

See also: Al-Assad, Bashar; Free Syrian Army; Hayat Tahrir al-Sham; Islamic State (Daesh); Qatar; Saudi Arabia, Kingdom of

Further Reading

Cheterian, Vicken. "ISIS and the Killing Fields of the Middle East." *Survival: Global Politics and Strategy* 57, no. 2 (March 2015): 105–18.

Jones, Seth G. "Syria's Growing Jihad." *Survival: Global Politics and Strategy* 55, no. 4 (September 2013): 53–72.

Yassin-Kasab, Robin, and Leila Al-Shami. *Burning Country: Syrians in Revolution and War.* London: Pluto Press, 2016.

AKP-PKK Peace Talks (2005–2015)

Negotiations between the Justice and Development Party (AKP) government in Turkey and the arrested PKK leader Abdullah Ocalan, seeking to resolve the long insurgency conducted by the PKK against the government of Turkey. The Turkish military used the ongoing armed conflict with the Kurdistan Workers' Party (PKK), which has claimed more than 40,000 lives since 1978, as partial justification for its status as the center of power and defender of Turkish national security.

The AKP came to power in 2002, promising to follow a moderate Islamist approach and to abolish 70 years of Kemalist military supervision and control over the government institutions in Turkey. As part of its efforts to curb the power and guardianship of the military, the AKP implemented a series of administrative reforms and legislation, to end terror and strengthen social integration. Since 2005, PKK leader Abdullah Ocalan (arrested in 1999) had been declaring his desire to end armed conflict. His proposals for a political solution created an opportunity for the Turkish government to begin a resolution process.

Between 2005 and 2010, the Turkish Intelligence Organization (MIT) and PKK representatives in Europe conducted clandestine talks. Between 2011 and 2015 the talks continued publicly as the government allowed the leading Kurdish politicians to visit Ocalan monthly in the Imrali prison, where he is serving a life sentence. In August 2015, then prime minister Recep Tayyip Erdogan declared the end of the ongoing talks, which the ruling party called a "resolution" or "Kurdish opening." Kurds and left-wing liberals in Turkey understood these talks as a "peace process." The Turkish left- and right-wing nationalists resolutely opposed these talks. Kurdish leaders accuse the Gülen Movement of sabotaging the talks as a way to cause difficulty for its former ally, the AKP.

Kumru F. Toktamis

See also: Erdogan, Recep Tayyib; Justice and Development Party (Turkey); Kurdistan Workers' Party (PKK); Kurds; Ocalan, Adbullah; Turkey, Republic of

Further Reading

Kadioglu, I. Aytac. "The Oslo Talks: Revealing the Turkish Government's Secret Negotiations with the PKK." *Studies in Conflict and Terrorism* (February 20, 2018): 1–19.

Özpek, Burak Bilgehan. *The Peace Process between Turkey and the Kurds: Anatomy of a Failure.* London: Routledge, 2018.

Toktamis, Kumru. "A Peace That Wasn't: Friends, Foes, and Contentious Re-entrenchment of Kurdish Politics in Turkey." *Turkish Studies* 19, no. 5 (July 22, 2018): 697–722.

Al-Abadi, Haider

An Iraqi politician and prime minister of Iraq (September 8, 2014–October 25, 2018). Haider Jawad Kadhim Al-Abadi, born on April 25, 1952, in Baghdad into a middle-class family, became an activist in the Islamist Shi'a Da'wa Party. Persecution by Saddam Hussein forced him to flee to exile in Britain. He earned a doctorate in electrical engineering from the University of Manchester and became fluent in English. After the fall of Hussein, he served as communications minister in the first government (2003–2004). When al-Maliki's policies provoked an insurgency, Iraqi officials and societal leaders, with approval from international partners, brokered Al-Abadi's rise to power. Iraqi president Faum Masoum named him prime minister, and the Council of Representatives (COR) approved on September 8, 2014.

Al-Abadi promised reconciliation, the curbing of Islamic State (Daesh) recruitment narratives, power-sharing within state institutions to address endemic corruption, and a balancing of the ethnic distribution within the Iraqi military. In late 2014–early 2015, protests over electricity blackouts prompted Al-Abadi to propose specific anti-corruption reforms in August 2015. The courts and vested interests within the government blocked these reforms, creating a bureaucratic stalemate, which led to criticisms of ineffectual leadership.

Al-Abadi has faced difficulties due to Kurdish demands for greater autonomy. The national government worked with the Kurdish Regional Government (KRG) in fighting the Islamic State and reached agreements on oil production and revenue in 2015–2016. However, the KRG's independence referendum on September 25, 2017, led to greater conflict. Al-Abadi called it unconstitutional and sent the national army to disputed territories in October 2017. He created the political environment for the military defeat of the Islamic State (Daesh) in December 2017, but inconsistent policy effectiveness has marred the government's legitimacy.

Ahead of the 2018 parliamentary elections, he sought to negotiate the withdrawal of American forces and limit Iranian influence, while sustaining security support from partner states. The active Shi'a political forces have splintered into five groups, leaving Al-Abadi without a sustained base of support. His *Nasr* alliance came in third place in the May 2018 referendum, behind Muqtada al-Sadr's *Sairoon* (Marchers) Alliance and Hadi al-Amiri's *Fatah* (Conquest) Coalition. At the beginning of September 2018, massive protests in Basra over the lack of drinking water and other government failures led to demands for Al-Abadi to resign. His term ended in October, and he did not run for a second term.

Melia Pfannenstiel

See also: Al-Maliki, Nouri; Al-Sadr, Muqtada; Iran, Islamic Republic of; Iraq, Republic of; Islamic State (Daesh); Kurdistan Regional Government (KRG); Shi'a

Further Reading

Al-Qarawee, Harith Hasan. "From Maliki to Abadi: The Challenge of Being Iraq's Prime Minister." *Crown Center for Middle East Studies: Middle East Brief* 11 (June 2016): 1–8.

Blanchard, Christopher. "Iraq: In Brief." Washington, DC: Congressional Research Service, March 5, 2018, 1–18.

Katzman, Kenneth. "Iraq: Politics, Security, and U.S. Policy." Washington, DC: Congressional Research Service, June 22, 2015, 1–47.

Al-Ahmar, Ali Muhsin

A Sunni military officer, one of the most powerful men in Yemen, serving since 2016 as the vice president of Yemen. Born in Sanhan, Yemen, in 1945, Ali Muhsin entered military service at the age of 16 and rose through the ranks to become commander of the First Armored Division (1987–2011) and then commander of the Northwestern Military District until 2012.

General Ali Muhsin played an instrumental role in bringing Ali Abdullah Saleh into power as president and in keeping him there for over 30 years. After working for Saleh as one of his strongest supporters, he later became his biggest rival. General Ali Muhsin survived Saleh's attempt to have him killed in 2009, when Saleh gave Saudi Arabian forces the coordinates to bomb General Ali Muhsin's headquarters as a "Houthi target" during Operation Scorched Earth; however, the Saudis called off the bombing. On March 21, 2011, General Ali Muhsin broke ties with Saleh, and sided with youth protesters calling for revolution. His defection caused a fracture in the regime, accelerating the end of Saleh's rule.

Despite General Ali Muhsin's long history of corruption, and even ties to Salafi groups, the Muslim Brotherhood, and al-Qaeda in the Arabian Peninsula, he retained a significant level of power. In 2012, Saleh's successor, President Abdu Rabbu Mansour Hadi, appointed him as his military adviser, and General Ali Muhsin has served since 2016 as the vice president of Yemen.

Rebecca Antecki

See also: Al-Qaeda in the Arabian Peninsula (AQAP); Hadi, Abdu Rabbu Mansour; Houthis (Ansar Allah); Muslim Brotherhood; Operation Decisive Storm; Salafism; Saleh, Ali Abdullah; Saudi Arabia, Kingdom of; Yemen, Republic of

Further Reading

Day, Stephen W. *Regionalism and Rebellion in Yemen: A Troubled National Union*. New York: Cambridge University Press, 2012.

Hill, Ginny. *Yemen Endures*. New York: Oxford University Press, 2017.

Al-Assad, Bashar

The ruler of Syria, who inherited the position from his father, the previous president, Hafez al-Assad, and continued many of his brutal policies, but without his shrewd political skills and discernment. Bashar al-Assad, born on September 11, 1965, attended medical school at Damascus University, conducted a residency in ophthalmology in a military hospital near Damascus, and in 1992 went to London for further medical studies. In 1994, his brother Bassel died in a car crash. His father called him home to prepare for political leadership.

Al-Assad entered the military academy and was promoted through the ranks to colonel in five years. During this time, he was given responsibility for an anti-corruption campaign, which he used to remove potential enemies from power. He advocated for modernization, and expanded access to the Internet and technical training, becoming president of the Syrian Computer Society. In 1998, he assumed responsibility for the Syrian military presence in Lebanon, and developed a strong relationship with Hassan Nasrallah, the leader of Hezbollah. On June 10, 2000, his father died. The government organized a referendum to elect Bashar as president. Initially, he promoted some economic liberalization, but the benefits went only to the elite inner circle of associates. After becoming president, he relaxed restrictions on the media and civic associations, which came to be called the Damascus Spring. However, after a year he tightened repression again.

He has personally expressed his commitment to resisting Israel and has supported Hamas and the Islamic Jihad Movement in Palestine. In Lebanon, Bashar's heavy-handed repression brought the Maronites, Sunni Muslims, and Druze into alliance against the Syrian military presence. After the assassination of the Sunni prime minister Rafik al-Hariri, massive Lebanese mobilization in the Cedar Revolution, supported by international pressure, forced Bashar to withdraw Syrian military forces. In 2007 and 2014, he was reelected to seven-year terms, in ceremonies considered as political theater by international observers.

In 2011, he ordered extremely harsh repression against protesters, which provoked even greater resistance, ultimately becoming a civil war, with dozens of groups seeking to overthrow his government. As commander in chief of the Syrian military, he bears the responsibility for the devastating war, including the use of chemical weapons. In response, the International Criminal Court at The Hague has indicted Al-Assad for war crimes.

Paul J. Springer

See also: Authoritarianism; Cedar Revolution; Corruption; Druze; Ghouta Chemical Weapons Attack of 2013; Hamas; Hezbollah; Israel; Lebanese Republic; Maronites; Nasrallah, Hassan Abdel Karim; Syrian Arab Republic; Syrian Civil War

Further Reading
Harris, William. *Quicksilver War: Syria, Iraq, and the Spiral of Conflict.* London: Hurst, 2018.
Lesch, David W. *Syria: The Fall of the House of Assad.* New Haven, CT: Yale University Press, 2013.
Zweir, Paul J. *Peacemaking, Religious Belief, and the Rule of Law: The Struggle between Dictatorship and Democracy in Syria and Beyond.* New York: Routledge, 2018.

Alawites (Nusayris)

A small, ethnically Arab, religious minority group living predominantly in rural areas of western Syria, with small numbers in southern Turkey and Lebanon, which rose to power in Syria. Although the Alawites share with the Shi'as a strong devotion to the Caliph Ali, the son-in-law and cousin of the Prophet Muhammad, the Alawi consider themselves a different branch of Islam. Traditionally, Sunnis have called the Alawites "Nusayri" after Ibn Nusayr, a student of the 11th Imam recognized by the dominant branch of Shi'a doctrine. A follower of Ibn Nusayr developed the new doctrine and brought it from Iraq to Aleppo and Latakia around 960 CE. In addition to professing an extreme glorification of Ali, they apply allegorical or mystical interpretations to Islamic law. They confess their faith differently and interpret the Five Pillars of Islamic practice as metaphorical moral lessons rather than literal, physical requirements. Their doctrine incorporates ideas from pre-Islamic paganism, and from Christianity. Because they celebrate many Christian festivals, and honor many Christian saints, historically some travelers have considered them derived from Christianity. The Alawites have exploited this image to gain political protection from the French. The Alawites do not publish their doctrines but restrict full knowledge of the faith to a relatively small core of religious leaders.

To escape persecution, from both Sunnis and Shi'as, they have often disguised their beliefs and claimed to follow an accepted path. In the 1920s, they adopted the name of *Alawiyya* ("followers of Ali")—meaning Shi'a. At times, various Sunni and Shi'a leaders have supported this claim for political reasons. In 1936, the Sunni Mufti of Jerusalem, Haj Amin al Husayni, declared that the Alawites qualify as Muslim, and in 1963, Ayatollah Hasan Mahdi al Shirazi accepted the Alawites as Shi'as. After the fall of the Ottoman Empire, when the French took control of Syria, the Alawites began working with the French authorities to gain political protection and status. The Alawites and other minorities, such as the Druze and the Ismailis, sought to serve in the military, as an opportunity for social mobility, while the Sunnis tended to shun military service. After the Sunnis won independence from France, the Alawites of Latakia initially resisted Sunni rule from Damascus. After the new government crushed a Druze revolt in 1954, they accepted Syrian citizenship.

The Ba'ath Party ideology of secularism and socialism offered the Alawites and other minorities potential economic improvement and relief from religious persecution. The Alawites benefited from the many military coups d'état between 1949 and 1963, in which Sunnis struggled for power and purged other Sunnis in the military. The Alawites in the military supported the Ba'ath revolution of March 8, 1963. As the Sunni leaders struggled to consolidate control, the Alawites in the military conducted their own coup in February 1966. This led to a struggle among Alawite officers, won by Hafiz al-Assad in November 1970. He made an alliance with the urban Sunni economic elite, which survived for 40 years.

Most rural poor Alawites have not benefited from the Alawite dominance in government and the military. Sunni religious antagonism to the Alawites, and grievances from government corruption and tyranny, have made the Alawites a target. This has fueled a variety of resistance movements, from the Muslim Brotherhood to the Islamic State (Daesh). The government has exploited the Syrian civil war to force the Alawite community to give its full commitment, knowing that losing the war will result in annihilation. The war has become an existential crisis for Alawites, Christians, and all those known as government supporters.

Jonathan K. Zartman

See also: Authoritarianism; Ba'athism; Druze; Islamic State (Daesh); Islamism; Military Coups; Minorities; Sectarianism; Syrian Arab Republic; Syrian Civil War

Further Reading

Fildis, Ayse Tekdal. "Roots of Alawite-Sunni Rivalry in Syria." *Middle East Policy* 19, no. 2 (Summer 2012): 148–56.

Friedman, Yaron. *The Nusayri-Alawis: An Introduction to the Religion, History and Identity of the Leading Minority in Syria.* Boston: Brill, 2010.

Goldsmith, Leon T. "The Alawites of Syria: The Costs of Minority Rule." In *The Routledge Handbook of Minorities in the Middle East,* edited by Paul S. Rowe, 185–96. New York: Routledge, 2019.

Zisser, Eyal. "The Alawis, Lords of Syria: From Ethnic Minority to Ruling Sect." In *Minorities and the State in the Arab World,* edited by Ofra Bengio and Gabriel Ben-Dor, 129–45. Boulder, CO: Lynne Rienner, 1999.

Al-Awlaki, Anwar

An American-born Muslim preacher of Yemeni heritage who created a vast library of YouTube videos to inspire Muslims to commit terrorism, and who became the first American citizen killed overseas without trial by a drone attack. Anwar Al-Awlaki (1971–2011) was born in Las Cruces, New Mexico, while his father studied agriculture, but he spent most of his youth in Yemen. He attended Colorado State University, where he earned a bachelor's degree in civil engineering. In college, he demonstrated increasing interest in politics and religion, and identified with the Taliban of Afghanistan. He served as an imam at mosques in San Diego and northern Virginia, where he met several of the September 11 hijackers, with no evidence that he knew of their plot. Al-Awlaki publicly condemned their attacks. He gained a reputation as an inspiring, charismatic speaker who communicated effectively with young people.

In 2002, Al-Awlaki gave a series of lectures in the United Kingdom, praising the concept of martyrdom, and supporting Muslims fighting against the United States and its allies in Afghanistan. Al-Awlaki returned to Yemen, where he taught at Iman University. In 2006, he was arrested for his role in kidnapping a Shiite teenager and remained in Yemeni custody until late 2007. Upon his release, Al-Awlaki increased his contacts with terrorist sympathizers and began broadcasting a series of lectures to inspire terrorism. His videos, many in English, offered a bridge between Muslims in traditional communities and those abroad, particularly the United States and Great Britain.

Investigators have found evidence that he inspired dozens of people to commit attacks, such as Umar Farouk Abdulmutallab, Sharif Mobley, and Faisal Shahzad, largely through e-mail messages. He corresponded repeatedly with Nidal Malik Hasan, who killed 13 fellow soldiers at Fort Hood in 2009. On July 16, 2010, top officials in the Obama administration placed him on the Specially Designated Global Terrorists list. Despite a lawsuit by his father, demanding his removal from the list, due to his American citizenship, the U.S. government sent remotely piloted aircraft to Yemen to track and attack Al-Awlaki. After at least one unsuccessful strike, on September 30, 2011, a Hellfire missile from an MQ-1 Predator killed Al-Awlaki. Two weeks later, another strike in Yemen killed his 16-year-old American-born son, Abdulrahman. Critics argue that, other than stopping his coaching activities and continuing production of propaganda, killing him further enhanced his reputation and credibility: his videos remain widely available.

Paul J. Springer

See also: Al-Qaeda Central; Al-Qaeda in the Arabian Peninsula (AQAP); Salafism; Yemen

Further Reading

Conway, Maura. "From al-Zarqawi to al-Awlaki: The Emergence and Development of an Online Radical Milieu." *CTX: Combating Terrorism Exchange* 2, no. 4 (2012): 12–22.

Powell, Jefferson. *Targeting Americans: The Constitutionality of the U.S. Drone War.* New York: Oxford University Press, 2016.

Shane, Scott. *Objective Troy: A Terrorist, a President, and the Rise of the Drone.* New York: Tim Duggan Books, 2015.

Alevis

Turkey's largest religious minority, constituting about a fifth of all Turkish Muslims, an internally diverse community that does not follow orthodox Sunni practices. Although a number of Alevi communities exist in other countries, mainly in the Balkans, most Alevis live in Turkey. The Alevi community has developed into two major approaches: Those who seek a secular state that would grant them the freedom to practice their cultural traditions, especially freedom from the state's imposing Sunni Islam; and the conservative, religious Alevis, who consider Sunni Islam a later corruption of their own pure understanding of Islam. They seek official recognition of their religious leaders, recognition of their meeting halls as places of religious worship, the right to list their religion as Alevi on their identification, and freedom from the mandatory classes in Sunni Islam in the schools.

Alevi beliefs developed as an oral tradition, which the community only recently began documenting as a single, formal doctrine. Although, like the Shi'as, they give high reverence to the trinity of Allah, Muhammad, and Ali, they differ significantly in all other aspects, as a highly syncretic faith that also includes elements of pre-Islamic Turkish belief, and even Christianity. They do not use a call to prayer, and do not pray five times a day; they pray in Turkish instead of in Arabic. Women and men pray together, instead of in separate places. They read the Qur'an in Turkish, interpret it as a mystical text, and use mystical poems and musical ballads as major parts of their worship. They fast during the first month of the Islamic lunar calendar—Muharram—instead of Ramadan. They believe that divine judgment does not rest on ritual participation, but on behavior in relating to other people. Alevis also follow Haji Bektash Veli, a Turkish Sufi dervish who came to Anatolia around 1230. They perform pilgrimage to the village in which he settled, instead of to Mecca. In many ways, orthodox Sunnis and Shi'as take offense at Alevi doctrines and practices, leading to discrimination and persecution.

The Alevis evolved as an intellectual and organizational movement in Turkey in the 10th century CE with influence from Shi'a Islam and Sufism. The Ottomans conquered them only with great difficulty, and at great cost suppressed their rebellions. Some Kurds are Alevi, and the Alevi rebellions sometimes coincided with Kurdish rebellions They initially supported Ataturk's secular politics as a way to escape the control of the Sunni religious leaders, but when he ordered the Sufi orders to disband in 1925, this prevented them from publicly expressing their community life. By the 1970s, many Alevis had developed secular views and pride in their communal identity, with some younger Alevis adopting leftist politics. The sporadic mob attacks by radical Sunnis have made the Alevis devoted to secularism. When the government was trying to control radical Sunni political activists, the Alevis provided crucial electoral support, and benefited from aligning with the central state. However, after Turkey's Justice and Development Party (AKP) became more openly Islamist, they have faced more adversarial conditions. Sunni religious forces attack the Alevis as disloyal, but Alevis reject the assertion that Turkish identity requires adherence to Sunni Islam. Alevi diaspora activists in Belgium and Germany continually raise the issue of Alevi religious freedom in Turkey with European human rights supporters.

Tom Dowling

See also: Islamism; Justice and Development Party (Turkey); Kurds; Minorities; Shi'a; Turkey, Republic of

Further Reading

Massicard, Elise. *The Alevis in Turkey and Europe: Identity and Managing Territorial Diversity.* London: Routledge, 2012.

Olsson, Tord, Elisabeth Ozdalga, and Catharina Raudvere. *Alevi Identity: Cultural, Religious and Social Perspectives.* Richmond, UK: Curzon Press, 1998.

Shankland, David. *The Alevis in Turkey—The Emergence of a Secular Islamic Tradition.* London: Routledge, 2003.

Soner, Beyram Ali, and Şule Toktaş. "Alevis and Alevism in the Changing Context of Turkish Politics: The Justice and Development Party's Alevi Opening." *Turkish Studies* 12, no. 3 (2017): 419–34.

Algeria, The People's Democratic Republic of

An authoritarian, oil- and gas-exporting, rentier state, with many political parties and regular elections. The people of this state suffer from economic grievances, lack of political representation, internal conflicts over the political and social role of Islam, and the language and collective rights of the Berber (Amazigh) minority. Most of the people speak local dialects of Arabic as the heritage of Arab rule since 711. Over time, as political rule fragmented, especially after the 1490s, contending groups sought support from different European states, or from the Ottoman Empire. The predations of maritime raiders and slave traders brought a number of European states, and the United States, to intervene in the area that would become Algeria.

The French occupation of Algeria, beginning in 1830, brought French governance and language and, more importantly, the impetus for Algerian nationalism. Algerians gained military experience fighting in the French Army. Following World War II, Algerians created popular nationalist groups calling for Algerian independence. By 1954, the Algerian National Liberation Front, known by its French acronym "FLN," began its fight against French occupation forces. For the next eight years, Algerian nationalists fought a guerrilla conflict, using terror tactics against political figures and French colonial citizens to coerce them to leave. The French use of torture and massive concentration camps in the desert created international support for the Algerian independence movement. The French negotiated their withdrawal. On July 5, 1962, the FLN declared Algerian independence.

The various revolutionary groups then competed to run the country. In 1965 Houari Boumédiène, the defense minister, ousted President Ahmed Ben Bella in a military coup. Boumédiène pursued a Soviet model of economic development, in which the state controlled the economy to develop capital-intensive industrialization, at the expense of labor-intensive economic sectors, such as agriculture. Oil and gas production enabled the government to expand education, health care, and infrastructure. The population grew dramatically, urbanization and literacy surged, but job creation lagged, leaving a large population of unemployed young men in the cities.

The military dominated the government and kept civilians and the FLN in a subservient position. The government created several military security agencies to control society, most importantly the Département du Renseignement et de la Sécurité (DRS). The government prohibited the formation of associations and political parties, inhibiting the development of civil society. The government closely controlled the mosques and other Islamic institutions but granted considerable freedom to women. The rulers maintained good relations with the Soviet Union and followed the Soviet economic model. The people regarded the military government as internally repressive. When Boumédiène died in 1978, the military replaced him with Colonel Chadli Benjadid, a military commander and competent administrator who introduced some economic liberalization but also allowed corruption to grow.

In the winter of 1979, the government launched an Arabization program to develop Algerian nationalism as Islamic and Arab. The Arabization program promoted disregard for the Berber language (Tamazight), identity, and history. Many Berbers had been using French as their second language for business, and many rural Berbers did not know Arabic, so the Arabization program created grievances that would fuel repeated conflicts. On March 10, 1980, the government blocked a public lecture by a Kabyle intellectual, which provoked student protests. On April 20, 1980, riot police stormed student dormitories, a factory, and a local hospital very early in the morning with clubs and tear gas. They arrested hundreds and wounded many more. This action gained great attention in the international press and from human rights organizations. This event became known as the Berber Spring, the start of the Berber Cultural Movement, and a symbol employed in future protests for language and cultural rights.

Many of the Arabic teachers that the government recruited from Egypt and Syria promoted Islamism, in opposition to the traditional practices of Sufism (Islamic mystical brotherhoods) common among the Berbers. They promoted more conservative social values, standards of dress, and roles for women. Until the administration of President Benjadid, Islamists did not challenge the state but developed large networks of followers. As cities grew, people started many mosques outside of state control, and these provided charitable and educational programs. In 1982, the state started to crack down on Islamists in the universities

DEMOCRATIC OPENING

From a peak in 1980, oil prices declined until, in 1986, they fell sharply. The government had to reduce imports and subsidies for many basic goods, causing inflation to rise. It stopped some big infrastructure projects, throwing many men out of work. Meanwhile, the flashy lifestyles of the well-connected people, and high government officials, stimulated popular fury. The army responded to demonstrations by firing on unarmed protesters, killing hundreds, which provoked large-scale rioting. In February 1989, the government decided to engage in political liberalization, allow the registration of new political parties, and introduce a new constitution.

In June 1990, in the first free elections for local assemblies, the Islamic Salvation Front (FIS) won overwhelmingly at the expense of the FLN. Abassi Midani, the leader of the FIS, employed very moderate, tolerant language. He sought to dispel fears of an Islamist victory, but his deputy used very fiery, intolerant language, antagonistic to democracy. The government responded by redesigning the electoral districts against the FIS. In April 1991, the Islamists launched protests, which the government suppressed harshly, arresting the two leaders and hundreds of members. Nevertheless, in the first round of elections for the National Assembly in December 26, 1991, the FIS won very dramatically. To prevent a final victory, the military forced the president to dissolve the parliament and then resign. The military appointed a five-member High State Council (HCE) to rule the country in the absence of a parliament. On February 9, 1992, the HCE declared a state of emergency. The next month it banned the FIS.

Meanwhile, the June 1989 military coup in Sudan brought radical Islamists to power, and they aided militants in Algeria. Algerians who had gone to fight in Afghanistan and returned, provided the leadership of militant Islamist groups. As government security forces arrested large numbers of people, including intellectuals with no Islamist affiliation, militants formed paramilitary groups to attack the government. Over the next year, these groups formed an association called the Armed Islamic Group (GIA). However, this group became very radical and eventually called anyone that did not support them infidels. The GIA attacked even the leaders and members of the FIS. This discredited Islamist ideology in the eyes of the general population. The FIS authorized the development of the Islamic Salvation Army (AIS) to fight back.

On January 30, 1994, the High State Council appointed the Defense minister General Liamine Zeroual as "State President." He advocated negotiating with all segments of society to resolve the civil conflict and led a segment of the military leadership known as "conciliators." However, other military officers called

Algeria, The People's Democratic Republic of

"eradicators" opposed and restrained these efforts. During 1994, Algeria began to gain some international economic support, even as violence continued. In January 1995, the main opposition parties agreed on the "Rome Platform," presenting criteria for negotiating an end to the conflict. To overcome hardline resistance to his program, President Zeroual first staged an election in which he won a respectable validation with strong turnout. At the same time, the GIA conducted a series of suicide attacks against targets in France.

The government engaged in both harsh repression and negotiations. The violence increased from late 1996 to 1998, including massacres of whole villages in which the perpetrators remained unknown. This drove the Islamic Salvation Army to order a unilateral cease-fire on October 1, 1997. In May 1998, a GIA commander rebelled against targeting civilians and created the Group for Salafist Preaching and Combat (GSPC), pledging a cleaner fight, strictly against security forces. On September 11, 1998, President Zeroual unexpectedly resigned.

On April 15, 1999, after a flawed election, the military chose Abdelaziz Bouteflika, a former minister of Foreign Affairs, as president. He promoted the Civil Concord Law, passed through a popular referendum, which gave amnesty to fighters who surrendered. Several thousand members of armed groups accepted this opportunity to demobilize.

After the terror attacks of September 11, 2001, the government of Algeria offered information to the United States in its campaign against al-Qaeda and in exchange received military equipment for counterterrorism operations. Like many other countries, Algeria sought to use the Global War on Terror to legitimize its own efforts against internal rebellion.

On September 29, 2005, a national referendum passed the Charter for Peace and National Reconciliation, granting amnesty to nearly all militants, and full amnesty to state officials. The robust government repression of militants had almost completely destroyed the GIA, but the GSPC continued to seek resources from al-Qaeda Central. On September 11, 2006, Ayman al-Zawahiri acknowledged this union. Shortly after, the GSPC committed several large suicide bombings against international targets. On January 24, 2007, the GSPC changed its name to Al-Qaeda in the Islamic Maghreb (AQIM). It continues to operate in Algeria, and in neighboring Tunisia, Libya, and Mali.

Bouteflika survived the political turmoil of the Arab Spring through government efforts to reduce food prices and increase supplies and subsidies, lifting the state of emergency while also applying police force against protesters. The DRS— military security organization—consistently employs harsh repressive policies, with significant violations of human rights. It has always acted very independently and began to challenge Bouteflika politically. After reelection to his fourth term in 2014, Bouteflika used bureaucratic restructuring and forced retirements to regain presidential control over military security in general. The 2016 Constitution made Tamazight both an official and national language and created the Algerian Academy of Berber Language. It also increased restrictions on the media. In sum, Bouteflika constructed a strong, centralized security state.

Algeria continues to face persistent economic problems, with a large unemployed youth population, increasingly connected to the rest of the world. On

February 22, 2019, Bouteflika announced that he would seek a fifth term, in spite of his advanced age and very poor health. Large persistent protests began, which eventually persuaded the army to force him to resign on April 2, 2019. The demonstrations continued because the protesters demanded a full purge of the people who kept Bouteflika in power and profited from his patronage. General Ahmed Salah ordered investigations of several prominent wealthy members of the elite, and has tried to manage the transition, which remains in the initial stages of a long-term process of government restructuring.

Sean Braniff

See also: Algerian Protests; Al-Qaeda Central; Al-Qaeda in the Islamic Maghreb (AQIM); Armed Islamic Group (GIA); Army of Islamic Salvation; Authoritarianism; Belmokhtar, Mokhtar; Black October Riots; Bouteflika, Abdelaziz; Islamic Salvation Front (FIS); Military Coups; Morocco, Kingdom of; National Liberation Front (FLN); Nezzar, Khaled; Rally for Culture and Democracy (RCD); Rentier State Politics; Salah, Ahmed Gaid

Further Reading

Ciment, James. *Algeria: The Fundamentalist Challenge.* New York: Facts on File, 1997.

Evans, Martin, and John Phillips. *Algeria: Anger of the Dispossessed.* New Haven, CT: Yale University Press, 2007.

Le Sueur, James D. *Uncivil War: Intellectuals and Identity Politics during the Decolonization of Algeria.* Philadelphia: University of Pennsylvania Press, 2001.

Quandt, William B. *Between Ballots and Bullets: Algeria's Transition from Authoritarianism.* Washington, DC: Brookings Institution Press, 1998.

Ruedy, John. *Modern Algeria: The Origins and Development of a Nation,* 2nd edition. Bloomington: Indiana University Press, 2005.

Tlemcani, Rachid. "The Purge of Powerful Algerian Generals: Civil-Military Reform or Presidential Power Grab?" Doha: Al Jazeera Center for Studies, February 12, 2017.

Algerian Protests (2011)

A relatively short series of protests that occurred in many Algerian cities in 2011, right after the beginning of protests in Tunisia. On January 3, 2011, youth began rioting, clashing with police in the east of the country, and in Oran. Over the next two days riots expanded in Algiers, as youths attacked the police with stones, attacked governmental buildings and commercial enterprises, and set fires in the streets. Police forces arrested a large number of demonstrators and tried to suppress the riots with tear gas. Over the next few days, protests continued in other cities through the country: Tizi-Ouzou, Béjaïa, Oran, M'sila, and Bou Ismail.

In this first phase, the revolts appeared spontaneous, as youths attacked private property, institutions that provide social services such as schools and medical facilities, and even random motorists, as well as government and Algerian National Liberation Front (FLN) buildings. This character of violence alienated the middle class. The attackers did not express any political demands, and had no alliances with political parties or other groups. Journalists speculated that they were protesting rising food prices in the context of high unemployment and housing shortages. However, prices had risen sharply the year before with no protests, and the government had warned about these price rises for several months. Complaints against government officials for treating people with contempt played a significant role.

On Saturday, January 15, Mohsen Bouterfif died from his burns after setting himself on fire in protest in front of the city hall in Boukhadra, in the far east of Algeria. In the following days, several other men engaged in self-immolation in protest. In general, the protests spread from the major cities outward, and the government repressed them severely, and relatively quickly, using only police forces and no army units. Only five people died, and no one reported torture. The 1,000 people reported injured included 800 policemen, indicating significant discipline and restraint by the police. After the government announced measures to reduce the prices of sugar, olive oil, flour, fruit, and vegetables, the protests diminished quickly.

On January 21, the Algerian League for the Defense of Human Rights formed a coalition with autonomous trade unions, human rights' activists, minor opposition political parties, and NGOs representing interest groups and professional associations called the *Coordination Nationale pour le Changement et Démocratie* (CNCD). This group claimed to represent people who felt that the political parties had failed them, especially the unemployed youth who had demonstrated. They demanded only that the government lift the state of emergency. On February 3, Bouteflika submitted a bill to that effect to parliament. On February 12 and February 19, the CNCD organized protest marches, but 30,000 riot police met 2,000 protesters. On February 23, the government lifted the state of emergency, but separate legislation still gave the army extensive powers, and protests remained banned. The government severely repressed the CNCD, and it split into two groups.

A broad variety of occupational groups began separate protest operations— more than 70 different movements took action in March 2011. As people learned that the government had raised the pay of police by 50 percent, backdated to January 2008, many other professions began demanding similar deals. The government responded selectively to some of these demands and overall granted significant economic support to a variety of groups. At the same time, it strongly suppressed demonstrations.

On March 19, 2011, President Bouteflika announced that he would introduce political reforms. Over the next several months the government consulted with political personalities and associations. On January 12, 2012, the parliament approved six new laws, but five of these tightened government control over society, and the sixth offered women a slight improvement in conditions. By April 2012, the government had approved 21 new political parties, so that a total of 44 political parties participated in the legislative election of May 10, 2012. The Islamist parties lost seats in these elections, while the parties aligned with the government gained seats, with a modest increase in turnout compared to that of previous parliamentary elections. Most parties received insufficient votes to get a seat in the parliament, so the top parties received most of the seats.

Observers sought to explain why Algeria avoided significant political change from the region-wide events. Primarily, they cite conflict fatigue among the Algerian population. In addition to the government's policies of selective appeasement and active repression of protests, the fresh memories of the assassinations and terror attacks in the 1990s caused a great aversion to escalating protests. The destructive character of ongoing conflicts in Libya and Syria also amplified the popular fear that militant Islamists would exploit any conflict. The regime's longstanding repression had left the political opposition weak and unorganized, so the people resisted any conflict, knowing that no organized party could pursue true political change. A perception that the government had manipulated the previous episodes of protest to create support for authoritarian policies kept people from belief in their own political effectiveness. Finally, they know that, while the government uses its vast oil wealth to appease those expressing economic grievances, it will simultaneously apply harsh repression.

Valentina Fedele

See also: Algeria, The People's Democratic Republic of; Bouteflika, Abdelaziz; Civil Wars; Grievance Model; Islamic Salvation Front (FIS); National Liberation Front (FLN)

Further Reading

Laachir, Karima. "Managed Reform and Deferred Democratic Rule in Morocco and Algeria." In *Democracy and Reform in the Middle East and Asia. Social Protest and Authoritarian Rule after the Arab Spring,* edited by Amin Saykal and Amitav Asharya, 43–64. London: I. B. Tauris, 2014.

Roberts, Hugh. "Algeria: The Negotiations That Aren't." In *Arab Spring: Negotiating in the Shadow of the Intifada,* edited by I. William Zartman, 145–81. Athens: University of Georgia Press, 2015.

Zoubir, Yahia H., and Ahmed Aghrout. "Algeria's Path to Reform: Authentic Change?" *Middle East Policy* 19, no. 2 (Summer 2012): 66–83.

Al-Islah (Reform Party)

A Yemeni political party that developed as a coalition of different elements in the north, including Yemeni intellectuals and tribal elements. The Al-Islah (Reform Party), formally known as the Yemeni Congregation for Reform, founded in September 1990, brought together a number of leaders with political experience in the northern Yemen Arab Republic. Under the new political conditions of unification, which inaugurated a multiparty system, more than 20 new political parties formed relatively quickly. Abdallah al-Ahmar, the sheikh of the Hashid tribal confederation, brought together tribal leaders, intellectuals, Islamist businessmen, and some activists with the Muslim Brotherhood. This created a broad movement of three wings: 1) members of the Muslim Brotherhood; 2) traditional tribal elites; and 3) business elites with ties to Saudi Arabia and the Gulf monarchies. It initially gained a reputation as a restrained, discreet, and intellectual Islamist party. Prominent personalities in the party range from Nobel Peace Prize winner Tawakkol Kamran, to Abd al-Majid al-Zindani, leader of the radical wing accused of supporting al-Qaeda.

The al-Islah party agreed to the democratic process and the multiparty system. From 1993 through 1997, it shared power with the General People's Congress (GPC), filling ministerial positions in the Justice, Education, Trade, and Religious

Affairs offices. After unification, the Islah party helped the GPC to consolidate rule over all of Yemen, in competition with the Yemeni Socialist Party (YSP), which also had supporters in the north. After the north defeated the YSP in the short civil war of 1994, the GPC did not need al-Islah anymore, and relations between the two parties deteriorated. In 2002, al-Islah joined the Joint Meetings Parties (JMP), a five-party coalition, to challenge the ruling GPC. After the Youth Revolution protests of 2011, the Houthis defeated the forces of al-Islah. Al-Islah's alignment with both Hadi and the Muslim Brotherhood has divided Saudi Arabia and the United Arab Emirates (UAE), the two largest participants in the coalition seeking to support President Hadi against the Houthis. Both countries call the Muslim Brotherhood a terrorist organization. Pragmatically, Saudi Arabia accepts al-Islah, while the UAE opposes the party.

Mark David Luce

See also: General People's Congress (GPC); Hadi, Abdu Rabbu Mansour; Houthis (Ansar Allah); Muslim Brotherhood; Operation Decisive Storm; Saleh, Ali Abdullah; Yemeni Socialist Party (YSP); Yemen Uprising

Further Reading

Bonnefoy, Laurent. *Salafism in Yemen: Transnationalism and Religious Identity.* London: Hurst & Company, 2011.

Yadav, Stacey Philbrick. "Yemen's Muslim Brotherhood and the Perils of Power-Sharing." Washington, DC: Brookings Institute, August 2015.

Al Jazeera

A media network located in Doha, Qatar, funded by the royal family, which began satellite television broadcasting in November 1996. Hamad al-Thani, the new emir of Qatar, began the project with British help. The television programming employed many former employees of *BBC News* and used most of its technical and production strategies. A staff of 3,000 people enables it to convey a highly professional image. It offers a narrative blending pan-Arabism with a moderate political Islam. The way in which it features debates communicates openness to previously taboo or censored ideas, a radical image with some liberalism, but tightly controlled by the host.

Al Jazeera also gained popularity by focusing on controversies affecting Islamic sensibilities, such as the French law against veiling in schools, which it portrayed as French persecution of Muslims, and the invasion of the Muslim community in France. It gave tremendous attention to the French riots of 2005, the Danish cartoon scandal, the 2012 attack on the Paris offices of *Charlie Hebdo,* and similar topics. This devotion to controversy appealed to the global Arab diaspora, especially guest workers in Europe, to convey a perception of Islam as suffering oppression.

Inspired by the recognition CNN earned from its coverage of the First Gulf War, Al Jazeera gained an equal global attention for its coverage of the 2001 U.S. invasion of Afghanistan and the 2003 invasion of Iraq. The station earned the enmity of the United States–led coalition for serving as the only media outlet used by Osama bin Laden and al-Qaeda to release his videos and announcements. Furthermore, Al

Jazeera helped al-Qaeda to professionalize its own media productions. It amplified the voice of Yusuf al-Qaradawi, a prominent religious preacher expelled from Egypt for his ties to the Muslim Brotherhood, by giving him a weekly call-in show called *Sharia and Life,* plus other guest appearances.

Al Jazeera brought together the forces of societal Islamization that had been growing since 1979, the growth in the youth population, and the rise of social media to create a greater acceptance of popular revolution. Quantitative studies of the most frequent topics covered in the 15 years before the 2011 protests reveal that it consistently gave the greatest attention to Tunisia, Egypt, and Gaza. Protesters in Tunisia credit Al Jazeera with sustaining and broadening the appeal of their movement and giving it the momentum to succeed. Its creativity in providing coverage in Egypt, even after the government closed its offices on January 30, 2011, also proved instrumental to the success of the protests in Tahrir Square. In Syria, Al Jazeera offers regular reports from the opposition side, but it did not cover protests in Bahrain, which provoked protests by the staff.

Because Al Jazeera calls for Islamist rebellion against secular dictatorships and representative government, many countries hate the network. This attitude played a crucial role in the decision by Saudi Arabia, the United Arab Emirates, Bahrain, Egypt, Jordan, and many other countries to impose an air and sea blockade on Qatar in June 2017. This resulted in a regional polarization, with Turkey, Iran, the Muslim Brotherhood, and a few other states supporting Qatar against that pressure. Although Al Jazeera has lost some popularity since 2013, its first two decades of operation instilled vitality in a neglected and repressed Arab media marketplace of ideas.

Jonathan K. Zartman

See also: Al-Qaeda Central; Authoritarianism; Bahrain, Kingdom of; Egypt, Arab Republic of; Jasmine Revolution; Modernization; Muslim Brotherhood; Qatar; Saudi Arabia, Kingdom of; Social Media; Tahrir Square Protests; Turkey, Republic of

Further Reading

Abdelmoula, Ezzeddine. *Al Jazeera and Democratization: The Rise of the Arab Public Sphere*. New York: Routledge, 2015.

Cherribi, Sam. *Fridays of Rage: Al Jazeera, the Arab Spring and Political Islam*. New York: Oxford University Press, 2017.

Zayani, Mohamed, ed. *The Al Jazeera Phenomenon: Critical Perspectives on New Arab Media*. London: Pluto Press, 2005.

Al-Maliki, Nouri

An Iraqi politician and prime minister of Iraq from May 20, 2006, until September 8, 2014. Nouri Kamil Mohammed Hasan al-Maliki was born on June 20, 1950, into a family known for political activism in the Karbala district of Iraq. He attended Usul ad-Din College in Baghdad in the early 1970s, majoring in Islamic studies, and earned a master's degree in Islamic literature from Salah ad-Din University in Kurdistan. He joined the Islamic Dawa Party in college, but then Saddam Hussein's persecution of party activists forced him to flee. He spent the next two decades in Syria and Jordan, living under the pseudonym Jawad al-Maliki. He served in modest roles in transitional governments until 2006. As violence rose, and the government failed to improve public services, American support turned toward al-Maliki to replace the prime minister.

The U.S. troop surge of 2007 and the cooperation of many Sunni factions against al-Qaeda in Iraq achieved some temporary stability. Maliki criticized U.S. forces at times for acts of violence against Iraqi civilians, and often argued for a faster U.S. withdrawal. Maliki successfully formed a second parliamentary government on December 22, 2010. Opposition politicians accused Maliki of constantly favoring the Shi'a majority and the Dawa Party over the interests of Iraqis as a whole, whether Sunnis, Shi'as, Arabs, or Kurds. The withdrawal of U.S. forces in 2011, and the regional protest movement, led to the rise of the Islamic State (Daesh). After many calls for his resignation, Maliki stepped down from office on August 14, 2014, but was later appointed to a largely symbolic post, as one of three vice presidents. In addition to his favoring the Shi'as, critics protested his restrictions on the press, his chipping away at constitutional provisions, his attempts to monopolize control over the Iraqi military, and his efforts to control Iraq's oil revenues.

Dan Campbell

See also: Al-Qaeda Central; Ba'athism; Iraq, Republic of; Islamic State (Daesh); Shi'a

Further Reading

Gordon, Michael R., and Bernard E. Trainor. *The Endgame: The Inside Story of the Struggle for Iraq, from George W. Bush to Barack Obama.* New York: Vintage Books, 2013.

Rayburn, Joel. *Iraq after America: Strongmen, Sectarians, Resistance.* Stanford, CA: Hoover Institution Press, 2014.

Al Manar Television

Hezbollah's television station based in East Beirut, Lebanon, founded in 1991, which has grown into a major communications presence in the Middle East. After steadily expanding its radio and TV coverage, Al Manar ("The Torch" or "The Lighthouse") began satellite service in May 2000, which gave it substantial international access and presence. It has sent foreign correspondents to most of the region and even parts of Europe and North America. In 2001, it added a daily English broadcast. However, while its technological and production capabilities have grown toward meeting international technical standards, its connections to Hezbollah have cost it access to a number of key markets.

Al Manar resolutely rejects adherence to journalistic balance and objectivity. Its executives consistently emphasize that, as part of Hezbollah, assigned to present its views, it must serve as the voice of the underdog such as the Palestinians. Arguing that all other news organizations advocate the views of governments, rival groups, or ideas like Zionism, Al Manar openly embraces its propaganda role. It gives priority to programming advocating antagonism to Israel, but after Syria withdrew from Lebanon in 2005, its programs have increasingly promoted Lebanese interests and development. In recent years, it has included Christians as experts on some subjects and as audience members, and non-veiled women dominate many programs, to signify Hezbollah's pragmatic turn as a Lebanese political party. By embracing the multiconfessional nature of the country, it asserts it national character.

Some networks denied Al Manar access from the start, or subsequently cut off its access. Over the years, French, German, and other authorities have ordered companies in their countries to cease transmitting Al Manar. In 2012, both Apple and Google withdrew applications assisting access to Hezbollah material. In 2004 the United States put Al Manar on its terrorism lists and has imposed sanctions since 2006. However, it remains available on the Internet. It exploits the opposition to its propaganda to claim the status of a sacrificial martyr in the Lebanese national struggle, and the voice of the Shi'as and the Palestinians against Israeli aggression and its international supporters.

Tom Dowling

See also: Hezbollah; Israel; Lebanese Republic; Palestine; Social Media

Further Reading

Baylouny, Anne Marie. "Not Your Father's Islamist TV: Changing Programming on Hizbullah's *al-Manar.*" *Arab Media and Society* no. 9 (Fall 2009).

Matar, Dina, and Farah Dakhlallah. "What It Means to Be Shiite in Lebanon: *Al Manar* and the Imagined Community of Resistance." *Westminster Papers in Communication and Culture* 3, no. 2 (2006): 22–40.

Yadav, Stacey Philbrick. "Of Bans, Boycotts, and Sacrificial Lambs: *Al-Manar* in the Crossfire." In *Culture Wars: The Arabic Music Video Controversy,* 172–77. Cairo: American University of Cairo, 2005.

Al-Qaeda Central

A militant, pan-Islamist organization, founded in 1988 by a rich Saudi named Osama bin Laden, which grew out of a broad, previously existing network of activists and organizations. The al-Qaeda (sometimes Al-Qa'ida) network formed as Arabs from many different countries went to fight against the Soviets after their invasion of Afghanistan in 1979. Beginning in 1984, bin Laden helped run a guest house in Peshawar, providing logistics for Arab volunteers, known as the *Maktam al-Khidmat.* He attracted the attention of an Egyptian doctor, Ayman al-Zawahiri, the founder of the Egyptian Islamic Jihad (EIJ), who became his ideological mentor and expanded bin Laden's campaign for political liberation into a global ambition. Al-Zawahiri argued for a systematic, confrontational, and rational use of inspirational slogans to mobilize the masses for a global war. His ideology promoted the use of suicide bombings, and the practice of denouncing other Muslims, whom he considered insufficiently pure in their doctrine and behavior.

Al-Qaeda effectively uses images of suffering Muslims to mobilize fighters. In short, al-Qaeda's ideology justifies terrorism as a tool to purify Islamic society and overthrow existing governments, to create a universal world government according to Islamic law. It uses terror as a tool for recruitment, internal discipline, and political coercion against governments. Al-Qaeda represents a vanguard, or core, of ideologically committed, educated activists seeking to mobilize large numbers of fighters. It employs the business model of a multinational corporation, with functional divisions for personnel, logistics, financing, targeting, military training, and counterespionage, as well as using independent cells of underground agents to avoid penetration by government intelligence services. Al-Qaeda provided training, arms, fighters, and money for campaigns in Algeria, the Balkans, Chechnya, and Southeast Asia. The men who had trained in its camps in Afghanistan before the 9/11 attacks developed similar organizations in Egypt, Iraq, Pakistan, Saudi Arabia, Syria, Yemen, and other countries.

Bin Laden and al-Zawahiri represent political entrepreneurs, rationally employing resources as instrumental tools, and strategically managing images to establish a new worldview. According to their strategic plan, Osama bin Laden and his associates sought to provoke the United States into attacking Muslims, believing that these attacks would mobilize ordinary Muslims to overthrow their own governments. Osama bin Laden's "Declaration of War against the Americans" carried little impact on the general American awareness. The 1998 bombings of the U.S. embassies in Kenya and Tanzania grabbed the attention of the American security community, but not the broader public consciousness. Similarly, the suicide bombing of the USS *Cole* in Aden Harbor, Yemen, failed to increase any understanding of the nature of al-Qaeda. Then the American reaction to the attack on September 11, 2001, forced al-Qaeda's leadership to seek protection in Pakistan's tribal areas from the U.S. military counterterrorism operations.

This also forced the central organization to shift operational control to independent cells working in loose communication as "franchise operations." Therefore, analysts distinguish between al-Qaeda Central (AQC), still located in Pakistan, and affiliate organizations such as al-Qaeda in the Islamic Maghreb (AQIM), Ansar al-Sharia in Libya, al-Qaeda in the Arabian Peninsula (AQAP), and al-Qaeda in the Indian Subcontinent (AQIS).

Even from his place of hiding in Abbottabad, Pakistan, bin Laden retained significant influence, and sent guidance to the different organizations by a trusted courier. After U.S. Navy SEALs killed him on May 2, 2011, al-Zawahiri succeeded him as al-Qaeda's emir, leading the organization with a few other key leaders. As counterterrorism operations prevent the central leadership of al-Qaeda from directly controlling operations, insubordinate commanders have caused significant problems, as seen in the case of Abu Musab al-Zarqawi, who split from AQC and developed the Islamic State (Daesh) in July 2014. As a result of its massive propaganda campaign and actions, Daesh effectively challenged al-Qaeda's authority and enticed its affiliates in Africa, the Middle East, and Southeast Asia to defect. The combination of the U.S. military campaign, and the ideological battle conducted on one side by Daesh, and by orthodox Sunni religious teachers on the other, has greatly degraded AQC. As al-Zawahiri struggles to overcome al-Qaeda's internal problems, Osama bin Laden's favorite son, Hamza, has now emerged as a likely successor to al-Zawahiri.

Mark David Luce

See also: Algeria, The People's Democratic Republic of; Al-Qaeda in the Islamic Maghreb (AQIM); Al-Qaeda in the Arabian Peninsula (AQAP); Egypt, Arab Republic of; Iraq, Republic of; Islamic State (Daesh); Islamism; Jihad; Saudi Arabia, Kingdom of; Syrian Arab Republic; Yemen, Republic of

Further Reading

Harmony and Disharmony: Exploiting al-Qa'ida's Organizational Vulnerabilities. West Point, NY: Combating Terrorism Center, United States Military Academy, 2006.

Orbach, Benjamin. "Usama bin Laden and al-Qa'ida: Origins and Doctrines." MERIA Journal 5, no. 4 (December 2001): 58–61.

Soufan, Ali. "Hamza bin Ladin: From Steadfast Son to al-Qa'ida's Leader in Waiting." CTC Sentinel 7, no. 8 (September 2017): 1–7.

Al-Qaeda in the Arabian Peninsula (AQAP)

A Salafi terrorist organization in Yemen, which has adopted the global objectives of al-Qaeda Central while relying on local tribal connections to attack the Houthis (Ansar Allah) and conduct an insurgency against the government of Yemen. Osama bin Laden drew many Yemeni volunteers to fight the Soviets in Afghanistan. They gained a commitment to impose their political vision on the world through terrorism. When these fighters returned from Afghanistan, President Saleh mobilized them to fight the more secular Yemeni Socialist Party and the Southern Movement. In December 1992, al-Qaeda (AQ) bombers hit a hotel in Aden formerly used by U.S. Marines. The United States began paying attention after the October 2000 suicide attack on the destroyer USS Cole in Aden. After September 11, 2001, the United States sought help from the government of Yemen to attack Al-Qaeda.

After AQ attacked Saudi Arabia multiple times in 2003 and 2004, Saudi security forces conducted a thorough campaign that drove the remnants into Yemen. In February 2006, 23 AQ leaders escaped from a prison, which led to renewed military action. In September 2008, AQ attacked the U.S. embassy with two suicide car bombs supported by snipers. In January 2009, the Yemeni and Saudi branches of AQ combined to form al-Qaeda in the Arabian Peninsula (AQAP). The organization took responsibility for the 2009 attempted Christmas Day bombing, parcel bombs over several years, and the Charlie Hebdo attacks in Paris in 2014.

In March 2011, AQAP took the name Ansar al-Sharia for its insurgent fighters, to highlight its governance operations. In May 2011, AQAP fighters took control of Zinjibar in southern Yemen and held it for a year. In February 2012, the group mounted a suicide attack on the presidential palace. As a Sunni Salafi group, AQAP has engaged in sectarian conflict against the Houthis, portraying them as part of a greater Shi'a campaign against the Sunnis. Many of the AQAP leaders come from well-known local families in the eastern region of the country. Taking the name "Sons of Hadramout," they have gained support from local tribes. These tribes played an important role in battles such as the April 2, 2015, conquest of the prosperous, eastern port city of al-Mukalla. It demonstrates significant political skill, as seen in the decision to withdraw from Mukalla on April 24, 2016, following negotiations, for the sake of saving the lives and property of civilians in the city. AQAP reflects the global priorities of AQ Central as seen in its sophisticated social media propaganda campaign, in spite of the low literacy rates and frequent lack of electricity in Yemen.

Jonathan K. Zartman

See also: Al-Qaeda Central; Houthis (Ansar Allah); Islamism; Salafism; Saudi Arabia, Kingdom of; Yemen, Republic of; Yemeni Socialist Party

Further Reading

Hull, Edmund J. *High-Value Target: Countering Al Qaeda in Yemen.* Washington, DC: Potomac Books, 2011.

Loidolt, Bryce. "Managing the Global and Local: The Dual Agendas of Al Qaeda in the Arabian Peninsula." *Studies in Conflict & Terrorism* 34, no. 2 (February 2011): 102–23.

Terrill, W. Andrew. *The Struggle for Yemen and the Challenge of Al-Qaeda in the Arabian Peninsula.* Carlisle, PA: Strategic Studies Institute, June 2013.

Al-Qaeda in the Islamic Maghreb (AQIM)

A terrorist organization originating in the Salafist Group for Preaching and Combat (GSPC), part of the militant Islamist struggle against the government of Algeria. The GSPC formed in 1998 to reject indiscriminate attacks on civilians conducted by the Armed Islamic Group (GIA). It consisted of a number of relatively autonomous groups, called *katibas* or brigades, operating independently due to personal rivalries among the leaders. Under severe pressure from the Algerian security services, the GSPC extended its operations from its bases in the mountainous Kabylie region, to establish brigades farther south in the under-governed areas of Algeria's neighbors, primarily in northern Mali.

As early as 2003, GSPC's leaders sought resources from former colleagues in Afghanistan and the global Islamist network. On September 11, 2006, Abdelmalek Droukdel (alias Abou Mossab Abdelouadoud), a trained engineer and explosives expert, formally affiliated with al-Qaeda Central (AQC). In 2007, it took the name Al-Qaeda in the Islamic Maghreb (*Maghreb* is Arabic for "West"). The group has operated throughout North Africa and the Sahel, the western region of the Muslim world. AQIM has gained significant wealth from trans-Saharan trafficking in drugs, weapons, and people, including high-profile kidnappings of Westerners for ransom. AQIM has experienced setbacks in Algeria, but its offshoots and affiliates in other parts of North Africa and the Sahel remain active.

AQIM's early vision focused on unseating the Algerian government and establishing a *sharia*-ruled state, drawing inspiration from the early Islamic conquest in North Africa and the Iberian Peninsula. However, AQIM supports the broader AQC pursuit of "rescuing Muslims from all corrupt, apostate regimes and their imperialist, crusader masters." In December 2007, it conducted suicide bombings against the United Nations, as well as Algerian government targets.

AQIM became a critical node in mobile terrorist networks that stretched across the Sahel and included Boko Haram in Nigeria, Al-Shabaab in Somalia, and AQAP in Yemen, with varying levels of communication, training, and even material support among these groups.

In 2011, AQIM exploited the chaos and power vacuum in Libya after the fall of Qaddafi to gain weapons, safe-haven areas of retreat, and recruits. The March 2012 coup in Bamako, Mali, and the Tuareg rebellion provided similar opportunities to seize territory and expand smuggling routes. AQIM activists expelled the more secular separatists and took over the newly declared independent state of Azawad in northern Mali. The French-led intervention in January 2013 largely reversed this expansion. The rise of the Islamic State caliphate in Iraq and Syria (Daesh), in competition with AQC, caused AQIM to lose funding and support and provoked internal contention. In early 2018, the Algerian army killed AQIM's chief propagandist Abu Rouaha al-Qassantini and gained a great deal of information from the captured electronic equipment, which enabled successful following operations. In March 2017, the remnants of AQIM's southern brigades joined with four other groups, and all gave their allegiance to AQ Central. The military pressure that originally provoked repeated splits in the militant opposition, and then greater international activity in the search for resources, has now led to organizational mergers for resources.

Scott Edmondson

See also: Algeria, The People's Democratic Republic of; Al-Qaeda Central; Armed Islamic Group (GIA); Belmokhtar, Mokhtar; Bouteflika, Abdelaziz; Islamic Salvation Front (FIS); Islamism

Further Reading
Filiu, Jean-Pierre. "Al-Qaeda in the Islamic Maghreb: Algerian Challenge or Global Threat?" *Carnegie Papers* no. 104 (October 2009).

Harmon, Stephen. "From GSPC to AQIM: The Evolution of an Algerian Islamist Terrorist Group into an Al-Qa'ida Affiliate and its Implications for the Sahara-Sahel Region." *ACAS Concerned Africa Scholars Bulletin* no. 85 (Spring 2010): 12–29.

Pham, J. Peter. "The Dangerous 'Pragmatism' of Al-Qaeda in the Islamic Maghreb." *Journal of the Middle East and Africa* 2 (2011): 15–29.

Al-Sadr, Muqtada

An Iraqi Shi'a religious leader, founder of a large military organization, and nationalist politician, born into a prominent family in Najaf, Iraq (approximately 1974). He enjoyed initial political success due to his father's reputation as a religious scholar, who served poor people in practical ways while courageously opposing the tyranny of Saddam Hussein. In 1999, Saddam responded to sharp criticism from Muqtada's father, Ayatollah Muhammad Sadiq al-Sadr, by arranging to kill him and two of his sons. Even under government surveillance, Muqtada secretly worked with his father's students to develop an organization, commonly called the Sadr Movement. Under persecution, the leaders of Shi'a dissident movements had fled into exile: the Da'wa Party, the Supreme Council for the Islamic Revolution in Iraq (SCIRI), and the Badr Organization. After the March 2003 coalition's invasion of Iraq, Muqtada and the Sadr Movement very quickly began mobilizing the urban poor and rural Shi'as into a movement of resistance against the occupation. With passionate oratory, Muqtada used his father's reputation, and the credibility of his supporters' presence on the ground, to quickly gain large numbers of motivated followers. His movement developed and effectively used radio, TV, the Internet, and newspapers. They competed with the other Shi'a parties, sometimes with assassination, violence, and open warfare.

On April 8, 2004, an Iraqi religious leader based in Iran, Ayatollah Kazem al-Haeri, appointed Muqtada his representative, giving him a substantial income, and urged the Iraqi Shi'a to seize power. On April 10, 2003, a mob of Muqtada's supporters killed Ayatollah Abdul Majid al-Khoei outside the Imam Ali Mosque. Then a mob besieged the home of Grand Ayatollah Ali al-Sistani, but nearby tribal leaders rescued him. Muqtada's movement established religious courts, with punishment committees employing summary executions and intimidation, to seize control of whole communities. In August 2003, he formed and began training the Jaish al-Mahdi (JAM, or the Mahdi Army). By 2004, his forces began engaging in open battles with the U.S. military. In late August 2004, Ayatollah Sistani brokered a truce in which Sistani gained greater public stature, the JAM lost, and Ayatollah Haeri removed his support. The JAM split into several factions, some financed by crime and some by Iran. In the preparations for the 2005 elections, Muqtada engaged in the political process with the Da'wa Party and SCIRI to form the United Iraqi Alliance, as a common Shi'a front, from which Nouri al-Maliki became prime minister. The Sadr Movement gained appointments to lead three ministries, which provided a source of jobs, incomes, and patronage. After the election, Iran worked through the Islamic Revolutionary Guard Corps–Quds Force and Lebanese Hezbollah to actively train and support Shi'a military forces in Iraq, including a splinter from JAM called the Khazali network, or the Asaib Ahl al-Haq (AAH). These groups created tremendous sectarian violence.

After the February 2006 bombing of the al-Askari Mosque in Samarra, Muqtada remobilized the Mehdi Army. The U.S. military accused JAM of running death squads, killing Sunni Arabs, and fighting with rival Shiite factions, such as the Badr Brigades, which then partnered with Iraqi security forces to fight the JAM. Criminal gangs within the JAM, and numerous splits funded and encouraged by Iran, undermined Muqtada's control.

Al-Maliki shielded the political leaders and military commanders of the Sadr Movement until November 30, 2006, when the Sadr Movement leaders withdrew from his government. With the support and agreement of the Da'wa Party and SCIRI leaders, and U.S. president Bush's January 10, 2007, announcement of a new plan to surge troops to Iraq, the government began a military operation against the Shi'a militias. As these operations gained success, in January 2007, Muqtada ordered his militia to stand down, and he fled to Iran to pursue further religious studies. He returned briefly in the summer of 2007 to try to regain control of his forces, but in August 2007, the JAM fought a big battle at Karbala with Iraqi security forces. Muqtada developed a strong antagonism against Nouri al-Maliki for targeting his supporters during this period. Nevertheless, he again declared a cease-fire with the Iraqi government, and later disbanded the Mehdi Army, which transitioned into the Saraya al-Salam (Peace Brigades). Ultimately, he sought to replicate the Hezbollah model, combining a social services organization, a political party, and a military force. While in Iran, throughout 2008, he tried and failed to regain control over the JAM. The Asaib Ahl al-Haq and other splinter groups continued fighting, and the Iraqi government twice sent delegations to Iran to negotiate peace.

In Iraq's 2010 elections, the Iraqi National Alliance Party of al-Sadr won 40 out of 325 seats. After months of political stalemate, at the urging of Iran, Muqtada agreed to enter Nouri al-Maliki's coalition, despite the open warfare between them from 2006 to 2008. Al-Maliki gained a second term as prime minister, and the Sadr Movement gained eight out of 32 cabinet seats. In January 2011, Muqtada al-Sadr returned to Najaf, Iraq, without finishing his program of education, striking a more conciliatory political tone, and pushing the government to include more technocrats and moderate Sunni elements.

By 2012, Muqtada claimed that he sought peace and sectarian harmony, but he also held rallies to protest al-Maliki's tyrannical policies. In August 2013, he announced that he was retiring from politics as well as dismantling the Mahdi forces. However, when Mosul fell to the Islamic State (Daesh) in June 2014, al-Sadr reformed his forces to fight the Islamic State and pressured al-Maliki to resign. In 2015, Muqtada formed an alliance called the Sairoon (Marching toward Reform) with the Iraqi Communist Party and other secular groups, reportedly to fight against corruption. In 2017, he made high-profile visits to both the UAE and Saudi Arabia to discuss regional issues and ask for economic investment in Iraq. In May 2018, the Sairoon electoral list won 54 seats in the Iraqi Parliament, the largest of any of the competing coalitions. Although Muqtada initially formed an alliance with Haider al-Abadi as the competing parties struggled to form a government, he later withdrew that support and reached a different compromise with his opposition. This completed his transformation from a sectarian warrior to a fully nationalist politician with cross-sectional appeal.

Jonathan K. Zartman

See also: Al-Abadi, Haider; Al-Maliki, Nouri; Hezbollah; Iran, Islamic Republic of; Iraq, Republic of; Islamic Revolutionary Guard Corps (IRGC); Quds Force; Sectarianism; Shi'a

Further Reading

Cochrane, Marisa. "The Fragmentation of the Sadrist Movement." *Iraq Report* 12. Washington, DC: Institute for the Study of War, January 2009.

Cockburn, Patrick. *Muqtada: Muqtada al-Sadr, the Shia Revival, and the Struggle for Iraq.* New York: Simon & Schuster, 2008.

Godwin, Matthew J. "Political Inclusion in Unstable Contexts: Muqtada al-Sadr and Iraq's Sadrist Movement." *Contemporary Arab Affairs* 5, no. 3 (July–September 2012): 448–56.

Raphaeli, Nimrod. "Understanding Muqtada al-Sadr." *Middle East Quarterly* 11, no. 4 (Fall 2004): 33–42.

Al-Sharif, Manal

A women's rights activist and one of the primary organizers of the Women2Drive campaign, which advocates for women's right to drive in Saudi Arabia. Manal

Al-Sharif, born on April 25, 1979, in Khobar, Saudi Arabia, grew up in a conservative society, which she attributes to the *Sahwa,* or "Islamic Awakening" Movement. She claims that she was beginning down the path to radicalism, even burning her brother's music tapes in the oven and burning her own artwork. On November 6, 1990, 47 courageous women challenged the ban on women's driving by driving in the streets of Riyadh. The women were detained, banned from leaving the country, and dismissed from their jobs. However, their actions stimulated women in Saudi Arabia to think about their status.

In 2002, Manal became one of the first Saudi women to specialize in information security, working for Saudi Aramco. A friend commented on the fact that Saudi Arabia does not have a law explicitly banning women from driving, but only refuses to grant women driving licenses. She posted a video of herself driving a car on May 21, 2011, in the Saudi city of Khobar, which the government quickly blocked. However, many people had already posted it many times to Facebook, ensuring that many people saw it. She was arrested and imprisoned for "disturbing public order" and "inciting public opinion." Other activists using social media spread the reports about her internationally, and the *New York Times* exerted pressure for her release. On May 30, 2011, she was released, after an international campaign on her behalf. She cofounded and led the #Women2Drive Movement, to challenge other women who held international drivers' licenses to drive on June 17, 2011. The government continued to punish harshly the women who participated in the following days. Although she later made Australia her home, she has continued to encourage women to pursue greater civil and social rights.

Jonathan K. Zartman

See also: Authoritarianism; Democracy Deficit; Development; Modernization; Saudi Sahwa (Islamic Awakening); Saudi Arabia, Kingdom of; Social Media; Women's Leadership in Protests

Further Reading

Al-Sharif, Manal. *Daring to Drive: The Young Saudi Woman Who Stood up to a Kingdom of Men.* London: Simon & Schuster UK, export edition, 2017.

Doumato, Eleanor Abdella. "Saudi Arabia." In *Women's Rights in the Middle East and North Africa: Progress Amid Resistance,* edited by Sanja Kelly and Julia Breslin, 425–57. Lanham, MD: Rowman and Littlefield, 2010.

Khondker, Habibul Haque. "Role of the New Media in the Arab Spring." *Globalizations* 8, no. 5 (2011): 675–79.

Ammar, Rachid

The Tunisian Army chief of staff (2002–2011) during the popular revolts of 2011, who played a pivotal role in Tunisia's subsequent governance, born in 1946 in Sayada, a small town on the coast. President Ben Ali had maintained the policy of his predecessor in keeping the army small and out of politics. He actively managed daily affairs, coordinating the army, air force, and navy, while keeping vacant the position of armed forces chief of staff. During the protests, on January

12, 2011, the government first deployed the army to the streets of Tunis to enforce a curfew. Conditions became chaotic, and communication within the government broke down. Some of the forces of the Interior Ministry started acting on their own interest without orders. Due to his fear of a coup, and distrust of General Ammar, Defense Minister Ridha Grira ordered him to go to the Interior Ministry to take control there, which he did, but this kept him away from the army command. A rumor had spread earlier that General Ammar had refused Ben Ali's orders to shoot at protesters. However, the opposition website that reported this later admitted that it was an act of propaganda to stimulate mistrust within the regime. On January 13, the army withdrew from some locations and even intervened between police and protesters to protect the people.

After Ben Ali fled the country on January 14, the army played a crucial role in restoring order, to control civilian looters and marauding members of Ben Ali's former security forces. For the next few weeks, the military repeatedly interceded to protect protesters from violence at the hands of police. Caravans of protesters came from the southern provinces to demand the resignation of Prime Minister Mohamed Ghannouchi, who represented the government of Ben Ali. On January 24, the government asked General Ammar to disperse the protesters. General Ammar worried that the protesters' impatience to throw out every member of the previous administration would create a dangerous lack of any political leadership. He made a highly publicized speech to more than 1,000 people in a square near his office, pledging to protect the revolution. He explicitly supported free elections and pledged to ensure a democratic result. This speech, combined with the "don't shoot" rumor and the army's behavior, made him the most popular leader in Tunisia, with significant influence.

Ammar's role as de facto interim ruler ended when National Council elections allowed a coalition government to form. General Ammar, who has stayed out of the public eye since Essebsi became prime minister, was promoted to armed forces chief of staff and remains the army commander, which gives him significant authority. Under his leadership, Tunisia appointed army officers to important civilian positions, including as governors of seven provinces in 2011. The new democratic civilian government has decentralized command of the military, transforming it from personal rule to institutional control. After the second Egyptian revolution raised fears that the army might use popular protests to justify a coup, the government changed military leaders and institutions, promoting officers from previously disadvantaged regions. General Ammar resigned from his position on June 27, 2013, claiming that, at age 67, he was far past retirement age.

Sean Braniff

See also: Authoritarianism; Jasmine Revolution; Military Coups; Tunisia, Republic of

Further Reading

Brooks, Risa. "Abandoned at the Palace: Why the Tunisian Military Defected from the Ben Ali Regime in January 2011." *The Journal of Strategic Studies* 36, no. 2 (2013): 205–20.

Grewal, Sharan. "A Quiet Revolution: The Tunisian Military after Ben Ali." Beirut, Lebanon: Carnegie Middle East Center, February 24, 2016.

Pachon, Alejandro. "Loyalty and Defection: Misunderstanding Civil-Military Relations in Tunisia during the 'Arab Spring.'" *The Journal of Strategic Studies* 37, no. 4 (2014): 508–31.

Ansar al-Sharia in Libya

A powerful Salafi militia in Libya seeking to establish an Islamic state by violence to implement *sharia* law. Several militant organizations in the Middle East–North Africa region use variations of the name *Ansar al-Sharia,* meaning "supporters of Islamic law." Ansar al-Sharia (ASL) emerged after the 2011 Libyan revolution, as a variety of actors struggled violently for local and regional control. Its operations began with an extensive program of outreach, or recruitment, that included providing social services as well as preaching. This group also sent shipments of relief goods to Sudan, Syria, and Gaza, revealing a sophisticated logistics capability and possible sponsorship from Sudan and Turkey. This movement includes two prominent groups within Libya: 1) the more prominent Ansar al-Sharia in Benghazi (ASB), led by Muhammad al-Zawahi until his death in late 2014; and 2) Ansar al-Sharia in Derna (ASD), led by former Guantanamo Bay–inmate Abu Sufyan bin Qumu. While these groups took root independently in their respective locales, they cooperated when possible for their shared ends. ASL gained international notoriety after members of the two groups conducted coordinated terrorist attacks on September 11, 2012, against the U.S. diplomatic facilities in Benghazi, Libya, killing four Americans, including U.S. ambassador J. Christopher Stevens. Although the ASL later denied involvement in these attacks, witnesses identified organization members at the scenes. On November 28, 2017, a U.S. District Court jury convicted Ahmed Abu Khattala, a senior leader of ASB, for his involvement in the attack on the diplomatic compound.

In 2014, as ASL's influence began to falter, the United States and the United Kingdom designated ASB and ASD as foreign terrorist organizations. The forces of General Khalifa Haftar fought the ASL intensively. Following al-Zawahi's death in 2014, along with heavy losses in the following years that killed most of ASL's leadership and its fighters, a significant number of the remaining members reportedly defected to the Islamic State (Daesh) in Libya. On May 27, 2018, Ansar al-Sharia in Libya formally dissolved. This signifies only that most of the members shifted to the Islamic State, or to al-Qaeda in the Islamic Maghreb (AQIM).

Melvin R. Korsmo

See also: Al-Qaeda in the Islamic Maghreb (AQIM); Benghazi Attack; Islamic State (Daesh); Islamism; Libya, State of; Qaddafi, Muammar

Further Reading

Gråtrud, Henrik, and Vidar Benjamin Skretting. "*Ansar al-Sharia* in Libya: An Enduring Threat." *Perspectives on Terrorism* 11, no. 1 (February 2017): 40–53.

Zelin, Aaron Y. "The Rise and Decline of *Ansar al-Sharia* in Libya." *Current Trends in Islamist Ideology* 18 (May 2015): 104–18.

Ansar Beit al Maqdis

A militant group based in the Sinai Peninsula formed after the 2011 Egyptian uprisings, responsible for numerous terror attacks in Egypt and Israel against government security forces, foreign tourists, Coptic and Muslim houses of worship, and oil infrastructure. The name, also spelled *Ansar Bayt al Maqdis,* translates as "Supporters of Jerusalem." It conducts periodic cross-border raids into Israel and has expanded into Egypt's Nile Valley region. Conflicting estimates of its size range from 500 to over 1,000. Initially focusing attention on local grievances, in November 2014 the group joined the Islamic State (Daesh), gaining the name Islamic State-Sinai Province (IS-SP, also ISIL-SP and ISIS-SP), but remains distinct from the group known as Islamic State Egypt.

The group displays increasingly sophisticated methods, such as armed assaults, rocket attacks, and bombings. Attacks attributed to the group include an October 2015 bomb on a Russian commercial jet, killing 224 on board, and the bombing of a mosque in north Sinai on November 24, 2017, killing 312 civilians.

Since 2015, Egyptian and Israeli counterterrorism efforts have expanded against IS-SP. The Egyptian government has produced new laws to implement repressive security measures in north Sinai, as exemplified in its "Right of the Martyr" and "Sinai 2018" operations. In April 2018, the Egyptian military announced it had killed the leader of IS-SP, Nasser Abu Zaqoul, but the group remains a key security threat in the region.

Melia Pfannenstiel

See also: Al-Qaeda Central; Coptic Orthodox Church; Egypt, Arab Republic of; Islamic State (Daesh); Islamism; Israel

Further Reading

Rank, Annette, and Justyna Nedza. "Crossing the Ideological Divide? Egypt's Salafists and the Muslim Brotherhood after the Arab Spring." *Studies in Conflict and Terrorism* 39, no. 6 (2016): 519–41.

Berman, Ilan. "The Once and Future Threat: Al-Qaeda Is Hardly Dead." *World Affairs* 177, no. 1 (May/June 2014): 76–85.

Ismail, Alexandrani. "Egypt's Revolutions." In *Sinai: From Revolution to Terrorism,* edited by Bernard Rougier and Stéphane Lacroix, 179–96. New York: Palgrave Macmillan, 2016.

April 6 Youth

A secular, Egyptian youth movement known for its use of social media to organize mass protests against the Hosni Mubarak regime during the 2011 Egyptian uprising. The April 6 Movement emerged from the *Kefaya* Youth Movement, comprised of nationalist, communist, and Islamist factions that participated in 2004 anti-Mubarak protests. In 2006, some *Kefaya* members allied with a labor movement established by textile-factory workers in Mahalla al Kubra. In March 2008, the April 6 Facebook group gained 100,000 members and mobilized thousands to support the textile workers with a national strike. Police repression of the strike provoked a significant riot. While the April 2008 strike did not lead to political change, it did draw attention to the potential for activists to use social media to organize a growing movement. The April 6 Youth leaders adopted a strategy of nonviolence, following the advice of the Center for Applied Non-Violent Action and Strategies (CANVAS), an organization founded by the Serbian resistance movement Otpor. April 6 Youth employed these tactics during the January 25, 2011, uprising, using social media to organize separate rallies to evade Egyptian security services.

Following President Mubarak's resignation in 2011, policy disagreements prevented secular youth activists from forming any political coalition. Although the April 6 Youth later supported the removal of President Morsi from power, under President Sisi the Egyptian security forces repressed and tightly regulated political activity, subjecting many April 6 Youth members, and leaders Ahmed Maher and Muhammad Adel, to repression.

Melia Pfannenstiel

See also: Egypt, Arab Republic of; El-Sisi, Abdel Fattah Saeed Hussein Khalil; Morsi, Mohamed; Mubarak, Muhammad Hosni Sayyid; Social Media; Tahrir Square Protests

Further Reading

Gelvin, James. *The Arab Uprisings: What Everyone Needs to Know.* New York: Oxford University Press, 2012.

Joffe, George. "The Arab Spring in North Africa: Origins and Prospects." *The Journal of North African Studies* 16, no. 4 (December 2011): 507–32.

Sharp, Jeremy. *Egypt: The January 25 Revolution and Implications for U.S. Foreign Policy,* CRS Report No. RL33003. Washington, DC: Congressional Research Service, 2011.

Arab Nationalism

An ideology driving political efforts for Arab unity and independence that initially developed in the Levant area of the Ottoman Empire as a result of the modernization/reform movement. In reaction to Napoleon's invasion of Egypt and the rising power of European states, a number of reformers (called Jadids) advocated nationalism, the development of newspapers, and an increase in literacy, as well as a renewal of education, to include math, science, engineering, and European languages. Jadids who promoted Turkic nationalism posed a challenge to the ideology sustaining the multiethnic, multiconfessional character of the Ottoman Empire. This stimulated a reaction by educated Arabic speakers, who defended the virtues of Arab culture. Arabs resentful of Turkish domination promoted Arab nationalism to demand greater rights and autonomy and, ultimately, the complete independence of the Arab provinces. Arab nationalists sought a united Greater Syria that would include Lebanon and Palestine. The British took advantage of these sentiments in supporting the great Arab Revolt of 1916, to weaken and eventually defeat the Ottoman Empire, the ally of Germany in World War I. That war discredited Ottomanism and pan-Turkism. After the war, Islamism and socialism competed with Arab nationalism as tools for social mobilization.

European colonization resulted in each major power's shaping the politics of different areas into different national forms. Each set of elites reacted primarily against their own colonial power, the French, the British, and the Zionists, thus creating local forms of nationalism. The political ambitions of competing Syrian, Palestinian, and Iraqi Arab nationalists undermined the prospects of a united Arab state. Nationalists also exploited the grievances of the people against the tremendous inequalities of wealth, almost all of which was in the hands of the monarchies created by the colonial powers. The Ba'ath Party promoted Arab nationalism with the language of socialism and political secularism, to bring in the non-Muslim Arabs. They saw Arab nationalism as an opportunity to escape from their second-class status and discrimination. For example, the Arab Christian George Antonius promoted this idea through literature in *The Arab Awakening* (1938). In some areas, activists exploited Arab nationalism to justify policies of forced assimilation and even warfare against non-Arab minorities, as seen in the 1933 massacre of a group of Assyrians in northern Iraq, and the later massive campaigns against the Kurds.

After the 1952 Free Officers Revolt in Egypt brought Gamal Abdel Nasser to power in Egypt, he promoted Arab nationalism. Egypt's victory in the 1956 Suez Crisis over Israel, France, and Britain strengthened the ideological appeal of his ideas. Israel's defeat of Egypt in the 1967 war greatly undermined the appeal of Arab nationalism. People throughout the region turned from Arab nationalism to Islamism to mobilize their resistance to Israel. As Arab nationalism lost its luster, in each country the leaders and the military created independent ideologies to exalt distinctive local virtues and mobilize loyalty to the state. Arab nationalists shifted their energies to support for Palestinian nationalism. Saddam Hussein initially tried to take the place of Egypt as a patron of Arab socialism through the Iraqi Ba'ath party, before renouncing the pan-Arab vision in 1982.

Jonathan K. Zartman

See also: Ba'athism; Egypt, Arab Republic of; Iraq, Republic of; Islamism; Palestine; Syrian Arab Republic

Further Reading

Ghazal, Amal N. "The Other Frontiers of Arab Nationalism: Ibadis, Berbers, and the Arabist-Salafi Press in the Interwar Period." *International Journal of Middle East Studies* 42, no. 1 (February 2010): 105–22.

Haddad, Mahmoud. "The Rise of Arab Nationalism Reconsidered." *International Journal of Middle East Studies* 26, no. 2 (May 1994): 201–22.

Kramer, Martin. "Arab Nationalism: Mistaken Identity." *Daedalus*, Summer 1993, 171–206.

Arab Spring Movements (2011)

A series of large-scale, protracted protest demonstrations in many Arab countries, beginning in 2011, that led to the replacement of governing elites in Tunisia and Egypt, intervention by other Gulf states in Bahrain, and complex civil wars with significant external involvement in Yemen, Libya, and Syria. The scale, consequences, and apparently contagious character of these protest movements, which caught regional experts by surprise, has stimulated significant research to explain the vulnerability of states to civil discord and instability. Observers of these movements offer a number of useful conclusions regarding the motivations of protesters, the supporting structural conditions for large protest movements, and any facilitating factors.

The traditional journalistic account begins on December 17, 2010, when the video of Tarek el-Tayeb Mohamed Bouazizi setting himself on fire, in protest against government abuse and humiliation, sparked demonstrations all over Tunisia. The dramatically growing protests, ultimately called the Jasmine Revolution, forced President Zine al-Abidine Ben Ali to flee to Saudi Arabia on January 14, 2011. People in many different Arabic-speaking countries watched these events on Al Jazeera and followed the social-media campaigns of activists. They noted their similar living conditions: political exclusion under highly corrupt, aged, authoritarian rulers; inflation; and high levels of unemployment, even for educated youth. On January 17, 2011, the initial Green March protests began in Oman. On January 24, 2011, Yemeni security forces arrested the well-connected and influential activist Tawakil Karman, which provoked peaceful protests that would last for a year. On January 25, 2011, protests began in Tahrir Square, Egypt. Egyptian president Hosni Mubarak resigned on February 11, 2011, after 18 days of revolution. This inspired millions of people to think that they also could remove their rulers by collective action. These events motivated protests in more countries, stimulating renewal in the "Regime Change Cascades" literature.

On February 14, 2011, both Sunni and Shi'a opposition groups occupied the Pearl Roundabout in Manama, Bahrain. Three days later, the February 17th Revolution began in Benghazi, Libya, and quickly spread. After another three days, an organized cycle of protests began in Morocco, called the February 20 Revolution. Liberals took encouragement from these events, hoping that they would lead to greater individual liberties and even the expansion of political rights. This led to the expression "The Arab Spring," an optimistic reference to the 1968 democratic opening in Czechoslovakia called the Prague Spring. However, governments raised their determination to deter and suppress any rebellion among their own residents. On March 6, 2011, Saudi Arabia deployed massive security forces against Shi'a protests in the east. On March 15, 2011, Gulf Cooperation Council troops entered Bahrain to support the king's security forces in crushing demonstrations. Three days later in Yemen, government supporters killed 52 protesters, causing major military leaders to defect to the opposition. On March 18, 2011, Syrian government forces shot five protesters in Dara'a, followed by many further provocations that eventually grew into the Syrian civil war.

In the three states where protests sparked civil war, international intervention has played a significant role. On March 19, 2011, the United States, Britain, and France led the UN-authorized Operation Odyssey Dawn assault on the forces of Muammar Qaddafi in support of the rebellion. In Syria, the government would call on Iran and Russia to support its side in the war, reinforced by Hezbollah from Lebanon. On the other side, the Gulf states and Turkey supported a variety of Islamist militias. In Yemen, a precarious, internally divided state finally collapsed under assault from competing ambitious militias and the grievances of a desperately poor population. For all its internal conflict, the Yemen civil war gained formal international recognition when Saudi Arabia led a coalition of neighboring states to begin fighting against the Houthis.

These movements took a different character in each state, reflecting local conditions, the historical development of local civic organizing capacity, and the varying levels of political skill, legitimacy, and resources possessed by the ruling elites. In general, the wealthy oil-exporting passed through the seasons of political passion without change. The monarchies lacking oil revenues to placate the grievances of the masses endured these conflicts by offering a small show of political opening, and then restrained application of coercive suppression.

In the final analysis, for the people of many states, this protest cycle brought only calamity. In Egypt, the replacement of elites, from the June 24, 2012, election of Mohammad Morsi as president of Egypt to his overthrow in a military coup after the Tamarod rebellion of 2013, has left the people in worse conditions than when protests began. Only in Tunisia have the political parties demonstrated political maturity and willingness to compromise. They have created a credible constitution and new political institutions, while not yet making progress on the economic grievances of the population. However, these 2011 protests have established the political agency of the people to express their grievances. Their example continues to inspire collective action, as seen in the 2019 protests in Algeria, Jordan, and Sudan.

Jonathan K. Zartman

See also: Authoritarianism; Civil Wars; Corruption; February 17th Revolution; February 20 Movement; Jasmine Revolution; Jordanian Protests; Oman Protests; Pearl Roundabout Protests; Regime Change Cascades; Saudi Arabian Protests; Social Media; Syrian Civil War; Tahrir Square Protest; Yemen Civil War; Yemen Uprising

Further Reading

Al-Sumait, Fahed, Nele Lenze, and Michael C. Hudson, eds. *The Arab Uprisings: Catalysts, Dynamics, and Trajectories.* Boulder, CO: Rowman & Littlefield, 2015.

Khatib, Lina, and Ellen Lust, eds. *Taking It to the Streets: The Transformation of Arab Activism.* Baltimore: Johns Hopkins University Press, 2014.

Zartman, I. William, ed. *Arab Spring: Negotiating in the Shadow of the Intifadat.* Athens: University of Georgia Press, 2015.

Armed Islamic Group (GIA)

A terrorist organization dedicated to the overthrow of the Algerian government. In 1992, after the Algerian military arrested large numbers of the Islamic Salvation Front (FIS) members and politicians, militants formed the Armed Islamic Movement (MIA), which sought to engage the government in negotiations. In contrast, a diverse collection of groups dedicated to combat, including many veterans of the war in Afghanistan, formed the Armed Islamic Group (GIA, from the French Groupe Islamique Armé). The GIA conducted a series of assassinations and attacks on journalists and intellectuals and even attacked other Islamist groups, such as the leaders of the FIS and MIA. The GIA rejected any compromise with any group or individual that did not subscribe to its exclusive Salafist ideology. At its height, the GIA attracted hundreds of new members each month and became a major force in the Algerian conflict (1991–2002). However, the Algerian government proved quite adept at capturing or killing the leaders of the GIA, which limited its effectiveness. The continued leadership changes led both to ideological splits and to even greater radicalization.

A number of massacres of civilians, including whole villages, for which observers could not attribute the guilt, created a severe war fatigue and discredited both the militant Islamist groups and the government. The high levels of total violence caused most of the civilian population to turn against the GIA. Large numbers of militants began to desert the GIA, due to the indiscriminate nature of attacks. For the same reason, a commander, Hassan Hattab, broke away from the GIA in 1998 to form the Salafist Group for Preaching and Combat (GSPC). In 2002, Algerian security forces killed the last commander of the GIA in a battle, effectively ending the GIA's existence as a terror organization. The GSPC eventually became Al-Qaeda in the Islamic Maghreb (AQIM), with many former members of the GIA, as evidence of the continuing appeal of Islamist ideology as a means of political opposition in Algeria.

Paul J. Springer

See also: Algeria, The People's Democratic Republic of; Algerian Protests; Al-Qaeda in the Islamic Maghreb (AQIM); Islamism

Further Reading

Evans, Martin, and John Phillips. *Algeria: Anger of the Dispossessed.* New Haven, CT: Yale University Press, 2007.

Filiu, Jean Pierre. *From Deep State to Islamic State: The Arab Counter-Revolution and Its Jihadi Legacy.* London: Hurst, 2015.

Le Suer, James D. *Between Terror and Democracy: Algeria since 1989.* New York: Zed Books, 2010.

Armenians

A historic Christian community of the Middle East, predominantly belonging to the Armenian Apostolic Church. The Armenians claim as their heritage the Kingdom of Armenia (321 BCE–428 CE) and very early acceptance of Christianity as a people (after the Assyrians). They constitute the indigenous population of the area stretching from the Caucasus Mountains diagonally southwest to the Mediterranean Sea. The Arab conquests, as well as the invasions of the Turks and Mongols, reduced their number and territory greatly. They suffered as a people on the boundary between the competing Ottoman Empire and the Persian Safavids.

In 1605, the Safavid shah Abbas I forcibly relocated thousands of Armenian families, ultimately to Isfahan, turning it into a center for craftsmanship and international trade. Because of Ottoman persecution of Armenians, they demonstrated loyalty to the government of Iran. They participated in the Constitutional

Revolution, but they also helped the shah develop his military and promoted modernization. The Armenians negotiated to gain relief from the shah's restrictions on Armenian education. Armenians took part in the Iranian Revolution, and many died as volunteers in the Iranian military in the war with Iraq, but the hard social restrictions of the Islamic government have driven significant emigration.

In the late 1800s Ottoman Empire, Armenians developed their education systems and national consciousness, which led to the formation of independence movements, some of which were conducted as insurgency. In 1894, Turkish forces massacred tens of thousands as a warning. In 1915, a very systematic and thorough genocide killed hundreds of thousands, and tens of thousands were driven into the deserts of Syria. Survivors sought refuge in any Western country. A vibrant community of Armenians developed in Beirut with connections to Armenians in big cities abroad. In the Lebanese environment of violence in the 1970s, young men formed two different terrorist organizations, which conducted global campaigns of assassinations of Turkish officials. This movement died down when the Soviet Union fell, and Armenia became an independent republic and called Armenians to help build the new state. Passionate young men from the Armenian diaspora went to fight in Karabagh against Azerbaijan.

Armenians in Syria, especially in Aleppo, gained the respect of the state for their business skills and contributions to the economy, but during the civil war militant Islamists targeted the Armenians for their steady support for Assad. After the destruction of many factories, homes, and churches, two-thirds have fled. Armenians in Lebanon, Egypt, and elsewhere enjoy good social-political conditions with their own schools and social institutions. Times of political instability have caused many Armenians to emigrate to Western countries, but approximately one and a half million remain in Lebanon, Iran, Syria, Jordan, Cyprus, Turkey, Palestine, Egypt, and Iraq. The diaspora actively and consistently supports the remaining communities in the Middle East.

Emanuela Claudia Del Re

See also: Egypt, Arab Republic of; Iran, Islamic Republic of; Iraq, Republic of; Islamism; Jordan, Hashemite Kingdom of; Lebanese Republic; Minorities; Palestine; Syrian Arab Republic; Turkey, Republic of

Further Reading

Nalbantian, Tsolin. "Armenians in the Middle East: From Marginalization to the Everyday." In *Routledge Handbook of Minorities in the Middle East,* edited by Paul S. Rowe, 272–86. New York: Routledge, 2019.

Panossian, Razmik. *The Armenians: From Kings and Priests to Merchants and Commissars.* New York: Columbia University Press 2015.

Yaghobian, David N. *Ethnicity, Identity and the Development of Nationalism in Iran.* Syracuse, NY: Syracuse University Press, 2014.

Army of Islamic Salvation (AIS)

The armed wing of the Islamic Salvation Front (FIS) founded by Madani Mezrag and Ahmed Benaicha on July 18, 1994. They united several different FIS-supporting, anti-government guerrilla forces that had been fighting since the interruption of the electoral process in Algeria in 1992.

Unlike other Islamic armed groups, the Army of Islamic Salvation (AIS) considered *jihad* as only one of several possible means to reestablish the electoral process, which would have led to establishing a proper Islamic state. As a consequence, it adopted a long-term, guerrilla strategy, mainly against the Algerian state and its representatives, explicitly avoiding suicide bombings against masses of civilians. AIS could gain only limited popular support, mostly in the peripheral regions and among the religious middle class.

In 1995, AIS declared its support for a negotiated political solution to the conflict with the government. Between 1995 and 1996 it directly attacked the GIA. After subsequent negotiations with the Algerian authorities, in 1997 the AIS unilaterally declared a cease-fire. Mezrag declared AIS dissolved on October 1, 1997, and both Mezrag and Benaicha have offered support to the government in the fight against different Islamic armed groups. Former AIS combatants obtained amnesty in 2000, within President Bouteflika's national reconciliation policies. However, the government arrested some former AIS militants in 2013, on charges that they recruited Algerians to fight under the banner of Jabhat al-Nusra in Syria and established ties with jihadist groups in Libya and Tunisia.

Valentina Fedele

See also: Algeria, The People's Democratic Republic of; Bouteflika, Abdelaziz; Islamic Salvation Front (FIS); Syrian Civil War

Further Reading

Hafez, Mohammed M. "Armed Islamic Movements and Political Violence in Algeria." *The Middle East Journal* 54, no. 4 (2000): 572–91.

Willis, Michael J. *The Islamist Challenge in Algeria: A Political History.* New York: New York University Press, 1997.

Ashrawi, Hanan

A prominent Palestinian woman who has earned high praise for her work as a human rights activist, legislator, and scholar. Hanan Mikha'il Ashrawi, born in Mandatory Palestine in 1946 to a Protestant Christian Palestinian family, attended the Ramallah Friends Girls School and earned her bachelor's and master's degrees at American University of Beirut, graduating in 1968. Ashrawi obtained her doctorate in medieval and comparative literature from the University of Virginia in 1971.

After her return to Palestine, Ashrawi took an academic position at Birzeit University. Educated in the American canon and the eminent writers of American English, Hanan Ashrawi served as an eloquent and internationally recognized spokesperson during the first Intifada, and during the Madrid Peace Process as the official spokesperson of the Palestinian delegation. She succeeded in raising global awareness of Palestinian rights and the Palestinian cause. Since the establishment of the Palestinian National Authority, Hanan Ashrawi has contributed as a human rights activist by leading the Preparatory Committee of the Palestinian

Independent Commission for Citizen's Rights between 1993 and 1995. In 1998, she resigned from the Palestinian government in protest against corruption. As a civil society activist, she established the Palestinian Initiative for the Promotion of Global Dialogue and Democracy (MIFTAH), which she continues to direct. She has held various political positions, including as minister of education for Palestine, and has served on the Palestinian Legislative Council. For her distinguished role as a politician and civil society activist, Hanan Ashrawi continues to receive worldwide awards.

Philipp O. Amour

See also: Corruption; Democracy Deficit; Intifadas (I, II, and Knife); Israel; Middle East Road Map; Palestine; Palestinian Liberation Organization; Women's Leadership in Protests

Further Reading

Ashrawi, Hanan. *This Side of Peace.* New York: Touchstone, 1996.

Ashrawi, Hanan. "Concept, Context and Process in Peacemaking: The Palestinian-Israeli Experience." Joan B. Kroc Distinguished Lecture Series, University of San Diego, November 4, 2004.

Authoritarianism

A political ideology justifying the concentration of power and authority in a leader or small set of ruling elites without any formal, legal means to hold them accountable for their behavior. This ideology tends to prevail under conditions of warfare, when insecurity drives the need for collective defense of society. It finds support in societies emphasizing the cultural values of collective action, hierarchy, and risk aversion. It inhibits individual freedom and egalitarian social organization. While stability in any society necessarily requires constraining individual freedom of action for the collective good, under the extreme forms of authoritarianism, the rulers demand submission even from the majority community.

The political history of the Middle East offers many examples of diverse forms of authoritarianism, whether monarchy, military dictatorship, or ideological autocracy. The prevalence of government authority with little constraint from public accountability or responsibility in the region gained the label "democracy deficit." Military coups epitomize the authoritarian seizure of power. Therefore, authoritarian regimes engage in a variety of practices called coup-proofing: dividing the security forces into multiple competing forces; keeping the military removed from the capital and poorly trained and equipped; and entrusting internal security only to special units connected to the ruler by family, religion, ideology, and region of origin. Authoritarians fear mass mobilization and, therefore, constrain civil society and channels of mass communication. They commonly promote a monolithic ideology, whether based on religion, nationalism, or economic ideas; and in the name of the general will, they persecute minorities and dissidents. Authoritarian leaders sustain the loyalty of the first and second circle of their subordinates by distributing material rewards and claim to serve as a father figure to their people, a practice called clientelism or patrimonial rule. When the government can monopolize the export of one or two natural resources and distribute revenues (called economic rents) to the population, this practice, called rentier politics, supports authoritarian rule.

Gowhar Quadir Wani

See also: Ba'athism; Clientelism (Patrimonialism); Democracy Deficit; Grievance Model; Military Coups; Rentier State Politics

Further Reading

Bellin, Eva. "Reconsidering the Robustness of Authoritarianism in the Middle East: Lessons from the Arab Spring." *Comparative Politics* 44, no. 2 (January 2012): 127–49.

King, Stephen. "Sustaining Authoritarianism in the Middle East and North Africa." *Political Science Quarterly* 122, no. 3 (Fall 2007): 433–59.

Sassoon, Joseph. *Anatomy of Authoritarianism in the Arab Republics.* Cambridge, UK: Cambridge University Press, 2016.

B

Ba'athism

A popular Arab movement seeking to unify the Arab world into a single nation that would glorify Arab civilization, protect Arab identity and culture, end European colonialism, and reestablish the global influence of Arabs. The Ba'ath (Rebirth) Movement, initially known as Ba'ath al-Arabi al-Ishtiraki (the Arab Socialist Resurrection Movement), originated in the early 1940s in the writings of three Syrian teachers: Michel Aflaq (a Greek Orthodox Christian), Salah al-Din al-Bittar (a Sunni Muslim), and Zaki al-Arusi (an Alawite Shi'a). The movement advocated the redistribution of land from the wealthy to peasants, the nationalization of industries and banks, improvements of social services (especially schools and health clinics), and democracy. During the 1940s and 1950s, the Ba'athist ideology held great appeal for peasants, urban laborers, the intelligentsia, the middle class, and young army officers.

By the late 1950s, Ba'athism had spread from Syria to Iraq, Jordan, Lebanon, and Egypt. Egyptian president Gamal Abdel Nasser admired Ba'athism and adopted its foundational principles. During the decade after Egypt's victory in the 1956 Suez Crisis, his program, with its Ba'athist principles, became known as Nasserism, due to his immense charisma and popularity. However, Nasserism significantly declined after Israel defeated the Arab armies in the Six-Day War of June 1967. After Nasser's death in October 1970, his successor, President Muhammad Anwar al-Sadat, opposed socialism, encouraged capitalism, and improved relations with the United States and Israel.

The Ba'athist regimes of Syria's Hafiz al-Assad and Iraq's Saddam Hussein engaged in rivalry, criticism, and low-scale aggression, from 1970 until the U.S.-led coalition overthrew President Hussein in March 2003. In Syria, the minority Alawites dominated the majority Sunni population, while in Iraq, the Arab Sunni minority oppressed the majority Shi'a Arabs.

Because of the suffering Saddam Hussein imposed on the people of Iraq—the war with Iran, the invasion of Kuwait, the slaughter of the Kurds, and the oppression of the Shi'a majority—initially in the name of Ba'athist ideology, people rejected Ba'athism. The U.S.-led invasion and occupation of Iraq dismantled the Ba'athist government, purged the high-ranking Ba'athists, and promoted the ideological refutation of Ba'athism. After Hafiz al-Assad died in June 2000, his son Bashar continued his father's despotic rule. His efforts to suppress nonviolent protests with brutality and slaughter provoked a horrendous civil war—and strongly affected the Arab popular mentality. Therefore, under these two Ba'athist regimes, the people have suffered enormous political, socioeconomic, and spiritual impoverishment. Ba'athism has lost any ideological credibility or support in the Arab world.

Mir Zohair Husain

See also: Alawites (Nusayris); Arab Nationalism; Authoritarianism; Egypt, Arab Republic of; Iraq, Republic of; Jordan, Hashemite Kingdom of; Kurds; Lebanese Republic; Shi'a; Syrian Arab Republic

Further Reading

Baram, Amatzia. *Culture, History and Ideology in the Formation of Ba'athist Iraq, 1968–1989*. New York: Palgrave Macmillan, 1991.

Omar, Saleh. "Philosophical Origins of the Arab Ba'th Party: The Work of Zaki Al-Arsuzi." *Arab Studies Quarterly* 18, no. 2 (March 1996): 23–38.

Terrill, W. Andrew. *Lessons of the Iraqi De-Ba'athification Program for Iraq's Future and the Arab Revolutions*. Carlisle Barracks, PA: Strategic Studies Institute, May 2012.

Badawi, Raif

A Saudi Arabian liberal blogger and human rights activist, arrested in June 2012, whose case provoked strong international protests and, ultimately, conflict between Canada and the Kingdom of Saudi Arabia. Raif Badawi, born on January 13, 1984, in Khobar, Saudi Arabia, had lived in Riyadh and Jiddah before working in construction in Jizan, where he met Ensaf Haidar. Both Raif and Ensaf held conservative values and followed religious practices carefully. After significant struggle, they got permission to marry, but conflict with family, especially opposition from Raif's father, forced them to move to Jeddah. Raif managed a training institute that taught women English and computer skills.

Through Internet discussions, Raif discovered the classical literature on liberalism and became an advocate of it. He began the Free Saudi Liberals website, which hosted strong debates on religious and social issues. His eloquence and skill in argument brought him an international audience and reputation. His growing commitment to liberalism and disenchantment with the social control exercised by Islamic teachers caused conflict with the morality police of the Kingdom of Saudi Arabia. His father resented these developments and reacted by making YouTube videos falsely accusing Raif of leaving Islam. This further stimulated the morality police, resulting in repeated investigations, persecution, and court cases. He faced a variety of charges, and on May 7, 2014, was sentenced to 10 years in prison and 1,000 lashes and was fined approximately $267,000.

His wife, Ensaf, and their three children escaped to Canada, where she gained help from Amnesty International in publicizing the persecution of her husband. A video of him receiving the first 50 lashes in front of the Juffali Mosque in central Jeddah on January 9, 2015, received greater international attention because it corresponded in time with the massive protests in Paris, France, on January 11, 2015, against the attack on *Charlie Hebdo* by Islamist militants. In June 2016, the Saudi supreme court upheld the sentence for insulting Islam but postponed, as of June

2019, subsequent rounds of punishment on medical grounds. In July 2014, the Kingdom of Saudi Arabia sentenced Raif's lawyer to 15 years in jail, and in June 2018, the government arrested his sister. In August 2018, Canadian protests regarding these cases caused Saudi Arabia to break relations and freeze trade with Canada.

Jonathan K. Zartman

See also: Al-Sharif, Manal; Democracy Deficit; Modernization; Salafism; Saudi Arabia, Kingdom of

Further Reading

Badawi, Raif. *1000 Lashes: Because I Say What I Think.* Berkeley, CA: Greystone Books, 2015.

Hoffmann, Andrea C. *Raif Badawi: The Voice of Freedom: My Husband, Our Story.* London: Little, Brown Book Group, 2016.

Wehrey, Frederic. "Saudi Arabia's Anxious Autocrats." *Journal of Democracy* 26, no. 2 (April 2015): 71–85.

Bahrain, Kingdom of

A conservative Sunni monarchy ruling over an archipelago of 33 islands located in the Arabian Gulf, known since ancient times for pearl fisheries, now for oil. In 1783, the Al Khalifa family and extended tribe defeated the Persians and their Omani governor to begin their long history of rule over the islands. In 1816, the British began trade relations, which grew into a form of tutelage creating a bureaucratic state. Bahrain declared independence in 1971.

The population of Bahrain became Muslim during the Prophet's lifetime in 628 when a local ruler, controlling a broad region around Bahrain, accepted Islam. After the death of the Prophet, Sunnis and Shi'as struggled for dominance in eastern Arabia. In this conflict, people on the Awal Islands, known today as Bahrain, rallied behind Ali, the Prophet's son-in-law, together with other rulers of eastern Arabia. From that development, Shiism became firmly established in the region.

The Abbasid Caliphate initially controlled Bahrain, but in 899, a group of Shi'a Ismaili dissenters called the Qarmatians created an independent state in eastern Arabia. Under their rule, this branch of Ismailism became popular in Bahrain. After 976, the Abbasids conquered the Qarmatians. A series of local Sunni and Shi'a tribes controlled eastern Arabia until 1602, when the Safavids occupied Bahrain. They promoted Twelver Shi'a Islam, which replaced Ismailism. After a century of Safavid rule, the Omanis conquered Bahrain, initiating a long period of instability, as various powers competed for control of the region.

The Sunni Al Khalifa tribe arrived in 1783 from central Arabia. They consolidated their rule through a series of treaties with Britain. Other Sunni tribal families followed the Al Khalifa, changing the character of the local population. They pushed the settled population of Shi'a farmers from the east coast of Bahrain to northern and western areas, with the exception of the island of Sitra and its surroundings. Al Khalifa created a new social hierarchy ruling over the Sunni tribal families, over the predominantly Sunni merchants, then the technocrats, then

Shi'as who had migrated from Iran (called Ajam), and, lowest of all, the native rural Arab Shi'as (*Baharna*). Under the patronage of Great Britain, the rulers initiated a state-building process with bureaucratic reforms in the 1920s. They centralized the ruler's authority, and his family monopolized high governmental positions. The discovery of oil made the ruling family financially independent, and thus politically independent from the merchants and society.

Since the 1920s, Shi'a and Sunni leaders have launched parallel efforts to pressure the rulers to open a constitutional assembly. They gained their demands in 1971, after the British withdrew and the Al Khalifa family proclaimed independence. Amir Isa Bin Salman Bin Hamad Al Khalifa (1961–1999) convened the Constituent Assembly, composed of elected and appointed members. In 1973, the government proclaimed the constitution, stipulating that the legislative power would be vested in a unicameral parliament elected in general elections, while the amir would control the executive directly and by appointing the prime minister and the cabinet. The first parliamentary elections took place in 1973. However, after two years, the amir dissolved the parliament due to its opposition on issues of foreign policy, the U.S. naval base presence in Bahrain, and especially the State Security Law.

The Al Khalifa had become clients of the Kingdom of Saudi Arabia even as the British were withdrawing from the region, not only for the sake of Sunni religious solidarity, but more importantly because they needed protection from Iran's periodic claims on Bahrain. On November 30, 1971, the shah seized three islands from the United Arab Emirates, which raised the significance of Iran's threat. In the absence of Britain, the Al Khalifa strengthened ties with the United States. Bahrain became the headquarters of the U.S. Navy's Fifth Fleet, which became a challenge in the eyes of the postrevolutionary leadership of Iran. When the Ayatollah Khomeini took power in 1979 and sought to export the revolution through terrorism, this also raised fear of Iran. In 1981, the government of Bahrain accused a revolutionary Shi'a group of plotting a coup with support from Iran's Islamic Revolutionary Guard Corps.

The Shi'as of Bahrain follow a variety of religious teachers: some follow teachers that avoid politics in Iraq; but others follow the Ayatollah Khomeini. Bahraini Shi'as could not receive advanced religious training in Iraq during the rule of Saddam Hussein, which forced aspiring teachers to study in Iran. When Shi'as in Bahrain would hold pictures of Khomeini during their religious processions, the Sunnis questioned their loyalty to Bahrain. The government exploits this context to blame all domestic protest on Iranian subversion.

Bahraini authorities claimed that a Bahraini Hezbollah branch with headquarters in Tehran orchestrated the wave of unrest that followed in the years 1994–1996. In this protracted upheaval, known as the intifada, in the final years of the amir's rule, security forces faced sharp resistance when they tried to enter Shi'a villages. Meanwhile, urban Sunnis and Shi'as petitioned the amir for change on several occasions. The regime answered with more coercion, incarcerations, and deportations of opposition leaders, primarily from the Shi'a population.

In 2000, the new amir, Hamad bin Isa Al Khalifa (1999–present), initiated a plan called the National Action Charter. After the people supported it in a referendum, on December 16, 2002, the ruler proclaimed a new constitution that called Bahrain a kingdom. It established a new parliament but with a reduced role compared to that provided in the Constitution of 1973. This provoked a sense of betrayal that led Shi'a political associations to boycott the 2002 parliamentary elections. Therefore, Sunni candidates dominated the parliament. Realizing that they gained nothing from the boycott, Al Wefaq, the largest Shi'a political association, announced it would participate in the 2006 elections. The Shi'a opposition denounced the gerrymandered voting districts that preserve Sunnis' dominance. In 2006, a leaked report confirmed Shi'a accusations that governmental officials promoted the naturalization of Sunni citizens from abroad to dilute the Shi'a population.

The opposition competed in the 2006 election, but radical splinter groups formed that disagreed with participation because it would serve to legitimize the government. They began acts of rebellion and sabotage. In response, government oppression of the opposition increased. On the eve of the 2010 elections, arbitrary arrests of peaceful opposition leaders increased, together with reports of torture. Economic conditions deteriorated, and corruption became a crucial source of public anger.

The reports of protests in Tunisia and Egypt motivated youth groups to call for protests on the anniversary of the National Action Charter referendum, February 14, 2011. Both Sunni and Shi'a opposition groups occupied a landmark, called the Pearl Roundabout, initially calling for reform and national unity without regard for religious identity. The rapid mobilization of tens of thousands panicked the government into responding with violence and sectarian accusations and appeals. Although the government made some initial concessions—a limited cabinet reshuffle, release of political prisoners, and an offer of dialogue—opposition groups set conditions that the government considered too high. Skirmishes between security forces and protesters during the month-long sit-in resulted in several casualties on both sides. On March 15, 2011, the king announced a state of emergency, and Gulf Cooperation Council troops entered Bahrain. On March 17, security forces suppressed the protest and cleared the roundabout. A heavy crackdown ensued, yet demonstrations continued in suburban areas. Thousands of activists were arrested; a few were executed or chose exile. All 18 Al Wefaq ministers resigned from the parliament in protest.

When the protesters rejected the government's concessions and the offer of dialogue in March, the balance of influence shifted within the Al Khalifa family to the benefit of hardliners. They considered the protests an organized act of Iranian subversion—denying the legitimacy of the protesters' complaints or even their status as loyal citizens. On the opposition side, the sense of betrayal from the reduction in political rights under the Constitution of 2002, and the severity of oppression and discrimination, raised distrust of the government. After the expiration of the state of emergency in July, the government again offered dialogue, but not with the main parties of the opposition, and not regarding any of their complaints against the government. The lack of government sincerity, or willingness to reform, further drove opposition distrust.

The king ordered an Independent Commission of Inquiry to assess the events. On November 23, 2011, the commission returned a thorough and objective report critical of the government's use of force. After one year, outside parties assessed that the government had implemented very few of the recommendations, and none of the most important ones. The 2011 protests have fractured both the Shi'a and the Sunni opposition. The levels of popular grievances have risen, and sporadic unrest continues. Further crackdowns have radicalized some youth groups, which have begun using car bombs. Shi'a opposition associations boycotted the 2014 parliamentary elections, citing the lack of a political solution. Sunnis widely participated, with newcomers dominating the parliament, to the detriment of well-established political associations. In sum, the 2011 protests and the government response strengthened the divisions in Bahraini society: the mostly Shi'a opposition challenges the political system, while most of the Sunni part of society supports the current rule.

Magdalena Karolak

See also: Authoritarianism; Gulf Cooperation Council (GCC); National Action Charter; Pearl Roundabout Protests; Rajab, Nabeel; Saudi Arabia, Kingdom of; Sectarianism; Shi'a

Further Reading

Bassiouni, Mahmoud Cherif, et al. *Report of the Bahrain Independent Commission of Inquiry.* Manama, Bahrain: Independent Commission of Inquiry, December 10, 2011.

Louër, Laurence. *Transnational Shi'a Politics, Political and Religious Networks in the Gulf.* New York: Columbia University Press, 2008.

Matthiesen, Toby. *Sectarian Gulf: Bahrain, Saudi Arabia, and the Arab Spring That Wasn't.* Stanford, CA: Stanford University Press, 2013.

Nakhleh, Emile A. *Bahrain: Political Development in a Modernizing Society.* Lanham, MD: Lexington Books, 2011.

Ulrichsen, Kristen Coates. "Bahrain's Uprising: Regional Dimensions and International Consequences." *Stability: International Journal of Security and Development* 2, no. 1 (May 2013): 1–12.

Bahrain Protests (2011). See Pearl Roundabout Protests

Barzani, Masoud

An Iraqi Kurdish military leader and politician, born on August 16, 1946, in Mahabad, Iran. His public life and career derived from the work of his father, Mustafa, as a leading Kurdish nationalist who fought against the monarchy and later against Saddam Hussein. His family follows Sunni Islam and the Naqshbandi Sufi spiritual order, which has played a major role in nationalist movements in Iraq. Mustafa rebelled against the Iraqi monarchy as a foreign, imposed, Arab-occupation force kept in power by the British. The Kurds established the Kurdistan Democratic Party (KDP) in 1946 after the Iraqi Kurdish forces suffered defeat. They fled to Iran for refuge and established the independent Republic of Mahabad. That republic, supported by the Soviet Union, lasted for one year, and then Iran crushed it, with the help of the United States. In 1947, his father fled with 500 men into exile in the Soviet Union, while the rest of the family returned to Iraq, where the government had forced many Kurds into concentration camps. Masoud Barzani grew up in Iraq with his mother, mainly under house arrest.

After the July 14, 1958, military coup, the leader, Abd al-Qasim, invited Mustafa Barzani to return with his men. Qasim broke his promises to allow the Kurds regional autonomy and provoked tribal warfare among the Kurds, which the Barzani faction won. In 1961, the Kurds began a war with the Iraqi government, seeking autonomy. In May 1962, Masoud Barzani quit school to join the Peshmerga forces. In 1967, he helped start the Parastin Agency, the intelligence service of the Kurdistan Democratic Party. Although the Kurds defeated the Iraqi government, in 1968 the Ba'athists took power in a coup and renewed the conflict. After fighting stalled, Iraq agreed to negotiate. In 1970, Masoud Barzani helped negotiate the March 11, 1970, agreement with Iraqi vice president Saddam Hussein, which gave the Kurds some autonomy and representation in government. The Kurds began an intensive development program that lasted until 1974, while Iraq provoked renewed warfare with aggressive Arabization policies. Both Israel and Iran helped the Kurds in this war, which lasted until 1975, when Iran made an agreement with Iraq. This prevented the United States and Israel from helping the Kurds. The KDP leadership fled to Iran for refuge.

Masoud spent most of the time between 1976 and 1979 with his father, who was receiving medical treatment in the United States. In 1979, he went to Paris to meet with the office of Imam Khomeini, and after the Iranian Revolution he returned to Tehran to seek help against Iraq. After his father's death in 1979, the KDP elected him as their leader. Throughout the 1980s he commanded the Peshmerga forces in the struggle for Kurdish rights and autonomy. In 1983, Saddam Hussein ordered the death of the Barzan tribe: Iraqi forces killed 8,000 Barzanis, including 37 members of Masoud Barzani's family.

In 1987, Masoud Barzani rebuked the violence of the Kurdistan Workers' Party (PKK) of Turkey and allied himself with Turkish political forces. He became personally antagonistic to the PKK leader Abdullah Ocalan and helped Turkey combat the PKK. Although in 1975 Jalal Talabani split from the KDP to create the Patriotic Union of Kurdistan (PUK), the Kurds worked together in their struggle against the genocidal campaign of Saddam Hussein. The Kurdish region gained autonomy following the 1991 defeat of Iraq in Operation Desert Storm.

After initially sharing authority in the government, the KDP and PUK forces began battling for control in mid-1994. Popular support for each party primarily represented tribal and clan loyalties and the home areas of supporters. As Iran supported the PUK, Masoud Barzani invited the military intervention of Iraqi forces to fight the PUK. In August 1998, the United States brokered a settlement. On October 4, 2002, Barzani and Talabani apologized to the families of the victims of their internal war. After the 2003 U.S. invasion of Iraq, the two Kurdish factions cooperated in establishing the Kurdistan Regional Government (KRG), and Masoud Barzani became a member of the Iraqi Governing Council.

The KRG parliament elected Masoud Barzani president in 2005 and reelected him in 2009. In February 2011, the Italian Atlantic Committee gave him the Atlantic Award for protecting the Chaldo-Assyrian communities and promoting religious tolerance in the region. After his elected term expired in 2013, the parliament extended it by two years. During his administration the GDP per capita rose from $800 to $5,600. When the Iraqi military retreated from the Islamic State (Daesh) in 2014, Barzani ordered his Peshmerga to take Kirkuk, where Kurds competed against Arabs and Turkmen. Without further legislative sanction, Barzani served another two years.

In 2017, against the strong warnings of his international partners, and against the PUK, he pushed for an independence resolution. Although the Kurdish people voted for it overwhelmingly, the Iraqi government rejected the results and, with support from the PUK, invaded and conquered the Kirkuk region. Under heavy criticism for provoking such a political loss, he resigned from his position as president of the KRG. His nephew Nechirvan Barzani serves as KRG prime minister, and his son Masrour Barzani serves as intelligence chief.

Although he claims to not have personal financial investments in Kurdish oil or other industries, the Barzani family does control many businesses, fueling criticism about the growth of corruption and lack of financial transparency. The KRG fails to protect freedom of the press, as journalists who criticize the KRG and the Barzani family's many obscure financial connections often get arrested, kidnapped, or murdered.

Tom Dowling

See also: Ba'athism; Corruption; Iran, Islamic Republic of; Iraq, Republic of; Islamic State (Daesh); Israel; Kurds; Kurdistan Regional Government (KRG); Kurdistan Workers' Party (PKK); Patriotic Union of Kurdistan (PUK); Turkey, Republic of

Further Reading

Barzani, Massoud. *Mustafa Barzani and the Kurdish Liberation Movement (1931–1961).* Edited with a general introduction by Ahmed Farhadi. New York: Palgrave Macmillan, 2003.

Gunter, Michael M. "The KDP-PUK Conflict in Northern Iraq." *Middle East Journal* 50, no. 2 (Spring 1996): 224–41.

Phillips, David L. *The Kurdish Spring—A New Map of the Middle East.* New York: Routledge, 2015.

Qadir, Kamal Said. "Iraqi Kurdistan's Downward Spiral." *Middle East Quarterly* 14, no. 3 (Summer 2007): 19–26.

Basij

An Iranian volunteer paramilitary group with local operations centers in every district of the country, founded in May 1980 by Ayatollah Khomeini, to suppress his domestic opponents. *Basij* means mobilization. The Basij Resistance Force (BRF) constitutes one of the five main forces of the Islamic Revolutionary Guard Corps (IRGC), besides the air force, army, navy, and Quds Force. The Basij consists of unpaid volunteers, plus active members who receive pay and have extensive ideological and political indoctrination, and special members, who serve in the IRGC ground force in addition to their work for the Basij. Observers estimate its active personnel at 90,000, with a reserve strength of around 300,000.

The Basij has three main armed wings. The Ashura (male) and Al-Zahra (female) Brigades are the security and military branches and defend neighborhoods in case of emergencies. The force has multiple branches with specialized functions serving professionals, labor groups, students, and so forth. Regular military and paramilitary training camps prepare members to defend against invasion, or for mass mobilization to provide disaster relief and assistance. The members lack extensive military training and carry only light arms. They receive a strong degree of ideological training, due to their focus on suppressing civil unrest and enforcing Islamic cultural codes of behavior. The IRGC has organized Basij units in all sectors of Iranian society: university students, local tribes, factory workers, and so on. The Basij include youths and elderly pensioners.

The force suppressed social unrest (1992–1994) during President Rafsanjani's second term. In 1997, the Basij received increased ideological and political training to counter reformist thought during President Khatami's presidency. President Ahmadinejad encouraged Basij members to run for parliament, and many were elected. The Basij took a central role in the suppression of the Green Movement in 2009, but their actions caused backlash. The Student Day protests in December 2009 challenged the Basij, who mobilized several thousand members but still could not control protests at campuses in Tehran, Shiraz, and Tabriz. The failure of Basij units during these protests led the IRGC to implement riot-control training for the force, to strengthen their future capabilities in repressing political opposition.

Mark David Luce

See also: Ahmadinejad, Mahmoud; Green Movement; Islamic Revolutionary Guard Corps (IRGC); Khomeini, Ayatollah Sayyid Ruhollah Mūsavi; Rafsanjani, Ali Akbar Hashemi

Further Reading

Golkar, Saeid. *Captive Society: The Basij Militia and Social Control in Iran.* Washington, DC: Woodrow Wilson Center Press, 2015.

Golkar, Saeid. "The Rule of the Basij in Iranian Politics." In *Politics and Culture in Contemporary Iran,* edited by Abbas Milani and Larry Diamond, 115–40. Boulder, CO, and London: Lynne Rienner Publishers, 2015.

Safshekan, Roozbeh, and Farzan Sabet. "The Ayatollah's Praetorians: The Islamic Revolutionary Guard Corps and the 2009 Election Crisis." *Middle East Journal* 64, no. 4 (Autumn 2010): 543–58.

Battle of Sirte in 2011

The last major conflict of the February 17th Revolution in Sirte, Muammar Qaddafi's hometown on the coast of the Gulf of Sidra, which lasted over a month. From September 15 to October 20, 2011, the National Liberation Army fought against Qaddafi's loyalist Libyan Army. In late August 2011, a UN-sanctioned

NATO airstrike had destroyed Qaddafi's compound in Tripoli. Soon after, Tripoli fell to the rebels. Qaddafi fled to his hometown, Sirte, with several other high-ranking officials. Although the rebels did not know where Qaddafi had fled, they needed to capture the last two regime strongholds, Sirte and Bani Walid, to complete the rebellion. On October 17, 2011, rebels captured Bani Walid.

In mid-September 2011, the rebel forces surrounded Sirte and pushed the regime loyalists into a relatively small neighborhood. Many of Qaddafi's senior military figures lived in that area, so their forces resisted with great vigor, knowing the rebels would show them no mercy. The rebels tried to break through three times and failed. On the fourth engagement, on October 20, the rebels broke the defensive line, which forced Qaddafi and some supporters to flee in a truck convoy. NATO forces spotted and engaged the convoy with airstrikes, which injured Qaddafi. He fled on foot, and rebels later captured him while he was hiding in concrete pipes under a major roadway. They beat and executed him and then took his body to Misarata to display as a war trophy. They also captured, beat, and executed Qaddafi's son, Mutassim, and put his body on display in Misarata. These events ensured the end of that regime's brutality, thus ending the rebellion.

Steven A. Quillman

See also: February 17th Revolution; Libya, State of; Qaddafi, Muammar

Further Reading

Chivvis, Christopher S. *Toppling Qaddafi: Libya and the Limits of Liberal Intervention.* New York: Cambridge, 2014.

Pargeter, Alison. *Libya: The Rise and Fall of Qaddafi.* New Haven, CT: Yale University Press, 2012.

Battle of Sirte in 2016

A major, bloody battle for the control of Sirte between the forces of the Government of National Accord (GNA) and the Islamic State (Daesh). The battle took place from May 12 to December 6, 2016. In 2014, the conflict between the Operation Dignity coalition forces of the east versus the Libya Dawn forces from around Tripoli created a gap in security and governance in Sirte, which had suffered extensive damage in the battle of 2011 and did not receive help to recover afterward. The Islamic State began sending fighters to Libya in 2014, where they competed with the Ansar al-Sharia. Local resistance forces expelled the Islamic State fighters from their first stronghold in Derna, and they began infiltrating Sirte. By the spring of 2015, Daesh fighters defeated the coalition of Ansar al-Sharia, Libya Dawn, and the Libyan National Army that controlled the city and then began using it to launch raids on many other towns. International supporters of Libyan independence did not want to help only one militia to defeat Daesh but rather pushed hard to persuade Operation Dignity to join with the Libya Dawn forces to form a Government of National Accord, as a condition for military support. The Libyan Political Agreement of December 17, 2015, established the conditions for international support, although the Operation Dignity forces later backed out.

On May 5 and 6, 2016, Daesh fighters attacked the Misratan Military Council with suicide bombers, which provoked a counterattack in the name of the GNA, an operation called "Al-Bunyan Al-Marsoos" (Solid Structure-BM) in mid-May 2016. Between May and July 2016, suicide bombers, booby traps, and heavy sniper fire prevented BM forces from achieving meaningful gains in Sirte. During this period, the Libyan Navy helped secure Sirte's coast, thus blocking Daesh fighters from escaping by sea. On July 25, 2016, the BM forces asked the Presidential Council to call for U.S. airstrikes. On August 1, in response to a request by Prime Minister Fayez al-Serraj, AFRICOM launched Operation Odyssey Lightning with airstrikes by U.S. Air Force and Marine Corps forces targeting Daesh fighters and their heavy equipment. Air strikes continued off and on from August until December 2016, giving priority to avoiding civilian casualties. AFRICOM reported that U.S. forces conducted 495 precision airstrikes during this period, in addition to the airstrikes and intense artillery shelling by the GNA.

During the remaining three months (September–December 2016), the GNA fought a slow and bloody offensive to retake the last remaining Daesh-held areas in Sirte. Daesh forces used the civilians as human shields, as well as booby traps and mines, which delayed the advancing GNA forces. By December 2016, Daesh fighters controlled only an area with 50 buildings. Several women pretending to surrender blew themselves up to kill and wound GNA forces. On December 6, 2016, the GNA forces completed their capture of Sirte after heavy fighting against the last Daesh fighters, who surrendered at night.

Steven A. Quillman

See also: Ansar al-Sharia in Libya; Battle of Sirte in 2011; Islamic State (Daesh); Libya, State of; Libyan Civil War; Libya Dawn Coalition

Further Reading

Chivvis, Christopher S. "Countering the Islamic State in Libya." *Survival* 58, no. 4 (August–September 2016): 113–30.

Pack, Jason, Rhiannon Smith, and Karim Mezran. *The Origins and Evolution of ISIS in Libya*. Washington, DC: Atlantic Council, June 2017.

Belhaj, Abdul Hakim

A Libyan, former Islamist fighter, and rebel commander, who became a politician and leader of Libya's al-Watan Party. Born in Tripoli in 1966, Belhaj developed a passion for Islamism in opposition to the regime of Muammar Qaddafi. By the time he entered adulthood, he sought to overthrow Qaddafi. Having been driven from the country, Belhaj joined the anti-Soviet jihadi movement in Afghanistan in 1988. He eventually returned to Libya in 1992, where he and others applied the mujahideen model from Afghanistan in founding the Libyan Islamic Fighting Group (LIFG). For much of the 1990s, he and the LIFG waged an insurgency campaign against the Qaddafi regime until Belhaj was forced to flee Libya again.

Following the September 11 attacks, American intelligence agents arrested Belhaj in 2001 and returned him to Libya, where he was subsequently imprisoned for seven years. In 2010, the Libyan government released Belhaj, due to his participation in a deradicalization initiative headed by Qaddafi's son, Saif al-Islam Qaddafi. Belhaj, with five other members of LIFG, wrote a 411-page book, published in 2009, disavowing terrorism. After civil war engulfed the country in March 2011, LIFG changed its name to Libyan Islamic Movement for Change and placed its several hundred members under the command of the National Transition Council (NTC). Belhaj became the commander of the rebel Tripoli Brigade, and on August 20, he led the assault on Qaddafi's compound. Ultimately, he rose to lead the Tripoli Military Council, which ruled the city following the defeat of government forces.

Since the conclusion of the civil war, Belhaj has been a prominent member of Libya's newly founded al-Watan (Homeland) Party, a nationalist-Islamist party supported by the cleric Ali al-Sallabi. His party won only two seats in the July 2012 General National Congress elections, and Libyans criticized him for taking support from Qatar outside of NTC control. He has faced accusations from rivals doubting the sincerity of his turn from terrorism and his willingness to share power with secular forces, even as he complains that secularists exclude Islamists from sharing power. In 2014, Belhaj and other former LIFG members backed Libya Dawn, a collection of Islamist militias that briefly seized control of Tripoli and proclaimed their own government. Saudi Arabia, Egypt, and the United Arab Emirates have placed him on a terrorist list due to the support he received from Qatar.

Sean Braniff

See also: Islamism; Libyan Civil War; Libya Dawn Coalition; Libya, State of; National Transition Council; Qaddafi, Muammar; Qatar

Further Reading

Chivvis, Christopher S., and Jeffrey Martini. *Libya after Qaddafi: Lessons and Implications for the Future.* Santa Monica, CA: RAND, 2014.

Serafimov, Alex. "Who Drove the Libyan Uprising?" *Interstate—Journal of International Affairs* 2011, no. 2 (2012): 1–2.

Belmokhtar, Mokhtar

An elusive, entrepreneurial leader of militant Salafi groups in the trans-Sahara region, born in Ghardaia, Algeria, in 1972. After fighting with the Taliban in Afghanistan for 18 months, after the Soviets had left, Mokhtar Belmokhtar returned to Algeria in 1993 to fight against the government. He established a militia as part of the Armed Islamic Group (GIA), which transitioned in 2006 to become Al-Qaeda in the Islamic Maghreb (AQIM). Mokhtar commanded one of two AQIM southern brigades, responsible for generating millions in dollars by kidnapping Westerners for ransom. From providing protection for smugglers, he built a successful smuggling business based on his knowledge of desert routes and connections to Arab, Berber, and nomadic Tuareg tribal groups, cemented with marriages to four women.

His feuds with other AQIM leaders, and his reputation for independent and entrepreneurial activities, brought him disfavor with the local supervising council of AQIM, as seen in a December 2012 letter of reprimand. In January 2013, to protest Algerian support for the French-led intervention in Mali, he organized the high-profile attack on a natural gas plant at In Amenas, Algeria, killing 37 workers. He claimed credit in the name of a group he called "Those Who Sign in Blood," while also claiming allegiance to Al-Qaeda Central (AQ). He then merged with the Mali-based group "Movement for Unity and Jihad in West Africa" to create Al-Mourabitoun ("the Sentinels"), a group he may still be leading, which remains loyal to AQ. These organizational changes represent adaptation to Algerian counterterrorism activity and French military support for the government of Mali. Terrorist groups in response have increased the transnational character of their operations, especially in exploiting instability in Libya.

Scott Edmondson

See also: Algeria, The People's Democratic Republic of; Al-Qaeda Central; Al-Qaeda in the Islamic Maghreb (AQIM); Armed Islamic Group (GIA); Islamism; Salafism

Further Reading

Boeke, Sergei. "Mokhtar Belmokhtar: A Loose Cannon?" The Hague: International Center for Counter-Terrorism, December 3, 2013.

Fowler, Robert R. *A Season in Hell: My 130 Days in the Sahara with Al Qaeda.* Toronto: HarperCollins, 2011.

Wojtanik, Andrew. "Mokhtar Belmokhtar: One-Eyed Firebrand of North Africa and the Sahel." West Point, NY: Combating Terrorism Center, 2015.

Ben Ali, Zine al-Abidine

A Tunisian military officer and politician, who served as president for 24 years, born on September 3, 1936, to a modest family in the city of Sousse. Ben Ali began his career in the Tunisian Army with training at France's St. Cyr Military Academy, then Senior Intelligence School in Maryland, and antiaircraft school in Texas. Returning to Tunisia in 1964, Ben Ali created the department of military security, which he then led for a decade. After short tours as a military attaché in Morocco and Spain, he became director of National Security, serving 1977–1980. A variety of senior positions followed, including ambassador to Poland, then interior minister in 1986 under President Bourguiba. In 1987, senior government leaders declared Bourguiba mentally unfit to govern, removed him from power, and replaced him with Ben Ali—a move called "the medical coup d'état."

Initially, his administration seemed to offer a remarkable liberalization, releasing thousands of political prisoners and increasing political institutions and legal protections. Ben Ali ran unopposed in his first two presidential elections. Other parties were allowed to run in subsequent elections, but Ben Ali continued to win more than 90 percent of the vote. While credited with initially successful economic management and progress on some social issues, Ben Ali became increasingly repressive and restricted freedoms of speech, assembly, and the press. Eventually, his government changed the constitution to allow him to run for a fifth term. He, his extended family, and his wife's family engaged in conspicuous consumption combined with thuggish property theft, which generated significant discussion and awareness while most Tunisians struggled just to survive. A 2014

World Bank study later confirmed the extent of the family's theft of Tunisia's wealth. When protests began in 2010, Ben Ali initially adopted a tough approach and moderated only after the revolution had engaged all sectors of society. Ben Ali and his family fled Tunisia to take refuge in Saudi Arabia under strict conditions.

Tom Dowling

See also: Authoritarianism; Bouazizi, Tarek al-Tayeb Mohamed; Corruption; Democracy Deficit; Demographics (Youth Bulge); Grievance Model; Jasmine Revolution; Military Coups; Saudi Arabia, Kingdom of; Tunisia, Republic of

Further Reading

Brooks, Risa. "Abandoned at the Palace: Why the Tunisian Military Defected from the Ben Ali Regime in January 2011." *Journal of Strategic Studies* 36, no. 2 (2013): 205–20.

Cavatorta, Francesco, and Rikke Hostrup Haugbølle. "The End of Authoritarian Rule and the Mythology of Tunisia under Ben Ali." *Mediterranean Politics* 17, no. 2 (2012): 179–95.

Murphy, Emma C. "Ten Years On—Ben Ali's Tunisia." *Mediterranean Politics* 2, no. 3 (1997): 114–22.

Schraeder, Peter J., and Hamadi Rediss. "The Upheavals in Egypt and Tunisia: Ben Ali's Fall." *Journal of Democracy* 22, no. 3 (July 2011): 5–19.

Benghazi Attack

Premeditated assaults on a U.S. diplomatic compound and a nearby Central Intelligence Agency (CIA) building in Benghazi, Libya, in September 2012, which killed the U.S. ambassador, two U.S. contractors, and a State Department employee. Overnight on September 11, 2012, large numbers of armed men attacked the consulate and set fire to its main building, in which key personnel took shelter during the attack. U.S. personnel responded from a nearby CIA annex, which subsequently came under mortar attack as well. Thirty Americans escaped from the compounds during the attacks.

The United States maintained a diplomatic presence in Benghazi, Libya's second biggest city, to promote postconflict reconstruction and development. The nearby CIA annex was reportedly assigned a surveillance mission targeting al-Qaeda affiliates, although some alleged that U.S. personnel also arranged the covert shipment of surplus arms from Libya to arm the Free Syrian Army fighting against Bashar al-Assad's regime in Syria.

Increasing violence prompted Britain to withdraw its diplomatic station in mid-2012. In the weeks preceding the attack, the U.S. ambassador repeatedly requested security improvements at the Benghazi facilities, which the State Department failed to provide. Following the attacks, President Barack Obama claimed the attack represented local displeasure, as portrayed in a virtually unknown, amateurish, anti-Islamic video that had appeared online. Within Libya, people protested against the armed militias' continuing violence. In the United States, investigations stalled amid political polarization.

Nicholas Michael Sambaluk

See also: Al-Qaeda Central; Free Syrian Army; Haftar, Khalifa Belqasim; Islamism; Libya, State of; Libyan Civil War

Further Reading

Burton, Fred, and Samuel Katz. *Under Fire: The Untold Story of the Attack in Benghazi.* New York: St. Martin's Press, 2013.

Select Committee on the Events Surrounding the 2012 Terrorist Attack in Benghazi. *The Benghazi Committee Report.* Washington, DC: CreateSpace, 2016.

Zuckoff, Mitchell. *13 Hours: The Inside Account of What Really Happened in Benghazi.* Boston: Twelve, 2014.

Benkirane, Abdelilah

Prime minister of Morocco from November 2011 to March 2017, head of the Justice and Development Party, editor of several publications such as *Al-Islah, Arraya,* and *Al-Tajdeed,* and member of parliament four times. Abdelilah Benkirane, born in Rabat on April 2, 1954, earned a bachelor's degree in physics, and taught at the teacher training school in Rabat. From his parents he gained interest in Sufism and Islamism. From 1976 to 1981, he participated in several different Islamic political societies, while also engaged in leftist political activism. As an eloquent negotiator in Arabic and French, he persuaded diverse Islamist groups to cooperate and form a broad Islamist movement—under various names—in the struggle to gain legal recognition, ultimately the Movement for Unification and Reform. His understanding of the political possibility for promoting Islamic values led him to join his movement with a relatively minor, but well-established political party, which became the Justice and Development Party (JDP) modeled after the Turkish party of the same name.

In July 2008, the JDP elected him as leader, replacing Saadeddine Othmani. Benkirane became prime minister on November 29, 2011. His government established ambitious economic growth and employment targets and worked actively to improve Morocco's ties with the European Union, its chief trade partner, as well as the six-member Gulf Cooperation Council. In 2017, Benkirane could not form a functioning government, in spite of intensive political negotiations. On March 15, 2017, after five months of postelection deadlock, King Mohammed VI ousted Benkirane as prime minister of Morocco and chose Saadeddine Othmani from the same party as prime minister. On April 12, 2017, Benkirane resigned from the Moroccan Parliament.

Amir Muhammad Esmaeili

See also: Development; Gulf Cooperation Council (GCC); Islamism; Justice and Development Party (Morocco); Mohammed VI, King of Morocco; Morocco, Kingdom of; Sufism

Further Reading

Bahaji, Kassem. "Moroccan Islamists: Integration, Confrontation, and Ordinary Muslims." *Middle East Review of International Affairs* 15, no. 1 (March 2011): 39–51.

El Hachimi, Mohamed. "Democratisation as a Learning Process: The Case of Morocco." *The Journal of North African Studies* 20, no. 5 (2015): 754–69.

Szmolka, Inmaculada. "Inter- and Intra-Party Relations in the Formation of the Benkirane Coalition Governments in Morocco." *The Journal of North African Studies* 20, no. 4 (2015): 654–74.

Berbers (Imazighen)

The indigenous people of North Africa, who speak variants of a single language, called Tamazight, belonging to the Afroasiatic language family. Activists consider the term *Berber* as pejorative and instead use *Amazigh* in the singular (and in the adjective form), which means "free man," and *Imazighen* in the plural. In total, approximately 20 million people live in Tamazgha, the name that activists use to describe the territory in most North African countries inhabited by the Imazighen, which extends from the Siwa Oasis in Egypt to the Atlantic Ocean, encompassing a great part of the Sahel and the Canary Islands. In the absence of official statistics, academics estimate that they represent between 30 and 40 percent of the population in Morocco, 20 and 30 percent in Algeria, 8 and 10 percent in Libya, around 1 percent in Tunisia, and around 20,000 people in the Egyptian Siwa Oasis.

The situation of the Amazigh population varies from one country to another. In Algeria and Morocco, a strong and consolidated activist movement has achieved constitutional recognition for Tamazight as an official language. Amazigh activism has flourished in Libya and Tunisia after the 2011 popular protests.

Ángela Suárez-Collado

See also: Algeria, The People's Democratic Republic of; Libya, State of; Morocco, Kingdom of; Tunisia, Republic of

Further Reading
Maddy-Weitzman, Bruce. *The Berber Identity Movement and the Challenge to North African States.* Austin: University of Texas Press, 2011.

Miller, Susan, and Katherine Hoffman, eds. *Berbers and Others: Beyond Tribe and Nation in the Maghrib.* Bloomington: Indiana University Press, 2010.

Black October Riots (1988)

A violent social upheaval in Algeria, which demonstrated the breakdown of rentier politics and led to a short period of dramatic political liberalization. A sharp fall in oil prices in 1986 led to a deteriorating economy, a rising unemployment rate, and rising prices for basic necessities. The people who prospered under the economic liberalizations introduced by President Chadli Bendjedid had begun to flaunt their prosperity, raising public consciousness about the magnitude of corruption. Meanwhile, austerity measures, such as dropping subsidies for basic food items, imposed in 1986 became fully effective in 1988. In September 1988, labor movements began organizing industrial strikes. On September 19, 1988, the president broadcast a speech calling on Algerians to work harder to reach economic goals. On the evening of October 4, gangs of teenagers in the Bab-El-Oued neighborhood of Algiers began to riot—burning cars, buses, state-owned shops, and offices of the ruling party, the Front de Libération Nationale (FLN). Rioting spread to all the major urban centers. On October 6, the government declared a state of siege, placing civil and administrative authorities under military command, and sent troops to all the major towns. The government appointed General Khaled Nezzar as head of military command, in charge of restoring order. On October 7, Abassi Madani and another veteran Islamist activist organized a peaceful protest of 6,000 supporters in central Algiers, but the military opened fire and killed approximately 50 unarmed people. On October 10, a younger, fiery preacher named Ali Belhadj organized a larger demonstration of 20,000 in central Algiers, despite the objections of Madani and older, conservative teachers. General Nezzar's men killed another 30 protesters. Over the 10-day period of rioting, the official figures reported between 169 and 176 people killed; other reports counted around 500 dead. Hundreds of young people were arrested and tortured.

The government negotiated with the Islamists to ask their help in reducing the violence of the protests, which made it appear as though they were the prime movers in events. This diminished the greater role of labor, youth, and women's rights protesters. On October 10, President Bendjedid announced his intention to hold a referendum on a new constitution that would give greater power to the parliament and create new freedoms. That constitution, adopted in February 1989, ended the single-party system and permitted political associations.

Saphia Arezki

See also: Authoritarianism; Corruption; Islamism; Nezzar, Khaled; Rentier State Politics

Further Reading
Le Sueur, James D. *Between Terror and Democracy: Algeria since 1989.* New York: Zed Books, 2010.
Roberts, Hugh. *The Battlefield Algeria, 1988–2002: Studies in a Broken Polity.* London: Verso, 2003.

Black September

A repression campaign by the Jordanian government against Palestinian expatriates September 17–25, 1970. After Israel inflicted a crushing defeat on the Arab states in the 1967 Six-Day War, around 300,000 Palestinian refugees flooded into Jordan. Several guerilla groups, including al-Fatah, the Popular Front for the Liberation of Palestine (PFLP), the Democratic Front for the Liberation of Palestine (DFLP), and others, gained a significant following within the refugee community. Many of these groups, referred to as *fedayeen* ("freedom fighters"), operated under the umbrella of the Palestine Liberation Organization (PLO), led by al-Fatah leader Yasser Arafat. These groups began to challenge the government of King Hussein bin Talal, who sought to maintain law and order. The guerillas, however, repeatedly disregarded Jordanian authority: rejecting local government control, conducting cross-border raids into Israel, which provoked military reprisals, and even attempting to assassinate the king several times.

When the PFLP hijacked four civilian airliners and landed three of them in Jordanian territory, tensions boiled over. The hijackers threatened harm to the hostages and the planes. King Hussein took this as a rejection of his authority. On

September 17, the Jordan Armed Forces (JAF) attacked Palestinian refugees without differentiating between civilians and guerillas. They bombarded refugee camps and chased the *fedayeen* across the country, until accepting a negotiated cease-fire on September 25. By that point, hundreds of guerillas and thousands of Palestinian civilians had died in the fighting. Despite this, the bloodshed continued into 1971, and the PLO leaders transferred their headquarters to Lebanon. During the following decade the PLO and its affiliates conducted a rising number of terrorist attacks in an effort to gain Arab world support for the Palestinian campaign to regain territories from which they had fled.

Benjamin V. Allison

See also: Fatah Party; Islamism; Israel; Jordan, Hashemite Kingdom of; Lebanese Republic; Palestine; Palestine Liberation Organization; Refugees

Further Reading

Cobban, Helena. *The Palestinian Liberation Organization: People, Power, and Politics.* Cambridge, UK: Cambridge University Press, 1984.

Sayigh, Yezid. *Armed Struggle and the Search for a State: The Palestinian National Movement, 1949–1993.* Oxford, UK: Oxford University Press, 1997.

Bouazizi, Tarek el-Tayeb Mohamed

A young street vendor in the provincial town of Sidi Bouzid, Tunisia, whose public suicide in protest of abusive police action sparked protests, which grew into a revolution to overthrow the government of Tunisia. Tarek el-Tayeb Mohamed Bouazizi (1984–2011) was forced to leave school to support his family before he could complete high school. His father had died of a heart attack when he was three, and his mother took work in the fields when she could get it. He sold fruits and vegetables from a pushcart, to earn the equivalent of five dollars a day to support his family with six siblings. However, he owed his suppliers $200.

Like all the other vendors, he suffered routine abuse from the police, who confiscated his goods and pressed for bribes, although Tunisia does not require a license to sell vegetables from a wheelbarrow. On the morning of December 17, 2010, a municipal police official confronted him, confiscated his scale, and dumped out his cart of vegetables. Bouazizi then went to the office of the local governor to protest and demand the return of his scales. The official refused to see him. He quickly returned with a can of lighter fluid and set himself on fire. Due to the severe burns over most of his body, the local clinic could not help him, so he was transferred to the larger city of Sfax, and then eventually to the capital, where the president did visit him in the hospital. He lingered in an intensive-care ward for 18 days, until dying on January 4, 2011.

After his initial action, hundreds of youths began protesting, to the extent of smashing cars and breaking shop windows, which police tried to suppress with tear gas. Another young man, Lahseen Naji, feeling the same despair, made a public protest of his suicide by electrocution, followed by another man also committing suicide. The powerful symbolism of Mohamed Bouazizi's death in protest against corruption, in the context of poverty and humiliation, gained power because so many people captured the events on video. Previously, protests through suicide that were not captured on video failed to catalyze a social movement. Protests initially spread as a result of outrage when people watched the videos, which were spread through social media. After the police killed Professor Hatem Baltahir in Douz, organized groups began moving to cities to attack government buildings.

Tom Dowling

See also: Authoritarianism; Corruption; Grievance Model; Jasmine Revolution; Social Media; Tunisia, Republic of

Further Reading

Angrist, Michele Penner. "Understanding the Success of Mass Civic Protest in Tunisia." *The Middle East Journal* 67, no. 4 (Autumn 2013): 547–64.

Ayeb, Habib. "Social and Political Geography of the Tunisian Revolution: The Alfa Grass Revolution." *Review of African Political Economy* 38, no. 129 (2011): 467–79.

Mabrouk, Mehdi. "A Revolution for Dignity and Freedom: Preliminary Observations on the Social and Cultural Background to the Tunisian Revolution." *The Journal of North African Studies* 16, no. 4 (December 2011): 625–35.

Bouteflika, Abdelaziz

Algerian politician and president of Algeria since 1999. Bouteflika was born on March 2, 1937, in Oudja, Morocco, into a family of Algerian immigrants. In 1956, he joined the armed wing of the Front de Libération National (FLN) to fight in the Algerian war for independence from France. After independence, he served in the cabinet of two presidents. In 1983, he was convicted of embezzling state funds from the accounts of the Algerian embassies but was given amnesty by President Bendjadid, and then he spent six years abroad. In 1989, the Algerian Army brought him back to serve in the Central Committee of the FLN. In 1999, as the military's candidate, Bouteflika became president, after an election with significant irregularities.

During his presidencies, he worked hard to regain international legitimacy, as well as bring internal peace. He promoted a legal amnesty program called "The Charter for Peace and National Reconciliation" of 2006. He engaged in bureaucratic struggles to overcome resistance from hardline advocates of a purely military solution to terrorism—known as "eradicators." Through the combination of military action, with persistent negotiations, and a second major amnesty program—the December 2009 Law on Civil Concord—his administration dramatically reduced the incidence of terrorist attacks. In the spring of 2001, excessive violence by the gendarmerie in the Kabila region provoked sharp protests by the Berber population, denouncing cultural, economic, and social exclusion. He stood for a third term in 2009 and was reelected, in spite of poor health and a mixed record. He promised reforms, and a deepening of democracy in the aftermath of the protests of 2010–2012, but apart from improving women's rights, the political changes further tightened the government's control over society and restricted political opportunity. He used General Ahmed Gaid Salah to bring the military security services (Département du Renseignement et de la Sécurité, the DRS) under civilian control, through restructuring and retirements. His administration continues to pursue massive infrastructure investments and tries to regain investor confidence and international support. After an enabling constitutional amendment, in spite of repeated, protracted hospitalizations in France, he ran for a fourth term and was reelected in 2014. The political opposition argues that the president's bad health disqualifies him from further leadership. When he announced that he would seek a fifth term, protests began on February 22, 2019, and under pressure from the army he resigned on April 2, 2019.

Valentina Fedele

See also: Algeria, The People's Democratic Republic of; Berbers (Imazighen); National Liberation Front (FLN); Salah, Ahmed Gaid

Further Reading

McDougall, James. *A History of Algeria*. Cambridge, UK: Cambridge University Press, 2017.

Mortimer, Robert. "State and Army in Algeria: The 'Bouteflika Effect.'" *The Journal of North African Studies* 11, no. 2 (June 2006): 155–71.

Tlemcani, Rachid. "Algeria under Bouteflika: Civil Strife and National Reconciliation." *Carnegie Papers* No. 7 (February 2008).

C

Cedar Revolution (2005)

A massive set of protests in Beirut, Lebanon, against Syrian military and political domination after the February 14, 2005, assassination of the Sunni billionaire businessman and politician Rafik Hariri. Throughout 2004, various groups had protested against the large occupation force of Syrian military soldiers and intelligence agents, even though Israel had withdrawn its forces in 2000. The September 2, 2004, UN Security Council Resolution 1559 called for the immediate withdrawal of Syrian troops and the disarming of all militias. Syrian president Bashar al-Assad coerced Prime Minister Rafik Hariri to allow the parliament to change the constitution and keep a Syrian agent in office as president of Lebanon. Under threats, Hariri submitted, but resigned on October 20, 2004. In opposition, a group of Christian political leaders formed a coalition called the Qornet Shahwan Gathering. Walid Jumblatt, the Druze leader and a good friend of Hariri, also strongly opposed Syria's domination. Fearful of the Christian/Druze/Sunni coalition that their aggression had provoked, Syria began a slander campaign against Hariri, who enjoyed enormous popularity for his charity work during the war and for the rebuilding of Beirut after the war.

When a massive car bomb killed Hariri and 21 others as their armored convoy passed by, the public shock and grief led to big demonstrations. Protesters blamed Syria, working through its large number of intelligence agents. Opposition groups looked to the 2003 Rose Revolution in Georgia and the 2004 Orange Revolution in Ukraine for inspiration, so they called their movement the Cedar Revolution. Hariri was close to French president Jacques Chirac and the Saudi Royal family and had good relations with many Arab leaders and credibility in the West for his moderate views and liberal economic policies, so these protests attracted global attention. Under this pressure, the prime minister resigned on live television, but the protesters demanded that the president also resign, and that the Syrians withdraw. In opposition, Hezbollah organized a rally on March 8 to thank Syria for its commitment to Lebanon and brought half a million people to that demonstration.

Those who opposed Syria protested on March 14 and attracted a crowd more than twice as large, more than a quarter of Lebanon's population. Their nonviolent, even festival atmosphere with flowers and sweets for the soldiers and friendly singing was broadcast globally on Arabic satellite television networks. Under strong international pressure, on April 26, 2005, Syria withdrew the last of its troops, and the United Nations launched an inquiry into the Hariri assassination. With a huge mobilization of local and international observers, in May 2005, the government allowed free parliamentary elections, which gave the opposition a majority. This event created political polarization, with a March 8 coalition of parties supporting Syria opposed by the March 14 coalition seeking national sovereignty and independence. A series of car-bomb assassinations of politicians critical of Syria followed over the next six months. With the help of pressure from Syria, the March 8 coalition held enough seats in parliament to block any action, creating a protracted political stalemate and forcing the March 14 coalition to make painful compromises for the government to operate even minimally in the face of severe economic and social problems.

Jonathan K. Zartman

See also: Druze; Hariri, Saad; Hezbollah; Jumblatt, Walid; Lebanese Republic; Maronites; Syrian Arab Republic

Further Reading

Arsan, Andrew. *Lebanon: A Country in Fragments*. London: Hurst and Co, 2018.

Kurtulus, Ersun N. "'The Cedar Revolution': Lebanese Independence and the Question of Collective Self-Determination." *British Journal of Middle Eastern Studies* 36, no. 2 (August 2009): 195–214.

Safa, Oussama. "Lebanon Springs Forward." *Journal of Democracy* 17, no. 1 (January 2006): 22–37.

Civil Wars

The highest level of violent intrastate political competition, usually representing the challenge by a nonstate party seeking: 1) the control of the territory, population, and resources of a country; or 2) independence for a region of the existing country; or 3) the creation of a different independent country (secession); or 4) joining with a neighboring country (irredentism).

Academics, such as J. David Singer in the Correlates of War Project, define a civil war as conflict within a state that results in 1,000 or more battle deaths per year. By this definition, 104 civil wars occurred between 1944 and 1997. In 2017, fourteen conflicts met this criterion. Most modern civil wars involve intervention by outside powers.

Scholars frequently use one or more of three theoretical perspectives, hereafter called "models," to explain civil wars: greed, grievances, and framing. Greed-based explanations emphasize that people fight because they think they can win. They hold fixed, unchanging interests in surviving and maximizing their personal wealth and power. They will adapt their identities to achieve their interests. This perspective emphasizes that all people calculate the risks, costs, and potential benefits of acting to gain material benefits. This perspective argues that people calculate their opportunity to rebel and seize economic benefits through pillaging, extortion of protection money, control of trade, and exploitation of labor. This includes explanations of conflict as a breakdown in bargaining behavior among important social actors.

The grievance model explains that people fight to overcome injustice, whether based on identity or broader social, economic, and political exclusion. The grievance model claims that people can change the way they define their interests over time, but they fight to protect and express their collective identity. Since people require institutions to protect their rights and provide services, the grievance model supports a liberal-institutional emphasis on the necessity for state-building to prevent civil war. This model argues that political inclusion and representation—democratization—can prevent and overcome grievances.

The framing model represents a synthesis between the greed and grievance models, while emphasizing the role of ideas, identity, symbols, social movements, and change. It argues that people fight for reasons of morality, justice, ideology, and religion, in ways constructed by the people who produce culture: teachers, journalists, artists, and activists. This model describes how activists and creative, ambitious ideological leaders exploit internal contradictions in the political ideology of a state, or conflicts between state ideology and the culture of the people. The framing model shows that cultural and ideological conflict precedes and motivates civil war. This model helps explain behavior that violates the propositions of the greed and grievance models, such as young, educated, middle-class men engaging in suicide terror attacks. It explains why countries with strong economies, strong leaders, strong external support, and relative tolerance of minorities may suffer a massive social revolution, while neighbors with less positive conditions struggle along for decades without civil conflict. In this perspective, competing incompatible narratives impede communication and trust, preventing political elites and civic leaders from bargaining to resolve their conflicts. This leads them to use violence to resolve the issues on which they cannot negotiate.

These three models do not independently explain every aspect of a conflict, or a civil war, but rather in combination they provide powerful explanations. A policy that relies on only one perspective to prevent civil war can fail. Not one of these perspectives alone can provide sufficient guidance to stop a civil conflict and build a durable peace. While approaches based on the greed model can lead to quick changes, the results will not be durable. Policies based on the framing model take more time but can lead to sustained stability.

Samuel S. Stanton, Jr., and Benjamin V. Allison

See also: Authoritarianism; Democratization; Framing Model; Greed Model; Grievance Model; Military Coups

Further Reading

Ahmad, Aisha. "Going Global: Islamist Competition in Contemporary Civil Wars." *Security Studies* 25, no. 2 (2016): 353–84.

Cederman, Lars-Erik, and Manuel Vogt. "Dynamics and Logic of Civil Wars." *Journal of Conflict Resolution* 61, no. 9 (2017): 1,992–2,016.

Fearon, James D., and David Laitin. "Ethnicity, Insurgency, and Civil War." *American Political Science Review* 97, no. 1 (February 2003): 75–90.

Hironaka, Ann. *Neverending Wars: The International Community, Weak States, and the Perpetuation of Civil War.* Cambridge, MA: Harvard University Press, 2005.

Clientelism (Patrimonialism)

A relationship with a patron with power, status, authority, and influence who provides benefits, such as material and political resources or protection, to a subordinate client in exchange for loyalty and labor. Although these relations develop in societies with many different cultural values, in every region of the globe, they reinforce cultural values of hierarchy. In addition to inequality of power and status, and the reciprocal exchange of benefits, they require face-to-face relationships and some degree of trust, because repayment may come at a much later date: each actor can thwart the goals of the other by short-run calculations of personal advantage. The relations can span generations, when sons inherit the patron or client position of their fathers. They can be very stable as long as the patron retains access to a reliable flow of resources. They become vulnerable when the patron becomes ill or close to losing legal status. In such cases, potential patrons compete for control of resources, sometimes to the point of civil war. As voluntary, informal relations, with no legal status, they prevail in conditions lacking the rule of law, giving them the taint of corruption (that is, the misuse of office for personal gain). In contrast, citizens in democracies hold a claim to individual, impartial benefits by law, and can hold the government accountable for deficiencies. In states with weak institutions, lacking democratic values, and especially under authoritarianism, people rely on personal connections to a patron to overcome bureaucratic bottlenecks. When political authorities distribute benefits based on personal relations—the patrimonial state—the people lack any capability to hold officials accountable. Therefore, corruption flourishes, creating grievances that motivate rebellion.

Clientelism as a system consists of rivalry between groups, each with members from different economic classes, occupations, and ethnic identities. Some patrons may be clients of more powerful patrons, in a hierarchy that constitutes a network of influence. International recognition as a state constitutes a huge pool of resources that supports large patronage networks. Therefore, in patrimonial states, politics consists of competition between patronage networks. While state elites seek to monopolize resources, to restrain the competition of their clients, when they fail, the competition of regional governors, rich businessmen, and charismatic religious leaders with large client networks of their own may escalate to the point of civil war.

Lindsay J. Benstead

See also: Authoritarianism; Corruption; Grievance Model; *Wasta*

Further Reading

Alamdari, Kazem. "The Power Structure of the Islamic Republic of Iran: Transition from Populism to Clientelism, and Militarization of the Government." *Third World Quarterly* 26, no. 8 (2005): 1,285–301.

Elvira, Laura Ruiz de, Christopher H. Schwarz, and Irene Weipert-Fenner, eds. *Clientelism and Patronage in the Middle East and North Africa: Networks of Dependency*. New York: Routledge, 2019.

Conflict, Theories of. *See* Civil Wars

Constitutional Drafting Assembly

A democratically elected body of Libyans holding the responsibility to design a constitution after the Libyan Revolution of 2011. On August 3, 2011, the National Transitional Council (NTC) issued an interim, provisional "Constitutional Declaration" to provide governing guidance until it could transfer authority to a legitimate, elected representative assembly, which could write a final constitution. The elections for the General National Congress (GNC), conducted in a spirit of enthusiasm, with strong turnout on July 7, 2012, initiated a phase of intensive social dialogue and education: civic associations prepared the people for their role as citizens who would need to approve any constitution. However, a number of armed militias exerted strong pressure on the GNC representatives, imposing their preferences on the constitution. In the context of kidnappings and assassinations, the GNC decided that instead of appointing the members of a commission to write it, they would delegate this task to a separate, elected Constitution Drafting Assembly (CDA).

Under pressure from militias from the eastern region of Cyrenaica, and from the south, the GNC decided on a commission of 60 members, 20 from each of the three major regions. Even though this violated the principle of population proportionality, it followed the pattern of the 60-member commission that prepared the constitution for independence in 1951. After this decision, but before the CDA elections, the GNC made three other decisions that provoked serious armed conflict: political exclusion of people associated with the Qaddafi regime; amnesty for crimes committed during the revolution; and criminalizing complaints about those crimes. The active combat that ensued inhibited voting. The Amazigh (Berber) population boycotted the February 2014 election for the CDA. Although successful constitution-writing requires an inclusive, participatory process, the conditions of civil war stopped all of the civic dialogue and education efforts.

In spite of insecure conditions, eventually 56 members met on April 21, 2014, in the far eastern town of Al-Bayda to negotiate. By that time Libya had devolved into a second civil war with two competing governments, but the CDA enjoyed widespread public support and worked in relative isolation. In August 2015, the representatives of the Tebu and Tuareg minorities began to boycott the negotiations. In January 2016, after the adoption of a new draft, 11 members from the western part of Libya started to boycott the proceedings. In February 2016, boycotting members filed suit in a local administrative court to get the chairman dismissed. This prompted the UN Support Mission in Libya to begin actively supporting the negotiations.

In spite of violent protesters breaking into the meeting and beating some of the members, the CDA approved the draft constitution on July 29, 2017, with a vote of 43 out of 44 remaining members. Members held several dialogue sessions in a number of cities to introduce it. However, the House of Representatives has rejected the constitution, and refused to allow a referendum on it, because the current constitution draft excludes certain individuals from power in the government, including Khalifa Haftar. In December 2018, the police forces even prevented the assembly members from holding presentations on the constitution. The assembly appealed to the international community for help in breaking the political blockade and considered other political strategies to proceed.

Dusty Farned

See also: February 17th Revolution; General National Congress; Haftar, Khalifa Belqasim; Libyan Civil War; Libya, State of; National Transition Council

70   Coptic Orthodox Church

Further Reading

Cross, Ester, and Jason Sorens. "Arab Spring Constitution-Making: Polarization, Exclusion and Constraints." *Democratization* 23, no. 7 (2016): 1,292–312.

Geha, Carmen, and Frederic Volpi. "Constitutionalism and Political Order in Libya 2011–2014: Three Myths about the Past and a New Constitution." *The Journal of North African Studies* 21, no. 4 (2016): 687–706.

Van Lier, Felix-Anselm. "Constitution-Making as a Tool for State-Building? Insights from an Ethnographic Analysis of the Libyan Constitution-Making Process." *Working Paper* No. 192. Halle/Saale, Germany: Max Planck Institute for Social Anthropology, 2018.

Coptic Orthodox Church

The primary Christian church in Egypt, and the largest Christian group in the Middle East, comprising an estimated 6–10 percent of the Egyptian population, whose adherents reside largely in the upper Nile Valley and major urban areas. The name *Copt* originates from the Greek word for Egyptian, *aigyptos,* and the Arabic word *qibt*. Following a fifth-century doctrinal dispute, the Alexandrian Copts separated from the rest of Christendom. They preserved the Coptic language, in spite of the Arab conquests and centuries of Arabic cultural influence. Churches in Jerusalem, Khartoum, Sudan, and throughout Australia and the United States provide an international network of support to the Cairo-based patriarch and affiliated educational institutions.

The government of Egypt gives Christians some rights as citizens, and Copts serve alongside Muslims in government and the military. Islamic law classifies them as officially protected but subordinate, effectively second-class citizens. During the Tahrir Square protests, the crowds demonstrated an inclusive nationalism, using the symbol of the cross and crescent intertwined, which originated in the 1919 Egyptian nationalist struggle for independence. The Christians protected Muslims in massive Friday prayers, and two days later Muslims protected Christians holding a Sunday Mass in Tahrir. However, this peaceful coexistence broke down relatively quickly. On October 9–10, 2011, a group of young, Coptic demonstrators protested the demolition of a church in Aswan in front of the Maspero television building. The military attacked the peaceful group, killing 27 and injuring another 200, and then denied responsibility.

In practice, militant Islamic groups frequently target churches, Copt-owned businesses, priests, and individual believers. Violence such as this increases during times of high political tension, as mobs have attacked Coptic Church institutions, gatherings of Copts, and individual families. The armed attacks in June and July 2016 on Coptic priests in Minya, Egypt, and North Sinai, as well as the December 2016 suicide bombing of a church that killed 29, illustrate the threats Copts face amid evolving social and political forces.

The leadership of the Coptic Church makes great efforts to prevent or reduce publicity of the incidents, affirm the government's support, seek a negotiated settlement of the conflict, and affirm the patriotism of Christians, all to avoid further inflammation of more systematic persecution. The government seeks to ensure that Copts remain disengaged from politics by holding the pope of the Coptic Church responsible for the community and giving him authority over family law. The military has patronized the Sawiris family, well known as Copts, through construction contracts and other business ventures, which have made it very wealthy, and then has used them as an example to claim that Copts do not suffer discrimination in Egypt. The government has also allowed this family to sponsor a political party called the Free Egyptians Party, which gained 14 seats in Parliament in the 2011–2012 elections.

Individual Copts who have fled to other countries for asylum from Islamist persecution in Egypt have become very nationalistic and seek to publicize the suffering of people hurt in these conditions. They hold great anger against the church hierarchy as well as the government. Some young people from a Coptic background have become secular and disaffected due to their anger at both the Coptic Church and the government.

Melia Pfannenstiel

See also: Corruption; Egypt, Arab Republic of; Islamism; Libya, State of; Minorities; Tahrir Square Protests

Further Reading

Ayalon, Ami. "Egypt's Coptic Pandora's Box." In *Minorities and the State in the Arab World,* edited by Ofra Bengio and Gabriel Ben-Dor, 53–71. Boulder, CO: Lynne Rienner, 1999.

Ibrahim, Vivian. *The Copts of Egypt: The Challenges of Modernization and Identity.* New York: I. B. Tauris, 2011.

Nisan, Mordechai. *Minorities in the Middle East: A History of Struggle and Self-Expression.* Jefferson, NC: McFarland & Co., 1991.

Corruption

The abuse of public power for private gain, a concept that rests on the distinction between public and private domains, which varies among differing societies. Corruption occurs when officials selfishly exploit their authority to appoint and purchase on behalf of the state, or when private individuals use their connections to political officials for private gain. Corruption includes petty bribery, the buying and sale of offices, the seeking of preferential treatment, and grand corruption such as embezzlement and fraud. Greater state access to resources, such as exportable natural resources, or even international development aid, can fuel systematic government corruption. Political corruption damages the public interest and weakens social cohesion. Corruption inhibits economic development and the equal provision of public services. Corruption progressively destroys the middle class and creates a vast population of poor people ruled by a few rich and powerful elites.

When people with influence steal resources by demanding bribes, or making their clients rich at the public expense, common citizens can develop tremendous anger, which can fuel insurgency and even terrorism. Criminal and terrorist organizations exploit the prevalence of corrupt officials to develop powerful, wealthy, and technologically sophisticated transnational networks that further undermine state sovereignty and promote regional conflict. When corrupt officials use state resources to develop a network of loyal clients, politics can devolve into a competition of clans. Competing elites seeking control of the state can instigate tremendous social destruction, such as organizing massive protest movements, even to the point of civil war.

The forms of political corruption depend on the type of political system, the level of economic development, and the freedom of the media. Corruption occurs in traditional and modern societies, in authoritarian regimes and democracies. Political corruption is associated with patronage, clientelism, and lobbying. Political corruption thrives in communities where the public lacks awareness, or exhibits indifference toward, corruption. People in states with a mixture of democratic and authoritarian rule—with inadequate bureaucratic procedures of internal accountability, and high levels of state control over the judiciary and media—face great difficulties in campaigning against corruption. High-level officials in some states keep official salaries for government employees low, forcing them to depend on bribes to survive. The state can then use the compromised status of employees to coerce their submission and also create a system in which people bid high prices for appointment to public office.

Anti-corruption efforts include a broad variety of strategies to strengthen legal institutions and capabilities for prosecuting state officials, and also to shape public opinion and social values and provide broader supporting factors in a case-specific approach. The global NGO Transparency International has helped raise awareness through its annual surveys and country rankings.

Philipp O. Amour

See also: Authoritarianism; Clientelism (Patrimonialism); Democracy Deficit; Development; Grievance Model; *Wasta*

Further Reading

Corruption: The Unrecognized Threat to International Security. Washington, DC: Carnegie Endowment of International Peace, 2014.

Rose-Ackerman, Susan, and Bonnie J. Palifka. *Corruption and Government: Causes, Consequences, and Reform,* 2nd ed. New York: Cambridge University Press, 2016.

Coup of 2016

An attempted coup by a small segment of the military against the government of President Erdogan of Turkey on the night of July 15, 2016, suppressed by the loyal majority of the military within about 12 hours. Around 4:00 p.m. that afternoon, Turkish military intelligence alerted the chief of staff that intercepted communications indicated a coup was planned. The president was vacationing at a resort, many senior officers were attending a wedding, and newspapers had been reporting that on August 1 the government would conduct a major reorganization and purge of the military. At 6:00 p.m. the military tried to avert the problem by ordering military units confined to their barracks and closing some airspace. This alerted the conspirators to the compromise of their plot, prompting them to move their plans up. At 9:00 p.m. the plotters moved to seize bridges, television stations, airports, and police headquarters. By 10:00, tanks had blocked traffic on the two Bosporus bridges, and shortly after 11:00, an announcer of the state television network read a statement in which the coup plotters referred to themselves using an archaic Kemalist formula.

At 11:00, the prime minister called a private TV station to appeal for public resistance to the coup. At 11:30, the commander of the First Army in Istanbul had appeared on television, declaring the coup illegitimate and informing the people that coup plotters had taken top commanders hostage. At the same time, jets attacked the headquarters of the national satellite station, the national intelligence building, the Ankara police department, and the Presidential Palace. Legislators rushed to the parliament to demonstrate their opposition to the coup attempt, and jets dropped three bombs on the building.

At 12:28 a.m. on July 16, Erdogan used Facetime to call CNNTurk and conducted an interview urging his supporters into the streets. Since he had been engaged in an open political war with the Hizmet Movement since 2011, he immediately identified the coup plotters as followers of Gülen, without allowing any time for gathering evidence. At the same time, the imams used the mosque loudspeakers to call people into the streets. Commandos attacked the resort where Erdogan had been staying but narrowly missed him. He went to the airport to fly to Istanbul. On his arrival, he further energized the massive public defense of the government. Millions of people demonstrated in defense of the government, the state, and its democratic independence, reinforced by anger at the destructive traitors, an enduring shared national experience. The trauma of the attacks on the central institutions of the state make this comparable to the September 11, 2001, attacks for Americans. The treachery of native Turk attackers, embedded in the government and military, increased the emotional power of the event. Therefore, these attacks destroyed social trust and completely discredited the Hizmet Movement inside Turkey

The coup failed due to lack of military support. All of the political parties denounced it, and public opinion massively opposed it. By 9:00 a.m. on July 16, 2016, the loyal military forces had thwarted the coup and taken 1,400 soldiers into custody. At least 272 people were killed and 2,200 wounded in the violence in the two major cities, including civilians run over by tanks and shot by soldiers. The government's chaotic and disorganized response indicates genuine surprise and, combined with the degree of the violence, undermines suspicions that it was a government deception operation to flush out disloyal elements. The people who accept the government's accusation that Gülen ordered the coup offer several points: First, Gülen did publicly support the Coup of 1980 on television, which undercuts any claim that he opposes all coups as a matter of principle. Second, exposure of false claims that caused the Ergenekon and Sledgehammer prosecutions to collapse created an image of the Hizmet Movement as engaged in an immoral, politically motivated prosecution. Third, a video of Gülen urging his followers to secretively infiltrate the system until they had the numbers to prevail and take over the system, discredits the movement and exposes its political ambitions. Fourth, the secretive, hierarchical, authoritarian administration of the

Hizmet Movement creates suspicion of its motives and contradicts the transparency necessary for democracy. Erdogan's political war on Gülen since 2013, through his control of the media, meant that people accepted Erdogan's accusation and came to his support.

However, the extraordinarily broad and massive purge of people with no discernible connection to either the Gülen Movement or to the coup plot itself undermines the government's portrayal of the event. The government detained almost half of Turkey's generals and admirals, of whom 99 were formally arrested, in addition to sweeping purges in the judiciary, police, schools, universities, and Turkey's national intelligence agency. The speed and the huge number of people purged, including a prosecutor who had died 57 days before the coup, suggest that the purge was planned well before the coup. The government jailed more than 100 journalists who questioned these actions and closed more than 100 media outlets. The ruling Justice and Development Party (AKP) has blocked impartial investigations, preserving perpetual elements of mystery. The AKP has also promoted the claim that NATO and the United States organized the coup to keep Turkey weak and divided. This has increased already strong antagonism to the United States and the West and raised Turkey's motivation to rely on Russia, China, and Iran to balance against the United States. Erdogan has successfully created much higher public support, strengthening his capability to suppress dissent, silence opposing voices, and exercise centralized control.

Jonathan K. Zartman

See also: Authoritarianism; Erdogan, Recep Tayyip; Hizmet (Gülen) Movement; Iran, Islamic Republic of; Justice and Development Party (Turkey); Military Coups

Further Reading

Berktay, Hilal, with Pinar Kandamir, eds. *History and Memory: TRT World in the Face of the July 15 Coup.* Istanbul: TRT World Research Centre, July 15, 2017.

Jenkins, Gareth H. "Post-Putsch Narratives and Turkey's Curious Coup." *Turkey Analyst,* July 22, 2016.

Tas, Hakki. "The 15 July Abortive Coup and the Post-Truth Politics in Turkey." *Southeast European and Black Sea Studies* (2018): 1–19.

Yavuz, M. Hakan, and Rasim Koc. "The Turkish Coup Attempt: The Gülen Movement vs. The State." *Middle East Policy* 23, no. 4 (Winter 2016): 136–48.

Dahiya Doctrine

An Israeli military strategy of asymmetric warfare named after Beirut's southern suburbs—the target of Israel's aerial bombardment during the Second Lebanon War of 2006. The originators announced the doctrine in a series of press interviews in 2008, and Israeli military strategists subsequently published analytical studies. The doctrine responds to the new and complex demands of Israel's asymmetric engagements with Hezbollah in the north and Hamas in the south. Both groups share a strategic conception that attacks on Israel's civilian rear can offset the Israel Defense Forces's (IDF) military superiority and achieve political success. Operationally, they use high-trajectory missiles capable of targeting Israeli civilian settlements.

In response, Israeli strategists advocate a military doctrine intent on inflicting severe damage on their opponent's infrastructure and civilian centers to achieve deterrence and avoid getting dragged into wars of attrition. The originators, Major General Gadi Eizenkot, chief of General Staff of the Israel Defense Forces since 2015, and Colonel (Ret.) Gabriel Siboni, now serving as the director of an important Israeli military think tank, argue that Israel must respond to enemy hostilities immediately, decisively, and with disproportionate force. By setting a painful and memorable precedent, quick military operations serve to shorten and intensify the period of fighting and lengthen periods of calm between rounds of fighting. Israel's explicit goals include increasing the cost of postwar recovery for the states and civilian populations that support and finance attacks on Israel. Israel's archenemies consider postwar recovery imperative and integral to any victory. They mobilize their financial and noncombat resources for large-scale reconstruction efforts aimed at the rapid alleviation of civilian suffering.

Since its inception, the Dahiya Doctrine has guided IDF military operations in Gaza in 2008, 2012, and 2014. In each of these wars, human rights groups and international organizations widely criticized Israel for its disproportionate use of force and for the scale of the devastation inflicted. For critics of the Dahiya Doctrine, this intention to inflict immense destruction, explicitly not distinguishing between civilian and military targets and the purposefully high damage inflicted on civilian property and infrastructure, constitute a breach of international conventions and laws of war, especially of the principle of proportionality.

Proponents of the Dahiya Doctrine justify its use in asymmetric engagements with enemies fighting out of uniform. They contend that the international community should revisit the laws of war in an era of nonstate actors and transnational terrorism.

Proponents of the Dahiya Doctrine attribute the calm on Israel's northern and southern fronts to the deterrence imposed by Israel's disproportionate use of force in Lebanon and Gaza.

Fouad Gehad Marei

See also: Hamas; Hezbollah; Israel; Israeli Invasion of Lebanon; Lebanese Republic; Palestine

Further Reading
Eizenkot, Gadi. "A Changed Threat? The Response on the Northern Arena." *Military and Strategic Affairs* 2, no.1 (2010): 29–40.

Hasian, Marouf, Jr. *Israel's Military Operations in Gaza: Telegenic Lawfare and Warfare.* New York: Routledge, 2016.

Siboni, Gabi. "Disproportionate Force: Israel's Concept of Response in Light of the Second Lebanon War." *Insight* No. 74. Tel Aviv: Institute for National Security Studies, October 2, 2008.

Demirtas, Selahattin

A Kurdish politician from Diyarbakir, Turkey, recently a presidential candidate from the Peoples' Democratic Party/Halkların Demokratik Partisi (HDP), which mostly represents Turkey's large Kurdish ethnic minority. After graduating from the Ankara University School of Law, he worked as a lawyer advocating for human rights. He became the mayor of Diyarbakir and a member of the Turkish National Assembly. His charisma, youthful looks, and progressive politics earned him the moniker "the Kurdish Obama" for his similarities to the former American president.

Between 2009 and 2011, he helped the ruling Justice and Development Party (AKP) negotiate with the Kurdistan Workers' Party (PKK) in secret talks, resulting in a truce that curbed violence and enabled Kurdish politicians, and the HDP, to function on the Turkish political scene separate from the PKK/terrorist label. However, in 2014, the rise of the Islamic State's (Daesh) threat to the population in northern Syria, and international support of the Kurdish Self-Protection Forces (YPK), created the potential for a Kurdish state in northern Syria to connect with the autonomous Kurdistan Regional Government in northern Iraq. While Demirtas advocated for changes in Turkish minority rights, Turkey's President Recep Tayyip Erdogan aggressively shifted the country's policy to prevent the development of a Syrian Kurdistan, and to contain Kurdish nationalism in the southeast, under the guise of combating terrorism.

In 2014, the HDP elected Demirtas as their coleader. He helped shift the party's image to appeal to secular, left-leaning Turks and the dispossessed urban poor. Despite being arrested on 142 different charges, along with 150,000 others, after the failed 2016 coup attempt against President Erdogan, the HDP named him the party's presidential candidate in 2018. Despite sitting in prison, the government allowed him the single, legally guaranteed 20 minutes of television time to communicate with the Turkish people. He managed to finish third in Turkey's 2018 presidential election, with over 8 percent of the vote. Demirtas remains in prison, but his case has prompted a November 2018 ruling from the European Court of Human Rights demanding his release from prison.

Andrew Zapf

See also: AKP-PKK Peace Talks; Erdogan, Recep Tayyip; Justice and Development Party (Turkey); Kurdistan Workers' Party (PKK); Kurds; Minorities; Turkey, Republic of

Further Reading

Celep, Odul. "The Moderation of Turkey's Kurdish Left: The Peoples' Democratic Party (HDP)." *Turkish Studies* 19, no. 5 (2018): 723–47.

Demirtas, Selahattin. "The Middle East, The Kurdish Peace Process in Turkey, and Radical Democracy." *Turkish Policy Quarterly* 13, no. 4 (Winter 2015): 27–33.

Democracy Deficit

The gap between the expectations and demands for participation in debate and even policy formation, stimulated by rising literacy and access to communication, versus the reality of closed political systems and the harsh repression of political speech and the right of assembly. This includes various barriers that prevent people from holding their government responsible for its policies, even in states that allow elections and political parties. The development of democracy in other regions of the world, in spite of barriers such as an authoritarian colonial heritage, ethnic diversity, persistent poverty, and inadequate education, has drawn attention to the contrasting lack of democratization in the Middle East and North Africa.

Since Turkey, Malaysia, and Indonesia, as predominantly Muslim states, have achieved significant progress in democratization, scholars reject Islam itself as the reason for a democracy deficit. Contrasting the wealth of the monarchic Gulf states versus the poverty of democratic India reduces the value of explanations based on income or modernization. The rentier politics model applies to oil-rich states but does not explain many other states in the region. The insecurity model claims that authoritarian states will provoke conflict, either against minorities or neighboring states, to justify their monopolization of power, using resistance to Zionism and imperialism to sustain popular support. Other states use the threat of radical Islamic militancy to justify very tight controls on society and media, which prevent activists from educating people on democracy. The 2011 wave of protests failed to overcome these factors that support authoritarian rule because diverse interest groups can mobilize people against tyranny, but they find great difficulty in formulating a political platform to shape a new government. Many of these groups discovered that democratization requires a clear perception of the relative power and interests of the important groups, a learning how to engage in sustained dialogue, and a willingness to compromise, factors often summarized as "political maturity."

Gowhar Quadir Wani

See also: Authoritarianism; Clientelism (Patrimonialism); Corruption; Development; Rentier State Politics

Further Reading

Eickelman, Dale F. "The Arab 'Street' and the Middle East's Democracy Deficit." *Naval War College Review* 4, no. 4 (Autumn 2002): 39–48.

Elbadawi, Ibrahim, and Samir Makdisi, eds. *Democracy in the Arab World: Explaining the Deficit.* New York: Routledge, 2010.

Gambill, Gary C. "Explaining the Arab Democracy Deficit, Part I." *Middle East Intelligence Bulletin* 5, no. 2 (February–March 2003).

Demographics (Youth Bulge)

A phenomenon in the developing world where the youth proportion of the population grows rapidly due to medical improvements that reduce infant mortality while the fertility rate remains high. Demographers define youth as ages 15 to 29, when young people become more socially active and ultimately expect to start families. If they find employment, they will create economic demand—buying houses, furniture, and other needs of a new family—and create an economic benefit for the country. In the Middle East and North Africa (MENA) oil-exporting countries, the oil sector requires a greater proportion of capital, rather than labor, creating fewer jobs. When the economy does not develop as fast at the population grows, the resulting unemployment leads to great frustration, even emigration to find work, or motivation to engage in rebellion. When a large percentage of young men cannot find work, they represent an available labor pool, a resource for recruitment into protests, or even a source of militia members. If food prices rise, and the supply of housing fails to meet the demand, which occurred in the MENA region in 2008–2010, grievances against the government will rise.

In 2011, people under age 30 in many MENA countries suffered unemployment at twice the rate of the general population. Many youth protesters of the Arab Spring had relatively high levels of education but few opportunities for employment and satisfactory income. When students graduate from a college without learning critical thinking skills, and employers won't hire them, they have high expectations that they cannot meet. The deficient quality of education left many people unqualified for the available jobs. Furthermore, the greater stability and privileges of public-sector employment motivated young people to avoid taking lower-paying private-sector work while waiting for a public-sector job, another recipe for frustration.

These conditions caused many observers to attribute the 2011 protests to this youth bulge. Historically, most civil conflicts occur in countries where more than half of the population is younger than 30. Although a higher percentage of younger people participated in the protests, academics have documented that people of all age groups protested, and the average age of protesters was over 30. The young people who provided a core nucleus of activists early in the process helped motivate their older family members and neighbors.

Autumn Cockrell-Abdullah

See also: Development; Foreign Fighters; Grievance Model; Labor Migration; Modernization

Further Reading

Hamanaka, Shingo. "Demographic Change and Its Social and Political Implications in the Middle East." *Asian Journal of Comparative Politics* 2, no. 1 (2017): 70–86.

Hoffman, Michael, and Amaney Jamal. "The Youth and the Arab Spring: Cohort Differences and Similarities." *Middle East Law and Governance* 4 (2012): 168–88.

Mulderig, M. Chloe. "An Uncertain Future: Youth Frustration and the Arab Spring." *The Pardee Papers* No. 16. Boston: Boston University, April 2013.

Development

A process of increasing capability for people to meet their needs, supported by access to infrastructure and sustaining institutions, which generally reduces popular grievances, but can also include the ability to mobilize collective action against a corrupt and illegitimate government. Great differences in access to food, shelter, health care, and education become symbols of the failure of development. Populations that suffer from famines, epidemics, and natural disasters symbolize the failure of development. The grievance model of conflict and the idea of relative deprivation explain conflict as a result of underdevelopment. This perspective informed the 1995 UN *Agenda for Development*. The UN Development Program operates a variety of programs in 170 countries to reduce conflict by promoting development. It creates annual Human Development Reports, reflecting this perspective, with health and education indices for most countries. In 2002, it released the first Arab Human Development Reports, as a platform for Arab scholars to highlight conditions in Arab countries, with annual updates devoted to different themes.

Improving health and education, together with the infrastructure for trade and communications, leading to higher incomes and well-being, constitutes economic development. Increasing job specialization, individualism, and the variety of social organizations as a result of urbanization and increased technology comprise social development, linked to modernization. In general, economic and social development have led to, and enabled, more representative rule, with rational bureaucratic government protecting individual rights—called political development.

Projects to improve health and education require not only financial investment and technical guidance but also sustained institutional support and protection. Therefore, outside interventions to implement projects designed to promote economic development have commonly failed due to the lack of security or government support, resistance from traditional elites fearful of the erosions of moral values, and failure to understand the local economic, social, and cultural environment. Analysis of the great number of failed development projects over the past two decades reveals that people adapt in creative, culturally specific ways to the appearance of the new resources embodied in a development project. This has led to a new appreciation for the value of local initiative, emphasizing that poor people choose how to find and use resources according to cultural values and can improve their lives by working together using community resources.

Therefore, socioeconomic development does not just require technological innovation to improve health and life expectancy; it requires enabling people to choose ways to increase their individual resources, and protecting their right to choose. Rising levels of education and growing access to information can lead to increasing incomes, but also increasing social complexity.

Sayed Hassan Akhlaq Hussaini

See also: Grievance Model; Modernization

Further Reading

Bin Talal, Hassan. "The Arab Human Development Report 2002: Review and Reform." *Arab Studies Quarterly* 26, no. 2 (Spring 2004): 5–20.

Kuhn, Randall. "On the Role of Human Development in the Arab Spring." *Population and Development Review* 38, no. 4 (December 2012): 649–83.

Welzel, Christian, Ronald Inglehart, and Hans-Dieter Kligemann. "The Theory of Human Development: A Cross-Cultural Analysis." *European Journal of Political Research* 42, no. 3 (May 2003): 341–79.

Druze

A small, monotheistic religious group with a reputation for military passion and skill, combined with a strongly cohesive sense of community within the faith. The Druze religion originated as a split from the Ismaili doctrine in Fatimid Egypt, due to their belief in the divinity of al-Hakim Bi-Amer Allah (996–1021 CE); over the years, they have added other doctrines from Islamic Sufism, and from Greek Gnosticism, such as reincarnation. Like the Alawites and the Ismailis, the Druze justify the relative ignorance of most of their members about doctrinal details, allowing only a few educated leaders access to their foundational texts. Instead of physical religious rituals, they follow seven spiritual principles that emphasize loyalty to the Druze community, monotheism, and the repudiation of other forms of belief. The religion gives women full legal and social equality, conditioned in practice by a patriarchal family relationship. Some Druze women have held high spiritual, political, and social positions. After the community moved to Lebanon and Syria, they stopped seeking conversions and marry only within the community.

For extended periods, under exceptional leaders, in partnership with the Maronites, the Druze carved out an autonomous emirate from the Ottomans. However, competition between leading families led to a bloody war, after which the losers moved to the mountains of south Syria. From 1840 to 1860, a series of wars between Druze and Maronites brought French intervention to establish a power-sharing government. After defeating the Druze, the French tried to use them to inhibit the rise of Arab nationalism, but failed. The Syrian Druze played an important part in anti-colonial efforts against the French, leading to national independence, but the first independent Syrian government proved hostile to the Druze.

The largest percentage of Druze live in Syria, constituting 3 percent of Syria's population, and about 6 percent of the population of Lebanon, living predominantly in rural mountainous areas, with no urban centers. The Druze tend to support revolutionary leftist political parties. Many joined Ba'athism as a defense against Sunni domination; some Druze advanced socially by serving in the Ba'athist regime. As

Bashar al-Assad developed a strong relationship with Hezbollah and alienated the Lebanese Sunni population, Druze leader Walid Jumblatt built good relations with the Sunni Hariri clan. The rising dominance of the Shi'a Hezbollah has forced the Maronites to make peace with the Druze. This reconciliation enabled the 2005 Cedar Revolution that forced Syria's military to leave Lebanon. However, the militant Islamist movements like the Islamic State (Daesh) pose a greater, existential threat, motivating the Druze to support Syria again.

The small community of Druze in Israel, approximately 70,000 people, had good relations with the early state, and Druze serve in the military and security forces. The Israeli invasion of Lebanon in support of Christians created real strains in this relationship. The Jewish character of the state alienates the Druze, while Palestinians appeal to their shared Arab language. Throughout the region, the small Druze population has survived by virtue of their high levels of military skill, as well as flexibility in alliances, and by feigning assimilation when necessary.

Nicholas Michael Sambaluk

See also: Alawites (Nusayris); Arab Nationalism; Ba'athism; Cedar Revolution; Hezbollah; Israel; Lebanese Republic; Maronites; Syrian Arab Republic; Syrian Civil War

Further Reading

Halabi, Abbas. *The Druze: A New Cultural and Historical Appreciation.* Reading, UK: Ithaca Press, 2015.

Hazran, Yusri. *The Druze Community and the Lebanese State: Between Confrontation and Reconciliation.* New York: Routledge, 2014.

Parsons, Laila. "The Palestinian Druze in the 1947–1949 Arab-Israeli War." *Israeli Studies* 2, no. 1 (1997): 72–93.

E

Economic Protests (2017–2018)

A series of massive protests in Iran, especially in smaller and poorer cities, reflecting the population's frustration with economic stagnation, inequality, unemployment, and mismanagement. Demonstrations started in late December 2017 in the city of Mashhad, the second largest city, and a bulwark of conservatism. Reformists claimed that hardliners organized the first protests to attack President Rouhani, but a conservative religious leader in Mashhad denied it. Protests quickly spread, through news conveyed on social media, but in each place protesters expressed different grievances. Protests took place in 72—mostly smaller—cities, and 29 of 31 provinces. The most violent, widespread, and longest-lasting occurred in Khuzestan and Isfahan, where people suffer severely from air pollution and lack of water. More protests, especially complaining about corruption, took place in areas with the highest unemployment, predominantly populated by ethnic minorities—Gilakis, Azeris, Arabs—who suffer from economic marginalization. In these primarily economic protests, two events triggered the demonstrations: the leak of a new financial budget plan to raise the domestic price of fuel to reduce government debt, and the astonishing jump in prices of essential goods. The protests also reflected growing impatience with the results of the Joint Comprehensive Plan of Action (JCPOA) nuclear deal. Despite initial optimism about the lifting of the international sanctions, the people saw no improvement in the economy.

In most cases, the Basij and police controlled the protests without the large-scale violence seen in the 2009 Green Movement. However, where the protesters overwhelmed the local police in smaller cities, the government deployed the Islamic Revolutionary Guard. Police suppressed the protests with brutality, reportedly killing 20. The fact that protesters directly and explicity challenged the Ayatollah Khamenei, and the system of government, represents a new development in the political culture. In contrast to the largely urban, middle-class character of the 2009 Green Revolution, these protests predominantly represented the poor and working-class laborers in the peripheral provinces. They were the biggest demonstrations since the 2009 Green Movement, but they lacked any central political platform, or leadership, and did not actually threaten the regime. They illustrate the challenge to the government, and particularly for moderates associated with Rouhani. The fact that a month later the parliament rejected the budget plan and promised no price increases in the current fiscal year shows concern by the political elite for large-scale populist disruption.

Luiza Gimenez Cerioli

See also: Basij; Development; Green Movement; Iran, Islamic Republic of; Islamic Revolutionary Guard Corps (IRGC); Khamenei, Ayatollah Sayyid Ali; Minorities; Rouhani, Hassan Feridun

Further Reading

Erdbrink, Thomas. "Hearts 'Full of Anger': Daily Dissatisfaction Fuels Protests in Iran." *New York Times* 167, no. 58046 (August 6, 2018): A7.

Saidi, Mike. "More Protests, No Progress: The 2018 Iran Protests." *Critical Threats.* Washington, DC: American Enterprise Institute, December 19, 2018.

Tawoos, Shannon, "Making Sense of the Iran Protests." *Washington Report on Middle East Affairs* 37, no. 2 (March/April 2018).

Egypt, Arab Republic of

A military dictatorship in the northeast corner of the African continent, at the intersection of Africa and Asia along the Nile Valley. Egypt has the largest population in the Arab world, estimated at 99 million in 2018, and its major population centers host universities, newspapers, and other media that exert cultural influence throughout the Arab world. This has made Egyptian Arabic a very widely understood dialect. Members of the Sunni Muslim majority (90 percent) and the predominately Coptic Christian minority (9 percent) both identify as ethnically Egyptian, and small numbers of Imazighen (Berbers) and Bedouins also live in Egypt. As the second country in which the mass protests of 2011 forced a ruler to resign, Egypt has retained its significance for the broader Middle East and North African (MENA) region.

Napoleon's 1798 invasion of Ottoman Egypt provoked later reforms by the Ottoman Albanian Army commander Muhammad Ali. Expanding European influence stimulated the development of modernist Islam and an Age of Enlightenment in Egypt, as well as in Turkey and Iran, the centers of three competing civilizations: Arabic, Turkic, and Persian. The opening of the Suez Canal in 1869 increased European intrusion in Egypt, leading to de facto British control over internal Egyptian affairs for decades. British military occupation began in 1882, which provoked large, sustained opposition called the Urabi Revolt, the first of three major revolutions in roughly three generations. It represented a temporary alliance of landlords, constitutionalists, and junior army officers.

The British allowed an Ottoman official to retain symbolic political control until 1914, when the British established the protectorate, while they fought World War I. The second major modern revolt against the British, from 1919 to 1922, forced them to grant Egypt nominal independence, but the British maintained leverage over Egypt's ruling regimes throughout World War II. While Britain steadily lost global power after the war, Egyptian nationalists unified in opposition to the British occupation, and against the creation of the Israeli state in 1947. Arab losses in the 1948–1949 Arab-Israeli war provoked the third major revolt, the 1952 Egyptian Revolution. This began with a military coup d'état, carried out by a small group known as the Free Officers on July 23, 1952.

The military officers, led by General Muhammad Naguib, spent many years planning the overthrow of the unpopular monarch, King Farouk. The military

Egypt, Arab Republic of

government sought several long-term goals, including an end to British influence, a stronger military, better wealth distribution between the rich and poor, and a more democratic political system. These reforms would require reorganizing the government during a transition period. By June 1953, they had established a new republic, banned political parties, and made General Naguib president and prime minister. In 1954, Colonel Gamal Abdel Nasser overcame the opposition of the other ruling officers to replace General Naguib. Under a new constitution in 1956, Nasser gained more centralized power, and he remained in the presidency until his death in 1970.

Nasser used the competition between the Soviet Union and the United States to gain financial and political support for planned economic reforms and infrastructure projects. After refusing to accept the conditions offered by the United States to help finance the construction of the High Dam in Aswan, Nasser strengthened relations with the Soviets and nationalized the Suez Canal in July 1956, taking all Suez Canal Company property. Israel, Britain, and France responded by invading the Sinai, but they retreated due to pressure from the United States, the Soviet Union, and the United Nations. The Suez Crisis strengthened Arab nationalism and Nasser's leadership role among other Arab countries.

In February 1958, Egypt and Syria formed a political union under the name United Arab Republic (UAR), an arrangement from which Syria withdrew in 1961, after growing Syrian dissatisfaction and a military coup. Egypt maintained the name UAR until adopting the current official name, Arab Republic of Egypt, in 1971. The country suffered a devastating military defeat in the June 1967 six-day Arab-Israeli War, leaving the country more reliant on external support from the Soviet Union. Israel occupied the Sinai, and the Suez Canal closed until 1975. Egypt suffered damage to the military, a decline in tourism, and, most importantly, the loss of oil fields in the Sinai, which hampered the economy and Nasser's socialist reforms.

Following Nasser's death in September 1970, Vice President Anwar al-Sadat became president, but he maintained many of Nasser's domestic and foreign policies until 1972. The October 1973 Arab-Israeli War resulted in political success, as Egypt eventually regained Sinai territory lost in 1967. However, Sadat's willingness to negotiate with Israel in the Camp David Accords, and to pursue better relations with the United States, provoked anger across the Arab world, especially among the militant Islamists in Egypt. Increasing violence in 1980–1981, amid stagnant economic growth and growing persecution of the Coptic Christians by Islamists, prompted Sadat to repress a range of political and religious leaders, in addition to scholars and journalists. Militant Islamists assassinated President Sadat on October 6, 1981.

Vice President Hosni Mubarak was sworn in as president the next week, following a referendum. In response to Sadat's assassination, Mubarak further centralized the power of the executive branch and increased repression of Islamists, including the influential Muslim Brotherhood. Mubarak strengthened the security apparatus and aggressively limited opposition, despite frequent promises to expand opportunities for political participation. Between 2005 and 2010, Mubarak allowed some political parties to form. He held elections but tightly restricted the Muslim Brotherhood and other religious-based social or political groups.

Inspired by the Arab Spring uprising in Tunisia, in a time of rising food prices and a declining economy, several secular Egyptian youth movements, later supported by religious factions, collectively launched a revolution to overthrow Mubarak's regime. The initial protests on January 25, 2011, led to the occupation of Cairo's Tahrir Square on January 28. The massive character of the protests, and the army's refusal to intervene, forced Mubarak to resign on February 11, 2011. He handed authority to the Supreme Council of the Armed Forces (SCAF), a group of senior military officers led by Field Marshall Mohammed Hussein Tantawi, who was named president of the transitional government.

The people of Egypt grew increasingly frustrated throughout 2011 and early 2012 with the slow progress toward reform and failure to improve domestic security. In March 2011, the SCAF rammed through a weak revision of the 1971 constitution, over the objections of the revolutionaries and opposition forces. Disagreements among secular reformers, Islamist parties, and the Copts regarding the future of Egypt frequently turned bloody. Dozens died, and thousands suffered injuries in the clashes. For example, on October 9, 2011, army forces killed peaceful Coptic Christian protesters at the Maspero state television building.

Through a series of closely contested elections, the more organized Islamist parties gained power throughout government. Mohamed Morsi, leader of the Freedom and Justice Party, the political arm of the Muslim Brotherhood, won the 2012 presidential referendum and took the oath of office on June 30. Dissenters from more conservative Islamic factions and secular youth immediately challenged Morsi, who then imposed limitations on speech and the press and attempted to rule by decree. Judges dissolved the lower house of parliament on a technicality. This left no way for Morsi to write a legitimate constitution, or even rule with legitimacy.

After operating as both executive and legislature, on November 22, Morsi claimed expanded powers beyond any appeal, similar to the status of a constitution, which provoked large demonstrations. Meanwhile, the military and Mubarak-era elites had been sabotaging the delivery of public services, fuel, and security. Eventually, protesters took to the street because they saw no parliament, no regional government, and little hope of improvement. Mohammed ElBaradei, working with the National Salvation Front and the youth organizers of the Tamarod (rebellion) campaign, organized massive protests against Morsi. On July 3, 2013, Defense Minister Abdel Fattah el-Sisi deposed Morsi in a military coup. Saudi Arabia, Kuwait, and the United Arab Emirates endorsed the coup and promised significant financial assistance. The SCAF initially transferred authority to an interim civilian government. The head of the Supreme Constitutional Court led a committee to write a new constitution.

In response, critics of the coup, especially the Muslim Brotherhood, staged nationwide protests. Brotherhood supporters occupied al-Nahda Square and a large square and intersection in front of the Rabi'a Al-Adawiya Mosque in Nasr City, disrupting life for large numbers of people, who complained of suffering violence from the protesters. Brotherhood supporters conducted sporadic attacks on police forces for six weeks. After weeks of trying to negotiate, and then warning people to clear those encampments, on August 14, 2013, Egyptian security forces conducted an operation to clear thousands of protesters, killing at least 1,000. The SCAF again effectively ruled the country. The new constitution, adopted in January 2014, formalized an increase in the military's political power.

In May 2014, Abdel Fattah el-Sisi resigned from his position as Defense minister to stand for election as a presidential candidate. He won that election on June 8, 2014, with 95 percent of the vote, amid reports of widespread voting irregularities. President el-Sisi ruled through decree until those elected in the 2015 parliamentary election were seated. Since 2016, el-Sisi has invoked the threat of terrorism and insurgency from the Sinai and western desert near Libya to justify restricting civil liberties and political opposition. In April 2018, Egyptian voters reelected el-Sisi to another term, set to expire in 2022. On April 23, 2019, a public referendum approved constitutional changes effectively enabling him to rule, with one more election in 2024, until 2030. It also gave more powers to the president and the military.

Continual political upheaval and a rise in terrorist activity between 2011 and 2018 have hindered successful implementation of democratic reforms, while President el-Sisi argues authoritarian measures remain necessary to secure the country. Egypt has good relations with Russia, China, Saudi Arabia, the United Arab Emirates, Bahrain, and Kuwait, while enduring bad relations and criticism from Turkey and Qatar. Civil liberties remain severely constrained, and most Egyptians suffer from precarious economic conditions. The government has begun some massive infrastructure projects and boasts that economic growth has reached 5 percent again. However, the lack of legal transparency and the military domination of the economy restrain the recovery. Egypt remains under the conditions of an International Monetary Fund (IMF) support package that mandated a currency devaluation, reduction of subsidies, and reduced social support for the population. Inflation, poverty, and unemployment remain high. Therefore, critics complain that conditions have not improved since 2011.

Melia Pfannenstiel

See also: Ansar Beit al Maqdis; April 6 Youth; Coptic Orthodox Church; Corruption; El-Sisi, Abdel Fattah Saeed Hussein Khalil; Ghonim, Wael; Grievance Model; Islamism; Morsi, Mohamed; Mubarak, Muhammad Hosni Sayyid; Muslim Brotherhood; Qatar; Rabi'a al-Adawiya Massacre; Saudi Arabia, Kingdom of; Tahrir Square Protests; Tamarod Movement; Turkey, Republic of; United Arab Emirates (UAE)

Further Reading

Faris, David M. "Deep State, Deep Crisis: Egypt and American Foreign Policy." *Middle East Policy* 20, no. 4 (Winter 2013): 99–110.

Gelvin, James. *The Arab Uprisings: What Everyone Needs to Know*. New York: Oxford University Press, 2012.

Ibrahim, Saad Eddin. "Anatomy of Egypt's Militant Islamic Groups: Methodological Note and Preliminary Findings." *International Journal of Middle East Studies* 12, no. 4 (December 1980): 423–53.

Letourneau, Jean-Francois. "The Perils of Power: Before and After the 2013 Military Coup in Egypt." *British Journal of Middle Eastern Studies* 46, no. 1 (2019): 208–13.

Roll, Stephan. "Managing Change: How Egypt's Military Leadership Shaped the Transformation." *Mediterranean Politics* 21, no. 1 (2016): 23–43.

Springborg, Robert. *Egypt*. Medford, MA: Polity, 2018.

Egyptian Protests (2011). *See Tahrir Square Protests*

El-Sisi, Abdel Fattah Saeed Hussein Khalil

President of Egypt, former field marshal, and Defense minister during the July 2013 military coup that deposed President Mohamed Morsi. Abdel Fattah el-Sisi was born on November 19, 1954, into a middle-class Cairo family. He attended professional military schools in Egypt, the United Kingdom, and the United States and rose through the Egyptian military ranks, serving as the youngest member of the Supreme Council of the Armed Forces (SCAF) to oversee the 2011 post-Mubarak transition. He served as the director of Military Intelligence and Reconnaissance.

Following the July 3, 2013, coup, el-Sisi remained closely involved in the transition. After a new constitution was adopted in January 2014, General el-Sisi resigned his position in the armed forces to stand in the May 2014 presidential election. He secured over 95 percent of the vote against the leftist candidate Hamdeen Sabbahi, although reports of voting irregularities brought the election's legitimacy into question. He took office on June 8, 2014, and ruled through decree until after the new parliamentary members were seated in 2016. During his administration, the government engaged in a very sustained prosecution of the Muslim Brotherhood activists and leaders. The government also arrested large numbers of civil society leaders, human rights activists, and journalists and sentenced them to substantial jail terms. Throughout 2017, critics accused him of using broad election laws to exclude viable opposition candidates from competing in the April 2018 presidential election.

President el-Sisi has taken sustained measures to promote reform and modernization in the education system, especially in regard to Islam. He worked with Al Azhar University to conduct high-profile public events to present a tolerant and moderate approach to religious belief and practice. He has engaged in effective diplomacy and strategic communications with the Coptic Christian community to overcome the legacy of persecution. El-Sisi has worked hard to manage the severe economic crisis in Egypt, in part through some big infrastructure projects. Since 2016, he has expended considerable government resources to counter terrorism and insurgency from the Sinai Peninsula. He has enjoyed warming relations with the United States over shared security concerns, despite rebukes for limiting civil liberties. In April 2018, El-Sisi was elected to another term, set to expire in 2022. On April 23, 2019, a public referendum approved constitutional changes extending his current term to six years, allowing him to run for a third six-year term in 2024, and giving more powers to the president and the military.

Melia Pfannenstiel

See also: Authoritarianism; Coptic Orthodox Church; Development; Democracy Deficit; Egypt, Arab Republic of; Muslim Brotherhood; Tahrir Square Protests; Tamarod Movement

Further Reading

Aly, Abdel Monem Said. "Deciphering Abdel Fattah el-Sisi: President of Egypt's Third Republic." *Middle East Brief* No. 82. Waltham, MA: Crown Center for Middle East Studies, July 2014.

Roll, Stephan. "Managing Change: How Egypt's Military Leadership Shaped the Transformation." *Mediterranean Politics* 21, no. 1 (2016): 23–43.

Rutherford, Bruce K. "Egypt's New Authoritarianism under Sisi." *The Middle East Journal* 72, no. 2 (2018): 185–208.

Ennahda Movement

The largest party in Tunisia's parliament, founded in 1989 from an earlier organization called the Tunisian Islamic Tendency Movement (MTI). Abdelfattah Mourou and Rachid Ghannouchi founded the MTI in 1981 as a Sunni organization to demand freedom of religion in Tunisia, influenced by the ideas of Egypt's Muslim Brotherhood. The MTI adopted the language and causes of international Islamist movements at the time but focused on demonstrations opposing the Tunisian government. Some MTI members were even accused of involvement with bombings of tourist facilities. The group's efforts to establish its political presence spurred police repression that jailed thousands and forced more into exile, including Rachid Ghannouchi, the movement's cofounder, an Islamist intellectual.

In 1989, MTI leaders formed a new, successor group called the Ennahda (Renaissance) Movement. The government blocked the movement from participating in that year's national elections, but the votes for members running as individuals constituted 13 percent of the total. The government responded with increased repression, which continued until 2011. The movement remained quietly active in social and cultural activities, seeking to serve poor people, which gave it a strong presence on the ground. During his over two decades abroad, Ghannouchi's views steadily evolved from Islamism in the early 1980s to a blend of Islam and democracy.

After the Ben Ali family left, the transitional government legalized Ennahda in March 2011. It won a large majority in the next election and yet made painful concessions to help write a new constitution that would protect democracy and human rights. After some politicians tried to blame Ennahda for some terrorist attacks by Salafi extremists, the party stepped down and gave power to a technocratic government. The party leaders demonstrated their pragmatism and commitment to compromise for the sake of national unity by joining a coalition government in 2014. The party has also shown commitment to gender equality by mandating equal gender representation on all party lists in elections. In late 2018, Ennahda held 67 parliamentary seats (having won 31 percent of the vote), while the strongly secular Nidaa Tounes Party held 46 seats with 21 percent of the vote.

Tom Dowling

See also: Authoritarianism; Ben Ali, Zine Al-Abidine; Democracy Deficit; Ghannouchi, Rachid; Islamism; Muslim Brotherhood; Salafism; Tunisia, Republic of

Further Reading

Boubekeur, Amel. "Islamists, Secularists and Old Regime Elites in Tunisia: Bargained Competition." *Mediterranean Politics* 21, no. 1 (2016): 107–27.

Cavatorta, Francesco, and Fabio Morone. "Moderation through Exclusion? The Journey of the Tunisian Ennahda from Fundamentalist to Conservative Party." *Democratization* 20, no. 5 (2013): 857–75.

Deeb, Mary Jane. "Militant Islam and the Politics of Redemption." *The Annals of the American Academy of Political and Social Science* 524, no. 1 (November 1, 1992): 52–65.

McCarthy, Rory. *Inside Tunisia's Al-Nahda: Between Politics and Preaching.* New York: Cambridge University Press, 2018.

Wolf, Anne. *Political Islam in Tunisia: The History of Ennahda.* London: Hurst & Company, 2018.

Erdogan, Recep Tayyip

A populist, Islamist Turkish politician who has led Turkey since 2003. Recep Tayyip Erdogan (born in 1954 in Istanbul) comes from a poor, devoutly Muslim family from the Caspian Sea coastal town of Rize, Turkey. He has oriented his political appeal to Turkey's conservative Muslims. He gained a reputation for his speeches promoting political Islam even in high school and then supported Necmettin Erbakan in his various political parties. In 1994, he was elected mayor of Istanbul under the Welfare Party and gained a good reputation for clean, effective, and competent management.

In 1998, he was convicted of inciting religious hatred by citing an Islamist poem by a famous Turkish nationalist. He served four months and then in 1991, with two friends, formed the Justice and Development Party (AKP), which won the 2002 parliamentary elections. A December 2002 constitutional amendment overturned the rule barring him from serving in parliament or as prime minister. In May 2003 he became prime minister.

Erdogan led the AKP in implementing a great array of political and economic reforms to satisfy the criteria to join the European Union. He implemented a number of infrastructure projects, increasing foreign investment and trade that revitalized Turkey's economy and raised the overall standard of living. Turkey's gross domestic product per capita has doubled since 2002. He also gained significant foreign policy successes with Ahmet Davutoglu, mediating international disputes, such as between rivals in Lebanon, between Hamas and Hezbollah, and between Israel and Syria, and pursuing reconciliation with the Kurds. Erdogan and Davutoglu sought to establish Turkey as the dominant power in the Middle East, extend Turkish influence as a power broker in the region, and make Turkey the leading state in a pan-Islamic movement. Erdogan led the gradual break in Turkey's relations with Israel, beginning in May 2004 and culminating in May 2010. A series of corruption allegations and prosecutions revealed the breakdown of his alliance with the Gülen (Hizmet) Movement. Both sides engaged in open political war, creating a highly polarized political environment, with increasing suppression of civil liberties.

During the Arab uprisings, in September 2011, Erdogan embarked on a speaking tour of the Middle East and North Africa to portray Turkey as a model of the compatibility of Islam and secular governance. He called for Egyptian president Hosni Mubarak to resign and objected to the Saudi intervention in Bahrain. Erdogan sought good relations with Syrian president Bashar al-Assad until 2011, when he objected to the brutality of Syria's repression of protesters. Erdogan began aiding Islamist fighters against Assad and improving relations with the Kurdistan Regional Government (KRG) of northern Iraq, as a means to oppose both Assad and the Shi'a government of Maliki. Erdogan's repressive measures in the wake of the Gezi Park protests of 2013 irritated liberals in the West, and this irritation increased as his policies became increasingly authoritarian. After three terms as prime minister, he gained election as president in August 2014. With the help of legislative actions, he has transformed the Turkish presidency from a largely symbolic office to an effective executive one and has consolidated control over the government. He transformed Turkey from the state controlling the public expression of religious faith toward the state promoting public conformity to conservative practices.

The confused and ambivalent Western reaction in the wake of the July 15, 2016, coup attempt drove Erdogan to improve relations with Russia and Iran—both allies of the Assad regime. He shifted Turkey's policy to focus its military efforts against Kurdish forces in Syria, committing Turkish ground forces to the fighting in August 2016. Erdogan has consistently aligned himself with Qatar in its proxy war with Saudi Arabia (2017–2018), an expression of his support for the Muslim Brotherhood and related organizations.

His survival of the 2016 coup attempt allowed him to consolidate his power, to become more autocratic while claiming the status of an elected populist. In April 2017, a constitutional referendum eliminated the post of prime minister and gave the president expanded executive powers. In 2018 he was reelected as president. He can run again in 2023 for a term ending in 2028. His grandiose construction projects, public monuments, and sponsorship of lavish dramas indicate a flair for the dramatic. With brilliant rhetorical skill he seeks to raise Turks' appreciation of their importance, and from this he has gained strong public support from half of the nation; so far, the other half remains badly divided among themselves.

Benjamin V. Allison

See also: Al-Maliki, Nouri; Coup of 2016; Gezi Park Protests; Hizmet (Gülen) Movement; Islamism; Israel; Justice and Development Party (Turkey); Kurdistan Regional Government (KRG); Muslim Brotherhood; Palestine; Qatar; Saudi Arabia, Kingdom of; Syrian Arab Republic; Turkey, Republic of

Further Reading

Cagaptay, Soner. *The New Sultan: Erdogan and the Crisis of Modern Turkey*. New York: I. B. Tauris, 2017.

Kuru, Ahmet T. "Turkey's Failed Policy toward the Arab Spring: Three Levels of Analysis." *Mediterranean Quarterly* 26, no. 3 (September 2015): 94–116.

Phillips, David L. *An Uncertain Ally: Turkey under Erdogan's Dictatorship*. London: Routledge, 2017.

Ergenekon Scandal

An extensive investigation by Turkish prosecutors into an alleged conspiracy against the state that began in June 2007, named after a mythical valley where Turks are said to have originated in Central Asia. This scandal exploited a common belief that some organized criminal groups operated in collusion with some members of the military and the government. Initially, observers in the West expressed hope that this investigation would promote a healthy cleansing of state corruption to enable greater democratization. Over the following years, prosecutors conducted over a dozen predawn raids and indicted over 200 people. The size of the indictments—nearly 2,000 pages each—inhibited defendants and independent investigators from understanding these cases. Although the investigation uncovered some crimes, the violations of judicial standards raised considerable suspicion regarding the political intention of the operations. The suspects arrested in the raids seem to have no logical connection to one another, except their opposition to the Justice and Development Party (AKP) and to Islamist conservatism. The suspects spent a very long time detained without formal charges of any crime, and the charges suffered from deep inconsistencies and internal contradictions. Prosecutors accused the suspects of every act of political violence in recent history. The police also systematically leaked evidence in a way that compromised the integrity of the investigation while intimidating the opposition.

The Ergenekon prosecutions resembled a subsequent set of prosecutions called the Sledgehammer (*Balyoz*) Case. Both represented conspiracies of great proportions, resulting in the arrest of large numbers of prominent secularists and many retired and active members of the military, based on forged evidence. Detractors called these actions political attacks on secular nationalists with links to the military. These trials began with the overt support of the AKP government during a time in which the Erdogan administration had good relations with the Hizmet (Gülen) Movement. Critics later accused the police and prosecutors in this case of acting on behalf of the Gülen Movement. The investigation has led to a climate of fear among people opposed to the AKP government and to conservative Islamism. In 2012 a large number of suspects received prison sentences, but in June 2014, after the Erdogan government had solidified its position against potential military intervention and had entered into open opposition to Fethullah Gülen, the courts overturned these convictions. The original judge was arrested in July 2016, and the prosecutor fled the country.

Jonathan K. Zartman

See also: Corruption; Justice and Development Party (Turkey); Erdogan, Recep Tayyip; Hizmet (Gülen) Movement; Islamism; Turkey, Republic of

Further Reading

Balci, Ali. "A Trajectory of Competing Narratives: The Turkish Media Debate Ergenekon." *Mediterranean Quarterly* 21, no. 1 (2010): 76–100.

Jenkins, Gareth H. "Between Fact and Fantasy: Turkey's Ergenekon Investigation." *Silk Road Paper*. Washington, DC: Johns Hopkins University, August 2009.

Rodrik, Dani. "Ergenekon and Sledgehammer: Building or Undermining the Rule of Law?" *Turkish Policy Quarterly* 10, no. 1 (2010): 100–109.

Yavuz, M. Hakan, and Rasim Koc. "The Turkish Coup Attempt: The Gülen Movement vs. The State." *Middle East Policy* 23, no. 4 (Winter 2016): 136–48

F

Fatah Party

A secular Palestinian national movement created by these members of the Palestinian diaspora in Qatar in 1959: Yasser Arafat, Mahmoud Abbas, Sakah Khalaf, Khalil al-Wazir, and Khaled Yashruti. Based in the reverse acronym of Harakat al-tahrir al-watani al-Filastini (Palestinian National Liberation Movement), Fatah began as a party in 1965, in leading the Palestinian revolution that started that year. The party became a dominant force after the Six-Day War in 1967. From that year on, Fatah joined the Palestine Liberation Organization (PLO). Fatah leader Yasser Arafat served as PLO chairman from 1969 until he died in 2004. Another member of Fatah, Mahmoud Abbas, replaced him. The party makes decisions through two groups, the Central Committee (executive body) and the Revolutionary Council (legislative body). Fatah has constituted the main faction in the PLO. It held the majority in the Palestinian Legislative Council (the legislature of the Palestinian Authority, which began in 1996) until 2006, when it lost its majority to the Islamist party Hamas. The Hamas legislative victory led to dispute between the two parties, which paralyzed the Legislative Council. Despite reconciliation efforts in order to negotiate an agreement on the formation of a unity government, and even an agreement signed in Cairo in 2017, relations between the parties demonstrate continued conflict.

On November 29, 2016, the Fatah General Congress held its seventh meeting attended by 1,400 delegates in Ramallah to elect its leader, and the members of the Fatah Central Committee and Revolutionary Council. Although Mahmoud Abbas, at 81, had been serving for 12 years as president of the Palestinian Authority, with sharp coercive measures he prevented any challenge and was elected to a five-year term.

Carolina Bracco

See also: Abbas, Mahmoud; Hamas; Israel; Palestine; Palestine Liberation Organization (PLO)

Further Reading
Gresh, Alain. *The PLO: The Struggle Within.* London: Zed, 1988.
Usher, Graham. "The Democratic Resistance: Hamas, Fatah, and the Palestinian Elections." *Journal of Palestine Studies* 35, no. 3 (Spring 2006): 20–36.

Fayyad, Salam

A Palestinian statesman, economist, independent politician, and former prime minister, who conducted energetic reform in the Palestinian Authority (PA) and developed effective institutions in the West Bank, in the aftermath of the Second

94 February 17th Revolution

Intifada (2000–2005) and the schism between Fatah and Hamas (2006–2007). Salam Fayyad, born on April 2, 1951, in the northern West Bank village of Deir al-Ghusun, earned a master's in business administration from Edwards University in 1980 and a doctorate in economics at the University of Texas at Austin in 1986. He worked for the International Monetary Fund, as its Palestine representative, 1995–2002. He served twice as Finance minister (2002–2005 and 2007–2012) and then as prime minister of the Palestinian Authority (June 15, 2007–June 6, 2013). He promoted the professional training of the PA's security forces, curtailed corruption, and advocated infrastructure construction in Israel-controlled Area C of the West Bank. He believed that such efforts would strengthen Palestine's negotiating position with Israel in pursuit of a "two-state solution."

As a passionate and persuasive advocate of rational argument, self-empowerment, and nonviolence, he offered a path to overcome many Israeli objections to Palestinian statehood. As prime minister, Fayyad won favor from the U.S. media and significant international support. He joined with Hanan Ashrawi on a slate of secular liberals called the Third Way Party in the 2006 parliamentary elections, but the party won only two seats and then disbanded. His work against corruption brought him into conflict with the established Fatah Party leaders and their distribution of patronage. Ultimately, Israel reduced its cooperation after the March 2009 election of Netanyahu as Israeli prime minister, which undercut Fayyad's message. At the same time, Mahmoud Abbas sought to go around Israeli obstruction by seeking greater international recognition, which similarly undermined Fayyad's strategy. Critics argue that his reforms increased Palestine's dependence on foreign aid and entrenched Israel's occupation.

Toward the end of his premiership, Fayyad's government faced a series of crises that highlighted the PA's dependence on external support, as well as Fayyad's political isolation due to the domination of President Mahmoud Abbas. He resigned on April 13, 2013. Since leaving office, Fayyad has joined the Harvard Kennedy School. He remains supportive of the "two-state solution" but openly criticizes the Oslo agreements.

Philip Leech-Ngo

See also: Abbas, Mahmoud; Ashrawi, Hanan; Fatah Party; Hamas; Hamas-Fatah Conflict; Intifadas (I, II, and Knife); Palestine

Further Reading

Danin, Robert M. "A Third Way to Palestine: Fayyadism and Its Discontents." *Foreign Affairs* 90, no. 1 (January/February 2011): 94–109.

Fayyad, Salam. "Farewell to Victimhood." *Atlantic Council* (January 2016): 1–8.

Leech, Philip. *The State of Palestine: A Critical Analysis.* New York: Routledge, 2017.

February 17th Revolution

The massive popular revolts in every region of Libya that began in the eastern city of Benghazi and spread rapidly west, ultimately resulting in the capture and death of Libyan leader Muammar Qaddafi. Protests began in Benghazi after the arrest of Jamal al-Hajji, a political activist, who called for protests through social media on February 1. The next day a small protest and riot took place but was quickly crushed by Libyan security forces. Then on February 15, 2011, Libyan authorities arrested Fathi Terbil, a popular human rights lawyer in Benghazi. Terbil and a coalition of activists, many of them young liberals, had been preparing for many weeks to hold protests on February 17 to commemorate the date that security forces used great violence to suppress protests in 2006. Crowds gathered outside the Benghazi police station, demanding his release. Security forces fired on the crowds. This brutality further fueled the rebellion. In response to the violence of the security services, protesters occupied the military barracks in Benghazi on February 18, and large numbers of the military defected. Protests began in Misrata, the third largest city, on February 19, and large-scale protests hit Tripoli on February 20. National protests spread rapidly, and Qaddafi recognized that his government was losing control. By the end of February, the mainstream opposition had formed a group called the National Transitional Council (NTC), which included some high-profile regime defectors claiming leadership of the movement. NTC asked for international help. However, it was not able to actually control anything on the ground because the revolution consisted of more than 100 widely scattered militias pursuing local agendas.

After the opposition made progress toward capturing important coastal towns of the oil-export region, Qaddafi's forces regained the offensive. In March, bolstered by African mercenaries, loyalist forces retook several coastal cities, as a UN resolution authorized member states to create a no-fly zone over Libya. On March 31, under UN auspices, NATO took control of air operations to "protect civilians and civilian-populated areas from attack or the threat of attack." Over the summer, the tide shifted against Qaddafi. An August rebel offensive, supported by NATO bombing, retook lost territory, including Tripoli. In September 2011, the United Nations recognized the NTC as Libya's government. On October 23, 2011, after Qaddafi's capture and death in Sirte, NTC chairman Mustafa Abdul Jalil declared the liberation of Libya—essentially the end of the war. However, Qaddafi loyalists continued to fight, local militias and tribes clashed periodically, and long-suppressed intertribal rivalries resurfaced. The NTC rejected the presence of any United Nations forces, effectively hindering the stabilization and reconstruction of the country.

Tom Dowling

See also: Authoritarianism; Battle of Sirte in 2011; Belhaj, Abdul Hakim; Grievance Model; National Transitional Council; Qaddafi, Muammar; Qatar

Further Reading

Cole, Peter, and Brian McQuinn. *The Libyan Revolution and Its Aftermath*. New York: Oxford University Press, 2015.

Mundy, Jacob. *Libya*. Medford, MA: Polity Press, 2018.

Pack, Jason, ed. *The 2011 Libyan Uprising and the Struggle for the Post-Qadhafi Future*. New York: Palgrave Macmillan, 2013.

February 20 Movement

A panoply of Moroccan civil society organizations, political groups linked to the secular left, members of the Islamist Al Adl Wal Ihsan (Justice and Virtue) Movement, and independent citizens, who organized the cycle of demonstrations across

Morocco beginning on February 20, 2011, and lasting to the spring of 2012. Under the inspiration of protest movements in Tunisia and Egypt, some young secular Moroccans used social media to organize a march, which led to a series of protests throughout Morocco. They sought to mobilize large-scale street protests to denounce present conditions and present a platform of seven clear, political, economic demands: 1) reform of the constitution; 2) resignation of the Abbas Al Fassi government; 3) dissolution of the parliament; 4) creation of an effective separation of powers; 5) liberation of political prisoners; 6) official recognition of Berber language and identity; and 7) prosecution of persons and authorities responsible for human rights abuses and corruption. In simultaneous demonstrations in 53 cities, hundreds of thousands of Moroccans united to protest for this platform.

Two weeks later, on March 9, 2011, the king made a dramatic speech promising to reform the constitution. Another massive set of protests held in 63 towns on March 20 gathered twice as many people. Again, another larger set of protests on April 24 occurred in 110 towns. However, by the middle of May the movement lost momentum, due in large part because of the dramatic preemptive action by the king, but also because the civil war in Libya, and the brutality of the battles in Syria, Yemen, and Bahrain, reduced the popular passion for revolution. On May 22, 2011, the government conducted a systematic and brutal campaign to suppress protests, with police beatings and arrests all over the country. In June, the government adopted a different strategy: hiring thugs to commit violence in the name of neighborhood defense associations.

The protests led to the creation of supporting groups, such as the National Committee to Support the February 20 Movement, with numerous local branches. The government held a constitutional referendum on July 1, 2011, and legislative elections concluded on November 25. Police repression increased, and the movement suffered internal divisions, which undermined the motivations of activists and thus the capabilities of the February 20 Movement. Two years after the beginning of the February 20 Movement, Moroccan human rights associations and local media reported nearly 70 activists in prison.

Currently, Moroccans only occasionally engage in protests against specific new repressive actions or decisions. Most of the previously active members of the movement in Casablanca and Rabat have reoriented their actions to cultural activism.

Ángela Suárez-Collado

See also: Grievance Model; Mohammed VI, King of Morocco; Morocco, Kingdom of; Regime Change Cascades; Social Media

Further Reading

Benchemsi, Ahmed. "Morocco's Makhzen and the Haphazard Activists." In *Taking to the Streets: The Transformation of Arab Activism,* edited by Lina Khatib and Ellen Lust, 199–235. Baltimore: Johns Hopkins University Press, 2014.

Fernández-Molina, Irene. "The Monarchy vs. The 20 February Movement: Who Holds the Reins of Political Change in Morocco?" *Mediterranean Politics* 16, no. 3 (2011): 435–41.

Hoffman, Anja, and Christoph Konig. "Scratching the Democratic Façade: Framing Strategies of the 20 February Movement." *Mediterranean Politics* 18, no. 1 (2013): 1–22.

Fikri, Mouhcine

A fish seller from the Rif region in northern Morocco, whose gruesome death came to symbolize the cruelty and corruption of government officials. Born in September 1985 in the small village of Imzouren, Mouhcine Fikri came from a modest and conservative family with nine brothers and sisters. In 2004, Fikri abandoned his studies to contribute to the family economy. He held a variety of different occupations, including salesman, fisherman, and taxi driver. In 2013, he became a traveling fish broker, eventually delivering his merchandise even in Fes.

When the maritime fishing authorities confiscated 500 kilos of swordfish caught in violation of the prohibition on swordfish fishing at that time of year, Mouhcine Fikri climbed into the trash compactor of the garbage truck to retrieve his property and was crushed to death. Despite the prohibition on catching swordfish at the time, government authorities had ignored illegal networks engaged in commercial fishing for swordfish throughout the year from the port of Al Hoceima.

Two days after Fikri died, protesters organized marches and held rallies in Al Hoceima city, demanding justice for his death and complaining against the *hogra* (humiliation by the authorities), corruption, and inequality. These collective actions, led by male and female activists, brought together all sectors of the population and generated a cycle of mass protests. Protesters formed the Hirak al-Shaabi, the Popular Movement of the Rif, to present specific local demands. The Hirak expanded until April 2017, as the response of the central security services lagged. At the end of March 2017, a new government coalition formed, which reacted to the social unrest by allocating nearly $700 million for projects to accelerate the economic and social development of the Al Hoceima province, deploying more security in the region, and launching various defamatory media campaigns. However, demonstrations and rallies grew in intensity and frequency until police arrested the leader, Nasser Zefzafi, on May 29, 2017. The government then greatly increased the severity of its repression, arresting more than 450 people and prohibiting demonstrations. The protest movement dissipated and finally disappeared by the end of August. On June 26, 2018, the Casablanca Court sentenced 53 Rifian activist leaders to long prison terms.

Ángela Suárez-Collado

See also: Berbers (Imazighen); Bouazizi, Tarek al-Tayeb Mohamed; Corruption; Development; Grievance Model; Morocco, Kingdom of; Social Media

Further Reading

Aouragh, Miriyam. "L-Makhzan al-'Akbari: Resistance, Remembrance and Remediation in Morocco." *Middle East Critique,* July 6, 2017.

Howe, Marvine. "Year-Old Hirak Protest Movement Galvanizes Northern Morocco's Neglected Rif Region." *Washington Report on Middle East Affairs* 36, no. 6 (October 2017): 50–53.

Lefèvrea, Raphaël. "'No to hoghra!': Morocco's Protest Movements and Its Prospects." *The Journal of North African Studies* 22, no. 1 (2017): 1–5.

Suárez-Collado, Ángela. "Territorial Stress in Morocco: From Democratic to Autonomist Demands in Popular Protests in the Rif." *Mediterranean Politics* 20, no. 2 (2015): 217–34.

Foreign Fighters

Nationals of one country recruited to fight in a rebellion or insurgency in another country, based on a perceived threat to the shared transnational identity that requires a collective defense.

Historically, insurgents seeking resources to confront a state portray themselves as part of a larger transnational community, and the state as a threatening enemy to every member of that community. Those who lead a persistent conflict will appeal to the diaspora generation born in exile to return and fight. The growth of transnational ideologies has created a pool of potential recruits in diverse countries. Globalization aids the transmission of recruiting appeals and the travel of those who go to fight. The long history of predominantly young men going to fight as insurgents in another country reveals some trends. Recruiters appeal to the qualities of shared community, whether defined by religion, ethnicity, or ideology, and effectively convey the threat to that community. Potential fighters identify closely with their community and participate in its activities actively, but also suffer disrespect or marginalization from the host society. Recruiters work through tight social networks to avoid legal restrictions on their activities.

The great success of the Islamic State (Daesh) in recruiting foreign fighters follows the pattern of Afghan insurgents recruiting support from Muslims all over the world, and every previous insurgency with a transnational connection. Because foreign fighters cause higher levels of violence than local insurgents, and insurgencies that recruit foreign fighters have greater success, the issue deserves the attention of policy makers. This danger raises the importance for states to provide a positive experience of integration for refugees, to prevent the next generation from growing up alienated and angry. Because Algerians who had fought in Afghanistan played a major role in the 1992 Algerian civil war, returning fighters can make state officials worried. Since some European Islamic State fighters committed terrorist attacks in Europe after returning, governments throughout the Middle East and North Africa (MENA) region will watch carefully when their citizens return from fighting in Syria.

Melvin R. Korsmo

See also: Algeria, The People's Democratic Republic of; Civil Wars; Grievance Model; Islamic State (Daesh); Islamism; Refugees; Social Media; Syrian Arab Republic

Further Reading

Malet, David. *Foreign Fighters: Transnational Identity in Civil Conflicts.* Oxford, UK: Oxford University Press, 2017.

Mishali-Ram, Meirav. "Foreign Fighters and Transnational Jihad in Syria." *Studies in Conflict & Terrorism* 41, no. 3 (2018): 169–90.

Framing Model

One of three models of conflict, based on the principle that people fight to promote their worldview, or "frame" their understanding of how the world should work, whether defined in terms of an ideology like Salafism, nationalism, or socialism, in terms of religion, or in terms of another dimension of identity. In this perspective, every governing system represents a dominant worldview, a frame, that includes a narrative describing the right way for government to work and for people to live and a set of norms defining the character of justice. This narrative requires men and women of ideas to explain it, defend it, and reproduce it through the schools, the media and political speeches, and actions. In this perspective, military power alone does not suffice to create a government or a society, but rather every government seeks to justify itself and to proclaim its virtues, as defined by "producers of culture," which include artists, journalists, writers, teachers, and politicians. When the people no longer accept the dominant narrative or frame, they will fight to create a society that promotes what they believe and consider just. When the leaders lose faith in the ideology that governed a state in the past, the government will collapse. The framing model offers a powerful explanation of suicide bombing, ethnic strife, and ideological conflicts.

The framing model argues that in most societies, people compete to promote the superiority of their narrative. Totalitarian states seek to monopolize the world of ideas to prevent this competition, while even more liberal states seek to control that competition to preserve consensus on liberalism—and sometimes fail. In the framing perspective, changes in social networks, material benefits, or popular experiences can undermine the appeal of a dominant worldview, opening the opportunity for conflict. Conflict begins with a struggle initiated by cultural elites who seek to impose their worldview and challenge the influence of the existing economic and political elites.

If the educated stratum of society splits into camps led by advocates of competing sets of cultural values or opposing ideologies, this competition can grow into strong conflict, even civil war. Each group uses its understanding of core culture, and its skill in manipulating emotionally powerful symbols, to attract popular support. When one group emerges from the ideological competition triumphant, and those who produce culture gain political and economic power, they create political stability. The resources and social position of those who produce culture can either sustain conflict or provide the means for stability. However, the persuasive power of a dominant worldview still faces pressure in today's global information space. The framing perspective sees a constant boiling ferment of competing ideas, but this also leads to advice for conflict resolution.

The constructivist perspective argues that peace results when the people and their leaders hold the same culture, worldview, and ideology: peace requires cultural hegemony within a society. If the producers of culture and ideology develop a consensus or a shared worldview and gain material resources and political power, they can bring peace in society. Conflict resolution necessitates not only formal negotiations to reach agreement on the distribution of power and material resources—as recommended by the rational perspective—but also the protection of freedoms of speech, assembly, and the press, so that intellectuals can collectively recreate a shared cultural identity. In the framing point of view, conflict resolution consists of a process in which competing parties redefine their interests and form new identities.

Jonathan K. Zartman

See also: Arab Nationalism; Civil Wars; Greed Model; Grievance Model; Islamism

Further Reading

Desrosiers, Marie-Eve. "Tackling Puzzles of Identity-Based Conflict: The Promise of Framing Theory." *Civil Wars* 17, no. 2 (2015): 120–40.

Rothman, Jay. "From Interests to Identities: Towards a New Emphasis in Interactive Conflict Resolution." *Journal of Peace Research* 38, no. 3 (2001): 289–307.

Tarrow, Sidney. "Mentalities, Political Cultures, and Collective Action Frames: Constructing Meanings through Action." In *Frontiers in Social Movement Theory,* edited by Aldon D. Morris and Carol McClurg Mueller, 174–202. New Haven, CT: Yale University Press, 1992.

Free Syrian Army

The armed movement combatting the Bashar al-Assad regime in Syria since the regime responded with extreme brutality to initial peaceful protests in early 2011. Defecting elements of the Syrian military who refused to participate in violent repression combined with armed dissidents to organize the Free Syrian Army (FSA) to protect protesters. Initially, Turkey provided a valuable safe haven.

International media sources claim approximately 10,000–15,000 defectors joined the FSA in the first months of the war, but both sides dispute the numbers. The Free Syrian Army grew to perhaps 40,000 during 2012, and its combat performance impressed visiting journalists as reflecting skilled officers' leadership and capable troops, but as lacking sufficient weapons and equipment. The FSA leadership expected that further defections would enable a successful guerrilla-warfare campaign to challenge the regime. Defectors seldom brought more than personal equipment and small arms, forcing the FSA to use guerrilla fighting tactics and procedures and to rely on commercially available technologies for command and control. The vast distances between the leadership in Turkey and the areas of combat, and the lack of communications equipment, forced units in combat to improvise and form allegiances with whoever could provide the funding and supplies to survive. The conditions prevented large-scale coordinated operations. People migrated to units with the best record of success in combat. The lack of funding for the FSA made it uncompetitive with the Islamist brigades with greater organizational cohesion and strong funding from Qatar, Saudi Arabia, or other sponsors.

The U.S. policy makers broadly sympathetic to the rebels resisted commitment to the conflict, but in 2013 the United States did provide over $100 million in non-lethal aid to "moderate rebel" groups comprising the FSA. By 2013, the FSA lost strength due not only to casualties, but also to defections to Islamist groups such as the Al-Nusra Front and subsequently also to the rising Islamic State (Daesh). FSA elements and other groups formed the U.S.-supported Syrian Democratic Forces in late 2015, but Russian aircraft and ground forces quickly attacked them on behalf of the al-Assad regime. Starting in 2016, forces self-identifying as a Turkish-backed FSA reentered Syria with the help of Turkish armored vehicles and aircraft, and eventually U.S. air support as well.

Nicholas Michael Sambaluk

See also: Al-Assad, Bashar; Syrian Arab Republic; Syrian Civil War

Further Reading

Hinnebusch, Raymond, and Omar Imady, eds. *The Syrian Uprising: Domestic Origins and Early Trajectory.* London: Routledge, 2018.

Lister, Charles. *The Free Syrian Army: A Decentralized Insurgent Brand.* Washington, DC: Brookings Institution, 2016.

Yassin-Kassab, Robin, and Leila Al-Shami. *Burning Country: Syrians in Revolution and War.* London: Pluto, 2016.

G

General National Congress

The legislative authority of Libya for two years following the end of the February 17th Revolution, elected by popular vote on July 7, 2012. The General National Congress (GNC) took power from the National Transitional Council (NTC) in August 2012. The GNC consisted of 200 members, 80 elected through a party-list system of proportional representation, and 120 elected as independents in multiple-member districts. On October 14, 2012, the General National Congress elected human rights lawyer Ali Zeidan as prime minister, after approving his cabinet. Conflicts between Islamists who wanted a parliamentary system and liberal republicans who wanted a presidential system paralyzed the GNC. Militias repeatedly attacked the Congress and imposed policy changes that ultimately provoked a civil war.

The NTC gave the GNC 18 months to guide Libya to a permanent democratic constitution, but it failed to meet the deadline. On February 14, 2014, Khalifa Haftar called for the GNC to dissolve, since its mandate had expired. The Congress was forced to organize elections for a new House of Representatives (HOR), which took place on June 25, 2014, with an election turnout of only 18 percent. On August 4, 2014, the HOR took power and gained international recognition as the government of Libya.

A minority of former GNC members rejected the new government. An armed group called the Libya Revolutionaries Operations Room (LROR) and the Central Shield armed groups met on August 25, 2014, and declared a National Salvation Government. The international community does not recognize this GNC as the legitimate parliament of Libya. Due to the political stalemate between competing governments in the eastern and western parts of Libya, the United Nations conducted protracted negotiation efforts to develop a consensus government. The Skhirat Agreement, or Libyan Political Agreement, of December 17, 2015, created a new Government of National Accord, but the HOR refused to recognize it. On April 1, 2016, the GNC announced its own dissolution.

Amir Muhammad Esmaeili

See also: February 17th Revolution; Haftar, Khalifa Belqasim; Libya, State of; Libyan Civil War; National Transitional Council

Further Reading
Mundy, Jacob. *Libya*. Medford, MA: Polity Press, 2018.
St. John, Ronald Bruce. *Libya: Continuity and Change*. New York: Routledge, 2015.

General People's Congress

A political party founded by former Yemeni president Ali Abdullah Saleh on August 24, 1982. From its creation in 1982 until 2000, the al-Mu'tamar al-Sha'abi al-'Am (General People's Congress; GPC) operated without a political challenger. As GPC chairman, President Saleh advocated for Yemeni and Arab nationalism. Using the GPC's dominance in Yemen's parliament, Saleh developed a complex patronage system based on a strategy of inclusion, in order to prevent potential opposition. In 2002, five opposition parties formed a coalition, the Joint Meeting Parties (JMP), to push for political and economic reforms.

In 2012, President Saleh was forced to resign, and his vice president, Abdu Rabbu Mansour Hadi, became Yemen's transitional president. Hadi also became secretary general of the GPC. Saleh stayed on as the nominal head of the GPC. In 2014, the GPC held 225 out of Yemen's 301 parliamentary seats.

In September 2014, when the Houthis took power, former president Saleh allied himself with them. This deeply divided the GPC membership. In November 2014, the GPC ousted Hadi from his GPC position as secretary general. In January 2015, Hadi and his cabinet fled to Aden. The Saleh-Houthi alliance ended on December 4, 2017, with the assassination of ex-president Saleh and leading members of the GPC. The GPC has now become scattered. Some members are held captive in Sana'a, where the Houthis dictate pronouncements in the name of the party. The rest of the party remains allied with President Hadi's government in exile.

Mark David Luce

See also: Hadi, Abdu Rabbu Mansour; Houthis (Ansar Allah); Saleh, Ali Abdullah; Yemen, Republic of

Further Reading

Dresch, Paul. *A History of Modern Yemen.* Cambridge, UK: Cambridge University Press, 2012.

Poirier, Marine. "Performing Political Domination in Yemen: Narratives and Practices of Power in the General People's Congress." *The Muslim World* 101, no. 2 (April 2011): 202–27.

Gezi Park Protests (2013)

A series of popular uprisings and demonstrations with no political affiliation in 79 out of 81 Turkish cities, mobilizing 2.5 to 3 million people (mainly the urban, educated, middle classes) against Justice and Development Party (AKP) rule, triggered by reports of police brutality against peaceful protesters in Gezi Park, also called the Taksim Square protests. The region is heavily populated by Alevis, and as a main connecting point for transportation links, people often chose it for parades, demonstrations, and protests. The monuments and names of the streets around Taksim Square promoted Turkey's heritage as a republic. People had been protesting against plans to destroy one of the few green spaces in Istanbul since April 2013, supported by a group of civic neighborhood organizations called Taksim Solidarity. In 2009, the AKP-led municipality had approved the construction of a shopping mall and the re-creation of an Ottoman military barracks in the park.

Critics accused the government of glorifying the Ottoman past at the expense of republican symbolism. The Union of Chambers of Turkish Engineers and Taksim Solidarity opposed the project from the beginning, organizing demonstrations, petitioning the courts, and holding vigils. When bulldozing started on May 27, 2013, activists used the hashtag #occupygezi on social media to call protesters.

On the morning of May 28, police violently evicted around 50 young people and then conducted early-morning attacks on four subsequent days. Social media played a central role in bringing activists together, to overcome the apparent blockade by the public media outlets. On May 29, the number of protesters grew, due to outrage at the excessive force used against protesters. Raids on the next two days led to even larger crowds. On Friday, May 31, protests spread across central Istanbul, and people in many other cities took up the same cause. The activists extended their demands for fundamental freedoms and rights and for the end of AKP's encroachments on a secular lifestyle. These peaceful protests used creative and defiant humor in the form of slogans, posters, and grafitti to counteract media censorship, irreverently transforming the political and social rhetoric of power politics.

On June 1, the police temporarily withdrew from Gezi Park itself, but police continued to attack protesters in other parts of the city, and protests spread to even more cities. At Gezi Park, a heterogeneous mixture of Kemalists, leftists, nationalists, LGBT activists, liberal Islamists, feminists, ethnic and religious minorities (Alevis, Kurds, Christians), and football fans assembled. In the next two weeks, Gezi Park became a small mutual-support community. Prime Minister Recep Tayyip Erdogan labeled protesters marauders and defended the construction plans based on the absolute majorities that the AKP gained in all legislative and local elections since 2002.

On the morning of June 11, police tried to clear Taksim Square with aggressive use of tear gas and water cannons, even attacking people who took shelter in nearby hotels and hospitals. This form of police action continued through June 15. On June 17, a silent, stationary protest called "the standing man" took place in the evening. The Turkish medical association reported almost 8,000 were wounded in the weeks of protests, 12 people died all over the country, and almost 5,000 were detained for various periods.

The Gezi Park protests constituted the most important form of political dissent against AKP rule, for four reasons: 1) the AKP lost its image as a liberal democratic party; 2) Turkish society, particularly the youth, became politicized; 3) antagonistic societal groups temporarily worked together; 4) the pro-Kurdish BDP (Peace and Democracy Party) began changing into the HDP (People's Democratic Party) as a big-tent opposition party to defy AKP hegemony.

Isabel David and Kumru F. Toktamis

See also: Alevis; Erdogan, Recep Tayyip; Islamism; Justice and Development Party (Turkey); Kurds; Turkey, Republic of

Further Reading

David, Isabel, and Kumru F. Toktamis, eds. *Everywhere Taksim: Sowing the Seeds for a New Turkey at Gezi.* Amsterdam: Amsterdam University Press, 2015.

Gurcan, Efe C., and Efe Peker. *Challenging Neo-Liberalism at Turkey's Gezi Park: From Private Discontent to Collective Class Action.* London: Palgrave Macmillan, 2015.

Hemer, Oskar, and Hans-Ake Persson, eds. *In the Aftermath of Gezi: From Social Movement to Social Change?* London: Palgrave Macmillan, 2017.

Tufekci, Zeynep. *Twitter and Tear Gas: The Power and Fragility of Networked Protest.* New Haven, CT: Yale University Press, 2018.

Ghannouchi, Rachid

A Tunisian politician, globally recognized, influential Islamist thinker, and cofounder of the Ennahda (Renaissance) Movement, born on June 22, 1941, to a rural family. In 1964, he went to Egypt without the permission of his own government, filled with idealistic support for Nasser's Arab Socialist movement, and began studying agriculture at Cairo University. However, Tunisia persuaded Egypt to send the Tunisians back, so he fled to Syria to pursue his education. In 1968, he graduated from the University of Damascus, with a degree in philosophy. In the middle of his studies he spent seven months touring Europe. On his return, through intensive student debates in the intellectual ferment of the time, he shifted from Arab nationalism to Islamism. He went to Paris to pursue postgraduate studies in philosophy at the Sorbonne. He gained an appreciation for Catholics who maintained conservative morality, while he was disgusted at the immorality of immigrants from Muslim countries, and his observations provided a foundation for his later promotion of religious tolerance. In France he became active in a group that preached Islam to the poor and laborers in the slums, and he became very effective as a public speaker, transforming from a philosophy teacher to a man who invited people to Islam.

In 1981, Ghannouchi helped found Tunisia's Islamic Tendency Movement (MTI). Explicitly nonviolent, the MTI espoused economic opportunity, democracy, and an end to one-party rule. Within a few months, he and his group were arrested and sentenced to prison. Despite significant public support, he remained in prison until 1984, as he studied and wrote his influential book *Al-Hurriyat al-'Ammah (Public Liberties)*. In 1987, the new Zine al-Abidine Ben Ali government opened the prospect of electoral competition. Ghannouchi and his friends decided to form the Ennahda Movement, but the government still refused to register it. Moreover, the government arrested him again in 1987. After the government released him in 1988, he moved to Britain and returned to Tunisia only after the 2011 revolution. On his return, he overcame the fears of the secular opposition by pledging no change to the Personal Status Code, which protects the rights of women.

Ghannouchi consistently refused any formal government position and guided Ennahda to a successful compromise that satisfied those seeking to create a fundamentalist Islamic state, those who continue to support a secular state and society, and a third group who want a secular state that allows a role for Islamic values in shaping political and social behavior. In 2012, Ennahda accommodated these groups by explicitly refusing to make *sharia* the basis of law and by repeatedly opposing Islamist extremists. After several high-profile assassinations of liberal public figures, Ghannouchi led the withdrawal of the party from the government and abstained from participating in the next election. He repeatedly said that even a 60 percent majority in a divided society where democracy had not become fully established could not justify monopolizing power. In 2016, Ghannouchi announced that Ennahda was now a party of Muslim democrats as "there is no longer any justification for political Islam in Tunisia."

Tom Dowling

See also: Arab Nationalism; Ben Ali, Zine al-Abidine; Egypt, Arab Republic of; Ennahda Movement; Islamism; Muslim Brotherhood; Syrian Arab Republic; Tunisia, Republic of

Further Reading

Ghannouchi, Rachid. "From Political Islam to Muslim Democracy: The Ennahda Party and the Future of Tunisia." *Foreign Affairs* 95, no. 5 (September–October 2016): 58–67.

Tamimi, Azzam. *Rachid Ghannouchi: A Democrat within Islamism*. New York: Oxford University Press, 2001.

Yildirim, Ramazan. "Transformation of the Ennahda Movement from Islamic Jama'ah to Political Party." *Insight Turkey* 19, no. 2 (2017): 189–214.

Ghonim, Wael

The head of marketing for Google in the Middle East and North Africa in 2011, born in Cairo in 1981, who had earned a computer engineering degree and a master's degree in business administration. Ghonim discovered, when Mohamed ElBaradei announced he might enter politics, that people commenting on his Facebook page thought as he did. He organized a "Silent Stand" protest, which did not initially draw many people, but the online community used to promote it grew consistently over time, raising his commitment to using the Internet for social protest.

On June 6, 2010, police officers physically removed Khaled Said from an Internet café and killed him. They had taken offense at a video he had posted earlier highlighting police brutality. As a normal, middle-class citizen, Said could have passed his life with little notice, but Ghonim created the Facebook page "We Are All Khalid Said," criticizing police brutality in Egypt. People spread the news about Khalid Said on social media and made him into a symbol of all their grievances against a corrupt authoritarian state. Human rights groups and opposition activists began using the Khalid Said page to publicize police abuse and other issues, culminating in the massive January 25 rally in Tahrir Square. On January 28, the police arrested Ghonim and held him for 12 days. After his release, he made multiple television appearances, expressing his support for the Egyptian street protests. Two days later, his speech to the huge crowd at Tahrir Square galvanized the determination and purpose of the crowds. Since the removal of Hosni Mubarak as president of Egypt, Ghonim started two organizations advocating technology education and wrote his memoirs covering the social revolution in Egypt. He is famous for writing that "if you want to free a society, just give them Internet access," but he later admitted that assessment was in error since the government learned how to counter many online strategies.

Sean Nicholus Blas

See also: April 6 Youth; Authoritarianism; Egypt, Arab Republic of; Grievance Model; Mubarak, Muhammad Hosni Sayyid; Social Media; Tahrir Square Protests

Further Reading

Ghonim, Wael. "Remaking Social Media for the Next Revolution." *MIT Technology Review* 113, no. 3 (May 1, 2016): 26–27.

Ghonim, Wael. *Revolution 2.0: The Power of the People Is Greater Than the People in Power: A Memoir.* New York: Houghton Mifflin Harcourt, 2012.

Khondker, Habibul Haque. "Role of the New Media in the Arab Spring." *Globalizations* 8, no. 5 (2011): 675–79.

Ghouta Chemical Weapons Attack of 2013

A barrage of rocket attacks releasing vast amounts of sarin gas on August 21, 2013, against the Eastern Ghouta suburb outside Damascus. Anywhere from 270 to 1,700 people died, with no official numbers available. At the time, the Assad government controlled much of the areas surrounding Damascus. However, the rebels controlled the predominantly Sunni area of Ghouta, denying Assad's forces freedom of movement in the area.

UN inspectors were present in the country at the time of the attack, to investigate other chemical-weapons incidents. These inspectors visited the site of the Ghouta attack within a week and concluded that sarin gas was undoubtedly used. Bashar Assad and his supporters cite the timing of the attack as suspicious, coinciding with the presence of UN inspectors, as a defense against claims accusing the regime of responsibility.

The attacks drew widespread condemnation, with several countries considering military intervention. The United States and the United Kingdom, among other countries, were convinced the Assad government was responsible for the attack, while the Russian government vehemently disputed that claim. As a result, the Syrian government, with Russia negotiating on its behalf, acceded to an agreement to destroy its chemical-weapons stockpiles and formally became the 190th member of the Chemical Weapons Convention. However, subsequent reports allege that the Assad government has continued in its use of chemical weapons.

Samanvya Singh Hooda

See also: Al-Assad, Bashar; Alawites (Nusayris); Ghouta Chemical Weapons Attack of 2018; Sectarianism; Syrian Civil War

Further Reading

Brown, James D. "'A Nightmare Painted by Goya': Russian Media Coverage of the Syrian Chemical Weapons Attacks in Comparative Perspective." *Problems of Post-Communism* 62, no. 4 (2013): 236–46.

Syzbala, Valerie. *Assad Strikes Damascus.* Washington, DC: Institute for the Study of War, 2014.

Zanders, Jean P., and Ralf Trapp. "Ridding Syria of Chemical Weapons: Next Steps." *Arms Control Today,* November 2013.

Ghouta Chemical Weapons Attack of 2018

Multiple attacks against the Ghouta region of Syria using chemical weapons, on January 22, 2018, killing at least 20 people, and on April 7, 2018, killing at least 42. Experts attribute these attacks to the Syrian government with Russian involvement. The Syrian and Russian governments claimed no chemical weapons had been used. Russia used its UN Security Council veto to hinder investigations into the attacks. The Syrian state media suggest that a group controlling the area concocted video footage of the attack aftermath to solicit support from the international community. The attacks comprise part of the Syrian government's efforts to recapture the rebel-held region of Ghouta, Syria. Journalists reported that the Syrian government used chemical weapons as early as December of 2012. Third-party intelligence sources report the use of sarin and chlorine gas against targeted rebels in April 2013, and Ghouta itself was also attacked in August 2013.

Stephanie Marie Van Sant

See also: Al-Assad, Bashar; Alawites (Nusayris); Ghouta Chemical Weapons Attack of 2013; Sectarianism; Syrian Civil War

Further Reading

Barmet, Céline, and Oliver Thränert. "Syria and the Chemical Weapons Ban." *Policy Perspectives* 4, no. 8. Zurich: Center for Security Studies, November 2016.

Pita, René, and Juan Domingo. "The Use of Chemical Weapons in the Syrian Conflict." *Toxics* 2 (2014): 391–402.

Greed Model

One of three major models of conflict, based on the principle that people fight when the value of what they want exceeds the cost of fighting to get it, considering the risk of failure. Cultural anthropologists and economists call this model "rational" due to the calculation of cost, risk, and benefit. In this model, the person who wants the benefits of wealth and status derived from leading a large group, sometimes called the "political entrepreneur," looks at people, ideas, weapons, and money as tools or "instruments" that he can use to gain his or her objective. Therefore, political scientists call this rational-instrumental thinking the "greed model" of conflict. Because leaders use ideas and the relationships among people to mobilize them into activity, this "resource mobilization" theory gives attention to the social networks among people.

This perspective offers a powerful explanation for the behavior of leaders but also describes how common people respond to insecurity caused by rising crime and violence: they rationally seek protection from an armed group and pledge their commitment of time, labor, and treasure for mutual defense. Activists naturally compete to trigger, manipulate, and appropriate this dynamic consequence of insecurity. Therefore, rational explanations of conflict include both the selfish interests of leaders and the fears people suffer. An attack driven by greed to exploit or oppress another group forces potential victims to calculate their risks of suffering attack versus the risks of responding aggressively. A low cost of surrender or submission, compared to the risk of losing a conflict, will lead to submission. In this model, conflict occurs only when both sides think that they have more power than their opponent. Therefore, preventing conflict requires deterrence, by the demonstration of defensive capability and political will.

Deterrence also applies to discouraging any aspiring leaders from starting a coup or insurrection. Therefore, the rational perspective tends to predict authoritarian rule. Conflict persists as long as the war enables people who can enforce their decisions (regional field commanders, warlords, or drug lords) to receive a continuous flow of benefits, whether from external allies, from exploiting natural resources, or from illicit trafficking networks. This model effectively explains conflict driven by competition for natural resources. Because social scientists can find numbers to represent quantities of resources, they can more easily measure greed as a factor in conflict, when set in opposition to the grievance model.

A rational conflict-resolution strategy expects peace negotiations to occur at a moment when both parties perceive that their conflict has reached a stalemate, in which they have lost hope of winning, while continuing to suffer losses. Successful negotiation requires finding a solution in which both parties believe that they will receive gains from a power-sharing agreement—proportional to their military and political capacities. In this framework, a state possessing the material means to impose control on society enjoys stability, despite the diversity of its constituent ethnic and religious groups. Typical recommendations for sustained peace include a "strong-man" leader, foreign political and military support, and economic resuscitation.

Benjamin V. Allison

See also: Authoritarianism; Clientelism (Patrimonialism); Corruption; Framing Model; Grievance Model; Military Coups; Rentier State Politics

Further Reading

Bensted, Roland. "A Critique of Paul Collier's 'Greed and Grievance' Thesis of Civil War." *African Security Review* 20, no. 3 (2011): 84–90.

Collier, Paul, Anke Hoeffler, and Dominic Rohner. "Beyond Greed and Grievance: Feasibility and Civil War." *Oxford Economic Papers* 61, no. 1 (January 2009): 1–27.

Vici, Anthony. "Greed-Grievance Reconsidered: The Role of Power and Survival in the Motivation of Armed Groups." *Civil Wars* 8, no. 1 (2006): 25–45.

Green Movement (2009)

A nonviolent movement protesting against the announced results of the Iranian presidential elections, in which the government claimed a landslide victory (62.63 percent) for President Mahmoud Ahmadinejad in June 2009. The protesters accused the government of voter fraud and ballot-box stuffing. Two presidential candidates, Mir Hussein Mousavi and Mehdi Karroubi, called for the nullification of the election results. The movement had no real leaders due to its origin as a spontaneous reaction to blatant fraud, so Mousavi and Karroubi became the de facto leaders. The Green Movement adopted Mousavi's campaign color of green.

The Green movement demonstrated Iranians' desire to assert the republican principle of popular sovereignty, as guaranteed in the Iranian constitution, and to undermine the legitimacy of the Iranian theocracy. The movement used the slogan "Where's my vote?" People demanded the release of political prisoners and respect for human rights.

Spontaneous demonstrations sprang up around the central squares and streets of Tehran and later spread to Tabriz, Shiraz, and other cities. Although this reaction took the government by surprise, it quickly used the Basij to brutally suppress the demonstrators, calling them "thugs, seditionists, and monarchists." Police arrested scores of protesters and forced them to confess at "show trials." The protests continued for more than six months. The government put both Mousavi and Karroubi under house arrest.

Pundits have called the movement the "Twitter Revolution" because protesters used Facebook, Twitter, blogs, e-mail, online newsletters, and short message service (SMS) to spread their messages and discuss slogans and strategies for the demonstrations. To aid the movement, Google and Facebook added Persian versions of their websites. Green Movement members posted the names, addresses, and phone numbers of the security force members featured in mobile phone broadcasts of photos and videos of women and children being beaten. After the government suppressed the first wave of protests, the movement exploited public observances of key events and religious holidays, to protest when large numbers of Iranians would customarily come out in public.

The political crisis alienated many of Iran's clerical elites, former presidents Akbar Hashemi Rafsanjani and Mohammad Khatami, and former Majles Speaker Mehdi Karroubi. It renewed Iran's constitutional struggle between the republican versus autocratic character of the state. Grand Ayatollah Hussein Ali Montazeri criticized the Supreme Leader, Ayatollah Ali Khamenei, and called the crackdown unholy and illegal.

Violent suppression of peaceful unarmed demonstrators at Montazeri's funeral, and later during Ashura demonstrations, caused five respected intellectuals in exile to release a manifesto. They referred to Montazeri as the Green Movement's spiritual leader, and to the regime as "religious despotism." They called the Supreme Leader the "tyrannical guardian." The manifesto demanded reform, democratization, the observance of human rights, religious tolerance, and recognition of pluralism in politics.

Mark David Luce

See also: Ahmadinejad, Mahmoud; Authoritarianism; Democracy Deficit; Islamic Revolutionary Guard Corps (IRGC); Khatami, Mohammad; Rafsanjani, Ali Akbar Hashemi; Social Media

Further Reading
Dabashi, Hamid. *Iran, The Green Movement and the USA: The Fox and the Paradox.* London: Zed Books, 2010.

Hashemi, Nader, and Danny Postel, eds. *The People Reloaded: The Green Movement and the Struggle for Iran's Future.* Brooklyn, NY: Melville House, 2010.

Milani, Abbas, and Larry Diamond, eds. *Politics and Culture in Contemporary Iran.* Boulder, CO, and London: Lynne Rienner Publishers, 2015.

Grievance Model

One of three models of conflict, based on the principle that people fight when they become angry, due to the violation of their basic human needs for security, identity, and recognition, as well as when they face threats to their means of survival. This model argues that people defend their identity, whether considered in terms of ethnicity, religion, or even language, as fixed and unchanging.

Although individuals can learn a second, third, and more languages, a group of people usually rebels against restrictions on the free and public use of their language, considering it a threat to the survival of their shared identity. Therefore, a minority group often develops a grievance against a state that seeks to impose a monolithic language in the public sphere. Although individuals do sometimes change their religion, groups usually resist fiercely any pressure to change their shared beliefs. The imposition of such pressure constitutes a strong grievance. On the other hand, individual members of a minority ethnic group may seek to assimilate to the dominant ethnicity to avoid persecution, only to suffer rejection due to their appearance or persistent adverse images of their group from the past. When minority ethnic groups face discrimination, whether they flee, or stay and suffer, they preserve their grievances.

Because cultural anthropologists document how individuals can change important aspects of their identity over time, they reject the concept of fixed identities, commonly called primordialism. Historians agree, because they trace changes in groups over long periods. However, observers should not let these academic complaints prevent them from understanding the contributions of this concept to a full understanding of conflict. Despite the academic disapproval, this perspective dominates the way the popular media approach conflict. An excessive emphasis on this perspective leads to a false portrayal of ethnic identity as "ancient hatreds" boiling in a pot, repressed by the authoritarian state. In fact, a global comparison of the great numbers of ethnic groups shows that ethnic conflict remains statistically rare, and therefore, conflict requires more factors than merely ethnic differences.

In addition to grievances based on identity, a whole population may develop grievances against their rulers, or the ruling class, based on a perception of relative deprivation. The vast masses of people excluded from the benefits given by an authoritarian ruler to an inner circle of supporters hold grievances against the ruler and those supporters, demanding justice and the prosecution of corruption. When they protest and the ruling authorities crush them, this strengthens and reinforces their grievances. According to the grievance perspective, any relaxation of central control would permit these grievances to generate a spontaneous, violent social movement. Sociologists refer to this perspective as breakdown theory, because when government control breaks down, people protest against the injustice they have suffered.

Authoritarian rulers can rely on the people of their own clan, tribe, and hometown, but often blame smaller groups for the problems in society, thus laying the foundation for tribal conflict and sectarian warfare. Furthermore, corruption inhibits business investment, which prevents economic growth, leaving a large

Gulf Cooperation Council (GCC)

percentage of the population unemployed. Their hunger adds to their grievances. In corrupt societies, education, health care, public utilities, and services all falter, creating a broad base of grievances in the general population. When political scientists discuss civil wars, they commonly contrast grievances with explanations based on rational calculations, or greed. Conflict mediation of grievances requires developing state institutions to protect the rights of groups suffering discrimination, provide justice, fight corruption, and provide social services. Peacebuilders conduct dialogues to help all sides of the conflict to understand the grievances of the other parties and to explore ways to resolve them.

Benjamin V. Allison

See also: Authoritarianism; Civil Wars; Corruption; Democracy Deficit; Framing Model; Greed Model; Minorities; Sectarianism

Further Reading

Burton, John. *Conflict: Resolution and Prevention.* New York: St. Martin's Press, 1990.

Gurr, Ted Robert. *Peoples versus States: Minorities at Risk in the New Century.* Washington, DC: United States Institute of Peace Press, 2000.

Vally, Koubi, and Tobias Böhmelt. "Grievances, Economic Wealth, and Civil Conflict." *Journal of Peace Research* 51, no. 1 (January 2014): 19–33.

Gülen, Fethullah. *See* Hizmat [Gülen] Movement

Gulf Cooperation Council (GCC)

An intergovernmental organization established in the Gulf region to foster the strategic, economic, and political integration of its members. In 1979, Iran's efforts to export its Islamic Revolution threatened its neighbors, especially the Sunni monarchies along the shore of the Arabian Peninsula. Iraq reacted to these activities by invading Iran on September 22, 1980. This amplified the shared perception of threat. On May 25, 1981, Saudi Arabia, Oman, and Kuwait organized a summit meeting with Qatar and Bahrain in Abu Dhabi, UAE (United Arab Emirates), to inaugurate the Gulf Cooperation Council (GCC). The initial reaction focused on economic cooperation to provide for mutual self-defense. The Unified Economic Agreement provided a framework to eliminate customs duties and promote the free movement of labor, capital, and entrepreneurs within member states. After the Iran-Iraq conflict shifted from land warfare to attacks on shipping, the member states more intensively integrated their defense coordination. In 1984 they decided to form a joint military force, the Peninsula Shield Forces; however, the member states failed to follow through with the necessary organizational, political, and material resources to create a competent force.

In 1991, the GCC states participated in—together with 85 other states—but did not lead the response to Iraq's invasion of Kuwait. In 2011, these states called for the international community to impose a no-fly zone in Libya during Qaddafi's efforts to suppress an uprising—ahead of the Arab League, an important push for the eventual operation. Although Qatar and the UAE started out supporting the mission in order to protect civilians, they supported opposing sides in the Libyan civil war. Saudi Arabia, Qatar, and the UAE deployed forces to protect infrastructure in Bahrain during protests in 2011. The GCC states, with the exception of Oman, formed the core of the March 2015 coalition assembled by Saudi Arabia for an intervention in Yemen, called Operation Decisive Storm. The June 2017 air, sea, and land blockade of Qatar by Saudi Arabia, the UAE, and Bahrain demonstrates the conflicting state perspectives and difficulties in achieving consensus in this organization. Oman and Kuwait have consistently worked to mediate disputes within the GCC, as well as those with Iran.

The states of the GCC face security threats posed by the wars in Yemen and Iraq and by Iranian ambitions. They claim to promote the political values of moderation, compromise, and patience in coexistence, but in practice they primarily protect the monarchical political system and values. The six smaller states use the GCC as one tool to restrain the ambitions of Saudi Arabia and Iran, while keeping the United States as an available but distant protector.

Philipp O. Amour

See also: Bahrain, Kingdom of; Iran, Islamic Republic of; Iraq, Republic of; Kuwait, State of; Libya, State of; Oman, Sultanate of; Operation Decisive Storm; Qaddafi, Muammar; Qatar; Saudi Arabia, Kingdom of; United Arab Emirates (UAE); Yemen, Republic of

Further Reading

Kechichian, Joseph A. *From Alliance to Union: Challenges Facing Gulf Cooperation Council States*. Brighton, UK: Sussex Academic Press, 2016.

Martini, Jeffrey, Becca Wasser, Dalia Dassa Kaye, Daniel Egel, and Cordaye Ogletree. *The Outlook for Arab Gulf Cooperation*. Santa Monica, CA: RAND, 2016.

Ramady, Mohamed A. *Political, Economic and Financial Country Risk: Analysis of the Gulf Cooperation Council*. Cham, Switzerland: Springer, 2014.

H

Hadi, Abdu Rabbu Mansour

A Yemeni soldier and politician who became president of Yemen through years of tumult and war after the protests of 2011, supported by an international coalition led by the Kingdom of Saudi Arabia. Abdu Rabbu Mansour Hadi, born on September 1, 1945, in Thukain, Abyan Governorate, Yemen, graduated from a military academy in the Federation of South Arabia (Aden). He received military scholarships to study in Egypt and the Soviet Union. Hadi served as a major general under President Ali Nasir Muhammad during the South Yemen civil war (1986), then fled to North Yemen for asylum before the unification of North and South Yemen in 1991. Hadi sided with President Saleh during the 1994 civil war. Saleh appointed him as minister of Defense to lead the war against the South and as vice president.

After the unrest of the Arab Spring, on February 21, 2012, Hadi was elected president to head a two-year transitional government until the conclusion of the National Dialogue Conference (NDC) and the ratification of a new constitution. After the Houthis took over Sana'a in September 2014, however, Hadi entered into a power-sharing arrangement with them. In November 2014, the General People's Congress (GPC) removed Hadi from his position as GPC's secretary general. In January 2015, Hadi resigned as president. After a brief period of house arrest, Hadi and his cabinet escaped to Aden and then to exile in Saudi Arabia. In March 2015, Saudi Arabia and the UAE formed a coalition to invade Yemen and restore Hadi and his cabinet to power. Hadi's internal support comes mainly from elements of the GPC, the al-Islah party, and forces from Yemen's elite Republican Guard led by Brigadier General Tariq Muhammad Abdullah Saleh, its former commander.

Mark David Luce

See also: Al-Islah (Reform Party); General People's Congress; Houthis (Ansar Allah); Saleh, Ali Abdullah; Saudi Arabia, Kingdom of; United Arab Emirates (UAE); Yemen, Republic of

Further Reading

Clark, Victoria. *Yemen: Dancing on the Head of Snakes.* New Haven, CT: Yale University Press, 2010.

"Yemen: Is Peace Possible?" *Middle East Report* No. 167. Brussels: International Crisis Group, February 9, 2016.

Haftar, Khalifa Belqasim

A Libyan political and military leader who played a driving role in the Libyan Civil War, beginning in 2014. Born in the city of Ajdabiya circa 1943, Khalifa Haftar completed his military education in 1966, graduating from the Benghazi

University Military Academy. As a junior officer he joined the Libyan Free Officers Movement led by Muammar Qaddafi and took part in the 1969 Libyan coup d'état that brought down the Senussi monarchy.

Khalifa Haftar held important political and military positions during Qaddafi's rule. As a member of the military junta, he served on the Revolutionary Command Council. He commanded the Libyan contingent in the 1973 Yom Kippur War. He also led Libyan forces in the Chadian-Libyan War (1978–1987). However, Chad defeated the Libyan forces and captured him. Qaddafi held him responsible for the defeat and disowned him. He moved to the United States and tried unsuccessfully to topple Qaddafi in the 1996 uprising. During the 2011 Libyan Revolution, Haftar returned to Libya and joined the opposition military in the eastern section of the country called Cyrenaica. The rebel forces did not readily welcome him due to his past history of working for Qaddafi, not to mention the support he received from the CIA in his plot to overthrow Qaddafi.

On February 14, 2014, he declared the GNC suspended because it had exceeded its term of office. In May 2014, Islamists were assassinating activists, politicians, journalists, security professionals, and army officers in Benghazi almost every day. Haftar launched an offensive he called Operation Karama (Dignity) on May 16, purportedly to cleanse Libya of terrorism. He built a military force with aid from Egypt, Russia, and the United Arab Emirates. On March 2, 2015, the House of Representatives (HoR) appointed him commander of the Libyan National Army (LNA), with the rank of lieutenant-general. In September 2016, the LNA captured the important oil terminals at Sidra and Ras Lanuf. The HoR then promoted him from lieutenant-general to field marshal. The LNA lost these areas in March 2017 but regained them in 2018. In December 2016 and January 2017, the LNA captured airfields in the south and by September 2017 finally consolidated control of Benghazi.

In April 2018, he went to Paris for three weeks of medical treatment. During five years of fighting he has assembled a heterogeneous coalition, gathering prominent secular politicians as well as army officers and militias from Zintan and Benghazi. On April 5, 2019, his forces moved to take control of Tripoli.

Taylan Paksoy

See also: General National Congress; Libya, State of; Libyan Civil War; Military Coups; Qaddafi, Muammar

Further Reading

Lacher, Wolfram. "Libya's Local Elites and the Politics of Alliance Building." *Mediterranean Politics* 21, no. 1 (2016): 64–85.

Tawil, Camille. "Operation Dignity: General Haftar's Latest Battle May Decide Libya's Future." *Terrorism Monitor* 12, no. 11 (May 30, 2014): 8–11

Wehrey, Frederic. *Burning Shores: Inside the Battle for the New Libya.* New York: Farrar, Straus and Giroux, 2018.

Hamas

A political party and militia with roots in the Muslim Brotherhood. Organized in 1987 to resist Israel, Hamas gained control over the Gaza Strip in 2006. The Ḥarakat al-Muqāwamah al-ʾIslāmiyyah (Hamas—Islamic Resistance Movement)

has frequently spent the bulk of its budget on social-welfare programs, in keeping with Islamic understandings of obligations to charity. The provision of social services has led people to define their loyalties to Hamas rather than to the formal political structure of the Palestinian Authority. This reflects the Muslim Brotherhood's strategy, which enabled it to endure for decades as a marginalized and illicit political party. Hamas gives money to Palestinians who lose their homes due to Israeli military actions and to the families of Palestinians who become casualties as a result of combat against Israeli forces and attacks on its citizens.

Hamas gained elected authority in the Palestinian parliamentary elections for Gaza in early 2006, reflecting popular disappointment with the politically dominant Fatah Party associated with the Palestine Liberation Organization (PLO). Fighting between Fatah and Hamas forces flared in 2007. However, independent polling efforts a decade later suggest that residents of Gaza do not generally support Hamas's ideological opposition to a two-state solution for the lands of the former Palestine Mandate. Until 2011, Egypt gave the appearance of cooperating with Israeli efforts to restrict the shipment of military supplies to the Gaza strip. However, hundreds of tunnels allowed massive amounts of smuggled goods to flow. After the collapse of Hosni Mubarak's regime in Egypt in 2011, the Muslim Brotherhood regime under Mohamed Morsi opened the Rafah Crossing to allow residents of Gaza into Egypt, but this stopped on July 5, 2013, after the fall of Morsi's government. Due to its tactics, frequently involving suicide bombing attacks targeting civilians, most states call Hamas a terrorist organization. Hamas works to disrupt initiatives toward any regional peace that involves a secure future for Israel. It depends greatly on financial support and military equipment from Iran, often channeled through Hezbollah. Qatar and Turkey have given Hamas strategic support.

Nicholas Michael Sambaluk

See also: Abbas, Mahmoud; Fatah Party; Hezbollah; Iran, Islamic Republic of; Muslim Brotherhood; Palestine Liberation Organization; Palestinian Islamic Jihad; Qatar; Turkey, Republic of; Primary Document: *The Arab Peace Initiative*

Further Reading
Jefferis, Jennifer. *Hamas: Terrorism, Governance, and Its Future in Middle East Politics.* Santa Barbara, CA: Praeger Security Studies, 2016.

Milton-Edwards, Beverley, and Stephen Farrell. *Hamas: The Islamic Resistance Movement.* Cambridge, UK: Polity Press, 2010.

Hamas-Fatah Conflict

An armed struggle between the two most significant factions in Palestinian politics in the aftermath of the Second Intifada (2000–2004), the death of Yasser Arafat in 2004, and Hamas's unexpected victory in the Palestinian legislative elections on January 25, 2006. The conflict, costing an estimated 600 Palestinian lives, included foreign clandestine forces and the use of extreme brutality on both sides. It led to a protracted division in Palestinian politics that resulted in authoritarian rule by the Palestinian Authority (PA), which lost any pretense of democratic legitimacy.

Following the death of Arafat and his replacement by Mahmoud Abbas as president in 2004, the British Intelligence Service drew up secret plans (later leaked to the press) for a military crackdown on Hamas and other armed groups by Palestinian Authority security forces. In 2005, Israel pulled its citizens and security forces from Gaza under strong attack from Hamas.

In the 2006 legislative elections, judged to be "free and fair" by independent observers, Hamas achieved an overwhelming victory, winning 74 of the 132 seats. Israel, the United States, and the European Union (as well as several other donors, including some Arab states) suspended foreign aid to Palestine, leading to significant economic distress in occupied territories.

Between March and December 2006, the rivalry between Hamas and Fatah gradually escalated, primarily over control of the Palestinian security forces. Hamas announced the creation of its own "Executive Force," while Abbas developed his own, expanded Presidential Guard. On December 14, Fatah-aligned militants attempted to assassinate Ismail Haniyeh, the leader of Hamas in Gaza and prime minister of the Palestinian National Authority. Abbas denied responsibility for the attack on Haniyeh. News of these events sparked widespread protests in the West Bank, which police repressed with brutality. Abbas called for fresh elections on December 16, 2006. The next day, militants attacked another top Hamas official.

Despite an agreement signed on February 8, 2007, in Mecca, sporadic violence continued. On June 14, Hamas fighters took over Preventative Security Forces headquarters in Gaza. Forces loyal to Fatah countered in the northern West Bank cities of Nablus and Jenin. President Abbas dissolved the government, declaring a state of emergency, and began to rule by decree. Abbas appointed a new government under Salam Fayyad on June 15, 2007. Foreign governments quickly recognized this new government and restored aid. The new government shut down Hamas's social and civil society infrastructure throughout the West Bank, arrested scores of Hamas members, and imposed censorship even in mosques. It also gradually moved against the al-Aqsa Martyrs' Brigades forces aligned to Fatah. Human Rights Watch alleged that both sides engaged in torture and other criminal behavior.

Hamas disputed the legitimacy of the West Bank government and consolidated its rule through violent attacks on Fatah-aligned groups and suppression of pro-Fatah demonstrators in October and November 2007. Despite several changes of key leaders on both sides and several attempts to reconcile every year since 2007, the situation remains in a stalemate.

Philip Leech-Ngo

See also: Fatah Party; Fayyad, Salam; Hamas; Intifadas (I, II, and Knife); Israel; Palestine

Further Reading

Brown, Nathan J. "The Hamas-Fatah Conflict: Shallow But Wide." *Fletcher Forum of World Affairs* 34, no. 2 (Summer 2010): 35–49.

Elgindy, Khaled. "Lost in the Chaos: The Palestinian Leadership Crisis." *The Washington Quarterly* 38, no. 4 (Winter 2016): 133–50.

Hoigilt, Jacob. "The Palestinian Spring That Was Not: The Youth and Political Activism in the Occupied Palestinian Territories." *Arab Studies Quarterly* 35, no. 4 (2013): 343–59.

Hariri, Saad

A Sunni, Lebanese billionaire businessman and politician. Saad al-Din Rafīq al-Ḥariri, born on April 18, 1970, in Riyadh, Saudi Arabia, became the heir to his father's political legacy and businesses, worth about four billion dollars. After receiving his education in France and Saudi Arabia, in 1992, he graduated with a degree in business administration from Georgetown University in Washington, DC. He then went to work for his father's construction business in Saudi Arabia, where he managed projects resulting in significant expansions of the business. He gained a good relationship with the Saudi royal family with his pleasant personality. On February 14, 2005, a huge car bomb killed his father and 21 other people. His brother declined to take up his father's political commitments but chose instead to focus on his own business interests, working from the family estate in Geneva.

In alliance with Walid Jumblatt and several Maronite Christian groups, Saad Hariri led the March 14 coalition, which protested against the assassination of his father during the Cedar Revolution and blamed Syria and Hezbollah. Over the next four years he developed his skills, connections, and reputation as a Lebanese politician engaged in managing the extensive patronage network built by his father. He successfully lobbied for financial aid for Lebanon from the United States and negotiated an agreement among political parties to form a government in 2007. In the June 2009 parliamentary elections, the March 14 coalition gained the most votes. After great difficulty, he formed a government in November, which collapsed in January 2011. He moved to Paris for safety amid tensions, assassinations, and threats from Syria, but returned to Lebanon in 2014.

After the absence of a president for over two years, Hariri overcame the political stalemate by supporting Michel Aoun, allied with Hezbollah, for president, who then appointed Hariri as prime minister in December 2016. His Saudi construction business had collapsed, and his wealth dropped to one and a half billion dollars. On November 2, 2017, the government of Saudi Arabia called him to come, but then Saudi officials held him without communication until November 4. Then he gave a televised resignation speech, which President Aoun refused to accept. On November 9, 2017, French president Emmanuel Macron went to Riyadh to negotiate his release. On November 22, 2017, he returned to Lebanon, rescinded his resignation, and claimed that he had good relations with Saudi Arabia. In the May 2018 parliamentary elections, his coalition lost many seats. Hariri made severe concessions to break the political stalemate of the previous years and was appointed as prime minister again.

Jonathan K. Zartman

See also: Cedar Revolution; Hezbollah; Jumblatt, Walid; Lebanese Republic; Maronites; Saudi Arabia, Kingdom of; Syrian Arab Republic

Further Reading

Arsan, Andrew. *Lebanon: A Country in Fragments*. London: Hurst and Co, 2018.

Khashan, Hilal. "Saad Hariri's Moment of Truth." *Middle East Quarterly* 18, no. 1 (Winter 2011): 65–71.

Vloeberghs, Ward. "The Hariri Political Dynasty after the Arab Spring." *Mediterranean Politics* 17, no. 2 (July 2012): 241–48.

Hayat Tahrir al-Sham (HTS)

An extremist Salafist militant group that has been fighting in the Syrian Civil War since 2011. Hayat Tahrir al-Sham (HTS; Organization for the Liberation of the Levant) formed as an offshoot of al-Qaeda in Syria. It emerged from the January 28, 2017, merger of Jabhat Fatah al-Sham (JFS)—previously known as Jabhat al-Nusra (JAN; or Al-Nusra Front)—with some other militias. Abu Muhammad Al-Golani began the Al-Nusra Front as a franchise and later spinoff from al-Qaeda. It claims to provide support—*nusra*—for "oppressed Muslims in Syria." The group conducts combat against the Syrian government and engages in noncombat activities in rebel-held areas. It appeals to a global community of zealous Salafi Islamists for additional fighters and financial support. They provide security and welfare services, deliver essential commodities, and administer food-basket programs in areas JAN controls. Its propaganda material mixes messages of commitment to combat with themes and vocabulary drawn from liberal humanitarianism, in an effort to evoke a global, militant, Islamist "duty of care" and "responsibility to protect."

Jabhat Al-Nusra competed with the Islamic State (Daesh) in Syria, in spite of efforts by mediators to prevent armed confrontation. In 2013, al-Golani publicly rejected an overture by his Daesh counterpart, Abu Bakr Al-Baghdadi. Despite the operational and strategic divergence between JAN and Daesh, discerning the difference on the ground becomes difficult. However, JAN recruits foreign fighters and establishes institutions for a temporary purpose, in contrast to the efforts of Daesh to establish a durable caliphate.

While al-Qaeda's influence persists, al-Golani recreated Jabhat al-Nusra as JFS to disavow links with external parties, al-Qaeda included. Until late 2016, JFS was close to Harakat Ahrar al-Sham al-Islamiyya (AS), which exercises similar military strength as JFS in northern Syria. Due to reports that talks between the two groups broke down, many AS members defected to JFS, and later to HTS. Abu Mohammad al-Golani, the first head of Jabhat al-Nusra, continues to lead HTS. The fighters of JAN/JFS hold the greatest operational capability of the groups in the alliance, and they now serve in the organization's senior leadership. The U.S. government, along with other countries, has designated HTS a terrorist organization. Estimates say HTS has between 10,000 and 20,000 fighters, and the group has conducted operations primarily in northern Syria, from its headquarters in the Idlib Governorate.

Fouad Gehad Marei and Samanvya Singh Hooda

See also: Al-Assad, Bashar; Al-Qaeda Central; Islamic State (Daesh); Islamism; Syrian Arab Republic

Further Reading

Cafarella, Jennifer. *Jabhat al-Nusra in Syria*. Washington, DC: Institute for the Study of War, 2014.

Heller, Sam. "The Strategic Logic of Hayat Tahrir al-Sham." *Perspectives on Terrorism* 11, no. 6 (December 2017): 139–52.

Lister, Charles R. *The Syrian Jihad: Al-Qaeda, the Islamic State and the Evolution of an Insurgency*. New York: Oxford University Press, 2015.

Hezbollah

A Shi'a Islamist organization founded in Lebanon in 1982 in response to the Israeli invasion of southern Lebanon. Hezbollah (Party of God) initially functioned as a guerrilla resistance against Israeli occupation, but the group's goals and forms of operation quickly expanded as it grew in size and power. Iran has funded Hezbollah throughout its existence and has also provided extensive access to high technology weaponry and logistics. After Israel withdrew from Lebanon in 2000, Hezbollah further expanded its methods of operation, becoming a political party that achieved moderate success in its electoral campaigns. It functions as a state-within-a-state: Hezbollah prohibits Lebanese government officials from entering areas under its control. Hezbollah's military wing has substantially greater fighting capability than the Lebanese Army and has engaged in many clashes with Israeli forces.

In 1975, religious and social schisms in Lebanon erupted into a civil war. The presence of millions of displaced Palestinians, coupled with existing tensions between Christian, Sunni, and Shi'a factions, created an extremely convoluted situation. Syria exploited this situation and occupied most of Lebanon in support of Shi'a militias. In 1982, Israeli Defense Forces (IDF) units invaded and occupied southern Lebanon, largely in support of the South Lebanon Army (SLA), a Christian militia. Hezbollah first began as a consolidation of smaller Shi'a militias in opposition to the Amal Movement. It immediately began conducting guerrilla warfare against the Israelis.

It also attacked the UN peacekeeping forces sent by the United States and France. On October 23, 1983, a pair of Hezbollah truck bombs struck the barracks housing U.S. and French troops, killing 241 U.S. and 58 French peacekeepers, as well as six civilians. This made Hezbollah the deadliest terrorist group in the world until September 11, 2011, and caused the U.S. Department of State to list Hezbollah as a foreign terrorist organization when creating the list on October 8, 1997. Later in the 1980s, Hezbollah operatives hijacked aircraft and launched a series of suicide attacks upon Israeli and SLA troops in Lebanon. Hezbollah repeatedly launched indiscriminate rocket attacks into northern Israel to hit Israeli citizens. Many pieces of evidence link Hezbollah to the June 14, 1985, hijacking of TWA Flight 847, which included the public murder of one U.S. sailor and triggered the release of over 700 Lebanese prisoners from Israeli jails. In the 1980s, Hezbollah operatives increasingly relied upon kidnapping for ransom: between 1982 and 1988, over 40 percent of all international kidnappings took place in Lebanon. Kidnappers targeted Westerners, both for ransoms and to persuade Western nations to withdraw their military and diplomatic personnel.

In 1985, Hezbollah released a manifesto identifying its goals: the eradication of the state of Israel, the end of Zionism, and the formation of a *sharia*-based state in Lebanon. It demanded that all foreign forces withdraw from Lebanon—while ignoring the 2,000 members of Iran's Revolutionary Guard advising and training Hezbollah operatives. To emphasize the value of martyrdom, Hezbollah established a Martyrs' Foundation to support suicide attacks with the necessary logistics and to reward the families of suicide attackers. During the 1990s, Hezbollah expanded geographically to develop a major presence in South America. In 1992, a Hezbollah suicide truck bombing against the Israeli Embassy in Buenos Aires killed 29 and injured 242. Two years later, Hezbollah attackers struck the Argentine-Israeli Mutual Association, killing 114, mostly Israelis.

Following the end of the Lebanese Civil War in 1990, and the Israeli withdrawal in 2000, Hezbollah modified its ideology while preserving its commitment to annihilating Israel. In particular, the group began emphasizing political activities and providing social services, following the pattern of Hamas and the Muslim Brotherhood, suggesting that Hezbollah might pursue international recognition. In 2000, Hezbollah operatives abducted three IDF soldiers patrolling the Lebanese border, and four years later exchanged their bodies for the release of Lebanese prisoners. In 2004, Hezbollah announced a new three-pillar vision for itself, calling for the establishment of *sharia* law in Lebanon, the obligation of *jihad* for all Shi'a Muslims, and the necessity of *velayat-e faqih* (the Iranian ideology of rule by the supreme religious teacher as a guardian). The Islamic Republic of Iran directed the last pillar.

In 2006, Hezbollah forces raided across the border and fired rockets at Israeli border towns and the city of Haifa. In retaliation, the Israelis launched an attack into Lebanon, backed by heavy artillery and airstrikes, with the aim of destroying Hezbollah's fighting capability. After 34 days of bloody conflict, characterized by thousands of rocket attacks upon Israel and almost unlimited airstrikes against Hezbollah positions, the two sides declared a cease-fire. Hezbollah declared victory in the conflict, on the grounds that the IDF failed to eradicate their paramilitary units.

Hassan Nasrallah serves as the secretary-general of Hezbollah, a position he has occupied since 1992, despite several assassination attempts ostensibly linked to Israel. Nasrallah has led the group into more aggressive attacks against civilian targets in Israel. In return, Iran has supplied Hezbollah with increasingly sophisticated military hardware, such as long-range rockets and unmanned aircraft, recently deployed against Israeli citizens. In addition to millions of small arms and vast quantities of ammunition, Hezbollah has also received anti-tank and anti-ship weapons from Iran. To date, the Israeli antimissile defense system, Iron Dome, has quite successfully intercepted Hezbollah rockets projected to hit inhabited areas. However, lack of recent successes has not deterred Hezbollah, which continues to launch missiles into Israel after almost any significant event.

Hezbollah consists of three functional divisions: 1) military and security functions; 2) political and administrative activities; and 3) the social services wing. The Leadership Apparatus Shura Council, headed by Nasrallah, includes representatives of each wing. At the regional level, Hezbollah also includes these three wings. The dual nature—social services and military—permeates Hezbollah. Despite the Shura Council's claims that Hezbollah consists of two entirely separate entities operating in Lebanon, the people cannot relate to the social services wing without supporting the military-terrorist operations.

In 2005, political leaders of Hezbollah directed military operatives in assassinating former Lebanese prime minister Rafic Hariri with a bomb that detonated as his motorcade passed the St. George Hotel in Beirut. The assassination sparked a series of protests that grew into the Cedar Revolution, a fundamental social shift that eventually forced Syria to withdraw its troops from Lebanese territory. Hariri's son Saad served as prime minister from late 2009 until June 2011 and resumed the office in December 2016. He has continually clashed with Hezbollah representatives in the parliament and has called for the ouster of Bashar al-Assad, Syria's president. As of the elections held on May 5, 2018, Hezbollah holds 13 of the 128 seats in the Lebanese Parliament, and two of 30 cabinet positions, and continues to oppose Hariri's rule. For his part, Hariri has demanded, in vain, that Hezbollah disband its paramilitary forces and disarm.

Hezbollah's extensive social services operations provide hospitals, schools, and media organizations for the Shi'a population of Lebanon. During the 2006 war, Hezbollah supplied humanitarian aid to citizens in Beirut, who were left without power and water due to Israeli attacks. The Hezbollah educational system promotes its strategy of attacks upon Israel with anti-Semitic and Holocaust-denying campaigns throughout the world. The Hezbollah-run media organizations include the influential satellite television station Al-Manar, which supports martyrdom operations by praising suicide bombers for their attacks against Jewish and Israeli targets. The social branch of Hezbollah consumes an increasing share of the organization's budget and personnel resources. Providing these services effectively generates support from the civilian population but creates expectations that these services will continue. Hezbollah boasts about providing key services in demanding international recognition.

In addition to extensive support in cash and supplies from the governments of Iran and Syria, Hezbollah also extracts funding from within Lebanon, through the contributions of business groups and private individuals. It solicits money from members of the Lebanese diaspora and through a variety of illicit sources, including cigarette smuggling, narcotics trade, and dealing in blood diamonds. Hezbollah engages in money-laundering, credit-card fraud, and cyberattacks upon businesses and banks.

In 2013, Nasrallah announced that Hezbollah had deployed forces to Syria to combat "Islamic extremists," in particular the Sunni terror organization the Islamic State (Daesh). Despite fighting against a common foe, the Hezbollah forces have not cooperated effectively with the Syrian Army. In July 2014, Nasrallah's nephew, Hamzah Yassine, was killed in the Syrian fighting.

Despite the severe attrition of Hezbollah's forces fighting in Syria, it still holds significant military capabilities and remains one of the most dangerous terror organizations in the world. Hezbollah's efforts to prop up the Al-Assad regime demonstrated its regional presence and willingness to export violence to other theaters offering opportunities. Nasrallah and the other leaders of Hezbollah have launched attacks against non-Shi'a civilians that they view as a hindrance to their greater control of power. Hezbollah trainers have given substantial help to the Houthis in their battles in Yemen. So long as Hezbollah remains the largest armed group in Lebanon, the Lebanese government cannot become a fully functioning representative of the Lebanese people. Rather, it will continue to exist largely at the sufferance of Hezbollah and its supporters.

Paul J. Springer

See also: Al-Assad, Bashar; Al Manar Television; Cedar Revolution; Hamas; Hariri, Saad; Houthis (Ansar Allah); Islamic State (Daesh); Israel; Lebanese Republic; Nasrallah, Hassan Abdel Karim; Palestine Liberation Organization; Refugees; Syrian Arab Republic

Further Reading

Azani, Eitan. *Hezbollah: The Story of the Party of God, from Revolution to Institutionalization.* New York: Palgrave Macmillan, 2011.

Blanford, Nicholas. *Warriors of God: Inside Hezbollah's Thirty-Year Struggle against Israel.* New York: Random House, 2011.

Daher, Aurlie. *Hezbollah: Mobilization and Power.* New York: Oxford University Press, 2016.

Deeb, Marius. *Syria, Iran, and Hezbollah: The Unholy Alliance and Its War on Lebanon.* Stanford, CA: Hoover Institution Press, 2013.

Gleis, Joshua L., and Benedetta Berti. *Hezbollah and Hamas: A Comparative Study.* Baltimore: Johns Hopkins University Press, 2012.

Harel, Amos, Ora Cummings, Moshe Tlamim, and Avi Isacharoff. *34 Days: Israel, Hezbollah, and the War in Lebanon.* New York: Palgrave Macmillan, 2009.

Harik, Judith. *Hezbollah: The Changing Face of Terrorism.* New York: I. B. Tauris, 2007.

Levitt, Matthew. *Hezbollah: The Global Footprint of Lebanon's Party of God.* Washington, DC: Georgetown University Press, 2013.

Norton, Augustus R. *Hezbollah: A Short History.* Princeton, NJ: Princeton University Press, 2009.

Qassem, Naim. *Hizbullah: The Story from Within.* London: Saqi, 2010.

Hizmet (Gülen) Movement

A conservative Turkish religious movement active in civil society, education, and business in over 150 countries. It embodies the teaching of Fethullah Gülen, who began his public life employed by the Directory for Religious Affairs (Diaynet) as a preacher in Izmir, Turkey. Gülen diagnosed the crisis in Turkish society, which took the form of political violence, extremism, and secularization. In response, he developed constructive and innovative solutions that convinced many people: instead of building mosques, the Hizmet (service) Movement invested in schools to broaden access to university education for religious students suffering exclusion under the secular Turkish state. Hizmet founded businesses and civil society organizations and promoted dialogue initiatives, while at the same time promoting the traditional family. Hizmet also built up a network of loyal members in the state bureaucracy. After growing into the strongest Turkish civil society movement, it allied itself with other Islamic activists in the 1990s to dislodge the authoritarian regime.

The movement consists of several layers, of which observers see only the outer layer composed of civil society organizations and businesses in the cultural and economic fields. The second layer consists of the religious students who receive Gülen's teachings and participate in discussion circles, at which the leaders collect donations to fund Hizmet activities. The hierarchical political structure of the movement centered around Gülen himself forms the inner core.

The organizations constituting the outer layer of civil society associations often deny their connection to the Gülen Movement. This "strategic ambiguity" helped

Hizmet (Gülen) Movement

the organization survive in the oppressive environment of Turkish secularism, but it contradicts the principles of accountability and transparency necessary for democratic governance. The success of the schools in preparing children for a university education has stimulated significant demand by parents worldwide. In the United States, Hizmet operates the largest network of charter schools. It provokes controversy by employing many teachers directly from Turkey, buying supplies from Turkish firms, and relying on Turkish construction firms. The schools help the globalization of Turkish society and help Turkish business firms establish offices globally. The movement's newspaper, *Zaman,* became Turkey's second most important newspaper; the TV and radio stations established an Islamic counterculture. Intercultural dialogue institutions both in Turkey and worldwide fostered conversations on issues such as multiculturalism, secularism, and religion. Hizmet sponsored many cultural activities that attracted members and gave it a positive image as a representative of the best of Islam.

In politics, the movement rejected the pursuit of power through competition in elections but, instead, taught its members to become loyal bureaucrats, especially in the army, the police, and the judiciary. After the 1997 military coup ended the Islamist Welfare Party, the Hizmet Movement allied with the Justice and Development Party (AKP) to dislodge the dominance of the secular military regime. In 1999, Fethullah Gülen came to the United States for medical treatment and moved into a large but rather remote estate in the mountains of Pennsylvania. In 2000, the government of Turkey accused him of setting up an illegal organization to undermine the secular structure of the state. In June 2008, the Turkish Supreme Court of Appeals upheld Gülen's acquittal. The military threat to intervene against the AKP brought Gülen closer to Erdogan, and Hizmet supported the AKP against the secular Kemalists in the military. This alliance succeeded in reducing military influence by passing legislation shifting power to the government bureaucracy. After the constitutional referendum of 2010 reduced the power of the military, the alliance broke apart as the two groups began an open struggle to control the state. Gülen had objected to Erdogan's growing antagonism to Israel. On top of these offenses, Erdogan interpreted the corruption probe that began in 2013 as an act of open political warfare by Gülen's followers in the judiciary. Erdogan exploited the failed 2016 coup to justify an extremely broad purge of anyone suspected of any kind of connection to the Hizmet Movement As a sign of the success of the government's message, all political parties in Turkey, including the opposition, blame Hizmet for involvement in the failed 2016 coup. The government strongly opposes Hizmet's claims for status as a civil society movement solely dedicated to fighting humanity's three enemies of ignorance, disunity, and poverty. On the contrary, Turkey calls it a failed contender for state power. Many in the West, and Gülen himself, deny involvement in the coup and accuse the government of overreach and human rights violations. The persecution in Turkey led to the closure of all its organizations and the jailing of tens of thousands of people. Increased emigration will strengthen Hizmet abroad, especially if Western governments continue their support, and if the movement does not disintegrate with the death of its founder, now in his late 70s.

Sabine Dreher

See also: Corruption; Democracy Deficit; Development; Erdogan, Recep Tayyip; Islamism; Justice and Development Party (Turkey); Military Coups; Modernization; Turkey, Republic of

Further Reading

Hendrick, Joshua D. *Gülen: The Ambiguous Politics of Market Islam in Turkey and the World*. New York: New York University Press, 2013.

Tittensor, David. *The House of Service: The Gülen Movement and Islam's Third Way*. Oxford, UK: Oxford University Press, 2014.

Turam, Berna. *Between Islam and the State: The Politics of Engagement*. Stanford, CA: Stanford University Press, 2007.

Watmough, Simon P., and Ahmet Erdi Öztürk. "From 'Diaspora by Design' to Transnational Political Exile: The Gülen Movement in Transition." *Politics, Religion and Ideology* 19, no. 1 (2018): 33–52.

Yavuz, M. Hakan, and Bayram Balci. *Turkey's July 15th Coup: What Happened and Why*. Salt Lake City: University of Utah Press, 2018.

Houla Massacre (2012)

The slaughter of civilians in the Sunni village of Houla, near Homs, Syria, in May 2012. The Bashar Assad government sought to destroy the rebellion in Homs, Syria's third largest city, which in late 2011 became a central coordination center for several rebel groups. After repeated failures to dislodge the entrenched opposition militias in the area, the Syrian government began one of the largest offensives ever committed in the civil war. The government would use the tactics used here many times again in the future.

After several hours of indiscriminate artillery bombardment by government forces, on May 25, 2012, military commanders sent the *shabiha,* government-aligned militias, into select villages in the Houla region (primarily Taldou), populated mostly by Sunni Muslims. The UN High Commissioner for Human Rights and other sources have prepared reports accusing government forces and the *shabiha* of "unlawful killing, torture, arbitrary arrest and detention, sexual violence, indiscriminate attack, pillaging, and destruction of property." The *shabiha* killed 108 people, of whom 49 were children. Consequently, 11 countries, including the United States, expelled Syrian diplomats from their countries. China and Russia vetoed a resolution at the UN Human Rights Council for an international criminal investigation into the matter. The Syrian government has not allowed any independent formal investigation but has instead blamed al-Qaeda–linked groups for the massacre.

Samanvya Singh Hooda

See also: Sectarianism; Shabiha Militias; Syrian Arab Republic; Syrian Civil War

Further Reading

Al-Saleh, Assad. *Dissecting an Evolving Conflict: The Syrian Uprising and the Future of the Country*. Washington, DC: Institute for Social Policy and Understanding, 2013.

Amster, Hillary W. "Report of the Independent International Commission of Inquiry on the Arab Syrian Republic." *International Legal Materials* 51, no. 6 (2012): 1381–466.

Houthis (Ansar Allah)

Yemeni religious and political military movement named after its founder, Husayn al-Huthi (1956–2004), which played a central role in the Yemeni Civil War that started in 2015. The Houthis, also known as Ansar Allah, emerged in the early 2000s in northern Yemen out of a cultural revival movement called the Shabab al-Mu'min (Believing Youth). From 2004 until 2011 the movement fought six wars against the Yemeni regime. After the government killed Husayn al-Huthi in September 2004, during the first round of the conflict, his younger brother Abd al-Malik assumed the leadership of the group. In 2011, the Houthis took part in the Arab Spring protests that ousted President Ali Abdullah Saleh. After its participation in the National Dialogue Conference, the movement, now in an alliance with Saleh, exploited the unpopularity and weakness of the government to expand southward. By the time the Saudi-led coalition began its intervention in Yemen in March 2015, the Houthis governed the most populous areas of the country. The movement's military successes have been widely attributed to the support it allegedly receives from Iran.

While the Houthi movement has not precisely defined its goals, its ideology promotes the renewal of Zaydi Islam in Yemen, political justice in the face of mismanagement and corruption, and opposition to the foreign policies of the United States, Israel, and, more recently, Saudi Arabia, which are seen as detrimental to Yemen and the wider region.

Alexander Weissenburger

See also: Ansar al-Sharia in Libya; Operation Decisive Storm; Saleh, Ali Abdullah; Saudi Arabia, Kingdom of; Yemen, Republic of; Yemen Uprising; Zaydi

Further Reading

Brandt, Marieke. *Tribes and Politics in Yemen: A History of the Houthi Conflict.* London: Hurst & Company, 2017.

Salmoni, Barak A., Bryce Loidolt, and Madeleine Wells. *Regime and Periphery in Northern Yemen: The Huthi Phenomenon.* Santa Monica, CA: RAND, 2010.

I

Ibadi Doctrine

A theological approach (Madhhab) in Islam distinct from both Sunni and Shi'a doctrine, which developed in the very early history of Islam. Three characteristics distinguish Ibadi doctrine. First, because Ibadi doctrine developed out of the political decision to reject the authority of the Caliphs Uthman and Ali, and of the Umayyads, this approach emphasizes the necessity that a community select its ruler based on merit. The scholars and notable figures select the righteous *imam* (leader) based on his leadership skills and devotion, not his lineage. This community of elites also holds the right and the duty to remove an *imam* who becomes unjust.

Second, the Ibadi position on God and the Qur'an aligns with the rationalist, and now extinct, eighth-century Mu'tazila school of theology. Ibadis believe that individual judgment dictates interpretation of the Sunnah (the path or example of Muhammad), which enables interpretation of the Qur'an. Ibadis shun a literal reading of God's descriptions in the Qur'an, refuse the separation of God's essence and attributes, and believe that even in eternity the righteous will not be able to see God. They agree with the Shi'as in objecting to the Sunni claim for the uncreated nature of the Qur'an. However, Ibadis side with the Ash'arite Sunnis on the important question of predestination, confirming that God creates all human deeds.

Third, Ibadis seek to disassociate from both *kuffar ni'ma*—ungrateful, sinning monotheists—and *kuffar shirk*—idolatrous nonbelievers. Ibadis may lawfully inherit from, marry, and live among people in the first category who remain Muslims. This policy of dissociation does not authorize aggression, but rather it constitutes a command to withhold friendship. Living among other communities, as they seek to pursue their rationalist orientation, Ibadis today promote harmonious relations with other religious groups. They do not believe in any obligation to fight against an unjust *imam,* as the radical Kharijites (Takfiris) believe. If a community lacks a qualified ruler, they can live without one. They can practice their faith in secrecy, or *taqiyah,* when living under the rule of tyrants. The Ibadi base their laws on their own authorized collection of hadith called *Al-Jami'i Al-Sahih,* also referred to as *Musnad Al-Rabi' bin Habib.*

The foremost living Ibadi authority, Mufti of Oman Shaikh Ahmad al-Khalili, leads Ibadi efforts in reconciling religious differences. Therefore, Ibadis consider their doctrine an internal issue that does not obstruct rapprochement with the two other major Islamic communities of practice. The Three Points of the Amman Message specifically include the Ibadis, who represent the majority of the population of Oman, where the state religion is Al-Ibadhiyah. Smaller groups of Ibadis also live in Zanzibar, in Jabal Nafusah and Zuwarah in Libya, on Jerba Island in Tunisia, and in Wadi Mzab in Algeria.

Bader Mousa Al-Saif

See also: Oman, Sultanate of; Sectarianism

Further Reading

Gaiser, Adam R. *Muslims, Scholars, Soldiers: The Origins and Elaboration of the Ibadi Imamate Traditions.* New York: Oxford University Press, 2010.

Ghubash, Hussein. *Oman: The Islamic Democratic Tradition.* New York: Routledge, 2006.

Hoffman, Valerie J. *The Essentials of Ibadi Islam.* Syracuse, NY: Syracuse University Press, 2012.

Wilkinson, John Craven. *Ibâdism: Origins and Early Development in Oman.* Oxford, UK: Oxford University Press, 2010.

Intifadas (I, II, and Knife)

The Arab word for "uprising," used to describe a series of Palestinian revolts that started on December 8, 1987, in the Gaza Strip, which expanded to all the Occupied Palestinian Territories (OPT). This first insurrection, after 20 years of Israeli occupation, combined civil disobedience, economic boycott, refusal to work in Israeli settlements, and refusal to pay taxes. Protesters also threw stones at Israeli tanks to show the inequality of forces. The images of kids throwing stones at tanks spread around the world and drew popular attention to the situation of Palestinians living under occupation. The Israeli Defense Forces (IDF) deployed thousands of its soldiers against the protesters. Almost 2,000 Palestinians were killed, many of them underage. The IDF sought to break the morale of the Palestinian people with a ferocious repression.

The First Intifada stimulated the emergence of a Palestinian leadership inside the OPT, in addition to all the major figures of the Palestine Liberation Organization (PLO) in exile abroad—mostly in Tunis. The Madrid Conference in 1991, which ultimately led to the Oslo Accords in 1993, created an interim government called the Palestinian Authority. The First Intifada strengthened the political connections between the PLO and the Palestinian people, but Islamist competitors to the PLO also gained credibility and support. The intifada created an image of Palestinians as resilient, politically effective agents, who established their own agenda. The PLO ultimately gained negotiations with the United States, and King Hussein withdrew his claim to represent West Bank Palestinians.

However, Palestinians living under Israeli occupation concluded that the Oslo Accords would not lead to any improvement in their political status or living conditions. After Israeli prime minister Ariel Sharon visited the Al Aqsa Mosque in September 2000, a new massive wave of protests and fighting erupted, known as the Second Intifada, or the Al Aqsa Intifada. Muslims called Sharon's presence in their sacred place a provocation, amplified by his complicity in the September 1982 massacres, by the Lebanese Maronite Phalange, at the Sabra and Shatila Palestinian refugee camps in Lebanon. In this second intifada, the Palestinians used suicide bombings and gunfire while the Israeli security forces responded with snipers, tank gunfire, and air attacks. The confrontation ended on February 8, 2005, when Palestinian president Mahmoud Abbas and Prime Minister Ariel Sharon met at Sharm el-Sheikh, Egypt, where they reaffirmed their commitment to the Road Map for Peace, which began at Madrid. The Israeli Human Rights Organization B'Tselem reported that 4,789 Palestinians and 1,053 Israelis had died during the uprising. As a result of the Second Intifada, and the negotiations between the parties, Israel withdrew from the Gaza Strip and started constructing a barrier wall in the West Bank, confiscating more Palestinian land.

In October 2015, individual Palestinians living in Jerusalem and the West Bank began committing a series of knife attacks, shootings, and attempts to run over Israeli citizens—called the "Knife Intifada." The attacks demonstrated individual initiative, without any coordination, central control, or formal political agenda. At the rate of more than one per day, by March 2016 more than 40 car attacks, 80 shootings, and 200 stabbings had injured more than 400 people but caused only about 30 deaths. Many family members of the attackers publicly took pride in the actions, and leading Palestinian figures often celebrated the attacks. The Palestinian side explained the attacks as caused by a lack of a political solution to their demands and a feeling of being under attack. The attacks have only caused Israelis to adjust their awareness and self-protection measures, but not to seek any political change.

Carolina Bracco

See also: Abbas, Mahmoud; Fatah Party; Israel; Middle East Road Map; Palestine; Palestine Liberation Organization

Further Reading

Ajluni, Salem. "The Palestinian Economy and the Second Intifada." *Journal of Palestine Studies* 32, no. 3 (Spring 2003): 64–73.

Baroud, Ramzy. *The Second Palestinian Intifada: A Chronicle of a People's Struggle.* London: Pluto Press, 2006.

Cobban, Helena. "The PLO and the 'Intifada.'" *Middle East Journal* 44, no. 2 (Spring 1990): 207–33.

Collins, John. *Occupied by Memory. The Intifada Generation and the Palestinian State of Emergency.* New York: New York University Press, 2004.

Pressman, Jeremy. "The Second Intifada: Background and Causes of the Israeli-Palestinian Conflict." *The Journal of Conflict Studies* 23, no. 2 (Fall 2003): 114–41.

Iran, "Girls of Enghelab Street." See Against Compulsory Hijab

Iran, Islamic Republic of

An autocratic state ruled by a Shi'a religious legal expert, which employs some democratic procedures, situated between Iraq and Pakistan, bounded on the south by the Gulf of Oman, and sharing land boundaries with Afghanistan, Armenia, Azerbaijan, Turkey, and Turkmenistan. Under favorable political conditions, Iran could exploit its geographic position for international trade. Its large, relatively well-educated population not only represents a significant potential market, but also a source of cultural influence on its neighbors. However, its diverse population suffers from strong internal divisions, made worse by an oppressive state apparatus.

Before the 1979 Islamic Revolution, the shah (king), Mohammad Reza Pahlavi, ruled Iran as a constitutional monarchy, promoting its heritage of 2,500 years of Persian civilization. He promoted modernization aggressively. His oppression and poor governance provoked a massive opposition movement that culminated in a revolution. Democrats, nationalists, socialists, and Islamists all contributed to the revolution to overthrow the shah. However, afterward, these different groups struggled to create a new state. The Shi'a Islamists, led by Ayatollah Ruhollah Khomeini, ruled with the nationalist and democratic leaders for the first year. The Ayatollah used the capture of American hostages from the embassy by students to further polarize society in his favor—against the nationalists and democrats—enabling him to get rid of them. The socialists (Mujahidin-e Khalq) fought back hard with terrorist attacks but lacked the numbers to prevail: the Islamists killed, captured, or expelled them.

After the first, transitional year in which the Islamists defeated the other major social forces, the supporters of Khomeini established a state in which the most highly qualified Shi'a religious jurist (called a *faqih*) would act as the guardian (*velayat*), with absolute authority. This doctrine represented a revolutionary departure from classical Shi'a political doctrine. That historically evolved doctrine acknowledged a difference between secular, political rule versus religious authority. Traditionally, the religious teachers believed that they had a duty to guide the rulers into moral governance but not to take political authority. In contrast, Khomeini's doctrine claimed that all people, in their religious ignorance, represented children needing a guardian (*velayat*) to control their lives, a classical expression of authoritarianism.

Most of the other highly esteemed Shi'a religious scholars rejected this political ideology in the name of religious doctrine. Therefore, Ayatollah Khomeini repressed many other ayatollahs, and provoked conflicts with Shi'a leaders in other states. Khomeini's supporters created a state that has elements of a republic but keeps real authority in the hands of a select group of about 100 religious scholars. The Islamic revolution derived its power from popular antagonism to the shah, westernization, and cultural alienation. The revolution, and the state today, opposes the United States as "The Great Satan" and the "Global Arrogance."

The Islamic revolution took control of a heavily armed state, due to the shah's lavish spending on the military as a way to gain regional influence. However, the Ayatollah quickly sought to export his revolutionary ideology to its neighbors through propaganda, targeted assassinations, terror attacks, and support for opposition movements. Khomeini did not trust the regular army and ordered large numbers of the officers killed. Iraq's Saddam Hussein interpreted these two conditions—the provocations and an army without its officers—as an opportunity to take control of Iran's oil rich province of Khuzistan. He invaded Iran on September 22, 1980.

Iran, Islamic Republic of

The newly formed Islamic Revolutionary Guard Corps (IRGC) lacked the training to fight a conventional war. The IRGC leaders had been trained by the Palestine Liberation Organization to fight an insurgent war. The new Iranian ideology favored martyrdom and sacrifice rather than military planning and strategy. On October 24, 1980, the Iraqis captured the Iranian city of Khorramshahr, and isolated the important cities of Abadan and Ahvaz. However, in January 1981, Iran successfully counterattacked. Iran's IRGC and Basij militias refused to fight integrated with the regular Iranian Army, but instead conducted human wave assaults, followed by the regular Iranian Army. By June 1982, Iran had pushed all Iraqi forces out of the country. Despite Iraq's seeking a cease-fire, Iran's leaders took the war to Iraq, thinking they could spread their revolution, that the Shi'a Iraqis would defect, but most remained loyal and fought hard for Iraq.

In 1983, Iraq began using chemical weapons to soften Iranian human wave assaults and to instill terror, but this tactic failed. The United States condemned the use of these weapons but still sided with Saddam Hussein. The United States feared that revolutionary Iran, with 60 million people at that time, could defeat Iraq with only 20 million people. In 1983, the United States shared satellite images of Iranian troop movements and began providing Iraq with aid via the Commodity Credit Corporation for the purchase of agricultural products. By 1987, this aid amounted to $652 million. As a heavily armed, anti-Western, anti-American state calling for revolution throughout the Muslim world, Iran frightened Saudi Arabia and other U.S. allies. Kuwait and the other Sunni Gulf states supported Iraq with loans and other aid.

Iraq increased its indiscriminate missile attacks on Iranian cities and internationalized the war by attacking Iranian oil installations on Kharg Island. Iran responded by attacking Iraqi oil tankers. After a Kuwaiti request, the United States reflagged Kuwaiti tankers and provided naval escorts. Iranian mines and attacks on shipping provoked a number of U.S. operations against Iranian ships and oil platforms. On July 3, 1988, the USS *Vincennes* shot down Iran Air Flight 655, an Iranian commercial aircraft, killing 290 passengers flying to Dubai. This raised Iranian fears that the Americans might enter the war more directly. Iranian leaders persuaded Ayatollah Khomeini to accept UN Resolution 598, which brought an immediate cease-fire. The war lasted eight years, killed almost one million Iranians, while wounding and maiming tens of thousands more.

During the Reagan administration, the Lebanese Hezbollah, a paramilitary group with ties to Iran's Islamic Revolutionary Guards, had taken seven American hostages. Senior Reagan administration officials secretly facilitated the sale of arms to Iran in exchange for Iran's releasing the hostages. This caused a great scandal that deeply harmed the Reagan administration.

After Iraq invaded Kuwait, Iran greatly benefited from Operation Desert Storm. Iraq withdrew troops from eight border enclaves and granted Iran border concessions on August 14, 1990, reverting to the borders of the 1975 Algiers Treaty. Both countries also resumed prisoner exchanges that released nearly 75,000 prisoners of war from both sides.

While engaged in its "War of Sacred Defense" against Iraq, Iran hosted over a million Afghan refugees—primarily Shi'a Hazaras—due to the Soviet invasion of Afghanistan. After the Taliban appeared in 1996, their intense aggression against the Hazara increased the refugee burden. In August 1998, when the Taliban conquered Mazar-i-Sharif, they killed eight Iranian diplomats and an Iranian journalist, which sparked a massive Iranian Army mobilization on the border. Intervention by the United States and the UN prevented war.

After the terror attacks on September 11, 2001, Iranian contacts helped the United States form a new Afghan government. The United States joined an existing coalition (India, Russia, Iran, and the Northern Alliance) to overthrow the Taliban. Iran used its influence with all elements of the Afghan opposition to help a new government form during the 10-day conference in Bonn, Germany.

Despite Iran's offers of cooperation in Afghanistan, the IRGC continued its support of international terrorism. On January 3, 2002, Israel intercepted a ship in the Red Sea, the *Karine A,* carrying Iranian weapons to Palestine. Combined with reports of Iranian cooperation with North Korea on missiles and nuclear technology, this provoked President George W. Bush to label Iran part of an "Axis of Evil." That undermined the relatively moderate administration of President Mohammad Khatami and prevented any negotiations.

After the U.S.-led coalition invaded Iraq, Iranian support for Shi'a militias strengthened American antagonism to Iran. Iran exported "explosively formed penetrators," which killed many Americans. Iran sustained the insurgency by supplying training, mortars, weapons, and money, transforming it into a sectarian civil war costing thousands of lives. The belligerent and provocative showmanship of the Ahmadinejad administration increased international tensions, and Iran's relations with its neighbors deteriorated. But even during the Ahmadinejad administration, the Sultanate of Oman kept good relations with Iran and facilitated the beginnings of its negotiations with the United States.

With the United States drawing down its forces from Iraq, and the 2008 election of Barak Obama as U.S. president, the United States made its first tentative efforts at secret negotiations. In 2009, Iranians staged massive protests, called the Green Revolution, against the fraudulent reelection of Ahmadinejad. Based on the recommendation of Iranian exiles that American support would discredit the protesters, and in spite of domestic pressure, the Obama administration adopted a very restrained approach. Protesters not only complained about government tyranny and corruption but also about the massive funds spent supporting Hamas and Hezbollah.

When the 2011 Arab uprisings began, Iran tried to call them Islamic uprisings, despite the initial absence of organized Islamist support. Iranian dissidents offered the lessons that they had learned from the Green Revolution and also from the 1979 Islamic revolution—to warn against Islamists hijacking their movements. Although the election of Mohamed Morsi in Egypt seemed to benefit Iran, after the military coup, Egypt rejected Iranian influence. Iran exploited the 2011 protests in Yemen to expand its covert assistance to the Houthis in their competition with the government. Similarly, Iran committed its resources wholeheartedly to defending the government of Bashar al-Assad in Syria. Iran persuaded Hezbollah to commit significant forces to support Syria. Iran recruited and trained Afghan refugees and Shi'a from Pakistan and sent them to fight in Syria. After the rise of the Islamic State (Daesh), which rapidly took a great deal of territory in Iraq and Syria, Iran funded and trained great numbers of fighters as part of the Popular

Mobilization Forces (PMF) in Iraq. This has led Iranian officials to boast of controlling the capitals of five countries and strengthened the sectarian character of these conflicts.

Under Hassan Rouhani, elected as president of Iran on June 14, 2013, the new foreign minister, Mohammad Javad Zarif, opened negotiations, beginning in November 2013, with Britain, China, France, Germany, Russia, and the United States. On January 16, 2016, Iran agreed in the Joint Comprehensive Plan of Action (JCPOA) to curb its nuclear program in order to gain relief from international sanctions, but this had no effect on its extensive missile-development program. In spite of the dropping of some sanctions by the United Nations and the United States, Iran's economy did not improve. After the election of Donald Trump as U.S. president, the United States reinstated many sanctions and tried to persuade its European partners not to do business with Iran. In 2017–2018 a series of major demonstrations in the peripheral provinces and secondary cities of Iran focused on economic issues.

Although Iran has many resources, natural, social, and cultural, that could support economic growth, and even though Iran has developed literacy, health care, urbanization, and rural electrification under the revolution, the economy remains hobbled. The large role of the Bonyads, large segments of the economy either state-controlled or controlled by the IRGC, the cost of Afghan refugees, high levels of corruption, and lack of legal business protections greatly inhibit economic growth. High unemployment, inflation, and government oppression fuel drug smuggling, the flight of educated, talented people, and rebellion. Multiple, strong, well-funded security forces, including an intrusive, experienced secret police apparatus, control the media, and the support of some powerful social classes reinforce authoritarian rule and give the appearance of stability. The 2009 and the 2017–2018 protests show that the government can expect repeated domestic disturbances.

Mark David Luce

See also: Against Compulsory Hijab; Ahmadinejad, Mahmoud; Authoritarianism; Basij; Corruption; Development; Economic Protests; Green Movement; Hamas; Hezbollah; Iraq, Republic of; Islamic Revolutionary Guard Corps (IRGC); Islamic State (Daesh); Khamenei, Ayatollah Sayyid Ali; Khatami, Mohammad; Khomeini, Ayatollah Sayyid Ruhollah Mūsavi; Kuwait, State of; Lebanese Republic; Modernization; Mujahedin-e Khalq (MEK); Oman, Sultanate of; Palestine Liberation Organization; Political Decision-Making in Iran; Quds Force; Rafsanjani, Ali Akbar Hashemi; Rouhani, Hassan Feridun; Sectarianism; Syrian Arab Republic; Yemen, Republic of

Further Reading
Amanat, Abbas. *Iran: A Modern History.* New Haven, CT: Yale University Press, 2018.

Ansari, Ali. *Iran.* New York: Routledge, 2004.

Bruinessen, Martin van. *Kurds and Identity Politics.* London: I. B. Tauris, 2001.

Cordesman, Anthony, and Abraham Wagner. *The Lessons of Modern War, Vols. I & II: The Iran-Iraq War.* Boulder, CO: Westview Press, 1990.

Jahanbakhsh, Forough. *Islam, Democracy and Religious Modernism in Iran, 1953–2000: From Bazargan to Soroush.* Leiden, The Netherlands, and New York: Brill Academic Publishers, 2001.

Wright, Robin. *In the Name of God: The Khomeini Regime.* New York: Simon and Schuster, 1989.

Iranian Azerbaijanis

The second largest ethnic group in Iran, sharing the same Turkic language and background as the majority of people in the former Soviet Republic of Azerbaijan. While estimates of their numbers range from 12 to 25 million, approximately three times as many Azerbaijani (adjective: Azeri) people live in Iran as in Azerbaijan itself. The Azerbaijanis derive in part from a heritage of Turkic rule over Iran, during most of the past 1,000 years. Iran adopted the Shi'a version of Islam under the rule of the Safavid Azerbaijani Turks beginning in 1500. The Turkic Qajar Dynasty (1779–1924) controlled all of present-day Iran and extensive territory in the Caucasus and Central Asia.

When Colonel Reza Khan Pahlavi overthrew the Qajars, he promoted Persian language, culture, and identity at the expense of Azeri Turkish. During World War II, the Soviets took control over northern Iran, where they established the Azerbaijani People's Republic. After the war, U.S. president Harry Truman forced the Soviets to withdraw. On December 15, 1946, the government of Mohammad Reza Shah Pahlavi retook control of Iranian territory. The government initially prohibited the use of the Azerbaijani language, even though the shah's mother and wife were Azerbaijani. The Ayatollah Khomeini used military force to crush opposition from the leading Azeri Ayatollah Shariat-Madari, who promoted separation of religion and state rather than Azeri identity. The Iranian Revolution of 1979 formally promoted a pan-Islamist ideology, but the government continued to impose Persian language usage. The government does not allow schools to use the Azerbaijani language, but stores can sell books in Azeri. The lack of education in their native language inhibits Azeris in professional development.

After 1990, Azerbaijani nationalists in the former Soviet Union campaigned to unify with Iranian "South Azerbaijan," which created a threat of secession. Therefore, the government of Iran allied with Christian Armenia against the predominantly Shi'a Azerbaijan in the Nagorno-Karabakh War. Azeris in Iran complain against continued neglect of their language, culture, and history. On May 12, 2006, the special edition of the children's magazine *Iran* portrayed Azeris as cockroaches, which provoked massive protests in Tabriz. On the other hand, large numbers of Azeris serve in high positions of the government and in religious offices and hold prominent positions in business. Azeri merchants predominate in the Tehran bazaar. Supreme Leader Ayatollah Ali Khamenei has recited Azeri poetry on television. Azeri opposition to the government takes a very liberal position of advocating democracy and human rights.

Tom Dowling

See also: Grievance Model; Iran, Islamic Republic of; Khamenei, Ayatollah Sayyid Ali; Minorities

Further Reading

Elling, Rasmus Christian. *Minorities in Iran: Nationalism and Ethnicity after Khomeini.* New York: Palgrave-MacMillan, 2013.

Riaux, Gilles. "The Formative Years of Azerbaijani Nationalism in Post-Revolutionary Iran." *Central Asian Survey* 27, no. 1 (March 2008): 45–58.

Shaffer, Brenda. *Borders and Brethren: Iran and the Challenge of Azerbaijani Identity.* Cambridge, MA: MIT Press, 2002.

Iraq, Republic of

A parliamentary, federal democratic republic suffering from significant political instability, located in the historic area called the Fertile Crescent along the Tigris and Euphrates Rivers. As an agriculturally productive area, it formed the heartland of many empires, most recently the Ottoman Empire since 1534. The British campaign against the Ottoman Empire in World War I took the area of the modern state of Iraq in stages, beginning with Basra in 1914. The British administration utilized former Ottoman elites, consisting mostly of Sunni government officials and military officers. In 1920, the League of Nations gave the British a mandate to develop the area, but local residents revolted against foreign occupation. Suppressing that revolt cost hundreds of lives, which convinced the British to seek alternative, less direct means of governance: a local monarchy with treaties of protection, retention of military bases, and extended use of airpower.

As part of the initial British bargain with Hussein bin Ali, the Hashemite ruler of Mecca, in 1921 they appointed his son Faisal as king of Iraq. The government of King Faisal inherited the ideology of Arab nationalism. The government promoted Arab identity and Iraqi nationalism in a secular state, which created conflicts. The Kurds rebelled against the denial of their identity and distinctive culture, and the Shi'as rebelled against the foreign protection of Sunni domination. After the state suppressed the Shi'a rebellion, the leaders took refuge in Iran.

In 1932, the mandate ended, and Iraq became independent, but the British retained some bases. Under the monarchy, Iraq began to develop as a modern state with a professional military. In 1933 the Assyrian community demanded the right to self-government. In response, the Iraqi military massacred large numbers of unarmed civilians. In 1936, the army staged its first coup to replace the prime minister, which lasted for a year. Six more coups occurred—against the cabinet— in the next six years. The outbreak of World War II in 1939 brought conflict between pro-British and pro-German factions. The latter removed their opponents by force, provoking the British to reoccupy the country until 1945.

Kurdish nationalism revived and motivated a full-scale revolt from 1943 to 1945, led by Mustafa Barzani. In September 1945, the Iraqi government persuaded several Kurdish tribes to defect and to attack the Barzani-led coalition. After battlefield defeat, the leaders retreated to Iran. After a year, Iran reasserted sovereignty over Kurdish areas, forcing the Barzanis to take refuge in the Soviet Union until the late 1950s. These struggles only further strengthened Kurdish identity.

Despite periodic protests and disturbances, the Hashemites ruled until 1958, amid a tide of growing pan-Arabism promoted by Egypt's Gamel Abdel Nasser. On July 14, 1958, a handful of nationalist senior military officers, led by Brigadier Abd al-Karim Qasim, conducted a successful coup d'état. The officers created a republic ruled by three leaders, one Sunni, one Shi'a, and one Kurd, with Qasim as prime minister. The cabinet included representatives of the major political currents. The new government developed good relations with the Soviet Union and the People's Republic of China, thus entering the international Cold War antagonistic to the United States, Britain, and the West. Iraqi politics became polarized between Arab nationalists versus the communists and the Kurds, led by Qasim. His government promoted an Iraqi national mythology that justified greater national boundaries than those set by the British. For example, in 1961, Qasim claimed control over Kuwait.

On January 8, 1963, the Iraqi Ba'ath Party and sympathetic nationalist officers and groups overthrew Qasim. The Ba'ath Party appealed to young, disenfranchised Shi'as. The government was overthrown again, but on July 17, 1968, the Ba'athists retook control of the state. In 1968, Saddam Hussein emerged as the dominant figure in Iraq. He initially negotiated with Kurdish leaders, to use them against Iran. In response, Iran gave support to the Iraqi Kurdish aspirations (not Iranian Kurds), while at the same time disputing the border along the Shatt al-'Arab. In 1969, as tensions mounted, Iraq expelled 20,000 ethnic Iranians and harassed the Shi'a population.

With the benefit of the 1973 oil price increase, the economy flourished while the government expanded the infrastructure and promoted development. The government engaged in open warfare against the Kurds, ultimately crushing the revolt in 1975. In the March 1975 Algiers agreement, Iran agreed to stop supporting Iraqi Kurds, and Iraq agreed to recognize the median line of the Shatt al-'Arab waterway as their international border. The Kurds split into two major parties, the Kurdistan Democratic Party (KDP) led by Massoud Barzani and the Patriotic Union of Kurdistan (PUK) led by Jalal Talabani. The Iraqi government forcibly relocated Kurds from the northern border with Turkey, bulldozed many villages, and encouraged Arabs to move to the historic Kurdish heartland and oil-producing region around Kirkuk, which provoked a renewed Kurdish revolt.

In 1979, Saddam Hussein assumed the presidency, purged the Ba'ath Party, and established his government based on patronage, with favoritism to people from his home region of Takrit. Saddam aspired to make Iraq a regional hegemon, in spite of its powerful neighbors—Iran, Turkey, and Israel. After the Iranian revolution, the Iranian government purged its military officers while also trying to export the revolution, using assassinations and bombings in neighboring states, thus committing aggression from a position of apparent weakness. On September 23, 1980, Iraqi forces invaded Iran. Iraq developed its chemical- and biological-weapons programs during this period. It used them against Iran during the war and against the Kurds in 1986. More than one million people would die during this war over the next eight years.

The conflict between Iraq and Iran ended with a cease-fire on August 20, 1988, with no change in the borders. Iraq incurred high levels of debt to the Sunni states that had supported it in the war. Saddam revived Iraqi claims on Kuwait in hopes of capturing its lucrative oil fields, as well as voiding its debt to Kuwait. The Iraqi Army invaded Kuwait in 1990, while also threatening Saudi Arabia. The UN Security Council declared an arms embargo. In response to a Saudi government

Iraq, Republic of

request for help, the United States mobilized over 500,000 American troops and a broad international coalition to force Iraq to withdraw from Kuwait. On January 16, 1990, the Allied attack defeated Iraqi forces, forcing survivors to retreat to Iraq. President George H. W. Bush stopped short of invading Baghdad, believing that this would only have led to regional destabilization. The United States declared a cease-fire on February 28, 1991.

Spontaneous revolts broke out throughout Iraq. Saddam's government created a humanitarian disaster in its attacks on the Shi'as in the south and the Kurds in the north. On April 5, 1991, UN Security Council Resolution 688 required Iraq to allow international humanitarian organizations to monitor and relieve the suffering. The United States, Britain, and France cited this decision to create two no-fly zones to protect Shi'a and Kurdish populations. Furthermore, the UN Special Commission (UNSCOM) applied strict standards to Iraq's weapons of mass destruction (WMD) program, which included chemical, biological, and nuclear weapons development. In 1999, in response to Iraq's banning of UNSCOM inspectors from Ba'ath Party headquarters, President Bill Clinton ordered airstrikes on military sites.

The government exploited the suffering of its people to lobby for the lifting of sanctions. In 1998, the U.S. Congress committed $100 million to assist Iraqi opposition groups, a move reflecting a desire for regime change. Following the departure of UNSCOM inspectors in 1998, Saddam maintained ambiguity regarding his WMD program, to deter aggression from Iran. Eventually, Iraq did permit inspections, but under a high degree of control and harassment. The United States failed to garner UN support for an attack on Iraq yet continued seeking regime change, ultimately invading in 2003. The war began with an air campaign on March 19, 2003, followed by ground forces entering from bases in Kuwait. By April 9, 2003, U.S. troops occupied Baghdad, and Saddam fled into hiding. The United States, Britain, and a coalition of 10 other states occupied Iraq and sought to establish a new government. Instead of Iraqis' reorganizing their government, incidents of massive looting and mobs attacking government ministry buildings eventually grew into an insurgency, for which the coalition had not prepared.

In May 2003, George W. Bush declared the end of major combat operations, but Sunni and Shi'a groups opposed to the U.S. occupation organized attacks against coalition forces—and one another. The decision to purge the government of Ba'athist Party members, and especially the top tiers of the military, created anger and grievances among large numbers of now unemployed, predominantly Sunni men with organizational and military skills and connections with militant movements abroad. The loss of experienced personnel in all governmental organizations caused the collapse of government services.

The initial U.S.-led Multinational Force devolved to a Coalition Provisional Authority, which appointed an Iraqi Governing Council composed of exiles and dissidents. Iraqi representatives wrote a Transitional Administrative Law, which established a federal, democratic, pluralistic republic. Most of the provisions of this law carried over into a constitution approved by referendum on October 15, 2005. Free elections were administered by the United Nations, and in 2009, voters elected Nouri al-Maliki as prime minister.

Syria facilitated the flow of foreign fighters, who supported the growth and development of a large Sunni insurgency. A group affiliated with al-Qaeda utilized improvised explosive devices (IEDs) and suicide bombers in an attempt to wear down U.S. occupation. At the same time, Iran provided weapons and technology to terrorist groups for use against coalition forces. Groups such as Jaish al-Mahdi, centered in the Shi'a section of southern Baghdad known as Sadr City, provided organized resistance.

The publicity regarding abuses of prisoners and mounting civilian deaths created a very negative perception of the war. In January 2007, the United States announced a new strategy and surged troop deployments by 30,000, hoping to buy time and space for the new government to take root. The new counterinsurgency strategy developed by U.S. Army general David Petraeus sought to improve Iraqi capabilities, move forces out from the large bases, integrating them more with the population, and improve quality of life for Iraqi citizens.

As the insurgency began to diminish, the United States began withdrawing its forces. In 2008, newly elected president Barak Obama ordered the end of the war. The U.S. mission shifted to "advise and assist," completed in 2011. The 2011 wave of political unrest that hit neighboring Syria also affected Iraq, fueling militant appeals to alienated Sunnis, who established the Islamic State in Iraq and Greater Syria (Daesh). The Islamic State seized Fallujah and Ramadi in January 2014, and then Mosul in June 2014, giving it tremendous financial resources as well as large numbers of American weapons abandoned by fleeing Iraqi forces. These conquests displaced over one million Iraqis and threatened Iraqi sovereignty. The United States, joined by other nations, responded by sending advisers and air support to assist the Kurdish Peshmerga and Iraqi forces to defeat the Islamic State. The United States blamed Prime Minister Nouri al-Maliki's policies promoting Shi'a power and influence at the expense of Sunnis for fueling the insurgency. Working through Iraqi officials and religious leaders, the United States persuaded al-Maliki to resign, and in August 2014, the Iraqi president appointed Haider al-Abadi to replace him.

The Iraqi government asked for volunteers to fight the Islamic State. The Ayatollah Sistani issued a fatwa, encouraging Iraqis to join the government's defense forces. A number of local militias took these events as an opportunity to gain funding and expand operations, with significant support from Iran. The Iraqi government recognized these groups as Hashd al-Shaabi ("Popular Mobilization Forces"; PMF), which even included Kurdish and Christian groups. Iranian support to many of these groups has increased their manpower and funding to the point that observers warn they might seek to dictate policy to the Iraqi government.

The severity of the civil war in Syria and the war in Yemen have caused many Iraqi Shi'as to become more nationalistic and seek to reduce Iran's influence. For example, Muqtada al-Sadr shifted away from his ardent Shi'a sectarian policies. As an Iraqi nationalist, he even went to the United Arab Emirates and Saudi Arabia to seek economic assistance in rebuilding Iraq. In the May 12, 2018, parliamentary elections, many parties emphasized a cross-sectarian national identity, while competing parties seek voters in each of the major groups. With accusations of fraud and relatively low turnout, the political situation remains fragmented. It took until October 2018 to form a new government. In December 2018, Iraq celebrated victory over the Islamic State.

The improved security allows Iraqis to focus on the debilitating corruption and the lack of economic recovery, electricity, and government services. In July 2018, large numbers of Iraqis protested in Basra against corruption and the lack of electricity, jobs, and water. In September, more violent protesters in Basra attacked and set fire to almost every government building, the Iranian consulate, the headquarters of the ruling Da'wa Party, and every Iranian-backed militia. While sectarian and ethnic divisions remain significant, government corruption and Iranian influence now pose strong threats to the government of Iraq. The Sunni tribes, the Shi'a religious hierarchy, the popular mobilization forces, and the government all hold significant power and compete with the others.

David R. Leonard

See also: Al-Abadi, Haider; Al-Maliki, Nouri; Al-Sadr, Muqtada; Arab Nationalism; Ba'athism; Barzani, Masoud; Civil Wars; Clientelism (Patrimonialism); Foreign Fighters; Islamic State (Daesh); Iran, Islamic Republic of; Islamism; Kurdistan Regional Government (KRG); Military Coups; Patriotic Union of Kurdistan (PUK); Popular Mobilization Forces (PMF); Sahwa (Sunni Tribal Awakening); Syrian Arab Republic

Further Reading

Marr, Phebe, and Ibrahim Al-Marashi. *The Modern History of Iraq,* 4th ed. New York: Routledge, 2017.

Metz, Steven. *Iraq and the Evolution of American Strategy.* Washington, DC: Potomac Books, 2008.

Rayburn, Joel Dawson. *Iraq after America: Strongmen, Sectarians, Resistance.* Stanford, CA: Hoover Institution Press, 2014.

Sky, Emma. *The Unraveling: High Hopes and Missed Opportunities in Iraq.* New York: Public Affairs, 2015.

Terrill, W. Andrew, III. *Lessons of the Iraqi De-Ba'athification Program for Iraq's Future and the Arab Revolutions.* Carlisle, PA: Strategic Studies Institute, May 2012.

Visser, Reidar. "Ethnicity, Federalism and the Idea of Sectarian Citizenship in Iraq: A Critique." *International Review of the Red Cross* 89, no. 868 (December 2007): 809–22.

Iraq, Surge. *See Sahwa Sunni Tribal Awakening*

ISIL, or ISIS. *See Islamic State (Daesh)*

Islamic Revolutionary Guard Corps (IRGC)

A large, well-funded Iranian military force capable of both external defense and major actions to suppress public protests, commonly called the Pasdaran (Guards). On May 5, 1979, Ayatollah Khomeini issued a decree to establish the Islamic Revolutionary Guard Corps (IRGC) to protect the state from a military coup. The Islamic Republic of Iran maintains a conventional army (IRIA, also called Artesh), air force, and navy, but the IRGC possesses four independent forces consisting of

Islamic Revolutionary Guard Corps (IRGC)

ground forces, an air force, a navy, and the Basij (a volunteer corps) as well as the Quds Force, an elite special operations corps of 15,000 troops. The government assigns the most modern equipment to the IRGC, while the regular forces receive only older technology. The IRGC functions as Iran's major internal security force, specializing in asymmetric and irregular warfare.

The Guard forces number up to 150,000 men divided into land, sea, and air forces. As a predominantly ground force, the IRGC's army consists of between 100,000 and 125,000 men. The IRGC's navy may total as many as 20,000. IRGC ground forces can operate in coordination with Iran's conventional forces or act independently, as needed. The IRGC's air and space force operates fixed-wing and rotary-wing aircraft and controls three intermediate-range ballistic-missile units. It also controls Iran's biological and chemical weapons.

The IRGC's navy trains in asymmetric warfare and maintains bases to provide coastal defense on islands in the Persian Gulf and along Iran's coast. The force includes four infantry brigades, about 10 patrol boats equipped with missiles, and a fleet of fast attack craft and minisubmarines. It can conduct amphibious landings and raids, as well as attacks against shipping in the Persian Gulf.

The Basij consists of volunteers operating under the IRGC to provide internal security and law enforcement, support special religious or political events, and serve as the morality police. Basij members can be young or old. In many instances, Basij organizations operate as NGOs in educational, professional, and labor cadres.

Through its Quds Force, the IRGC has trained Hezbollah in Lebanon, the Mahdi Army in Iraq, and part of the Taliban movement in Afghanistan. It also supports Hamas in the Gaza Strip and the Houthis in Yemen. The Quds Force engages in extensive operations in Syria and Iraq.

The IRGC's mission emphasizes indoctrination, training, and media activities through a massive network that includes Basij university-student groups, paramilitary training, monthly bulletins, and newspapers. It instructs cadres on morality, ideology, and political preaching on the theory of *vilayat-e faqih* (rule of the supreme jurist) that governs the Islamic Republic of Iran. The IRGC and the Basij operate throughout the Iranian education system at the university and the high school levels.

The Pasdaran conducts paramilitary training throughout the country to cultivate loyalty to the regime. Basij armed units provide a large manpower pool (600,000) for home defense, disaster relief, and protest control. Additionally, the IRGC and the Basij offer scholarships, loans, technical job training, and a degree of social mobility. Specialized IRGC websites, newspapers, and news media of the Islamic Republic of Iranian Broadcasting (IRIB) provide 24-hour radio and television programming. The IRGC also plays a major role in the censorship of the press and the Internet.

ECONOMIC CLOUT

After the Iran-Iraq War in 1988, the Majles (parliament) allowed the IRGC to use its engineering expertise for reconstruction efforts without oversight. The

IRGC established a headquarters known as Khatam al-Anbia. It established companies in the agriculture, oil, industry, mining, road building, transportation, import/export, and education sectors. As the IRGC's engineering arm, it has completed thousands of industrial and mining projects based on multibillion-dollar no-bid contracts. The IRGC undertakes rural development projects that include building railroads, gas pipelines, dams, public buildings, and schools. The Construction Basij implements many projects with small manufacturing and training units in rural areas.

The IRGC controls two large and important *bonyads* (charitable foundations): the Foundation of the Oppressed and the Foundation of Martyrs and Veterans Affairs. Despite their technically nongovernmental status, the Supreme Leader, Ayatollah Khamenei, appoints IRGC members or former members to lead them. These foundations own and operate businesses in agriculture, industry, transportation, tourism, and telecommunications. They also solicit contract work in the Middle East, Europe, Africa, and South Asia.

Ayatollah Khomeini preferred an apolitical military and, therefore, banned the IRGC and the Basij from political participation. However, as the IRGC grew economically and ideologically in the 2000s, its veterans entered politics and filled many important political positions, including speaker of the parliament, and became close associates of the Supreme Leader. President Ahmadinejad (2004–2014) encouraged IRGC members to enter politics, and many gained seats in parliament. President Rouhani (2014–present) has worked to reduce the power of the IRGC both politically and economically.

Mark David Luce

See also: Ahmadinejad, Mahmoud; Basij; Green Movement; Hamas; Hezbollah; Houthis (Ansar Allah); Iran, Islamic Republic of; Iraq, Republic of; Khamenei, Ayatollah Sayyid Ali; Quds Force; Rouhani, Hassan Feridun; Syrian Arab Republic; Yemen, Republic of

Further Reading

Alfoneh, Ali. "How Intertwined Are the Revolutionary Guards in Iran's Economy?" *Middle Eastern Outlook* No. 3. Washington, DC: American Enterprise Institute, October 22, 2007.

Khalaji, Mehdi. "Iran's Revolutionary Guard Corps, Inc." *PolicyWatch* No. 1273. Washington Institute for Near East Policy, August 17, 2007.

Uskowi, Nader. *Temperature Rising: Iran's Revolutionary Guards and Wars in the Middle East.* Lanham, MD: Rowman and Littlefield Publishers, 2018.

Wehrey, Frederic. *The Rise of the Pasdaran: Assessing the Domestic Roles of Iran's Islamic Revolutionary Guards Corps.* Santa Monica, CA: RAND Corporation, 2009.

Islamic Salvation Front (FIS)

An Algerian Islamist political organization founded by Abassi Madani on February 18, 1989. The Islamic Salvation Front (FIS) enjoyed official registration status as a political party from September 6, 1989, until March 4, 1992, when a military coup dismantled and banned it.

To overcome the legacy of 130 years of French colonization, the government leaders promoted Arabization, using teachers imported from Egypt and Syria. Many of these teachers brought a political ideology of Islamism, and a strategy for promoting socially conservative values in the population. Islamist activists rapidly expanded their influence through a network of associations throughout the country, assisting the poor and promoting opposition to the government during Friday prayers. This Islamist movement started to grow rapidly in the 1970s among college students and the unemployed urban population. Although the government crushed an initial Islamist rebellion from 1982 to 1987, it also employed appeasement, instituting a Family Code in 1984 that restricted the rights and freedoms of women.

In 1989, in the first free elections for local, municipal, and regional assemblies, the FIS won a great proportion of the towns, and 32 of 48 provinces. Although the leader, Abassi Madani, claimed support for multiparty democracy, cooperation with France and the West, and only gradual employment of *sharia,* his running mate, Ali Ben Hadj, engaged in fiery rhetoric against the government and the National Liberation Front (FLN), calling democracy unbelief. However, most of the people who voted for the FIS considered this party their best hope to punish the FLN and the brutal security services. In the national parliamentary elections on December 26, 1991, the FIS won 188 seats out of 231, leaving the ruling FLN Party in third place with 15 seats.

The prospect that the FIS would win enough seats in parliament to change the constitution, combined with the rhetoric of Ben Hadj, created great fear that an FIS victory would stop democratic progress and force a radical purge of the government. Before the second round of elections could take place, the army compelled President Chadli Benjedid to dissolve parliament and then resign. The military leaders blocked elections, imprisoned the FIS leaders, and put thousands of Islamists into prison camps in the Sahara Desert. Upon release, some activists joined militants organizing in remote places, who started a guerrilla campaign to force the government to return to democracy. In 1994, the FIS acknowledged an armed wing, the Islamic Salvation Army (AIS), which formed in reaction to the indiscriminate violence of the Armed Islamic Group (GIA). Madani and Belhadj remained in jail until July 2003, when President Abdelaziz Bouteflika released them as part of his bargaining strategy.

Carolina Bracco

See also: Algeria, The People's Democratic Republic of; Armed Islamic Group (GIA); Bouteflika, Abdelaziz; Islamism; National Liberation Front (FLN)

Further Reading

Kapil, Arun. "Algeria's Elections Show Islamist Strength." *Middle East Report* no. 166 (September–October 1990): 31–36.

Roberts, Hugh. "The Islamists, the Democratic Opposition and the Search for a Political Solution in Algeria." *Review of African Political Economy* 22, no. 64 (June 1995): 237–44.

Willis, Michael. *The Islamist Challenge in Algeria: A Political History.* New York: New York University Press, 1996.

Islamic State (Daesh)

A Salafi Islamist militia based in Syria and Iraq, commonly called ISIS or ISIL, that emerged as a franchise of al-Qaeda, with the distinctive vision to establish a territorial state under strict *sharia* law. Arabs who despise the group calling itself al-Dawla al-Islamiya fi al-Iraq wa al-Sham (The Islamic State in Iraq and Greater Syria) use the acronym *Daesh* because it sounds close to the Arabic word *daes,* meaning, "one who crushes something underfoot."

Daesh originated as a terror organization founded by Jordanian-born Abu Musab al-Zarqawi in Iraq, exploiting the chaos caused by the U.S.-led coalition invasion to depose Saddam Hussein. Zarqawi despised the majority Shi'as in Iraq as heretical and directed his forces to launch a series of suicide bombings against Shi'a gatherings and shrines. In 2004, he pledged loyalty to Osama bin Laden, and his group took the name Al-Qaeda in Iraq (AQI). For two years, Zarqawi directed insurgent operations against the occupation forces, until he was killed in an airstrike on June 7, 2006. After his death, an Egyptian, Abu Ayyub al-Masri, led his organization to join with other groups to establish the Islamic State of Iraq (ISI), led by Abu Omar al-Baghdadi.

In response to its attacks on the population of Iraq, coalition forces targeted the group, and within two years nearly eradicated it with airstrikes and ground operations. On April 18, 2010, a special operations raid killed Al-Masri and Abu Omar al-Baghdadi, creating a leadership vacuum. Ibrahim Awad Ibrahim al-Badri, taking the name Abu Bakr al-Baghdadi, took control of the group and gave it a new purpose and energy. He appointed former Ba'athist Iraqi military and intelligence officers to leadership positions. They brought a sophisticated understanding of military operations, as well as access to major weapons caches throughout Iraq. During the summer of 2011, while the group prepared for major operations, protests in Syria against President Bashar al-Assad intensified, triggering the Syrian Civil War. In May 2011, U.S. forces killed Osama bin Laden, creating a struggle for leadership in al-Qaeda. Abu Bakr Al-Baghdadi announced that his organization had merged with Jabhat al-Nusra (JAN) to form the Islamic State of Iraq and the Levant (ISIL). Both bin Laden's successor, Ayman al-Zawahiri, and the JAN disagreed. Daesh formally broke with al-Qaeda, took most of JAN's foreign fighters, and expelled the group from Raqqa.

Unlike al-Qaeda, Daesh resolved to hold territory, establish permanent institutions, redefine national borders, and proclaim the existence of a caliphate. Its open defiance of the al-Qaeda leadership triggered heated debate among militant Islamists over the value of establishing the caliphate. Daesh argues that only a militant Islamist state can purify and promote Islam. Daesh recruited thousands of foreign fighters through a sophisticated online operations campaign.

In Iraq, Daesh raided prison facilities, freeing hundreds of prisoners from the Iraqi insurgency. This aided recruitment to the group, while international fighters streamed into Iraq and Syria to join attacks against both governments. Daesh soon had more than 10,000 trained fighters and in 2014 captured Fallujah and Mosul, driving out elements of the Iraqi Army and threatening to seize Baghdad. Fresh from these victories, al-Baghdadi proclaimed the Islamic State as a caliphate and declared himself Caliph Ibrahim, with political, military, and religious authority over his followers and their territory. Daesh has engaged in human smuggling, systemic rape, public executions, and mass killings and has used every available means of violence, including chemical weapons, to gain and control territory.

Sunni terror organizations in Libya, Saudi Arabia, Uzbekistan, and Yemen pledged allegiance to the Islamic State, expanding its reach and deadly capacity, in competition with al-Qaeda. In early 2015, Nigerian-based Boko Haram, the deadliest terror organization in Africa, swore formal allegiance to al-Baghdadi's group, making it the most prominent Sunni terrorist group in the world. The United States formed a coalition to fight Daesh, which began a major aerial campaign in Iraq and Syria, and trained military forces in both nations to conduct ground offensives against Daesh. At the height of its power, Daesh controlled an area with more than 10 million people in eastern Syria and northwestern Iraq. Although the combined efforts of airpower and ground attacks have eradicated any Islamic State claims to hold territory, it remains a large and deadly international terror organization, due to the number of allied organizations. Abu Bakr al-Baghdadi remains at large, and in May 2019 released a video declaring his intention to continue building his global caliphate, regardless of the forces arrayed against him.

Fouad Gehad Marei

See also: Al-Qaeda Central; Foreign Fighters; Iraq, Republic of; Islamism; Salafism; Sectarianism; Syrian Arab Republic; Syrian Civil War; Takfiri Doctrine; Turkey, Republic of

Further Reading

Fishman, Brian H. *The Master Plan: ISIS, Al-Qaeda, and the Jihadi Strategy for Final Victory.* New Haven, CT: Yale University Press, 2016.

Gerges, Fawaz A. *ISIS: A History.* Princeton, NJ: Princeton University Press. 2016.

Lister, Charles R. *The Syrian Jihad: Al-Qaeda, The Islamic State and the Evolution of an Insurgency.* New York: Oxford University Press, 2015.

Moubayed, Sami. *Under the Black Flag: At the Frontier of the New Jihad.* New York: I. B. Tauris, 2015.

Warrick, Joby. *Black Flags: The Rise of ISIS.* New York: Anchor Books, 2015.

Islamism

The ideology, sometimes called "political Islam," that seeks to establish a state that would implement only policies derived from Islamic law. Advocates of this ideology, called Islamists, regard *sharia* law as divine and immutable and believe that it speaks to almost every aspect of a Muslim's life. Islamism includes a great variety of philosophical and political positions regarding not only how to achieve such a state, but also what it would look like in practice. Liberal Islamists seek to create a perfect political society through education in peace and security. Most Islamist leaders—often enlightened professionals, including teachers, preachers, and scholars—want to establish an "Islamic Order."

The achievement of justice in Islam through the application of *jihad,* meaning "to struggle in the way of God," plays a central role in Islamism. The Qur'anic

Islamism

promise, that one who dies while fighting a *jihad* will earn the title of *shaheed* (martyr), and be rewarded with Paradise, makes *jihad* popular among Muslims.

Six aspects characterize Islamism. First, Islamism promotes the application of Islamic values in the mainstream sociocultural, legal, economic, and political domain of everyday life. Second, Islamists promote greater debate of Islamic issues in the mass media, including Islamic Internet sites, and a proliferation of books and articles. Third, Islamism appeals to the Muslim masses who regard their nonpracticing Muslim elites as autocratic, inept, and corrupt. Islam emphasizes honesty as well as socioeconomic equity and justice. Islamists pledge to institute the *sharia* and break the dominance of capitalists, landlords, tribal leaders, generals, and bureaucrats. They believe their polices hold the answer to widespread unemployment, soaring inflation, increasing poverty, blatant corruption and nepotism, rising debt, and growing disparity of wealth between the elite and the impoverished. Fourth, Islamists reject all the imported secular "isms" (nationalism, capitalism, socialism, communism, pan-Arabism, Ba'athism, and Nasserism) that have failed to end the many problems in Muslim societies. Fifth, Islamism strongly opposes outside influence. Muslim educational institutions emphasize the greatness of past Islamic civilizations and the long conflict with the Western Christian world. Islamists want Muslim countries to end their dependence on the great powers, which exploit Muslim resources, leaving Muslim societies indebted, divided, and weak. Instead, Islamists advocate developing a united Islamic bloc of Muslim states, which could exert greater influence in world affairs. Finally, Islamists reject and despise cultural Westernization, including the excessive freedom, individualism, consumerism, and hedonism promoted by Western entertainment and mass media. They believe that the spread of Western culture increases the generation gap between young and old; it leads to sexual infidelity, drugs, and violence. They fear that a new era of uncivilized culture will spread.

The modern, global manifestation of Islamism began in Egypt, after the Arabs suffered a humiliating defeat in the 1967 Arab-Israeli War. Islamism then spread to the rest of the Muslim world, helped by the oil boom and influx of petrodollars in the predominantly Muslim, oil-exporting countries, as well as by the 1978–1979 Islamic Revolution in Iran, the invasion of Afghanistan (1979–1989), and the work of the Organization of the Islamic Conference (OIC) to institutionalize pan-Islamism.

Islamism inspires government policies and programs in Iran, in Saudi Arabia, in Afghanistan by the Taliban (1996–2001), in Sudan, and in Pakistan. This shows how Islamists disagree on the content and character of *sharia* law. In addition, peaceful Islamic movements and political parties seek to establish an Islamic political system, by social and political means, such as the Justice and Development Party in Morocco and the Ennahda Party (Renaissance Party) in Tunisia. The most legalistic Islamists denounce secularists and the West with great energy. Other Islamists employ pacifism in their conservative adherence to Islamic doctrine. The Progressive Islamists—variously referred to as apologists or revisionists—endeavor to reconcile religious doctrine with scientific rationalism, while asserting the continuity of Islamic tradition and modernity.

Islamism also includes radical organizations that wage violent campaigns to gain power, such as the infamous al-Qaeda (The Base) and the Islamic State (Daesh), which conquered huge parts of Syria and Iraq in 2014. They justify killing other Muslims they do not consider pure enough, as a means to impose their vision of a state on their society.

While Islamists have spread their ideology worldwide and influenced international relations, the ideology remains polycentric and multifaceted. Islamism today results from not only the interaction among diverse forms of Islamism, but also from the activities of secularist elites. Consequently, Islamism cannot create a unified Muslim *ummah* or Islamic bloc. While the violence of militants discredits Islamism, most Muslims hold on to the peaceful facets of Islamism.

Mir Zohair Husain

See also: Al-Qaeda; Islamic State (Daesh); *Jihad;* Sahwa (Sunni Tribal Awakening); Salafism; Saudi Arabia, Kingdom of

Further Reading

Husain, Mir Zohair. *Global Studies: Islam and the Muslim World.* Dubuque, IA: McGraw-Hill, 2006.

Osman, Tarek. *Islamism: What It Means for the Middle East and the World.* New Haven, CT: Yale University Press, 2016.

Strindberg, Anders, and Mats Warn. *Islamism: Religion, Radicalization, and Resistance.* Cambridge, UK: Polity Press, 2012.

Israel

A parliamentary democracy in the Levant (eastern coast of the Mediterranean Sea) that proclaimed its statehood in May 1948, after a war of independence against the British. After independence, Israel also fought wars against its Arab neighbors in 1956, 1967, and 1973. In 1979, at the conclusion of the Camp David negotiations, Israel signed a peace treaty with Egypt. That agreement eventually provided the basis for security cooperation against militant Islamist groups and helped to limit Iran's regional influence. Egyptian society retained a strong antagonism to Israel, while Jews remain suspicious of all their Arab neighbors. Their shared border remained stable, and Israeli warships regularly use the Suez Canal. The 1979 treaty effectively removed an existential threat to Israel, since no array of Arab states could destroy Israel without Egyptian help. Since 2003, when the U.S.-led coalition overthrew Saddam Hussein in Iraq, Israel has defined its security threats as follows: first, Iran; then Hezbollah and Hamas, which Iran supports; and finally, the Arab populations of the West Bank.

The 2011 Arab protests did not lead to a new intifada, but young Palestinians did organize mass protests to demand reconciliation between Fatah and Hamas. In Israel, between July 14 and October, 2011, large numbers of leftist youth staged urban protests, developing tent cities in open urban areas, to protest the high cost of living, escalating prices for housing, and diminishing state support for social programs. After establishing the initial tent city in a wealthy area of Tel Aviv, activists claim that the movement spread to 70 tent cities all across Israel and became a mass protest of half a million people at its peak. Protests in a second phase expressed the grievances of the immigrants from Arab countries who feel excluded by the predominantly Ashkenazi European Jewish elite. The protesters created a thorough set of proposals, and a government commission also developed a response plan. In October, as the protests began to diminish, the government demolished the encampments by force and ultimately made no policy changes.

Israeli relations with Jordan, governed by a peace treaty since October 1994, did not suffer due to demonstrations in Jordan. Some Palestinian and Islamist groups did protest over economic difficulties, governmental corruption, and Jordan's relations with Israel. King Hussein shuffled his cabinet ministers numerous times while suppressing the demonstrations, and overall stability remained. Protests in Egypt caused the Israeli leadership grave concern that the overthrow of Mubarak would enable the Muslim Brotherhood to rise to power, which it did, for one year. This represented a real risk, since the Brotherhood, as well as the Egyptian public, opposed the Egyptian peace treaty. Israel also expected Egypt would support Hamas, a branch of the Brotherhood, and engage Iran in cooperation, causing a dramatic deterioration in Israel's security. Mohamed Morsi did negotiate a peace agreement between Hamas and Fatah, in spite of strong Israeli opposition and pressure on Fatah, but ultimately both sides violated the agreement.

After the Egyptian military overthrew Morsi, it quickly made clear that it would meet all its obligations under the peace treaty with Israel and reestablished a close working relationship with Israel. Islamist militants exploited the chaos in Libya and the internal upheaval in Egypt to bring a flood of weapons into the Sinai region to attack Egyptian forces and Israel. This reinforced Egyptian motives to cooperate in security issues.

Events in Syria created the greatest security threats. The civil war in Syria has deepened Syrian dependence on Iran and Hezbollah. Based on the previous years of conflict between Israel and Hezbollah, most recently in 2006, another round of fighting seemed inevitable. Hezbollah's battles in Syria against the Sunni opposition have kept it from attacking Israel from Lebanon. The seven years of warfare as Hezbollah, Syria, and Iran battled militant Sunni Islamists has not given Israel a clear benefit. Despite its losses in personnel, Hezbollah has become stronger, with an experienced, battle-hardened force, Russian technology, and advanced Iranian missiles. Although Hezbollah has acquired many thousands more rockets and missiles, more accurate and larger than before, Israel has launched hundreds of airstrikes into Syria to disrupt the delivery of weapons to Hezbollah and to degrade Iran's growing presence in the country. In time, Hezbollah's forces will return to Lebanon and increase Israel's level of security concern.

Israel has suffered sporadic problems at the border into the Golan Heights. In response to requests from the United Kingdom and the United States, on July 22, 2018, the Israel Defense Forces (IDF) evacuated over 400 members of the Syrian "White Helmets" civil rescue and medical support NGO, bringing them through the Golan Heights to Jordan. The Israeli government has given free medical care to thousands of Syrians coming to the border. On September 23, 2014, the IDF shot down a Syrian fighter jet.

Israel has tried to keep good relations with Russia, while Russia provides airpower support to keep Bashar al-Assad in power. In the fall of 2015, Israel and Russia set up communications channels to avoid conflicts between Israeli strikes against Hezbollah and Iran versus Russian operations against Syrian rebels. After Assad recovered large parts of Syria, Israel's policy shifted, from containing Iranian forces to driving them out by military means. On February 9, 2018, after Syria shot down an Israeli F-16 returning from bombing an Iranian position in Syria, the Israeli Air Force struck a Syrian base with Russian military advisers present. Netanyahu went to Russia and won its recognition of Israel's security interest in the withdrawal of Iranian forces. Israel accepts Russian airstrikes close to its border in southern Syria against Syrian rebels. Israel has restrained its Druze citizens from crossing the border to aid Syrian Druze attacked by Jabhat al-Nusra.

Israel worries more about the thousands of Iranian troops building permanent basing capabilities in Syria, which Israel considers unacceptable. Israel has attacked these sites multiple times, reportedly killing over 20 Iranian military personnel as of June 2018. Israel has sought Russian assistance to reduce Iran's longterm presence. Russian officials have since repeatedly insisted all foreign fighters should leave post-conflict Syria, but Iran's presence in Syria remains a reason for concern.

Israel does not worry about Assad's pending victory, since Bashar Assad and his father before him ensured peace along the Israel-Syrian border since the 1973 war. Israel insists on retaining control over the Golan Heights, with its 20,000 Jewish settlers and freshwater sources. Israel will not tolerate adversarial forces on this strategic plateau, which overlooks much of northern Israel.

On December 6, 2017, President Trump publicly recognized Jerusalem as Israel's capital, and on May 14, 2018, moved the U.S. embassy there. Most of the international community denounced both acts, since Palestinians claim sovereignty over East Jerusalem. On March 25, 2019, the United States recognized the Golan Heights as part of Israel through a presidential proclamation signed by President Trump.

Israelis have long complained against what they perceive as a lack of genuine commitment to negotiating in good faith by the Palestinians, based on the various offers refused and resurgent initiation of violence. The independent political existence of Hamas also undercuts confidence that the Palestinians could enforce on their side any deal they might reach. The rising political upheaval after the protests of 2011 has also raised Israel's strategic uncertainty regarding the risks associated with a two-state solution. They argue that giving up control of the West Bank would allow terrorists a base from which to attack Israel. More importantly, Israeli leaders have to fear the domestic consequences from citizens who reject a deal they perceive as giving up too much security. Memories of the assassination of Prime Minister Yitzhak Rabin in 1995 provide a strong warning. Furthermore, most proposals for a two-state solution would require large-scale settler evacuations. Israeli officials have good reason to fear widespread civil strife in protest of such evacuations. Since Israel captured the West Bank in the 1967 war, every Israeli government has supported the settler movement in Israel, which has become an influential political force. Now over 600,000 Israeli Jews live in occupied territory. As that number rises, the political will to restrain or reverse the settler movement shrinks.

Since the 2003 Iraq War and the 2011 Arab protests, Iran has exploited insecurity in Syria and Yemen to assert its regional influence. This raises significant fears in many Arab countries, especially those in the Gulf region. They have begun working quietly with Israel to counter that threat. In return, Israel encourages these Arab states to persuade the Palestinians to accept a peace deal. The Trump administration has been applying similar pressure on Arab states. After dismantling the nuclear deal with Iran, to which Israeli and Arab leaders objected, Trump administration officials now press Arab countries to induce the Palestinians to accept its coming proposal. They compare the Palestinian position to stockholders in a failing company who should make a deal now while they have some equity left, rather than be forced to accept an even worse deal later. Palestinian leaders reject efforts to push them into abandoning their national aspirations.

With help from the United States, Israel has blocked Palestinian efforts to gain full membership in the United Nations. Israel devoted considerable diplomatic energy to combating the international Boycott, Divest, and Sanctions (BDS) Movement initiated by Palestinians in 2005. Modeled after the fight against apartheid in South Africa, the BDS Movement seeks to place international pressure on Israel until it ends its occupation, allows the return of Palestinian refugees, and treats Palestinian citizens of Israel with full equality. Israel insists BDS is an existential threat incompatible with preserving the state as a refuge for Jews. Most see BDS as a demand for a binational one-state solution. Palestinians fear that Israel will impose its own one-state solution by unilaterally annexing parts or all of the West Bank, while offering Palestinians political rights short of citizenship, encouraging large-scale emigration, and treating the Gaza Strip as the de facto, rump state of Palestine.

Robert C. DiPrizio

See also: Dahiya Doctrine; Egypt, Arab Republic of; Hamas; Hezbollah; Intifadas (I, II, and Knife); Iran, Islamic Republic of; Israeli Invasion of Lebanon (2006); Jordan, Hashemite Kingdom of; Lebanese Republic; Middle East Road Map; Operation Cast Lead; Palestine; Palestine Liberation Organization (PLO); Syrian Arab Republic; Primary Document: *The Arab Peace Initiative*

Further Reading

Abadi, Jacob. "Saudi Arabia's Rapprochement with Israel: The National Security Imperatives." *Middle Eastern Studies* 55, no. 3 (2019): 433–49.

Amour, Philipp O. "Israel, the Arab Spring, and the Unfolding Regional Order in the Middle East: A Strategic Assessment." *British Journal of Middle Eastern Studies* 44, no. 3 (2017): 293–309.

Byman, Daniel. "Israel's Pessimistic View of the Arab Spring." *The Washington Quarterly* 34, no. 3 (Summer 2011): 123–36.

Marteu, Elisabeth. "Israel and the Jihadi Threat." *Survival* 60, no. 1 (2018): 85–106.

Peters, Joel, and Rob Geist Pinfold, eds. *Understanding Israel: Political, Societal and Security Challenges.* New York: Routledge, 2019.

Smith, Charles D. *Palestine and the Arab Israeli Conflict: A History with Documents,* 9th ed. Boston: St. Martin's Press, 2016.

Israeli Invasion of Lebanon (2006)

An invasion of Lebanon in July 2006 intended to reduce attacks by Hezbollah against northern Israel. While the Israeli military was engaged with trying to recover a soldier kidnapped by Hamas on June 25, 2006, an intrusion by Hezbollah fighters on July 12, 2006, killed three Israel Defense Forces (IDF) soldiers and captured two others. Hezbollah was seeking to exchange them for Lebanese prisoners that Israel held. The initial quick operation to recover the soldiers failed. On July 13, Israel imposed an air, land, and sea blockade against Lebanon, arguing it would hold the government of Lebanon responsible for the security violations. For nine days, Israel struck Lebanon's infrastructure with air and naval strikes, even bombing the Beirut International Airport, inflicting heavy damage. One million Lebanese civilians fled north during the conflict. Israel launched more than 7,000 bomb and missile strikes against Lebanon, while Hezbollah fired more than 3,000 rockets at Israel.

On July 22, 2006, Israel commenced a ground offensive. Hezbollah drew Israeli forces into tight urban areas where it fought tenaciously and skillfully, and then fell back, drawing the Israeli military deep into Lebanon, beyond its supply lines. Israeli ground forces pressed all the way up into Beirut. On August 11, 2006, the UN Security Council unanimously approved UN Resolution 1701, with the approval of both the Lebanese and Israeli governments. However, Israel lifted its air and sea blockade only on September 8, 2006. International observers accused both Hezbollah and Israel of violating international humanitarian law during the conflict.

The conflict revealed that both sides misjudged the other. Although Hezbollah had prepared thoroughly for Israel's attack by developing very sophisticated communications systems, tunnels, large munitions depots, anti-tank mines, and well-hidden fighting positions, they still failed to anticipate the severity of Israel's response. In spite of watching the extensive buildup of Hezbollah's personnel, facilities, and logistics, Hezbollah's strategy and tactics, especially its Russian-made, long-range, anti-tank missiles with double, phased-explosive warheads, still surprised the Israeli military. Hezbollah remained able to fire Katyusha rockets into Galilee until the last day of the war.

The IDF did not accomplish any of its objectives. The Israeli government had to face public anger for strategic failure and lack of proper training for the military. This led to investigations and personnel changes at the top. Because Israel had attacked Lebanon as a state, Hezbollah gained greater Lebanese public support as a defender of all of Lebanon. Two years later, Hezbollah exchanged the bodies of the two captured Israeli soldiers for five of its fighters alive and the remains of 200 more, which gave Hezbollah a significant propaganda victory.

The war did create a sense of deterrence on both sides. Hezbollah gained a reputation as a regional power able to humble the military of an advanced industrial state. Over the 10 years since this war, Israel has improved its training, surveillance, and planning, while Hezbollah has increased the number of its rockets by more than 10 times and greatly increased their range and accuracy.

Jonathan K. Zartman

See also: Hezbollah; Israel; Lebanese Republic

Further Reading

Harel, Amos, and Avi Issacharoff. *34 Days: Israel, Hezbollah, and the War in Lebanon.* New York: Palgrave Macmillan, 2009.

Matthews, Matt M. *We Were Caught Unprepared: The 2006 Hezbollah-Israeli War.* Fort Leavenworth, KS: Combat Studies Institute Press, 2008.

Salem, Paul. "The After-Effects of the 2006 Israel–Hezbollah War." *Contemporary Arab Affairs* 1, no. 1 (January 2008): 15–24.

J

January 25 Revolution. *See Tahrir Square Protests*

Jasmine Revolution

A protest movement in Tunisia, which grew into a massive revolt throughout the country, encompassing a broad array of groups and sectors of society during the winter of 2010–2011. The success of the movement in toppling the regime of President Zine el Abidine Ben Ali catalyzed a series of protest movements, which erupted in other countries across northern Africa and the Middle East, commonly called the "Arab Spring."

Outside observers had generally considered Tunisia a stable and prosperous country, compared to other states in the region, and friendly to Western powers, including the United States. The European Union and the United States sought primarily to promote trade and economic growth with various agreements and failed to enforce the conditions in these agreements requiring progress toward human rights and democracy. Ben Ali demonstrated commitment to robust authoritarian rule. After the September 11, 2001, terrorist attacks, in spite of an official democracy-promotion policy, the United States primarily focused on economic liberalization and security assistance. In 2002, al-Qaeda attacked foreign tourists at a synagogue on the island of Djerba. In December 2006 Tunisian security forces uncovered a terrorist plot by men associated with al-Qaeda called the Soliman group and arrested 40 activists. The aggressive Tunisian response to events like these reassured its international partners. Meanwhile, the United Nations and NGOs were praising Tunisia's National Solidarity Fund as an effort to alleviate poverty. These factors, and the repression of protests prior to 2010, kept outside observers from understanding the depth of despair and anger in the country.

The December 17, 2010, video of Tarek el-Tayeb Mohamed Bouazizi setting himself on fire to protest the official abuse by city officials caused a wave of revulsion, anger, and humiliation in those who saw it, and they spread it very widely. The city in which he lived, Sidi Bouzid, lies in the rural western part of the country, between the capital and the mining center of Gafsa, a site of several major labor strikes and riots. The government had not initiated any new projects in the Gafsa region after 2000. Government neglect and economic marginalization of the central and southern provinces of the country made local distress worse. Bouazizi's character, as a very poor but generous and friendly man, strengthened the sense of tragedy and grief felt by the people who knew him. Millions of Tunisians could identify with him, feeling the pain of poverty, lack of employment, and abuse from corrupt government officials. The recent dramatic rise in the cost of food strengthened the crisis. The UN Food and Agriculture Organization Food Price Index shows a dramatic spike in prices in 2010 and 2011.

Local protests escalated and spread in the days following Bouazizi's immolation, with at least one protest-suicide by electrocution and a mounting number of deaths from riot police confronting protesters. The first protester died on December 24. As protests mounted, more demonstrators joined the movement, and the range of grievances increased. Repression and official corruption remained central complaints. On December 20, 2010, the minister for development visited Sidi Bouzid, while President Ben Ali remained in Dubai with his family on vacation. The interior minister did not inform the president about the protests until December 26, and demonstrators reached Tunis on December 27. On December 28, Ben Ali returned to have his picture taken at the bedside of Bouazizi and make a television address. He fired two ministers, called the demonstrators "terrorists and thugs," and ordered police to fire.

Protests became larger and more violent in January, while professional groups such as the nation's lawyers, and especially the Tunisian General Labor Union, supported the protesters, demanding more change to the regime. Diaspora cyberactivists, called Takrizards, working with militant soccer fans, also helped the protesters in their confrontations with the police. Tunisia employed a relatively large number of people in several competing, well-funded agencies for internal security, which did not coordinate their activities. Only on January 9 did the Ministries of Interior and Defense start working together.

On January 10, Ben Ali finally realized that the protests represented a serious problem, and he started taking more dramatic action. On January 12, the government imposed a curfew and deployed army troops on the streets. On January 13, he made another address to the nation, promising reforms and jobs and declaring a state of emergency. The public reacted with only more fury, which convinced the people around him to stop supporting him. While the head of the Presidential Guard began to fear a coup by the Department of Defense, the police began giving their guns to the newly deployed army, to prevent demonstrators from taking them. The army withdrew from some locations and even intervened between police and protesters to protect the people. Although several reports credit the chief of staff of the military, General Rachid Ammar, for refusing an order to fire on the protesters, the reports lack evidence.

The extended family of the president's second wife, called the Trabelsi clan, became fearful and went to the airport to seek airline tickets to leave. Conditions within the administration became extremely confused, and communication broke down. The head of the counterterrorism unit of the Ministry of the Interior went to the airport, angry that the Trabelsi family was trying to leave, and blocked their departure. This created a chaotic confrontation between several different military and security agencies, which helped convince the president to flee. The breakdown of communication caused the head of the Presidential Guard to tell the president that he could not guarantee his safety, which further convinced Ben Ali to flee with his family. On January 14, he fled the country for Saudi Arabia, and a state of emergency was declared in Tunisia.

Ben Ali's abrupt departure caused confusion in Tunisia. The prime minister briefly announced his own succession to the presidency, but then Tunisia's high court invalidated the succession arrangement that Ben Ali had ordered before his departure. Fouad Mebazaa, the speaker of the National Parliament, became interim president. While protests continued during the next week, the prime minister, the new interim president, and all the other cabinet members repudiated their affiliation with the ruling Democratic Constitutional Rally (RCD) party, in an effort to assuage popular unrest. The national police sought to join the winning side of a tectonic shift in Tunisia's power structure. Within days, Ben Ali was being charged in absentia with illegally using power to amass wealth. In March, the prime minister resigned, plans were announced to dissolve the secret police, and the RCD was officially suspended as a political party.

Although a journalist coined the term "Jasmine Revolution," only the international media adopted it. The people of Tunisia occasionally say the Sidi Bouzid Revolution, or more commonly the Dignity Revolution. The nonprofit pro-media organization Reporters Without Borders gave an award to the Tunisian bloggers of Nawaat.org for their work in reporting on the protest movement, which fueled its growth when Tunisia's official media tried to minimize recognition of the protests.

Nicholas Michael Sambaluk

See also: Ammar, Rachid; Authoritarianism; Ben Ali, Zine el Abidine; Bouazizi, Tarek el-Tayeb Mohamed; Corruption; Democracy Deficit; Grievance Model; Social Media; Takrizards; Tunisia, Republic of; Tunisian General Labor Union

Further Reading

Ayeb, Habib. "Social and Political Geography of the Tunisian Revolution: The Alfa Grass Revolution." *Review of African Political Economy* 38, no. 129 (September 2011): 467–79.

Fraihat, Ibrahim. *Unfinished Revolutions: Yemen, Libya, and Tunisia after the Arab Spring.* New Haven, CT: Yale University Press, 2016.

Mabrouk, Mehdi. "A Revolution for Dignity and Freedom: Preliminary Observations on the Social and Cultural Background to the Tunisian Revolution." *The Journal of North African Studies* 16, no. 4 (December 2011): 625–35.

Schraeder, Peter J., and Hamadi Redissi. "Ben Ali's Fall." *Journal of Democracy* 22, no. 3 (July 2011): 5–19.

Tadros, Samuel. "The Story of the Tunisian Revolution." Stanford, CA: The Hoover Institution, 2014.

Teti, Andrea, Pamela Abbott, and Francesco Cavatorta, eds. *The Arab Uprisings in Egypt, Jordan and Tunisia: Social, Political, and Economic Transformations.* New York: Palgrave Macmillan, 2018.

Jihad

The Arabic word for "struggle" or striving, understood in both a spiritual and physical sense, with a deep history in Islam, preserved in both the Qur'an and *hadith* literature. The earliest *suras* (chapters) of the Qur'an counseled patience and nonviolence toward those who persecute Muslims. Following the Muslim *Hegira* (migration) from Mecca to Medina in 622 CE, Muslims used the term *jihad* to describe both violent, defensive struggles, in their wars with the Meccans, and the internal struggle of each Muslim against sin. The classical doctrine of *jihad* describes four progressive developmental forms: 1) *jihad* of the heart, to understand and submit to Islamic doctrine in full; 2) *jihad* of the tongue, to invite others to Islam; 3) *jihad* of the hand, to serve others and increase the appeal of Islam; and 4) *jihad* of the sword, to defend the Muslims as a community. The classical doctrine restricted physical *jihad*, permitting war only in defense of Muslims, when declared by a head of an Islamic state; or by a consensus of Islamic scholars, when they agree on a clear threat to Islam or Muslims by external forces. The *hadith* reporting Muhammad's orders to his fighters constitute a set of restrictions very similar to the Western doctrine of a just war.

The contrast between the internal, spiritual struggle to master the internal appetites and passions versus the struggle of military defense derives from a *hadith* that states, "We have returned from the lesser *jihad* to the greater *jihad* (i.e. the struggle against the evil of one's soul)." Although scholars dispute the authenticity of this tradition, due to defects in its chain of transmission, Muslims and scholars alike have accepted it. Historically, the Medina-based Muslims engaged in an intense struggle against the Meccans who resisted Muhammad's claims, which led to interpretations of verses dealing with *jihad* in more explicitly martial terms. Revelations during this period also clearly specify a requirement for fighting. After the death of the Prophet in 632 CE, the Arab armies spread out from Arabia to establish a vast and expanding empire. Muslims used terms like *jihad* and tribal raiding (*Gazwa*) to describe combat against non-Muslims who resisted conquest. The Islamic conception of *jihad* also offers elaborate promises to those who die in battle as a martyr, which modern-day recruiters for military combat use to create emotionally powerful appeals.

Contemporary militant Islamist interpretations of *jihad* rely on the views of past thinkers, such as Ibn Taymiyyah and Sayyid Qutb, and convey a Manichean view of the world as composed of two warring parts. The contemporary Islamist understanding of *jihad* emphasizes the writing of Dr. 'Abdullah 'Azzam (1941–1989), a Palestinian scholar who wrote a great deal based on his experiences in fighting against the Russians in Afghanistan. His work shaped the thinking of Osama bin Laden and al-Qaeda's conception of waging war against the Near Enemy, the regimes of the Islamic world, and the Far Enemy, the United States and its Western allies. Azzam changed the conception of modern *jihad* from independent local struggles to a single universal *jihad* against false Muslims and un-Islamic regimes. Today, most Islamist groups embrace the idea of a universal *jihad* in terms drawn from Dr. 'Azzam, who personified the joining of the "pen of the scholar and the blood of the martyr."

Jeffrey Kaplan

See also: Al-Qaeda Central; Framing Model; Islamism

Further Reading

Cook, David. *Understanding Jihad.* Berkeley: University of California Press, 2015.

McGregor, Andrew. "'Jihad and the Rifle Alone,' Abdullah 'Azzam and the Islamist Revolution." *Journal of Conflict Studies* 23, no. 2 (2006): 92–113.

Robinson, Glenn E. "The Four Waves of Global Jihad, 1979–2017." *Middle East Policy* 24, no. 3 (2017): 70–88.

Jordan, Hashemite Kingdom of

A constitutional monarchy located south of Syria, north of the Kingdom of Saudi Arabia, west of Iraq, and east of the Jordan River, originally established as an emirate by the British in 1921. The British aided Abdullah bin Hussein in establishing his rule in this area, in partial fulfillment of their promise to Hussein bin Ali, the Hashemite sharif and emir of Mecca, to gain his leadership in the 1916 Arab Revolt. Abdullah entered from the Hejaz in November 1920 and faced difficulty in gaining the loyalty of the local residents. British funding enabled him to spread patronage among the tribes of the southern part of present-day Jordan, and British military advisers and supplies enabled him to suppress initial revolts, as well as invasions from Syria and by the religious militia of the Saudis. Abdullah built his kingdom on the Bedouins as the social base of his authority. Today, 90 percent of the labor force in the southern tribal areas serves either in the military or in other government offices.

In April 1921, the British established the Emirate of Transjordan, in distinction from the areas remaining under British mandate Palestine. Jordan gained its independence on May 25, 1946, under the official name "The Hashemite Kingdom of Jordan." In 1951, an assassin killed King Abdullah at the entrance to the Al-Aqsa Mosque in Jerusalem. His son, Talal bin Abdullah, ruled for only one year, due to his mental illness. Abdullah's grandson, King Hussein, then ruled until his death in 1999.

Due to a failed coup against King Hussein in 1956, the kingdom imposed martial law and banned political parties in 1957. In the late 1950s and early 1960s, Jordan came under significant ideological and political pressure from Egypt and President Gamel Abdel Nasser's promotion of Arab nationalism. Even before independence, the Muslim Brotherhood of Egypt had good relations with the monarchy, as both struggled to resist the growth of Israel. From its original base of support among East Bank merchants, the brothers gained influence among the West Bank Palestinians and gave them a channel for greater political influence.

The population of the area at independence, called Transjordanians or East Bankers, which formed the base of the monarchy, preserves its distinction from the people of Palestinian origin, or West Bankers. During the 1948 Arab-Israeli War, 70,000 Palestinians moved to Jordan—adding to a population of only 440,000 at the time. In 1950, King Abdullah took control of the West Bank and granted citizenship to the Palestinians there, as well as those who came to Jordan. Thus by the end of the decade, 700,000 Palestinians had gained Jordanian citizenship. The king retained tribal loyalty by distributing patronage—titles, subsidies, land, tax exemptions, and jobs—to the rural southern tribes, while restricting the Palestinians, the majority of the population, from government service and the upper ranks of the military. While most of the rural, poor Palestinians who came as refugees have struggled in their new country, some of the educated, urban

160   **Jordan, Hashemite Kingdom of**

Palestinians became wealthy entrepreneurs. In general, Palestinians have predominated in the private sector.

With the loss of the West Bank in 1967, the Palestine Liberation Organization (PLO) established camps in several parts of Jordan, particularly in the northern city of Irbid. Palestinian attacks on Israel provoked reprisals. After severe conflicts, the government suppressed the PLO with sustained warfare during 1970, an event known as Black September, or the Jordanian Civil War. In the period 1973–1983 Syria and the PLO still sought to regain the use of Jordanian territory to strike Israel. During Israel's attack on Lebanon in 1983–1984, fringe radical groups committed a number of attacks in Jordan. The Kingdom of Jordan reacted against the rhetoric of the Israeli Likud Party that "Jordan is Palestine" by deciding to officially disengage from West Bank territories on July 31, 1988.

In 1986, oil prices fell sharply, causing a recession in Jordan. Oil-producing countries in the Gulf reduced their grants to Jordan and stopped much of their construction work, forcing Jordanian laborers to return home. Jordan lacks natural resources but relies on grants and aid, initially from Britain, and later from the United States, and remittances from Jordanians working abroad. Under the financial pressure of the recession, the kingdom could not sustain the previous levels of social support and patronage, which led to protests and riots in the southern city of Maan, the center of political support for the monarchy. In 1989, the government responded with a process of liberalization, holding free elections and opening the parliament. Political parties remained banned, so candidates ran as independents. Islamists won 35 seats in the 80-member parliament.

In early 1991, when the United States and the international coalition entered Kuwait to expel the Iraqi military, Jordan did not support the coalition but remained a close ally. A variety of previously unknown groups committed more than a dozen terrorist attacks, with no discernible pattern to the tactics and targeting but reflecting anger against Jordan's relations with the United States.

In 1992, the king inaugurated a National Charter that legalized the political parties. This initiated the era of political pluralism. The Brotherhood established the Islamic Action Front (IAF) as its political wing, one of the key opposition parties in the kingdom. In 1993, the king revised the electoral law to favor the southern areas in the country like Maan, Salt, and Tafila, which support the monarchy most strongly, at the expense of Amman, Irbid, and Zarqa, where most of the Palestinians live. The Muslim Brotherhood rejected the 1993 Oslo Accords, in which the PLO recognized the existence of Israel. The kingdom's decision to normalize its ties with Israel in 1994 led to large-scale demonstrations in the streets of Amman by a diverse coalition of groups including Islamists, leftists, liberals, socialists, and former public officials.

Continuing financial difficulties, as Jordan complied with International Monetary Fund (IMF) and World Bank conditions, resulted in protests for the lack of greater social support. This added another level of grievance to the ongoing opposition to normalization. In 1997, in an effort to reduce protests, the government imposed more restrictions on the press. Again, the government changed the election laws to favor the southern, rural tribal areas, at the expense of the urban areas that give greater support for the Islamist parties. The Muslim Brotherhood boycotted the 1997 elections. In February 1999, King Hussein died, and his son Abdullah II

Jordan, Hashemite Kingdom of

became king. Although he initially indicated a desire for liberalization, he limited public opposition to the peace agreement with Israel. The government had allowed Hamas to operate from Jordan relatively freely, but after 1994, Hamas began inciting violence. In September 1999, the government cracked down on the Jordanian offices of Hamas and expelled four leaders.

When the Second Intifada began in September 2000, Jordan did not tolerate protests in support. In May 2001 and April 2002, the government used force to break up demonstrations in Amman. On October 28, 2002, two men, reportedly paid by the Islamist militant leader Abu Musab al-Zarqawi, killed the U.S. diplomat Laurence Foley in Amman.

After the 2003 U.S. invasion of Iraq led to rising levels of sectarian violence next door in Iraq, Jordan hosted large numbers of Iraqi refugees. The king organized a conference with leading scholars of all the major branches of Islam to refute the arguments of those promoting sectarian warfare. The document they produced in 2004, called the Amman Message, helped promote tolerance and undermined the ideology of radicals. The IAF participated in the 2003 parliamentary elections, winning 16 seats.

On November 9, 2005, terrorists trained by Al-Zarqawi struck three hotels in Amman. This caused the kingdom to shift its policy from promoting Jordanian identity to promoting security first. After Zarqawi was killed by an airstrike on June 7, 2006, Jordan entered a period of relative calm. The government arrested two IAF leaders for visiting Zarqawi's house to offer condolences. The government asked the IAF to nominate moderate candidates for the 2007 elections, and they won six seats, while complaining bitterly about election fraud. The government revised the electoral law again, continuing its effort to ensure a parliament elected by supporters of the monarchy.

When the people of Jordan saw the events in Tunisia, the first reaction came from the cities of the southern tribal core of support for the government. Then later, the young educated urban liberals began a campaign of demonstrations. These protests never mobilized numbers as large as in Tunisia or Egypt, and the protesters demanded only reform, rather than the overthrow of the regime. The government adopted an initial policy of restraint, with promises of financial help and policy change, and used enough violence to suppress the protests without provoking a greater conflict. The government stalled for time. Then the civil wars in Syria, Libya, and Yemen created a greater desire for stability rather than confrontation.

Under the pressure of changing government policies, the Muslim Brotherhood has fragmented. The Kingdom of Jordan has resisted international pressure to ban all of its different operational branches, preferring to keep a legally registered political party. Some of the protests and opposition seen since 2011 consist of groups of East Bank Jordanians fearful that the government's policies of economic liberalization will reduce the patronage that they have been receiving and give greater bargaining power to Jordanians of Palestinian descent. At the same time, the West Bank groups demand reduction of corruption and greater resistance to Israel.

By September 2018, the king had appointed seven different prime ministers since 2011. After the civil war erupted in Syria, new groups like Jayeen (We're Coming) and Hirak (Movement) have mobilized partly in response to the huge number of Syrian refugees, which governmental sources claim reaches more than one million. Under the pressure of the huge numbers of refugees, prevailing social divisions, unemployment, and other economic problems have increased.

Nur Köprülü

See also: Abdullah II, King of Jordan; Black September; Clientelism (Patrimonialism); Hamas; Israel; Jordanian Protests; Muslim Brotherhood; Palestine Liberation Organization; Rentier State Politics; *Wasta*

Further Reading

Abu Rish, Ziad. "Protests, Regime Stability and State Formation in Jordan." In *Beyond the Arab Spring: The Evolving Ruling Bargains in the Middle East,* edited by Mehran Kamrava, 277–312. New York: Oxford University Press, 2014.

Clark, Janine A. *Local Politics in Jordan and Morocco: Strategies of Centralization and Decentralization.* New York: Columbia University Press, 2018.

Köprülü, Nur. "Consolidated Monarchies in the post-Arab Spring Era: The Case of Jordan." *Israel Affairs* 20, no. 3 (2014): 318–27.

Robins, Philip. *A History of Jordan.* Cambridge, UK: Cambridge University Press, 2004.

Worman, John G., and David H. Grey. "Terrorism in Jordan: Politics and the Real Target Audience." *Global Security Studies* 3, no. 3 (Summer 2012): 94–111.

Yaghi, Mohammed, and Janine A. Clark. "Jordan: Evolving Activism in a Divided Society." In *Taking to the Streets: The Transformation of Arab Activism,* edited by Lina Khatim and Ellen Lust, 236–67. Baltimore: Johns Hopkins University Press, 2014.

Jordan, King. *See* Abdullah II, King of Jordan

Jordanian Protests (2011)

A series of protests in 2011 in the Hashemite Kingdom of Jordan against corruption, demanding political reform rather than questioning the legitimacy of King Abdullah II or the monarchy itself. The protests in other Arab countries affected Jordanians who suffer similar levels of youth unemployment, corruption, and authoritarian rule. In May 2010 a group of 140,000 army veterans released a petition warning against an Israeli plot to expel Palestinians from the West Bank. They represented one of four new forces, together with the Transjordanian youth, tribal leaders, and reformists elites, who played prominent roles in these protests. On January 7, 2011, several hundred people gathered in Theiban, in southern Jordan, to protest unemployment and poverty. The initiative for the growing protest cycle came from cities of the tribal south, which had provided a core base of support for the monarchy. Under pressure from their youth members, the Supreme Coordinating Committee for the seven opposition parties started to organize protests after Friday prayers in Amman. The government reacted by passing a $169 million plan for subsidizing fuel and food prices, followed quickly by a $422 million package of subsidies and civil salary raises. On January 21, 5,000 people gathered in Amman to protest economic problems. By then, protests had spread to all the major cities. The king even met for the first time with Muslim Brotherhood leaders. On March 24, a large number of youths tried to set up a permanent sit-in demonstration at the Gamel Abdel Nasser Circle near the Interior Ministry, but the government used plain-clothes thugs to conduct beatings and then cleared the area forcefully. The scale of the violence deterred the further growth of the protest movement, although protests continued in a wide array of places. The civil wars in Syria, Yemen, and Libya further demoralized those who might have pressed harder for political change. In general, the protests dwindled because they exposed the divisions between policies sought by the Jordanians of Palestinian descent versus the demands of the tribal conservatives of the East Bank. The public protests in Jordan lacked the distribution, durability, or violence seen in other countries of the broader region. New groups like Jayeen (We're Coming) and Hirak (Movement) have mobilized partly in response to the huge number of Syrian war refugees.

Nur Köprülü

See also: Abdullah II, King of Jordan; Corruption; Grievance Model; Jordan, Hashemite Kingdom of; Palestine; Refugees; Syrian Arab Republic; Yemen, Republic of

Further Reading
Ryan, Curtis R. *Jordan and the Arab Spring: Regime Survival and Politics beyond the State.* New York: Columbia University Press, 2018.

Yaghi, Mohammed, and Janine A. Clark. "Jordan: Evolving Activism in a Divided Society." In *Taking to the Streets: The Transformation of Arab Activism,* edited by Lina Khatim and Ellen Lust, 236–67. Baltimore: Johns Hopkins University Press, 2014.

Jumblatt, Walid

Lebanese politician, leader of Lebanon's Druze community, and president of the Progressive Socialist Party (PSP). Walid Jumblatt, born in Moukhtara on August 7, 1949, inherited the legacy of his father, Kamal Jumblatt, founder of the Progressive Socialist Party, who was assassinated in 1977, probably by the Syrians. His grandfather Prince Shakib Arslan, a Druze politician, writer, poet, and historian, suffered exile from Lebanon under the French Mandate.

Walid Jumblatt studied political sciences and public administration at the American University of Beirut. In 1983, in the middle of the Lebanese civil war, Jumblatt founded the National Salvation Front with the Sunni statesman Rashid Karami and the Maronite politician Suleiman Frangieh: a coalition of leftist, Syria-supporting Sunni Muslims, Druze, and some Christians. They opposed the official Lebanese Armed Forces supported by the Lebanese Forces militia (a coalition of primarily Christian parties led by Amin Gemayel, the Kataeb Party leader). During the 1983 Mountain War, the Druze forces of Walid Jumblatt conducted a strong war against the rural Maronites.

After almost 20 years as a client and supporter of Syria, after the death of Syrian president Hafez Assad in 2000, Jumblatt became critical of Bashar al-Assad, and of his alliance with the Lebanese Shiite party Hezbollah. In 2005, after the assassination of Rafik Hariri, Jumblatt reconciled with the Maronites to join the March 14 Coalition that created the Cedar Revolution to expel the Syrian military from Lebanon. His defiance of Syria gave him a reputation as a pan-Lebanese nationalist. The government formed after the Syrian withdrawal appointed Walid Jumblatt as the minister in charge of encouraging Christians to return to the homes they had fled in the war. After the beginning of the Syrian war in 2011, Jumblatt and the PSP accused Assad of having created the radical jihadist al-Nusra Front. However, after the development of the Islamic State (Daesh), in 2014, he reversed his position to again support Syria.

Although Jumblatt left Parliament in 2009, he remains an important political figure. He confirmed his son Taymour as his political heir on March 19, 2017, the 40th anniversary of the assassination of Kamal Jumblatt.

Emanuela Claudia Del Re

See also: Al-Assad, Bashar; Cedar Revolution; Druze; Hariri, Saad; Hezbollah; Islamic State (Daesh); Lebanese Republic; Maronites; Minorities; Syrian Arab Republic

Further Reading
Harris, William. "Bashar al-Assad's Lebanon Gamble." *Middle East Quarterly* 12, no. 3 (Summer 2005): 33–44.
Moubayed, Sami. "Syria Loses Its Former Ally in Lebanon, Druze Leader Walid Jumblatt." *Washington Report on Middle East Affairs* 20, no. 1 (January/February 2001): 35–36.
Rowayheb, Marwan G. "Walid Jumblatt and Political Alliances: The Politics of Adaptation." *Middle East Critique* 20, no. 1 (2011): 47–66.

Justice and Development Party (Morocco)

A legally registered, Islamist political party in Morocco that derived from the merger of the Popular Democratic Constitutional Party (PDCP) and the Harakat al-Islah wa al-Tajdid (Reform and Renewal Movement; MRR) in 1996. The MRR did not disappear; rather, the movement merely split into two organizations serving different objectives. The MRR changed its name to the Movement for Unification and Reform (MUR), which continues to promote Islam through preaching, teaching, and social-service activities.

In 1998, the new combined political party changed its name to al-Adala wa al-Tanmiyya (Justice and Development Party; JDP). This enabled the Islamists to engage in explicitly political activity, rather than merely religious or social pursuits, but it required them to 1) accept the constitutional monarchy; 2) reject the use of violence; and 3) accept democracy and human rights within Islam. Through this party they protest against negative Western influences, corruption, indifference, moral decay, and tolerance of official cruelty. They compete in elections for the Moroccan Parliament and participate in educational activities to promote justice, equality, dignity, and equal opportunity. Legal registration allows the party to rent official facilities for large meetings and gain greater media exposure. Participation in the parliament and in local councils gives the party leaders some influence on policies and some benefit from the distribution of political patronage. In local districts where the JDP won 30 percent or more of the vote, it exerted a positive effect on investment and reduced corruption. Throughout its behavior in government, the party negotiated governing coalitions, even with socialist parties promoting antithetical ideologies, for the sake of some shared goals, such as greater transparency and democratization.

Some individuals remain members of both the MUR and the JDP, even as they keep the two sets of objectives separate. The party publishes its own newspaper in competition with that of the MUR. Both the party and the movement compete ideologically with the Al-Adl wa al-Ihsan (Justice and Virtue) Movement, which rejects the king's claim to religious status and rejects becoming a political party. The JDP did not participate in the February 20 Movement but did endorse its platform. In the November 2011 elections, the Justice and Development Party became the first Islamist party to lead a Moroccan government: in October 2016, it won the second parliamentary elections since the Arab Spring.

Jonathan K. Zartman

See also: Authoritarianism; Benkirane, Abdelilah; Corruption; February 20 Movement; Islamism; Morocco, Kingdom of

Further Reading

Bahaji, Kassem. "Moroccan Islamists: Integration, Confrontation, and Ordinary Muslims." *Middle East Review of International Affairs* 15, no. 1 (March 2011): 39–51.

Buehler, Matt. "Safety-Valve Elections and the Arab Spring: The Weakening (and Resurgence) of Morocco's Islamist Opposition Party." *Terrorism and Political Violence* 25, no. 1 (2013): 137–56.

Howe, Marvine. *Morocco: The Islamist Awakening and Other Challenges.* New York: Oxford University Press, 2005.

Pellicer, Miquel, and Eva Wegner. "The Justice and Development Party in Moroccan Local Politics." *Middle East Journal* 69, no. 1 (Winter 2015): 32–50.

Justice and Development Party (Turkey)

An Islamist, populist, and socially conservative political party in Turkey, promoting centralized authoritarian rule. In August 2001, Recep Tayyip Erdogan, Abdullah Gül, and Bülent Arınç formed the *Adalet ve Kalkınma Partisi*/Justice and Development Party (AKP) as the successor to the Virtue Party. Erdogan has led the party from its beginning. In the aftermath of the 2001 financial crisis, the AKP surprised many observers by winning nearly 35 percent of the seats in the Grand National Assembly, in the general election of 2002. This victory made Abdullah Gül the prime minister, followed by Erdogan from 2003 to 2014. In the general election of 2007, the AKP gained nearly 46 percent of the vote. In 2007, the AKP won a constitutional referendum to select the president by direct popular vote, rather than by the Grand National Assembly. In the general election of 2011, the AKP received nearly 50 percent of the vote, in part due to Turkey's surging economy. In 2012, the AKP's social policies created a lot of anger and indirectly led to the 2013 Gezi Park protests, which the government repressed with violence.

With Erdogan's election to the presidency in 2014, Ahmet Davutoğlu became the prime minister until 2016. Tension grew between Davutoğlu and Erdogan, along with public opposition to increasing abuse of power. During the general election of June 2015, the AKP vote percentage dipped to just under 41 percent. Amid growing violence in southeastern Turkey, the AKP called another general election in November 2015, which gave the AKP just below 50 percent. Davutoğlu resigned as party leader and prime minister in May 2016.

Erdogan exploited the July 2016 failed military coup to conduct a widespread purge of government, the military, the media, and the education system under the cover of a state of emergency. The government attacked Kurdish political activities, including the People's Democratic Party (HDP). These actions have effectively eliminated the AKP's rivals. This created a political climate that enabled the AKP to pass a constitutional referendum in April 2017, with 51 percent of the vote, that abolished the office of prime minister and created an executive presidency. This gave the AKP and Erdogan extraordinary power to reshape the political structure of Turkey. In February 2018, in response to some renewed opposition, the AKP formed an electoral alliance called the People's Alliance/Cumhur İttifakı with the Nationalist Movement Party and a few smaller parties. This electoral block took over 52 percent of the vote in the general election of June 2018. Although on March 31, 2019, the AKP officially lost the mayoral races in Ankara, Izmir, and Istanbul, the party challenged the results and demanded a new vote in Istanbul, which it lost. The electoral commission disallowed victories by the HDP in eight electoral districts. In the big cities, the AKP still controls the local councils, media, judiciary, and powerful patronage networks, making any mayor's race less consequential.

James Tallon

See also: Democracy Deficit; Erdogan, Recep Tayyip; Islamism; Turkey, Republic of

Further Reading

Baser, Bahar, and Ahmet Erdi Öztürk. *Authoritarian Politics in Turkey: Elections, Resistance and the AKP.* London: I. B. Taurus, 2017.

Cizre, Ümit. *Secular and Islamic Politics in Turkey: The Making of the Justice and Development Party.* London: Routledge, 2008.

Hale, William M., and Ergun Özbudun. *Islamism, Democracy and Liberalism in Turkey: The Case of the AKP.* London: Routledge, 2011.

Khamenei, Ayatollah Sayyid Ali

Iran's supreme religious and political leader since June 1989. Khamenei was born in 1939 into a family of Islamic scholars in Mashhad, Iran, where he studied in Islamic schools. After one year in Najaf, Iraq, to study under eminent Shi'a *ulema* (scholars-teachers), he went to Qom to study under Ayatollah Ruhollah Khomeini. In 1963, he joined Khomeini in protesting Shah Muhammad Reza Pahlavi's aggressive modernization programs. The shah's regime crushed the protests, and Khomeini was exiled in 1964. That same year, Khamenei became a *hojatolislam* (authority on Islam), the rank directly below ayatollah, and continued with his religious studies. The shah sentenced him to prison several times between 1964 and 1975, but ultimately his efforts in organizing nationwide protests forced the shah into exile on January 16, 1979. Ayatollah Khomeini returned to govern Iran on February 1, 1979.

In 1979, Khamenei became a commander in the Islamic Revolutionary Guards Corps (IRGC). After Iraq invaded in September 1980, Khomeini appointed Khamenei to lead the Supreme Defense Council and serve as commander-in-chief of the armed forces. For eight years, Khamenei helped lead Iran's war effort. In 1981 and 1985, Khamenei was elected as Iran's president. Khamenei persuaded Khomeini to accept the 1988 UN cease-fire, ending the eight-year war with Iraq. As president, he made a concerted effort to rebuild Iran's private sector. After Khomeini's death in 1989, Khamenei did not have the necessary credentials of religious scholarship to become the supreme leader, but he had a reputation as an effective politician and leader. Ali Akbar Hashemi Rafsanjani persuaded the Assembly of Theological Experts to promote 49-year-old Ali Khamenei to ayatollah and elect him as Vilayat-e-Faqih (supreme religious and political leader). Thereafter, Khamenei's worldview became more conservative and more antagonistic to the West; he increased media censorship and abolished the prime minister position.

In the 2009 presidential election, he injected himself directly into the political conflict, removing the pretense of religious authority, which hurt the legitimacy of the state. He openly sided with then-president Ahmadinejad. When security forces fired on peaceful protesters, many Iranians blamed Khamenei. In June 2014, after the Islamic State (Daesh) captured significant portions of Syria and northern Iraq, Khamenei sent Iranian Shi'a recruits, including Afghan labor migrants in Iran, to fight. He agreed to the removal of Iraqi prime minister Nouri al-Maliki, who had lost favor with Iraqi Sunni Arabs and the United States, and agreed to support Haidar al-Abadi as Iraq's new prime minister.

Despite reluctance toward nuclear negotiations with Western powers, Khamenei accepted negotiations with the United States from 2002 to 2003 and 2013 to 2015. On July 14, 2015, after the negotiators agreed on the Joint Comprehensive Plan of Action (JCPOA), Khamenei endorsed the nuclear deal. In his international policy he seeks to assert the primacy of Shi'a Islam in competition with Sunni leaders. He tries to claim the status of "Supreme Spiritual Leader," not just of Iran but of the entire Muslim world, in his pronouncements criticizing the United States, Israel, and the enemies of Islam.

Mir Zohair Husain

See also: Ahmadinejad, Mahmoud; Al-Abadi, Haidar; Al-Maliki, Nouri; Iran, Islamic Republic of; Iraq, Republic of; Islamic State (Daesh); Islamic Revolutionary Guard Corps (IRGC); Khomeini, Ayatollah Sayyid Ruhollah Mūsavi; Rafsanjani, Ali Akbar Hashemi; Syrian Arab Republic

Further Reading

Buchta, Wilfried. *Who Rules Iran: The Structure of Power in the Islamic Republic.* Washington, DC: Washington Institute for Near East Policy, 2000.

Khalaji, Mehdi. *The Last Marja: Sistani and the End of Traditional Religious Authority in Shiism.* Washington, DC: Washington Institute for Near East Policy, 2006.

Wright, Robin. *The Last Great Revolution: Turmoil and Transformation in Iran.* New York: Alfred A. Knopf, 2000.

Khatami, Mohammad

An Iranian religious leader, reformist, and politician who served as president of Iran for two consecutive terms (1997–2005). Mohammad Khatami, born in 1943 in Yazd province, grew up in a conservative religious family; his father was well known as a Shi'a religious teacher. After earning his bachelor's degree in philosophy and studying for a master's degree in education at Tehran University, he completed his religious studies in Qom, earning the title *Hojatolislam*. He studied under Ayatollah Khomeini and became close friends with his other students.

In 1980, Khatami was elected as a representative in the Iranian parliament. In 1982, Prime Minister Mir Hossein Musavi appointed him to serve as minister of Culture and Islamic Guidance. In 1983, he married a granddaughter of Ayatollah Khomeini, who became a women's rights activist. During the Iran-Iraq War, Khatami served as deputy and then head of the joint Command of the Armed Forces and chair of the War Propaganda Headquarters. After the end of the war and the rise of Khamenei, protests in 1992 by conservative clerics against some materials Khatami had allowed into circulation forced him to resign as minister of Culture and Islamic Guidance, so President Hashemi Rafsanjani appointed him director of the National Library.

In 1997, Khatami ran for president with a political message of support for freedom of expression, advancement of women's rights, and a freer market. He appealed to moderates, leftists, younger voters, women, and businessmen. This helped him win a landslide victory and appoint a progressive cabinet. However, hardline, conservative Islamists opposed him relentlessly. Even the Iranian parliament, controlled by progressive Islamists, could not implement reforms, due to the conservatives who held all the positions of true political control. Khatami promoted the first elections for local officials, held in 1999. Khatami won a landslide victory in the 2001 national election. During his second presidential term, he carried out parts of his platform, continuing Rafsanjani's efforts to end Iran's isolation and improve relations with other states. Instead of a "clash of civilizations," Khatami promoted a "dialogue of civilizations" in several international societies and the United Nations. The United Nations proclaimed 2001 as the Year of the Dialogue of Civilizations. Despite his efforts toward dialogue, as well as support for the United States in the initial invasion of Afghanistan, he could not control the Islamic Revolutionary Guard Corps, which raised international opposition through its support for terrorism abroad. He also could not control the Basij forces that were attacking and oppressing his supporters, so they lost hope in democratic elections and political activity. They failed to turn out to support reformists in 2005, but the conservatives campaigned aggressively and won the next set of elections.

After leaving the presidency in August 2005, Khatami founded and still directs two private organizations. First, the International Institute for Dialogue among Cultures and Civilizations, registered as a foundation, or *bonyad*. Second, the BARAN Foundation, focused on domestic activities. *Baran* means "rain," an acronym in Persian for "Foundation for Freedom, Growth and Development."

Mir Zohair Husain

See also: Basij; Democracy Deficit; Iran, Islamic Republic of; Islamic Revolutionary Guard Corps (IRGC); Modernization; Political Decision-Making in Iran; Rafsanjani, Ali Akbar Hashemi

Further Reading
Ansari, Ali M. *Iran, Islam, and Democracy: The Politics of Managing Change,* 2nd ed. London: Royal Institute of International Affairs, 2006.

Ehteshami, Anoushiravan, and Mahjoob Zweiri, eds. *Iran's Foreign Policy: From Khatami to Ahmadinejad*. Reading, UK: Ithaca, 2012.

Tazmini, Ghoncheh. *Khatami's Iran: The Islamic Republic and the Turbulent Path to Reform*. London: Tauris Academic Studies, 2009.

Khomeini, Ayatollah Sayyid Ruhollah Mūsavi

Leader of a militant Shi'a Islamist movement that took control of a popular revolution in Iran, which had forced the shah to flee in 1979. His followers played a major role in that massive movement, which also included socialist and nationalist coalitions, protesting against the shah's corruption and dictatorial policies.

Sayyid Ruhollah Mūsavi Khomeini (1902–1989) was born in Khomeyn and later moved to Qom, where he studied the Qur'an, Islamic law, philosophy, and mysticism. Khomeini wrote more than 40 books and taught at the seminaries in Najaf and Qom before entering active politics in 1963. Khomeini condemned the rapid modernization and increased rights for women in Mohammad Reza Pahlavi Shah's "White Revolution." He compared the shah to the infamous tyrant Yazid, triggering a series of protests throughout the nation. In 1964, he led another set of protests against the shah for granting diplomatic immunity to American military personnel. In November 1964, the Iranian government sent him into exile, first to Turkey; then he moved to Iraq and, finally, to Paris. In exile, Khomeini developed his distinctive ideology of Vilayat-i Faqih (rule of the supreme religious lawyer) and continued to denounce the Iranian government, gradually building a massive following that grew into an open revolt.

After the shah fled the country in 1979 and Khomeini returned from exile, his followers defeated the socialist groups, including the Mujahidin-e Khalq, in street combat. Khomeini used the student takeover of the American embassy to further mobilize Islamic support against the democratic and nationalist parties and leaders who served in an interim government. His coalition developed a new constitution, overwhelmingly supported in a popular referendum, to create an Islamic republic ruled by a religious legal scholar. Khomeini became the first Supreme Leader of Iran, ruling until his death. He pursued autarchic economic policies, implemented a strict interpretation of Islamic law, and actively promoted revolution in the Muslim world, especially in neighboring states with large Shi'a populations.

Due to Iran's aggressive propaganda campaigns, combined with targeted assassinations and support for militants, Iraq launched an invasion of Iran, leading to a bloody eight-year war (1980–1988) that featured missile attacks against cities and the use of chemical weapons. Under Khomeini's leadership, the government exploited the doctrine of martyrdom in Shi'a Islam. This resulted in tactics that dramatically increased the human cost of the war.

He died in 1989 after a series of heart attacks. His funeral attracted three million mourners passionately seeking to touch Khomeini's body or take a piece of his burial shroud. He was succeeded by Sayyid Ali Hosseini Khamenei, who continued his repression, imposing a strict interpretation of religious law.

Paul J. Springer

See also: Iran, Islamic Republic of; Islamic Revolutionary Guard Corps (IRGC); Islamism; Khamenei, Ayatollah Sayyid Ali; Modernization; Mujahidin-e Khalq (MEK); Sectarianism

Further Reading

Moin, Baqer. *Khomeini: Life of the Ayatollah*. New York: St. Martin's Press, 1999.

Taheri, Amir. *The Spirit of Allah: Khomeini and the Islamic Revolution*. Bethesda, MD: Adler and Adler, 1986.

Wright, Robin. *In the Name of God: The Khomeini Decade*. New York: Simon and Schuster, 1990.

Kurdistan Regional Government (KRG)

The official governing structure of the Kurdish region in northern Iraq. Following the U.S.-led coalition intervention to protect the Kurds in Iraq in 1990, after their revolt against Saddam Hussein, a coalition of Kurdish political parties initially agreed to form a united parliament. In May 1992, the Kurdistan National Assem-

Kurdistan Regional Government (KRG)

bly formed the Kurdistan Regional Government (KRG), with the political offices evenly divided between the two main parties. Following the 2003 Iraq War, the Transitional Administrative Law (TAL) promoted the development of the 2005 Iraqi Constitution, which recognized the autonomy of the KRG in the Kurdish region of a newly federated Iraq. Under the Iraqi Constitution, each region manages its own domestic affairs while the federal government in Baghdad manages international affairs.

The government consists of a president, prime minister, parliament, and various governmental ministries. Popular elections select both the president of the KRG and the Iraqi Kurdistan Parliament, located in Erbil, the capital of the region. The president heads the cabinet and acts as chief of state and commander in chief of the Peshmerga Armed Forces. The majority party selects the prime minister and members of the cabinet. While the president heads the executive branch, the prime minister heads the legislative branch of government, and both share executive powers. Historically, the two largest political parties, the Kurdistan Democratic Party (KDP) and the Patriotic Union of Kurdistan (PUK), have dominated the cabinet and parliament.

As a land-locked, semi-autonomous area, it suffers from the competition of antagonistic neighbors, who cynically exploit its internal political divisions. The KDP waged a sustained war against the Kurdistan Worker's Party (PKK) based in Turkey. This gives it good relations with Turkey, which holds antagonism toward the PUK for its alliance with Iran and attempt to control Kirkuk, where many Turkmen live. The whole region depends on exporting oil to Turkey for financing. The 2014 invasion by the Islamic State (Daesh) inflicted serious losses, exposing the weakness of the separate Peshmerga military forces, and left a long-term problem in caring for the huge numbers of refugees. The American air support that enabled Kurdish and Iraqi forces to defeat the Islamic State showed the mutual dependence of U.S. policy and the Kurdish forces. The 2017 Kurdistan independence referendum, the aggressive response from Iraq, the opposition of the international community, and the withdrawal of Kurdish forces to avoid a major conflict weakened the political bargaining power of the region. The internal corruption of the two major parties, which propelled the creation of the Goran Party, shows that the KRG must make greater progress in democratic consolidation and internal cohesion to become more politically independent. The future security of Iraqi Kurds depends on that.

Autumn Cockrell-Abdullah

See also: Authoritarianism; Barzani, Masoud; Clientelism (Patrimonialism); Corruption; Democracy Deficit; Iran, Islamic Republic of; Iraq, Republic of; Islamic State (Daesh); Kurds; Patriotic Union of Kurdistan (PUK); Turkey, Republic of

Further Reading

King, Diane E. *Kurdistan on the Global Stage: Kinship, Land and Community in Iraq.* New Brunswick, NJ: Rutgers University Press, 2014.

Natali, Denise. *The Kurdish Quasi-State: Development and Dependency in Post-Gulf War Iraq.* Syracuse, NY: Syracuse University Press, 2010.

Toperich, Sasha, Tea Iranovic, and Nahro Zagros, eds. *Iraqi Kurdistan Region: A Path Forward.* Washington, DC: Center for Transatlantic Relations, 2017.

Kurdistan Workers' Party (PKK)

A Kurdish nationalist party established on November 27, 1974, in Turkey by Abdullah Ocalan using Marxist-Leninist ideology, with some influence of Maoist doctrine. The Kurdish Workers Party (*Partiya Karkeren Kurdistan*; PKK) emerged out of the ferment of leftist parties and the development of Kurdish nationalism in Turkey in the 1960s. The Turkish government suppressed the initial parties and movements effectively by 1969. Its policy sought to force the Kurds to assimilate to Turkish language and culture. The 1970 agreement between the Kurdistan Democratic Party (KDP) of Iraq and the government of Iraq not only raised Kurdish aspirations in Turkey, it also caused great alarm in the Turkish government, which launched a campaign of severe repression and collective punishment. After the March 1971 army coup, this campaign intensified.

During the years of martial law after the September 1980 military coup, Turkish government repression crushed the Kurdish parties, and the PKK fled to Syria and Lebanon to regroup. On August 15, 1984, the PKK began acting as a militia, attacking and bombing Turkish government forces. The Turkish government recruited Kurds to serve as guards to defend each village. The PKK attacked even these people without discrimination, which justified the government of Turkey in calling them terrorists. Turkish policy has involved occasional raids into Iraqi Kurdistan and huge depopulation campaigns in Kurdish areas of Turkey, destroying villages and killing and displacing thousands of people. Large numbers of Kurds moved to cities, but this also fueled the PKK's recruitment efforts. By 1996 the PKK had become one of the largest guerilla organizations in the world. The indiscriminate character of PKK warfare also provoked opposition from the KDP in Iraq, leading to a long-running war.

By the summer of 1999, the combination of Turkish and KDP war against the PKK had reduced it to only about 1,500 fighters inside Turkey. After the Turkish government captured Ocalan in February 1999, the PKK declared a cease-fire, which ended under continued Turkish repression at the end of 2003. Over the next decade, the government of Turkey continued to arrest various Kurdish politicians, lawyers, and civil society leaders on charges of belonging to a terrorist organization. The Turkish state has tried to negotiate with the PKK through Ocalan. In 2009, Ocalan's trial revealed the basic points of his 160-page road map for solving the Kurdish problem through democratization and decentralization in Turkey. Although defeated militarily, the PKK organized a parliament in exile in Europe, special branches for women, and a popular-front Kurdistan People's Congress. Its branches in Syria and Iran remain active. Its media operations, recruitment, fundraising, and training continue. In addition to legitimate business activities, it also engages in drug trafficking, smuggling, extortion, and money laundering.

In 2013, the PKK declared a cease-fire but in 2015 announced the cease-fire ended and stated that only a cease-fire guaranteed by the United Nations or the United States would be acceptable. The North Atlantic Treaty Organization (NATO), the European Union (EU), the United States, and many other European countries recognize the PKK as a terrorist organization.

Sarah Fischer

See also: AKP-PKK Peace Talks; Iran, Islamic Republic of; Iraq, Republic of; Kurdistan Democratic Party (KDP); Lebanese Republic; Ocalan, Abdullah; Syrian Arab Republic; Turkey, Republic of

Further Reading

Kutschera, Chris. "Mad Dreams of Independence: The Kurds of Turkey and the PKK." *Middle East Report* No. 189 (July–August 1994): 12–15.

Olsen, Robert. *Blood, Belief and Ballots: The Management of Kurdish Nationalism in Turkey, 2007–2009.* Costa Mesa, CA: Mazda Publishers, 2009.

Wilgenburg, Wladimir van. "Kurdish PKK Using PJAK to Isolate Turkey." *Terrorism Monitor* 8, no. 33 (August 19, 2010): 3–5.

Kurds

A stateless ethnic group speaking several different dialects, living primarily in southern and eastern Turkey, northern Iraq, northern Syria, and northwestern Iran, with a diaspora in Europe and North America. Scholars can only estimate the total number of Kurds—around 30 million—due to the lack of any appropriate census in the countries where they live. Some Kurds speak only the language of the host society but retain their cultural heritage. In addition to their linguistic diversity, Kurds include a diverse array of religious groups.

The Ottoman Empire (1299–1922) ruled most of the Kurdish homeland, called Kurdistan. After the Allies defeated the Ottomans in World War II, they negotiated the division of the empire. Despite an initial early effort to create a state for the Kurds, Mustapha Kemal Ataturk led Turkish nationalists in fighting to conquer the Kurds, which created the present boundaries of the new Republic of Turkey. Then the French and the British divided the remaining territory, based roughly on the 1916 Sykes-Picot Agreement. The outside major powers excluded Kurdish representation in their negotiations and divided the historic Kurdish homeland among the four major states.

Today, over one-quarter of Kurds live in Turkey, where they represent one-fifth of Turkey's population. Kurds did not immediately face trouble in the new Republic of Turkey, but after the Sheikh Said Rebellion in 1925, Turkey aggressively promoted Kurdish assimilation. The state denied Kurdish identity while asserting the prestige of Turkish identity. The government prohibited Kurdish political parties, Kurdish names, broadcasts in Kurdish, and even the speaking of Kurdish in public. The laws, politics, and economic decisions all served to keep Kurds powerless.

For decades, the Kurds periodically rebelled against the state. In 1978, Kurdish rebellion in Turkey led Abdullah Ocalan to establish an insurgent group, the Kurdistan Workers Party, or Partiya Karkarên Kurdistanê (PKK), to oppose state violence. From 1984 to 1999, the war between the PKK and the government of Turkey resulted in the deaths of tens of thousands and the destruction of hundreds of villages, and massive numbers of Kurds fled to the cities and to Europe. War fatigue and exhaustion have prompted many cease-fires, which all eventually collapsed. When the Justice and Development Party (AKP) began its rise to power, negotiations with Ocalan led to some relaxation of the rules governing Kurdish life. Nonetheless, the state's violence and discrimination against the Kurds has not ceased.

In Iraq, the first significant Kurdish rebellion occurred in 1975. Because some Iraqi Kurds supported Iran during the Iran-Iraq War of the 1980s, Iraqi president Saddam Hussein saw the Kurds as traitors. Near the end of the war, he used chemical weapons against whole villages of civilian Kurds near the Iranian border, a genocidal campaign called *"al-Anfal"* (Spoils of War). The Kurds rebelled against the Iraqi government again in 1991. After this, the United States helped to establish a no-fly zone for the Kurds between the 36th Parallel and Iraq's northern border. Since the establishment of this area, Iraqi Kurds have enjoyed significant autonomy. Yet within the no-fly zone, two Kurdish factions fought a bitter conflict.

The no-fly zone was the precursor to the Kurdistan Regional Government (KRG). More recently, under the leadership of Masoud and Nechirvan Barzani, the KRG has struggled with Iraq's central government and has sought greater Kurdish autonomy. The KRG has a sizeable military and provides limited public services to its citizens, such as education and health care. In 2014, the Islamic State (Daesh) came within 20 miles of Erbil, capital of Iraqi Kurdistan. That threat motivated Kurds to reduce their political infighting in the KRG and increase their efforts to establish an independent Kurdish state. The Kurds, backed by the U.S. military, defeated Daesh.

Syria's Kurds, who constitute about one-tenth of Syria's population, mainly occupy the northernmost part of the country, which has both fertile farmland and petroleum reserves. Most of these Kurds descended from those who fled Turkey after the failed Kurdish uprisings of the 1920s. In Syria, Kurds living in rural areas developed different attitudes than those living in urban areas: many urban Kurds adopted Arabic; others became more committed to Kurdish nationalism. They hoped for greater autonomy after World War II, but after ethnic violence in the 1960s, the Syrian government stripped many Kurds of their citizenship, their ability to work, or their access to public resources, such as education. The Syrian government expropriated land from Kurds living near the Turkish border and established a belt of Arabs to prevent contact between Kurdish communities. Textbooks and other official materials began to deny Kurds existed. After 2000, the government banned Kurdish cultural events and materials published in Kurdish, and violence against Kurds in Syria increased. The Partiya Yekîtya Demokratic (Democratic Union Party; PYD) has fiercely resisted the Islamic State in Syria, but the Kurds refused to align with Arab Syrian rebels. As of June 2019, the PYD controlled a part of northern Syria.

Kurds constitute approximately 11 percent of Iran's population. Most Kurds live in five northwestern Iranian provinces, although many have migrated to Tehran to find work. In 1946, Kurds attempted to establish a Kurdistan State with Soviet help and launched guerilla warfare on Tehran in the 1960s. These attempts failed, both due to the state's strength and to divisions among Kurdish factions, split by tribes, religious groups, and locations. The two Kurdish parties at the time of the Iranian Revolution opposed Ayatollah Khomeini, and he executed hundreds of Kurds after he came to power. Remnants of the political parties continue in exile in the KRG. In the late 1980s and early 1990s, Iran assassinated two of these party leaders in Europe. In the early 2000s, Turkey's PKK helped Iranian Kurds form the Parti Jiyani Azadi Kurdistan (Free Life Party of Kurdistan; PJAK). The Iranian government has banned Kurdish literature and presses, Kurdish names for children, and education in Kurdish. Iranian Kurds face discrimination for both their ethnicity and their Sunni beliefs.

In their struggle for self-determination, Kurds face many barriers. Fighting among Kurds has prevented them from developing internally legitimate self-government. Most notably, each state where they reside has repressed their cultural and political self-determination. Yet Kurdish groups often work across borders to support one another. As a sign of progress, in Iraq and in the Syrian Civil War, the Kurds' success in fighting the Islamic State has won greater external support for Kurdish self-governance.

Sarah Fischer

See also: Barzani, Masoud; Iran, Islamic Republic of; Iraq, Republic of; Islamic State (Daesh); Kurdistan Regional Government (KRG); Kurdistan Worker's Party (PKK); Patriotic Union of Kurdistan (PUK); Syrian Civil War; Turkey, Republic of

Further Reading

Gunter, Michael. *The Kurds: A Modern History.* Princeton, NJ: Markus Wiener Publishers, 2016.

Jwaideh, Wadie. *The Kurdish National Movement: Its Origins and Development.* Syracuse, NY: Syracuse University Press, 2006.

Marcus, Aliza. *Blood and Belief: The PKK and the Kurdish Fight for Independence.* New York: New York University Press, 2009.

Phillips, David L. *The Kurdish Spring: A New Map of the Middle East.* New Brunswick, NJ: Transaction Publishers, 2015.

Kuwait, State of

A tiny, wealthy city-state located between Iraq and Saudi Arabia at the northern tip of the Gulf, ruled for more than two and a half centuries by the Al-Sabah family as a hereditary, patriarchal emirate. Kuwait covers an area smaller than Connecticut or New Jersey, with a natural harbor that shelters an excellent port. In 1756, a group of families appointed as their ruler the first ruler of the Al-Sabah family, who preserved the autonomy of the region by managing relations with more powerful patrons, such as the Ottomans and then the British. This external patronage gave the emir more wealth and promoted his influence at the expense of the wealthy merchant families.

The Al-Sabah family controlled markets, fishing, and pearling, backed by maritime trade relations with the outside world. It gained prosperity as a thriving independent trading community under the tutelage of the Ottoman Empire. The Ottoman Turks did not directly rule the country but, rather, served as a patron for the Al-Sabah family. Near the end of the 1800s, the Ottomans tried to impose more direct control, which prompted Sheikh Mubarak I Al-Sabah to seek British protection. The Anglo-Kuwaiti Agreement of 1899 between Sheikh Al-Sabah and the British government in India began a strong relationship in which Britain controlled Kuwait's foreign affairs until its independence in 1961. Even after independence, the alliance and the British defensive shield continued.

Citizen opposition to authoritarian rule began before the discovery of oil, but the people understood the political consequences of oil wealth, which stimulated a greater commitment to constraining the ruler's autocratic power with a constitution. To prevent the emir from keeping all of the oil revenue for himself, Kuwaiti merchants created a political movement that established a representative parliament (1938–1939) to advise and direct the ruler. They created government agencies, reformed the tax code, and wrote a constitution, with British support. Although Sheikh Mubarak shut the parliament down, he called for a new one, but the British withdrew their support, and the sheikh closed it down again. This started a pattern of contentious politics, in which the emir would respond to significant protests by alternating concessions and oppression.

The next emir, Abdallah al-Salim, opened up the political system as a way of competing with other members of his family and defending his rule against the pan-Arab and socialist activists of the early 1960s. On November 11, 1962, Kuwait adopted a constitution defining the country as a hereditary emirate, with an appointed government and an elected parliament. The emir serves as the head of state and selects his successor in consultation with the members of the Sabah family. He appoints the prime minister, normally the crown prince and heir apparent. The emir exercises his power through an appointed cabinet of ministers, also mostly members of the Sabah family. The elected parliament (Majlis al-Umma) consists of 50 members directly elected by popular vote with a four-year term limit.

The emirs who followed Abdallah al-Salim tried to restrain the civil liberties of the people and weaken the parliament. When the parliament would demand to question a minister regarding his corruption, such as in 1976 and in 1986, the emir could suspend the parliament. In the second incident, the parliament shifted to meeting in private homes for political discussions and planning. The emir responded by surrounding the house of the next host with soldiers and, one time, with riot police, tear gas, stun grenades, and tanks.

The discovery of huge oil reservoirs in the early 20th century made Kuwait a target of acquisition by powerful neighbors. Rising from a state of poverty, due to the world's sixth largest oil reserves Kuwait has become a very modern and prosperous country. Kuwait has considerable gas reserves, produced together with the crude oil. The relatively small population of Kuwait enjoys a high per capita income and has achieved a high Human Development Index score. More than half of all Kuwaitis reside in urban settlements bordering the Persian Gulf. Of the more than four million people living in Kuwait, only 1.3 million have Kuwaiti citizenship; the rest consist of foreign guest workers. Although the government allows the foreign workers to practice their faith, Islamists have protested against this. The 15 to 20 percent of the population that follows Shi'a Islam also faces antagonism from the hard-core Sunni Islamists.

Though formal political parties do not technically exist under Kuwaiti law, numerous political groups work as de facto political parties during elections, and parliamentary voting blocs exist. Progovernment nationalists compete against secular reformers and Islamic traditionalists, both Sunni and Shi'a. Numerous political and social organizations enjoy a certain degree of autonomy from the government, creating an active civil society. Despite this relative autonomy of social and political organizations from the government, the emir exercises ultimate authority, and the executive branch routinely tramples on the political and civil rights of citizens.

After the collapse of the Soviet Union, the 1990–1991 Iraqi invasion forced Kuwait to build closer ties with the United States and other supporting countries that worked together to liberate Kuwait. During the Iraqi occupation, the political opposition, leading merchants, and professionals confronted the emir in two meetings in Jeddah, Saudi Arabia, to demand a restoration of their political rights. He made promises but after liberation declared martial law. The people suffered massive human rights violations, and death squads targeted dissidents. However, the coalition parties insisted that Kuwait hold elections, which it did in October 1992.

Political activism expanded greatly after liberation, as activists formed civil society organizations supported by international connections. Among the many human rights issues, women's rights rose in prominence. Revelations of embezzlement by high government officials in 1999 drove widespread popular demonstrations. Emir Jabar al-Ahmad dissolved parliament and called for new elections. In the absence of parliament, the emir issued a decree granting women full rights to vote and run for office. The new parliament voted down the emir's decrees. This pushed a variety of interest groups to support the feminists in their campaign for political rights. With intensive political activity and pressure the parliament passed the supporting bill on May 16, 2005.

Activists picked up lessons from the women's rights movement to campaign for another cause—reducing the number of electoral districts from 25 to five as a way to reduce the emir's political control over disproportionate districts. The activists sold this policy change as a way to fight corruption. The government used force to block the protests and ultimately dissolved parliament and called for snap election in 2006. The government also manipulated relations between the urban population and the Bedouins.

In the beginning of 2011, the transition of rulers resulted in a prime minister who became the focus of public anger over corruption. News of events in Kuwait and Egypt stimulated public protests, parliamentary action, and civil strikes in Kuwait. In February 2011, the government announced that every citizen would receive $3,500 and that basic food items would be free until March 2012. It also set aside a record budget to subsidize the cost of fuel and raise public-sector salaries. After the parliament demanded to question three members of the royal family, the whole government resigned. While the government tried to suppress demonstrations, the number of protesters and the issues at stake increased. The government did crush demonstrations by the stateless Bedouins. The government increased salaries, housing programs, and support to religious organization in June, but substantial labor strikes hit in September and October. The mounting evidence of corruption stimulated a great expansion of the protest movement. On November 16, 2011, members of the parliamentary opposition together with a large number of young men stormed the National Assembly building to convey their protest against corruption. The prime minister and his cabinet did resign, which satisfied one demand of the opposition. The parliament soon resumed efforts to question the new prime minister, who was named in December, after five years of protest that resulted in three snap elections and four cabinet reshuffles.

The protests during this year also brought tribal religious conservatives who previously supported the government into the opposition. The tribal and Islamist opposition prevailed in the February 2012 election, but the Constitutional Court decided in June 2012 that the election was unconstitutional and reinstated the 2009 parliament. This blocked any effective progress on popular demands. After the Constitutional Court approved the new five-district plan, the emir dismissed the parliament and changed the election law again. Security forces disrupted a rally on October 15, 2012. This provoked very large protests estimated at more than 50,000 people on October 20, but special forces and national guard met the marchers to attack and arrest them. For a second March for Dignity on November 5, the protesters shifted locations more quickly than security could respond. The Islamist and tribal groups argued for a boycott of the December 2012 election, which resulted in a more regime-friendly parliament and a large number of Shi'as elected.

The Shi'as of Kuwait earned respect through their resistance to Iraqi forces during the occupation. Although the hard-core Sunni activists have caused the Shi'as some difficulties, the emir has acted as their protector. The Shi'as have very clearly shown their antagonism and resistance to Iranian plots and strategies. The 2011 events in Bahrain and Syria have stirred sectarian passions in Kuwait on both sides, which the government of Kuwait has worked to restrain.

Another parliament was elected on July 27, 2013, which included more youths. The progression of all these opposition movements has led to a greater political maturity. The political parties have begun pursuing broader political consensus, to overcome the politics of division used by the ruling elites. So far, these demands for political reforms, for a more representative electoral system, and for wider popular participation in the formation of the government have not affected the country's political structure.

Given the threat from Iraq, Kuwait's diplomacy sought to gain powerful allies and to maintain strong relations with most countries, particularly in the Arab world. Thus, for the sake of security, stability, and sustainable economic prosperity, Kuwait has historically pursued a pragmatic and balanced approach, based on a degree of neutrality and quiet diplomacy. During and after the 2003 Iraq War, Kuwait participated in coalition operations and donated generous economic and political assistance to the reconstruction efforts in postwar Iraq. Besides the United States, Kuwait made efforts to secure allies in the UN Security Council and concluded defense agreements with Russia, France, and the United Kingdom. Kuwait plays a pivotal role in the Gulf Cooperation Council to promote cooperation and coordination among the Gulf emirates.

Muhammed Kursad Ozekin

See also: Authoritarianism; Gulf Cooperation Council (GCC); Democracy Deficit; Iran, Islamic Republic of; Iraq, Republic of; Islamism; Labor Migration: Sending Countries; Rentier State Politics; Sectarianism

Further Reading

Casey, Michael S. *The History of Kuwait.* Westport, CT: Greenwood Press, 2007.

Crystal, Jill. *Kuwait: The Transformation of an Oil State.* New York: Routledge, 2016.

Herb, Michael. "A Nation of Bureaucrats: Political Participation and Economic Diversification in Kuwait and the United Arab Emirates." *International Journal of Middle East Studies* 41, no. 3 (August 2009): 375–95.

Isiorho, Solomon A. *Kuwait.* Philadelphia: Chelsea House Publishers, 2002.

Tétreault, Mary Ann. "Political Activism in Kuwait: Reform in Fits and Starts." In *Taking It to the Streets: The Transformation of Arab Activism,* edited by Lina Khatib and Ellen Lust, 268–97. Baltimore: Johns Hopkins University Press, 2014.

L

Labor Migration: Receiving Countries

Immigration creates a security issue for the Gulf states due to the great numbers of guest workers compared to the citizens. International labor migrants in the Gulf states constitute from 37 percent of the population in Saudi Arabia to 88 percent in the United Arab Emirates (UAE). The Gulf states define citizenship based on blood on the paternal side: only the children of an Emirati father receive Emirati citizenship. Concern for security and for the protection of the privileges of the citizens causes all of these states to very tightly regulate the labor market. Noncitizens require a citizen sponsor, who can order them expelled at any time. Workers who attempt to protest for any reason get sent home quickly. This represents a form of support for authoritarianism.

Labor migrants often work under extraordinarily difficult conditions, receive very little protection for their rights, and suffer exploitation and abuse. This attracts the attention of Amnesty International and Human Rights Watch, which seek to generate political pressure on the receiving countries. The grievances of the migrant workers give them a motivation to protest, which governments fear. Many of the Gulf states originally recruited Arabic-speaking Muslim workers from neighboring countries. However, pan-Arab nationalists—who rejected national borders and expected better treatment as Muslims—sometimes protested and caused trouble. The receiving countries found that small cultural differences and attitudes caused big problems. After the 1967 Arab-Israeli War, the Gulf states began replacing Arab workers with men from Asian countries. After the 1979 Islamic Revolution in Iran, receiving countries became more fearful of Shi'a workers from Lebanon, Yemen, and other countries, so the replacement trend accelerated. After the 1990 Gulf War, governments expelled workers from countries that supported Iraq. In exchange, India, Pakistan, Bangladesh, the Philippines, and other Asian countries organized the recruitment of workers to fill the needs in the Gulf. The Asian workers often received lower pay and worked in more difficult conditions than Arab workers. The receiving countries recognize a number of cultural and security threats created by very large percentages of foreign workers and have begun developing programs to train citizens to replace foreign workers, so far with relatively little success. Moreover, since the 2011 Arab protests, the Gulf states have also directed their security concerns to the arrival of refugees, either from Yemen or Syria.

Kristin Kamøy

See also: Authoritarianism; Bahrain, Kingdom of; Grievance Model; Iraq, Republic of; Kuwait, State of; Lebanese Republic; Oman, Sultanate of; Qatar; Saudi Arabia, Kingdom of; Shi'a; Syrian Arab Republic; United Arab Emirates (UAE); Yemen, Republic of

Further Reading

Kapiszewski, Andrey. *Arab Versus Asian Migrant Workers in the GCC Countries.* Beirut: United Nations Secretariat, May 22, 2006.

Lori, Noora. "National Security and the Management of Migrant Labor: A Case Study of the United Arab Emirates." *Asian and Pacific Migration Journal* 20, nos. 3–4 (2011): 315–37.

Naufal, George S. "Labor Migration and Remittances in the GCC." *Labor History* 52, no. 3 (August 2011): 307–22.

Labor Migration: Sending Countries

Large numbers of people travel in search of work from areas with few job opportunities to areas needing more workers. From North Africa, workers have commonly gone to Europe in search of greater social and political freedom, as well as jobs. Common trends for those who went to Europe before the protests of 2011 include the following: most found jobs through an extended social network, except the well-educated; one-third originally went as students; they do not represent the very poor but the urban unemployed, with resources to fund the trip; they stayed an average of 10 years; only half sent remittances; and they returned wealthier than those who did not go. After 1973, the oil-exporting countries of the Gulf embarked on massive programs to develop their infrastructures and construct modern urban areas, which require a lot of imported labor. The Gulf states initially drew Arabic-speaking workers from lower-income, neighboring states: Egypt, Jordan, Lebanon, Palestine, Syria, and Yemen. These workers sent home remittances that provided a crucial safety net for their families and economic benefit to their home society, a factor for stability. Their absence while working abroad reduced the labor pool available for a revolution, reducing the potential threat to their authoritarian governments. To the extent that these workers gained exposure to more modern equipment and technology, when they came home they stimulated development in their home countries.

The very difficult work environment, lacking protection of human rights, has two effects on the workers: 1) some become more receptive to radical ideologies that justify rebellion; and 2) some return home demoralized and intimidated by security services. Those who adopted different religious and ideological perspectives have contributed to civil discord when they returned. Having a large percentage of men working in another country creates a form of dependence, or political leverage, that the receiving country can use against the sending country. For example, Iraq expelled one million Egyptian workers on the eve of the 1991 Gulf War in retaliation for Egypt's entering the Gulf War coalition. Similarly, Kuwait and Saudi Arabia expelled 300,000 Palestinians and 700,000 Yemenis due to their leaders' taking sides with Saddam Hussein.

When large numbers of men leave to work in other countries, the women left behind have to assume new roles and responsibilities, altering the gender relations of the sending countries. In response to the extensive publication of abuse of migrant workers, some labor-exporting countries have banned their citizens from traveling to Gulf Cooperation Council countries, and some have successfully lobbied for their citizens' rights.

Autumn Cockrell-Abdullah

See also: Authoritarianism; Demographics (Youth Bulge); Development; Egypt, Arab Republic of; Gulf Cooperation Council (GCC); Jordan, Hashemite Kingdom of; Lebanese Republic; Modernization; Palestine; Syrian Arab Republic; Yemen, Republic of

Further Reading

Brand, Laurie A. *Citizens Abroad: Emigration and the State in the Middle East and North Africa.* New York: Cambridge University Press, 2006.

David, Anda, and Mohamed Ali Marouani. "The Impact of Emigration on MENA Labor Markets." *Policy Brief* No. 21. Gaza, Egypt: Economic Research Forum, October 1, 2016.

Lebanese Republic

A multiconfessional republic on the mountainous eastern coast of the Mediterranean Sea bordered on the north and east by Syria and on the south by Israel. Since its formal independence in 1943, Lebanon has often suffered sectarian violence and civil war, recently made worse by battles between Hezbollah and Israel, and by Syrian intervention. The diverse ethnic and religious composition of Lebanese society has created multiple dimensions of competition: the Sunnis have disputes with the Shias, and both reject the Druze. The five separate Christian denominations—Maronite, Greek Orthodox, Greek Catholic, Armenian Orthodox, and Syriac—also compete politically. Each of these groups carved out a place of refuge in the mountains from the invasions of the neighboring great powers—the Egyptians to the south, the Ottoman Turks to the north, the Bedouin Arab raiders and the Syrian Arab state to the east, and then the European imperial powers occupying the region after defeating the Ottomans in World War I. Forced by history to share the same geography, each group developed its martial virtues and diplomacy to evolve a form of coexistence and sometimes even power-sharing.

The French established Lebanon as a state separate from Syria to protect the Maronite Catholics but included in that territory additional diverse populations to create an economically viable territory, joining the agricultural region of the Bekaa Valley and the seaports of the coast. At the time of independence in 1943, the Maronites and the Sunni Muslims agreed to an unwritten National Pact that reserves the presidency and the army for the Maronites, the office of prime minister for the Sunnis, and the speaker of the House to the Shi'as. The Sunnis agreed not to seek Syrian intervention, and the Maronites agreed not to seek French influence. The Shi'as and the Druze did not participate in this agreement and felt cheated because of it. In this form of government, called consociational democracy, each religious community determines its own family status laws, and community membership governs political participation. As the Maronites used state resources as patronage to distribute to their clients, this stimulated competition within each community for control over the allocation of resources.

184   Lebanese Republic

Educational institutions established by the French and by missionaries around Beirut appealed mostly to the Maronites and other Christian groups. At the time of independence, the Christians collectively made up about 52 percent of the population. Maronites dominated in economic, political, and military power; the Sunni Muslims around Beirut had some economic power, while the Shi'as in the south and Sunnis in the north felt neglected. This badly fractured Lebanese society and led to an increasingly ineffective government.

After the 1948–1949 Arab-Israeli War, some 300,000 Palestinians sought refuge in Lebanon and began staging raids into Israel. Many more Palestinians came after the 1967 war, and then in September 1970 the Hashemite Kingdom of Jordan expelled many Palestinians, and the Palestine Liberation Organization moved its offices to Lebanon. The influx of mostly Sunni Palestinians disturbed the demographic balance of the Muslim population and provoked conflict. Because Maronites with education and initiative left whenever they found opportunities abroad, and their birthrate was lower, the Christian proportion of the population fell. This raised grievances against the now smaller Christian population holding disproportionate political power.

On April 13, 1975, a gunman opened fire on a Christian church in East Beirut, killing four people. Later that same day, in apparent retaliation, members of the Christian Lebanese Phalanges Party murdered 27 Palestinians on a bus in Ayn ar Rummanah. From such beginnings a civil war grew to encompass the whole country, lasting for 15 years and killing more than 110,000 people, injuring twice as many, and causing almost a million people to emigrate.

The civil war did not represent any simple Christian versus Muslim conflict, but rather each of the major groups splintered and also fought one another. Even two Armenian militias fought each other. In May 1976 the Syrian Navy blockaded Lebanon's ports to prevent the resupply of arms, and in June President Suleiman Franjieh invited Syria to send troops to assist the Maronites against their leftist and Palestinian enemies. In October, a massive offensive by regular infantry and armored units conquered central Lebanon. In response to a Palestinian incursion that killed 34 Israelis, on March 15, 1978, Israel invaded, in alliance with a Christian militia. Several thousand Lebanese died during the invasion, and the Israelis withdrew. More Palestinian raids and rocket attacks by Palestinians led to retaliation on both sides until June 1982, when Israel invaded southern Lebanon and lay siege to Beirut. As a result, Iran helped the local Shias to form a militia called Hezbollah.

Efforts by various other states to stop the civil war repeatedly failed, including the ill-fated U.S. military mission to Lebanon. On October 23, 1983, the two suicide truck bombings in Beirut killed 241 U.S. Marines and 58 French troops and wounded scores of others. In the so-called War of the Camps in 1985–1986, several thousand Palestinians died in refugee camps. In 1989, the United States and Saudi Arabia, working through the Arab League, persuaded Syria to accept the Taif Accords, which redistributed power in Lebanon, setting conditions for ending the civil war. The United Nations established and still operates an "Interim Force in Lebanon" (UNIFIL).

The Taif Accords reaffirmed the political role of sectarian affiliation, consolidated the role of Syria, and allowed Hezbollah to keep its militia, while all the

Lebanese Republic

other militias had to disarm. Taif disseminated and diffused power. It led to both paralysis of decision-making and lack of accountability. Political power-sharing according to sectarian affiliation represented not just a social contract but also formalized the distribution of spoils, leading to corrosive corruption inhibiting state efficiency.

In 1993, and again in 1995, Israel attempted to stop Palestinian rocket attacks against Israeli civilians by attacking Palestinian strongholds in southern Lebanon, killing hundreds and displacing several hundred thousand civilians. In 1998, President Hafiz al-Assad of Syria gave his son Bashar responsibility for relations with Lebanon. Since the Taif Accords, Syria had controlled political events in Lebanon by distributing favors and threats, reinforced by thousands of Syrian troops and an extensive intelligence organization. Bashar grew very close to Hassan Nasrallah, the secretary general of Hezbollah, and developed a dislike for Prime Minister Rafik Hariri, the popular billionaire Sunni prime minister, who had sustained the Lebanese education system during the civil war with thousands of scholarships and had then redeveloped Beirut after the war. In May 2000, Israel withdrew from Lebanon, and in June, Hafez al-Assad died. In the 2000 parliamentary elections, Hariri's supporters replaced the supporters of President Emile Lahoud, Syria's agent. Bashar and Lahoud determined to stop Hariri's political career.

In 2003, the United States invaded Iraq, making Bashar feel that he might be next. In September 2004 the UN Security Council passed Resolution 1559, which called for Syria to withdraw from Lebanon and for Hezbollah to disarm. All of this made Bashar al-Assad feel threatened. He wanted the Lebanese parliament to amend the constitution to extend the term of his agent President Lahoud. He called Rafik Hariri to Damascus and threatened him. Hariri complied but then resigned. On February 14, 2005, a huge, carefully planned car-bomb attack killed Hariri and 20 other people. This raised Sunni anger against the Syrian occupation and Hezbollah, which supports Syria's activities in Lebanon. Shock and fury drove a large protest movement called the Cedar Revolution, which gained international support and forced Syria to withdraw its forces. The government did not interfere with the next elections, won by the anti-Syrian coalition called the March 14 Movement. Over the next six months, a steady succession of car bombings killed politicians opposed to Syria. In parliament, pro-Syrian representatives from Hezbollah and other parties could block any government action. The international investigation into the assassination of Rafik Hariri at first identified four generals linked to Syrian intelligence, and they spent four years in jail. Then under a new authorization and leadership, the investigation identified four members of Hezbollah.

In 2006, Hezbollah raided a border village and captured two Israeli soldiers. The Israelis retaliated with an extensive bombing campaign for a month, killing hundreds of militants and even more Lebanese civilians, while up to one million Lebanese civilians fled to other regions. In spite of these losses, Hezbollah claimed victory and with Iranian financing worked to rapidly rebuild and rearm, acquiring a larger and more lethal arsenal. In 2008, Walid Jumblatt, the Druze leader, exposed Hezbollah's private communications system and surveillance of the Beirut airport. Hezbollah occupied Beirut by force of arms and successfully pressured parliament to prevent any restrictions. Sustained political and military pressure from Syria and Hezbollah has driven politicians to defect from the anti-Syria coalition. Even Saad Hariri, who had taken up his father's political commitments, was forced to go to Syria to beg for relief. After intervention by Saudi King Abdullah, the pro-Syrian politicians allowed Saad Hariri to form a government from 2009 to 2011.

The civil war in Syria caused fear in Lebanon regarding the consequences. The government has tried to stay neutral, even as the Sunnis felt great sympathy for the rebellion and Hezbollah sent hundreds of fighters to support Bashar al-Assad. More than a million refugees have come to Lebanon, which lacks the resources to care for them. The people of Lebanon face great despair over the dysfunction of their own government. For example, when the government failed to find a means to dispose of garbage after the existing facilities filled up in July 2015, the large protests called "You Stink" degenerated into street fights, forcing the government to deploy the army. To overcome this political stalemate, Saad Hariri returned from exile and supported the Maronite ally of his enemy Hezbollah, Michel Aoun, for president, who then named him prime minister. Hariri faces extraordinarily difficult challenges: Syrian government antagonism; political deadlock and government corruption; lack of electricity; a million Syrian refugees; a more heavily armed and confident Hezbollah; high government debt; and the need for foreign economic aid. The most important security threat comes from the rising grievances of the Sunni population, who feel excluded from government and oppressed by Syria and Hezbollah.

Jonathan K. Zartman

See also: Al Manar Television; Cedar Revolution; Druze; Hariri, Saad; Hezbollah; Israel; Jumblatt, Walid; Maronites; Nasrallah, Hassan Abdel Karim; Palestine Liberation Organization; Shi'a; Syrian Arab Republic

Further Reading

Arsan, Andrew. *Lebanon: A Country in Fragments*. London: Hurst & Company, 2018.

Hurst, David. *Beware of Small States: Lebanon, Battleground of the Middle East*. New York: Nation Books, 2010.

Rabil, Robert. *Embattled Neighbors: Syria, Israel, and Lebanon*. Boulder, CO: Lynne Rienner, 2003.

Salamey, Imad. *The Government and Politics of Lebanon*. New York: Routledge, 2013.

Winslow, Charles. *Lebanon: War and Politics in a Fragmented Society*. New York: Routledge, 1996.

Libya, State of

A large, Sunni, Arab state suffering significant civil discord after protests fueled a rebellion that overthrew the dictator, Muammar Qaddafi. Libya consists of three major regions of mostly desert, oil-rich territory on the northern coast of Africa between Egypt and Algeria. The political conflicts in Libya derive from its history after the Italians occupied three Ottoman Empire provinces in 1911. In 1943, Britain defeated the Italian and German forces in Libya, making the country a British

Libya, State of

and French protectorate. Britain supported Idris al-Sanussi, the leader of a Sufi religious brotherhood, which had resisted the Italians and given aid to the British, to become Libya's first king. However, as a Bedouin Arab, from the eastern province of Cyrenaica, he could not get the support of Berbers in Tripolitania, the western area. Libya won independence in 1951, but the constitutional monarchy remained economically weak, dependent on Western aid to keep the country united.

After the discovery of oil in 1959 created an economic boom, King Idris tightened his political control, refused to allow social and political reforms, but tolerated corruption. Arab socialism and nationalism gained great appeal. After the defeat of Arab armies in the 1967 war against Israel, public anger at his pro-Western policy further increased the revolutionary potential. On September 1, 1969, Colonel Muammar Qaddafi, a 27-year-old army officer and disciple of Nasser's Arab nationalism, led a bloodless coup that removed Idris from power. Qaddafi implemented reforms that included free health care, free education, and subsidized housing. By 2010, the people of Libya had gained relatively high levels of literacy, high life expectancies, and relative freedom for women. Qaddafi introduced a political philosophy blending Marxist social reforms with Islamic and pan-Arab nationalism, codified in the *Green Book,* published in 1975.

Qaddafi's government banned all political parties and opposition groups and nationalized the oil sector. Oil exports enabled his social reforms, as well as an active foreign policy. Qaddafi also used this wealth to form alliances by patronizing several important tribes: his own Qaddafi tribe; the Magariha, allied to him by marriage; and the Warfalla, the largest. Tribes and prominent personalities neglected in this distribution of the wealth objected to this corruption and tried six times—in 1969, 1970, 1975, 1984, 1993, and 2008—to overthrow Qaddafi, but failed due to his efficient internal-security system.

Qaddafi used several strategies to prevent a successful coup: he kept military units divided and poorly trained and equipped, rewarding loyalty and punishing initiative. The government shifted officers to different assignments frequently, to prevent them from developing any strong relations with the people they commanded. He recruited nomadic Tuareg into the military because their desperate economic background and lack of local tribal attachments made them loyal to him personally. The special state security services received the best funding and equipment. The total intolerance for dissent resulted in tens of thousands of political prisoners.

Qaddafi organized the government as a series of people's committees and congresses that controlled the people instead of representing them. Due to the lack of institutions, and Qaddafi's pattern of chaotic, personalized rule, after the revolution the new government lacked either the personnel, procedures, or cultural standards to create a government that could make decisions and enforce them. He created a political culture that distrusted both political parties and executive leadership. These conditions now impede the development of an effective bureaucratic state.

Qaddafi engaged in conflict with Chad, seeking to take a strip of land with valuable resources, and was defeated. In 1977 he attacked Egypt but was defeated in four days. As a vocal critic of Zionism, he supported the Palestinian cause financially and militarily. His support for revolutionary guerilla movements around the world led to direct confrontation with the United States. On December 3, 1979, a huge mob attacked and burned the U.S. embassy, leading to a break in relations. In 1981, two Libyan jets fired on two U.S. warplanes, which then shot them down. In 1982, Reagan imposed an embargo on Libyan oil. In 1986, the United States blamed Qaddafi for bombing a nightclub in Berlin that killed two American soldiers and set plans to bomb Qaddafi's military assets in Tripoli and Benghazi.

The investigation into the Pan Am Lockerbie Bombing in 1988 led to Libyan agents, strengthening international anger against Libya's support for revolutionary terrorist groups. Qaddafi's dramatic and demanding personality made enemies even in the Muslim world. After the fall of the Soviet Union, Libya began to change its foreign policy to regain relations with Western countries. On April 6, 1999, after protracted diplomacy and bargaining, Qaddafi turned two Lockerbie suspects over to The Hague for trial in the bombing of Pan Am Flight 103. Qaddafi agreed to pay $2.7 billion in compensation to the families of the Pan Am victims. In December 2003, Qaddafi decided to give up his weapons of mass destruction and sought diplomatic and economic relations with the United States. In 2004, the United States lifted the freeze on $1.3 billion in Libyan assets and reestablished diplomatic relations. At the same time, Saif al-Islam Qaddafi, Qaddafi's Western-educated son, introduced new economic, political, and social reforms, but resistance from hardliners within the regime prevented their implementation. Western countries accepted Libya's efforts to rebuild relations. Libya reintegrated with the international economy. Western businessmen flocking to Libya in search of opportunity.

Despite Qaddafi's efforts to promote Libyan nationalism, Libyans gave greater weight to their local and tribal identities. Libyans depend on their tribal connections for protection and for finding a job. Many people in Cyrenaica felt excluded from the political and economic process. On February 1, 2011, protests began in Benghazi, Libya's second biggest city and the capital of the Cyrenaica region, but Libyan security forces quickly crushed them. Two weeks later, new protests began again in Benghazi and then spread. Sporadic fighting also broke out in Qaddafi's stronghold of Tripolitania. On February 26, the UN Security Council (UNSC) adopted Resolution 1970, imposing an arms embargo and freezing regime assets. Then in Cyrenaica, on February 27, 2011, a group of elites formed the Transitional National Council (TNC), claiming to represent the political face of the revolution. The European Union, the United States, the Arab League, and the United Nations quickly recognized the TNC. The Libyan government increased its efforts to crush the revolt, using violence against unarmed protesters. The Arab League and the Gulf Cooperation Council responded to the shocking language of Qaddafi's speeches and reports of attacks on civilians by calling on the United Nations to protect civilians. On March 17, 2011, the UN Security Council passed Resolution 1973 to impose a no-fly zone over Libya and provide support and humanitarian assistance to the Libyan people.

With the help of senior army officers who defected, and coalition airstrikes against Libyan government military forces, the rebels took control of the east and south and then focused on Tripoli. The city fell on September 1, but two Qaddafi strongholds, Bani Walid and Sirte, held out with fierce resistance. On October 20, 2011, rebels found Qaddafi hiding in Sirte, chased him down, and killed him.

The TNC organized elections held on July 7, 2012, and on August 8, 2012, formally transferred power to the newly elected General National Congress (GNC). However, the GNC lacked the institutional capability to exert initiative and leadership, to demobilize and reintegrate fighters, and to reconstitute the military and security forces, much less to provide essential government services. The September 11, 2012, attack on the U.S. diplomatic compound brought international attention to the strength of violent Islamist militias in Libya. Instead of disarmament, the weapons continued to flow, and the militias kept recruiting new members. By 2013, observers estimated rebel groups could count on 200,000 fighters in roughly 300 militias. Multiple militias competed to control Tripoli. Conflict between secularists and Islamists led to paralysis in the GNC. Multiple attacks by militias, even the kidnapping of the prime minister, forced the GNC to make decisions that led to the following civil war. On May 5, 2013, the Islamist alliance forced through a controversial "Political Isolation Law," which excluded the service of many experienced, secular-leaning politicians. It failed to protect those who had defected many years before and led the opposition to Qaddafi. It destroyed the majority party, the National Forces Alliance, giving Islamists control over the GNC and the government.

On June 25, 2014, Libya held elections to form a new assembly, called the House of Representatives (HoR), but due to insecurity, only 18 percent of the people voted, and the Islamists fared very poorly. Rejecting the results, an alliance of Islamist, Misratan, and Berber militias called Libya Dawn launched a six-week assault on Tripoli. The high level of violence forced the HoR to establish its operations in Tobruk, far to the east. In this context of insecurity and social disorder, on May 16, 2014, Khalifah Haftar, a former general, led his Libyan National Army (LNA) in a campaign against the Islamist militias called Operation Dignity.

In the security vacuum created by the competition between two governments in opposite ends of the country, the Islamic State (Daesh) began sending fighters to Libya. In 2015, these fighters took control of Sirte, where a coalition of Western forces engaged in a long battle against them. In December 2015, the United Nations negotiated a power-sharing "Libyan Political Agreement" between the HoR government based in Tobruk and the Libya Dawn Coalition in Tripoli, to create a Government of National Accord (GNA), recognized by the UN Security Council as the legitimate government of Libya. However, Haftar refused to accept the people appointed to cabinet ministries. The mandate of that government expired in December 2017, and the competition between the HoR and the GNA for control of the Central Bank and the export of oil continued with sporadic militia battles.

While Haftar's Libyan National Army controls many of the oil ports, the international community buys oil only from the National Oil Company based in Tripoli. Due to this interdependence, the two parties cooperated to some extent in 2018, and the leaders on both sides have met several times in other countries to negotiate their differences. The UN Security Council has provided political support in the form of advice and mediation called the Support Mission in Libya

(UNSMIL) with a mandate extended until September 15, 2019. The Special Representative appointed by the UN Secretary General has held dozens of dialogue sessions across Libya to facilitate a negotiated resolution to the internal conflict.

Meanwhile, instability continues among the militias competing for control of Tripoli, such as the Benghazi Defense Brigades, reportedly supported by Qatar and Turkey. In 2019, Field Marshal Haftar's LNA began a military campaign that conquered first the southern part of the country and then swung north toward Tripoli. The LNA receives support from the United Arab Emirates, Egypt, and Russia. Therefore, Libya has become a field of combat among proxy forces. In seven years of war, an estimated 500,000 people have fled their homes, and many have ended up as refugees in Europe.

Alexander Shelby

See also: Ansar al-Sharia in Libya; Battle of Sirte in 2011; Battle of Sirte in 2016; Belhaj, Abdul Hakim; Benghazi Attack; Constitutional Drafting Assembly; February 17th Revolution; General National Congress; Haftar, Khalifa Belqasim; Libya Dawn Coalition; Libyan Civil War; National Transition Council; Qaddafi, Muammar

Further Reading

Chivvis, Christopher S., and Jeffrey Martini. *Libya after Qaddafi: Lessons and Implications for the Future.* Santa Monica, CA: RAND, 2014.

Cole, Peter, and Brian McQuinn, eds. *The Libyan Revolution and Its Aftermath.* New York: Oxford University Press, 2016.

Joffé, E. George H. *Insecurity in North Africa and the Mediterranean.* Rome, Italy: NATO Defense College, 2017.

Pack, Jason, ed. *The 2011 Libyan Uprising and the Struggle for the Post-Qadhafi Future.* New York: Palgrave Macmillan, 2013.

Wehrey, Frederic M. *The Burning Shores: Inside the Battle for the New Libya.* New York: Farrar, Straus and Giroux, 2018.

Libya Dawn Coalition

A coalition of Libyan militias supporting the National Salvation Government, composed of politicians opposed to the government of the House of Representatives (HoR) and claiming to still represent a General National Congress (GNC). The mandate of the GNC had expired, and it ceased its legal existence with the election of the HoR, but some Islamist former members tried to claim government authority by creating a coalition of several Islamist militias, including the Libyan Shield Force, Libyan Revolutionary Operation Room, and Mistrata revolutionaries. During August 2014, those groups rebelled against the HoR and launched Fajr Libya (Libya Dawn) and quickly captured the capital, Tripoli, and its international airport. This seizure of Tripoli allowed these militias to declare themselves the government of Libya. The HoR, under the protection of General Khalifa Haftar's Libyan National Army (LNA), remained the internationally recognized, legitimate government of Libya, based in Tobruk, an eastern city in Libya. The LNA launched Operation Dignity to destroy the terrorist groups within Libya, which implicitly included the regional Islamist groups. The power struggle between

Libya Dawn and the LNA enabled the rise of the Islamic State (Daesh), which fought against everyone. International support helped both sides defeat the Islamic State. However, Libya Dawn's coalition has weakened due to internal power struggles, and by the summer of 2019, General Haftar's forces had swept the south of Libya and advanced on the capital.

Steven A. Quillman

See also: Battle of Sirte in 2016; General National Congress; Haftar, Khalifa Belqasim; Islamic State (Daesh); Libyan Civil War

Further Reading

Bradley, Megan, Ibrahim Fraihat, and Houda Mzioudet. *Libya's Displacement Crisis: Uprooted by Revolution and Civil War.* Washington, DC: Georgetown University Press, 2016.

Lacher, Wolfram. "Libya's Local Elites and the Politics of Alliance Building." *Mediterranean Politics* 21, no.1 (2016): 64–85.

Libyan Civil War

A complex, multiparty armed conflict that emerged in Libya in 2014 after the legitimately elected General National Congress (GNC) failed to find a consensus, or resolve competing claims by different regions, ethnic groups, tribes, and ideological factions. The elections to the GNC, conducted in freedom and fairness with a large turnout, marked a high point of optimism. However, the GNC could not control the dozens of armed militias, which each considered themselves entitled to spoils of war from defeating Qaddafi. Islamist militias threatened and intimidated GNC representatives to exclude prominent liberal politicians and military leaders. In 2014, after its mandate expired, the GNC organized elections for a replacement House of Representatives (HoR), in which liberals gained significant influence. High levels of violence forced the HoR to relocate to Tobruk, in eastern Libya.

The conflict became a full civil war when a rejectionist movement supported by Islamist militias—the Libya Dawn Coalition—captured control of the capital, calling itself a National Salvation Government and claiming the name of the GNC, which most other states did not recognize, aside from Turkey, Sudan, and Qatar. However, this government never gained control over the multitude of militias in Tripoli. Due to the threat of the Islamic State (Daesh), both sides received international support. In addition, many other militias continued to exercise control over their regions and compete for greater resources. This created a general condition of chaos, amplified by international parties taking conflicting sides. Egypt, Russia, and the United Arab Emirates have steadily helped the HoR and Field Marshall Khalifa Haftar's Libyan National Army (LNA).

By 2015, the battle between the LNA and the opposing Islamist militias seemed to reach a stalemate. In December 2015, the United Nations persuaded representatives from both sides to sign the Libyan Political Agreement, to form a Government of National Accord (GNA). The UN Security Council then recognized the GNA as Libya's legitimate government. However, the HoR refused to accept the GNA, and parts of the GNC have withdrawn support. In addition to the main competition between the Tobruk government (HoR) versus the GNA and the GNC, other Islamist militias operate against both sides. The Misrata Brigades, the Benghazi Defense Brigades, scattered independent remnants of the Islamic State, and a range of small, armed groups with shifting allegiances complete the confusing picture. From 2017 to 2019, Field Marshall Haftar captured substantial areas in the south and had control over the oil fields on the coast, and in April 2019, he moved to take control over Tripoli, with fighting continuing through June 2019.

Tom Dowling

See also: Battle of Sirte in 2016; Benghazi Attack; February 17th Revolution; General National Congress; Haftar, Khalifa Belqasim; Islamic State (Daesh); Islamism; Libya Dawn Coalition; National Transition Council; Qaddafi, Muammar

Further Reading

Joffé, E. George H. *Insecurity in North Africa and the Mediterranean.* Rome, Italy: NATO Defense College, 2017.

Mundy, Jacob. *Libya.* Medford, MA: Polity Press, 2018.

Wehrey, Frederic M. *The Burning Shores: Inside the Battle for the New Libya.* New York: Farrar, Straus and Giroux, 2018.

Libyan Protests (2011). *See February 20 Revolution*

Local Coordination Committees

A loose umbrella network of local committees established during the Syrian uprising to coordinate nonviolent resistance countrywide and enhance the efficacy and visibility of on-the-ground activism. More than half of the local coordination committees (LCCs) that emerged in Syrian neighborhoods, cities, and villages since 2011 have joined the Local Coordination Committees of Syria (LCCSyria) network led by prominent Syrian lawyer Razan Zeitouneh.

Committed to nonviolent resistance, the LCCs assumed responsibility to coordinate protests, organize strikes, document war crimes and human rights violations, carry the voices of the protesters to Arab and international media, and coordinate relief and aid delivery. They vary in composition and ideological leaning. Some LCCs consist predominantly of young tech-savvy media and human rights activists; some are dominated by local elites, Islamic preachers, and tribesmen; some uphold secular and liberal-democratic viewpoints; and some take inspiration from Islamic notions of freedom, human dignity, and social solidarity.

The militarization of the Syrian uprising created a serious challenge for the LCCs. Despite their official statements discouraging opposition forces from taking up arms, activists associated with LCCs joined armed factions and engaged in military operations against regime forces and rival factions. Moreover, the humanitarian cost of the conflict, and the vacuum created by the withdrawal of government forces and services, required LCCs to assume new responsibilities. LCCs acted as centers of civic authority, managed humanitarian and relief aid, provided medical and legal services, and administered social initiatives including food basket programs. LCCs activists played an important role in the formation of Local Administrative Councils in opposition-held territories.

Decentralized committees and executive, media, and relief offices supervised their activities. Modern communication technologies enabled activists to breach the regime's media blackout to coordinate their activities. Due to their apparent alignment with the views of Western governments, the LCCs received support from numerous governments, NGOs, and conflict-stabilization practitioners, including capacity building, training, funding, program incubation, and expensive technologies and equipment.

Recognizing their importance as key in-country actors, opposition groups in exile sought to include LCC representatives. The Syrian National Council and its successor, the National Coalition, included LCCSyria activists. Although they made up a third of the votes in the council, LCC activists accused the coalition of underrepresenting civilian, nonpartisan, and in-country opposition forces. Faced with rebel infighting, the expansion of violent Islamist groups, and military victories by regime forces, the LCC's role has gradually dwindled as many activists fled the country or hid.

Fouad Gehad Marei

See also: Free Syrian Army; Syrian Arab Republic

Further Reading

Alvarez-Ossorio, Ignacio. "Syria's Struggling Civil Society." *Middle East Quarterly* 19, no. 2 (Spring 2012): 23–32.

Brown, Frances Z. "Dilemmas of Stabilization Assistance: The Case of Syria." Washington, DC: Carnegie Endowment for International Peace, October 2018.

Hajjar, Bahjat, et al. *Perceptions of Governance: The Experience of Local Administrative Councils in Opposition-Held Syria.* Bern: Swiss Peace Foundation, January 2017.

Maronites

A patriarchal, Lebanese Christian group in full communion with the Roman Catholic Church, claiming the early church at Antioch as its heritage. Leaders trace their history back to Saint Marun, a fourth-century hermit. Under pressure after the Arab conquest, almost all of the community moved to Mount Lebanon. This church developed around monasteries in rural mountainous areas as a closed, hierarchical society. The group received little outside notice until the Crusaders passed through, which the Maronites saw as a source of outside support. They used Aramaic until the 15th century and preserved it as a language for worship until recently. The small community in Israel identifies as ethnically Aramean or Arab. Consistent efforts over the centuries to gain recognition and support from the Catholic Church attracted some French Jesuit commitments.

The French intervened in Ottoman policy, demanding the right to protect the Maronites. After suffering a massacre from the Druze in 1860, the French intervened to impose a power-sharing agreement. Connections with the French led to a European orientation and a strong focus on education. After the defeat of the Ottoman Empire, the Maronites lobbied the French to create the State of Lebanon and then formed a power-sharing deal with the Sunni Muslims, called the National Pact, to gain independence from the French. Due to their higher levels of education and international trade connections, the Maronites began to dominate the economy, politics, and the security forces. Education and greater Western perspective also enabled greater emigration, and birth rates fell, leading to a declining Maronite population. The Maronites exercised disproportionate power for 20 years and used control of state patronage to seek more.

During the Lebanese civil war, the Maronite community fragmented, and different Maronite militias even fought one another. When one militia leader invited Syria to intervene and end the war, this further strengthened the divisions. As a result of declining population, internal division, strategic errors, loss of legitimacy from atrocities during the civil war, and Syrian domination, the Maronites have become politically marginalized. On February 6, 2006, Michel Naim Aoun, a Maronite Christian, signed a memorandum of understanding with Hezbollah secretary general Hassan Nasrullah to pursue national dialogue and coexistence and reduce the intrusion of foreign powers. This affirmed Hezbollah's right to keep its arsenal of weapons. After protracted negotiations, in 2016 the parliament elected Aoun as president of Lebanon.

After losses due to emigration, the Maronites remain the second largest Christian group in the Middle East and still constitute a quarter of the Lebanese population. Maronites live in Syria, Cyprus, Palestine, and Israel, with a diaspora in Western countries.

Emanuela Claudia Del Re

See also: Civil Wars; Druze; Hezbollah; Lebanese Republic; Minorities; Nasrallah, Hassan Abdel Karim; Syrian Arab Republic

Further Reading

Abraham, Paul. *The Maronites of Lebanon, the Staunch Catholics of the Near East.* Piscataway, NJ: Gorgias Press, 2011.

Nisan, Mordechai. *Minorities in the Middle East: A History of Struggle and Self-Expression.* London: McFarland & Company, 2015.

Zamir, Meir. "From Hegemony to Marginalization: The Maronites of Lebanon." In *Minorities and the State in the Arab World,* edited by Ofra Bengio and Gabriel Ben-Dor, 111–28. Boulder, CO: Lynne Rienner, 1999.

Middle East Road Map (2003)

A plan devised by representatives of the United Nations, the European Union, the United States, and Russia, which became known as the "Middle East Quartet," first floated at a foreign ministers' meeting in Madrid in April 2002. The outbreak of the Second Intifada, with Israeli military incursions into Palestinian territory and repeated Palestinian suicide bombings, gave a sense of urgency to the process. The collapse of previous attempts at negotiation at Camp David II and at Taba in January 2001 added to a strong desire to find a new creative solution—through a multilateral approach of great powers—to an extremely difficult political problem. The negotiators accepted the Arab Peace Initiative and sought to give new momentum to the Oslo peace process, to complement American mediation with support from three critical players: the United Nations, the European Union, and Russia—with Israeli and Palestinian consultation.

The road map sets up a series of steps to create an independent Palestinian state that exists peacefully with Israel through a three-year period. Both sides accepted the basic outlines after it was proposed by former U.S. president George W. Bush in 2003. The plan proposed three stages. The first demands an immediate cessation of Palestinian violence, the reform of Palestinian political institutions, the normalizing of Palestine life, the dismantling of Israeli settlement outposts built since March 2001, and a progressive Israeli withdrawal from the occupied territories. It establishes an independent Palestinian state in the West Bank and Gaza Strip, alongside Israel. The second phase focuses on the transition from May to June 2003. The last stage sought a permanent status agreement and end of the Israeli-Palestinian conflict.

Despite the formal support of powerful states and organizations, the Quartet failed to address several extremely difficult problems: final borders, the status of Jerusalem, the disposition of Israeli settlements, and future prospects for Palestinian refugees. Critics charge that the Quartet sought to motivate U.S. engagement with the peace process when the American administration had other priorities, then when the United States did engage, it used the Quartet to legitimize its own actions. American antagonism to Hamas and opposition to a Palestinian declaration of statehood impeded effective negotiations. Ultimately, after 2006 the Quartet merely issued supportive statements as other parties made independent initiatives.

Jonathan K. Zartman

See also: Fatah Party; Hamas; Intifadas (I, II, and Knife); Israel; Palestine; Palestine Liberation Organization; Primary Document: *The Arab Peace Initiative*

Further Reading

Elgindy, Khaled. "The Middle East Quartet: A Post-Mortem." *Analysis Paper* No. 25. Washington, DC: The Saban Center for Middle East Policy at Brookings, February 2012.

Salem, Walid. "The Arab Peace Initiative and the International Community: Concerted Efforts for Its Implementation." *Palestine-Israel Journal* 20, no. 23 (2015): 79–85.

Tocci, Nathalie. "The Middle East Quartet and (In)effective Multilateralism." *Middle East Journal* 67, no. 1 (Winter 2013): 29–44.

Military Coups

The seizure of executive authority by some portion of the military, to change the executive leadership, without necessarily changing the nature of the government or its methods of governing. The term derives from the French phrase *coup d'état,* a disabling strike against the state. From 1945 to 2017, the Middle Eastern and North African (MENA) region experienced 27 successful coups. Half of all the successful coups occurred in just Syria (eight coups) and Iraq (six coups). Although relatively common in the MENA region, military coups occur more often in Latin America or sub-Saharan Africa. Globally, over half the coups attempted between 1946 and 1969 succeeded. From 2010 to 2018, only six out of 29 attempts have succeeded. Military coups rarely occur in liberal democracies and free societies. The highest risk factors for a military coup include 1) a previous history of a coup; 2) poverty that inhibits the development of political institutions; and 3) extreme political polarization, social alienation from elites, demands for rule by a simple majority, without consideration for the values of large minorities, populism, and frequent massive rallies and demonstrations. A leader facing potential disloyalty in his government can stage a theatrical coup to flush out his enemies and justify a thorough purge of the government. Military leaders who expect that they will suffer arrest and torture may attack the president, to go down fighting rather than endure public shame.

Military coups can be divided into two pathways. First, where the military is relatively united, but separate from society, while society suffers from strong internal divisions and the government is young or lacks legitimacy, then the military as an institution can impose its vision for solving the major social division. Many of the coups in the early history of postcolonial states in the MENA region fall into this pattern. In the second pathway, a smaller group seeks to create a bandwagon effect, with a display of shocking force, seeking to compel the majority to feel that they have to join. Leaders have to convince other officers and soldiers that success is already assured, so that joining becomes necessary for survival. The leaders face great difficulty in assessing the willingness of other officers to join the plotters, who must organize in secret. The display of shocking force at the beginning can create an image of the plotters as enemies of civil society. Therefore, the plotters must consider the high cost of failure—usually death, sometimes after interrogation under torture.

To prevent coups, states employ a variety of strategies, commonly called "coup-proofing." These can include bribery of generals, ideological indoctrination, and establishment of parallel military organizations, such as the Islamic Revolutionary Guard Corps of Iran. Creating multiple parallel security organizations, as in prerevolutionary Tunisia, can hinder their conspiring to overthrow the state. Usually, a leader will create a bodyguard unit that is highly paid, trained, and well-equipped, with unquestionable loyalty, like Saddam Hussein did, relying on people from his home region of Tikrit. However, promotion based on loyalty rather than military strategic skill undermines the military's effectiveness in a conventional war. Coup-proofing inhibits other qualities, such as small-unit initiative, complex training, and information-sharing, necessary for modern conventional warfare. It creates factional strife in the military and distrust, which distorts decision-making.

After a successful coup, the military usually lacks the experience in economics, education, or social and political policy to overcome the problems that led to social polarization and the military intervention. If it does not quickly arrange an orderly transition back to civilian political rule, it will create extensive grievances that fuel long-term social disorder. Governments that suffer an attempted coup usually become more authoritarian. The development of international norms against military coups, reinforced by aid conditionality, motivate powerful dissident groups in government to use alternative strategies that disguise the violation of political process, such as judicial coups and the organization of mass protest movements to remove a chief executive and his supporters.

Tom Dowling

See also: Authoritarianism; Democracy Deficit; Egypt, Arab Republic of; Grievance Model; Iran, Islamic Republic of; Iraq, Republic of; Islamic Revolutionary Guard Corps (IRGC); Syrian Arab Republic; Tunisia, Republic of; Turkey, Republic of

Further Reading

Khuri, Fuad. "The Study of Civil-Military Relations in Modernizing Societies in the Middle East: A Critical Assessment." In *Soldiers, Peasants and Bureaucrats: Civil-Military Relations in Communist and Modernizing Societies,* edited by Roman Kolkowitz and Andrzej Korbonski, 9–27. Boston: George Allen and Unwin, 1982.

Klaas, Brian. "Why Coups Fail." *Foreign Affairs,* July 17, 2016.

Luttwak, Edward. *Coup d'État: A Practical Handbook.* Cambridge, MA: Harvard University Press, 2016.

Singh, Naunihal. *Seizing Power: The Strategic Logic of Military Coups.* Baltimore: Johns Hopkins University Press, 2014.

Minorities

Numerically smaller groups within a larger population, claiming a distinct character based on their ethnic, cultural, religious, or linguistic identity. The rise of nationalism, as an ideology in which one people claims the authority of the state, reduces the status of other groups. The form of nationalism determines the relations between dominant and subordinate groups. Similarly, Islamism justifies excluding and discriminating against religious minorities. The development of nationalism connects cultural identity with the rights and powers of state authority, therefore, minorities become significant in struggles between states and struggles for power within states. Historically, Islam classified Christians, Jews, and Zoroastrians as protected "People of the Book," a secondary status subject to payment of a poll tax. Nevertheless, Zoroastrians suffered significant persecution. Other religions such as the Alawites, Alevis, and Druze often suffered more. The rise of pan-Arab nationalism led to discrimination against Berbers, Kurds, and other non-Arab Muslims. Arabs in Iran suffer discrimination, both for their language and for their Sunni faith.

Because the Islamic Republic of Iran chose to use Shi'a identity as a political tool, this affects the conditions of life for Shi'as living as minorities in other states. Authoritarian states often use minorities as scapegoats—accusing them of disloyalty, inviting foreign intervention, or blaming them for problems. The existence of Israel made the position of the Jewish minority in Arab countries almost impossible, causing most of them to flee. All minorities recognize the danger that their country of residence will consider them potential agents of a foreign power. For this reason, the Copts of Egypt have rejected the label of minority, and the church leaders have rejected outside publicity of the persecution that they suffer. Similarly, the Armenians in Iran deny their persecution to outsiders and proclaim their loyalty to the state. By preemptive assertions of loyalty, the Circassians of Jordan have prospered, but in Syria they became part of a struggle among minorities, and like the Druze, they lost to the Alawites. Because authoritarian states tend to engage in disproportionate and indiscriminate reprisals, any rebellion can put the survival of the whole group at risk. For example, the Armenian insurgency of 1890 in the Ottoman Empire led to genocide. Kurdish rebellions have provoked a similar response. Relatively small groups can survive in austere terrain if they develop exceptional political and martial skills, as seen in the Druze.

Relatively small Muslim populations differing only in ethnicity often choose to assimilate to the host nation where possible. Religious minorities tend to resist converting. International law mandates that states protect minorities, although protection often leads to greater persecution. The persecution of minorities activates the humanitarian sensibilities of the international community, as seen in the support given to the Kurds who fled to Turkey from Saddam Hussein's persecution, and the support given to the Yazidis under assault by the Islamic State (Daesh). Nadia Murad, a member of the Yazidis persecuted by the Islamic State, won the Nobel Peace Prize in 2018.

Emanuela Claudia Del Re

See also: Alawites (Nusayris); Alevis; Armenians; Authoritarianism; Berbers (Imazighen); Coptic Orthodox Church; Druze; Egypt, Arab Republic of; Iran, Islamic Republic of; Islamic State (Daesh); Islamism; Israel; Jordan, Hashemite Kingdom of; Kurds; Maronites; Shi'a; Syrian Arab Republic; Turkey, Republic of; Yazidi

Further Reading

Castellino, Joshua, and Cavanaugh, Kathleen. *Minority Rights in the Middle East: A Comparative Legal Analysis*. Oxford, UK: Oxford University Press, 2013.

Longva, Anh Nga, and Anne Sofie Roald, eds. *Religious Minorities in the Middle East: Domination, Self-Empowerment, Accommodation*. Boston: Brill, 2015.

Nisan, Mordechai. *Minorities in the Middle East: A History of Struggle and Self-Expression*. Jefferson, NC: McFarland, 2012.

Modernization

The progression from traditional, agrarian societies into urban, industrial societies, which requires technological development and education, and which commonly leads to changes in social values. Beginning in the early 1800s, states in the Middle East began a process of modernization, sometimes provoking rejection and revolution. Beginning with Napoleon's invasion of Egypt, and continuing with increasing European colonialization, Muslims asked, "Why was this possible, since we have the true religion?" Those who blamed laxity, innovation, and departure from religious purity developed into the Salafist Movement. The other common answer looked at specific factors supporting European power. Reformers, called the Jadids, based on the Arabic word for "new," observed that Muslims had led the world in technology, science, and military power in the past. They concluded that Muslims could regain their military advantage by promoting education, nationalism, newspapers, science, and engineering and by learning European languages.

Initially, modernizing reformers had some success in Egypt, Turkey, and Iran in a form of defensive modernization: to increase military competitiveness. They faced opposition from conservative, traditional forces. For example, the Ottomans started the modernization of the state, but after the collapse of the empire, the military success of Kemal Ataturk enabled him to thoroughly reshape the Turkish state and society. The Turkish modernization endured, due to the autonomous military occasionally intervening to maintain Ataturk's vision.

Similarly in Iran, the Persian Constitutional Revolution from 1905 to 1911 began the political modernization. Mohammad Reza Pahlavi overturned the constitution but forced a great deal of policy change in the name of modernization. In response to economic change and forced secularization, large landowners and religious teachers led a revolution that mobilized the economic grievances of the working class and students. Although militants may initially seek to block technological change, under the pressure of military competition with the state, they often prove remarkably adaptive in exploiting technology. Therefore, their anger represents a rejection of the changing social values that modernization can bring.

Social scientists have studied the changes in social values due to modernization. Over generations, people living in urbanized, industrial conditions tend to become more individualistic, direct in their communication, egalitarian, task-oriented, and risk acceptant. To the extent that they either reject or fail to submit to traditional authority figures and the values of their grandparents' village, feelings of mutual alienation will motivate conflict. Technological change, which enables globalization, creates an awareness of how much better people live in other parts of the world. Modernization allows elites to engage with the global economy, often sending their money to other countries to purchase luxury goods or to send their children to university abroad. They lose the motivation to recycle their finances within their community, to sustain their local reputation. All of this creates a sense of relative deprivation that fuels anger and conflict.

Modernization, and often the decline in rural economic conditions, draws young men from the villages to the city, where they face many needs—for jobs, housing, education, health care, and, ultimately, a wife. Without the support network of extended family in their home village, they find the support offered by religious organizations of all types, which seek to meet their needs. Religious organizations also give them a way to understand their suffering and a vocabulary and narrative in which to express their grievances. Therefore, modernization creates social stresses, even to the point of personal emotional crises. Under the forces of modernization, levels of religious devotion and activism have risen, contrary to the expectation of the modernization theorists of the 1960s. While states must improve their levels of education and technological capacity to compete militarily, preserving internal stability requires carefully managing the social stress created by changing cultural values and meeting the needs of young men displaced by economic change.

Ali A. Olomi

See also: Demographics (Youth Bulge); Development; Egypt, Arab Republic of; Framing Model; Grievance Model; Iran, Islamic Republic of; Labor Migration: Sending Countries; Turkey, Republic of

Further Reading

Dekmejian, R. Hrair. "The Rise of Political Islamism in Saudi Arabia." *Middle East Journal* 48, no. 4 (Autumn 1994): 627–43.

Hinnebusch, Raymond. "Authoritarian Persistence, Democratization Theory and the Middle East: An Overview and Critique." *Democratization* 13, no. 3 (2006): 373–95.

Inglehart, Ronald, and Wayne E. Baker. "Modernization, Cultural Change, and the Persistence of Traditional Values." *American Sociological Review* 65, no. 1 (February 2000): 19–51.

Mohammed VI, King of Morocco

The hereditary monarch of the Kingdom of Morocco, holding the religious title Commander of the Faithful, and one of the richest businessmen in Africa. Mohammed VI, born on August 21, 1963, in Rabat, into the royal family of Morocco, which claims descent from the Prophet Muhammad, received an education in Islam and politics to prepare him for his future role as king. Mohammed VI studied law at the Mohammed V University in Morocco and in 1993 received a doctorate in Law from the University of Nice-Antipolis.

Mohammed VI became king after the death of his father, King Hassan II, on July 23, 1999. Many of Mohammed VI's early actions as monarch sought to overcome the legacy of his father's repressive policies. These reforms include granting increased civil liberties and women's rights, creating a council on reparations that addressed the claims of former political prisoners, and dismissing his father's interior minister Driss Basri. In 2006, he worked with a coalition of feminists and moderate Islamists to get the parliament to pass a progressive family code. He has built good relations with liberal Western leaders and promoted environmental consciousness.

In response to the Arab Spring, Mohammed VI instituted further reforms, including a new constitution in July 2011, which enhanced the power of the prime minister and parliament and increased judicial independence. It gave Tamazight (the Berber language) official recognition. The king retains the power to appoint and control the Ministries of Defense, Interior, Foreign Affairs, Justice, and Religion, and various provisions still allow the king the ability to appoint the prime minster and the cabinet. He can dissolve parliament at any time. These reforms appeared to temporarily reduce demands for greater changes, but they did not fundamentally reduce the grievances that drove the February 20 Movement or the Al Hociema Protests.

Critics and human rights activists charge that the government has responded to the protests in northern Morocco with a punitive strategy, in spite of the economic nature of the protester's demands, which the state could meet. Complaints about the scale and pervasive character of corruption and human rights abuses continue. The king owns a large and very successful holding company and extensive agricultural land in Morocco. He has used his wealth and businesses as economic leverage to enhance his political negotiations, exemplified by his success in bringing Morocco back into the African Union. The king promotes the competition of political parties, while staying above that competition and serving as the mediator.

The king controls a very powerful patronage network that gives him even great informal but effective power. The combination of formal and informal practical influence, exercised through a network of about 20 families closely tied to the royal family, called the Makhzen in Morocco, remains firmly in control.

Andrew Harrison Baker

See also: Authoritarianism; Clientelism (Patrimonialism); Corruption; February 20 Movement; Fikri, Mouhcine; Morocco, Kingdom of; Party of Authenticity and Modernity

Further Reading

Boussaid, Farid. "The Rise of the PAM in Morocco: Trampling the Political Scene or Stumbling into It?" *Mediterranean Politics* 14, no. 3 (November 2009): 413–19.

Campbell, Patricia J. "Morocco in Transition: Overcoming the Democratic and Human Rights Legacy of King Hassan II." *African Studies Quarterly* 7, no. 1 (2003): 38–58.

Sheline, Annelle. *Royal Religious Authority: Morocco's "Commander of the Faithful."* Houston, TX: Baker Institute for Public Policy, March 2019.

Stepan, Alfred, Juan J. Linz, and Juli F. Minoves. "Democratic Parliamentary Monarchies." *Journal of Democracy* 25, no. 2 (April 2014): 35–51.

Moroccan Protests (2011). *See* February 17th Revolution

Morocco, King. *See* Mohammed VI, King of Morocco

Morocco, Kingdom of

A hereditary monarchy ruling over an Arab and Amazigh (Berber) Sunni Muslim population on the northwestern Mediterranean coast of the African continent. Officially the al-Mamlakah al-Maghribiyyah, the Kingdom of the West, using the Arabic term *Maghreb,* referring to the western region of the North African coast, which includes Morocco, Algeria, and Tunisia. Although joined by religion and language to the countries of the Arab world, Morocco engages with its neighbors in Europe, the African Union, the Arab League, and the Union for the Mediterranean. Morocco depends on these intersecting alliances to generate trade and investment, as well as to manage security threats, emigration, and the transit of Africans to Europe.

The Kingdom of Morocco has modified its constitution several times to reduce domestic tensions. It allows a number of registered political parties to compete for seats in the parliament, but the ruling authorities, called the Makhzen, actively manage that competition to preserve the independence of the king. Several different forms of conflict fill the domestic political arena. Rising levels of urbanization, education, and employment in factories have enabled the rise of socialist and nationalist movements. The heritage of French and Spanish influence has created a more cosmopolitan way of life in the cities, which creates a sense of insecurity for leaders of traditional, conservative segments of society. The tension between the secular liberals and the Islamist activists constitutes one dimension of domestic conflict. The demands for cultural recognition by Amazigh (Berber) activists creates a second form of internal pressure. Third, the grievances of people in the underdeveloped and neglected northern Rif mountain region also draw government attention. Fourth, a legacy of corruption and underdevelopment derives from the decades of authoritarian rule through patronage, benefiting relatively few families.

In addition to these four dimensions of domestic conflict, Morocco engaged in decades of conflict after its 1975 invasion and occupation of Western Sahara. In 1971 and 1972, King Hasan survived two assassination attempts and then purged the military, creating a vulnerable condition for the state. He also struggled to suppress a leftist uprising in the countryside, while negotiating with the nationalist opposition. In 1973, in the territory of Western Sahara, ruled by Spain as a colony since 1884, a group of Sahrawi students influenced by socialist ideas founded a popular liberation front for the region called the Polisario.

Under pressure from the Sahrawi independence movement, Spain decided to leave the territory. King Hasan pursued international recognition of Moroccan sovereignty in the region through intense diplomatic efforts and sought a ruling from the International Court of Justice, which, on October 16, 1975, gave only an ambiguous answer. The next day, he called for volunteers to march into Western Sahara carrying their Qur'ans, a campaign called the Green March. The marchers arrived at the border on November 9, 1975. To avoid an open confrontation, Spain signed the Tripartite Agreement of November 1975, giving Morocco the northern two-thirds of the territory and Mauritania the rest. The troops of both countries encountered stiff resistance when they entered, while half of the Sahrawi population left for exile in Tindouf, Algeria. Mauritania eventually gave up its portion, and Morocco fought the Polisario resistance until a cease-fire in 1991, though continued tension remains.

The Moroccan effort to secure UN recognition for its sovereignty over Western Sahara has become the pivot for its foreign policy. Morocco works hard to keep good relations with Europe as a market for its agricultural produce. The rural elites constitute a durable source of domestic support for the monarchy, making these exports very important politically as well as for the economy as a whole. To strengthen its support from Europe, Morocco has adopted a discourse of human rights. This has also helped Morocco keep good relations with the United States, for the sake of arms supplies and security assistance. Morocco has signed a free-trade agreement with the United States and has supported peace negotiations, but within the constraints of Arab consensus. Moroccan troops have protected Saudi Arabia and served in the conflict in Yemen.

The current king, Mohammed VI, reigning since 1999, dramatically opened politics and expanded freedoms of speech and the media—compared to the policies of his father, King Hassan II. In 2001, the government recognized the Amazigh population and heritage by creating the Royal Institute of Amazigh Culture (IRCAM). In 2003, the government reformed the Moudawana, Moroccan Family Code, to expand women's rights in marriage, divorce, and child custody. The king had already taken steps to manage the influence of Islamists, first by helping the Justice and Development Party (JDP) to compete with the very large and effective Islamist movement called *al Adl wal Ihsan* (Justice and Charity). Second, in 2002, he appointed a well-known and highly educated Sufi as minister for Religious Endowments and Islamic Affairs. With state support, the Sufi Movement has grown even stronger over the following years.

In February 2003, Osama bin Laden issued a statement calling Morocco an unjust, apostate government. On May 16, 2003, 12 suicide bombers attacked five Western and Jewish targets in Casablanca, killing 33 and injuring more than 100. Morocco embarked on a comprehensive strategy against terrorism, including counter-radicalization educational initiatives. In 2005, the king launched the National Initiative for Human Development (INDH) to address poverty. By the beginning of 2011, Morocco had become one of the more politically liberal states in the Arab world.

In November 2010, security forces crushed demonstrations near Western Sahara's regional capital Laayoune, but this did not affect the country as a whole. Morocco has a very large civil society sector: almost all of these organizations serve basic social, health, and educational needs and stay clear from politics. The Moroccan Association for Human Rights (AMDH), with 10,000 members, represents the largest and most significant association in Morocco. The AMDH gained a reputation for courage by holding large numbers of sit-ins to protest injustice and demand the release of political prisoners, in the face of consistent brutal repression. Morocco also has 34 legally recognized political parties, 30 of which accept the government and the legitimacy of the king. The remaining four radical leftist parties poll only 1 percent of the vote. Three of these created the Democratic Alliance of the Left (DAL). Some young Internet activists with strong secular convictions met in person when they protested against police enforcement of Ramadan fasting in public. This group also protested the police torture and killing of a young laborer on September 15, 2010. This protest gained the support of the AMDH and the DAL and generated enough publicity that the government finally charged the policemen involved in that death. This gave the Internet activists confidence that they could promote political change.

After the events in Tunisia, the Internet activists formulated a platform of seven demands and started planning a protest on February 20, 2011. The DAL offered their offices and logistical support for a set of protests, combined with the AMDH. Despite the aversion between Islamists and the leftist political parties, some of the independent bloggers invited participation from the youth of the Justice and Charity Movement, on the condition that they adhere to the seven-point platform only, with no religious slogans. This collaboration of disparate groups carried tremendous energy and initial optimism, mobilizing large crowds of protesters in almost all of the major towns, which grew larger on the second and third days of protest.

However, the activists made decisions in large assemblies by consensus, rather than voting, without any formal leadership, to avoid giving the government a target for future persecution. Therefore, internal differences and the lack of leadership left the movement unable to respond to the king's speech of March 9, 2011, promising some constitutional reforms. After enthusiasm for the movement fell in mid-May 2011, the government began attacking and arresting protesters. The government drafted a new constitution, which the people approved in a referendum in July 2011.

In the November 2011 elections, the Justice and Development Party (JDP) won the largest number of seats in the House of Representatives, and its leader, Abdelilah Benkirane, formed a coalition government. King Mohammed VI supported this development so that he could claim to lead reform by promoting an opposition party with a clean reputation. The JDP had to implement policies that it disliked, due to the other parties in the coalition and the government's subordinate position under the king. The king took many functions under his direct control, leaving the elected officials with little authority and often only ceremonial roles. Prime Minister Benkirane continued to support the king and carried out difficult policies. Through political skill and charisma, he retained his personal popularity.

Despite these reforms, the king retains ultimate authority and does not tolerate any rivals in government, military, judiciary, or religious affairs. Morocco passed through the tumult of early 2011 with slightly better political openness, and many women's rights, and Amazigh civil rights groups have grown. In 2014, the government revised the law used to force rape victims to marry their rapists. Constitutional reforms have remained, but improvements in local governance have lagged. For example, the al-Hoceima demonstrations lasted for months, protesting against the abusive contempt of the authorities, including violence and bribe-taking. They reveal a continuing sense of social despair and political disenfranchisement, as well as low wages and high youth unemployment, which drive high rates of labor migration. The kingdom faces problems similar to those of its neighbors: grievances created by corruption and authoritarian government have fueled Islamist rebellion, and the changing role of technology and media has brought global debates over social values into Moroccan conversations. With limited natural resources, a growing population, and a mounting budget deficit, the government faces difficult economic challenges. However, the events in the region since 2011 have only increased Morocco's value to Europe and the United States in counterterrorism activities and managing the migration of sub-Saharan Africans.

In the 2016 elections, the JDP again received the largest number of votes, competing mostly against the Party of Authenticity and Modernity, which had support from King Mohammed VI. Through diverse political manipulations, the king prevented Benkirane from forming a governing coalition, then dismissed him as prime minister, and appointed another JDP leader in his place in March 2017.

Kristin Hissong

See also: Authoritarianism; Benkirane, Abdelilah; Berbers (Imazighen); Corruption; February 20 Movement; Fikri, Mouhcine; Islamism; Justice and Development Party (Morocco); Morocco, Kingdom of; Mohammed VI, King of Morocco; Party of Authenticity and Modernity

Further Reading

Benchemsi, Ahmed. "Morocco's Makhzen and the Haphazard Activists." In *Taking to the Streets: The Transformation of Arab Activism,* edited by Lina Khatib and Ellen Lust, 199–235. Baltimore: Johns Hopkins University Press, 2014.

Howe, Marvine. *Morocco: The Islamist Awakening and Other Challenges.* New York: Oxford University Press, 2005.

Lefevre, Raphael. "'No to hoghra!': Morocco's Protest Movement and Its Prospects." *The Journal of North African Studies* 22, no. 1 (2017): 1–5.

Sater, James N. *Morocco: Challenges to Tradition and Modernity.* New York: Routledge, 2016.

Spiegel, Avi Max. *Young Islam: The Politics of Religion in Morocco and the Arab World.* Princeton, NJ: Princeton University Press, 2015.

Willis, Michael J. *Politics and Power in the Maghreb: Algeria, Tunisia and Morocco from Independence to the Arab Spring.* Oxford, UK: Oxford University Press, 2014.

Zeghal, Malika. *Islamism in Morocco: Religion, Authoritarianism and Electoral Politics.* Translated by George Holoch. Princeton, NJ: Markus Wiener Publishers, 2009.

Morocco, Movement for Unification and Reform. See Justice and Development Party (Morocco)

Morsi, Mohamed

A leader in the Muslim Brotherhood, and the first elected civilian president of Egypt from June 30, 2012, to July 3, 2013. Mohamed Morsi was born on August 8, 1951, in El Adwah, a village north of Cairo, the son of a farmer. He studied engineering at the University of Cairo, receiving a master's degree in 1978. He earned a doctorate from the University of Southern California in 1982 and served on the faculty of California State University, Northridge, until returning to Egypt in 1985 to teach at Zagazig University.

In 1977 Morsi joined the Muslim Brotherhood and rose in authority. He served in Parliament from 2000 to 2005, officially as an independent. Despite lacking charisma, as the chairman of the Freedom and Justice Party he had organizational support. After the 2011 protests, Egyptian voters elected Morsi as president. He won 52 percent of the vote, with a 51 percent turnout. His initial statements indicated a possible genuine turn to democracy and respect for ethnic and religious minorities. As the first Islamist head of state he struggled to overcome the constraints imposed by the military. He annulled measures previously passed by the Supreme Council of the Armed Forces (SCAF) to limit presidential power, purged the top ranks of the SCAF, and chose Abdel Fattah el-Sisi for Defense minister. His opponents strongly objected to his November 2012 presidential declaration denying judicial oversight of the Constituent Assembly, after which he drafted a new constitution. He made a variety of statements and political decisions that provoked fear that he was creating a religious dictatorship. His perceived power-grab—while the government failed to provide basic services—provoked a youth-led movement to replace Morsi, known as Tamarod (Rebellion).

Millions of protesters gathered on June 30, 2013, demanding his resignation. On July 3, the military, led by General Abdel Fattah el-Sisi, arrested him. The military coup d'état enjoyed wide popular support. Although General el-Sisi violated democratic procedure, the undemocratic character of Morsi's rule created a problem for his supporters as well as his opponents. He faced criminal trials from 2013 to 2015 for abusive treatment of protesters and alleged ties with terrorist organizations. An Egyptian court sentenced Morsi to death, but the courts overturned the sentence in 2016. On June 17, 2019, he died in a Cairo courtroom.

Dan Campbell

See also: Egypt, Arab Republic of; El-Sisi, Abdel Fattah Saeed Hussein Khalil; Military Coups; Mubarak, Muhammad Hosni Sayyid; Muslim Brotherhood; Tahrir Square Protests; Tamarod Movement

Further Reading

Bassiouni, M. Cherif. *Chronicles of the Egyptian Revolution and Its Aftermath: 2011–2016.* New York: Cambridge University Press, 2017.

Brown, Nathan. "The Transition: From Mubarak's Fall to the 2014 Presidential Election." In *Egypt After the Spring: Revolt and Reaction,* edited by Emile Hokayem and Hebatalla Taha, 15–31. New York: Routledge, 2016.

Sallam, Hesham. "The Egyptian Revolution and the Politics of Histories." *PS: Political Science and Politics* 46, no. 2 (April 2013): 248–58.

Mubarak, Muhammad Hosni Sayyid

An Egyptian Air Force officer who became president of Egypt in 1981 and ruled until February 2011. Mubarak, born on May 4, 1928, joined the Egyptian Air Force after attending the Air Force Academy. He gained national recognition as commander of the air force during the October 1973 Yom Kippur War. Anwar

Sadat chose him to serve as vice president in 1975. In this position, Mubarak gained experience as diplomatic liaison between Egypt and its neighbors, Saudi Arabia in particular. He sought regional acceptance of Egypt's early postwar diplomacy with Israel. He did not favor Sadat's Camp David Accord with Israel. Islamists who disapproved of the peace agreement assassinated Sadat, and Mubarak, although wounded, succeeded Sadat as president.

Once in office, Mubarak kept good relations with the United States and sought to overcome Egypt's isolation from the Arab world. He built relations with Iraq during its war with Iran, but in 1990 he opposed the Iraqi invasion of Kuwait and joined the coalition to drive Iraq out. This gained Egypt debt relief from the G8 countries and increased aid from the United States. He successfully mediated talks among Hamas and Fatah, and even Israel. Mubarak retained power through a combination of harsh political repression and some economic liberalization. His failing health and his efforts to groom his son Gamal to succeed him stimulated a persistent opposition movement. High unemployment, significant economic disparity between the few very rich and great masses in poverty, rampant corruption, and police brutality created a massive social revolution against him and his government. As police violence against the protesters in the Tahrir Square protests escalated, the military forced him to resign.

Through corruption during his career as a high-ranking air force officer and three decades as president, he accumulated a family fortune estimated at $40 billion. In trials starting in mid-2011 and extending into mid-2012, judges convicted Mubarak of corruption, abuse of power, and failing to prevent his security forces from killing protesters. Between 2013 and 2017, as his health deteriorated, and leadership of Egypt passed to Mohamed Morsi and then to the army under Abdel Fattah El-Sisi, courts overturned many of those convictions.

Nicholas Michael Sambaluk

See also: Authoritarianism; Corruption; Egypt, Arab Republic of; El-Sisi, Abdel Fattah Saeed Hussein Khalil; Fatah Party; Hamas; Iraq, Republic of; Israel; Morsi, Mohamed; Saudi Arabia, Kingdom of; Tahrir Square Protests

Further Reading

Amin, Galal. *Egypt in the Era of Hosni Mubarak, 1981–2011*. New York: American University in Cairo Press, 2011.

Arafat, Alaa Al-Din. *Hosni Mubarak and the Future of Democracy in Egypt*. New York: Palgrave Macmillan, 2009.

Blaydes, Lisa. *Elections and Distributive Politics in Mubarak's Egypt*. New York: Cambridge University Press, 2011.

El-Bendary, Mohamed. *The Egyptian Revolution: Between Hope and Despair: Mubarak to Morsi*. New York: Algora, 2013.

Mujahedin-e Khalq (MEK)

A militant Islamic Marxist student group formed at Tehran University in 1965 to lead an armed revolt against the shah, Muhammad Reza Pahlavi. The Mujahedin-e Khalq (MEK; People's Holy Warriors), also known as the Mujahedin-e Khalq

Organization (MKO), attacked and killed U.S. military personnel and U.S. civilians working in Tehran (in 1973, 1975, and 1976). The MEK initially aligned with the Islamic Revolution but split from the regime in 1981 and bombed the headquarters of the Islamic Republic Party (IRP), killing 70 high-ranking Iranian officials, including Iran's chief justice (Ayatollah Beheshti), its president, and its premier.

Massoud Rajavi, MEK's emerging leader (born in Tabas, Iran, in 1947), joined the MEK in 1967. After he broke with the Iranian regime in 1981, he fled to France with his wife, Maryam, former president Bani Sadr, and other MEK leaders, where they formed the National Council of Resistance of Iran (NCRI). Other members established communes in Iraq or fled to Iranian Kurdistan. Members remaining in Iran formed an underground network and executed anti-regime attacks. In 1986, MEK leaders relocated to Iraq, financed and armed by Saddam Hussein. The MEK fought Iranian forces during the Iran-Iraq War (1980–1988), causing most Iranians to hate them with great passion. Saddam Hussein also utilized MEK forces to suppress Kurdish unrest in northern Iraq, and among Shi'ites in southern Iraq after the Gulf War of 1991. In other countries, MEK forces attacked Iranian assets, launching terrorist attacks against Iranian embassies throughout the 1990s. In 1997, the United States classified the MEK as a terrorist organization. Until 2003, MEK fought Iranian forces along the Iran-Iraq border.

After the coalition invasion of Iraq in 2003, U.S. forces—unaware of MEK's past activities—on April 15, 2003, agreed to a truce with the MEK, which claimed neutrality. The coalition disarmed its members and moved them to Camp Ashraf near Baghdad. Under the Fourth Geneva Convention, the United States extended "protected person" status to 3,800 detainees between 2004 and early 2009. In December 2011, the UN High Commissioner for Refugees (UNHCR) designated them as "persons of concern" needing international protection and by the end of 2013 had relocated most of them to foreign countries.

The MEK has maintained a clandestine network inside Iran, which intelligence agencies credit with exposing Iran's nuclear facilities in Natanz and in Arak. Some observers also accuse them of helping assassinate Iranian nuclear scientists.

After the MEK moved to France, it developed into a cult of personality as Massoud and Maryam Rajavi demanded complete loyalty and embraced feminism. Most of the MEK's commanders were women. Massoud disappeared in 2003, believed dead. The organization elected Maryam Rajavi, who runs the Paris headquarters, as president-elect of Iran.

The organization promotes itself as a democratic group to gain political support and money under false pretenses. In 2001, investigators in the United States, Great Britain, and Germany exposed MEK money-laundering activities. After an extensive lobbying campaign, on September 28, 2012, the U.S. State Department formally removed the MEK and the National Council of Resistance from the list of Specially Designated Global Terrorist groups.

Mark David Luce and Ali A. Olomi

See also: Iran, Islamic Republic of; Iraq, Republic of; Khomeini, Ayatollah Sayyid Ruhollah Mūsavi; Women's Leadership in Protests

Further Reading

Abrahamian, Ervand. *The Iranian Mojahedin,* 2nd ed. New Haven, CT: Yale University Press, 1992.

Khodabandeh, Massoud. "Bulgarians to Dismantle Iranian Terrorist Group MKO in Iraq." *Terrorism Monitor* 4, no. 3 (February 9, 2006).

Sheehan, Ivan Sascha. "Challenging a Terrorist Tag in the Media: Framing the Politics of Resistance and an Iranian Opposition Group." *Digest of Middle Eastern Studies* 22, no. 2 (2013): 229–61.

Muslim Brotherhood

The transnational, Sunni, Islamist political organization founded by Hasan al-Banna (1906–1949) in 1928 at Ismailia, Egypt, dedicated to the promotion of Islamic law as the proper basis of government. The Muslim Brotherhood (al-Ikhwān al-Muslimūn) has become the most significant and effective Islamic revivalist organization of the 20th-century Arab world. This movement originated in efforts to oppose the Westernization of Muslim society in general, and Egyptian society in particular. The movement spread quite rapidly within Egypt and beyond, inspiring a huge number of Muslims living in Palestine, Jordan, Syria, Kuwait, Sudan, Lebanon, and North Africa.

Claiming Islam as a universal message and remedy for all challenges and problems, the Brothers reshaped their societies through education, preaching, and charity works. Al-Banna defined the organization's comprehensive nature, strategy, and program as "a Salafi message, a Sunni way, a Sufi truth, a political organization, an athletic group, a cultural-educational union, an economic company, and a social idea." They built mosques; operated small hospitals, schools, and industries; and opened social clubs. The movement combined social and political activism, which generated rapid membership growth and influenced other Islamist movements around the world. From its base as a religious organization focused on spirituality, morality, education, welfare, and social activities, it expanded into a transnational organization addressing issues such as Palestine, natural resources management, Marxism, social inequalities, Arab nationalism, and the weakness of the Islamic world on the international scene. In reaction to the socio-economic crisis and growing secularism of Egypt, it began to function as a political organization opposed to the country's ruling Wafd Party, as well as against the Zionists, the government, and the British. It established an armed branch known as the Secret Apparatus (al-Jihāz al-Sirrī). Between 1948 and 1949, the Brothers sent volunteers to fight Zionists and support the cause of Palestine. After the assassination of the Egyptian prime minister, in December 1948, the government seized the movement's assets, imprisoned scores of its members, compelled others to go underground or live in exile, and had Hasan al-Banna killed.

The Brothers supported the Free Officers' Coup of 1952, but after a failed attempt to assassinate Nasser in October 1954, the government crushed the movement. Throughout the 1960s and 1970s the Brotherhood remained largely clandestine. Its conditions improved under Anwar al-Sadat, who released thousands of Brotherhood members from prison and permitted them to resume their activities, to combat the influence of the socialists. In the 1980s, the organization made alliances with secular political parties to compete in elections. Although banned from open elections, individual members won 17 seats in the 2000 elections and five years later gained 88 seats.

After the uprising of 2011, the government lifted the ban on the organization's open participation in Egyptian politics. The Brothers established the Freedom and Justice Party (FJP), which won nearly half the seats in the lower house of the Egyptian parliament in the first elections after the protests of 2011. Mohamed Morsi, the leader of FJP, became Egypt's first democratically elected president in June 2012. By late 2012, Morsi attempted to rule by decree to circumvent the courts and legislature and to limit speech and press freedoms. Amid protests in July 2013, the military ousted President Morsi, dissolved the upper house, and suspended the constitution. In 2013, the Egyptian government banned the Muslim Brotherhood, labeled it a terrorist organization, and dissolved the Freedom and Justice Party in 2014. Since Mohamed Morsi's 2013 arrest, human rights groups report mass arrests and extrajudicial killings of Muslim Brotherhood and Freedom and Justice Party members.

Mohammad Dawood Sofi

See also: Democracy Deficit; Egypt, Arab Republic of; El-Sisi, Abdel Fattah Saeed Hussein Khalil; Islamism; Morsi, Mohamed; Salafism; Tamarod Movement

Further Reading

Al-Awadi, Hisham. *The Muslim Brothers in Pursuit of Legitimacy.* London: I. B. Taurus, 2014.

Obaid, Nawaf. *The Muslim Brotherhood: A Failure in Political Evolution.* Cambridge, UK: Belfer Center for Science and International Affairs, 2017.

Wickham, Carrie Rosefsky. *The Muslim Brotherhood: Evolution of an Islamist Movement.* Princeton, NJ: Princeton University Press, 2013.

Muslim Brotherhood in Jordan

The key Islamist movement in Jordan, which has a strong reputation as a reformist, legally recognized movement. It has provided a channel for Palestinians to overcome political exclusion. The Muslim Brotherhood of Jordan (Ikhwan) began in 1945 with East Bank merchants who resisted the development of Israel. Official toleration and good relations with the Brotherhood as a loyal opposition supported the Islamic legitimacy of the monarchy. The Brotherhood played a crucial role in defending the government under pressure from pan-Arab, Ba'athist, and Nasserist ideological activists throughout the 1950s and 1960s, and in supporting the kingdom's policy of uniting the East and West Banks in 1950. Due to the Ikhwan's nonconfrontational strategy, the king allowed them to work as a charity organization, prior to the legalizing of political parties in 1992. Its historically moderate, nonviolent character makes the Jordanian Ikhwan distinct from other branches of the Muslim Brotherhood across the Middle East. However, the war in Syria has driven the radicalization of the Islamist movement regionwide. Thus, rather than allowing greater liberalization, the kingdom has intensified its monitoring of dissident groups. The Ikhwan suffered significant political persecution from 2007 to 2010 after complaining against the conditions for the 2007 parliamentary elections.

The Brotherhood's political party, the Islamic Action Front (IAF), boycotted elections in 2010 and 2013. In 2012, a coalition led by previous moderate and reformist Brotherhood leaders formed a moderate Islamist organization called the ZamZam Initiative. In 2014, Saudi Arabia, Egypt, and the United Arab Emirates condemned the Brotherhood as a terrorist organization and put pressure on Jordan to outlaw the Brotherhood completely. In 2015, the organization split over how to adapt its strategies in response. The government declared the existing Ikhwan illegal, confiscated its assets, and turned them over to a newly licensed split called the Muslim Brotherhood Society (MBS). In 2016, the IAF ran candidates for parliament as part of the National Coalition for Reform (NCR), which also included nationalists, Christians, and other minorities. The NCR won 15 of 130 seats, of which 10 were IAF members, and three of these were women. The IAF also performed very well at the local-level elections in August 2017.

Nur Köprülü

See also: Egypt, Arab Republic of; Islamism; Jordan, Hashemite Kingdom of; Jordanian Protests; Muslim Brotherhood

Further Reading

Bar, Shmuel. *The Muslim Brotherhood in Jordan.* Tel Aviv: The Moshe Dayan Center for Middle Eastern and African Studies, 1998.

Boulby, Marion. *The Muslim Brotherhood and the Kings of Jordan, 1945–1993.* Atlanta: Scholars Press, 1999.

Schwedler, Jillian. *Faith in Moderation: Islamist Parties in Jordan and Yemen.* Cambridge, UK: Cambridge University Press, 2006.

Nakhla, Rami

A Syrian democracy activist of Druze ancestry born in Sweida, in southern Syria. Nakhla studied political science while living near Damascus before the outbreak of the Syrian civil war. He engaged in a great deal of online activism under the guise of Malath Aumran, to protect his personal life from repercussions from his online activities. He played a key role in organizing nonviolent protests in Syria. He served as a technological guide to help Syrian activists connect online while protecting themselves from government persecution. As death threats against him increased, he fled the country to live in Beirut, Lebanon, where he collected extensive evidence from networks within Syria of the disproportionate violence employed by the Assad government. Syrian intelligence agencies employed their influence in Lebanon to search for Rami Nakhla, forcing him to flee for asylum in the United States in late 2011.

He briefly attended Yale University, followed by work as a program specialist at the U.S. Institute of Peace. In this role, he facilitated the development of "The Day After," a nongovernmental organization funded primarily by the U.S. Department of State, to discuss and define proposals for the future of Syrian politics after the departure of Bashar Assad. This NGO has brought together diverse groups, such as representatives from the Muslim Brotherhood, secularists, and ethno-religious minorities from Syria. He serves as a spokesperson for the Local Coordination Committees (LCC) of Syria and a member of the Syrian National Council. In 2018, Nakhla went to Turkey to document war crimes committed during the Syrian civil war.

Samanvya Singh Hooda

See also: Lebanese Republic; Local Coordination Committees; Social Media; Syrian Arab Republic; Syrian Civil War

Further Reading

Bahrampour, Tara. "Out of Hiding to Build Tomorrow's Syria." *The Washington Post,* August 29, 2012: B.1.

El-Hibri, Hatim. "The Cultural Logic of Visibility in the Arab Uprisings." *International Journal of Communication* 8 (2014): 835–52.

Lynch, Mark, Deen Freelon, and Sean Aday. *Syria's Socially Mediated Civil War.* Washington, DC: United States Institute of Peace, 2014.

Nasrallah, Hassan Abdel Karim

A Lebanese Shi'a military and political leader, famous for his oratorical skills, who has served as secretary general of Hezbollah since 1992. Hassan Abdel Karim Nasrallah, born on August 31, 1960, to a vegetable vendor, grew up in a poor neighborhood of East Beirut. In 1976, he went to study in a seminary in Najaf, Iraq, where he gained favor with one of the leading teachers, Muhammad Baqir al-Sadr, and met Sayed Abbas Musawi. In 1978, Iraq expelled the Lebanese Shi'a students, so Nasrallah and Musawi returned to Lebanon. Nasrallah joined the Lebanese Shi'a Amal Movement and became a member of the central political office.

After the Israeli invasion of 1982, Nasrallah joined the Hezbollah militia, which adopted a more strident, uncompromising approach and had excellent funding and logistics supplied by Iran. In 1987, Nasrallah gained respect for his military leadership in hard battles that Hezbollah fought with Amal in Beirut. Syria intervened to support Amal, so Nasrallah went to Qom, Iran, for theological study until 1989, when he returned to lead Hezbollah in new battles against Amal. Hezbollah also suffered internal conflict over future strategy. Nasrallah rejected the Taif Accords and sought to establish an Islamic state like Iran. He fought with his mentor Musawi and lost. Iran temporarily pulled Nasrallah out, while Syria asserted its hegemony over Lebanon; when he returned, he submitted to Syria's point of view.

In February 1992, after an Israeli helicopter assault killed Musawi, Nasrallah became the Hezbollah secretary general. Nasrallah has effectively played the traditional Lebanese role of a chieftain distributing patronage through a very large array of schools, medical facilities, social-welfare organizations, and infrastructure construction. In his public presentations and media appearances, his skillful use of different styles of speech elicits a potent emotional response. Hezbollah took part in the 1992 elections in Lebanon and gained a reputation for pragmatic policy changes and even ideologically inconsistent parliamentary alliances. For instance, in February 2006, he formed an alliance with the Christian militia leader Michel Aoun, famous for his savage battles against Syrian domination. Nasrallah seeks to portray Hezbollah as a defender of Lebanon, rather than as the Islamist agent of Iranian and Syrian interests. In 2008, Hezbollah gained 11 out of 30 cabinet seats and veto power, and in 2009, parliament passed a bill allowing Hezbollah to keep its weapons. In the May 6, 2018, election, Hezbollah's March 8 coalition gained significant influence.

Under his leadership, Hezbollah has consistently harassed Israel in a campaign of psychological warfare, by which he gained a highly exalted reputation among the Shi'as. The timing of some of his provocations of Israel reflect the needs of Iranian foreign policy messaging, but other attacks have helped Hezbollah's domestic political competition. He claims credit for Israel's withdrawal in 2000, success in a 2004 prisoner-exchange deal with Israel, and even the defeat of Israel in the 2006 Lebanon war. These successes gave him an extremely high reputation among the Shi'as.

Jonathan K. Zartman

See also: Hezbollah; Iran, Islamic Republic of; Israel; Lebanese Republic; Shi'a; Syrian Arab Republic; Primary Document: *The Taif Agreement*

Further Reading
Khashan, Hilal. "Lebanon's Shiite-Maronite Alliance of Hypocrisy." *Middle East Quarterly* 19, no. 3 (Summer 2012): 79–85.

Matar, Dina. "Hassan Nasrallah: The Cultivation of Image and Language in the Making of a Charismatic Leader." *Communication, Culture & Critique* 8, no. 3 (2015): 433–47.

National Action Charter

A document of constitutional reforms in Bahrain put forward in 2001 by Amir Hamad bin Isa Al Khalifa (1999–present). The charter promised far-reaching political reforms and guarantees of civil and property rights and equality of all citizens. The work on the charter started in 2000. It marked a break from the authoritarian rule of Amir Isa Bin Salman Al Khalifa (1961–1999), who had suspended the parliament in 1975, implemented a restrictive state security law, and established state security courts. The kingdom submitted the document to a national referendum, and the people approved it overwhelmingly. As the government restored civil rights and allowed political dissidents to return, they formed political associations and NGOs. The opposition groups were initially pleased. The kingdom then published a new constitution. On December 16, 2002, Bahrain became a constitutional monarchy. Nonetheless, the outcomes of reforms remained disappointing for some. The charter failed to give specific details to guarantee the separation of powers and the democratic basis of government. Because it reduced the role of parliament compared to the Constitution of 1973, the people considered it a betrayal. In a show of discontent, Shia political associations boycotted the parliamentary elections in 2002. Ultimately, the implementation of the charter contributed to a growing division within Bahraini society.

Magdalena Karolak

See also: Authoritarianism; Bahrain, Kingdom of; Democracy Deficit; Shi'a

Further Reading

Mohammed, Nadeya Sayed Ali. "Political Reform in Bahrain: The Price of Stability." *Middle East Intelligence Bulletin* 4, no. 9 (September 2002).

Peterson, J. E. "Bahrain: Reform—Promise and Reality." In *Political Liberalization in the Persian Gulf,* edited by Joshua Teitelbaum, 157–85. New York: Columbia University Press, 2009.

National Council of Resistance of Iran.
See Mujahedin-e Khalq (MEK)

National Liberation Front (FLN)

A socialist political party, founded in Algiers on November 1, 1954, by the Revolutionary Committee of Unity and Action, to unify diverse competing factions into a nationalist movement against the French colonial occupation. The National Liberation Front (FLN) gained significant public legitimacy as a revolutionary body that directed, and won, the war for independence in 1962. In March 1962,

France and the FLN signed the cease-fire. After overwhelming public support in a referendum, the FLN declared independence on July 3. Ahmed Ben Bella, with two other leaders—Houari Boumedienne and Muhammad Khidr—created the Political Bureau of the FLN, and became the first premier in May 1963. In 1965, Boumedienne overthrew Ben Bella and suspended the constitution of 1963.

The Boumedienne government relegated the FLN to a secondary position of providing propaganda, selecting government employees, and serving as a kind of political police. Therefore, the party did not hold national conferences or interfere with the operation of the state. After Boumedienne died in 1978, the FLN picked Chadli Benjedid to rule the state. As the only constitutionally legal party in Algeria until 1989, the FLN actively suppressed competing mass organizations, such as the labor unions, Islamist parties, democratic forces, and Berber cultural activists. After the October 1988 riots, the government approved a new constitution that eliminated the one-party political system, as well as the country's socialist ideology. The FLN lost its primacy in the violence of the 1990s but recovered under the leadership of Abdelaziz Bouteflika, who won the presidency in 1999.

Carolina Bracco

See also: Algeria, The People's Democratic Republic of; Black October Riots; Bouteflika, Abdelaziz

Further Reading

Jackson, Henry F. *The FLN in Algeria: Party Development in a Revolutionary Society.* Westport, CT: Greenwood Press, 1977.

Seddon, David. "Elections in Algeria." *Review of African Political Economy* 17, no. 49 (Winter 1990): 70–73.

National Transition Council

The de facto government of Libya for a period beginning during the February 17th Revolution, in which rebel forces overthrew the government of Muammar Qaddafi. Under the leadership of Mahmoud Jibril, the National Transition Council (NTC) announced its formation in Benghazi on February 27, 2011, to act as the "political face of the revolution." In August 2011, the NTC issued a Constitutional Declaration to set up a road map for the transition to a constitutional democracy with an elected government. The council gained international recognition as the legitimate governing authority in Libya and occupied the country's seat at the United Nations. However, it consisted initially of defectors from the regime and educated exiles who had returned. It lacked control over the huge number of militias that conducted the revolutionary fighting. Due to its origins in the east, where the revolution began and where the first area to gain some stability were located, critics in other parts of the country accused it of submitting to domination by easterners. Although the council tried to expand its membership to represent a broader section of the national population, it also lacked the legitimacy of an elected congress. Due to these defects, when pressured by militia violence, it accommodated the demands of federalists. This set a destructive precedent that the General National Congress (GNC) followed.

The NTC governed Libya for a period of 10 months after the end of the war, holding elections to the GNC on July 7, 2012. The high rate of participation and the free and fair conditions of that election, supported by large numbers of international observers, generated a period of significant optimism for the future of Libya. In a ceremony on August 8, 2012, the NTC formally transferred power to the newly elected GNC, the first peaceful transition of power since the end of the monarchy.

Amir Muhammad Esmaeili

See also: February 17th Revolution; General National Congress; Qaddafi, Muammar

Further Reading

Chivvis, Christopher S., and Jeffrey Martini. *Libya after Qaddafi: Lessons and Implications for the Future.* Santa Monica, CA: Rand, 2014.

Filiu, Jean-Pierre. *The Arab Revolution: Ten Lessons from the Democratic Uprising.* Oxford, UK: Oxford University Press, 2011.

Nezzar, Khaled

A former Algerian general of the National People's Army (ANP), born in 1937 in eastern Algeria. In April 1957, he deserted the French Army to become an instructor in the National Liberation Army. After independence in 1962, Algeria sent him as one of the first military officers to receive training in the Soviet Union. He fought in the Israeli-Arab War in 1967. In 1984, he was promoted to general of the ANP and gained recognition for modernizing the army and raising its professionalism. Promoted in 1987 to commander of land forces and deputy chief of staff, in October 1988, he led the military effort to quell the riots, which killed nearly 500 people. He then became military chief of staff until promoted to minister of National Defense in 1990. After the Islamic Salvation Front (FIS) organized a general strike in protest against the government's changing the electoral rules, Nezzar led the decision to declare a state of siege on June 5, 1991. He pressed for harsher treatment of the FIS and for stopping the elections, to both provoke and discredit the FIS. After the FIS won strongly in the parliamentary elections of December 1991, Nezzar and four other generals forced President Chadli to dissolve the parliament, then resign—effectively a coup d'état. From 1992 to 1994, he served on the High Council of State (HCE), the new center of administrative power in Algeria.

He retired in 1994, after narrowly surviving an assassination attempt. In 2001, he filed a libel suit in Paris against the publication of a book accusing him of war crimes and lost. The testimony of witnesses in the trial became another book, printed by a reputable French publisher. In 2012, the Swiss Federal Criminal Court indicted him for war crimes and crimes against humanity. He wrote several books including *Mémoires du général Nezzar.*

Saphia Arezki

See also: Algeria, The People's Democratic Republic of; Black October Riots; Islamic Salvation Front (FIS); Salah, Ahmed Gaid

Further Reading

Aboul-Enein, Youssef H. "Algerian Defense Minister General Khalid Nezzar: Memoirs." *Military Review* 83, no. 2 (March 1, 2003): 89–90.

Le Suer, James D. *Between Terror and Democracy: Algeria since 1989.* New York: Zed Books, 2010.

Nezzar, Khaled. *Mémoires du Général Nezzar.* Alger: Chihab, 1999.

Roberts, Hugh. "Algeria between Eradicators and Conciliators." *Middle East Report* no. 189 (July–August 1994): 24–27.

Ocalan, Abdullah

The official founder and leader of the Kurdistan Workers Party (PKK), until his capture and imprisonment by Turkey on February 16, 1999. Abdullah Ocalan (known as Apo, "uncle") was born in 1948 in Omerli village near Urfa, Turkey. Educated in Turkish (his first language), he joined the Political Science Faculty of Ankara University, after failing the army entrance exam. Within academic circles, Ocalan embraced socialist ideology to promote Kurdish nationalism. On November 1978, he formed the PKK in a village near Diyabakir. After the 1980 military coup, Ocalan went to Lebanon and Syria; since 1984, the PKK has conducted armed operations against Iraq, Iran, and Turkey to establish an independent Kurdish state.

In January 1995, the PKK abandoned Marxism and denounced Soviet communism to adopt a humanitarian political ideology. After leaving Syria, Ocalan sought refuge elsewhere to direct his operations. In November 1998, he was arrested in Rome, but the Italian government did not extradite him, to avoid the death penalty established by Turkey. After the rejection of many European countries, Ocalan went to Kenya where he was kidnapped, arrested, and transported back to Turkey. In June 1999, he was sentenced to death for terrorist crimes; this sentence was commuted to life imprisonment in 2002. Ocalan is currently detained, alone, in the island-prison of İmralı. Recently, he significantly changed his ideology and theorized his ideal society as a "democratic-ecological society," later redefined as a "liberationist society on gender" and describing himself as a democrat-ecologist.

Gianfranco Bria

See also: AKP-PKK Peace Talks; Iraq, Republic of; Kurdistan Workers Party (PKK); Kurds; Lebanese Republic; Syrian Arab Republic; Turkey, Republic of

Further Reading

Gunter, Michael M. *The Kurds Ascending: The Evolving Solution to the Kurdish Problem in Iraq and Turkey.* New York: Palgrave Macmillan, 2011.

Kiel, Stephanie Lynne. "Understanding the Power of Insurgent Leadership: A Case Study of Abdullah Ocalan and the PKK." PhD dissertation, Georgetown University, 2011.

Özcan, Ali Kemal. *Turkey's Kurds in Perspective: A Theoretical Analysis of the PKK and Abdullah Ocalan.* New York: Routledge, 2006.

Oman, Sultanate of

An absolute monarchy with a reputation for mediating conflicts and adopting an independent foreign policy, located on the southeastern coast of the Arabian

Peninsula adjoining the Gulf of Oman. Oman shares land borders with Saudi Arabia to the northwest, the United Arab Emirates to the northeast, and Yemen to the West, and controls the Musandam Peninsula, one side of the Strait of Hormuz, directly opposite Iran.

Although often described as somewhat isolated from the main currents of political conflict in the Arab world, Oman has a heritage as a mercantile state with strong international connections. These two major aspects of the Omani state reflect the influence of two important regions and two forms of authority. The deserts and mountains around the oases of the inner area protected a theocratic state founded upon the Ibadi Doctrine of Islam. Since 730 CE, an elected Ibadi *imam* has usually ruled over the interior, although different coalitions have engaged in major conflicts over succession, and sometimes a ruler could claim only political authority. The coastal cities flourished on trade with the coasts of Africa and India, and both regions depended on each other.

The Portuguese destroyed Muscat in 1507 and controlled the coastal areas. In 1624, as expanding British influence weakened the Portuguese, the leading Ibadi religious teachers (*ulema*) of the interior elected an *imam,* who reunited the country politically. By 1650, the Ibadis had brought peace and stability to the interior, expelled the Portuguese, and then took Zanzibar, Baluchistan, and Bahrain. From 1650 to 1810, the Omanis were the principal maritime power of the Indian Ocean. In 1724, a civil war broke out between the leading personalities of two inner cities. In 1737, the sultan, ruling from Muscat, asked for Persian help to regain the Imamate. However, by 1745, Ahmad al-Busa'id, the governor of the coastal city of Sohar, defeated the other parties. In 1749 he expelled the Persians and in 1753 was elected *imam* by the leading Islamic teachers. He began the al-Bu'said Dynasty that rules the country today. His dynasty focused primarily on trade and governing the empire that included the island of Zanzibar, Mombasa, and ports on the coast of Iran and present-day Pakistan. Therefore, the population of Oman includes the descendants of the merchant families from this period.

British trade competition and the prohibition of the slave trade caused that empire to collapse. The British signed a treaty of protection with the al-Bu'said, as they did with the emirs of Kuwait, Bahrain, and the emirates of the Gulf. As a result of economic decline, the country of Oman split between the Ibadi *imams* of the interior versus the sultan of the coastal areas. In 1920, the British brokered a peace agreement between the two, in which the sultan accepted the autonomy of the interior. In 1932, Sultan Taimur abdicated the throne in favor of his 20-year-old son Said, who then struggled for several years to persuade his own relatives to accept his rule. He developed a good relationship with the ruling *imam* and appealed to the principles of rule by imamate law to gain popular legitimacy. He promoted personnel from key tribes of inner Oman and modeled his sultanate on the best aspects of the imamate. He became effective as a mediator among tribal conflicts and never pressed any claim to the imamate when he had the opportunity.

The prospect of oil at the Buraimi oasis in the interior drew Saudi efforts to claim it, while the tribes of the interior sought greater autonomy. In 1946, the British refused to help Sultan Said gain control over the interior. In 1952 the Saudis occupied the Buraimi oasis, and in 1955 they supported an *imam* from Nizwa, in the interior, in challenging the sultan's authority. Sultan Said ultimately prevailed in that struggle with British help, shrewd political negotiations, and a flair for dramatic but gracious presentation. However, he failed to show real concern for the hardships of the people and failed to promote health and education, supporting only the infrastructure necessary for oil exploration. Furthermore, he offended some tribal sheikhs by refusing to see them when they came for consultations. In the 1957 Jebel Akhdar War, the Saudis supported the imamate and some tribes against the sultan. Then the British gave very substantial help to the sultan's armed forces in the major battles of the war, mostly won in 1959. Although some leaders escaped, small skirmishes, sabotage, and roadside bombings continued until 1962. However, this allowed the exploration for oil to continue.

Sultan Said settled in Salalah, the major coastal town of the Western Dhofar region, and married a local woman from one of the largest tribes. However, he failed to rule by consensus, with a shared understanding with the tribal leadership, as he had done with his initial capture of authority in the interior. Instead, he imposed such heavy taxes that the economy withered, forcing large numbers of men to seek work in Kuwait, Bahrain, and other Gulf states. In 1963, a small tribal revolt called the Dhofar Liberation Movement began, and it grew much larger with support from socialist forces in Yemen and ultimately from other communist states. In 1964, a revolutionary movement overthrew Omani political control over Zanzibar, forcing most of the remaining Omani-origin ruling class to flee into exile—most came back to Oman. In 1965, Sultan Said recalled his son Qaboos, who had finished his military training in Britain and even served as a British officer for a while in Germany. However, when he returned, his father kept him relatively isolated in Salalah for five years. Oil production began in 1967 and stabilized in 1969, providing the State of Oman with revenue 40 times higher than in previous years.

In June 1969, a radical Marxist wing of the National Liberation Front (NLF) in Yemen gained power, turning the country into the communist People's Democratic Republic of Yemen (PDRY) with support from China and the USSR. The government of PDRY supported the Dhofar rebels with weapons, personnel, and financing and also imposed communist ideology. After the communists forced the British to leave Aden, they renewed their commitment to preventing communists from taking over Oman. The British had a political consul at the Omani court and use of facilities for the Royal Navy. The Dhofar rebels appeared to be winning the struggle, but the rebels' shift toward using communist ideology cost them local support. The evident failure of Sultan Said's detached and remote approach provoked his brother to plot to depose him.

In this context, Qaboos bin Said took the initiative to force his father to abdicate. He took the throne with British knowledge, but not as a British coup. Enabled by the new flow of oil money, he quickly launched an active nationwide program of development, including economic, social, and educational reforms and reforms in the military and civil administration. The sultan's new government also introduced a series of international diplomatic initiatives, seeking legitimacy as a modern Arab state. Oman entered the Arab League in 1971, receiving recognition from other Arab states.

The sultan's extensive health care and agricultural development programs in Dhofar, combined with a sophisticated political campaign promoting commitment to Islam, and the sultan's identity as the son of a local woman, undermined the appeal of the Dhofar rebels. He employed political and social liberalization with narrowly targeted counterinsurgency tactics. To aid resistance to the spread of communism, Saudi Arabia, Jordan, and the United Arab Emirates sent military support. In 1973, the shah of Iran began sending military helicopters and troops to support the sultan, all of which enabled Sultan Qaboos bin Said to triumph.

Over the next 30 years, Oman has greatly developed its education and health care facilities and programs. The government has used oil revenue to build infrastructure and promote economic diversification and industrialization. Lacking the really huge oil revenues of some of its neighbors, Oman has taken a gradual approach that has avoided debt and reduced the cultural shock of rapid modernization. Despite extremely impressive progress in education, from a very low base, Oman still could not produce the numbers of skilled workers needed for industrialization. Although the government has tried to entice previously departed workers to return, Oman has still needed large numbers of labor migrants to keep the economy growing. Therefore, Oman provides a source of labor for its neighbors and receives labor migrants from India, Pakistan, and other Asian states.

Government policy seeks to prevent internal conflicts from the three major directions seen in recent history: 1) struggles within the ruling family for control of the state; 2) rebellion of tribes in the interior; and 3) separatist movements in Dhofar. To prevent competition within the family, the sultan has not allowed close family members to hold positions of great influence or prosperity but instead has relied on the leaders from tribes in the northern coastal cities and descendants of merchant families with connections to Iran, Pakistan, India, and Africa to promote trade and economic development. Many families from outside Oman, after living for multiple generations in Oman, have considerable wealth and influence. Oman actively ensures freedom of religion so that the Shia Liwatiyya, from the Sind in Pakistan, and the Hindu Banyan, originally from Mandvi, have government-protected places for worship. This supports Oman's international reputation for religious tolerance. But complaints about the political connections and wealth of these families also fuels a discourse of corruption.

To prevent disaffection and rebellion among tribes in the interior, the government appoints tribal leaders to positions of authority, making them clients, dependent on the patronage of the sultan. To the extent that leaders fail to distribute resources from the government equally to members of their tribe, the people at the bottom often blame the government. Oman also promotes development and infrastructure to tie the country together. While the government protects Ibadi Islam, the faith of approximately two-thirds of the people, and generally governs according to its principles, the education system tends to promote a form of generic Islam to reduce offense to the Sunnis. Nevertheless, the government remains sensitive to the fact that rebels may try to exploit Ibadi Doctrine to justify their political program. In 1994, one month after an Israeli delegation visited to participate in a meeting of the Water Resources Working Group, the government arrested 430 people on charges of conspiring to overthrow the government to establish an

Islamist state. In 1998 the government closed four institutes for Islamic studies and brought all of them into the Sultan Qaboos University. The government supervises mosque-based religious education, but some people still seek private study groups.

In 1995 the sultan was seriously injured in a car accident that killed a very wealthy businessman. In November 1996, the sultan issued the first written constitution, which spelled out the procedure to follow in choosing his successor. It added an appointed upper chamber to the parliament to provide technocratic advice from a nontribal perspective, which he uses as an opportunity to appoint an increasing number of women.

To prevent Dhofar separatism, or similar forms of rebellion, the government has developed large, effective, and fast-acting security services. For example, in January 2005, the government arrested a group of well-educated Ibadi men employed in educational and religious organizations, with no international connections, on charges of planning to attack the Muscat Festival and seeking to re-create the Ibadi Imamate. They were convicted and sentenced but then received royal pardons on June 9. Oman has avoided problems with Islamist radicalization and has not contributed foreign fighters to any of the various regional conflicts, a very unique accomplishment.

Oman continues to rely on large numbers of Baluchi soldiers in the military, supported mostly by officers from the tribes of the northern coastal plain. Meanwhile, tens of thousands of Omani men serve in the armed forces of the various emirates, especially Abu Dhabi. Oman plays an active role in the Gulf Cooperation Council (GCC), urging greater cooperation but resisting Saudi domination and antagonism to Iran. The sultanate has mediated diplomatic crises between Iran and several Arab states, as well as functioning as a platform for negotiations between member countries of the GCC. Oman seeks to balance the interests of both Saudi Arabia and Iran to advance Omani national interests. Oman has also negotiated with Iran on behalf of the United States and facilitated the direct negotiations over Iran's nuclear program.

Regarding Yemen, Oman did not participate in military operations and tries to support the government of Yemen. Oman has refused to accept refugees, although the country has provided humanitarian and medical assistance to Yemeni civilians. In March 2018, Saudi Arabia and the United Arab Emirates (UAE), with backing from the United States, accused Oman of allowing Iranian weapons to flow through Oman and into Yemen.

Falling oil prices present serious challenges for the Omani government because depleted revenues make it increasingly difficult for the government to meet its budget. The Omani economy has suffered the most among the member countries of the GCC. The government is making serious efforts to diversify its economy away from oil. Although Oman did have some protests in 2011, the government was able to suppress them with relatively low cost. Initially, the government took a more relaxed approach to these protests and revived previous economic, social, and political reform programs. However, by March 2011, protests increased and also became more violent. Riot police dispersed violent protesters, and the government cracked down on Internet criticism. The GCC gave both Bahrain and

Oman $10 billion in aid over a period of 10 years to finance social and economic measures to meet some of the demands.

The failing health of the aging Sultan Qaboos, who has no living brothers, no children, and no designated heir, causes outsiders concern. However, the sultan has kept his choice of successor secret to prevent open contention ahead of time, and the constitution puts the decision in the hands of the Ruling Family Council of about 50 men. The next sultan will lack the legitimacy of Sultan Qaboos and will struggle to secure enough support from the country's centers of power. The economy will continue in the hands of an oligarchy of the principal merchant families with a network of connections to political leaders. The sultan has organized his state in a very centralized manner to manage the problems of tribalism, religious authority, and competing regional ambitions. Over his long life and rule, Sultan Qaboos has shaped the political culture, creating a brand, or reputation, of the state for promoting gradual development and modernization with stability, which motivates minority groups to fervently pledge their commitment. Oman's unique foreign policy and strategic geographic location make it a significant geopolitical player in Middle East politics and diplomacy.

Autumn Cockrell-Abdullah

See also: Authoritarianism; Bahrain, Kingdom of; Clientelism (Patrimonialism); Development; Gulf Cooperation Council (GCC); Ibadi Doctrine; Iran, Islamic Republic of; Kuwait, State of; Oman Protests; Qaboos bin Said bin Taimur Al Said; Rentier State Politics; Saudi Arabia, Kingdom of; United Arab Emirates (UAE); Yemen, Republic of

Further Reading

Allen, Calvin H., Jr., and W. Lynn Rigsbee II. *Oman under Qaboos: From Coup to Constitution, 1970–1996.* Portland, OR: Frank Cass, 2000.

Barrett, Roby C. *Oman: The Present in the Context of a Fractured Past.* MacDill AFB, FL: Joint Special Operations University, August 2011.

Eickelman, Dale F. "From Theocracy to Monarchy: Authority and Legitimacy in Inner Oman: 1935–1957." *International Journal of Middle East Studies* 17, no. 1 (February 1985): 3–24.

Jones, Jeremy, and Nicholas Ridout. *A History of Modern Oman.* New York: Cambridge University Press, 2015.

Katzman, Kenneth. *Oman: Reform, Security and US Policy.* RS21534. Washington, DC: Congressional Research Service, April 26, 2016.

Kechichian, Joseph. *Oman and the World: The Emergence of an Independent Foreign Policy.* Santa Monica, CA: RAND, 1995.

Valeri, Marc. *Oman: Politics and Society in the Qaboos State.* New York: Columbia University Press, 2009.

Worrall, James. "Oman: The 'Forgotten' Corner of the Arab Spring." *Middle East Policy* 19, no. 3 (September 2012): 98–115.

Oman Protests (2011)

A series of demonstrations in Oman, beginning relatively small on January 17, 2011, but escalating and spreading at the end of February. Demonstrators complained about rising unemployment among the youth bulge. They blamed the rising cost of living on corruption among government officials and demanded better working conditions and salaries. The rise of social media only increased the popular capabilities to organize. In the second Green March, in Muscat on February 23, participants submitted a petition to the government. Some carried banners with slogans supporting the sultan. They explained that they rejected violence and felt the sultan was handling events well. They claimed that his ministers, advisers, and men of wealth and influence had deceived him and used the government for corrupt advantage.

On February 28, protests hit Dhofar. The next day, larger, more serious demonstrations hit Sohar, a port city with a refinery, petrochemical plants, a steel mill, two power plants, and a water-desalination plant. Protesters set up a camp at the Globe Roundabout, blocking traffic and demanding a "real parliament." They attacked and burned the governor's office, a police station, and some cars. The police and army broke up the protest camps and arrested an unknown number of persons, and one person was killed. The protesters in Sohar expressed particular resentment against rich Indians and Pakistanis making excessive profits and driving up the cost of living, while poor people struggled to find jobs. The protests soon spread to other cities such as Haima, Sur, and Salalah. On March 1, the army began clearing blockages in Sohar, and the tone shifted to a more peaceful expression of political demands in Muscat, the capital.

The demonstrators also called for greater civil and political rights, greater power for the advisory Shura Council, judiciary independence, the installation of anti-corruption mechanisms in the government, and guaranteed freedom of expression. Sultan Qaboos responded to the protests by reshuffling the cabinet, promising investment to create new jobs, and separating the public prosecutors' office from the police. He established a consumer protection agency and sacked two senior ministers. Although the government arrested its critics, after they were convicted and sentenced, they were all pardoned.

In the spring of 2012, protests reemerged over unemployment and the slow pace of reforms, signifying dissatisfaction with the limited political and social reforms. A wave of arrests targeted human rights activists, bloggers, and journalists who had criticized the government. In 2012, a total of 35 activists were sentenced to prison for protesting and expressing their views on social media, according to Human Rights Watch.

Sultan Qaboos ultimately made more substantial reforms than other Gulf monarchs. At the end of 2013, the government took significant moves against corruption; in a number of trials against high officials convicted of taking huge bribes, the government ensured a lot of publicity. The government also initiated elections to provincial councils, held for the first time in 2012. Although the sultan managed to avoid further crisis, the government increased its repression of activists and further restricted freedom of expression and assembly.

Jonathan K. Zartman

See also: Authoritarianism; Clientelism (Patrimonialism); Corruption; Development; Grievance Model; Oman, Sultanate of; Qaboos bin Said bin Taimur Al Said; Rentier State Politics

Further Reading

Jones, Jeremy, and Nicholas Ridout. *A History of Modern Oman.* New York: Cambridge University Press, 2015.

Katzman, Kenneth. *Oman: Reform, Security and U.S. Policy.* RS21534. Washington, DC: Congressional Research Service, April 26, 2016.

Worrall, James. "Oman: The 'Forgotten' Corner of the Arab Spring." *Middle East Policy* 19, no. 3 (September 2012): 98–115.

Operation Cast Lead

A 22-day Israeli combined arms attack on Gaza. After a cease-fire in mid-2008, in November 2008 an Israeli raid killed several Hamas members and reignited tensions. Hamas began firing an extensive barrage of missiles into southern Israel. On December 27, Israel opened the initial phase of Operation Cast Lead with a week of air attacks. The second phase began on January 3, 2009, when Israeli Army units entered Gaza. Palestinian authorities claimed 1,430 Gazans died, with another 5,300 wounded. Israel lost three civilians and 10 soldiers, four of whom were reportedly killed by friendly fire, and had 519 wounded. The high number of casualties, the destruction of infrastructure, and the use of white phosphorous in populated areas, as well as the Palestinians' firing over 500 rockets during the operation, contributed to growing international pressure on Israel to end the operation. On January 18, Israel and Hamas each announced unilateral cease-fires that ended the fighting.

The UN Human Rights Commission created a fact-finding mission under Richard Goldstone. Despite Israeli refusal to cooperate, on September 16, 2009, the Goldstone mission issued a 569-page report critical of both sides' conduct and largely rejected by both. The operation strengthened the bitterness and desire for revenge by the people of Gaza. Israel did not gain the release of a captured soldier, but only a protracted series of negotiations and international criticism for indiscriminate and disproportionate operations. Israel's relations with Turkey in particular suffered serious damage.

Tom Dowling

See also: Hamas; Israel; Palestine; Turkey, Republic of

Further Reading

Blecher, Robert. "Operation Cast Lead in the West Bank." *Journal of Palestine Studies* 38, no. 3 (September 2009): 64–71.

Cohen, Stuart A. "The Futility of Operation Cast Lead." *BESA Center Perspectives* No. 68. Begin-Sadat Center for Strategic Studies, Bar Ilan University, February 16, 2009.

"Gaza's Unfinished Business." *Middle East Report* No. 85. Brussels, Belgium: International Crisis Group, April 23, 2009.

Operation Decisive Storm

A 2015 coalition effort in Yemen, led by the Kingdom of Saudi Arabia (KSA), to restore the internationally recognized government of President Abdu Rabbu

Mansour Hadi to power. The coalition included Bahrain, Egypt, Jordan, Kuwait, Morocco, Qatar, Sudan, and the United Arab Emirates. Additionally, the United States provided logistics and intelligence support for the effort. In September 2014, the Houthis, with the support of former president Saleh, took control of Sana'a, Yemen. In spite of efforts in negotiations, they rejected power-sharing agreements and put President Hadi under house arrest. In February 2015, after one month of captivity in Sana'a, Hadi escaped and fled to Aden. After the Houthis began attacks by air on Aden, the KSA built this coalition to act in defense of its own borders.

On March 26, 2015, the first strikes targeted air-defense capabilities: fighter aircraft, ballistic missiles, and antiaircraft weapons that the Houthis had seized in Sana'a. In addition, the coalition imposed a complete embargo on Yemen ports to prevent resupply to the Houthis. On April 21, 2016, the coalition declared the operation complete and expressed the desire to transition to a reconstruction effort, named Operation Restoring Hope. However, some members of that coalition continued to bomb targets associated with the Houthis, up until June 2019.

Rebecca Antecki

See also: Hadi, Abdu Rabbu Mansour; Houthis (Ansar Allah); Saleh, Ali Abdullah; Saudi Arabia, Kingdom of; Yemen, Republic of

Further Reading

Lackner, Helen, and Daniel Martin Varisco, eds. *Yemen and the Gulf States: The Making of a Crisis*. Berlin, Germany: Gerlach Press, 2018.

Willis, John M. "Operation Decisive Storm and the Expanding Counter-Revolution." *Middle East Research and Information Project,* March 30, 2015.

Operation Restoring Hope. *See Yemen Civil War*

P

Palestine

The area of coastal plains, foothills, and mountains on the eastern coast of the Mediterranean Sea up to the deserts of Arabia, in historical terms described as southern Greater Syria (Shams). Present-day usage refers more narrowly to areas between the Mediterranean and the Hashemite Kingdom of Jordan, between Lebanon and Egypt, not part of Israel proper, but captured by Israel during the 1967 Arab-Israeli War. Currently, this area consists of the West Bank, East Jerusalem, and the Gaza Strip. The Arab population, both Christian and Muslim, of the first two areas, governed by the Palestinian Authority and the Fatah Party, protests against Israeli occupation whenever conditions allow. The population of the Gaza Strip, under the control of the Islamist militia Hamas, does not have Israeli residents, but both Israel and Egypt try to control its borders.

The secular, nationalist party Fatah dominates the Palestinian Authority (PA), established by the Oslo Accords to govern Palestinians under occupation until a negotiated final agreement. The PA rules Palestinian cities and towns in the West Bank and shares security responsibilities with Israel in the surrounding areas. The PA has no authority over the remaining 60 percent of the West Bank, where Israelis live in settlements protected by a variety of security measures.

The current president of the PA, Mahmoud Abbas, has promoted nonviolent resistance to occupation and negotiations in order to establish a two-state solution. Since 2006, the PA has worked closely with Israel to limit anti-Israeli violence in the West Bank. After Hamas broke away in 2007, Abbas declared a state of emergency and has ruled by decree ever since. His refusal to step down at the end of his term in 2009, or even to hold elections, has given him an autocratic reputation. Failure to make progress toward independence, corruption, and unresponsive government has made him unpopular. Most Palestinians now see the PA as corrupt, ineffective, and co-opted by Israel.

Hamas has consistently dominated the Gaza Strip ever since Muslim Brotherhood activists established it there during the first Palestinian uprising (1987–1991). Its original charter calls for the destruction of Israel and the establishment of an Islamic regime in all of Palestine. Hamas opposed the Oslo Accords and conducted many suicide bombings in the second uprising (2000–2005), in which over 1,100 Israelis and nearly 5,000 Palestinians died. Because Hamas commits suicide bombings against civilians, the United States, Israel, and many other states call it a terror group. In 2005, Israel decided to unilaterally withdraw its troops and 9,000 settlers from the Gaza Strip. A few months later, Hamas won parliamentary elections, giving it the right to appoint its members to top PA positions. The United

States and Israel have refused to accept a Hamas-dominated government and encouraged Fatah to seize power. After a severe but brief civil conflict, in which more than 100 Palestinians died, Hamas established itself as the de facto government in Gaza, while the Fatah-dominated PA has ruled Palestinian towns in the West Bank. After Hamas captured an Israeli soldier, Gilad Shalit, on June 25, 2006, Israel began severely restricting what it allowed in and out of Gaza, and Egypt has largely cooperated. Israel faces great difficulty in reducing access to weapons and missiles. Hamas developed hundreds of tunnels to smuggle materials in from Egypt. Israel has eased its blockade over time due to criticisms over the living conditions for the two million Palestinians living in Gaza.

The 2011 protests in Arab countries took international attention away from the Palestinian protest movements. Inspired by the mass uprisings elsewhere, Palestinians in Gaza and the West Bank demonstrated in large numbers in March 2011, calling for Hamas and Fatah to reconcile. Numerous attempts to bridge the Hamas-Fatah divide have failed. Hamas took great hope on June 30, 2012, when Mohamed Morsi from the Muslim Brotherhood took power in Egypt. Morsi negotiated a peace agreement between Hamas and Fatah, but both sides violated it. Both parties remain unwilling to overcome their differences, to work together to improve the living conditions of their constituents and achieve Palestinian independence.

When the Egyptian military retook the government, it coordinated with Israel to strangle Hamas, sealing off Gaza from Egypt and repeatedly flooding Hamas's smuggling tunnels. Egyptian president Abdel Sisi has since tried a number of times to broker deals that would expand PA authority to the Gaza Strip. Hamas updated its charter in early 2017, accepting the idea of a negotiated two-state solution based on the 1967 borders, implicitly recognizing Israel's right to exist. It also disassociated itself from the Muslim Brotherhood. These changes helped ease tensions with Egypt and shrank the political gap between Hamas and Fatah on the issue of Israel (both now accept partition), but the two remain at odds.

In late 2017, Egypt brokered another reconciliation agreement, but disagreements persist over the control of internal security in Gaza and over when new parliamentary and presidential elections should occur. In an effort to force Hamas to cede control of the Gaza Strip, President Abbas retired many PA government officials serving in Gaza, made deep cuts to the salaries of those that remain, restricted social-welfare payments to hundreds of Gazan families, and has even coordinated with Israel to reduce the flow of electricity and fuel. These efforts have yet to force Hamas to submit, but they further undermined the humanitarian situation in Gaza. The United Nations and NGOs warn against the falling living conditions for the two million Palestinians stuck there. Unemployment hovers around 50 percent, and people often struggle to find basic necessities like food, drinkable water, medicines, building materials, and electrical power. Combat operations destroyed significant parts of the territory's infrastructure during the 2008, 2012, and 2014 wars with Israel. Both the PA and Hamas have lost much of their legitimacy for many Palestinians since they refuse to reconcile and fail to improve living conditions or advance the Palestinian national cause. They see no clear path to reconciliation and no clear process for replacing the elderly Mahmoud Abbas as PA president.

The regional instability that developed from the 2011 protests has reduced the influence of the Palestinian cause for many Arab leaders. They give most of their attention to maintaining internal security, combating militants, and restraining Iran's growing influence in the region. This insecurity has given Israel opportunities to pursue backdoor diplomacy with its Arab neighbors and drive a wedge between Palestinians and their major Arab benefactors. In Egypt, the political upheavals, economic struggles, and rising terrorist threats have forced President el-Sisi to focus on internal affairs, such as the attacks by militants in the Sinai Peninsula. Egypt now works closely with Israel to combat these groups and restore stability to the Egyptian-Israeli border.

This reliance on Israel hampers Egypt's ability to promote pro-Palestine policies. Jordanian leaders have also focused much of their attention on domestic concerns since 2011. King Abdullah struggles to manage the economic and security challenges of hosting over two million refugees from Iraq and Syria. The civil war in Syria interrupted its support for Hamas and gave Iran greater regional influence. Arab states increasingly rely on the Jewish state to fight their common enemies and to support their good relations with Washington. Many Israelis now argue that Arab states should not require progress on the Palestinian issue to normalize relations.

Israelis point to the rejection of past "generous" offers and repeated Palestinian attacks to argue that the Palestinians do not represent a partner for peace. They also argue that the divisions between Hamas and the PA make negotiating a deal impossible. The Arab protests in 2011 created further strategic uncertainty and raised the perception of danger associated with a two-state solution. These risks include losing control of the West Bank, which serves as a strategic buffer from external attack, and affording terrorists territory from which to operate. Israelis often point to the hundreds of rocket attacks that have followed their unilateral withdrawals from Gaza and southern Lebanon as examples of what happens when they give up territory in hopes of peace.

As of May 2019, all the states of the region nervously anticipate the Trump administration's proposal for restarting negotiations to settle the Israeli-Palestinian conflict. Despite some consultations with Israel and some neighboring Arab states in preparing the proposal, the United States has largely ignored the Palestinian leadership. Palestinians reject American mediation as biased, due to President Trump's recognizing Jerusalem as Israel's capital, his decision to cut Palestinian aid, and his decision to appoint pro-Israel partisans to head up his negotiating team. Israel and the United States have pressed Palestine's Arab patrons to push Palestinian leaders to accept a deal. Palestinian officials have declared the proposal dead on arrival. Any plan that does not create a viable Palestine with East Jerusalem as its capital has no chance, since this issue resonates strongly among the masses in the Arab and Islamic world.

Most Palestinians have lost hope in a two-state solution, given Israel's extensive colonization of East Jerusalem and the West Bank (where some 600,000 Israeli Jews live in hundreds of settlements) and the shift of Israel's establishment to the political right. Palestinian leaders have gone to the United Nations to demand an end of the occupation, but the United States has vetoed such efforts in the Security Council. Still, Palestine enjoys broad support in the UN General

Assembly, which has approved Palestine to join a number of international institutions, including the International Criminal Court.

Israel actively opposes such efforts but concentrates its greatest effort to fight the Boycott, Divest and Sanctions (BDS) Movement, organized by Palestinian citizens in 2005. Modeled after the fight against apartheid in South Africa, this movement seeks to put international pressure on Israel until it ends its occupation, allows the return of Palestinian refugees, and gives Palestinian citizens of Israel full equality. Israel calls the BDS Movement an existential threat and anti-Semitic at its core.

An increasing number of Palestinians reject partition as an unjust solution that would give Palestinians sovereignty over only 22 percent of historic Palestine, would not improve the plight of the 1.7 million Palestinian citizens of Israel, and would not offer help to five million Palestinian refugees. Therefore, they argue for a single binational state giving full citizenship and equal rights under the law to all Jews and Palestinians living in Israel, Gaza, East Jerusalem, and the West Bank. Zionists cannot accept this because Israel would cease to exist as a Jewish state. Alternative forms of an "Israeli solution" have even less plausibility.

Robert C. DiPrizio

See also: Abbas, Mahmoud; Ashrawi, Hanan; Egypt, Arab Republic of; Fatah Party; Fayyad, Salam; Hamas; Hamas-Fatah Conflict; Intifadas (I, II, and Knife); Iran, Islamic Republic of; Islamism; Israel; Muslim Brotherhood; Palestine Liberation Organization; Palestinian Islamic Jihad; Salafism

Further Reading

Brown, Nathan J., and Daniel Nerenberg. *Palestine in Flux: From Search for State to Search for Tactics.* Washington, DC: Carnegies Endowment for International Peace, 2016.

Elgindy, Khaled. "Lost in the Chaos: The Palestinian Leadership Crisis." *Washington Quarterly* 38, no. 4 (October 2015): 133–50.

El Kurd, Dana. "Palestinian Protests: Jerusalem's Shifting Fortunes." *Contemporary Arab Affairs* 11, no. 4 (December 2018): 19–40.

Høigilt, Jacob. "The Palestinian Spring That Was Not: The Youth and Political Activism in the Occupied Palestinian Territories." *Arab Studies Quarterly* 35, no. 4 (2013): 343–59.

Natil, Ibrahim. "Palestinian Youth Movements and 'the Arab Spring.'" In *Non-Western Social Movements and Participatory Democracy,* edited by Ekim Arbatli and Dinah Rosenberg, 33–42. Cham, Switzerland: Springer, 2017.

Robinson, Glenn E. "Palestinian Tribes, Clans and Notable Families." In *Strategic Insights.* Monterey, CA: Naval Postgraduate School, 2009.

Smith, Charles D. *Palestine and the Arab-Israeli Conflict,* 9th ed. Boston: Bedford/St. Martin's Press, 2017.

Palestine Liberation Organization

A coalition of Palestinian political parties and movements seeking the liberation of Palestine, founded in Jerusalem on May 28, 1964, at the first meeting of the Palestinian National Council (PNC). In 1974, the Arab Summit recognized the Palestine Liberation Organization (PLO) as the sole legitimate representative of the Palestinian people. The PLO consists of multiple political factions that represent the diversity of the Palestinian political arena.

From an early stage, the center-right Fatah Party has exercised predominant influence. Yasser Arafat (1929–2004), the Fatah Party leader, became the visible face of the Palestinian struggle worldwide in the 1960s. In 1969, the PLO Executive Committee elected Arafat as chairman. Other major factions include the Popular Front for the Liberation of Palestine (PFLP), the Democratic Front for the Liberation of Palestine (DFLP), the Palestinian People's Party (PPP), and the Palestinian Democratic Union (FIDA), among others. The PLO does not include Islamist parties such as Hamas and Islamic Jihad.

The Fundamental Law of the PLO defines the functions of the three leading parts of the organization: the PNC, the Central Council, and the Executive Committee. The PNC holds the highest authority and formulates its policies and programs; it represents all Palestinians and sectors and should meet every two years. The Central Council serves as a legislature when the PNC is not in session. The Executive Committee provides four primary executive functions: to represent the Palestinian people, to supervise the various PLO bodies, to execute the policies and decisions set out by the PNC, and to handle the PLO's financial issues through the Palestine National Fund.

The Palestinian National Charter establishes the ideological position and political objectives of the organization. In 1988, after the success of the First Intifada, in which independent local resistance took the initiative, the PLO decided to negotiate with Israel in order to regain leadership of the movement. At its 19th PNC session in Algiers in November 1988, the PLO proclaimed the State of Palestine and recognized UN Resolutions 181, 242, and 338: by doing so, it implicitly acknowledged Israel's right to exist. This paved the way for the peace talks that ultimately led to the Oslo I and II Accords (1993–1995). As a condition to the Accords, Israel insisted that the PLO revise its National Charter. The PNC met in Gaza in April 1996 and declared that it would change the charter to recognize the State of Israel, but the charter itself has not yet been amended. In December 1998, the PNC met again in Gaza, with U.S. president Bill Clinton present, to reaffirm the annulment of those parts of the charter that denied Israel's right to exist. In those Accords, Israel recognized the PLO as the representative of the Palestinian people. They also created the Palestinian National Authority (PA), a temporary, transitional body of interim self-government. Yasser Arafat was the first president of the PA (1994–2004), and after his death, Mahmood Abbas took office. He serves as both chairman of the PLO and president of the PA. In 2009, Abbas convened an extraordinary session of the PNC to replace some members of the Executive Committee. On May 1, 2018, the PNC met in Ramallah to discuss breaking ties with Israel and transforming the PA to assert the full functions of a state, as well as discussing reconciliation between Hamas and Fatah. The fact that the PNC had not met in regular session for 20 years illustrates the diminished relevance of the organization. The operation of the PA's bureaucracy has reduced the significance and political power of the PLO.

Carolina Bracco

See also: Abbas, Mahmoud; Fatah Party; Intifadas (I, II, and Knife); Israel; Palestine

Further Reading

Baracskay, Daniel. *The Palestine Liberation Organization: Terrorism and the Prospects for Peace in the Holy Land.* Santa Barbara, CA: Praeger, 2011.

Rubenberg, Cheryl Ann Snyder. *The Palestine Liberation Organization: Its Institutional Infrastructure.* Belmont, MA: Institute of Arab Studies, 1983.

Palestinian Islamic Jihad

A Palestinian Islamist militia established in 1979, known for its strict discipline, claiming inspiration from Ayatollah Khomeini's Islamic Revolution in Iran. The Palestinian Islamic Jihad (PIJ), developed by former members of the Egyptian Muslim Brotherhood Fathi Shaqaqi and Abd al-Aziz Awda, defines its purpose as removing the Israeli government and establishing an autonomous Islamic state based on *sharia* (Islamic law) in all the land currently comprising Israel, the West Bank, and Gaza. In 1989, the PIJ established its headquarters in Syria and keeps offices in Beirut, Tehran, and Khartoum. The secretary general of the PIJ, Ramadan Abdullah Shallah, holds a doctorate in economics and taught for several years in the United States. He manages the PIJ's relations with Iran, its major source of funding. Iran considers the PIJ its proxy in an axis of resistance to Israel and the United States. PIJ refuses to negotiate with Israel and rejects a two-state solution to the Israeli-Palestinian conflict. It conforms to the policy of Iran, which has declared the government of Israel an enduring enemy.

The PIJ is the second-largest group in Gaza today, after Hamas. Like Hamas, it portrays the Israeli-Palestinian conflict as a religious clash, not merely a territorial dispute. Therefore, it claims that eradicating Israel and establishing an Islamic state constitutes an Islamic religious obligation. To achieve this goal, the PIJ argues that only through military struggle can Muslims achieve their liberation. The PIJ has gained a reputation for using suicide bombers, beginning in the early 1990s, and since 2003 has recruited a number of women for these attacks. Unlike Hamas, the PIJ does not participate in the political process. Until recently, it did not provide social services, but it now operates some elementary schools and offers alternative dispute resolution. After some initial conflict with Hamas over the PIJ's promoting of Iranian ideology, its military arm called the Al Quds Brigades cooperates with Hamas, with the Fatah Movement's Tanzim faction, and with the al-Aqsa Martyrs Brigades in conducting terror attacks. The PIJ maintains relations with Egypt and has tried to mend relations between Hamas and Syria. The PIJ claims an elite image as a relatively smaller group that appeals to more educated recruits. When it conducts terror attacks in Israel without coordinating with Hamas, it provokes reprisals that cause political difficulties that Hamas may wish to avoid.

Sean Nicholus Blas

See also: Egypt, Arab Republic of; Fatah Party; Hamas; Iran, Islamic Republic of; Islamism; Israel; Muslim Brotherhood; Palestine; Syrian Arab Republic

Further Reading

Moghadam, Assaf. "Palestinian Suicide Terrorism in the Second Intifada: Motivations and Organizational Aspects." *Studies in Conflict & Terrorism* 26, no. 2 (March 2003): 65–92.

Strindlberg, Anders. "The Damascus-Based Alliance of Palestinian Forces: A Primer." *Journal of Palestinian Studies* 29, no. 3 (Spring 2000): 60–76.

Party of Authenticity and Modernity

An anti-Islamist Moroccan political party founded in 2008 by Fouad Ali El Himma, a close associate of Morocco's King Mohammed VI, which rapidly became one of the largest parties in Morocco's parliament. In August 2007, El Himma resigned from his role as deputy minister of Interior and ran for a seat in the legislature. Following his election, El Himma created two groups in early 2008, a parliamentary group named Authenticity and Modernity, and the Movement for All Democrats, which attempted to increase voter turnout and mobilize politically inactive elites. These two groups served as the foundation for the Party of Authenticity and Modernity, which registered in August 2008. The party seeks to promote modernization in Morocco's political system and economy. It opposes Islamist parties such as the Justice and Development Party, advocating instead a clear separation between Islam and politics. Opponents call it a monarchist party and have accused the government-controlled press of favoring it. After the 2016 elections, the Party of Authenticity and Modernity became the second largest party in the Moroccan parliament.

Andrew Harrison Baker

See also: Authoritarianism; Clientelism (Patrimonialism); Corruption; Democracy Deficit; Development; Islamism; Modernization; Morocco, Kingdom of

Further Reading

Boukhars, Anouar. *Politics in Morocco: Executive Monarchy and Enlightened Authoritarianism.* London: Routledge, 2010.

Eibl, Ferdinand. "The Party of Authenticity and Modernity (PAM): Trajectory of a Political *deus ex machina*." *The Journal of North African Studies* 17 (2012): 45–66.

Patriotic Union of Kurdistan (PUK)

A Kurdish political party in Iraq that exercises de facto control over the Kirkuk, Erbil, Dohuk, and Sulaymaniyah area, established in 1975 after the Iraqi government crushed the 1973–1975 uprising by Mulla Mustafa Barzani. In 1975, a coalition of leftist intellectuals and academics with core support in the Sulaymaniyah region among the Sorani-speaking Kurds broke away to create the Patriotic Union of Kurdistan (PUK), in protest over the Barzani tribe's dominance over the Kurdistan Democratic Party (KDP). Jalal Talebani emerged as the top PUK leader, and the party gained good relations with Iran. After the PUK returned to Iraq, the two parties worked together during the Iran-Iraq war in resisting the 1987–1988 Iraqi genocide campaign.

After the international coalition forced the Iraqi Army to withdraw from Kuwait in 1991, the Kurds rebelled, in hope of achieving their own state. The ferocious Iraqi government response forced two million Kurds to flee to the mountains of Iran and the Turkish border. The United States, Britain, and France established a no-fly zone in the north to stop another massive slaughter. In May 1992, both parties formed a parliament to govern the region. However, from 1994 to 1998 the KDP and the PUK fought a civil war over land and customs revenue in which 4,000 people died. Fearing Iran's support of the PUK, the leader of the KDP, Masoud Barzani, asked Saddam Hussein to intervene militarily. In August 1996, the Iraqi Army crushed the PUK and expelled the party from Erbil. In 1996–1997 both parties expelled tens of thousands of supporters of the other party from the territory that they controlled. In 1998, a U.S.-mediated agreement led to a formal peace treaty between the KDP and the PUK.

In 2005 and 2009 the two parties ran as a united party in the Iraqi parliamentary elections. In 2009, a new party called Gorran (Change) split from the PUK, complaining against nepotism, corruption, and clientelism in both the KDP and the PUK. This pushed the PUK to third place in the subsequent Kurdistan Regional Government elections. However, Gorran remains less powerful than the other two parties because it controls neither its own military forces nor patronage networks.

The Kurdish parties ultimately seek a federal government as a final goal; but through this goal, the Patriotic Union of Kurdistan has focused particularly on equality, human rights, self-government, and political autonomy. The PUK sought control over its own militia and parliament, asserted that the oil-rich Kirkuk area (over which they already exercise considerable informal control) should be formally incorporated into the Kurdish zone, and insisted that the "Arabization" policies of the former Ba'athist regime should be reversed. When the PUK Peshmerga, supported by the Kurdistan Workers' Party (PKK), seized Kirkuk, the Turcoman minority in the province protested strongly. The Turkish government warned that they would intervene to prevent the "Kurdification" of the city. Both the PUK and KDP have powerful militias (the Peshmerga) and intelligence functions (the Zanyari and Parastin, respectively).

Jonathan K. Zartman

See also: Arab Nationalism; Ba'athism; Barzani, Masoud; Clientelism (Patrimonialism); Corruption; Iraq, Republic of; Islamic State (Daesh); Kurdistan Regional Government (KRG); Kurds; Turkey, Republic of

Further Reading

"Arming Iraq's Kurds: Fighting IS, Inviting Conflict." *Middle East Report* No. 158. Brussels, Belgium: International Crisis Group, May 12, 2015.

Gunter, Michael M. "The KDP-PUK Conflict in Northern Iraq." *Middle East Journal* 50, no. 2 (Spring 1996): 224–41.

Jude, Johannes, "Contesting Borders? The Formation of Iraqi Kurdistan's de facto State." *International Affairs* 93, no. 4 (2017): 847–63.

Pearl Roundabout Protests

A series of sit-in protests that began on February 14, 2011, on the Pearl Roundabout, a former central monument in Manama, Kingdom of Bahrain. Following the success of the Tunisian revolution, some young Bahraini activists organized a movement they called the February 14 Youth Coalition, using social media, and sought to peacefully occupy a centrally located landmark. In January 2011, they established the Facebook page "February 14th Revolution in Bahrain," calling for mass protests throughout Bahrain. This date marked the 10th anniversary of the referendum on the National Action Charter. The activists remained anonymous but posted several demands for reforms of the political system, release of political prisoners, guarantee of freedom of speech, and evaluation of the politically motivated naturalization of foreigners. Then other youth groups joined, to form the Coalition Youth of 14 Feb Revolution.

On February 15, after protests had begun throughout the country, tens of thousands of Sunnis and Shi'as, including families with children, occupied the Pearl Roundabout where they remained in tents. The initial organization of the protest worked hard to appeal across the Shi'a-Sunni divide. Despite the protesters' commitment to peace, conflicts with security forces resulted in the deaths of two people in disputed circumstances. The authorities adopted uncompromising antagonism to the protests. On February 17, security forces removed families camped there and their makeshift tents. They shot several protesters at close range who attempted to reoccupy the roundabout. The crowd tried to retaliate, and this resulted in deaths among policemen. Security forces prevented wounded protesters from getting medical treatment. They arrested large number of medical personnel for treating the wounded. The opposition named the events of February 17 "Bloody Thursday." Ultimately, the government employed sectarian appeals and accusations, which combined with the violence drove the Sunnis from the protests.

Security forces allowed protesters to return to the Pearl Roundabout on February 19. The established opposition political societies responded to the movement later than the youth. On February 20, seven opposition political societies issued a joint statement calling for progressive political reforms. On February 21 and again on March 2, 2011, the government organized an estimated 120,000 pro-government Sunnis, including the Muslim Brotherhood, the Salafis, and both urban and tribal Sunnis, to demonstrate their support for the government. In response, on February 25, an estimated 200,000 people marched to demand democracy. However, violent attacks by the security forces, and lack of political gains by the protesters, gave credibility to radical political associations. On March 7, 2011, three previously outlawed societies formed a coalition seeking to topple the monarchy and establish a republic.

The government claims that it released political prisoners and withdrew troops from the streets, and on March 12, 2011, Crown Prince Salman offered negotiations on the important issues, but the opposition refused to negotiate without much greater concessions. Violence by the opposition escalated on March 13 and 14. On March 14, Gulf Cooperation Council troops entered to support the government. On March 15, the government declared a state of emergency, and security forces immediately began to clear protesters from the Pearl Roundabout. On March 18, 2011, the government demolished the Pearl Monument. The protests, and the government suppression, did not lead to any political liberalization, but rather the government has increased its security operations and restricted social freedoms. Sporadic protests continued in suburban areas. The political opposition in general has become ineffective, due to divisions and the growth of competing radical and militant groups.

Magdalena Karolak

See also: Bahrain, Kingdom of; Gulf Cooperation Council (GCC); National Action Charter; Rajab, Nabeel; Shi'a; Social Media

Further Reading

Neumann, Ronald E. "Bahrain: A Very Complicated Little Island." *Middle East Policy* 20, no. 4 (Winter 2013): 45–58.

Ulrichsen, Kristen Coates. "Bahrain's Uprising: Regional Dimensions and International Consequences." *Stability: International Journal of Security and Development* 2, no.1 (May 2013): 1–12.

Zunes, Stephen. "Bahrain's Arrested Revolution." *Arab Studies Quarterly* 35, no. 2 (Spring 2013): 149–64.

Political Decision-Making in Iran

The process by which leaders in Iran make decisions that can affect the security of the leadership, the governing ideology, the territory, and the people of Iran. This process reflects the operation of informal networks of allegiance, as well as the bureaucratic apparatus of the state—the institutions created and defined by the constitution. In 1906, the people of Iran created one of the first constitutions and parliaments in the Middle East, and on this foundation an educated, liberal strata of the population opposed the shah and contributed to the revolution. The followers of the Ayatollah Khomeini did not all agree that Iran should be a dictatorship by one religious teacher. Therefore, leaders of the Islamic revolution created a constitutional system that combined strong centralized authority with some aspects of a representative republic.

This design seeks to restrain any change in the system or in the ideology of its origination. However, over time, two contending approaches have evolved. The principlists, or hardline conservatives, strongly resist any greater popular representation, or pluralism. They defend socially conservative morality and a more aggressive foreign policy. In contrast, reformists argue that the security of the state requires improving economic conditions, which in turn requires more social freedom and a less antagonistic international posture.

To insulate the state from any future weakening of the ideology of Khomeini, the constitution relies on an Assembly of Experts for Leadership, a body of experts in the interpretation of Shi'a religious law—jurists—to designate and dismiss the leader of Iran. Its members must have social insight and moral purity in addition to high reputations as religious legal scholars. The 88 members of the Assembly of Experts, who serve eight-year terms, hold some power but rarely meet to exercise that power. The history of the assembly shows two significant decisions: In 1985, the Assembly of Experts chose Ayatollah Montazeri to succeed Ayatollah Khomeini as the leader, but Khomeini removed him from consideration a year later. Second, the Assembly chose Ali Khamenei to succeed Ayatollah Khomeini after he died in June 1989. The principlists disagree with the reformists on whether the Assembly of Experts has the right to supervise the leader and continually confirm that he meets the qualifications.

Although the people elect these men, they can select only from among candidates approved in advance by the Guardian Council of the Constitution, consisting of 12 legal scholars. The Supreme Leader appoints six of these men, and the head of the judiciary appoints the other six, with approval of the popularly elected Parliament. In other words, the power to appoint flows in a circle among the Shi'a legal scholars. The Guardian Council has the responsibility to interpret the Constitution, supervise elections, approve candidates for the Assembly of Experts, the presidency, and the Parliament, and ensure the compatibility of legislation with Islam and the Constitution. The Iranian principlists and reformists disagree on how to recognize the qualifications of candidates. Iran still has an elected Parliament, but the Guardian Council severely restricts who can run for election. In spite of this control, the overall political orientation of the Parliament has shifted from conservative to reform and back twice.

During the presidency of Mohammad Khatami, the conflict between the reformist-dominated Parliament and the conservative Guardian Council became quite severe. Rather than intervene personally and bear the consequences of favoring one side or the other, Ayatollah Khamenei created a new group he called "the council for discerning the expediency of the system," commonly called the Expediency Council. He appointed men to resolve conflicts between the Parliament and the Guardian Council and to provide him with advice. He chooses its members every five years. This council can even ignore the *sharia* law, if required for reasons of expediency, to protect the country or its political system.

This complex system of institutions, under the supervision of the Supreme Leader, performs the legislative, executive, and judicial functions of government. In this system, voting occurs frequently, and voters do determine the membership of the Assembly of Experts, giving it the appearance of democratic procedures to preserve an essentially autocratic system. Since the system was designed for stability, to resist reform, advocates of pluralism and popular representation will face continued difficulties.

Sayed Hassan Akhlaq Hussaini

See also: Iran, Islamic Republic of; Khamenei, Ayatollah Sayyid Ali; Khatami, Mohammad; Khomeini, Ayatollah Sayyid Ruhollah Mūsavi

Further Reading

Alamdari, Kazem. "The Power Structure of the Islamic Republic of Iran: Transition from Populism to Clientelism, and Militarization of the Government." *Third World Quarterly* 26, no. 8 (2005): 1,285–301.

Brumberg, Daniel, and Farideh Farhi. *Power and Change in Iran: Politics of Contention and Conciliation.* Bloomington: Indiana University Press, 2016.

Goodman, Adam. "Iran: Informal Networks and Leadership Politics." *Middle East Series* 08/12. Shrivenham, England: Defence Academy of the United Kingdom, April 2008.

Popular Mobilization Forces (PMF)

A large set of relatively independent Iraqi militias brought into a state-supported status by Prime Minister Nouri al-Maliki, in response to the 2014 collapse of the Iraqi Army and the conquests of the Islamic State (Daesh). On June 10, 2014, the

240 Popular Mobilization Forces (PMF)

Islamic State captured Mosul, prompting al-Maliki to issue an emergency declaration creating the Al-Hashd al-Shaabi (Popular Mobilization Forces; PMF). On June 13, 2014, the Grand Ayatollah Ali al-Sistani, the most highly respected Iraqi Shi'a leader, issued a religious legal ruling encouraging Shi'as to enroll in the Iraqi security forces to defend their country from the advancing forces of the Islamic State. The leaders of many independent militias mobilized their supporters to form combat units. Tens of thousands joined these militias, instead of the Iraqi Army, due to its reputation for severe corruption and lack of capability.

After the 2003 U.S.-led invasion, Iran activated its existing network of Iraqi militias, called the Islamic Resistance, that it had developed in the 1980s to conduct guerilla warfare against Saddam Hussein. More militias formed to resist the international coalition, such as the Mahdi Army (Jaish al-Mahdi; JAM), led by Muqtada al-Sadr. By the time al-Maliki took office and overcame doctrinal resistance to informal militias, he could call on seven different groups, which he used not only for defense but also against his political enemies. By 2014, approximately 20 core militias already existed. Five of these protected important Shi'a shrines. The largest forces, Kata'ib Hezbollah and Asa'ib Ahl al-Haq, operated as Iranian proxies during the coalition occupation of Iraq. The commander of the most powerful force, the Badr Organization, fought on the side of Iran during the Iran-Iraq War.

On November 26, 2016, the Iraqi Parliament passed legislation incorporating the PMF into Iraq's security forces, subject to military law, with equal status to the army, but remaining apolitical, nonsectarian, and separate from nongovernmental militias. Analysts report that by 2014 an estimated 67 militias had joined the PMF, of which 40 received some degree of funding, equipment, and training from Iran through the Quds Force. Based on the payroll records, the government estimates approximately 110,000 fighters in these groups. They include a diverse array of forces: the Babylon Brigades, a Christian militia; Sinjar Resistance Units (Yazidis); Liwa al-Shabak (Shabak); the Nineveh Guards, the Salaheddin Brigade, and the Tribal Mobilization Forces (Sunni militias); and the Peshmerga Kurdish militias.

The largest Shi'a groups consist of four major political orientations. Some give their loyalty to the Ayatollah Sistani, and some to the officials at Shi'a shrines. Both of these categories of militias reject the ideology of Iran and its control. After meeting the emergency needs caused by the Islamic State conquests, they want to either disband or join the regular Iraqi Army and police. A third group supports Muqtada al-Sadr in pursuing an independent, nationalist, Shi'a path. Militias in the fourth group openly give allegiance to Iranian leaders, who even sent some of these militias to Syria after 2011, to defend Shi'a shrines and fight against Sunni opposition groups.

According to law, the PMF commanders report to the Iraqi prime minister, as commander in chief, through the Hashd Commission, of which the deputy chairman, Jamal Jaafar Mohammed, also known as Abu Mahdi al-Mohandis, serves as the operational commander. However, in practice al-Mohandis serves alongside Qassem Soleimani, the head of the Quds Force, the section of Iran's Revolutionary Guards Corps that operates internationally. The two men have worked collaboratively for

Popular Mobilization Forces (PMF)

20 years, along with the other commanders of the oldest Iraqi militias. Militia leaders have become deeply embedded in the bureaucracy of the Iraqi government, especially the Ministry of the Interior. However, some of the militias boast that they do not always obey the government. Furthermore, the credible reports that Shi'a militias have committed repeated, gross human rights abuses against Sunni populations serves as a point of caution. It also highlights the problems that the government faces with large armed forces that it does not completely control.

Politically, the militias aligned with Iran have begun following the Hezbollah pattern of developing extensive social services and community outreach as a foundation for political influence. In general, the Shi'a community regards their own militias very favorably, as uncorrupt, heroic volunteers. Twenty PMF militias joined the Fatah Alliance election list to compete in the 2018 parliamentary elections; this alliance came in second, winning 47 seats in Parliament, after Muqtada al-Sadr's Sairoon Alliance. After the Iraqi government officially announced victory over the Islamic State on December 9, 2017, outside parties advised the Iraqi government to begin a process of demobilization and reintegration of the militias, followed by reconciliation programs and judicial mechanisms. Such a process will expose the conflict between the nationalist militias and those with a long-term vision of advancing the interests of Iran.

Jonathan K. Zartman

See also: Al-Maliki, Nouri; Al-Sadr, Muqtada; Corruption; Hezbollah; Iran, Islamic Republic of; Iraq, Republic of; Islamic Revolutionary Guard Corps (IRGC); Islamic State (Daesh); Quds Force; Shi'a

Further Reading

Harari, Michal. "Status Update: Shi'a Militias in Iraq." In *Backgrounder*. Institute for the Study of War, August 16, 2010.

Heras, Nicholas A. "Iraq's Fifth Column: Iran's Proxy Network." *Policy Paper* 2017-02. Washington, DC: Middle East Institute, October 2017.

Mansour, Renad, and Faleh A. Jabar. "The Popular Mobilization Forces and Iraq's Future." Beirut, Lebanon: Carnegie Middle East Center, April 2017.

Qaboos bin Said bin Taimur Al Said

The sultan of Oman, born in the port city of Salalah in Dhofar, southwestern Oman, on November 18, 1940, as the only son and heir to a dynasty ruling Oman since 1744. His father had pursued a policy of isolation, seeking to avoid international debt, but sent Qaboos to study in England at the Royal Military Academy Sandhurst. He joined the British Army after graduation. His father called him home in 1965. In 1970, he removed his father from office in a bloodless coup and sent his father into exile. At the time, the ruling elite in the coastal cities did not have authority over the inner desert areas, and Marxist rebels had hijacked a separatist rebellion in the southern Dhofar region, next to Yemen. Qaboos used a very effective policy of promoting development, providing security, and entering negotiations combined with an amnesty program to resolve the rebellion. Similarly, through consultation and dialogue, he gained control of the desert regions, the historical center of the Ibadi Imamate.

Sultan Qaboos began a reform and modernization program that has dramatically increased the level of education, improved health care, and developed infrastructure. He has also effectively promoted protection of the environment. He has engaged in careful, gradual efforts to promote political reform, introducing first a cabinet of ministers, and then a Majlis al-Shura that gives the government advice but does not legislate. He has pursued a policy of international engagement with an understated tone. More importantly, he has kept good relations with Iran and mediated conflicts without seeking publicity. In 1985, he established a symphony orchestra. He has promoted greater gender equality through education for girls and has appointed women to ministerial positions and other high government offices.

Sultan Qaboos has no children, and his advancing age raises questions about who will follow him as the ruler of Oman. The government has kept plans for his succession secret, believing that advance knowledge of the next ruler's identity would trigger palace intrigues, meddling and pressure by regional powers, and even conflict among Omani tribes. The people of Oman celebrate the sultan's birthday, November 18, as their National Day, and July 23, the day he came to reign in 1970, as Renaissance Day.

Autumn Cockrell-Abdullah

See also: Development; Ibadi Doctrine; Iran, Islamic Republic of; Oman, Sultanate of; Oman Protests; Yemen, Republic of

Further Reading

Cafiero, Giorgia, and Theodore Karasik. "Can Oman's Stability Outlive Sultan Qaboos?" *MEI Policy Focus 2016-10.* Middle East Institute, April 2016.

Kéchichian, Joseph A. "A Vision of Oman: State of the Sultanate Speeches by Qaboos bin Said, 1970–2006." *Middle East Policy* 15, no. 4 (Winter 2008): 112–33.
Plekhanov, Sergey. *A Reformer on the Throne: Sultan Qaboos bin Said Al Said.* London: Trident Press, 2004.

Qaddafi, Muammar

A Libyan military officer and long-serving ruler, who developed a distinctive, Arab socialist, absolute dictatorship in the name of the masses. Muammar Mohammed Abu Minyar Qaddafi, born on June 7, 1942, into a tribal family, joined the military at an early age and prospered in that environment. On September 1, 1969, he led the Libyan Free Officers in a military coup against King Idris I. After the coup, Qaddafi consolidated his power by purging the Libyan government of Idris loyalists. He nationalized large numbers of residential properties and businesses for redistribution to peasants, who displaced the country's business class. He also nationalized the oil industry and used the country's vast oil resources to implement social reforms such as improving health care and education and granting women equality. However, throughout the 1970s, he also supported many foreign militant organizations, including the Palestine Liberation Organization. He gained popularity in the Arab world for his support for Palestine and antagonism to the West. Throughout the 1980s, the United States confronted Libya in a series of incidents that culminated in the April 15, 1986, airstrikes on Libyan political and military targets.

Qaddafi became known for his eccentric and arrogant diplomatic behavior and for his three-volume statement of political philosophy mixing Islam, revolutionary socialism, and glorification of Bedouin culture. Islamist militants tried to rebel, but his oppressive security state with multiple aggressive intelligence agencies thwarted their efforts. After the U.S.-led invasion of Iraq in 2003, Qaddafi renounced his weapons of mass destruction. His failed economic and social policies, and his humiliating abuse of the Libyan people, provoked an uprising in February 2011, as part of the regional mass-protest movements. This resulted in Qaddafi's downfall and death on October 20, 2011. Because he did not allow any civil society organizations, political parties, or even government bureaucratic institutions to develop, Libya has faced great difficulties in building a new state. Because he used politicized tribal connections as channels for patronage distribution and as targets of exclusion, the post-Qaddafi Libya suffers from the continuing competition of tribal-based militias.

Alexander Shelby

See also: Arab Nationalism; Authoritarianism; Battle of Sirte in 2011; February 17th Revolution; Islamism; Libya, State of; Military Coups; Palestine Liberation Organization

Further Reading
Emadi, Hafizullah. "Libya: The Road to Regime Change." *Global Dialogue* 14, no. 2 (Summer/Autumn 2012): 128–42.
Pargeter, Alison. *Libya: The Rise and Fall of Qaddafi.* New Haven, CT: Yale University Press, 2012.

Qatar

A constitutional monarchy, located on a small peninsula protruding into the Gulf, between Bahrain and the United Arab Emirates, ruled since its inception by the Al Thani family. On September 3, 1971, Qatar gained its independence from protectorate status as a consequence of the general British withdrawal from the region. As a small country surrounded by bigger neighbors, Qatar has sought to balance positive relations with the majority of regional actors to achieve some degree of autonomy. Based on its control over the world's third largest natural gas resources and as the second largest gas exporter in the world, Qatar is the fifth largest economy in the Arab world. This wealth has given Qatari citizens a high income and enabled the country to conduct a vigorous foreign policy. The Qatari government has developed Doha, the capital, into a significant global financial center.

The current leader, the emir of Qatar, Sheikh Tamim, took power on June 25, 2013, after his father, Hamad, abdicated the throne. Under Hamad's reign, Qatar mastered the art of converting gas into clean-burning gas-to-liquid fuels (GTL) and became the leading exporter, expanding its market to all of Asia and Europe. By selling large volumes of GTL to the United Kingdom, China, India, and Japan, Doha made itself indispensable to the global economy. This created an economic boom enabling Hamad to make social reforms, as well as unprecedented economic investments in infrastructure. In 1996, the state-owned news network, Al Jazeera, began broadcasting in English and soon became one of the most influential media outlets in the Arab world. In 1997, Qatar launched its own airline to stimulate innovation in the global air-travel market.

Emir Hamad worked to promote his vision of Qatar as a moderate, internationally connected, and developed country. To attract foreign investments and the international spotlight, particularly during the first decade of 2000, Qatar began to build a brand as a business-orientated, modern country. It increased its investments in the West, particularly in the United States, and established satellite campuses of American universities in Doha, such as Georgetown University and Carnegie Mellon University. Qatar donated millions of dollars to the victims of Hurricane Katrina in the United States. To foster investments in areas beyond the energy sector, Hamid founded the Qatar Investment Authority in 2005, which holds investments in the United Kingdom, Germany, France, and beyond. For example, it became famous for buying the Paris Saint-Germain football team in 2012. The government has been creating the necessary infrastructure for hosting the FIFA World Cup in 2022.

Emir Hamid used his personal connections to engage in a growing, proactive foreign policy, raising his country's regional and international profile. He aimed to project a diplomatic image as a mediator for the greater Middle East, such as his efforts in the Darfur conflict in 2008 and in Lebanon in 2009, to promote regional stability and avoid escalation of domestic struggles. Between 2005 and 2010, Qatar attempted to mediate internal disputes in Yemen, Lebanon, Sudan, and Gaza. However, these efforts yielded only short-term agreements, later broken, or lacking sufficiently robust implementation. This interest in mediation relied on

Qatar's financial resources and its reputation as a neutral actor. Throughout several decades, the country managed to establish a multidirectional, balanced foreign policy: it pursued good relations with regional actors in conflict, such as Israel and Hamas, or Iran and Saudi Arabia.

Beyond the desire to gain a higher status, Qatar seeks to maintain its security and regional stability. In 1971, when the United Kingdom decided to withdraw the protection it had extended to the smaller monarchies in the Gulf since 1912, Qatar become vulnerable to its larger and more powerful neighbors. Qatar had to manage the consequences of Saddam Hussain's ambitions toward Kuwait, the Iranian shah's desire to dominate Bahrain and his seizure of the Gulf islands of Abu Musa and the Tunbs, and several disagreements with Saudi Arabia about border delimitation. Therefore, Qatari foreign policy seeks international recognition to protect itself from the hazards of vulnerability. During the first decade after the British pullout, Qatar remained under Saudi protection, relying on its security guarantees toward other regional threats.

The 1979 Iranian Revolution created a government opposed to all monarchies, which sought to export its revolutionary ideology to other Muslim countries. On September 22, 1980, Iraq invaded Iran, starting the long Iran-Iraq War. In May 1981, the Gulf monarchies founded the Gulf Cooperation Council (GCC), as a clearly defensive reaction. The organization aimed for greater cooperation in all possible fields; however, it lacked effective collective decision-making institutions. Furthermore, the far greater economic capability and geographic size of Saudi Arabia made the other GCC countries fearful that, although they depended on Saudi protection, they also feared that Riyadh could abuse its authority in the organization.

Having very small armed forces of its own, Qatar must depend on foreign partners. In 1990, when Saddam Hussain invaded Kuwait, the United States and its allies responded quickly, in August 1990, by starting Operation Desert Storm to halt Iraq's expansion. Qatar promptly helped this effort and later, in June 1992, signed a defense cooperation agreement, initiating close military coordination with the United States that endures until today. In 2003, the American Combat Air Operations Center moved from Saudi Arabia to the Qatari Al Udeid airbase, southwest of Doha. The nearby camp, As Sayliyah, hosts prepositioned U.S. military equipment and command facilities. American and allied forces use Al Udeid and other facilities in Qatar as basing hubs for regional operations.

Furthermore, the United States also supports Qatari military modernization, through arms sales, joint training, cooperative defense exercises, and military-construction activities. Americans and Qataris also cooperate in counterterrorism efforts in the region, especially after the *9/11 Commission Report* reported that private Qatari citizens and individuals based in Qatar had provided support to many terrorist cells, including al-Qaeda. Since then, both governments have worked together in controlling and monitoring the bank transfers of individuals and charitable institutions. However, Qatar's open-doors policy creates some international relations ambiguity, which can draw American criticism. In December 2013, the U.S. Secretary of Defense, Chuck Hagel, visited the new Emir Tamim, and they signed a renewed, 10-year defense-cooperation agreement.

The fast economic changes at the beginning of Hamad's reign attracted a great number of labor migrants. Today, they constitute more than 90 percent of Qatar's workforce and around 70 percent of the population. The non-Qataris, the majority from South Asia and India, work at low-paying jobs, mainly for contractors, often in poor and insecure working conditions, without any welfare entitlements. Migrants cannot work without a sponsor, typically their employer, who can withdraw this sponsorship at any time, forcing their deportation. These conditions have received significant international criticism, especially after a new massive wave of migrants came to construct the projects necessary for the 2022 World Cup. For example, a 2017 Amnesty International report denounced the human rights abuses against hundreds of migrant workers and urged supporters to pressure Qatar and FIFA to change the labor law.

Furthermore, the drop in the oil price since 2014 has led Qatar—like other oil-producing countries—to seek to diversify its economy and modernize its private sector, to cautiously reduce the population's dependence on state welfare funded by gas exports. Qatar has embarked on a series of national development strategies as part of a comprehensive national project called Vision 2030. While presently the overwhelming majority of Qataris work in the public sector, this plan seeks to encourage Qataris to enter the private sector. Vision 2030 promises to increase the employment of nationals, especially in the private sector, and to restrict the recruitment of migrant workers. In sum, Qatar faces significant challenges in labor, national infrastructure, economy, and social cohesion due to the previous rapid pace of economic development.

In addition, Qatar must deal with international challenges due to Emir Hamad's decision to engage in the so-called Arab Spring and support protesters in Libya, Egypt, Syria, and Tunisia. This destroyed Qatar's previous reputation for a neutral foreign policy. In contrast to the other Gulf monarchies in the GCC, Doha did not feel threatened by the wave of protests but supported many Islamist actors, directly with funding or indirectly with favorable media coverage by Al-Jazeera. By openly supporting the Muslim Brotherhood after 2011, Qatar damaged its traditional relations with Saudi Arabia and the United Arab Emirates. Both Emiratis and Saudis developed great antagonism toward the Brothers, calling them a source of regional instability. As the Muslim Brotherhood began to make political gains in Tunisia and Egypt in 2012, Dubai and Riyadh toughened their position and became more public about their dissatisfaction with Doha.

When Tamim ascended to the throne, he tried to reduce the enmity of his neighbors and recalibrate Qatar's foreign policy. For example, after Muslim Brotherhood president Morsi lost power in Egypt in 2013, Qatar supported this change, together with the Saudis and Emiratis. But other GCC countries kept expressing their disapproval of Qatar's international behavior. Growing scepticism toward the Qatari motivations led to small disagreements in 2013 and 2014. In 2014, reports leaked by a hack on the Qatar News Agency (QNA) website alleged that the emir had expressed support to Iran and Hamas. This created the biggest crisis in the history of the GCC.

In June 2017, Saudi Arabia, the Emirates, Egypt, Bahrain, and Mauritania cut ties with Qatar, accusing it of supporting terrorism and criticizing its close relations with Iran. Their air, sea, and land blockade forced Qatar into closer reliance on Iran and brought signifiant support from Turkey. The blockading countries, led by Riyadh, presented a list of 13 demands, including closing Al Jazeera, paying reparations, closing the Turkish military base, and cutting ties with Iran. Qatar has no choice in keeping good relations with Iran since they share a vast gas field in their bordering territorial waters. In response to the regional sanctions, Turkey has sent troops to protect Qatar from any neighboring attacks, and Iran has been providing aid and diplomatic support. This rift has imposed high financial and diplomatic costs on all the parties.

As one of the biggest economies in the region, and especially as the sponsor of Al Jazeera, Qatar draws a lot of attention and has long been considered a very successful small country. Now observers claim that its assertive foreign policy exceeded its diplomatic and military capacity. Since it has abandoned its neutral, open-door diplomacy, it faces some larger strategic descisions for its future.

Luíza Gimenez Cerioli

See also: Al Jazeera; Bahrain, Kingdom of; Gulf Cooperation Council (GCC); Iran, Islamic Republic of; Iraq, Republic of; Kuwait, State of; Labor Migration: Receiving Countries; Muslim Brotherhood; Saudi Arabia, Kingdom of; United Arab Emirates (UAE)

Further Reading

Barakat, Sultan. "Qatari Mediation: Between Ambition and Achievement." Analysis Paper No. 12. Doha: Brookings Doha Center, 2014.

Bel-Air, Françoise de. "Demography, Migration, and Labour Market in Qatar." *Gulf Labour Markets and Migration Note* 3 (February 2018).

Blanchard, Christopher. "Qatar: Background and U.S. Relations." RL31718. Washington, DC: Congressional Research Service, 2014.

Khatib, Lina. "Qatar's Foreign Policy: Limits of Pragmatism." *International Affairs* 89, no. 2 (2013): 417–31.

Robert, David. "Understanding Qatar's Foreign Policy Objectives." *Mediterranean Politics* 17, no. 2 (2012): 233–89.

Ulrichsen, Kristian Coates. "Implications of the Qatar Crisis for Regional Security in the Gulf." *Al Sharq Forum* (2017): 1–8.

Quds Force

A paramilitary organization under the Intelligence Directorate of the Islamic Revolutionary Guard Corps (IRGC), with an estimated strength of 15,000 men. Former president Ali Akbar Hashemi Rafsanjani formed the Quds (also spelled Qods), meaning "Jerusalem" Force, during the Iran-Iraq War (1980–1988) to conduct extraterritorial covert operations and external intelligence efforts and to strengthen Iran's influence abroad. In addition to direct action, it also provides financial support, arms, and training to foreign groups. Under the command of Major General Qasem Soleimani, it has greatly expanded its technological sophistication and geographic range of activity. The IRGC has organized the force according to geographical areas of responsibility. It operates from Iranian diplomatic missions, charities, and religious and cultural institutions. The U.S. Treasury Department designated the Quds Force a supporter of terrorism in 2007.

Quds Force commanders helped train and organize militant Lebanese Shiites in Lebanon to form Hezbollah during Israel's 1982–1985 occupation of Lebanon. Hezbollah trains with the Quds Force and coordinates its military activities with them in Syria and elsewhere. In Iraq, the Quds Force trained and assisted the Mahdi Army, a Shi'ite militia group led by Muqtada al-Sadr. In the summer of 2003, it waged war in Iraq against Sunnis and U.S. and Iraqi forces. It has assisted the Taliban in Afghanistan and supported Hamas in the Gaza Strip. Militant groups come to Iran for training by the IRGC, and then the Quds Force provides financial aid, missiles, explosives, and weapons.

Since the rise of the Islamic State (Daesh) in Iraq in July 2014, the Quds Force has funneled massive military and financial support to Shi'a, Iraqi state, and Kurdish forces and has moved thousands of IRGC and Basij troops into the country. Quds Force fighters have coordinated operations, collected intelligence, and fought alongside Iraqi forces. The Quds Force has provided leadership and support for a number of Iraqi Shi'a militias and parties with a long history of cooperation from the decades before the U.S. invasion. Operating through Shi'a militias of the Popular Mobilization Forces (PMF), Iran has gained considerable influence over the Iraqi government.

In Syria, the Quds Force provided military and financial aid and trained thousands of pro-Assad militiamen. It concentrates on training proxy Shi'ite militias from neighboring countries in Iran, then sending them to Syria under the pretext that they will defend Shi'ite religious shrines. The Quds Force has been instrumental in assisting the Houthis in Yemen and Shi'ite groups in Bahrain as part of Iran's propaganda and proxy war with Saudi Arabia.

Mark David Luce

See also: Al-Sadr, Muqtada; Bahrain, Kingdom of; Foreign Fighters; Hamas; Hezbollah; Houthis (Ansar Allah); Iran, Islamic Republic of; Iranian Revolutionary Guard Corps (IRGC); Iraq, Republic of; Islamic State (Daesh); Lebanese Republic; Popular Mobilization Forces (PMF); Rafsanjani, Ali Akbar Hashemi; Sectarianism; Syrian Arab Republic; Yemen, Republic of

Further Reading

O'Hern, Steven. *Iran's Revolutionary Guard: The Threat That Grows While America Sleeps.* Washington, DC: Potomac Books, 2012.

Ostovar, Afshon. *Vanguard of the Imam: Religion, Politics, and Iran's Revolutionary Guards.* New York: Oxford University Press, 2016.

Uskowi, Nader. *Temperature Rising: Iran's Revolutionary Guards and Wars in the Middle East.* Lanham, MD: Rowman and Littlefield Publishers, 2018.

Rabi'a al-Adawiya Massacre

A clearance operation conducted on August 14, 2013, by the Egyptian military, assisting the national police, against supporters of Mohamed Morsi who had staged a six-week protest in the square in front of Rabi'a al-Adawiya Mosque in Nasr City. After the Egyptian military removed Mohamed Morsi as president on July 3, 2013, his supporters conducted major sit-in demonstrations that became large encampments, which severely disrupted the whole neighborhood. In addition, his supporters attacked police and security forces, killing hundreds. Complaints about Muslim Brotherhood activists detaining, torturing, and killing people who disagreed with them, or who complained about the disruption, reached a high level. The government first tried to negotiate, but protesters rejected those offers. Then the government spent several days in warning the protesters that they would be removed. On August 14, 2013, the police moved in to dismantle the barricades and structures installed in the roads. The protesters dispersed fairly quickly from the al-Nahda Square camp in Giza near Cairo University. However, at Rabi'a al-Adawiya Square, some protesters shot at the police, killing seven. The ferocious security force attack eventually led (according to the Ministry of Health) to the deaths of 638 people, of whom 595 were peaceful protesters, with at least 3,994 injured. The Human Rights Watch report claims more than 1,000 people were killed, and violent incidents also occurred in other cities.

News of the massacre at the mosque reportedly triggered retaliatory attacks on churches and police stations by Brotherhood supporters. This massacre marked the fall of the Muslim Brotherhood in Egypt; its leadership has been jailed or fled, and its charity work ended. The group has been banned, and many of its assets seized.

Mark David Luce

See also: Egypt, Arab Republic of; El-Sisi, Abdel Fattah Saeed Hussein Khalil; Morsi, Mohamed; Muslim Brotherhood; Tamarod Movement

Further Reading

"All According to Plan: The Rab'a Massacre and Mass Killings of Protesters in Egypt." New York: Human Rights Watch, 2014.

Chandler, Matthew J. "Civil Resistance Mechanisms and Disrupted Democratization: The Ambiguous Outcomes of Unarmed Insurrections in Egypt, 2011–2015." *Peace & Change* 43, no. 1 (January 2018): 90–116.

The Egyptian Revolution against the Muslim Brotherhood. London: 9 Bedford Row International Practice Group, December 10, 2015.

Rafsanjani, Ali Akbar Hashemi

A student and supporter of Ayatollah Ruhollah Khomeini, who became a high-level Iranian politician, known for his wealth and business orientation. Ali Akbar Hashemi Rafsanjani (1934–2017) was born into an upper-middle-class family of pistachio farmers. When Khomeini was exiled, Rafsanjani informed Khomeini about developments within Iran and delivered Khomeini's letters and sermons. Khomeini appointed Rafsanjani to the Council of the Islamic Revolution, and Rafsanjani cofounded the Islamic Republican Party. He also played a role in shaping the Islamic Republic's constitution. From 1980 to 1989, he was speaker of the Majles (Parliament). Khomeini appointed Rafsanjani to the interim presidential council, head of the Supreme Defense Council, and deputy commander in chief of the armed forces.

Throughout his political career, Rafsanjani sought a less confrontational relationship with the West (including the United States). In 1985, Rafsanjani persuaded the Lebanese Shi'a militias to peacefully end their hijacking of an airliner and release American and other Western hostages. In 1986, he influenced Lebanese Hezbollah militants to release Western hostages in order to acquire much-needed spare parts for American-made weapons. In 1988, he persuaded Khomeini to accept UN Security Council Resolution 598, ending the Iran-Iraq War.

After the war with Iraq, Rafsanjani spearheaded the economic reconstruction of Iran's devastated cities. When Khomeini died in 1989, Rafsanjani, an influential member of the Assembly of Experts, engineered Khamenei's elevation to Supreme Leader. As president for two four-year terms, Rafsanjani fostered a free market economy, encouraged family planning (by promoting contraceptive use), placed women in prominent positions, improved economic relations with the West, and expanded oil exports, while remaining a paternalistic autocrat. He promoted better relations with the Gulf states, especially Saudi Arabia and Kuwait. State policy elevated technical competence and economic liberalization without any political reforms. He also engaged in privatizations to quasi-state organizations, crony capitalism, and corruption. In the process he became extraordinarily wealthy and gained a reputation as obsessed with power and making deals.

During the two terms of Khatami (1997–2005), Rafsanjani favored the conservatives rather than the reformers. He blocked some of the reform efforts of the Majles. His priority of economic liberalization did not match Khatami's priority of political liberalization. In 2002, Rafsanjani became chair of the Expediency Council, and in 2005 he ran for another presidential term but lost to Mahmoud Ahmadinejad. In the contentious national election of 2009, Rafsanjani enthusiastically supported progressive candidates and criticized President Ahmadinejad. In 2013, when Rafsanjani registered as a presidential candidate, the Guardian Council disqualified him due to media criticism of his corruption. Therefore, he supported Hassan Rouhani, who brought many Rafsanjani protégés into his cabinet.

In sum, due to his close association with Khomeini and his considerable political talents, Rafsanjani held a record number of high-level positions and prevailed in several confrontations against conservative and fundamentalist clerics. Thanks to Rafsanjani's tutelage and support, two of his protégés, Mohammad Khatami and Hassan Rouhani, served as two-term presidents of Iran.

Mir Zohair Husain

See also: Ahmadinejad, Mahmoud; Corruption; Iran, Islamic Republic of; Iraq, Republic of; Khamenei, Ayatollah Sayyid Ali; Khomeini, Ayatollah Sayyid Ruhollah Mūsavi; Khatami, Mohammad; Kuwait, State of; Lebanese Republic; Modernization; Rouhani, Hassan Feridun; Saudi Arabia, Kingdom of

Further Reading

Esfandiari, Haleh, and Shaul Bakhash. "The Long Career of Ali Akbar Hashemi Rafsanjani: From Revolutionary to Establishment Power-Broker." *The Atlantic,* January 8, 2017.

Goodman, Adam. "Iran: Informal Networks and Leadership Politics." *Advanced Research and Assessment Group Middle East Series 08/12.* Shrivenham, England: Defense Academy of the United Kingdom, April 2008.

Koolaee, Elaheh, and Yousef Mazarei. "Modernization and Political Parties: A Case Study of the Hashemi Rafsanjani Administration." *International Studies Journal* 15, no. 1 (Summer 2018): 81–102.

Rajab, Nabeel

A Bahraini human rights activist, winner of the 2011 Ion Ratiu Democracy prize from the Woodrow Wilson Center, and deputy secretary general of International Federation for Human Rights, born into a middle-class family in 1964. Nabeel Ahmed Abdulrasool Rajab earned a bachelor's degree in history at the University of Pune in India, but on his return to Bahrain, he became a building contractor. A series of uprisings in Bahrain between 1994 and 1999, in which liberals, leftists, and Islamists joined to support democratic reforms in Bahrain, activated his passion for human rights. In 2000 he joined with several others to establish the Bahrain Human Rights Society and later served as president of the Bahrain Centre for Human Rights (BCHR). He has worked to improve protections for migrant workers' human rights.

In March 2009, he joined Twitter and posted a profile description in English. However, he tweets in Arabic and has gained over 300,000 followers. His involvement in the Bahraini uprising of 2011 gained him international prominence, especially for his steadfast promotion of nonviolence and equality. He sent messages before February 14 and then during the protests from the Pearl Roundabout. The BCHR carefully avoids sectarian terminology but works to combat racial and religious discrimination.

The Kingdom of Bahrain has accused him of a variety of vague offenses and sentenced him to jail several times. He has suffered severe medical conditions from solitary confinement for long periods in difficult conditions. In February 2018, Bahrain gave him another five years, in spite of mounting international pressure for his release.

Sean Braniff

See also: Bahrain, Kingdom of; Pearl Roundabout Protests; Sectarianism

Further Reading

Kirkpatrick, David D. "Bahrain Activist Gets Five-Year Sentence for 'Insulting' Tweets." *New York Times* 167, no. 57881 (February 22, 2018): A6.

"Opinion No. 13/2018 Concerning Nabeel Ahmed Abdulrasool Rajab (Bahrain)." Opinions adopted by the Working Group on Arbitrary Detention at its 81st session, 17–26 April 2018. Human Rights Council Working Group on Arbitrary Detention, August 13, 2018.

Rally for Culture and Democracy (RCD)

An Algerian political party also called the Rassemblement pour la Culture et la Démocratie (French; RCD), which won nine seats in Algeria's National Popular Assembly (Assemblée Nationale Populaire; APN) in 2017. As a center-left party, the RCD strongly promotes secularism, drawing electoral support from the Kabylie, a region east of Algiers, the homeland of the Imazighen (Berbers). Recent initiatives have included promoting Maghrebi unity and protecting the Sahraouian refugees in the western Algerian province of Tindouf. Some Algerians consider the RCD an ethnic party that does not represent the majority of Arab, Muslim Algerians.

Saïd Sadi, a human rights activist, launched the RCD in 1989 when it split from the Socialist Forces Front (FFS). The RCD ran in the first round of parliamentary elections in 1990–1991, winning almost 3 percent of the votes. Then the military canceled the elections, and the civil war began. The RCD won 4 percent (19 seats) in multiparty elections in 1997 but boycotted in 2002, accusing the regime of manipulation and electoral rigging. It participated in elections in 2007, winning 3 percent of votes nationally for 19 seats. In 2012, its share fell to 1 percent of the vote nationally, yielding nine parliamentary seats. In 2014, the RCD called for a boycott of the presidential elections won by the ailing 77-year-old President Bouteflika. The RCD joined other Islamist and secular opposition parties to call for the fall of the regime, which enjoys support from powerful army factions, business elites, and the dominant political parties.

Lindsay J. Benstead

See also: Algeria, The People's Democratic Republic of; Berbers (Imazighen); Bouteflika, Abdelaziz; Islamic Salvation Front (FIS)

Further Reading

Entelis, John P. "Islamic Democracy vs. the Centralized State." In *Civil Society in the Middle East*, volume 2, edited by Augustus Richard North, 45–86. New York: Brill, 2001.

Roberts, Hugh. *The Battlefield: Algeria, 1988–2002: Studies in a Broken Polity*. London: Verso, 2003.

Refugees

People who have left their own country due to violence, persecution, and the serious violation of their human rights, with no way to find protection in their home country, as defined by international law, especially in the 1951 Geneva Convention.

The Convention's 1967 Protocol expanded the concept of refugee and the forms of protection and assistance a refugee should receive from the countries that have ratified the Convention. The Convention also specifies the refugee's obligations toward the hosting country. Status as a refugee with legal protection requires a formal, individual Refugee Status Determination by a host government or by the UN High Commissioner for Refugees (UNHCR). The UNHCR will intervene where states, who hold the primary responsibility, cannot. Statistics from the UNHCR in 2018 report approximately 25.4 million refugees in the world.

In the Middle East, Lebanon and Jordan host the highest number of refugees per capita worldwide, due to their borders with Syria and Iraq. They also hold refugee camps for Palestinians, which originated as temporary shelters for fleeing populations. Palestinians demanding repatriation to the area under Israeli control represent a major issue in peace negotiations. Turkey and Iraq also host large number of refugees, especially from the war in Syria, which has forced more than five million Syrians to flee. Only nine of the 22 member states of the Arab League have signed the 1951 Geneva Convention and its related protocol; none has ratified it. In 1965, the Arab League adopted the Casablanca Protocol for the Treatment of Palestinians in Arab States, which advocates for their rights, although they often cannot exercise the right to employment and freedom of movement. Since 2014, Middle Eastern countries have tightened border restrictions, and this has forced refugees to employ human-trafficking networks. Due to the large numbers of refugees who arrived in Europe in 2015, or who lost their lives while trying, in 2016 the European Union and Turkey signed a statement of cooperation to control refugees and migrants from crossing Turkey to the Greek islands.

Refugees represent a claim on the humanitarian ethics of a Western audience. Providing food, sanitation, education, health care, and jobs for them imposes a very heavy burden on the main receiving states, such as Lebanon, Turkey, and Jordan, from the crisis in Syria. Brutal dictatorships exploit their power to generate refugee flows to extract payments from international partners. Militias and governments use refugees as human shields to protect their warriors and sometimes to disguise the movement of agents. Host countries find it difficult to separate the combatants from the noncombatants. States find it very hard to protect vulnerable populations in a refugee camp, and women often continue to suffer brutality; religious minorities face continuing persecution. Host populations, often barely surviving themselves, can resent the international aid given to refugees. Life in a refugee camp constitutes a huge bundle of grievances, which militants exploit to recruit fighters. Host countries and NGOs face great difficulty in providing a humane education, in contrast to militants who claim to educate but instead indoctrinate into extremism.

Those who reach refuge in the advanced industrialized states face huge cultural adjustment problems and often rejection by host societies, sometimes leading youth into alienation and radicalization. Refugees often create a diaspora that can be more nationalistic even than those who remain. Their remittances not only alleviate human suffering in their home country, they also often fund the continuation of conflict.

Emanuela Claudia Del Re

256   **Regime Change Cascades**

See also: Coptic Orthodox Church; Foreign Fighters; Grievance Model; Iraq, Republic of; Jordan, Hashemite Kingdom of; Lebanese Republic; Libya, State of; Minorities; Palestine; Syrian Arab Republic; Turkey, Republic of

Further Reading

Boulby, Marion, and Kenneth Christie. *Migration, Refugees and Human Security in the Mediterranean and MENA*. London: Palgrave Macmillan, 2018.

Chatty, Dawn. *Displacement and Dispossession in the Modern Middle East*. New York: Cambridge University Press, 2010.

Mencütek, Zeynep Şahin. *Refugee Governance, State and Politics in the Middle East*. New York: Routledge, 2018.

Ullah, AKM Ahsan. *Refugee Politics in the Middle East and North Africa: Human Rights, Safety and Identity*. London: Palgrave Macmillan, 2014.

Regime Change Cascades

The sequential outbreaks of contentious politics—protests, revolts, insurgencies, or civil wars—in states with some conspicuous, shared features, that convey a sense of contagion. Historical episodes of seemingly related political changes attract analytical attention to the supporting conditions and the mechanisms of transmission. In regime change, a society, or set of powerful elites, replaces one government, or set of institutions, with a new one. Regime change cascades can go from freedom to tyranny, as well as the reverse. Cascading political changes can occur through demonstration effects and active mediation. Both common external causes and domestic triggers can cause similar events in countries that seem related. Political change rises in probability as unpopular leaders become lame ducks, either through constitutional limitations or by age and illness. When several countries share similar forms and conditions of leadership, any dramatic political event in one may potentially affect the others. Mass mobilization becomes more common when competing elites lack a focal point, such as an election or a charismatic personality, to coordinate their defection to a new leader or institutional arrangement. Sometimes, shared economic and technological conditions support a different regime type, such as globalization, international banking, electronic commerce, and Internet-based social media.

Contagion can occur through emulation, as activists in one country take inspiration, and learn by observation, from the success of a popular revolt in a similar state. For example, the Egyptian activists felt motivated by pride to achieve what people in Tunisia had accomplished, to follow that demonstration effect. They also benefited from the active coaching of activists from Serbia and Qatar. Individuals gain confidence for their own dissent by witnessing the dissenting actions of others, causing a chain reaction. Each successful revolt, in turn, builds psychological momentum for the activists in similar countries. Activists in the first successful protest hold an advantage because they take the state by surprise with their pioneering mobilization strategies and revolutionary message. The neighboring governments, watching and learning, quickly find ways to overcome those protest strategies. A protest movement in one country may not spread quickly to other countries more geographically separated, with more differences in social conditions. Nevertheless, activists actively seek to propagate their messages and strategies, leading to similar events after a delay.

In the sequence of protest movements in the Middle East and North Africa (MENA), a broad diversity of social groups mobilized to call for justice and reform, "bread and dignity," to hold people in power accountable at multiple levels of society. Beginning with protests in Tunisia, the series of anti-government demonstrations spread across the region, sparking successive uprisings in other countries. These revolts only sometimes shifted leaders from power, but they still transformed the way that citizens defined their identity, their ideology, and their relations to government, to their society, and to members of other religious and ethnic communities.

The uprisings and rebellions of the Arab Spring stimulated academic interest in the mechanisms of contagion, looking for historical precedents. Similar apparent contagions include the 1848 protests in Europe, the 1989 collapse of European Communism, and the 1998–2005 Color Revolutions. A broader level of generalization would include the so-called third wave of democratization (1974–1988), and in 1990–1994, protests in African states led to transitions. Going in the opposite direction, the wave of communist takeovers after World War II led to a sequence of disastrous interventions. Just as many states feared that the 1979 Iranian Revolution would lead to theocratic revolts throughout the Muslim world, now observers worry that Russian intervention in Syria could inspire authoritarian leaders elsewhere.

Governments suffering related protests drew different lessons. Some states offered at least a show of liberalizing reforms while providing greater welfare payments, but others embarked on a wave of resurgent authoritarianism, as well as cascades of militarization and domination. Overthrown elites who physically survive, perhaps taking shelter in another state, can gather courage, allies, and resources to return to power and repress the revolution. Therefore, a series of massive protests can lead to an even more repressive autocratic government or to a hybrid regime. The crisis in Egypt, as the military removed Mohamed Morsi, the crises in Iraq, and the ongoing civil wars in Syria, Yemen, and Libya all exemplify a contagion effect. The government of Syria provoked nonviolent reform movements into violent revolution; al-Qaeda cells in Iraq provoked conflict between Shi'a and Sunni communities; and al-Qaeda in Iraq moved into Syria, creating civil war. All these events have created an enormous migration and refugee crisis, raising the dangers of further contagion.

Autumn Cockrell-Abdullah

See also: Algerian Protests; Al-Qaeda Central; Authoritarianism; Cedar Revolution; Civil Wars; Economic Protests; February 17th Revolution; February 20 Movement; Gezi Park Protests; Green Movement; Jasmine Revolution; Jordanian Protests; Military Coups; Oman Protests; Pearl Roundabout Protests; Saudi Arabian Protests; Social Media; Syrian Civil War; Tahrir Square Protests; Tamarod Movement; Yemen Uprising

Further Reading

Bank, André, and Mirjam Edel. "Authoritarian Regime Learning: Comparative Insights from the Arab Uprisings." *GIGA Working Papers* No. 274. Hamburg: German Institute of Global and Area Studies (GIGA), 2015.

Hale, Henry E. "Regime Change Cascades: What We Have Learned from the 1848 Revolutions to the 2011 Arab Uprisings." *Annual Review of Political Science* 16 (May 2013): 331–53.

Lake, David A., and Donald Rothchild. *The International Spread of Ethnic Conflict: Fear, Diffusion, and Escalation.* Princeton, NJ: Princeton University Press, 1998.

Wayland, Kurt. "The Arab Spring: Why the Surprising Similarities with the Revolutionary Wave of 1848?" *Perspectives on Politics* 10, no. 4 (December 2012): 917–34.

Rentier State Politics

An explanation for the persistence of authoritarianism in states that have natural resources to export to earn hard currency (economic rents), to fund state operations without relying on taxing the domestic populations. Classical economics uses the term *rent* to describe income derived from the ownership of land and other natural resources. In political science, the term includes income derived from geographical position, such as control over maritime checkpoints, or the path of major pipelines. When a state does not rely on revenue from taxes but instead delivers health care, education, access to housing, security, and often subsidized basic food, then the state repeatedly shows citizens that they depend on the government. The state becomes a patron distributing benefits to the residents as clients. In these conditions, a ruler can claim to represent a father figure to his people, as in a patrimonial state.

Some analysts include revenue generated from foreign aid as rent. A state presiding over an unstable society, such as after a civil war, can market the threats of militants to its neighbors and great powers, as a form of blackmail to extract foreign aid. The export of conflict to extract aid then enables the ruler to claim the status of patron to his supported clients and the population. If the flow of income declines, such as when the price of oil falls, and the government must reduce its welfare spending, poor people commonly engage in "bread riots." If the government cannot find the means to resume spending, it may offer some superficial tokens of political opening and representation. Rentier state politics derive from the "resource curse": when governments use the money from natural resources to fund multiple, brutal security services to repress the population and prevent the promotion of democracy.

Autumn Cockrell-Abdullah

See also: Authoritarianism; Clientelism (Patrimonialism); Democracy Deficit

Further Reading

Beblawi, Hazem. "The Rentier State in the Arab World." *Arab Studies Quarterly* 9, no. 4 (Fall 1987): 383–98.

Girod, Desha M., and Megan A. Stewart. "Mass Protests and the Resource Curse: The Politics of Demobilization in Rentier Autocracies." *Conflict Management and Peace Science* 35, no. 5 (2018): 503–22.

Rouhani, Hassan Feridun

An Iranian lawyer, politician, and religious leader, born into a religious and politically engaged family as Hassan Feridun, on November 12, 1948. He attended Shi'a seminaries in Semnan and Qom in the 1960s and changed his last name to Rouhani, meaning "spiritual." He also studied in the modern University of Tehran and graduated in 1972 with a law degree. He performed his compulsory military service in Nishapur from 1973 to 1975. He traveled around Iran, making speeches against the shah, but eventually fled to France where he joined Ayatollah Khomeini in 1978. After the Iranian Revolution (1978–1979), he served in a variety of leadership capacities during the Iran-Iraq War (1980–1988): he was a member of the High Council for National Defense and served as the commander of Iran's air defenses. In 1989, he became Iran's secretary of the Supreme National Security Council. During all of this time, he also served as a member of the Majles (parliament) from 1980 to 2000.

He served as national security adviser to President Hashemi Rafsanjani (1989–1997). In 1999, Rouhani completed a doctorate in constitutional law from Glasgow Caledonian University in the United Kingdom. He came back to serve as national security adviser to Mohammad Khatami (2000–2005). Rouhani served as Iran's chief negotiator with the International Atomic Energy Agency concerning Iran's nuclear program from October 2003 until August 2005.

On June 15, 2013, Rouhani won a landslide victory to become president, having campaigned as a moderate who criticized Ahmadinejad's economic policies and confrontational foreign policies. Former presidents Khatami and Rafsanjani supported him, while other moderates dropped out or were disqualified. Following his inauguration in August, he launched a diplomatic campaign to engage with the West. After a phone call with U.S. president Barak Obama, he immediately tweeted about it, marking a milestone in the development of Iranian digital diplomacy. Rouhani's efforts led to the Joint Comprehensive Plan of Action (JPOAC) in July 2015, a 10-year agreement in which Iran pledged to keep its nuclear program peaceful.

Although Gross Domestic Product (GDP) rose, and inflation dropped with the lifting of sanctions, most Iranians did not see their welfare improve much. The lack of greater economic improvement raised popular awareness of the way that corruption, government policies, and the dominance of the Islamic Revolutionary Guard Corps (IRGC) in business greatly restricted the economy. During his time in office, the government of Iran has not relaxed its social controls but has, rather, increased the repression of journalists, human rights activists, dissidents, and religious minorities. These policies, implemented by the judiciary and other branches of government beyond the president's control, illustrate the limitations of the president under Iran's system of political decision-making. In May 2017, Rouhani was elected to a second term as president, with 57 percent of the vote. Since taking office, Rouhani has worked to reduce the political and economic power of the IRGC.

Mark David Luce

See also: Iran, Islamic Republic of; Islamic Revolutionary Guard Corps (IRGC); Khatami, Mohammad; Khomeini, Ayatollah Sayyid Ruhollah Mūsavi; Political Decision-Making in Iran; Rafsanjani, Ali Akbar Hashemi

Further Reading

Boroumand, Ladan. "Iran's 2017 Election: Waning Democratic Hopes." *Journal of Democracy* 28, no. 4 (2017): 38–45.

Harris, Melanie. "Leadership Analysis: Iranian President Hassan Rouhani." *Journal of Public and International Affairs* (2014): 73–87.

Mohsen, Milani. "Rouhani's Foreign Policy: How to Work with Iran's Pragmatic New President." *Foreign Affairs,* June 25, 2013.

Sherrill, Clifton W. "Why Hassan Rouhani Won Iran's 2013 Presidential Election." *Middle East Policy* 21, no. 2 (2014): 64–75.

S

Sahwa (Sunni Tribal Awakening)

A counterinsurgency effort by Iraqi Sunni Arab tribes against the Islamic State of Iraq (ISI, formerly Al-Qaeda in Iraq), beginning in late 2006, known as the Sahwa ("Awakening" in Arabic). In the wake of the American invasion of Iraq (March 2003), significant numbers of Sunni Arabs had supported Al-Qaeda in Iraq (AQI), the leading Sunni insurgent group. By 2006, however, many Sunnis grew angry at AQI's brutal and often indiscriminate tactics, its promotion of sectarian conflict, and its efforts to take local women as wives. Furthermore, AQI interfered with the tribes' regular sources of income from trade and even smuggling. The Sunni tribes of the al-Anbar province made several abortive attempts to rid themselves of AQI, dating back to late 2005, and finally succeeded with a campaign, proclaimed as the "Awakening," in September 2006. The grassroots "Anbar Awakening" Movement gained funding from the Iraqi government, supported by the United States. American commanders sought to expand it into a countrywide counterinsurgency campaign. With the beginning of the American "Surge" strategy under U.S. Army general David Petraeus, the United States began funding an initiative known as the "Sons of Iraq" (SOI) Movement, which paid and armed Sunni Arabs to combat the AQI. These former insurgents helped American and Iraqi forces quell the insurgency, thereby reducing violence and driving AQI underground. The movement rapidly grew to a major armed force of more than 80,000 members.

The Sahwa greatly reduced sectarian violence in Iraq in the 2007–2008 period. In 2008 and 2009, the United States reduced the numbers of its troops and delegated this program to the Iraqi government. However, the Shi'a and Kurdish parties did not trust this movement, and even some Sunni elites feared that it could become a competing independent political force. The government failed to incorporate the Sons of Iraq into the security services or other government jobs, as promised, and even those brought into the government did not receive their salaries regularly. In the summer of 2009, AQI increasingly committed reprisal assassination attacks against members of the Awakening Councils and their families. The combination of ISI's attacks with the Maliki government's repressive measures pressured many Sunnis into rejoining ISI and other insurgent groups. Thus, just as they had done before, ISI drew upon Sunni grievances to gather strength, eventually becoming the insurgency known as the Islamic State (Daesh).

Benjamin V. Allison

See also: Al-Maliki, Nouri, Al-Qaeda Central; Grievance Model; Iraq, Republic of; Islamic State (Daesh); Kurds; Sectarianism; Shi'a

Further Reading

Benraad, Myriam. "Iraq's Tribal 'Sahwa': Its Rise and Fall." *Middle East Policy* 18, no. 1 (Spring 2011): 121–31.

Cottam, Martha L., Joe W. Huseby, and Bruno Baltodano. *Confronting Al Qaeda: The Sunni Awakening and American Strategy in al Anbar.* New York: Rowman & Littlefield, 2016.

Lynch, Marc. "Explaining the Awakening: Engagement, Publicity, and the Transformation of Iraqi Sunni Political Attitudes." *Security Studies* 20, no. 1 (2011): 36–72.

Salafism

An umbrella term for efforts to restore ideal Islamic practice, based on the Arabic term *salaf,* meaning ancestors. Islamic doctrine argues that the first three generations of Muslims, the *"al-salaf al-salih"* (the pious predecessors), exemplified the practice of pure Islam, without any harmful innovations. This approach strengthened in response to the expansion of Western political, economic, and intellectual influence. Muslims asked why other non-Muslim people had gained military and political power to invade Muslim countries, since Muslims were following the true religion. In contrast to the modernist, or *Jadid,* movement that argues that Muslims need to study engineering, science, math, and foreign languages and promote education in the local language and nationalism, Salafis argue that Muslims should return to pure Islam to regain God's favor, and then He will restore them to military dominance.

From the end of the 1800s, in their effort to emulate the example of the Prophet Muhammad as closely as possible, Islamic scholars increasingly began to reassess the development of Islamic philosophy, doctrine, and law, to reject ideas developed after the first three generations of Muslims. In practice, Salafis emphasize a literal interpretation of Islamic texts; they frequently refer to specific medieval theologians such as Ibn Taymiyya, often reject a rationalist approach to scripture, and give great importance to ritual purity. Due to its critical approach toward historically developed legal opinions, observers often call Salafism a reform trend.

The "Salafi call to action" constituted one of eight major goals of the Egyptian Muslim Brotherhood, which used an effective organizational strategy and appealing model of activism to spread this ideology into many other Muslim countries. After the huge increase in revenue from higher oil prices in 1973, Saudi Arabia dramatically expanded its international funding for mosques and schools to teach its version of the Hanbali Salafi doctrine. The huge numbers of labor migrants who came to work in Saudi Arabia spread this doctrine when they returned home. When Arab men went to fight against the Soviets in Afghanistan, they gained exposure to an intolerant, revolutionary doctrine called Deobandism. The combination of these three different approaches created a militant doctrine of warfare to promote Salafism.

Contemporary Salafism consists of three quite different approaches: 1) quietist Salafism, the largest and most popular form, focused on proselytism and learning, which strongly rejects violence; 2) political Salafism, emphasizing peaceful political participation; and 3) militant Salafism (sometimes called jihadi Salafism), advocating the use of violence and warfare to create an Islamic state.

In general, Salafism represents a growing trend within contemporary Islam. Its egalitarian promotion of individual readings of Islamic scripture make it accessible and attractive for young Muslims feeling culturally disenfranchised in an increasingly globalized world. Muslim critics of Salafism complain that the early advocates rejected the use of scholarly consensus and analogy, the methodological foundations for deriving and following qualified judgment, and justified declaring Muslims who believe differently as unbelievers.

Alexander Weissenburger

See also: Egypt, Arab Republic of; Islamism; *Jihad;* Muslim Brotherhood; Saudi Arabia, Kingdom of

Further Reading

Cavatorta, Francesco, and Fabio Merone, eds. *Salafism after the Arab Awakening: Contending with People's Power.* London: Hurst & Company, 2017.

Lauziere, Henri. *The Making of Salafism: Islamic Reform in the 20th Century.* New York: Columbia University Press, 2016.

Meijer, Roel, ed. *Global Salafism: Islam's New Religious Movement.* New York: Oxford University Press, 2013.

Salah, Ahmed Gaid

The current deputy minister of Defense of Algeria, born on January 13, 1940, in the Batna area of East Algeria. He joined the National Liberation Army (ALN) in August 1957. During the Algerian Independence War, he trained in a camp near the Tunisian border under Khaled Nezzar. After independence in 1962, he trained in Algeria for two years, then in 1968 he participated in the Algerian campaign in Egypt against Israel. From 1969 to 1971, he went to the Soviet Union for military training in the Vystrel Academy.

He gradually rose in the hierarchy of the Algerian National People's Army (ANP) until he was promoted to general-major in 1993, in 2004 to chief of staff, and to the highest rank of the ANP *"general de corps d'armée"* in 2006. The government considered the 2013 terrorist attack on the gas-production facility near In Amenas a failure of the military security services (Departement du Renseignement et de la Securite, known as the DRS). In response, Algeria assigned General Gaid Salah to conduct a "Special Security Commission." From September 2013 to January 2014, the government conducted a purge of the DRS to bring it under the direct control of the army and the presidency. In this struggle, General Salah served as President Bouteflika's agent. In 2019, when massive protests erupted against Bouteflika's plan to run for a fifth term, General Salah forced him to resign. Then he became the public face of the transition, promoting corruption prosecutions but also pushing for July 2019 elections, in spite of resistance from the opposition.

Saphia Arezki

See also: Algeria, The People's Democratic Republic of; Bouteflika, Abdelaziz; Corruption; Nezzar, Khaled

Further Reading

Gaub, Florence. "Algeria's Army: On Jihadist Alert." *Issue Brief* 6. European Union Institute for Security Studies, March 2015.

Tlemçani, Rachid. "The Purge of Powerful Algerian Generals: Civil-Military Reform or Presidential Power Grab?" *Al Jazeera Centre for Studies,* February 12, 2017.

Saleh, Ali Abdullah

A Yemen nationalist politician and military leader known for his shifting alliances, management of tribal and ideological divisions, and elaborate patronage system. Ali Abdullah Saleh (born on March 21, 1942, in Bayt al-Ahmar, North Yemen; died on December 4, 2017, in Sana'a, Yemen) joined the army at age 16. In 1974, he supported a military coup, which later led to his appointment as military commander of Taiz Province. In 1977, after several assassinations created a political vacuum, the leaders of North Yemen appointed Saleh as president on July 17, 1978, and again in 1983. As a major, Saleh benefited from an agreement with Abdallah al-Ahmar, the sheikh of the powerful Hashid tribal confederation, and Brigadier General Ali Mohsen al-Ahmar, commander of the armored forces, in which he would serve as the political figurehead for the Hashid. He developed the General People's Congress (GPC) as a means to incorporate a broad section of different tribes and ideological movements and as an institution legitimating his rule.

On May 22, 1990, Saleh became president of a united Yemen. He and the GPC won the first elections in April 1993. His government fought a short civil war against the South (May 5–July 7, 1994) and defeated the Yemen Socialist Party. Prior to the 2011 "Youth Revolution" protests, Saleh and his family controlled all branches of the military, major Yemeni businesses, and the GPC party. In 2009, he broke his covenant with General Ali Muhsin al-Ahmar, who then turned against him in 2011, by defecting to the side of the protesting youth. Those protests also won the allegiance of the al-Islah Party and the major tribal forces, who ultimately forced him to resign. He was seriously wounded in a bomb attack on his palace on June 3, 2011. Under pressure from the protests, he negotiated his departure from power, finally signing an agreement on November 22, 2011. He extracted immunity from the prosecution, retained leadership of the GPC, and continued to reside in Yemen.

In 2014, he aligned himself with the Shi'ite Houthis (against whom he had previously waged war six times) and fought against his former vice president, Abdu Rabbu Mansour Hadi, and the Saudi-led coalition fighting to support Hadi in Yemen. In late 2017, Saleh began talks with the Saudi coalition to end the conflict. On December 4, 2017, Houthi forces killed Saleh in Sana'a.

Mark David Luce

See also: Al-Ahmar, Ali Muhsin; Al-Islah (Reform Party); General People's Congress; Hadi, Abdu Rabbu Mansour; Houthis (Ansar Allah); Yemen Uprising

Further Reading

Clark, Victoria. *Yemen Dancing on the Head of Snakes.* New Haven, CT: Yale University Press, 2010.

Knights, Michael. "The Military Role in Yemen's Protests: Civil-Military Relations in the Tribal Republic." *The Journal of Strategic Studies* 36, no. 2 (February 2013): 261–88.

Salman, Mohammad bin

The crown prince of Saudi Arabia, first deputy prime minister, president of the Council for Economic and Development Affairs, and minister of Defense. Mohammad bin Salman bin Abdulaziz Al Saud, born on August 31, 1985, in Riyadh, known colloquially as MBS, was appointed crown prince (heir apparent) in June 2017, following his father's decision to remove Muhammad bin Nayef from all positions. He graduated with a law degree from King Saud University and then established a number of firms working in the private sector.

He worked for the Saudi Cabinet as a consultant for the Experts Commission. In 2007, he became a full-time adviser to the Council of Ministers. On December 15, 2009, he became a special adviser to his father, who was serving as the governor of Riyadh Province. During this time, he quickly rose from one position to another, gaining attention for his political activities, while continuing to offer advice part-time to the Experts Commission until 2013. He was the secretary-general of the Riyadh Competitive Council, special adviser to the chairman for the King Abdulaziz Foundation for Research and Archives, and a board of trustee's member for the Albir Society in Riyadh.

In March 2015, he played a major role in the Saudi decision to lead a coalition of countries against the Houthi forces of Yemen to restore President Hadi to power. In April 2016, Prince Mohammed bin Salman announced his intention to restructure Saudi Arabia's economy and introduced Vision 2030 as the country's strategic orientation for the next 15 years. It details various measures to develop non-oil revenues, privatize some assets, develop e-government, and promote sustainable development.

He has led several serious reforms, including restricting the powers of the religious police and removing the ban on female drivers. Under his reign, the presence of women in the workforce increased, a Saudi sports stadium admitted women, and a female singer gave a public concert. Despite some international praise for his domestic liberalization, commentators criticize the intervention in Yemen and the escalation of the diplomatic crises with Qatar and with Lebanon, as well as his November 2017 arrests of members of the Saudi royal family. Despite promised reforms, the government has increased its persecutions of human rights activists under Mohammad bin Salman. Amnesty International and Human Rights Watch continue to criticize the Saudi government for its violations of human rights, including the detention and torture of human rights activists.

Amir Muhammad Esmaeili

See also: Authoritarianism; Development; Islamism; Modernization; Operation Decisive Storm; Saudi Arabia, Kingdom of

Further Reading

Hill, Ginny. *Yemen Endures: Civil War, Saudi Adventurism and the Future of Arabia.* Oxford, UK: Oxford University Press, 2017.

Mabon, Simon. "It's a Family Affair: Religion, Geopolitics and Rise of Mohammed bin Salman." *Insight Turkey* 20 (2018): 51–66.

Stenslie, Stig. "The End of Elite Unity and the Stability of Saudi Arabia." *The Washington Quarterly* 41, no. 1 (2018): 61–82.

Saudi Arabia, Kingdom of

A conservative dynastic monarchy ruling over most of the Arabian Peninsula, the birthplace of Islam. The Saudi kings claim the important title of "Guardian of the Two Holy Mosques," referring to the Grand Mosque in Mecca, which houses the Qa'ba, the sacred center of the Islamic faith, and the Prophet's Mosque in Medina. Saudi Arabia provides facilities and organizational logistics for millions of Muslims each year, from every part of the world, to perform their religious duties in the Hajj, or Pilgrimage. In addition, many more pilgrims come to the kingdom for the Umrah, or Lesser Pilgrimage. The Saudi Ministry of Hajj and Umrah issued more than six million visas for Hajj and Umrah visitors in 2017. In addition to its historical and religious significance, Saudi Arabia produces more than 11 million barrels of oil a day, giving the kingdom significant wealth.

The location of Riyadh, the Saudi capital in the Nejd, a scrub desert region in the geographic center of the country, gives the Nejdi tribes a disproportionate amount of political and economic power. The holy cities of Mecca and Medina as well as the cosmopolitan port city of Jeddah in the arid Hijaz attract most of the religious visitors. The kingdom also has mountains in the southern region of Asir toward the Yemen border with a more pleasant climate. Most of the Shi'ite population live in the East Province, the location of the vast oil resources along the Arabian Gulf coast. Finally, the Rub al-Khali (the Empty Quarter) in the southeast consists of the largest contiguous sand desert in the world.

The roots of the kingdom date to the early years of the 18th century CE when the conservative religious scholar Muhammad ibn 'Abd al-Wahhab (1703–1792) allied with the Emir Muhammad ibn Saud (d. 1765), who granted al-Wahhab protection and saw a power in his religious zeal that would help him build a kingdom. In exchange for al-Wahhab's religious authority, Mohammad ibn Saud would lead the Muslim community as the *imam* and wage *jihad* against all unbelievers (whether Muslim or not). They recruited a military force from settled tribes living in towns and villages of the Nejdi. Through preaching (*da'wa*) and military raids, the alliance spread the faith and expanded the lands under al-Saud control. The campaign expanded out of Arabia into Iraq and Syria, provoking resistance from the Ottomans, who crushed it. In January 1813, the Egyptian ruler Mohammad Ali captured Mecca, Taif, and Jedda, destroyed many towns, and took important leaders captive to Egypt.

In 1824, the Saudi family recovered and established a Second Saudi Kingdom. Defeated in 1891, they went into exile in Kuwait. In 1905 King Abdul Aziz ibn Saud returned from exile in Kuwait and began his campaign to conquer Arabia. In

1912, he allied with a Bedouin tribal unit called the Ikhwan (Brotherhood), that followed the doctrine of al-Wahhab with zeal. In 1924, with that support he conquered the Najd and, in 1924, the Hijaz with its holy cities, thus establishing the third and current Saudi Kingdom. Within three years, the Ikhwan's numbers exceeded 60,000 and became difficult to control. Their ruthless war within Arabia culminated in considerable violence against the Shi'ites in the east, but it brought all of Arabia under central control. Bedouin austerity and antipathy toward modernity soon created a crisis. King Abdul Aziz knew the importance of telephones, telegraphs, and radio for running a government, which the Ikhwan and many religious scholars saw as innovations contrary to Islam, and they hated the oil industry with its foreign technical managers.

In 1926, the Ikhwan rebelled, but King Abdul Aziz recruited tribal militias, and with British help, he defeated them in major battles. King Abdul Aziz then began building a modern state, balancing the influence of competing regions, with the military entrusted primarily to Nejdi elites, while relying on the Asiri tribes for the internal security force of the National Guard.

In 1932, King Abdul Aziz granted oil-exploration rights to present-day Chevron, which with several other oil companies formed a partnership with the kingdom called the Arabian American Oil Company (ARAMCO). King Abdul Aziz died in 1953, giving his heirs a state that rested on religion, oil, and American might. His first successor, King Saud, committed some missteps in domestic and foreign policy that forced him to cede executive power to his brother, Prince Faisal. Faisal reformed finances, restored harmony with the *ulama* (the religious scholars), and established the modern Saudi welfare state.

After the 1973 Middle East War, the Saudis supported the oil embargo that quadrupled oil prices and brought tremendous wealth from the developed world to the oil-producing states. By the late 1970s, the people of Saudi Arabia depended on oil and became vulnerable to its price fluctuations. In 1976, King Faisal took the first steps to diversify the Saudi economy by forming the Saudi Basic Industries Corporation (SABIC), to train young Saudis for employment in a modern diversified economy. In 1975, a disgruntled junior member of the royal family assassinated Faisal.

King Khaled continued Faisal's modernization policies, seeking both to diversify the Saudi economy and to increase political openness. The United States began its Twin Pillars Policy, pushing the kingdom to cooperate with Iran in security. Both countries bought advanced American military technology to exercise joint responsibility for Gulf security, with American support only if needed— "over the horizon." However, in 1979, the Islamic Revolution in Iran overthrew Shah Mohammad Reza Pahlavi, stirring revolutionary hopes to a fever pitch among Shi'a and Sunni Islamists alike.

On November 20, 1979, Juhayman al Utaybi and almost 500 followers seized the Grand Mosque of Mecca immediately following the Hajj. These fighters held thousands of pilgrims hostage while Juhayman declared himself the *mahdi,* a religious leader that Muslims expect in the Last Days to cleanse the world. The Saudi security forces faced great difficulty dislodging the rebels, who had hidden weapons in the myriad chambers of the Grand Mosque.

The Iranian Revolution stimulated a Shi'ite uprising in the Eastern Province in November 1979, in which protesters burned a number of important facilities. More than 20,000 Saudi National Guardsmen responded with considerable violence, killing hundreds of Shi'as. The Shi'ite uprising and the takeover of the Grand Mosque in Mecca created a perception of serious internal crisis. Elites concluded that popular rejection of the modernization process required a radical policy change to regain stability. As a result, Saudi Arabia became much more socially restrictive. In sum, Saudi Arabia turned inward from 1979 through the 1980s, as an ideologically harder Salafist interpretation of Islam prevailed.

After the 1979 invasion of Afghanistan, the kingdom encouraged young men to fight the Soviets. The United States and Saudi Arabia agreed to match dollars contributed to support the Afghan resistance. Wealthy individuals throughout the Arab world contributed to this effort. The men who traveled to Afghanistan passed through Pakistan, where they learned about the form of Islamism promoted by the Deobandi Islamic schools and developed a distinctive militant ideology. Many Arabs who returned from Afghanistan brought a commitment to create a pure Islamist state, and they demanded political changes in their home governments. One of these, the very wealthy Osama bin Laden, had developed a network among the Arab fighters who had passed through his guesthouse, a "base" of support operations and logistics in Pakistan.

After the 1990 Iraqi invasion of Kuwait, bin Laden demanded that the Saudi government rely on his fighters to defend the kingdom. The kingdom refused but gained a fatwa to allow U.S. troops to defend them. Bin Laden would use the presence of non-Muslim, American troops in the "Land of the Two Mosques" to justify his war against America and the West. After 1990, a movement of religious leaders, with some influence from the Muslim Brotherhood, called the Islamic Awakening (*Sahwa*), criticized the government for allowing non-Muslims to defend the kingdom. After 1979 they had become the dominant voice within the kingdom. In response to this criticism, and the belief that the Muslim Brotherhood had betrayed Saudi Arabia by taking the side of Iraq, the kingdom launched a purge of religious teachers holding views identified as part of the Sahwa.

After the terrorist attacks of September 11, 2001, the kingdom faced popular American antagonism that blamed Saudi Arabia and its ideology for creating the forces committing those attacks. Americans accused the kingdom of exporting its discontented young men to fight in other countries. Although the Bush administration worked hard to support good relations with the kingdom, before the 2003 invasion of Iraq, the U.S. government did not listen to Saudi warnings on the dangers of removing Saddam Hussein. Therefore, angry at the Bush administration's policies of promoting liberalization and democracy, and especially at destabilizing the region, the kingdom gave support for marginalized Sunnis in Iraq.

Between March 2003 and 2006, al-Qaeda hit Saudi Arabia with a wave of terrorist attacks, leaving more than 100 dead and several hundreds wounded. For example, on May 12, 2003, suicide attackers struck three Riyadh housing compounds, killing 35 and wounding over 200. From 2006 to 2009 Saudi security forces conducted dozens of raids on militant safe houses, achieving significant success in reducing the network and killing high-profile militants. In 2011, the kingdom avoided protests in the main Sunni cities but suppressed protests in the eastern Shi'a cities with great force.

After the 2014 development of the Islamic State (Daesh), its fighters also targeted Saudi Arabia. In March 2014, the Interior Ministry formally designated the Islamic State as a terrorist group, with Jabhat al-Nusra, the Muslim Brotherhood, Yemen's Houthi rebels, and the Saudi Hezbollah. In 2015, terrorists conducted eight sporadic attacks at borders against security forces, and they also attacked a mosque in May 2015.

Saudi Arabia finds its ideology under attack from three sources: Iran's Revolutionary Shia doctrine; terrorists seeking to establish a caliphate; and liberal secular materialism.

The greatly expanded security services engage in a battle of ideas, as well as a war of weapons with religious extremists. The kingdom has developed effective monitoring of the formal financial sector to block suspect donations and monitors social media intensively. In religious and security terms, the kingdom advertises its devotion to "moderate Islam" and seeks to assert its primacy in Sunni doctrine against the rising assertiveness of Turkey in its alliance with Qatar and the Muslim Brotherhood. The kingdom has given strong support to the moderate Tunisian Ennahda Party and to Field Marshal Haftar Khalifa in Libya. The kingdom has opposed Iran's interventions in Yemen, Bahrain, Lebanon, Iraq, and Syria. However, low oil prices, combined with the high cost of the wars, have created financial perils.

Mohammad bin Salman became the heir apparent by 2015 and was formally named crown prince in 2017. He announced, on April 26, 2016, an ambitious set of reforms, titled "Vision 2030," that aimed to reduce Saudi dependence on oil exports by curbing public spending, diversifying the economy, promoting modernization, and attracting foreign investment. The Saudization plan hopes to replace foreign workers with Saudis in key sectors of government and the economy. He embarked on an anticorruption campaign that included arrests and financial demands on senior members of the royal family. Western governments have also applauded a ruling that would allow Saudi women to drive by June 2018. The pace of reforms has created unease, but the degree to which the kingdom will actually implement its proposals remains unknown.

Jeffrey Kaplan

See also: Al-Sharif, Manal; Badawi, Raif; Haftar, Khalifa Belqasim; Iran, Islamic Republic of; *Jihad;* Khomeini, Ayatollah Sayyid Ruhollah Mūsavi; Operation Decisive Storm; Salafism; Salman, Mohammad bin; Saudi Arabian Protests; Saudi Sahwa (Islamic Awakening); Shi'a

Further Reading

Al-Atawneh, Muhammad. "Is Saudi Arabia a Theocracy? Religion and Governance in Contemporary Saudi Arabia." *Middle Eastern Studies* 45, no. 5 (2009): 721–37.

Al-Munajjed, Mona. *Women in Saudi Arabia Today.* London: Springer, 1997.

Al-Rasheed, Madawi. *A History of Saudi Arabia.* Cambridge, UK: Cambridge University Press, 2010.

Ansary, Abdullah F. "Combating Extremism: A Brief Overview of Saudi Arabia's Approach." *Middle East Policy* 15, no. 2 (2008): 111–42.

Hegghammer, Thomas, and Stéphane Lacroix. "Rejectionist Islamism in Saudi Arabia: The Story of Juhayman Al-ʿutaybi Revisited." *International Journal of Middle East Studies* 39, no. 1 (2007): 103–22.

Jones, Toby Craig. "Rebellion on the Saudi Periphery: Modernity, Marginalization, and the Shia Uprising of 1979." *International Journal of Middle East Studies* 38, no. 2 (2006): 213–33.

Lacey, Robert. *Inside the Kingdom: Kings, Clerics, Modernists, Terrorists, and the Struggle for Saudi Arabia.* New York: Viking, 2009.

Saudi Arabian Protests (2011)

A series of protests in the predominantly Shi'a populated Eastern Province of Saudi Arabia, beginning in early 2011 and continuing sporadically for the next two years, after efforts to mobilize protests among the Sunni population failed. Although a coalition including both Islamists and non-Islamists had been submitting petitions and manifestos for a constitutional monarchy, carefully using Islamic terminology and arguments since 2003, these did not gain significant traction. After the general population failed to react when the government arrested 10 of these activists, they decided to change their tactics. They formed the Saudi Civil and Political Rights Association to defend the rights of political prisoners, thousands of whom were held without charges or trial.

On February 10, 2011, 10 of these activists announced the creation of a political party, and the next day they issued a statement that the kingdom needed constitutional reform to avoid revolution. They developed two petitions seeking political change, referencing the changes in the region. At the same time, a number of youths active on the Internet began promoting human rights in Saudi Arabia through a variety of forums, such as the "Monitor of Human Rights in Saudi" Facebook page and the "Free Youth Coalition," which planned for a "Day of Rage" on March 11, 2011. The government infiltrated these groups and hijacked them by calling the planned event the "Hunayn Revolution." Because the Sunnis interpreted this as a Shi'a reference, this discredited the movement. On February 24, King Abdulla returned from getting back surgery abroad and announced a $37 billion domestic-aid program to build more housing units, create more state jobs, and increase housing subsidies and unemployment benefits. On March 11, the government deployed massive numbers of security agents to prevent people from getting to the location advertised for the protest. One man showed up, gave an interview expressing his grievances, and was arrested. On March 18, the government announced an even more massive funding package worth $97 billion. In sum, protest efforts among the Sunni population fizzled.

At the same time in the Eastern Province, where the Shi'as have extensive experience in protesting against official discrimination and oppression, demonstrators demanded the release of prisoners and proclaimed solidarity with protests in Bahrain, which began on February 14. Demonstrations began in Awamiyya, the hometown of well-known teacher Nimr al-Nimr, on February 17. After Saudi troops intervened in Bahrain on March 14, 2011, the protests increased dramatically in size on the streets of cities with a majority Shi'a population. Women became a driving force of the Shi'a protest movement. The government arrested large numbers of protesters and negotiated with the notable families and religious leaders. From late March to September 2011, this strategy succeeded in greatly reducing the size and number of protests.

During October and November 2011, the Saudi government increased the repression and sectarian accusations of foreign involvement, calling the Shi'as puppets of Iran, while religious teachers increased their inflammatory and insulting sermons against the Shi'as. On November 23, 2011, 20,000 people protested on the streets of Qatif, the largest protests since 1979. However, the level of repression also convinced the leaders of the Shi'as to call for calm, especially seeking to avoid violence during the month of Moharram, in which Shi'as conduct important rituals. Despite a large protest in Qatif on January 22, 2012, security improved for the next six months, while the government conducted raids on various locations, seeking individuals on a target list of 23 people.

On July 8, 2012, the government arrested Nimr al-Nimr, the most outspoken and assertive Shi'a teacher, which sparked renewed youth protests that turned violent. The Shi'a religious leaders of all of the main political groups issued a statement condemning violence and asserting their loyalty to the kingdom. This split between the notable leaders reaching out to the government to appease the king versus the anger of the protesters became a trend.

The Saudi intervention in Bahrain, together with the use of sectarian language and accusations of foreign involvement, exerted an intimidating, deterrent effect on Sunnis who sought political reform. In addition, the government gained religious rulings from high-level Sunni scholars prohibiting even protests and petitions. The government has prosecuted peaceful protesters as terrorists and has called agreeing with these protests "supporting terrorism." Increased government funding for the institutions in which Saudi Islamists work has reduced the protest motivation by religious scholars. By using its control of the religious institutions, expanding funding for social support, and resolute coercive force, the Saudi government stopped any significant Sunni protest movement.

Jeffrey Kaplan

See also: Authoritarianism; Bahrain, Kingdom of; Grievance Model; Islamism; Rentier State Politics; Salafism; Saudi Arabia, Kingdom of; Sectarianism; Shi'a; Social Media

Further Reading

Al-Rasheed, Madawi. "Saudi Regime Resilience after the 2011 Arab Popular Uprisings." *Contemporary Arab Affairs* 9, no. 1 (2016): 13–26.

Lacroix, Stéphane. "Is Saudi Arabia Immune?" *Journal of Democracy* 22, no. 4 (October 2011): 48–59.

Mathiesen, Toby. "A 'Saudi Spring?' The Shi'a Protest Movement in the Eastern Province 2011–2012." *Middle East Journal* 66, no. 4 (Autumn 2012): 628–59.

Saudi Sahwa (Islamic Awakening)

A revivalist Islamic renewal movement composed of various groups with slightly different viewpoints opposing Westernization and arbitrary rule, that became the most powerful social and political movement in Saudi Arabia. Islamists argue that the Saudi al-Sahwa al-Islamiyya (Islamic Awakening) groups represent a national manifestation of the broader set of global movements that developed the modern narratives of Islamism. In the 1960s exiles from Nasser's repression of the Muslim Brotherhood came to Saudi Arabia. The government allowed many to teach, because their doctrine was not that different from the ideology of the kingdom. In the 1970s Saudis who held to the kingdom's religious doctrine, but who were also influenced by the Brotherhood's political and social approaches, developed teaching circles and social groups. They resisted the major social reforms planned by Crown Prince Fahd bin Abdulaziz. After 1979, when Juhayman al-Otaybi seized the Grand Mosque, and the Iranian Revolution occurred, the government used these religious teachers to promote the image of the Saudi monarchy as properly Islamic, to persuade the wealthy to finance fighting in Afghanistan, and to encourage young men to go and fight. However, after the Iraqi invasion of Kuwait threatened the kingdom, the Sahwa strongly resisted King Fahd's decision to seek American protection for Saudi Arabia, a perspective also advanced by the Egyptian Muslim Brotherhood. The government concluded that the Sahwas were linked to the Brotherhood and felt betrayed.

The Sahwa also gained a reputation from two petitions, the first created in May 1991, and another in September 1992 called the Memorandum of Advice, which called for a Consultative Council to advise the government. The Saudi government threw many of the prominent Sahwa leaders in jail for a few years. In 1999, the government released most of the Sahwa leaders from jail. Some preached against the dangers of liberalism, but some recognized the growing threat of militant Islamism. The attacks of September 11, 2001, forced the government to reassess the influence of religious teachers on political and social affairs. After al-Qaeda in the Arabian Peninsula terrorists started striking targets in the kingdom in 2003, the Sahwa reinforced and supported government efforts to suppress the militants. In 2007, the prominent Sahwa teacher Salman al-Awda wrote a passionate open letter to Osama bin Laden, denouncing his actions.

After the fall of the rulers of Tunisia and Egypt in 2011, the well-known Sahwa personalities did not endorse demonstrations in Saudi Arabia, but rather they actively denounced the protests in Bahrain starting on February 14, 2011. They later supported the battles in Syria against Bashar al-Assad. The fall of Mubarak created the perception that a historic opportunity for reform had appeared. Members of the Sahwa, especially those born after 1979 and those with Western university degrees, developed petitions calling for a constitutional monarchy and for protections of human rights.

The government considers the size and influence of the Sahwa Movement a potential threat. In 2013, the Sahwa leaders signed a petition to protest Saudi government support for the July 3 military coup in Egypt. The government has responded with harsh repression, arresting Salman al-Ouda, who had written the king an open letter calling for reforms and charging him with dozens of crimes that can lead to the death penalty.

Jeffrey Kaplan

See also: Al-Qaeda in the Arabian Peninsula (AQAP); Bahrain, Kingdom of; Democracy Deficit; Egypt, Arab Republic of; Islamism; Muslim Brotherhood; Salafism; Saudi Arabia, Kingdom of; Syrian Arab Republic; Tunisia, Republic of

Further Reading

Al-Rasheed, Madawi. *Contesting the Saudi State: Islamic Voices from a New Generation.* New York: Cambridge University Press, 2007.

Berenek, Ondrej. "Divided We Survive: A Landscape of Fragmentation in Saudi Arabia." *Middle East Brief* No. 33. Waltham, MA: Brandeis University, January 2009.

Lacroix, Stéphane. "Saudi Islamists and the Arab Spring." *Kuwait Programme Research Paper* No. 36 (May 2014).

Sectarianism

All doctrines justifying the disparaging of other sets of religious doctrines within a broader religious tradition, promoting division within one religion, sometimes to justify criminal violence or open political conflict. Sectarianism in the Middle East and North Africa most frequently refers to conflict between Sunnis and Shi'as but can include militant Salafis' killing of other Muslims belonging to any other form of doctrine. Throughout the centuries of Islamic history, Muslims following different doctrinal forms have lived together peacefully in many places for protracted periods. However, competing leaders sometimes appeal to differences in religious doctrine to justify their battles in pursuit of power. For example, Shah Ismail I, the first Safavid ruler, forced his Azerbaijani Turkish army to convert to Jafari (Twelver) Shi'a doctrine, to use the difference in his battles against the Sunni Ottoman Turks. He then promoted Shi'a doctrine throughout Iran.

The Iranian Revolution gave great power to sectarian competition. The Ayatollah Khomeini threatened his neighbors and sought to export his revolution in the name of Shi'a Islam. Khomeini sought credibility as an Islamic leader. Iran supports not only the Shi'a Hezbollah movement of Lebanon but also the Sunni group Hamas in Gaza, as well as the Christian Armenians against the Shi'a Azerbaijanis. This shows that sectarianism alone cannot explain Iranian policy. Although in purely religious terms, Shi'as despise the Alawites of Syria as following a corrupt religion, for political reasons—the value of the alliance with Syria—Iran disregards this antipathy.

On the Sunni side, Salafi doctrine justifies antagonism to Shi'as and Sufis. The extent to which individual preachers or states use this antagonism to motivate violence varies according to political conditions. While at some times in their history the Ba'athists in Syria and Iraq promoted official impartiality between Sunnis and Shi'as, when insecurity rose, both states deliberately exploited sectarian loyalties. On January 13, 1991, Iraq added *"Allahu Akbar"* (God is greatest) to the flag and in 1993 launched a "faith campaign" to get international Sunni support for lifting sanctions. At the beginning of the civil war in Syria, the government released Sunni Salafi militants, knowing they would stir up sectarian strife. Bashar al-Assad believed this would solidify his political base of support, because the alternative to his government would be extinction.

In contrast to these examples of instrumental exploitation of sectarian loyalties, the king of Jordan, Abdullah II bin Al-Hussein, organized a conference of leading scholars from 50 countries to defend the consensus Islamic position of the unity of Muslims in different schools of legal interpretation and practice. They created the Amman Message to signify their rejection of sectarianism as well as the extremism of militants.

Fouad Gehad Marei

See also: Hezbollah; Iran, Islamic Republic of; Islamism; Khomeini, Ayatollah Sayyid Ruhollah Mūsavi; Salafism; Saudi Arabia, Kingdom of; Saudi Sahwa (Islamic Awakening); Shi'a; Syrian Arab Republic; Primary Document: *The Amman Message*

Further Reading

Abdo, Geneive. *The New Sectarianism: The Arab Uprisings and the Rebirth of the Shi'a-Sunni Divide*. New York: Oxford University Press, 2017.

Gause, F. Gregory, III. "Beyond Sectarianism: The New Middle East Cold War." Analysis Paper No. 11. Doha, Qatar: Brookings Doha Center, July 2014.

Hashemi, Nader, and Danny Postel. *Sectarianization: Mapping the New Politics of the Middle East*. London: Hurst & Company, 2017.

Shabiha Militias

Pro–Bashar Assad militias operating throughout Syria as a well-trained, well-supplied, and efficient extension of Syrian military operations. The *shabihas* developed out of various criminal gangs that Hafez al-Assad used to assist in the Syrian occupation of Lebanon in 1976. Beginning from the town of Latakia, they consolidated power through smuggling operations. Most of the *shabiha* members come from the Alawite community, closely tied to the Assad family. While observers noted the existence of these pro-government militias before the start of the 2011 civil war, these groups became much more organized, strategic, and political in their operations.

The "Popular Committees" that formed in Alawite neighborhoods to safeguard against attacks by Sunnis gradually evolved into pro-government militias that committed several atrocities across the country, including the Houla Massacre of May 25, 2012. The *shabihas* work closely with government forces and commit criminal violence after government forces have concluded military operations in an area. In addition to the direct military effects of their activities, they provide follow-up intimidation to deter dissent. Their targeted attacks against Sunni Muslims, especially in northern Syria, contributed to the rise of Salafi militias in response, therefore increasing the ethno-sectarian nature of the Syrian conflict. Their operations resemble those of the Iranian Basij paramilitary group as well as Hezbollah and receive support from both organizations.

Samanvya Singh Hooda

See also: Basij; Hezbollah; Houla Massacre; Syrian Arab Republic; Syrian Civil War

Further Reading

Cepoi, Ecaterina. "The Rise of Islamism in Contemporary Syria from Muslim Brotherhood to Salafi-Jihadi Rebels." *Studia Politica: Romanian Political Science Review* 13, no. 3 (2013): 549–60.

Chapman, Andrew. "Defining and Dangerous? An Examination of the Assad Regime's Use of the Shabiha Militia in the Syrian Conflict." In *CISD Yearbook of Global Studies*, 98–119. London: SOAS, University of London, 2014.

Phillips, Christopher. "Sectarianism and Conflict in Syria." *Third World Quarterly* 36, no. 2 (March 2015): 357–76.

Shi'a

The largest minority in Islam, consisting of several variants, constituting the majority form of practice in Iran, Iraq, and Bahrain. Historically, the people known as the *"Shi'at 'Ali"* (partisans of Ali, the cousin and son-in-law of the Prophet Muhammad) have formed ruling dynasties in several regions: the Buyids ruled Iran 934–1062; and the Ismaili Fatamid Caliphate ruled Egypt 909–1171. Although the doctrines of the Shi'as took codified form only 200 years after the beginning of Islam, the Shi'as point back to the contested succession to the Prophet as leader of the Islamic community to explain the origins of their faith.

The two largest communities of Muslims have developed contrasting political principles. The majority, or dominant, form of Islam, called "Sunni," derives from the expression *Ahl al Sunna wa'l Jama'a* (The people of the Prophet's way and the community). They believe that leadership passes to the most qualified, based on the consensus of the leaders. In contrast, the Shi'as believe that political and religious authority passes through the descendants of the Prophet, through Ali. They tend to favor a more formal, hierarchical structure of religious authority, requiring decades in study to advance from one level to the next. The Shi'as consist of several groups. The majority population of Iran, Iraq, and Bahrain who ascribe religious authority to a leader (an *imam*) 12 generations down from Muhammad are called the *Ithna Ashari* (Twelver Shi'a). Other smaller groups attribute spiritual authority to a man in the fifth generation (the Zaydis of Yemen), or to a man in the seventh generation (the Ismailis; widely scattered, but some live in Syria and Lebanon).

Jonathan K. Zartman

See also: Alawites (Nusayris); Hamas; Hezbollah; Ibadi Doctrine; Minorities; Sectarianism

Further Reading

Cole, Juan Ricardo. *Sacred Space and Holy War: The Politics, Culture and History of Shi'ite Islam.* New York: I. B. Tauris, 2005.

Fuller, Graham E. *The Arab Shi'a: The Forgotten Muslims.* New York: St. Martin's Press, 1999.

Haider, Najam Iftikhar. *Shi'i Islam: An Introduction.* New York: Cambridge University Press, 2014.

Social Media

Networking platforms used during political demonstrations and upheaval across the Middle East and North Africa (MENA), leading to regime changes in Tunisia, Egypt, and Yemen and to the eruption of civil war in Libya and Syria during 2011.

Before the uprisings, political analysts neglected the impact of social media technologies on protest movements, considering them as merely the fashion of the younger generation. By focusing on physical collective action to achieve a goal, they failed to consider the necessity of communication for social mobilization. Protest organizers used social media to collect and focus grievances against the government and to overcome the inherent hesitation to take risks.

In 2010, as the political unrest in the Arab world started to boil, the Oxford Internet Institute reported that 60 percent of the MENA's population had at least intermittent Internet access during this period. In many Arab countries, multiple people share Internet devices, which greatly increases the number of people with potential access. However, access does not correlate with social mobilization. Despite some of the highest levels of social media penetration, the United Arab Emirates, Bahrain, Qatar, Lebanon, and Kuwait experienced only low levels of unrest during the spring of 2011.

Social media provided a means for assorted civil groups to collaborate in developing the protest narrative, the "frame" explaining and justifying collective activity. A clear, emotionally powerful narrative justifying resistance ensured a wide base of support on the streets. This affected the strategy of the various civil efforts to force political concessions. It provided a crucial unifying element, holding groups together in a shared commitment to resisting the old regimes. With a common purpose, the networks of activists shared experiences, organized joint efforts, and survived their government's efforts to disrupt and suppress their activity.

People in the MENA region, on average, suffer under some of the highest rates of government censorship, a historical pattern of strong-arm tactics to limit physical organizations. Internet activists initially escaped this form of repression because the broader movements in each country lacked a hierarchical structure. Instead, small local groups networked with one another and also with distant groups throughout the world. As Internet-savvy youth promoted their message via social media, even groups with long-standing disputes set aside their differences to agree on a common platform. Information released on social media shaped the narrative by appealing to shared anger against the government.

The propagation of a resistance narrative on social media did not automatically create the physical means for organization. Already existing civic groups effectively filled this role, such as the labor union in Tunisia. In the short run, connections with other groups with experience and skills in confronting the police proved crucial, such as the Takrizards in Tunisia. In the longer run, the mosque and Islamic institutions provided the physical and social space for activists to organize resistance against the old regimes. Social media enhanced the speed of the wider movement, but at times cyber activists saw their objectives overtaken by existing physical movements that did not need them, once the passion of the protest became widely distributed.

Formulating effective policies in the current world requires understanding the interaction between social media and mobilization. Contemporary social-mobilization strategy relies on activism through multiple media formats. The continued spread of devices with Internet access accentuates the importance of understanding the effects of this medium. The 2011 protests have motivated many governments to establish control over social-media content. In response, networked activists search for ways to evade those restrictions. Social media is agnostic regarding content. The rapid distribution of information can cause short periods of societal change, producing a temporary surge of stimulus, but established governments have a similar ability to utilize the medium and reassert their control.

Sean Nicholus Blas

See also: Algerian Protests; Badawi, Raif; Civil Wars; Economic Protests; February 17th Revolution; February 20 Movement; Framing Model; Gezi Park Protests; Green Movement; Grievance Model; Jasmine Revolution; Jordanian Protests; Nakhla, Rami; Oman Protests; Pearl Roundabout Protests; Regime Change Cascades; Saudi Arabian Protests; Syrian Civil War; Tahrir Square Protests; Takrizards; Yemen Uprising

Further Reading

Esposito, John, Tamara Sonn, and John Voll. *Islam and Democracy after the Arab Spring.* Oxford, UK: Oxford University Press, 2016.

Joffe, George. "The Arab Spring in North Africa: Origins and Prospects." *The Journal of North African Studies* 16, no. 4 (December 2011): 507–32.

Salem, Fadi. *The Arab Social Media Report 2017: Social Media and the Internet of Things: Towards Data-Driven Policymaking in the Arab World* 7. Dubai: MBR School of Government, 2017.

Tawil-Souri, Helga. "It's Still About the Power of Place." *Middle East Journal of Culture and Communications* 5, no.1 (2012): 86–95.

Syria, Jabhat al-Nusra. *See Hayat Tahrir al-Sham*

Syrian Arab Republic

A multiconfessional, Arab, socialist dictatorship located in the Levant, at the heart of the area known historically as al-Sham, or Greater Syria, with Damascus as its capital. After the defeat of the Ottoman Empire, the French occupied the area south of the new Republic of Turkey, and north of the area of Iraq and Palestine. In July 1922 the League of Nations granted France a mandate to prepare the territory it governed in the Levant for independent statehood. Although France did engage in some infrastructure development and started creating state institutions, it also exploited the region economically, and the Arab population demanded independence. Syria acquired its independence in 1946, under a nationalist leadership composed of urban and Sunni notables who had been active in the political and administrative spheres since the Ottoman rule over the region.

From 1946 to 1963 the Syrian State suffered many military coups, and the army controlled society. In 1963, the Ba'ath Party took power, but battles between different factions of the party produced frequent changes of government and additional military coups. In 1967, Israel defeated the Arab states, and Syria lost the Golan Heights. In 1970, the minister of Defense, Air Force general Hafiz al-Assad, organized the last military coup. He consolidated his power over Syria and developed a strong and centralized state. The 1973 Constitution establishes the predominance of the president in an authoritarian system based upon the Ba'ath Party, the bureaucracy, and the army.

Under Assad's rule, the Ba'ath Party became a mass party and performed several political functions: it provided the official state ideology; it selected the bureaucratic elite; and it served as an instrument of control and a patronage network. People found that to perform basic tasks, they needed the mediation of the party. The public sector controlled the most important parts of the economic system and employed a high percentage of the Syrian population.

The government maintained a permanent state of war with Israel to justify sustained martial law and a state of emergency, as well as expansion of the military. By advocating stalwart resistance to Israel, and hosting a variety of leftist and terrorist groups, it sought broader Sunni Arab acceptance. Although Iraqi forces blocked Israel from capturing Damascus in 1973, Syria supported Iran in its war with Iraq. After the Islamic Revolution in 1979, Syria formed an alliance with Iran and worked through Hezbollah in Lebanon to threaten Israel indirectly. Syria was a reliable Soviet client state throughout the Cold War and has kept good relations with Russia after 1990.

Syrian society suffered under the pervasive control of the state intelligence. Hafiz al-Assad controlled society and the state with a mix of repression and cooptation policies. For example, he created the Progressive National Front (PNF), which allowed some leftist parties to engage in strictly limited political activity and gave them representation in the parliament. The state banned other parties or movements. Significant personalities outside the PNF could run for election only as independents. Assad harshly repressed the Muslim Brotherhood. In 1982, when the Brotherhood organized a rebellion, Assad responded by destroying a significant part of the city of Hama, killing an estimated 20,000 people.

When Hafiz died, his son Bashar took his place, presenting himself as a reformer promoting modernization. He announced reforms in the political field to open the system and reform the Ba'ath Party. After the first positive speeches of the young president, intellectuals, dissidents, activists, businessmen, academics, and former opposition leaders started discussion forums and human rights organizations, a movement described as the "Damascus Spring." They asked for reforms through public petitions, the end of the state of emergency, the release of political prisoners, comprehensive political reforms, and the freedom of press and speech. The regime responded to these movements with repression, closing the forums and arresting activists. In 2005, opposition leaders created a document entitled the "Damascus Declaration," to establish a unified platform for democratic change.

After the 2003 invasion of Iraq, Syria supported the Sunni resistance to the coalition by funneling large numbers of foreign fighters into the conflict, providing a safe haven and logistics. After the assassination of Rafik Hariri in Lebanon in 2005, the United States withdrew its ambassador. However, in April 2007, U.S. representatives visited Assad to encourage Syria in its negotiations with Israel, which Turkey was mediating. On September 6, 2007, Israel destroyed a suspected nuclear reactor in the Deir al-Zor region of Syria. Prominent members of the U.S.

Congress continued to advocate engagement with Syria, in opposition to the policy of the George Bush administration.

With regard to the economic sector, Bashar al-Assad implemented some liberalization measures inspired by the Chinese model, which theoretically combined capitalist logic with the social role of the state. Under a previous effort to create a mixed economy in the 1970s, Hafiz al-Assad had developed patronage relations with Sunni factory owners and merchants, giving them a monopoly in some economic sectors, to reduce their antagonism to the Alawites ruling through the military. In the more open economic policies of the 1980s and 1990s, a new group of elites formed, an oligarchy composed of high-ranking officials and their offspring. After Bashar became president, the sons of these important families tied to the regime became key players, with monopoly control in the new sectors created by Bashar's economic liberalization.

The government opened the domestic market to Chinese products and other low-cost imports, which hurt the business of the traditional merchants and industrialists. Therefore, these middle- and small-scale merchants turned against the regime. Furthermore, the rural population lost government subsidies during the worst drought in centuries. This forced large numbers of peasants to flee to the urban areas, creating dramatic growth in the peripheries of Damascus and Aleppo. By the end of 2010, the economic situation for most of Syria had become quite difficult, at the same time a very small elite displayed its wealth. Therefore, during Bashar's era, economic liberalization did not lead to either growth or job opportunities, while large segments of the population lost benefits they had previously received from the state. Bashar al-Assad lost the broad social base and alienated the key constituencies that his father had attracted.

The first protests broke out in Dara'a, a rural southern region that had traditionally supported the regime, an indication of the severity of increasing rural discontent. In 2011, the first protests called only for the civil and political rights claimed in earlier petitions. The people created local coordination committees (LCCs) to organize demonstrations and formulate demands. The grassroots civil resistance represented by committees and local councils supported the material survival of their communities, providing humanitarian aid and medical care.

The government responded to the nonviolent protests with heavy repression and a military escalation. The government's official narrative denied the spontaneous, authentic character of the protests but blamed foreign governments for manipulating people and called the protesters Sunni warriors. In October 2011, the Syrian government released 1,500 militant Islamists. They formed the leadership of local militias, like Jaysh al-Islam and Aḥrar al-Sham, and were the founding members of Jabhat al-Nuṣrah (the Syrian branch of al-Qaeda-JAN).

The protesters held to their nonsectarian, peaceful protest strategy for a year, while suffering brutal attacks from security forces. In spite of the military escalation, which increased over time, the government lost significant parts of its territory. After 2012, external actors became involved, transforming the conflict in Syria into a proxy war. Qatar and the Gulf states contributed funds and guns. Preachers throughout the Arab world exhorted young men to fight in Syria, and thousands poured in through Turkey. Iran and Hezbollah provided military support to the government, while China and Russia gave political support by blocking UN resolutions advanced by Western countries. On June 12, 2012, a UN official called the conflict in Syria a civil war.

The central government's strategy sought to maintain control of the territories encompassing the major urban areas of Damascus, Homs, Hama, Latakia, and Tartus. Some regions at the border with Turkey and with Jordan and some other little enclaves fell under the control of a collection of militias named Free Syrian Army (FSA), which received some inconsistent support from the Arab Gulf states, Turkey, and Europe. The vast number of independent groups and the Islamist character of some of them deterred support from the United States. In the north-eastern region of the country, the government disengaged and left some districts under the direct control of Kurdish parties and militias.

In 2014, an Islamist militant group with the ambition to control territory, rather than merely conduct hit-and-run guerrilla attacks, formed out of Al-Qaeda in Iraq. It took the name al-Dawla al-Islamiya fi al-Iraq wa al-Sham, meaning "The Islamic State in Iraq and Greater Syria," but local people use the Arabic acronym *Daesh*. With the escalation of violence, JAN and Daesh greatly increased their recruiting capacity. They became better equipped and financed and better organized and observed strict discipline. They became a strong second enemy to the civil and democratic resistance.

The United States avoided military intervention in 2013, after the Syrian government attacked Ghouta with chemical weapons. But international attitudes strongly changed after the beheading of Western hostages that began in August 2014 and then the November 13–14, 2015, terrorist attacks in Paris, claimed by Daesh. The United States, with European and Gulf countries, created an international coalition to attack the Islamic State, which had by then conquered a large part of the Syrian territory. However, the success of the opposition put at risk Russia's continued access to its naval base at Tartus and its use of Khmeimim Air Base near Latakia. Russia began providing direct air support for Syria, enabling the government to recapture the territories lost in the past years.

The Syrian political opposition failed in its effort to overthrow the Assad government due to its internal diversity and the lack of unified external support. Several different political coalitions formed, which the ferocity of the war forced to operate from outside the country. Then the activists remaining inside claimed the external politicians lacked credibility. Some groups were willing to negotiate with Assad, but others refused. Some tried to hold to a purely nonviolent political stance, but they could not represent the militant parties inside the country. While the Unites States wanted to back a secular or moderate opposition, Qatar and Turkey supported the Islamists. Because the Kurds provided a safe haven for persecuted minorities fleeing from Daesh, they won popular support in the United States. Furthermore, they demonstrated political will, military competence, and internal cohesion, making them an effective partner in defeating Daesh, but U.S. support for the Kurds aroused the anger of Turkey.

Since 2016, with Iranian and Russian help, Syria has gradually recaptured much of the territories previously lost. Although diplomatic negotiations continue, the government holds such a position of strength that it has no motivation to concede anything. Without the replacement of the regime, many external parties will not fund reconstruction, and much of the opposition will remain in rebellion.

Valentina Zecca

See also: Ahrar al-Sham Brigades; Al-Assad, Bashar; Alawites (Nusayris); Authoritarianism; Ba'athism; Civil Wars; Druze; Free Syrian Army; Ghouta Chemical Weapons Attack of 2013; Ghouta Chemical Weapons Attack of 2018; Hayat Tahrir al-Sham (HTS); Houla Massacre; Iran, Islamic Republic of; Islamic State (Daesh); Local Coordination Committees; Military Coups; Nakhla, Rami; Sectarianism; *Shabiha* Militia; Syrian Civil War

Further Reading

Baczko, Adam, Gilles Dorronsoro, and Arthur Quesnay. *Civil War in Syria: Mobilization and Competing Social Orders.* New York: Cambridge University Press, 2018.

Harris, William. *Quicksilver War: Syria, Iraq, and the Spiral of Conflict.* London: Hurst, 2018.

Hinnebusch, Raymond, and Omar Imady, eds. *The Syrian Uprising: Domestic Origins and Early Trajectory.* London: Routledge, 2018.

Kassab, Robin Yassin, and Leila al-Shami. *Burning Country. Syrians in Revolution and War.* London: Pluto Press, 2016.

Lesch, David W. *Syria: The Fall of the House of Assad.* New Haven, CT: Yale University Press, 2013.

Lister, Charles R. *The Syrian Jihad: Al-Qaeda, The Islamic State and the Evolution of an Insurgency.* New York: Oxford University Press, 2015.

Van Dam, Nikolaos. *Destroying a Nation: The Civil War in Syria.* New York: I. B. Tauris, 2017.

Syrian Civil War

A complex conflict in Syria that began in 2011 as a protest movement that expanded and intensified into a sectarian and proxy war involving hundreds of state and nonstate groups—killing more than 500,000 people and displacing more than half of the country's population. In March 2011, police arrested 15 young boys for spray-painting reform slogans on a school building, and then tortured and killed them. Syrians began peaceful protests against this injustice. The government responded with excessive violence, further enraging the people. The popular protest movement grew rapidly, as people complained against oppression, corruption, and poor economic conditions. The state also countered with pro-government rallies and gave citizenship to some Kurds previously kept stateless, to placate protesters. However, the government also deliberately released hard-core radical Islamist political prisoners, knowing that they would threaten and attack the minority populations.

Government violence escalated to using siege tactics, barrel bombs, and tanks to control opposition-held areas. After security forces killed thousands of civilians, several officers of the Syrian Army defected, forming an organization called the Free Syrian Army (FSA). Tens of thousands of soldiers deserted, filling the ranks of more than 1,200 opposition groups. Government propaganda blamed Sunni groups for the conflict. The government formed civilian gangs of common thugs called the *Shabiha* Militias, who tortured, raped, and killed many civilians. Security efforts concentrated on Damascus and Aleppo, leaving large areas of the country vulnerable to armed groups.

As the opposition movement grew, a network of Local Coordination Committees (LCC) formed to promote nonviolent and nonsectarian protest, but violence by the government drove the opposition to resist with force. While the Free Syrian Army, with its headquarters in Turkey, tried to gain international support, it could not actively guide or coordinate the combat operations of widely scattered brigades. By 2012, the United Nations classified the conflict as a civil war between the Assad government and largely uncoordinated militias. As the conflict expanded, the rebels sought outside support, arms, and funding, but they did not get immediate international support.

The government actively promoted the idea that the opposition constituted a Sunni attack on Alawites, Druze, and Christians, to force members of those groups into greater loyalty. In 2013, as the conflict became more sectarian in nature, several Islamist groups banded together to form the Islamic Front. These groups desired a government based on Islamic law but were more moderate than the al-Qaeda–derived Jabhat al-Nusra (Nusra Front—JN) or the new and more violent Islamic State (Daesh) formed in Iraq. As Islamist preachers throughout the Middle East recruited young men to defend the Sunnis of Syria from Assad, great amounts of men, money, guns, and ammunition poured into the Islamist fighting groups, at the expense of the moderate and secular FSA groups. In 2014, Daesh declared itself a caliphate, imposing an extreme form of brutal governance, keeping the population under its control in a state of fear. Daesh attacked the FSA more than the Syrian government and then launched a wave of conquest into Iraq in 2014, relatively quickly conquering Mosul and extracting significant amounts of modern weaponry and money, as well as control of oil. Kurds in the north defended themselves against the spread of Daesh, forming highly effective defense forces.

The conflict grew beyond a civil war to a proxy theater for multiple international interests. In 2013, Assad used mustard gas on opposition enclaves. While the United States discussed whether and how to respond, ultimately Russia announced a deal in which Assad would get rid of his chemical weapons in 2014. However, the April 2017 chemical attack on Khan Shaykhun and the 2018 chemical attack on Ghouta showed the fraudulent nature of Syria's claim of destroying these chemical stocks.

The United States engaged belatedly in some efforts to support the FSA, but delays and difficulties in trying to select recipients who would not promote Islamism caused the whole program to fail. Daesh and the other Islamist militias quickly defeated or captured the small numbers trained and equipped. The United States also tried to establish coordination with Qatar, Saudi Arabia, and the United Arab Emirates, but those efforts did not produce fruit until the rise of Daesh, which threatened the whole region. Small teams of special forces, combined with air force surveillance, provided the capability for precision airstrikes to support opposition forces, primarily the Kurds, to defeat Daesh.

Conversely, Russia provided arms and air support to the Assad regime in an effort to protect its own strategic interests. Iran and Lebanese Hezbollah provided money and seasoned fighters to fight for Assad. Turkey allowed foreign fighters to travel freely across its border to join various groups in Syria, and also attacked Kurdish forces. In late 2014, U.S.-backed Kurds attacked Daesh and JN forces, pushing them out of the Turkish border areas. In late 2016, the Turkish military, partnering with Syrian proxy forces, launched operation Euphrates Shield to clear Daesh and the Kurdish militia from Aleppo Province, establishing a Turkish protectorate in the area. In the southwest, the United States, Russia, and Jordan negotiated a cease-fire. In 2018, believing that the major armed groups loyal to Daesh had been defeated, the United States declared its intent to withdraw troops. This evoked protests from the opposition Syrian Democratic Forces, an alliance of local militias led by the Kurds, which controls northeast Syria. The regime maintains its power base in the west. Essentially, Assad has survived an eight-year civil war but cannot yet retake the disputed territories. Some refugees have begun to return, but the United States will not fund reconstruction until the political order becomes stable.

The militant Islamist opposition groups have fled to and remain in control of Idlib Province. Turkey and Russia have engaged in extensive diplomacy to limit the regime's attacks in the area, which holds three million people.

David R. Leonard

See also: Ahrar al-Sham Brigades; Al-Assad, Bashar; Alawites (Nusayris); Civil Wars; Free Syrian Army; Ghouta Chemical Attack of 2013; Ghouta Chemical Attack of 2018; Hayat Tahrir al-Sham (HTS); Houla Massacre; Islamic State (Daesh); Local Coordination Committees; *Shabiha* Militias

Further Reading
Lister, Charles R. *The Syrian Jihad: Al-Qaeda, the Islamic State and the Evolution of an Insurgency.* New York: Oxford University Press, 2015.
Ratney, Michael. "Post-Conflict Stabilization: What Can We Learn from Syria?" *PRISM* 7, no. 4 (2018): 48–63.
Van Dam, Nikolaos. *Destroying a Nation: The Civil War in Syria.* New York: I. B. Tauris, 2017.
Zisser, Eyal. "The End of the Syrian Civil War: The Many Implications." *Middle East Quarterly,* June 16, 2019.

Syrian Protests (2011). See Syrian Civil War

T

Tahrir Square Protests (2011)

A series of demonstrations that started on January 25, 2011, in Cairo and all major Egyptian cities, such as Alexandria and Suez (also known as the January 25 Revolution), inspired by the revolt in Tunisia that overthrew the Tunisian president Ben Ali. After small protests the previous weeks, youth organizations chose the date January 25 to denounce endemic police brutality. The young, creative protesters organized through online networks, initiating a series of demonstrations, marches, strikes, and acts of civil disobedience centered on the Tahrir Square in the center of Cairo.

The protesters organized their own security system because they often found infiltrators—either police officers or criminals released by the government to create chaos and justify repression by the security forces. The police and the infiltrating criminals violently attacked the protesters, took random detainees, tortured, and even raped female demonstrators, inside the Egyptian museum used as an operations center, due to its proximity to the square. Almost 900 people died, and more than 6,000 were injured. The protesters demanded the end of police brutality, the removal the state-emergency law, free elections, and free speech. Above all, they called for the overthrow of President Hosni Mubarak due to the prevalence of torture and disappearances, as well as corruption and fraud. He finally resigned on February 11, 2011, after 18 days of revolution.

After Mubarak's resignation, the military assumed power—with the support of the Egyptian people, who celebrated in the streets. The military suspended the constitution and dissolved Parliament, as well as the ruling National Democratic Party and the State Security Investigation Centre. Criminals looted most buildings and set them on fire.

Carolina Bracco

See also: April 6 Youth; Corruption; Egypt, Arab Republic of; El-Sisi, Abdel Fattah Saeed Hussein Khalil; Ghonim, Wael; Grievance Model; Mubarak, Muhammad Hosni Sayyid

Further Reading

Hassan, Abdalla F. *Media, Revolution and Politics in Egypt. The Story of an Uprising.* London: Tauris, 2015.

Sowers, Jeannie, and Chris Toesing, eds. *The Journey to Tahrir: Revolution, Protest, and Social Change in Egypt.* London: Verso, 2012.

Tawil-Souri, Helga. "It's Still About the Power of Place." *Middle East Journal of Culture and Communication* 5, no.1 (2012): 86–95.

Takfiri Doctrine

An Arabic term meaning to denounce for unbelief, based on the term *kafir* for non-Muslim. The term originated in the literature by the Khawārij (Kharajites), who denounced both Sunni and Shi'ite Muslims as *kafir* (unbelievers) to justify waging war against both. Ibn Taymiyya (d. 1328) championed the doctrine in his early writings but warned against it later in life, saying that Muslims cannot call each other unbelievers. The Egyptian scholar Sayyid Qutb, the ideologist of the Egyptian Muslim Brotherhood, revived the use of the term. He argued that all modern Muslim polities, failing to enforce *sharia,* protect their borders from *kafir* powers, or respect the men of religion, have forced Muslims to live under a state of *jahaliyya* (pre-Islamic ignorance and moral depravity), making the practice of *takfir* a necessity. In the 1980s, small terrorist organizations emerged to translate Qutb's ideas into violent action by waging war against the Egyptian state. One such group called itself Takfir wa'l Hijra, meaning "denounce and take flight" or *takfir,* and emigrate from any territory under the authority of non-Muslims.

Today, Sunni Islamist groups commonly use the term, and contemporary Islamist thinkers have developed Qutb's thought considerably. The leadership of groups who most passionately espouse the right to denounce other Muslims have a modern, secular education, not the traditional education of the madrassa and such great institutions as Egypt's Al Azhar. The opposing orthodox doctrine, called *Irja,* meaning "postponing," argues that faith is a matter of the heart, which only Allah can evaluate, not other human beings. Therefore, true piety combined with the humility that honors Allah as the only judge of men postpones the question of who is a true Muslim until the afterlife.

Jeffrey Kaplan

See also: Egypt, Arab Republic of; *Jihad;* Muslim Brotherhood

Further Reading

Adang, Camilla, Hassan Ansari, Maribel Fierro, and Sabine Schmidtke. *Accusations of Unbelief in Islam: A Diachronic Perspective on Takfīr*. Leiden, the Netherlands: Brill, 2015.

Cozzens, Jeffrey B. "Al-Takfir Wa'l Hijra: Unpacking an Enigma." *Studies in Conflict & Terrorism* 32, no. 6 (2009): 489–510.

Ramadan, Abdel Azim. "Fundamentalist Influence in Egypt: The Strategies of the Muslim Brotherhood and the Takfir Groups." In *Fundamentalisms and the State: Remaking Polities, Economies and Militance,* 152–83. Chicago: University of Chicago Press, 1993.

Takrizards

Members of Takriz, a Tunisian online cyber-hacking activist group opposed to the regime of Ben Ali, which formed a collaborative alliance with violent soccer fans. The Takriz, taking a name from Tunisian street slang, began in the late 1990s as a cyber think tank. They employed their hacking skills to mock the government and to publicize its abuse of human rights. In 1999, some Takrizards (or Taks) began to see the value of allying with the most violent fans, after a savage riot at a Tunisian soccer game left several fans dead. Angry, unemployed young men in the cities formed tightly knit, motivated groups of soccer fans, known as "ultras," who relished using dramatic displays of intimidation and aggression. Due to their battles with the police almost every weekend, they became battle-hardened and adept in using synchronized swarming behavior. The Taks created Internet fora that allowed "ultra" fans to link with one another and eventually with political activists. Over time, this new form of social linkage spread to their counterparts in Algeria, Egypt, Libya, and Morocco.

Ben Ali's policies had produced a large number of educated youth without any prospects for good jobs. In the decade preceding the revolution, Internet usage in Tunisia grew significantly. By the spring of 2011, the World Bank estimated roughly 35 percent of the population had Internet access, while other sources claim 20 percent of the population used Facebook. This created very favorable circumstances for individuals and groups to use social media to convert anger and grievances into action. When the crisis came, a hacker group shut down the government's websites while Takriz functioned as an information source, providing news and videos from all over Tunisia. The "ultra" forums also provided ways to quickly mobilize and direct crowds of tough, aggressive regime opponents. Other platforms also enabled people interacting anonymously on social networks to transfer their passions into action in the real world, on the street. The Takrizards created a template for political activists to work with cyber activists to create massive demonstrations that could endure and defeat the police repression.

Tom Dowling

See also: Egypt, Arab Republic of; Grievance Model; Jasmine Revolution; Modernization; Social Media; Tunisia, Republic of

Further Reading

Dutta, Mohan. "Communication, Power and Resistance in the Arab Spring: Voices of Social Change from the South." *Journal of Creative Communications* 8, no. 2–3 (July and November 2013): 139–55.

Hoffman, Michael, and Amaney Jamal. "The Youth and the Arab Spring: Cohort Differences and Similarities." *Middle East Law and Governance* 4, no. 1 (January 2012): 168–88.

Honwana, Alcinda. *Youth and Revolution in Tunisia*. London: Zed Books, 2013.

Pollock, John. "Streetbook: How Egyptian and Tunisian Youth Hacked the Arab Spring." *Technology Review* 114, no. 5 (September/October 2011): 70–82.

Tamarod Movement (2013)

A peaceful grassroots Egyptian movement strongly opposed to the rule of President Mohamed Morsi. In late April 2013, five activists, aged 22 to 30, with experience in the Egyptian Movement for Change (Kifaya), decided to conduct a petition campaign called Tamarod (Rebellion). The petition listed a number of grievances against the Morsi administration for its failures to provide security, justice, dignity, and economic recovery. As Egypt's first elected civilian president, Morsi carried the presumption of legitimacy; however, in office he behaved in a very autocratic manner. Because the military and officials remaining in office from the Mubarak era inhibited the restoration of full government operations, instability and continuing violence prevented economic recovery. The people began blaming Morsi for the lack of any improvement in their daily lives since the revolution of 2011.

On May 1, 2013, a core group of 50 persons began circulating a petition stating that the nation lacked any confidence in Morsi's ability to govern. The campaign aimed to collect 15 million signatures by June 30, 2013, with a simple message, "Irhal!" (Leave!). The petition demanded the president's resignation, the establishment of an interim government, the rewriting of the constitution, and early presidential elections. By early June, activists and political parties gained support from businessmen, members of the Muslim and Christian religious establishments of Al-Azhar and the Coptic Church, members of the security services, and later members from the army itself. Tamarod activists claimed that they had established offices in all of Egypt's 27 governorates. They used social networking effectively, and their Facebook page listed more than 500,000 followers. They adopted a tactic of "print, copy, sign, and collect," which mobilized thousands of teenagers and university students to collect signatures, reaching out to all political factions.

On June 19, they announced that they had 15 million signatures, approximately two million more than the votes President Morsi had received in the election. Ultimately, they would claim more than 22 million signatures, but no outside party ever audited these claims. Supporters of President Morsi mounted a counter campaign called Tagarod (Impartiality), which claimed that it had collected 11 million signatures by June 20, 2013, but that movement lacked the support to compete with Tamarod. At the end of June, Tamarod announced the formation of the June 30 Front, a coalition of opposition groups that had developed a road map for the transition.

On June 30, 2013, over 30 million Egyptians demonstrated. The Egyptian military opened negotiations with the political opposition parties. Tamarod supporters solicited the military's help in removing Morsi and the Muslim Brotherhood from power. On July 3, 2013, the Egyptian military, led by Abdel Fattah el-Sisi, took control of the government and arrested President Morsi and Muslim Brotherhood leaders. The military negotiations with the June 30 Front reached consensus and met many of the opposition parties' demands, a remarkable accomplishment for a group that included the Coptic Pope and the conservative Salafi Al Nour Party.

After the ouster of Morsi, Egyptian-U.S. relations suffered strain because, since 2012, the United States had conditioned its military and economic aid on steps to support democracy and improve human rights. These disruptions subsided relatively quickly.

Mark David Luce

See also: Authoritarianism; Coptic Orthodox Church; El-Sisi, Abdel Fattah Saeed Hussein Khalil; Grievance Model; Military Coups; Morsi, Mohamed; Muslim Brotherhood; Social Media

Further Reading

Chandler, Matthew J. "Civil Resistance Mechanisms and Disrupted Democratization: The Ambiguous Outcomes of Unarmed Insurrections in Egypt, 2011–2015." *Peace & Change* 43, no. 1 (January 2018): 90–116.

Housden, Oliver. "Egypt: Coup d'Etat or a Revolution Protected?" *The RUSI Journal* 158, no. 5 (2013): 72–78.

"Marching in Circles: Egypt's Dangerous Second Transition." *Middle East/North Africa Briefing* No. 35. Brussels, Belgium: International Crisis Group, August 7, 2013.

Tunisia, Republic of

A fledgling democracy on the northern coast of Africa between Algeria and Libya, distinguished by the pragmatic compromise among contending social forces that has enabled a working constitutional order. Tunisia's modern history shows a strong effort to modernize. Unfortunately, in the early 1800s excessive spending in that effort led to bankruptcy, and debt to European lenders, which led to European domination. In 1881, France took control of Tunisia. The French treated Tunisia as a protectorate, with the appearance of limited sovereignty under local ruling families. The French controlled the courts, finances, education, security, and agriculture.

Following World War I, young nationalists formed the Destour (Constitution) Party, but it remained just a party of the educated elite, lacking support from the rural masses. In 1934, a young, French-trained lawyer named Habib Bourguiba led a more aggressive breakaway faction called the Neo-Destour, focused on social and economic issues—and demanding independence. The French arrested him and other activists to stop the independence movement.

The German and Italian armies occupied Tunisia in World War II until the British, French, and American forces liberated the country in May 1943. Although Bourguiba advocated a gradual process of gaining autonomy, the French threw him in prison again (1952–1954). He spent a total of 10 years in French prisons. Meanwhile, Neo-Destour Party leaders built a national party, mobilizing Tunisians across all classes, regions, and ideologies. The party, allied with the Tunisian General Labor Union (UGTT), built strong international support for their cause. They instigated strikes, mass demonstrations, and small-scale violence intended to influence French public opinion and maintain pressure on the government. In March 1956, Tunisia declared formal independence, with Bourguiba initially as prime minister. He became president in 1957, declaring Tunisia a republic.

After the successful struggle for independence, the Neo-Destour Party split. Bourguiba and his allies represented a progressive wing of the party that reflected the influences of French socialism and its associated secular values. They pursued policies intended to generate economic growth and distribute it equitably. However, more traditional socialists on their left advocated state control of the economy, and a conservative, religious wing on the right opposed the state policies of secularism and affiliation with European ideals. Bourguiba embarked on efforts to reduce the social and public role of religion, to control religion to serve state purposes, even discouraging fasting during Ramadan. He pursued a pragmatic rather than hard-core socialism.

In the early 1960s, concern about the conservative opposition and the failure of the private sector to generate sufficient growth prompted Bourguiba to shift toward the socialist position. In 1964 the Neo-Destour changed its name to the Destourian Socialist Party (PSD), and its policies became more authoritarian. The government outlawed all other parties while tightly controlling the lower levels of government, the media, and civil society organizations. Because Tunisia distrusted Algeria, in 1974, the Tunisian government considered union with rich Libya, but later quickly turned away. This made Libyan leader Muammar Qaddafi angry, so periodically Libya made threats and caused trouble. In response, Tunisia tripled its defense budget and asked Western countries for help.

From 1971 to 1972 the government cracked down on leftist student organizations. In response, Islamists began recruiting in secondary schools and universities. At the same time, Anwar Sadat began releasing Muslim Brothers from Egyptian jails; some of them traveled to Tunisia. In 1975, Bourguiba was appointed "President for Life."

During a UGTT Labor Union general strike in 1978, security forces fired on striking workers and arrested much of the union leadership. The police were not able to stop the rioting that they had provoked, forcing the army to intervene. Director of National Security Ben Ali suppressed the protests with great violence. The bloodshed created a durable public antagonism to the government. Islamists exploited these conditions to organize and present the grievances of the people. In 1979, the Iranian Revolution provided an Islamic vocabulary for discussing economic and social issues. Libya also contributed to the troubles by sending trained commandos to attack Gafsa in 1980. In 1984, Libya expelled 32,000 Tunisian workers, while the International Monetary Fund (IMF) forced the government to stop subsidizing bread prices. People rioted in anger, but the police and national guard failed to stop the resulting riots. The army suppressed the protests, killing dozens, injuring hundreds.

By the 1980s, Bourguiba and the PSD had lost much of their historic legitimacy. In the fall of 1987, Tunisia teetered on the brink of civil war, but the president had become very erratic in his behavior. On the night of November 7, 1987, the cabinet ministers arranged for Prime Minister Ben Ali to replace Bourguiba on medical grounds.

Ben Ali began his administration with promises of democratization. He renamed the Socialist Destourian Party as the Democratic Constitutional Rally (RCD). In his first year he released thousands of political prisoners, invited exiles to return home, met with opposition-party leaders, eliminated unpopular institutions like presidency-for-life and the state security court, ratified the United Nations' anti-torture convention, and relaxed press restrictions. But his repression intensified with time, and Tunisia's internal-security apparatus grew ever larger. Surveillance, censorship, dirty tricks campaigns to incriminate opposition figures, arrests, and torture became the hallmarks of the government.

The Ben Ali government was forced to follow some IMF and World Bank conditions for reducing deficits. However, whenever the government privatized some assets, they went to the president's family. Ben Ali allowed the extended Trabelsi family of his wife, Leïla, and a few other loyal families to dominate the economy, as a way to control society. Under these conditions of widespread economic repression and intimidation, powerful families could force others to sell their property, while opponents of the regime could not get government jobs. Although the government claimed 5 percent growth for 20 years, the development plans neglected the south and the interior.

Internationally, Tunisia worked to promote dialogue and peace in international disputes. The government adopted an anti-Soviet, pro-West orientation, and tried to moderate the positions of the Palestine Liberation Organization (PLO) while hosting the PLO leaders from 1982 to 1993. However, in the preparation for the World Summit on the Information Society held in Tunis in November 2005, human rights activists sharply criticized Tunisia's repression of domestic society. Human rights groups joined with secular, communist, and Islamist political parties to form the 18 October Coalition for Rights and Freedoms, to show their opposition to the government's policies. They conducted a 52-day general strike, and significant personalities conducted a 32-day hunger strike, demanding freedom of association, information, and expression.

By 2011 the population growth rate was slowing, but economic growth was slowing faster. Tunisia ranked in the middle for the rate of urbanization, compared to other countries of the region. The national income per capita was just below the average for the Arab world. Labor migration had been stable for two years. The rate of basic literacy was not much higher than the average for the region. However, Tunisia ranked highest in the region for freedom of women. In higher education, Tunisians ranked second highest after Kuwait for the number of publications per million inhabitants, second place after Jordan for the number of researchers per million, and second place after Qatar for the quality of research institutions. Tunisia also ranked in the middle for Internet usage statistics. However, the government sources claimed 150,000 unemployed college graduates. In sum, large numbers of capable people in Tunisia could not get a job because the government and the president's family had created too many barriers to starting a business, which restrained investment.

Few anticipated a revolution in Tunisia, but under the surface an increasingly active civil society worked to free the nation from the arbitrary rule of Ben Ali and his close supporters. Rebellious acts proliferated, such as a "silent" protest for Internet freedom in Tunis in 2010, in which participants came together wearing white. This quiet opposition grew in capacity until December 17, 2010, when Mohamed Bouazizi set his own body ablaze in front of a government office in Sidi Bouzid.

In the years leading up to the revolt, Tunisia's economy struggled with successive years of drought and intense competition in global textile markets. Unemployment rates rose very high. Public awareness of corruption, and the degree to which Ben Ali's family was robbing the economy, increased the anger over poor economic conditions. Activists waited and watched for some incident they could exploit to protest against the government. As the protests occurred, marchers and bystanders used cell phone cameras to record clashes with security forces and posted the videos on Facebook. Then Al Jazeera began broadcasting the story and images internationally. This created a shared experience, a common narrative that cut across classes and regions and—ultimately—spread to other countries. The people who created the so-called Jasmine Revolution lacked any coherent organizational structure or political program to apply after they succeeded.

After Ben Ali and his family fled to Saudi Arabia, Tunisian parties and associations began the painstaking process of negotiating a new political order. After some initial confusion, parliamentary speaker Fouad Mebazaa became the interim president and sought to restore government operations. The army struggled to regain control while rioters and looters caused extensive damage and confusion. By February 27, violence still continued, so Prime Minister Mohammed Ghannouchi resigned. From January through March 2011, the interim government granted amnesty to political prisoners, invited exiles to return home, froze the RCD's assets, and began legalizing new political parties, including the Islamist party Ennahda. The government also created commissions to design political reforms and investigate the former regime's crimes.

Tunisians held elections for the Constituent Assembly on October 23, 2011—the first free and fair elections ever held in the country. Just over 40 percent of voters supported Ennahda, giving it the largest share of seats. Two secular parties that had participated in the October 18 Coalition received the next greatest number of votes and agreed to join a coalition government with Ennahda. The coalition partners worked to create a provisional constitution through the Constituent Assembly.

The radical Islamists felt betrayed by Ennahda's compromises. On September 14, 2012, Ansar al-Sharia, linked to al-Qaeda, attacked and burned the U.S. embassy in Tunis and a nearby school. In the midst of increasing instability, and public dissatisfaction with the lack of progress on the economy and growing insecurity, Nida' Tounes, a big-tent party led by incumbents from the Ben Ali era, obtained legal status in 2012. In 2013, terrorists assassinated two very prominent secular politicians, which Tunisians blamed on Ennahda. So Ennahda stepped down from government to avoid a coup.

The politicians writing this constitution debated with great vigor but ultimately reached a stalemate. The Tunisian General Labor Union joined with the Employers Union, the Bar Association, and the Human Rights League, called The Quartet, to negotiate and propose a path forward, which broke the political stalemate and created a constitution that the people could accept. The constitution declared Tunisia a democratic-republican system and advanced women's rights, even by contemporary global standards. It passed on the first vote in early 2014. In the October 2014 parliamentary election, Nida' Tounes won the greatest shares of seats, and that November its leader, Beji Caid Essebsi, won the presidential election. The 2014 constitution commits the state to promoting gender parity in elected assemblies, enabling women to win 47 percent of seats in local councils in May 2018. New parliamentary and presidential elections are slated for late 2019.

Tunisia faces continued concerns over economic challenges and insecurity and the government's responses to these issues. After a series of terrorist attacks on tourist sites killed more than 60 people in 2015, the government declared a state of emergency and extended it again in 2019. Dozens of jihadists attacked security facilities in Ben Guerdane near the Libyan border in 2016, and a woman detonated a bomb in Tunis in 2018, killing herself and injuring 20. Human rights groups criticize the state of emergency powers used by the state to curtail freedoms.

The four-year mandate of the Truth and Dignity Commission concluded in May 2018. Although the tribunal received over 62,700 complaints, the Essebsi government severely hampered the commission's work with numerous roadblocks, resulting in few trials. The commission has tried to deliver the report to the government, which has refused to receive it, effectively blocking its further publication.

Tunisia has not solved any of the economic problems that led to the protests, and its dependence on tourism represents a clear vulnerability for future attacks. The painful concessions made by Ennahda offer real hope that its pragmatic political strategy can enable Tunisia to navigate the sharp divide between secularists and Islamists. However, outside parties have the capability and interests to disrupt Tunisia's negotiated agreement. Large numbers of Libyan refugees in camps on the border also represent a potential threat.

Lindsay J. Benstead

See also: Ammar, Rachid; Authoritarianism; Ben Ali, Zine al-Abidine; Bouazizi, Tarek el-Tayeb Mohamed; Corruption; Ennahda Movement; Ghannouchi, Rachid; Grievance Model; Jasmine Revolution; Social Media; Takrizards; Tunisian General Labor Union; Tunisian National Dialogue Quartet; Women's Leadership in Protests

Further Reading

Benstead, Lindsay J. "Tunisia." In *The Government and Politics of the Middle East and North Africa,* 8th ed, edited by Mark Gasiorowski and Sean Yom, 463–90. Boulder, CO: Westview Press, 2016.

Boukhars, Anouar. "The Geographic Trajectory of Conflict and Militancy in Tunisia." Washington, DC: Carnegie Endowment for International Peace, July 2017.

Cavatorta, Francesco, and Rikke Hostrup Haugbølle. "The End of Authoritarian Rule and the Mythology of Tunisia under Ben Ali." *Mediterranean Politics* 17, no. 2 (July 2012): 179–95.

Hamdi, Mohamed Elhachmi. *The Politicisation of Islam: A Case Study of Tunisia.* Boulder, CO: Westview Press, 2001.

Pickard, Duncan. "Challenges to Legitimate Governance in Post-Revolution Tunisia." *The Journal of North African Studies* 16, no. 4 (December 2011): 637–52.

Stepan, Alfred. "Tunisia's Transition and the Twin Tolerations." *Journal of Democracy* 23, no. 2 (July 2012): 89–103.

Tunisian General Labor Union

The largest, best-organized, independent, nationalist organization in Tunisia, composed of labor unions initially organized in 1924 during the French colonial administration. Despite repeated repression by the French, it endured and in 1946 became the Tunisian General Labor Union. The union combined a dedication to both social and political struggles: it coordinated with the Destour (Constitution) Party in organizing major strikes in January 1952, which brought more French repression. This cooperation with the Destour Party continued until independence in 1958. Emphasizing "independence" and improved conditions for workers, the union did advocate nationalizing key economic sectors. The union now represents more than one million members out of Tunisia's total population of 10 million, with branches in every province.

While pressing for workers' interests, the Union also cooperated with the Bourguiba and Ben Ali governments, maintaining it had no desire for political power and sought only improved living standards and guaranteed political freedoms. Local branches of the union quickly joined in organizing the protest actions of the Jasmine Revolution and persuaded the central union to take the side of the protesters. This constituted a crucial source of organizational strength for the movement and psychological pressure on the Ben Ali administration to surrender. Despite its earlier record of good relations with the government, the public still trusted the Union, enabling it to survive the political upheaval after the 2011 revolution. By late 2012, as Tunisia seemed heading to anarchy or even civil war, the Union began working with its long-time opponents in the Tunisian Union of Industry, Trade and Handicrafts, as well as the National Order of Lawyers and the Tunisian League for Human Rights, comprising a Quartet to create a national consensus on a political solution. Their proposal enabled politicians to overcome the crisis and create political stability. In 2015, the Nobel Committee awarded its Peace Prize to the Quartet "for its decisive contribution to the building of a pluralistic democracy in Tunisia."

Tom Dowling

See also: Ben Ali, Zine al-Abidine; Jasmine Revolution; Tunisia, Republic of; Tunisian National Dialogue Quartet

Further Reading

Bishara, Dina. "Labor Movements in Tunisia and Egypt." *SWP Comments* 1. Berlin: Stiftung Wissenschaft und Politik, January 2014.

Ly Netterstrøm, Kasper. "The Tunisian General Labor Union and the Advent of Democracy." *The Middle East Journal* 70, no. 3 (Summer 2016): 383–98.

Zemni, Sami. "From Socio-Economic Protest to National Revolt: The Labor Origins of the Tunisian Revolution." In *The Making of the Tunisian Revolution: Contexts, Architects, Prospects,* edited by Nouri Gana, 127–46. Edinburgh: Edinburgh University Press, 2013.

Tunisian National Dialogue Quartet

A collaboration among the Tunisian General Labor Union, the Tunisian Confederation of Industry, Trade and Handicrafts, the Tunisian Human Rights League, and the Tunisian Order of Lawyers, which overcame a severe stalemate in the political competition after the flight of the Ben Ali family and created the basis for a national consensus on a political solution. In the October 23, 2011, election, the Ennahda Movement gained a central power position, and the political situation deteriorated. Islamist extremists increasingly pressed for political and social changes rejected by most Tunisians. Negotiators faced great difficulty in writing a new constitution. Assassinations of moderate politicians further escalated tensions. By mid-2013, the murder of another politician prompted opposition parties to withdraw from parliament and form a new, multiparty opposition coalition. The entire political system appeared headed for collapse.

In late July, the Tunisian General Labor Union began talks with political parties that accepted the need for a new approach. The Union developed close cooperation with other major institutions, most critically with the Tunisian Confederation of Industry, Trade and Handicrafts, which represents Tunisian business interests. Given long-engrained labor-capital antagonism, this cooperation demonstrated an extraordinary shared patriotism. In September, two other major organizations—the Tunisian Human Rights League and the Tunisian Order of Lawyers—joined them to propose a basis for a political solution. That proposal included firm dates for elections, concrete steps toward democratic government, installation of a technocratic interim government, and a commitment to preserving national identity. Based on the proposal, 21 parties of all sides agreed to negotiate. Meeting regularly, the parties agreed to a new government, ratified a new constitution, and set new presidential elections. In 2015, the Quartet was awarded the Nobel Peace Prize for "its decisive contribution to the building of a pluralistic democracy in Tunisia."

Tom Dowling

See also: Authoritarianism; Ennahda Movement; Ghannouchi, Rachid; Islamism; Jasmine Revolution; Tunisia, Republic of; Tunisian General Labor Union

Further Reading

Abassi, Hassine, Mohamed Fadhel Mahfoudh, Abdessatar Ben Moussa, and Ouided Bouchamaoui. "Nobel Lecture." Stockholm: The Nobel Foundation, December 10, 2015.

Ben Salem, Maryam. "The National Dialogue, Collusive Transactions and Government Legitimacy in Tunisia." *The International Spectator* 51, no. 1 (2016): 99–112.

M'rad, Hatem. *National Dialogue in Tunisia.* Tunis: Nirvana, 2015.

Somer, Murat. "Conquering versus Democratizing the State: Political Islamists and Fourth Wave Democratization in Turkey and Tunisia." *Democratization* 24, no. 6 (2017): 1–19.

Tunisian Protests (2011). *See Jasmine Revolution*

Turkey, Republic of

A large presidential democracy governing the Anatolian Peninsula between the Mediterranean and Black seas, and the southeast tip of Europe known as Thrace, spanning the Bosporus, the Sea of Marmara, and the Dardanelles. As the heir of the Ottoman Empire, the majority Sunni Muslim Turkish people claim the accomplishments of 16 historical Turkish states. Mustafa Kemal Ataturk led the foundation of the Republic of Turkey in 1923, with a program of state-directed industrialization and secular modernization, which included extensive language reform, such as changing the alphabet from the Arabic script to Latin-based characters.

Turkey engages in rivalry with its neighbor Greece, but each has supported the other in times of famine or earthquake. At the beginning of the Cold War, Turkey and Greece both joined the North Atlantic Treaty Organization (NATO) and, along with Yugoslavia, signed a pact that required mutual support in defense against the Soviet Union. Turkey allowed the United States to use the İncirlik Air Base near Adana for military reconnaissance missions during the Cold War. The Turkish military overthrew Turkey's civilian government in 1960 to roll back some Islamization measures, and again in 1971 to suppress leftist violence, both times returning to civilian rule within a few years. After a coup d'état in Cyprus by a group advocating for unity with Greece, on July 20, 1974, Turkey invaded the northeastern part of the island. While Greece and Turkey avoided major war, Turkey still controls the northeastern part of Cyprus, which it calls the Turkish Republic of Northern Cyprus, not recognized by any other country.

During the 1970s, domestic politics deteriorated in Turkey as members of Turkey's Nationalist Movement Party (MHP) exchanged violent attacks and assassinations with the followers of a Marxist-Leninist Party. During the same period, Kurds began to complain of increased violence and discrimination. In 1978, Abdullah Ocalan and a small group of university students started the Kurdistan Workers' Party (PKK), melding Marxism with Kurdish nationalism and attacking the Turkish state. In 1980, the military government took power to suppress this conflict and banned the speaking of Kurdish. This led to a cycle of escalating violence. The government declared a state of emergency in 1987 and enacted an anti-terror law aimed at curtailing the PKK in 1991.

Turkey's concern about local Kurds gaining reinforcements from other Kurds in Syria, Iraq, and Iran motivated its tacit support for violence against Kurds abroad, including the al-Anfal genocide in northern Iraq in the late 1980s. In 1999, Turkey had captured the PKK leader Abdullah Ocalan, who was tried and sentenced to death. However, the government converted Ocalan's sentence to life in prison due to justice system reforms required for European Union membership.

In 2002, the Justice and Development Party (AKP) won the largest share of votes for the Parliament, campaigning on joining the European Union, establishing peace with the Kurds, and promoting good governance. Many AKP leaders were known for their Islamist values but as mayors of Istanbul and other cities had demonstrated competence and effective governance, giving credibility to the party. During its initial years in power, the AKP had strengthened many of Turkey's democratic practices, and international trade expanded. The accomplishments of the party in reducing tensions with the Kurds, strengthening international relations, improving the economy, and pushing for European integration gave the party credibility and helped inhibit pressures from the military dominated by secularists.

The Persian Gulf War and the arrival of two million Kurds fleeing retribution from Saddam Hussein caused Turkey considerable problems. After protesting, Turkey allowed planes enforcing the no-fly zone to depart from İncirlik Air Force Base to protect the Kurds. Turkey opposed the U.S. invasion of Iraq in 2003 and would not let the United States use air bases in Turkey to support the invasion. American operations in Iraq caused greater protracted antagonism to the United States, which has increased over time. On July 4, 2003, American forces arrested Turkish special operations troops in northern Iraq trying to assassinate an elected Kurdish official in the region, which caused anger in Turkey. In September 2003, the PKK renounced its cease-fire. However, due to Masoud Barzani's antagonism to the PKK, his Kurdistan Democratic Party (KDP) allowed and even helped Turkey conduct military strikes against PKK forces in the Sinjar Mountain area of northern Iraq. Turkey established an extremely strong trade relationship with the Kurdistan Regional Government (KRG) of Iraq.

As Turkey was building its relationship with the KRG, its application for European Union (EU) membership was advancing. Improved relations with Kurds helped promote Turkey's EU membership. In 2004, Turkey legalized the speaking of Kurdish, allowed Kurdish names for cities and individuals, and allowed Kurdish political parties. In 2009, Turkey allowed a Kurdish-language television channel and radio and started Kurdish-language institutes at a handful of its public universities.

In the first eight years of AKP rule, Turkey played a very positive role in international relations. First as ambassador-at-large, until May 2009, and then as foreign minister, Ahmet Davatoglu joined with Prime Minister Recep Tayyip Erdogan to mediate a number of disputes and even enter into negotiations with Armenia. The AKP even delivered Turkish and Cypriot agreement to the UN reunification plan for Cyprus. In 2007, the military threatened to intervene against the AKP. Secular Turks organized a huge rally against the AKP on May 14, 2007, just before early general elections. The Hizmet Movement of Fethullah Gülen gave support to the AKP during this difficult time. At the same time a political scandal and judicial investigation called the "Ergenakon Terror plot" began, which ultimately targeted a great number of military and government officials. The prosecution removed many secular military leaders, reducing the threat to both the AKP and the Hizmet Movement.

In the meantime, Turkey's relations with Israel shifted from alliance to antagonism. Prime Minister Erdogan condemned Israel's May 2004 raid on the Rafah refugees camp in the Gaza strip as "state terrorism," but he still went to Israel in 2005 to promote trade, and in November 2007, Israeli president Shimon Peres addressed the Grand National Assembly of Turkey. Turkey harshly condemned Israel's Operation Cast Lead in the winter of 2008–2009, which really broke their relations. In January 2009, Erdogan engaged in a harsh confrontation with Israeli president Peres at the World Economic Forum in Davos Switzerland, and then received a hero's welcome when he returned. In May 2010, Turkey organized a shipment of relief supplies to Gaza on a freighter called the *Mavi Marmara,* to go directly to Gaza in violation of Israel's naval blockade. When Israeli commandos boarded the ship, nine Turkish passengers were killed and dozens were wounded, and nine Israeli soldiers were wounded. Fethullah Gülen criticized this as a needless provocation, which brought him into open conflict with Erdogan.

After the constitutional referendum of 2010 reduced the power of the military, Turkey's internal political situation entered a period of democratic decline. By 2010, Turkey's proposed Kurdish opening had begun to close. In the general election of 2011, the AKP received nearly 50 percent of the vote, in part due to Turkey's surging economy.

Erdogan tried to cultivate good relations with Syria, depending on Syria to suppress any activity by Kurds, and to show support for Syria's stance against Israel. When demonstrations in Dara'a, Syria, began to spread, he urged President Bashar al-Assad to negotiate and compromise. When Assad responded with ferocious state violence, Turkey began to host and train leaders of the Free Syrian Army, providing some with arms. Throughout the early part of the war, Turkey argued for multilateral and then unilateral military intervention. Other than some covert aid to the rebels, the international community did not accept.

However, by 2012, the AKP social policies had created a lot of anger and indirectly led to the 2013 Gezi Park protests. Then the government became more repressive in general, and state violence against the Kurds increased. A cease-fire negotiated with the PKK failed. The rise of the Islamic State (Daesh) in 2014 forced Kurdish militias in Iraq and Syria into increased activity in their fight against Daesh, which caused Turkey alarm. In 2014, Turkey began to pursue an openly declared regime-change policy in Syria. Since Iran and Russia have committed a lot of resources to help the Syrian government keep power, this brought Turkey into direct conflict with them. On November 24, 2015, a Turkish F-16 shot down a Russian aircraft near the Syria–Turkey border.

On October 13, 2014, Turkey agreed to allow the U.S.-led coalition to use its military bases for operations against the Islamic State and to use its territory to train Syrian opposition fighters. From January 2015 to August 2017, Turks suffered a series of terrorist attacks, not always with clear attribution. On June 5, 2015, Daesh attacked Kurds at a political rally in Diyarbakir, killing four and injuring 100. The Turkish government blamed Daesh for an attack on July 20, 2015, against Kurds in Surac that killed 32. In August 2015, Turkey agreed to participate in U.S.-led coalition airstrikes against Daesh, but most of its actions consisted of bombing Kurdish forces who were fighting against Daesh. On October 10, 2015, two Daesh suicide bombers attacked a peace rally at Ankara that killed 103 and wounded 250.

As the war in Syria expanded, massive numbers of both Kurdish and Arab refugees fled to Turkey. Their numbers reached approximately 3.5 million by 2018. Turkey has treated these people as merely passing through to permanent resettlement in a third country after the United Nations gives them refugee status. European Union member countries fear an influx of migrants if Turkey declares it will no longer host them. Based on this fear, they signed an agreement on March 18, 2016, in which Turkey promised that it would contain refugees, in exchange for visa liberalization, reactivation of the EU accession process, and substantial financial support.

The July 15, 2016, attempted coup deeply traumatized Turkish society, not only from the violence and sense of betrayal by the plotters, but also from the government's reaction, purging massive numbers of people from their employment, with huge numbers of people arrested. The crushing of the media, along with civil liberties and human rights, hurt Turkey's relations with Europe and liberal countries. It also strengthened Turkish antagonism to the United States and the West, while bringing Turkey into closer relations with Russia. In August 2016, Turkey launched an invasion of northwestern Syria it called Operation Euphrates Shield against Daesh. On January 20, 2018, Turkey attacked the Kurd-administered region of Afrin in Operation Olive Branch. This has forced the Kurdish People's Protection Units (YPG) to divert its forces from fighting Daesh to trying to defend Kurds from the Turkish military. Turkey justified its attacks by calling the YPG a terrorist group.

Sarah Fischer

See also: Academics for Peace; AKP-PKK Peace Talks; Alevis; Authoritarianism; Coup of 2016; Democracy Deficit; Erdogan, Recep Tayyip; Ergenekon Scandal; Gezi Park Protests; Hizmet (Gülen) Movement; Islamic State (Daesh); Islamism; Justice and Development Party (Turkey); Kurdistan Workers' Party (PKK); Military Coups; Syrian Civil War

Further Reading

Findlay, Carter V. *Turkey, Islam, Nationalism, and Modernity: A History, 1789–2007.* New Haven, CT: Yale University Press, 2010.

Finkel, Andrew. *Turkey: What Everyone Needs to Know.* New York: Oxford University Press, 2012.

Linden, Ronald H., et al. *Turkey and Its Neighbors: Foreign Relations in Transition.* Boulder, CO: Lynne Rienner, 2012.

Pope, Nicole, and Hugh Pope. *Turkey Unveiled: A History of Modern Turkey.* New York: The Overlook Press, 2011.

Tüfekçi, Özgür. *The Foreign Policy of Modern Turkey: Power and Ideology of Eurasianism.* London: I. B. Tauris, 2017.

White, Jenny B. *Islamist Mobilization in Turkey: A Study in Vernacular Politics.* Seattle: University of Washington Press, 2002.

Zürcher, Erik. *Turkey: A Modern History.* London: I. B. Tauris, 2017.

U

United Arab Emirates (UAE)

A federation of seven emirates on the western coast of the Gulf across from Iran, with Saudi Arabia to the west and Oman to the south. In 1971 six of the emirates—Abu Dhabi, Ajman, Dubai, Fujayrah, Sharjah, and Umm al-Qaywayn—formed the United Arab Emirates (UAE), and Ras al-Khaymah, which is also ruled by the same family as Sharjah, joined the UAE in 1972. The emirates differ greatly in size and resource endowments and vary somewhat in their domestic policy orientation but share a common external foreign policy. Due to their greater size and wealth, Abu Dhabi and Dubai exert greater influence in the federation. They have a larger, more cosmopolitan, expatriate, urban population and have promoted tolerance and some civic freedoms. The other five more homogenous emirates hold more religiously and politically conservative values. The ruler of Abu Dhabi serves as the president, while the ruler of Dubai serves as the vice president and prime minister. Crown Prince Shaikh Mohammad bin Zayid al-Nuhayyan of Abu Dhabi and Shaikh Muhammad of Dubai have provided the key strategic guidance for the UAE foreign and defense policies.

The UAE escaped the regional turmoil in 2011. The government committed $1.55 billion to infrastructure improvements and made arrangements to keep food prices low. Although youth activism increased and some intellectuals produced petitions, the government arrested and prosecuted the activists. The government increased the number of eligible voters from 6,000 to nearly 130,000 for the September 2011 elections to the Federal National Council, an advisory body with no real power. In March 2011, the UAE and Saudi Arabia used the Peninsula Shield Force to support Bahrain in suppressing protests.

The security threats to the UAE fall into four categories. First, Iran seized the Greater and Lesser Tunbs and Abu Musa islands on November 30, 1971, leading to the formation of the UAE two days later. In the face of a much larger, heavily armed Iran, these emirates could only protest through diplomacy and political arguments. After the Islamic Revolution of 1979, Iran tried to export revolutionary ideas using propaganda, assassinations, and bombings. In 1981, the UAE joined with five neighboring states to create the Gulf Cooperation Council (GCC) as the starting point for collective security. In 2000, the member states signed a "GCC Joint Defense Convention" emphasizing collective defense against threats. However, the emirates, especially Dubai, have a significant Persian population, and Iran engages in substantial non-oil trade through Dubai. In spite of this economic interdependence, the ideological and subversive threat of a revolutionary Shi'a state, on top of other regional threats, motivates exceptional military mobilization.

302 United Arab Emirates (UAE)

In the latest available estimate, the UAE spends 5 percent of its Gross Domestic Product on the military; its defense spending ranked as the second largest in the Middle East. In 1994, the UAE signed a bilateral defense agreement with the United States, which allows it to station troops in Al-Dhafra outside Abu Dhabi, and U.S. warships to use Dubai's Jebel Ali port. The UAE also has defense agreements with the United Kingdom and France and buys substantial amounts of weapons from both. In addition to building defense alliances, the UAE has also hired defense contractors, who have brought significant numbers of noncitizens into the armed forces. Academics fear that this reduces the cost of conflict and makes it more protracted, while hindering accountability for war crimes.

Second, the extremely rapid development in Dubai and Abu Dhabi required millions of guest workers, tightly controlled by the sponsorship policy. The UAE government recognizes that the presence of such a huge number of foreign noncitizens—80 percent of the population—represents a threat to the culture of the Emirates. Furthermore, the rapid development of the trade, transportation, hospitality, and tourism sectors of the economy brings many millions of people through every year. The UAE has adopted an exceptionally advanced and thorough system of identifying, monitoring, and tracking everyone who passes through or lives in the Emirates.

Third, the Emirates have taken an increasingly strong stand not only against extremism and terrorist groups, but also against Islamist groups such as the Muslim Brotherhood. Although they have a record of supporting quietist conservative Muslim groups that preach obedience to the ruler, after the administration of Mohamed Morsi in Egypt, the UAE had committed money and military power to opposing the Brotherhood and associated Islamist organizations. The UAE fought in cooperation with Qatar in the NATO-led military intervention in Libya in 2011 to overthrow Colonel Qaddafi. Qatar backed the Justice and Construction Party of the Muslim Brotherhood, but the UAE supported the Libyan National Transitional Council. After the overthrow of Morsi, the UAE worked with Egypt to support General Haftar against his Islamist opponents, especially the Islamic State (Daesh), which had set up operations in Sirte. The development of the Islamic State raised the stakes in the struggle to resist militant extremist groups. The UAE, with the other GCC states, demanded that Qatar cut its support, funding, and hosting of the Muslim Brotherhood and support of the Islamic State. On June 5, 2017, the UAE together with Saudi Arabia and several other states cut off ties with Qatar, triggering the most serious crisis in the GCC since the Kuwaiti invasion in 1990.

Fourth, the UAE engaged in military operations in Yemen through Operation Decisive Storm, which became Operation Restoring Hope, led by Saudi Arabia. These operations sought to stop the advancement of the Houthi tribal movement that ousted Yemeni president Abdu Rabbu Mansour Hadi. The UAE combined its military operation with a humanitarian effort, providing almost a billion dollars in aid to Yemen. The ongoing military engagement in Yemen motivated increased cooperation with the African Republic of Djibouti—basically right next door to Yemen. Djibouti serves as military base and point of entry for aid supplies to Yemen. In November 2015, the UAE established an annual Commemoration Day (originally Martyr's Day) and a memorial park beside the Sheikh Zayed Mosque in Abu Dhabi to recognize the soldiers killed in Yemen.

Kristin Kamøy

See also: Bahrain, Kingdom of; Gulf Cooperation Council (GCC); Iran, Islamic Republic of; Islamic State (Daesh); Libya, State of; Muslim Brotherhood; Oman, Sultanate of; Qatar; Saudi Arabia, Kingdom of; Yemen, Republic of

Further Reading

Almezaini, Khalid S., and Jean-Marc Rickli. *The Small Gulf States: Foreign and Security Policies before and after the Arab Spring.* New York: Routledge, 2017.

Guéraiche, William. *The UAE: Geopolitics, Modernity and Tradition.* London: I. B. Tauris, 2017.

Herb, Michael. "A Nation of Bureaucrats: Political Participation and Economic Diversification in Kuwait and the United Arab Emirates." *International Journal of Middle East Studies* 41, no. 3 (August 2009): 375–95.

Lori, Noora. "National Security and the Management of Migrant Labor: A Case Study of the United Arab Emirates." *Asian and Pacific Migration Journal* 20, no. 3–4 (2011): 315–37.

Ulrichsen, Kristian Coates. *The United Arab Emirates: Power, Politics and Policymaking.* New York: Routledge, 2017.

Washington Consensus

A range of broadly free-market policy recommendations promoted for developing countries by international financial institutions such as the World Bank, the International Monetary Fund (IMF), and the U.S. Treasury Department. As originally formulated in 1989 by John Williamson, the Washington Consensus included 10 sets of relatively specific policy measures to help crisis-ridden, less-developed countries to move toward stability, growth, and economic prosperity. These policy measures required deregulation of the economy, elimination of obstacles to international trade and investment, privatization of state-owned enterprises, currency devaluation to reduce imports and stimulate exports, and reduction of public spending.

Many developing countries, including those in the Middle East and North Africa, tried to modernize rapidly in the postcolonial period and incurred significant debt for big infrastructure projects and industrialization. They kept the currency exchange rate high to make it cheaper to import the materials needed for these projects, as well as luxury items for the elites. This created current account—trade—deficits. They also ran budget deficits by promoting the expansion of health care and education and by subsidizing bread and other essentials. As many countries suffered similar problems, this general debt crisis of the 1980s forced countries to seek help from the IMF and the World Bank, both with headquarters in Washington, DC, and both staffed with economists trained in classical neoliberal economics. The prescriptions of the Washington Consensus, usually imposed as conditions on aid to countries in financial distress due to their trade and budget deficits, prevailed as a development paradigm of the 1990s. However, these policies imposed high social costs as poor people suffered from the reduction of subsidies and the contraction of public funding for health care and education. Currency devaluation caused the price of imported goods to rise, creating inflation, which hurt poor people even more. Reduction of trade barriers often meant that mass-produced imported products became cheaper than local products produced by hand in very labor-intensive industries. Therefore, local businesses went bankrupt, raising unemployment. It can take several years for currency devaluation to stimulate production for export. Furthermore, states often implemented the required privatization by transferring state assets to the families and supporters of the ruler at below market prices, thus increasing the wealth of the rich and keeping most of the population poor. This corruption adds to popular anger against the state, motivating conflict and revolution.

These social costs for a transition to export-led growth turned the Washington Consensus into a pejorative term for neoliberalism. Sometimes the aid

306 *Wasta*

conditionality included policies other than the original 10 policy prescriptions. Most countries could not comply with all of the conditions due to the social costs—grievances—created by the inflation, unemployment, and poverty they produced, which led to continuing financial crises across the developing world. Therefore, many critics argue for a Post–Washington Consensus that emphasizes support for the poor, preserving education and health care, improving property rights, and reducing the cost of starting a business.

Muhammed Kursad Ozekin

See also: Corruption; Development; Grievance Model; Modernization

Further Reading

Naím, Moisés. "Washington Consensus or Washington Confusion?" *Foreign Policy* 118 (2000): 86–103.

Stiglitz, Joseph E. "More Instruments and Broader Goals: Moving toward the Post-Washington Consensus." In *Wider Perspectives on Global Development,* edited by Anthony B. Atkinson et al., 16–48. New York: Palgrave Macmillan, 2005.

Williamson, John. "What Washington Means by Policy Reform." In *Latin American Adjustment: How Much Has Happened,* edited by John Williamson, 5–20. Washington, DC: Institute of International Economics, 1990.

Wasta

The social practice of using *wasta* (meaning connections, an intermediary) to solve problems and meet important needs originated as a way of solving conflicts between families, clans, and tribes, through the mediation of powerful figures, such as the heads of the groups involved in conflict. During such negotiations, the leader would seek a solution beneficial to his group, while cementing the group's unity and his status. Indeed, the word *wasta* stems from *waseet* (middleman). In other words, people use loyalty to tribe, ethnic group, or religious party to achieve mutually beneficial exchanges of interests. A *wasta* can be a private citizen or official—anyone with the interest and ability to resolve problems, such as accessing public services in exchange for status, votes, or favors.

In the modern Arab world, *wasta* has taken on a different meaning. While it still plays a role in negotiations, its functions also extend to a broad variety of problems facing the applicant, particularly seeking benefits from government. The middleman who helps his client does not require an immediate reciprocal benefit from the client but may seek a favorable action of equivalent value in the future. The client has *wasta* when he can confidently receive help when he asks for it. Because some people use *wasta* to bypass lengthy bureaucratic procedures, obtain jobs, or get promoted, the illegitimate reception of preferential treatment carries a social cost because candidates lacking qualifications take the place of more capable candidates. The social acceptance, and expectation, that people will seek to develop *wasta,* and use it when they need to, provides a cultural support for corruption. The person in a position of influence who does favors for people he knows, and who protects them in exchange for their loyalty in voting or in conflict with other groups, acts as a patron to his clients. This leads to a pattern of politics

that inhibits the development of institutions, which is called "clientelism" or patrimonialism.

Magdalena Karolak

See also: Clientelism (Patrimonialism); Corruption; Development

Further Reading

Al-Ramahi, Aseel. "*Wasta* in Jordan: A Distinct Feature of (And Benefit for) Middle Eastern Society." *Arab Law Quarterly* 22, no. 1 (2008): 35–62.

Cunningham, Robert B., and Yasin K. Sarayrah. "Taming *Wasta* to Achieve Development." *Arab Studies Quarterly* 16, no. 3 (Summer 1994): 29–41.

Women's Leadership in Protests

In a number of states, women applied their creativity and zeal to motivate a greater
cross section of their society to demand respect for human rights and overthrow
corrupt autocratic governments that deny them, and thus earned respect for their
leadership. In the uprisings that sprang up across the region, women played prominent roles using new communication, activism, and networking technologies.
During the uprisings, Cairo's Tahrir Square, Manama's Pearl Square, and the
streets of Tunis, Sana'a, and Tripoli were not segregated by gender, and women
stood, marched, and united for regime change.

In Tunisia, Saida Sadouni led the February 2011 Qasaba protests that forced
Prime Minister Mohamed Ghannouchi out of office, and Lina Ben Mhenni and
Raja bin Salama worked through social media to bring international attention to
human rights abuses. In Egypt, Israa Abdel Fattah cofounded the April 6 Youth
Movement, Aliaa Magda Elmahdy uploaded photos with the words "Sharia is not
a constitution," and Nawal Elsaadawi revived the Egyptian Women's Union. In
Libya, Salwa Bugaighis helped to organize the February 17 protests that drove the
army out of Benghazi. In Bahrain, activists such as Maryam al-Khawaja and
Zainab al-Khawaja worked to advocate for Bahraini protesters and organize
through Twitter. In Saudi Arabia, Samar Badawi filed lawsuits against the male
guardianship system, and many others fought for the right-to-drive action. Tawakkol Karman won the Nobel Peace Prize for her work in Yemen in promoting freedom of the press and human rights. As regimes fell and protests dispersed,
however, momentum was lost, and women suffered harassment and prison.

In Tunisia, women continue to play an important role in the transition since the
uprisings. Tunisia has enacted a progressive Personal Status Code, and the state
gives emphasis to girls' education and female employment. It seeks to counter the
trend of highly educated but rarely employed women. Women's NGOs successfully pushed the government to recognize the Convention on the Elimination of
All Forms of Discrimination against Women. As of now, Tunisia has become
exceptional. As the wave of Arab protests continued, triumphed, and failed, many
people, including women's rights activists, suffered from resigned complacency.
In Egypt, activist Nehad Abo Alomsan organized the "Million Women March" in
Cairo to mark International Women's Day, March 8, 2011, which drew only a few
hundred participants. Police and counter-protesters beat them and, when they

were arrested, subjected them to groping. Again in December 2011, women marched in protest against police brutality and suffered more violence.

While the uprisings gave women an increased opportunity in public life and leadership, the subsequent crackdowns of law enforcement following the uprisings reinstated the status-quo marginalization. Women's commensurate participation in the aftermath of these events remains lacking.

Kristin Hissong

See also: Al-Sharif, Manal; April 6 Youth; February 17th Revolution; Jasmine Revolution; Libyan Civil War; Oman, Sultanate of; Pearl Roundabout Protests; Tahrir Square Protests; Yemen, Republic of

Further Reading

Alvi, Hayat. "Women's Rights Movements in the 'Arab Spring': Major Victories or Failures for Human Rights." *Journal of International Women's Studies* 16, no. 3 (2015): 294–318.

Moghadam, Valentine M. "Women and Democracy after the Arab Spring: Theory, Practice, and Prospects." In *Empowering Women after the Arab Spring. Comparative Feminist Studies,* edited by Marwa Shalaby and Valentine M. Moghadam, 193–206. New York: Palgrave Macmillan, 2016.

Yazidi

A monotheistic religious community speaking Kurmanji Kurdish and Arabic, practicing a syncretic belief system based on Zoroastrianism. Kurds generally accept the Yazidis as Kurds, while many Yazidis seek to assert their separate status as a minority group. The Yazidi (also Ezidi, Ezi, or Izid) have historically lived in Iraq, Turkey, Syria, Armenia, Georgia, and Iran. Although their numbers have declined since the end of the 20th century, today the Yazidis claim approximately 1.4 million members in the world. Persecution has forced large numbers to seek refuge in Western countries, especially Germany. Different governments across history have imposed assimilation programs, such as forcibly relocating many Arabs into their home region. In self-protection, Yazidis have sought strict separation from outsiders, applying binding marriage rules to preserve their cohesion and a caste system. They lament receiving only one seat in the 2018 Iraqi parliamentary elections.

Yazidi religious doctrine includes significant elements of ancient Zoroastrian belief, with some adaptation of ideas from Christianity and Islam. They believe in one Creator, who designated seven angels to rule the world, the first of whom they call Melek Ta'us (Peacock Angel) who decides the destiny of individuals for good or evil. Outsiders often misinterpret Melek Ta'us as the Devil and use this claim to justify the systematic marginalization of the Yazidis as Devil worshippers. The Yazidi doctrine also reflects the teaching of Sheikh Adi (d. 1162), an Arab Sufi who reformed their faith. They venerate his shrine in Lalish, Iraq.

They have survived many massacres, the last perpetrated by the Islamic State (Daesh) in 2014, when those forces captured the strategic Yazidi stronghold of Mount Sinjar, Iraq. The Yazidis had cooperated with the Kurdish Peshmerga forces, but when the Islamic State attacked, the Iraqi Peshmerga withdrew. After slaughtering thousands of men, the Islamic State militants kidnapped many Yazidi women and sold them into sexual slavery. Ultimately, Syrian Kurdish militias rescued 130,000 Yazidis trapped on Sinjar Mountain. They have created their own militia, the Sinjar Alliance, registered as part of the Iraqi Popular Mobilization Forces, but Kurdish officials arrested a Yazidi leader that sought weapons and aid from Iran.

The 2014 Islamic State attacks forced around 500,000 Yazidis to flee to other areas of Kurdistan. Approximately 40,000 Yezidis have since fled to Germany, joining an existing community. The United Nations and other parties have pronounced the attacks of the Islamic State against Yazidis as an act of genocide. The Nobel awards committee gave their 2018 Peace Prize to Nadia Murad, a young

Yazidi woman who was kidnapped and enslaved by the Islamic State and miraculously rescued.

Emanuela Claudia Del Re

See also: Iran, Islamic Republic of; Iraq, Republic of; Islamic State (Daesh); Kurds; Minorities; Popular Mobilization Forces (PMF); Refugees; Syrian Arab Republic; Turkey, Republic of

Further Reading

Acikyildiz-Sengul, Birgul. *The Yezidis. The History of a Community, Culture, and Religion.* New York: I. B. Tauris, 2010.

Guest, John S. *Survival among the Kurds: A History of the Yezidis.* New York: Routledge, 2015.

Oehring, Otmar, *Christians and Yazidis in Iraq: Current Situation and Prospects.* Berlin: Konrad Adenauer Stiftung, 2017.

Yemen, Ansar al-Sharia. *See* Al-Qaeda in the Arabian Peninsula (AQAP)

Yemen, Republic of

A poor, mountainous, war-torn country south of the Kingdom of Saudi Arabia and west of Oman, with a very long history of civilization and heritage as an independent Arab state. The mountains of the southwest corner of the Arabian Peninsula occupied by Yemen receive more rainfall than other areas and have historically supported much higher populations. Historically, trade from Africa to Arabia, and to urban areas north and east, has passed through Yemen and the strategic Bab el Mandeb Strait.

The people of the area now called Yemen submitted to Islam during the life of the Prophet Muhammad and became part of the rapidly growing Islamic realm under the Umayyads. In 893, the Imam Al-Hadi ila'l-Haqq Yahya came to Yemen and introduced the Zaydi doctrine. Four years later, the Zaydis separated politically from the Abbasid Caliphate but could not sustain a durable state. Various neighboring states conquered the area. Finally, the Ottomans conquered Yemen in 1538. In 1635, a Zaydi leader expelled the Ottomans and established an Imamate. However, a Sunni group established an independent state in the south, with Aden as its capital. In 1839, the British seized Aden, and the Ottomans retook Northern Yemen in 1849. After the fall of the Ottoman Empire in World War I, in 1918, the Zaydi Imamate regained its independence. The leaders of the north part of Yemen founded a theocratic monarchy with its capital at Sana'a.

In 1962, a military coup against the Zaydi Imam triggered the North Yemen Civil War. Egypt sent an army to support the rebels, who proclaimed the name Yemen Arab Republic (YAR) in their fight against the monarchy. Saudi Arabia and Jordan supported the forces of the Zaydi Imam. The war bogged down into a stalemate, until in 1967 Egyptian president Nassar agreed to withdraw his troops. However, the republican side ultimately prevailed.

The British resisted an insurgency in the south, until they granted South Yemen independence in 1962. The Soviet Union gave this new state substantial aid, to expand its string of client states, as part of its Cold War competition with the West. In 1970, under Marxist control, South Yemen changed its name to the People's Democratic Republic of Yemen (PDRY).

From 1970 to 1980, North and South Yemen clashed repeatedly at their borders. In 1978, Ali Abdullah Saleh became president of the YAR. In 1986, fighting within the South became a civil war. In 1986, the discovery of new oil reserves boosted exports and provided a growing source of foreign capital. That instigated some development reforms, which brought a wave of migrants to the cities. Because Yemen did not support the Coalition Forces that expelled the Iraqi invasion of Kuwait in 1990, the Gulf Cooperation Council (GCC) countries deported an estimated 800,000 Yemeni labor migrants. This repatriation led to very high unemployment and the proliferation of slums.

In May 1990, after the collapse of the Soviet Bloc, the YAR and the PDRY announced a unified state. However, in 1994, the south again separated from the north, complaining of exploitation. This led people to move to the north and urban centers. In the ensuing conflict, the north defeated the separatist southerners, and Saleh sought concentrated power. Saleh ruled the new unified Yemen using a complicated patronage system. He regularly manipulated social divisions to exploit domestic and international fear of instability. He constantly shifted alliances with local groups and used bribes, coercion, blackmail, and threats to maintain power. He appointed many of his family members to high positions of power. The administration engaged in corruption, reallocating resources to buy off the opposition. He created an image as the only force that could balance the highly factional and tribal politics of the country.

In 1990, Yemeni veterans of the fight against the Soviet Union in Afghanistan began coming home, carrying the ideology of the Islamist struggle. Saleh recruited some of these fighters in his struggle against the south but then faced difficulty controlling the variety of Islamist extremists. In October 2000, some militants associated with al-Qaeda attacked the USS *Cole* as it was refueling in Aden, killing 17 sailors. In February 2002, the government expelled more than 100 foreign Islamic teachers. In June 2004, the Houthis began to revolt against the government forces in North Yemen, complaining of discrimination and religious pressure from the Sunnis. They count their campaigns each year until 2010 as six different wars.

As a low-income nation, Yemen has depended on remittances by migrant workers; oil revenues, which have fallen due to depletion of reserves; and agriculture, which is vulnerable to global prices changes. Rising economic difficulties after 1995 forced President Saleh to seek help from the International Monetary Fund (IMF), but their reforms have not helped. Moreover, since the beginning of 2000, many of the farming regions have suffered from a water shortage crisis. Farmers use 30 percent of their cropland to grow a narcotic called qat, which requires a lot of water but brings in greater profit than food crops. Therefore, Yemen depends heavily on imported food.

In 2009, Salafi militants took the name Al-Qaeda in the Arabian Peninsula (AQAP). Starting in 2010, the United States began launching attacks on the AQAP in the south, which has continued for years. Therefore, the government of Yemen suffered from three concurrent conflicts: 1) Houthis versus the government of Ali Abdullah Saleh; 2) AQAP versus the government; and 3) southern secessionists versus the government.

Yemen faces multiple pressures: plummeting revenues; high levels of inequality, unemployment, and illiteracy; and a looming shortage of water and energy supplies. The government has failed to respond to the needs of the people, who suffer under high levels of corruption. By 2010, Yemen became the most impoverished country in the Arab world. In the context of these overlapping social and economic crises, inspired by the demonstrations in Tunisia and Egypt, Yemeni young people began protesting in January 2011. They demanded political changes, economic reforms, and the removal of Saleh.

Many local and tribal groups quickly started supporting the demonstrations, especially after Saleh's administration decided to repress the protests physically. In March, violent army action toward the protesters caused substantial numbers of the military to defect, a significant strike against Saleh's legitimacy. Among the groups that joined the protesters were the Houthis (or Ansar Allah), the Islamic Zaydi group from the north. During the protests, the Houthis grew beyond their northern base of support, participating in mainstream politics and calling for reforms. Through these actions they gained greater popular approval.

The threat of a possible civil war in Yemen led the international community, mainly the Gulf Cooperation Council (GCC), to pressure Saleh to resign. In June 2011, he survived an attempted assassination and went to Riyadh for medical treatment. Under Saudi pressure, he negotiated his departure, giving the power to his vice president, Abdu Rabbu Mansour Hadi, in exchange for immunity and the right to return to Yemen. In Sana'a, Hadi organized a National Dialogue Conference by 2013 to find a comprehensive solution among the many political factions in the country. However, the coalition government excluded the Houthis and the Southern movement and gave them little representation in the conference. The economic aid promised by the international community after Saleh resigned did not reach the people, and the country kept sinking into deeper economic crisis. Hadi's government had even less legitimacy and popular support than the previous one.

Many groups started to compete for influence in Yemen: the southern separatists; Islamist groups backed by the Muslim Brotherhood; pro-Hadi forces; Houthis; Saleh's loyalists; and Al-Qaeda in the Arabian Peninsula. This has created a very complex political situation. However, Hadi considered the Houthis his greatest threat and has portrayed them as an Iranian proxy. In February 2015, the Houthis took over the capital, Sana'a, put Hadi under house arrest, and occupied governmental institutions. One month later, Hadi escaped and fled to Aden. When the Houthis started attacking Aden, he fled to Saudi Arabia and asked for help to restore his government. In response, on March 26, 2015, Saudi Arabia organized a coalition that included the United Arab Emirates, Jordan, Egypt, Morocco, Sudan, and the other GCC countries, except for Oman. They began Operation Decisive Storm to attack the Houthis.

The coalition considered the Houthis part of a bigger international scheme by Iran to destabilize the region, by financing, training, and arming local groups.

Because of the Iranian-Saudi rivalry in the Gulf, both countries see themselves as engaged in a zero-sum competition for regional influence. Saudi Arabia finds Iranian involvement in the region a threat to its power and capacity to guarantee the status quo.

Saudi Arabia miscalculated in thinking it would win quickly. On April 21, 2015, the coalition changed the name of its campaign to Operation Restoring Hope, but hope for ending the conflict has not yet appeared. The United States supported this effort, in which Saudi Arabia has invested millions of dollars, with very limited results. Despite large numbers of airstrikes in Yemen, the Houthis have maintained their hold on Sana'a and other strategic areas and even struck back at Saudi Arabia with missiles and drones. Iranian support, which analysts thought was minor in 2015, grew in scope and size—the opposite of the intervention's goals.

The war brought disaster in Yemen, increasing the economic crisis. Yemen has become one of the greatest humanitarian crises of the 21st century. The people of Yemen suffer from preventable diseases like cholera; more than 10 million people need food assistance, and the number of deaths from famine keeps rising. Southern separatists increase their demands, and Al-Qaeda continues to expand.

Luíza Gimenez Cerioli

See also: Al-Ahmar, Ali Muhsin; Al-Qaeda in the Arabian Peninsula (AQAP); General People's Congress; Gulf Cooperation Council (GCC); Hadi, Abdu Rabbu Mansour; Houthis (Ansar Allah); Iran, Islamic Republic of; Operation Decisive Storm; Saleh, Ali Abdullah; Saudi Arabia, Kingdom of; Yemen Civil War; Yemeni Socialist Party (YSP); Yemen Uprising; Zaydi Doctrine

Further Reading
Clark, Victoria. *Yemen: Dancing on the Heads of Snakes.* New Haven, CT: Yale University Press, 2010.

Gasim, Gamal. "Explaining Political Activism in Yemen." In *Taking to the Streets: The Transformation of Arab Activism,* edited by Lina Khatib and Ellen Lust, 109–35. Baltimore: Johns Hopkins University Press, 2014.

Hill, Ginny. *Yemen Endures: Civil War, Saudi Adventurism and the Future of Arabia.* New York: Oxford University Press, 2017.

Phillips, Sarah. *Yemen and the Politics of Permanent Crisis.* London: International Institute for Strategic Studies, 2011.

Salisbury, Peter. *Yemen: Stemming the Rise of a Chaos State.* London: Chatham House, May 2016.

Yemen Civil War (2015)

A complex war in Yemen that drew intervention by a coalition of regional states, featuring the bombardment of many civilian targets, the use of ballistic missiles, missile attacks on shipping, and accusations of sectarian mobilization, resulting in a severe humanitarian crisis. Many observers begin their discussion of the civil war with the March 26, 2015, announcement by the Kingdom of Saudi Arabia (KSA) that it would intervene to restore the government of President Hadi. This decision derived from a long-developing crisis, most immediately from the August 2014 decision by the Houthi rebels to seize control of Sana'a. They put Hadi under house arrest and began expanding their military operations. After Hadi escaped and fled to Aden, on March 22, 2015, the Houthis advanced on Aden, seized the international airport, and bombed Hadi's headquarters. Hadi fled to Saudi Arabia and asked for international help. The Saudi government, together with eight Arab states, began a campaign called Operation Decisive Storm, consisting of a naval blockade and airstrikes against the Houthi's leadership, air force, and air defenses. The United Arab Emirates (UAE) contributed the second largest contingent of planes and men and led the first ground operations. The April 14, 2015, UN Security Council Resolution 2216 codified Saudi Arabia's ambitious, maximal objectives as not only the restoration of the Hadi government and the withdrawal of the Houthi forces, but also their disarmament, which implies their complete defeat.

When former president Ali Abdullah Saleh allied with the Houthis against his former vice president Hadi, the Houthis gained control over Yemen's air force, which included approximately 300 ballistic missiles. The coalition's bombing campaign destroyed Yemen's planes but not all of the missiles. After achieving control of the air, on April 21, 2015, the Saudis announced the end of Decisive Storm and the transition to Operation Restoring Hope, claiming that they would transition to delivering humanitarian assistance. However, combat operations on both sides continued without change. In July 2015, the coalition conducted an amphibious landing of conventional ground forces at Aden. In September another ground offensive from the Saudi border drove south toward Merib. In January 2016, the coalition launched a third ground assault from the Saudi border that captured the Yemeni port of Midi. By the spring of 2016, the war had become a stalemate. The first of many attempts to negotiate a resolution to the conflict began in April 2016 in Kuwait.

Instead of a clear competition between two sides, local tribes and militias controlled large areas of the country. Al-Qaeda and the Islamic state (Daesh) have taken advantage of the absence of strong central control, especially in the east and south, to mobilize for terrorist attacks, occasionally striking the Houthis. The Saudi-led coalition consists of a fragmented alliance. The UAE supported different tribes and proxy forces in Yemen than Saudi Arabia, leading to some tensions. In Yemen, Saudi Arabia supported the Islah Party, associated with the Muslim Brotherhood, and did not attack al-Qaeda, in spite of declaring the former a terrorist organization and suffering significant attacks from the latter. The coalition has employed a large number of contractors and mercenaries in the ground campaign, including forces from Colombia and Sudan.

The participation of Sunni forces loyal to the patronage network of former president Saleh in the Houthis' alliance undercuts the Saudi claim that it acts to defend Sunnis from the expansionist ambitions of Shi'a Iran. Before 2015, analysts claimed a lack of evidence for the direct, large-scale supply of arms from Iran to the Houthis but acknowledged that Iran provided light arms, with training primarily by Hezbollah. However, neither domestic manufacturing nor residuals of the Yemeni government arsenals can explain the sophisticated missiles that the Houthis have used against shipping or in attacking Saudi Arabia.

The Saudi-led coalition receives significant international criticism for the large numbers of airstrikes on civilian targets—schools, hospitals, markets, refugee camps, funerals, and places of worship. Critics also argue that despite the long history of siege warfare, the strategy of collective punishment against large populations violates international law and rarely succeeds as a strategy of coercion. This has undermined the legitimacy of the Hadi government, the campaign in general, and the coalition itself. For example, the U.S. Congress has put strong pressure on the Trump administration to stop its arms sales to Saudi Arabia. In July 2019, the UAE announced that it was beginning to withdraw its own forces but would sustain operations in Yemen, transitioning to "training and assisting" local soldiers. It claims to have trained 90,000 local fighters.

This intervention achieved one goal: blocking the Houthis from controlling Aden and denying them the possibility of taking control of the whole country. By July 2019, the United Nations had negotiated the withdrawal of militias from the port of Hudaydah, to allow the import of humanitarian aid, but any deal to end the war remains elusive. The United Nations describes the war as consisting of 30 active frontlines across the country. The Houthis still control most of Yemen, including the capital Sana'a. The cost of the war, which left half the population in severe need for food and resulted in an outbreak of half a million cases of cholera, has created a severe humanitarian crisis. The coalition has made some promises for reconstruction, but prospects for that remain distant.

Jonathan K. Zartman

See also: Al-Qaeda in the Arabian Peninsula (AQAP); Hadi, Abdu Rabbu Mansour; Houthis (Ansar Allah); Operation Decisive Storm; Saleh, Ali Abdullah; Saudi Arabia, Kingdom of; United Arab Emirates (UAE); Yemen, Republic of; Yemen Uprising

Further Reading
Darwich, May. "The Saudi Intervention in Yemen: Struggling for Status." *Insight Turkey* 20, no. 2 (Spring 2018): 125–41.
Hill, Ginny. *Yemen: Civil War, Saudi Adventurism and the Future of Arabia.* Oxford, UK: Oxford University Press, 2017.
Shield, Ralph. "The Saudi Air War in Yemen: A Case for Coercive Success through Battlefield Denial." *The Journal of Strategic Studies* 41, no. 3 (2018): 461–89.

Yemeni Socialist Party (YSP)

A socialist political party in Yemen, and the sole party in the People's Democratic Republic of Yemen (PDRY). The Yemeni Socialist Party (YSP) began in Aden in 1978 from a succession of movements and militias resisting British authority, as the "vanguard party" required by Marxist-Leninist theory. In 1990, after the fall of the Soviet Union, the YSP arranged the union of the PDRY (South Yemen) with the Yemen Arab Republic (YAR) and constituted one of the three major parties in the new state. However, the elections of 1993 led to a civil war between the YAR and southern elites. In May 1994, the YSP leaders declared a new Democratic Republic of Yemen in the south. Pressure from the central government forced the party's leaders into exile. The party's northern branch elected a new leadership, none of whom had experience in the PDRY government.

In the late 1990s, the other two major parties in the unified Yemen sought to give the YSP a role in the government due to its continued influence in the south. The YSP boycotted the 1997 elections, but some of its members gained election as independents. By the 1999 presidential election, northern members of the YSP had gained some political positions.

In 2000, the YSP joined a bloc of opposition parties to create the Supreme Opposition Council, and in 2003 it participated in the parliamentary elections, gaining 8 percent of the seats. They want real democracy, in a peaceful way. However, the party has been unable to control the lawless activities of southern secessionists, revolutionary socialists, and terrorist organizations such al-Qaeda.

Arhama Siddiqa

See also: Al Qaeda in the Arabian Peninsula (AQAP); Saleh, Ali Abdullah; Yemen, Republic of

Further Reading

Browers, Michaelle. "Origins and Architects of Yemen's Joint Meeting Parties." *International Journal of Middle East Studies* 39, no. 4 (2007): 565–86.

Burrowes, Robert D. "Prelude to Unification: The Yemen Arab Republic, 1962–1990." *International Journal of Middle East Studies* 23, no. 4 (1991): 483–506.

Yemen Uprising (2011)

A series of youth protests against the corruption and autocratic rule of President Saleh in Yemen, which endured for more than a year with support from tribal confederations, defecting military units, and an Islamist political party. These protests drew international intervention from most of the Gulf Cooperation Council (GCC) states, who ultimately persuaded the president to resign but did not solve any of the problems motivating the protests.

Activists protesting against the political discrimination and exclusion of people from the southern part of Yemen had acquired skills in nonviolent protest since 2007. Camps filled with people displaced by poverty, rapacious landlords, and conflict in the north had been growing near the major cities of Yemen. On January 23, 2011, Tawakkol Karman, a journalist and liberal activist, and the daughter and niece of prominent leaders in the Islamist wing of the Islah (Reform) Party, organized a march with young people in Sana'a to congratulate the people of Tunisia on overthrowing their president. The government arrested her, but this stimulated massive protests, so they released her after two days. Because the government blocked off Tahrir Square, the protesters set up a large encampment in the large open area near Sana'a University, which they renamed Taghyeer Square (Change Square).

On January 27, 10,000 people gathered at Change Square to demand the departure of President Saleh. This crowd grew larger on February 3. Protests in huge numbers continued throughout February in Sana'a, Aden, Taiz, and other cities. On February 25, the numbers of protesters in Sana'a for another "Day of Rage" reached 180,000. The next day, the leaders of the two largest tribal confederations announced that they would join the opposition forces. On March 1, Abdul-Majid al-Zindani, the head of the Council of Islamic Clerics, made a speech of support to the protesters. On March 11, 2011, security forces fired on the 40,000 protesters. On March 18, the government used plainclothes gunmen to kill 52 people and injure hundreds. This massacre prompted 11 senior military commanders to defect to the opposition, including the important brigadier general Ali Mohsen al-Ahmar, commander of the 1st Armored Division, who pledged on March 21 to protect the protesters. Despite the lack of accurate casualty counts, even more people died on March 25, 2011. In sum, the protesters drew to their cause influential and powerful tribal, military, and Islamist forces. These protests continued for the whole year while President Saleh promised three times to resign and then refused.

Although the government avoided big, direct battles with opposition military forces, this conflict carried two consequences: 1) The Houthis in the north took advantage of the absence of any restraining force to expand the territory they controlled; 2) the radical Islamist Al-Qaeda in the Arabian Peninsula similarly filled the absence of security forces in the south by conquering territory.

Saudi Arabia and the Gulf Cooperation Council states intervened in the chaotic conditions they saw, but they worked only with the government of President Saleh and the formal political opposition, called the Joint Meeting Parties (JMP). The youth who had been protesting and suffering the government assaults did not have any political representation or voice in the negotiations. Similarly, the formal negotiations did not include members of the southern movement, or the Houthis. The deal that the GCC negotiated with Saleh on November 23, 2011, gave him and his family immunity from prosecution, the right to keep his assets, and even the ability to return to Yemen. Only the JMP accepted that deal; the other parties rejected it. He returned to undermine the government of his successor President Abdu Rabbu Mansour Hadi and ultimately even joined with his former enemies, the Houthis, to bring the country into total civil war.

The youth who endured great sacrifices and armed attacks from their own government for a year did not gain any improvement in the political or economic conditions that drove their movement. Already the poorest Arab country before the protests, Yemen has collapsed economically, with minimal capabilities to meet basic human needs. The people find themselves caught between four major conflicts: Houthis versus the state; AQAP against everyone else; the family and loyalists of former president Saleh against the government; and the Saudi-led coalition against the Houthis.

Tom Dowling

See also: Al-Ahmar, Ali Muhsin; General People's Congress; Hadi, Abdu Rabbu Mansour; Houthis (Ansar Allah); Operation Decisive Storm; Saleh, Ali Abdullah; Yemeni Socialist party; Yemen, Republic of

Further Reading

Gasim, Gamal. "Explaining Political Activism in Yemen." In *Taking to the Streets: The Transformation of Arab Activism,* edited by Lina Khatib and Ellen Lust, 109–35. Baltimore: Johns Hopkins University Press, 2014.

Hill, Ginny. *Yemen Endures: Civil War, Saudi Adventurism and the Future of Arabia.* New York: Oxford University Press, 2017.

Juneau, Thomas. "Iran's Policy Towards the Houthis in Yemen: A Limited Return on a Modest Investment." *International Affairs* 92, no. 3 (May 2016): 647–63.

Peterson, J. E. *Yemen: The Search for a Modern State.* London: Routledge, 2017.

Rugh, William A. "Problems in Yemen, Domestic and Foreign." *Middle East Policy* 22, no. 4. (Winter 2015): 140–52.

Z

Zaydi Doctrine

A form of Shi'a doctrine, commonly known as the Fiver Shi'a, considered close to the Hanafi approach in Sunni Islam, in contrast to the Shafi'i approach held by the rest of Yemen. Zaydi doctrine emphasizes its political theory of the Imamate. Unlike the Jafari Doctrine (Twelver) and Ismaili (Sevener) Shia, the Zaydis consider Zayd ibn Ali to be the legitimate fifth Imam but also regard anyone in the house of Ali as eligible for the Imamate. The contender to the Imamate must possess certain qualities, primarily that of promoting justice, and must take the office by force from any unjust incumbent. They reject the doctrine of the Hidden Imam and the return of the Mahdi. They do not consider their Imam either infallible or capable of performing miracles. They follow a rationalist approach to religious and philosophical interpretation, while rejecting Sufism.

Originating in Iraq, Zaydism originally spread in northern Iran, but after defeats in battle, the remnants of that community eventually adopted the Jafari Doctrine. The Zaydi now live only in the mountains of northern Yemen, where they constitute 40 percent of the population. Zaydi Imams have ruled over Northern Yemen from the introduction of Zaydism in 897 until an army coup deposed the Imam and established the Yemen Arab Republic in 1962. From the 18th century onward, Zaydism became increasingly close to Sunni Islam, and the office of the Imamate became often hereditary.

Since 1962, the office of Imam has remained vacant, while scholars discuss its necessity. Several scholars were willing to give up the office, or interpret it in democratic ways. The political failure of Republican Yemen, and the spread of militant Salafism in the north have sparked a Zaydi revival trend, from which the Houthi Movement emerged.

Alexander Weissenburger

See also: Al-Qaeda in the Arabian Peninsula (AQAP); Houthis (Ansar Allah); Shi'a; Yemen, Republic of

Further Reading

Haider, Najam. "Zaydism: A Theological and Political Survey." *Religion Compass* 4, no. 7 (2010): 436–42.

King, James Robin. "Zaydi Revival in a Hostile Republic: Competing Identities, Loyalties and Visions of State in Republican Yemen." *Arabica* 59 (2012): 404–45.

Salmoni, Barak A., Bryce Loidolt, and Madeleine Wells. *Regime and Periphery in Northern Yemen: The Huthi Phenomenon.* Santa Monica, CA: RAND Corporation, 2010.

PRIMARY DOCUMENTS

1 Excerpts from *The Taif Agreement*, Ta'if, Saudi Arabia (October 22, 1989)

The Lebanese political system, based on a sectarian division of constitutional powers and positions, guaranteed the representation of important minority groups, but the flaws of this system also led Lebanon into civil war. The Lebanese parliament, with mediation by Saudi Arabia, negotiated this agreement to end the civil war, reaching agreement on October 22, 1989. The parliament ratified it on November 5. While recognizing Syria's contribution toward ending the civil war, it provided a framework for the withdrawal of Syrian forces. It extended Lebanese sovereignty and authority in South Lebanon, occupied by Israel. The accords transferred the power away from the presidency and vested it in a cabinet equally divided between Lebanese Muslims and Christians. It includes a Syrian-Lebanese security agreement to bring about the withdrawal of Israeli forces from Lebanese territory and calls for the disarmament and disbandment of all Lebanese and non-Lebanese militia.

First, General Principles and Reforms:

I. General Principles

A. Lebanon is a sovereign, free, and independent country and a final homeland for all its citizens.

B. Lebanon is Arab in belonging and identity. It is an active and founding member of the Arab League and is committed to the league's charter. It is an active and founding member of the United Nations Organization and is committed to its charters. Lebanon is a member of the nonaligned movement. The state of Lebanon shall embody these principles in all areas and spheres, without exception.

C. Lebanon is a democratic parliamentary republic founded on respect for public liberties, especially the freedom of expression and belief, on social justice, and on equality in rights and duties among all citizens, without discrimination or preference.

D. The people are the source of authority. They are sovereign and they shall exercise their sovereignty through the constitutional institutions.

E. The economic system is a free system that guarantees individual initiative and private ownership.

F. Culturally, socially, and economically-balanced development is a mainstay of the state's unity and of the system's stability.

G. Efforts (will be made) to achieve comprehensive social justice through fiscal, economic, and social reform.

H. Lebanon's soil is united and it belongs to all the Lebanese. Every Lebanese is entitled to live in and enjoy any part of the country under the supremacy of the law. The people may not be categorized on the basis of any affiliation whatsoever and there shall be no fragmentation, no partition, and no repatriation [of Palestinians in Lebanon].

I. No authority violating the common co-existence charter shall be legitimate.

II. Political Reforms

A. Chamber of Deputies:

The Chamber of Deputies is the legislative authority which exercises full control over government policy and activities.

. . .

5. Until the Chamber of Deputies passes an election law free of sectarian restriction, the parliamentary seats shall be divided according to the following bases:

a. Equally between Christians and Muslims.
b. Proportionately between the denominations of each sect.
c. Proportionately between the districts.

6. The number of members of the Chamber of Deputies shall be increased to 108, shared equally between Christians and Muslims. As for the districts created on the basis of this document and the districts whose seats became vacant prior to the proclamation of this document, their seats shall be filled only once on an emergency basis through appointment by the national accord government that is planned to be formed.

7. With the election of the first Chamber of Deputies on a national, not sectarian, basis, a senate shall be formed and all the spiritual families shall be represented in it. The senate powers shall be confined to crucial issues.

B. President of Republic:

The president of republic is the head of the state and a symbol of the country's unity. He shall contribute to enhancing the constitution and to preserving Lebanon's independence, unity, and territorial integrity in accordance with the provisions of the constitution. He is the supreme commander of the armed forces which are subject to the power of the cabinet. The president shall exercise the following powers:

1. Head the cabinet [meeting] whenever he wishes, but without voting.
2. Head the Supreme Defense Council.
3. Issues decrees and demand their publication.

. . .

C. Prime Minister:

The prime minister is the head of the government. He represents it and speaks in its name. He is responsible for implementing the general policy drafted by the cabinet. The prime minister shall exercise the following powers:

1. Head the cabinet.
2. Hold parliamentary consultations to form the cabinet and co-sign with the president the decree forming it.

. . .

D. Cabinet:

The executive power shall be vested in the Cabinet. The following are among the powers exercised by it:

Primary Documents

1. Set the general policy of the State in all domains, draws up draft bills and decrees, and takes the necessary decisions for its implementation.
2. Watch over the implementation of laws and regulations and supervise the activities of all the state agencies without exception, including the civilian, military, and security departments and institutions.
3. The cabinet is the authority which controls the armed forces.
4. Appoint, dismiss, and accept the resignation of state employees in accordance with the law.

. . .

E. Minister:

The minister's powers shall be reinforced in a manner compatible with the government's general policy and with the principle of collective responsibility. A minister shall not be relieved from his position unless by cabinet decree or unless the Chamber of Deputies withdraws its confidence from him individually.

. . .

G. Abolition of Political Sectarianism:

Abolishing political sectarianism is a fundamental national objective. To achieve it, it is required that efforts be made in accordance with a phased plan. The Chamber of Deputies elected on the basis of equal sharing by Christians and Muslims shall adopt the proper measures to achieve this objective and to form a national council, which is headed by the president of the republic and which includes, in addition to the prime minister and the Chamber of Deputies speaker, political, intellectual, and social notables. The council's task will be to examine and propose the means capable of abolishing sectarianism, to present them to the Chamber of Deputies and the cabinet, and to observe implementation of the phased plan. The following shall be done in the interim period:

a. Abolish the sectarian representation base and rely on capability and specialization in public jobs, the judiciary, the military, security, public, and joint institutions, and in the independent agencies in accordance with the dictates of national accord, excluding the top-level jobs and equivalent jobs which shall be shared equally by Christians and Muslims without allocating any particular job to any sect.
b. Abolish the mention of sect and denomination on the identity card.

III. Other Reforms

A. Administrative Decentralism:

1. The State of Lebanon shall be a single and united state, with a strong, central authority.
2. The powers of the governors and district administrative officers shall be expanded and all state administrations shall be represented in the administrative provinces at the highest level possible so as to facilitate serving the citizens and meeting their needs locally.

. . .

5. A comprehensive and unified development plan capable of developing the provinces economically and socially shall be adopted and the resources of the

municipalities, unified municipalities, and municipal unions shall be reinforced with the necessary financial resources.

B. Courts:

[1] To guarantee that all officials and citizens are subject to the supremacy of the law and to insure harmony between the action of the legislative and executive authorities on the one hand, and the givens of common coexistence and the basic rights of the Lebanese as stipulated in the constitution on the other hand:

. . .

[2] To ensure the principle of harmony between religion and state, the heads of the Lebanese sects may revise the constitutional council in matters pertaining to:

1. Personal status affairs.
2. Freedom of religion and the practice of religious rites.
3. Freedom of religious education.

[3] To ensure the judiciary's independence, a certain number of the Higher Judiciary Council shall be elected by the judiciary body.

D. Parliamentary Election Law:

Parliamentary elections shall be held in accordance with a new law on the basis of provinces and in the light of rules that guarantee common coexistence between the Lebanese, and that ensure the sound and efficient political representation of all the people's factions and generations. This shall be done after reviewing the administrative division within the context of unity of the people, the land, and the institutions.

E. Creation of a socioeconomic council for development:

A socioeconomic council shall be created to insure that representatives of the various sectors participate in drafting the state's socioeconomic policy and providing advice and proposals.

F. Education:

1. Education shall be provided to all and shall be made obligatory for the elementary stage at least.
2. The freedom of education shall be emphasized in accordance with general laws and regulations.
3. Private education shall be protected and state control over private schools and textbooks shall be strengthened.
4. Official, vocational, and technological education shall be reformed, strengthened, and developed in a manner that meets the country's development and reconstruction needs. The conditions of the Lebanese University shall be reformed and aid shall be provided to the university, especially to its technical colleges.
5. The curricula shall be reviewed and developed in a manner that strengthens national belonging, fusion, spiritual and cultural openness, and that unifies textbooks on the subjects of history and national education.

G. Information:

All the information media shall be reorganized under the canopy of the law and within the framework of responsible liberties that serve the cautious tendencies and the objective of ending the state of war.

Primary Documents 325

Second, spreading the sovereignty of the State of Lebanon over all Lebanese territories:

Considering that all Lebanese factions have agreed to the establishment of a strong state founded on the basis of national accord, the national accord government shall draft a detailed one-year plan whose objective is to spread the sovereignty of the State of Lebanon over all Lebanese territories gradually with the state's own forces. The broad lines of the plan shall be as follows:

A. Disbanding of all Lebanese and non-Lebanese militias shall be announced. The militias' weapons shall be delivered to the State of Lebanon within a period of 6 months, beginning with the approval of the national accord charter. The president of the republic shall be elected. A national accord cabinet shall be formed, and the political reforms shall be approved constitutionally.

. . .

C. Strengthening the armed forces:

1. The fundamental task of the armed forces is to defend the homeland, and if necessary, protect public order when the danger exceeds the capability of the internal security forces to deal with such a danger on their own.
2. The armed forces shall be used to support the internal security forces in preserving security under conditions determined by the cabinet.
3. The armed forces shall be unified, prepared, and trained in order that they may be able to shoulder their national responsibilities in confronting Israeli aggression.
4. When the internal security forces become ready to assume their security tasks, the armed forces shall return to their barracks.
5. The armed forces intelligence shall be reorganized to serve military objectives exclusively.

D. The problem of the Lebanese evacuees shall be solved fundamentally, and the right of every Lebanese evicted since 1975 to return to the place from which he was evicted shall be established. . . .

Third, liberating Lebanon from the Israeli occupation:

Regaining state authority over the territories extending to the internationally-recognized Lebanese borders requires the following:

A. Efforts to implement resolution 425 and the other UN Security Council resolutions calling for fully eliminating the Israeli occupation.
B. Adherence to the truce agreement concluded on 23 March 1949.
C. Taking all the steps necessary to liberate all Lebanese territories from the Israeli occupation, to spread state sovereignty over all the territories, and to deploy the Lebanese army in the border area adjacent to Israel; and making efforts to reinforce the presence of the UN forces in South Lebanon to insure the Israeli withdrawal and to provide the opportunity for the return of security and stability to the border area.

Fourth, Lebanese-Syrian relations:

Lebanon, with its Arab identity, is tied to all the Arab countries by true fraternal relations. Between Lebanon and Syria there is a special relationship that derives its strength from the roots of blood relationships, history, and joint fraternal interests. This is the concept on which the two countries' coordination and cooperation is founded, and which will be embodied by the agreements between the two countries in all areas, in a manner that accomplishes the two fraternal countries' interests within the framework of the sovereignty and independence of each of them. Therefore, and because strengthening the bases of security creates the climate needed to develop these bonds, Lebanon should not be allowed to constitute a source of threat to Syria's security, and Syria should not be allowed to constitute a source of threat to Lebanon's security under any circumstances. Consequently, Lebanon should not allow itself to become a pathway or a base for any force, state, or organization seeking to undermine its security or Syria's security. Syria, which is eager for Lebanon's security, independence, and unity and for harmony among its citizens, should not permit any act that poses a threat to Lebanon's security, independence, and sovereignty.

Source: "Lebanon: National Reconciliation Accord—Taif Agreement (1989)," November 5, 1989, United Nations Department of Political Affairs. Available from: https://peacemaker.un.org/lebanon-taifaccords89.

2   *The Arab Peace Initiative,* Beirut Arab League Summit (March 28, 2002)

Crown Prince Abdullah of Saudi Arabia announced the Arab Peace Initiative *at the Beirut Arab League Summit in March 2002, as a proposal for the Arab world to fully recognize the State of Israel. The 22 member states of the Arab League initially endorsed it when presented, and later the 57 member states of the Organization of Islamic Cooperation endorsed it. (Also re-endorsed at the 2007 and 2017 Arab League Summits.) This proposal came in a time of high tension for Israel during the Second Intifada, which initially interpreted it as a non-negotiable demand. However, support for it, as a basis for negotiations, has gained great momentum. The Quartet Road Map for Peace documents reference it. It was confirmed by UN Security Council Resolutions (UNSC) 1850 (2008) and 1860 (2009). Supporters claim it has elevated Palestine to a symmetrical position with Israel. They have created committees to develop and debate it and seek another, more rigorous UNSC resolution to enforce it.*

The Council of Arab States at the Summit Level at its 14th Ordinary Session, reaffirming the resolution, taken in June 1996 at the Cairo Extra-Ordinary Arab Summit, that a just and comprehensive peace in the Middle East is the strategic option of the Arab countries, to be achieved in accordance with international legality, and which would require a comparable commitment on the part of the Israeli government;

Having listened to the statement made by His Royal Highness Prince Abdullah bin Abdul Aziz, Crown Prince of the Kingdom of Saudi Arabia, in which His Highness presented his initiative calling for full Israeli withdrawal from all the Arab territories occupied since June 1967, in implementation of Security Council

Primary Documents

Resolutions 242 and 338, reaffirmed by the Madrid Conference of 1991 and the land-for-peace principle, and Israel's acceptance of an independent Palestinian state with East Jerusalem as its capital, in return for the establishment of normal relations in the context of a comprehensive peace with Israel;

Emanating from the conviction of the Arab countries that a military solution to the conflict will not achieve peace or provide security for the parties, the Council:

1. Requests Israel to reconsider its policies and declare that a just peace is its strategic option as well.

2. Further calls upon Israel to affirm:

I- Full Israeli withdrawal from all the territories occupied since 1967, including the Syrian Golan Heights, to the June 4, 1967 lines, as well as the remaining occupied Lebanese territories in the south of Lebanon.

II- Achievement of a just solution to the Palestinian refugee problem, to be agreed upon in accordance with UN General Assembly Resolution 194.

III- The acceptance of the establishment of a sovereign independent Palestinian state on the Palestinian territories occupied since June 4, 1967 in the West Bank and Gaza Strip, with East Jerusalem as its capital.

3. Consequently, the Arab countries affirm the following:

I- Consider the Arab-Israeli conflict ended, and enter into a peace agreement with Israel, and provide security for all the states of the region.

II- Establish normal relations with Israel in the context of this comprehensive peace.

4. Assures the rejection of all forms of Palestinian patriation which conflict with the special circumstances of the Arab host countries.

5. Calls upon the government of Israel and all Israelis to accept this initiative in order to safeguard the prospects for peace and stop the further shedding of blood, enabling the Arab countries and Israel to live in peace and good neighbourliness and provide future generations with security, stability and prosperity.

6. Invites the international community and all countries and organizations to support this initiative.

7. Requests the Chairman of the Summit to form a special committee composed of some of its concerned member states and the Secretary-General of the League of Arab States to pursue the necessary contacts to gain support for this initiative at all levels, particularly from the United Nations, the Security Council, the United States of America, the Russian Federation, the Muslim states and the European Union.

Source: Beirut Declaration on Saudi Peace Initiative. March 28, 2002. Israel Ministry of Foreign Affairs, Yearbook 2002. Available online at https://mfa.gov.il/MFA/ForeignPolicy/MFADocuments/Yearbook2002.

---

3   *The Amman Message* (July 26, 2005)

This document derived from a statement released on November 9, 2004, by H. M. King Abdullah II bin Al-Hussein in Amman, Jordan, declaring what Islam included

328   **Primary Documents**

and prohibited. In an effort to gain greater credibility, he sent three questions to 24 of the most senior religious scholars representing all branches of Islam. Based on the official rulings of religious law (fatwas) *he received in response, in July 2005, he convened a conference of 200 of the leading Islamic scholars from 50 countries. They released the following document emphasizing three fundamental issues. This statement represented a clear ideological defense of the consensus Islamic position in refuting the claims of al-Qaeda. On November 9, 2005, suicide bombers attacked three hotels in Amman, killing 60 people and injuring 115 others.*

In the Name of God, the Merciful, the Compassionate.

Peace and blessings upon His chosen Prophet, and upon his household, his noble blessed companions, and upon all the messengers and prophets.

God Almighty has said:

> O humankind! We created you from a male and female, and made you into peoples and tribes that you may know each other. Truly the most honored of you before God is the most pious of you. (49:13)

This is a declaration to our brethren in the lands of Islam and throughout the world that Amman, the capital of the Hashemite Kingdom of Jordan, is proud to issue during the blessed month of Ramadan in which the Qur'an descended as guidance to humankind and as clarifications for guidance and discernment. (2:185)

In this declaration we speak frankly to the [Islamic] nation, at this difficult juncture in its history, regarding the perils that beset it. We are aware of the challenges confronting the nation, threatening its identity, assailing its tenets (*kalima*), and working to distort its religion and harm what is sacred to it. Today the magnanimous message of Islam faces a vicious attack from those who through distortion and fabrication try to portray Islam as an enemy to them. It is also under attack from some who claim affiliation with Islam and commit irresponsible acts in its name.

This magnanimous message that the Originator—great is His power—revealed to the unlettered Prophet Muhammad—God's blessings and peace upon him, and that was carried by his successors and the members of his household after him, is an address of brotherhood, humanity and a religion that encompasses all human activity. It states the truth directly, commands what is right, forbids what is wrong, honors the human being, and accepts others.

The Hashemite Kingdom of Jordan has embraced the path of promoting the true luminous image of Islam, halting the accusations against it and repelling the attacks upon it. This is in accordance with the inherited spiritual and historical responsibility carried by the Hashemite monarchy, honored as direct descendants of the Prophet, the Messenger of God—peace and blessings upon him—who carried the message. For five decades, his late Majesty King Hussein Bin Talal—God rest his soul—demonstrated this way with the vigorous effort that he exerted. Since the day he took the flag, His Majesty King Abdullah II has continued this effort, with resolution and determination, as a service to Islam, fortifying the solidarity of 1.2 billion Muslims who comprise one fifth of humanity, preventing their marginalization or extrication from the movement of human society, and affirming their role in building human civilization and participating in its progress during our present age.

Islam is founded upon basic principles, the fundamentals are attesting to the unity of God (*tawhid Allah*); belief in the message of His Prophet; continuous connection with the Creator through ritual prayer (*salat*); training and rectifying the soul through the fast of Ramadan; safeguarding one another by paying the alms tax (*zakat*); the unity of the people through the annual pilgrimage (*hajj*) to God's Sanctified House, [performed] by those who are able; and [observing] His rulings that regulate human behavior in all its dimensions. Over history these [basic principles] have formed a strong and cohesive nation, and a great civilization. They bear witness to noble principles and values that verify the good of humanity, whose foundation is the oneness of the human species, and that people are equal in rights and obligations, peace and justice, realizing comprehensive security, mutual social responsibility, being good to one's neighbor, protecting belongings and property, honoring pledges, and more.

Together, these are principles that provide common ground for the followers of religions and [different] groups of people. That is because the origin of divine religions is one, and Muslims believe in all Messengers of God and do not differentiate between any of them. Denying the message of any one of them is a deviation from Islam. This establishes a wide platform for the believers of [different] religions to meet the other upon common ground, for the service of human society, without encroaching upon creedal distinctions or upon intellectual freedom. For all of this we base ourselves upon His saying:

> The messenger believes in what has been revealed unto him from his Lord as do the believers. Each one believes in God, and His angels, and His scriptures, and His messengers. We make no distinction between any of His messengers—and they say: "We hear, and we obey. [Grant us] Your forgiveness, our Lord. Unto You is the journeying." (2:285)

Islam honors every human being, regardless of his color, race or religion: We have honored the sons of Adam, provided them transport on land and sea, sustained them with good things, and conferred on them special favors above a great part of our creation. (17:70)

Islam also affirms that the way of calling [others] to God is founded upon kindness and gentleness: Call to the path of your Lord with wisdom and a beautiful exhortation, and debate with them in that which is most beautiful (*ahsan*). (16:125) Furthermore, it shuns cruelty and violence in how one faces and addresses [others]:

> It is by some Mercy of God that you were gentle to them. Were you severe— cruel-hearted—they would have broken away from you. So pardon them and ask forgiveness for them and consult with them in the conduct of affairs. And when you are resolved, put your trust in God; truly God loves those who trust [in Him]. (3:159)

Islam has made clear that the goal of its message is realizing mercy and good for all people. The Transcendent has said, We did not send you [Muhammad] but out of mercy for all creatures. (21:107) And the Prophet Muhammad—blessings and peace upon Him—said, "The Merciful has mercy upon those who are merciful, be merciful to those on earth, He who is in heaven will be merciful unto you."

Islam calls for treating others as one desires to be treated. It urges the tolerance and forgiveness that express the nobility of the human being: The recompense for an evil is an evil equal thereto, but who forgives and reconciles, his recompense is from God. (42:40) Good and evil are not equal. Repel with what is most virtuous. Then he, between whom and you there is enmity, will be as if he were an intimate friend. (41:34)

Islam confirms the principle of justice in interacting with others, safeguarding their rights, and confirms that one must not deny people their possessions: And let not the hatred of others make you swerve to wrong and depart from justice. Be just: that is closer to piety; (5:8) God commands you to return trusts to their owners, and if you judge between people, you shall judge with justice; (4:58) So give [full] measure and [full] weight and do not deny the people their goods, and work no corruption in the land, after it has been set right. (7:85)

Islam requires respect for pledges and covenants, and adhering to what has been specified; and it forbids treachery and treason: Fulfill the covenant of God when you have entered into it, and break not oaths after they have been confirmed and you have made God your surety; truly God knows what you do. (16:91)

Islam recognizes the noble station of [human] life, so there is to be no fighting against non-combatants, and no assault upon civilians and their properties, children at their mothers' bosom, students in their schools, nor upon elderly men and women. Assault upon the life of a human being, be it murder, injury or threat, is an assault upon the right to life among all human beings. It is among the gravest of sins; for human life is the basis for the prosperity of humanity: Whoever kills a soul for other than slaying a soul or corruption upon the earth it is as if he has killed the whole of humanity, and whoever saves a life, it is as if has revived the whole of humanity. (5:32)

The primordial religion of Islam is founded upon equanimity, balance, moderation, and facilitation: Thus have we made of you a middle nation that you might be witnesses over the people, and the Messenger a witness over yourselves. (2:143) The Prophet Muhammad—peace and blessings upon him—said: "Facilitate and do not make difficult, bear good tidings and do not deter." Islam has provided the foundation for the knowledge, reflection and contemplation that has enabled the creation of this deep-rooted civilization that was a crucial link by which the West arrived at the gates of modern knowledge, and in whose accomplishments non-Muslims participated, as a consequence of its being a comprehensive human civilization.

No day has passed but that this religion has been at war against extremism, radicalism and fanaticism, for they veil the intellect from foreseeing negative consequences [of one's actions]. Such blind impetuousness falls outside the human regulations pertaining to religion, reason and character. They are not from the true character of the tolerant, accepting Muslim.

Islam rejects extremism, radicalism and fanaticism—just as all noble, heavenly religions reject them—considering them as recalcitrant ways and forms of injustice.

Primary Documents

Furthermore, it is not a trait that characterizes a particular nation; it is an aberration that has been experienced by all nations, races, and religions. They are not particular to one people; truly they are a phenomenon that every people, every race and every religion has known.

We denounce and condemn extremism, radicalism and fanaticism today, just as our forefathers tirelessly denounced and opposed them throughout Islamic history. They are the ones who affirmed, as do we, the firm and unshakeable understanding that Islam is a religion of [noble] character traits in both its ends and means; a religion that strives for the good of the people, their happiness in this life and the next; and a religion that can only be defended in ways that are ethical; and the ends do not justify the means in this religion.

The source of relations between Muslims and others is peace; for there is no fighting [permitted] when there is no aggression. Even then, [it must be done with] benevolence, justice and virtue: God does not prevent you, as regards those who do not fight you in religion's [cause], nor drive you from your homes, from dealing kindly and justly with them: truly God loves the just. (60:8) Then if they cease, let there be no aggression, save against the oppressors. (2:193)

On religious and moral grounds, we denounce the contemporary concept of terrorism that is associated with wrongful practices, whatever their source and form may be. Such acts are represented by aggression against human life in an oppressive form that transgresses the rulings of God, frightening those who are secure, violating peaceful civilians, finishing off the wounded, and killing prisoners; and they employ unethical means, such as destroying buildings and ransacking cities: Do not kill the soul that God has made sacrosanct, save for justice. (6:151)

We condemn these practices and believe that resisting oppression and confirming justice should be a legitimate undertaking through legitimate means. We call on the people to take the necessary steps to achieve the strength and steadfastness for building identity and preserving rights.

We realize that over history extremism has been instrumental in destroying noble achievements in great civilizations, and that the tree of civilization withers when malice takes hold and breasts are shut. In all its shapes, extremism is a stranger to Islam, which is founded upon equanimity and tolerance. No human whose heart has been illumined by God could be a radical extremist.

At the same time, we decry the campaign of brazen distortion that portrays Islam as a religion that encourages violence and institutionalizes terrorism. We call upon the international community to work earnestly to implement international laws and honor the international mandates and resolutions issued by the United Nations, ensuring that all parties accept them and that they be enacted without double standards, to guarantee the return of rights to their [rightful] holders and the end of oppression. Achieving this will be a significant contribution to uprooting the causes of violence, fanaticism and extremism.

The way of this great religion that we are honored to belong to calls us to affiliate with and participate in modern society, and to contribute to its elevation and progress, helping one another with every faculty [to achieve] good and to comprehend, desiring justice for all peoples, while faithfully proclaiming the truth [of our religion], and sincerely expressing the soundness of our faith and beliefs—all of

332   **Primary Documents**

which are founded upon God's call for coexistence and piety. [We are called] to work toward renewing our civilization, based upon the guidance of religion, and following upon established practical intellectual policies.

The primary components of these policies comprise developing methods for preparing preachers, with the goal of ensuring that they realize the spirit of Islam and its methodology for structuring human life, as well as providing them with knowledge of contemporary culture, so that they are able to interact with their communities on the basis of awareness and insight: Say, "This is my way. I, and those who follow me, call for God with insight." (12:108); taking advantage of the communication revolution to refute the doubts that the enemies of Islam are arousing, in a sound, intellectual manner, without weakness or agitation, and with a style that attracts the reader, the listener and the viewer; consolidating the educational structure for individual Muslims, who are confident in their knowledge and abilities, working to form the integral identity that protects against corrupting forces; interest in scientific research and working with the modern sciences upon the basis of the Islamic perspective that distinguishes between creation, life and the human being; benefiting from modern achievements in the fields of science and technology; adopting an Islamic approach for realizing the comprehensive development that is founded upon [maintaining] the delicate balance between the spiritual, economic and social dimensions [of life]; providing for human rights and basic liberties, ensuring life, dignity and security, and guaranteeing basic needs; administering the affairs of society in accordance with the principles of justice and consultation; and benefiting from the goods and mechanisms for adopting democracy that human society has presented.

Hope lies in the scholars of our Nation, that through the reality of Islam and its values they will enlighten the intellects of our youth—the ornament of our present age and the promise of our future. The scholars shield our youth from the danger of sliding down the paths of ignorance, corruption, close-minded-ness and subordination. It is our scholars who illuminate for them the paths of tolerance, moderation, and goodness, and prevent them from [falling] into the abysses of extremism and fanaticism that destroy the spirit and body.

We look to our scholars to lead us in partaking of our role and verifying our priorities, that they may be exemplars in religion, character, conduct, and discerning enlightened speech, presenting to the nation their noble religion that brings ease [in all matters] and its practical laws in which lie the awakening and joy of the nation. Among the individuals of the nation and throughout the regions of the world, they disseminate good, peace and benevolence, through subtle knowledge, insightful wisdom and political guidance in all matters, uniting and not dividing, appeasing hearts and not deterring them, looking to the horizons of fulfillment to meet the requirements and challenges of the 21st century.

We ask God to prepare for our Islamic Nation the paths of renaissance, prosperity and advancement; to shield it from the evils of extremism and close-mindedness; to preserve its rights, sustain its glory, and uphold its dignity. What an excellent Lord is he, and what an excellent Supporter.

God Almighty says: This is My straight path, so follow it. And follow not the [other] ways, lest you be parted from His way. This has He ordained for you, that you may be God-fearing. (6:152-153)

Primary Documents

And the last of our supplications is that praise be to God, Lord of the worlds. (10:10)

Amman-Ramadan 1425 Hijri
The Hashemite Kingdom of Jordan—November 2004 A.D.

The Three Points of The Amman Message
HM King Abdullah II
Amman, July 26, 2006

In the Name of God, the Compassionate, the Merciful

May peace and blessings be upon the Prophet Muhammad and his pure and noble family.

(1) Whosoever is an adherent to one of the four Sunni schools (*Mathahib*) of Islamic jurisprudence (Hanafi, Maliki, Shafi'i and Hanbali), the two Shi'i schools of Islamic jurisprudence (Ja'fari and Zaydi), the Ibadi school of Islamic jurisprudence and the Thahiri school of Islamic jurisprudence, is a Muslim. Declaring that person an apostate is impossible and impermissible. Verily his (or her) blood, honor, and property are inviolable. Moreover, in accordance with the Shaykh Al-Azhar's fatwa, it is neither possible nor permissible to declare whosoever subscribes to the Ash'ari creed or whoever practices real *Tasawwuf* (Sufism) an apostate. Likewise, it is neither possible nor permissible to declare whosoever subscribes to true Salafi thought an apostate.

Equally, it is neither possible nor permissible to declare as apostates any group of Muslims who believes in God, Glorified and Exalted be He, and His Messenger (may peace and blessings be upon him) and the pillars of faith, and acknowledges the five pillars of Islam, and does not deny any necessarily self-evident tenet of religion.

(2) There exists more in common between the various schools of Islamic jurisprudence than there is difference between them. The adherents to the eight schools of Islamic jurisprudence are in agreement as regards the basic principles of Islam. All believe in Allah (God), Glorified and Exalted be He, the One and the Unique; that the Noble Qur'an is the Revealed Word of God; and that our master Muhammad, may blessings and peace be upon him, is a Prophet and Messenger unto all mankind. All are in agreement about the five pillars of Islam: the two testaments of faith (*shahadatayn*); the ritual prayer (*salat*); almsgiving (*zakat*); fasting the month of Ramadan (*sawm*), and the Hajj to the sacred house of God (in Mecca). All are also in agreement about the foundations of belief: belief in Allah (God), His angels, His scriptures, His messengers, and in the Day of Judgment, in Divine Providence in good and in evil. Disagreements between the *'ulama* (scholars) of the eight schools of Islamic jurisprudence are only with respect to the ancillary branches of religion (*furu'*) and not as regards the principles and fundamentals (*usul*) [of the religion of Islam]. Disagreement with respect to the ancillary branches of religion (*furu'*) is a mercy. Long ago it was said that variance in opinion among the *'ulama* (scholars) "is a good affair."

(3) Acknowledgement of the schools of Islamic jurisprudence (*Mathahib*) within Islam means adhering to a fundamental methodology in the issuance of fatwas: no one may issue a fatwa without the requisite personal qualifications

which each school of Islamic jurisprudence determines [for its own adherents]. No one may issue a fatwa without adhering to the methodology of the schools of Islamic jurisprudence. No one may claim to do unlimited Ijtihad and create a new school of Islamic jurisprudence or to issue unacceptable fatwas that take Muslims out of the principles and certainties of the *Shari'ah* and what has been established in respect of its schools of jurisprudence.

Source: Available online at The Amman Message, The Royal Aal Al-Bayt Institute for Islamic Thought, Amman Jordan, 2009, http://ammanmessage.com/the-amman-message-full/.

4   *The Damascus Declaration for Democratic National Change,* **Damascus, Syria (October 16, 2005)**

This historic initiative represents the first time since the Ba'ath Party seized power that the majority of Syrian opposition parties, together with the Kurdish parties, secular and religious, declared a consensus political position. Initially formulated and signed by five parties and nine very prominent individuals, it was signed by other smaller groups and individuals soon after. It proves the existence of popular forces with a long history of democratic struggle and a program for national change in the spirit of modernity. It offers a coherent alternative to both the Assad regime and the claims of radical Islamists.

Syria today is being subjected to pressure it had not experienced before, as a result of the policies pursued by the regime, policies that have brought the country to a situation that calls for concern for its national safety and the fate of its people. Today Syria stands at a crossroad and needs to engage in self-appraisal and benefit from its historical experience more than any time in the past.

The authorities' monopoly of everything for more than 30 years has established an authoritarian, totalitarian, and cliquish [*fi'awi*] regime that has led to a lack of [interest in] politics in society, with people losing interest in public affairs. That has brought upon the country such destruction as that represented by the rending of the national social fabric of the Syrian people, an economic collapse that poses a threat to the country, and exacerbating crises of every kind, in addition to the stifling isolation which the regime has brought upon the country as a result of its destructive, adventurous, and short-sighted policies on the Arab and regional levels, and especially in Lebanon. Those policies were founded on discretionary bases and were not guided by the higher national interests.

All that—and many other matters—calls for mobilizing all the energies of Syria, the homeland and the people, in a rescue task of change that lifts the country out of the mold of the security state and takes it to the mold of the political state, so that it will be able to enhance its independence and unity, and so that its people will be able to hold the reins of their country and participate freely in running its affairs. The transformations needed affect the various aspects of life, and include the State, the authorities, and society, and lead to changing Syrian policies at home and abroad.

In view of the signatories' feeling that the present moment calls for a courageous and responsible national stand, that takes the country out of its condition of weakness and waiting that is poisoning the present political life, and spares it the dangers that loom in the horizon, and in view of their belief that a clear and cohesive line on which society's various forces agree, a line that projects the goals of democratic change at this stage, acquires special importance in the achievement of such change by the Syrian people and in accordance with their will and interests, and helps to avoid opportunism and extremism in public action, they have reached an accord on the following bases:

Establishment of a democratic national regime is the basic approach to the plan for change and political reform. It must be peaceful, gradual, founded on accord, and based on dialogue and recognition of the other.

Shunning totalitarian thought and severing all plans for exclusion, custodianship, and extirpation under any pretext, be it historical or realistic; shunning violence in exercising political action; and seeking to prevent and avoid violence in any form and by any side.

Islam—which is the religion and ideology of the majority, with its lofty intentions, higher values, and tolerant canon law—is the more prominent cultural component in the life of the nation and the people. Our Arab civilization has been formed within the framework of its ideas, values, and ethics and in interaction with the other national historic cultures in our society, through moderation, tolerance, and mutual interaction, free of fanaticism, violence, and exclusion, while having great concern for the respect of the beliefs, culture, and special characteristics of others, whatever their religious, confessional, and intellectual affiliations, and openness to new and contemporary cultures.

No party or trend has the right to claim an exceptional role. No one has the right to shun the other, persecute him, and usurp his right to existence, free expression, and participation in the homeland.

Adoption of democracy as a modern system that has universal values and bases, based on the principles of liberty, sovereignty of the people, a State of institutions, and the transfer of power through free and periodic elections that enable the people to hold those in power accountable and change them.

Build a modern State, whose political system is based on a new social contract, which leads to a modern democratic Constitution that makes citizenship the criterion of affiliation, and adopts pluralism, the peaceful transfer of power, and the rule of law in a State all of whose citizens enjoy the same rights and have the same duties, regardless of race, religion, ethnicity, sect, or clan, and prevents the return of tyranny in new forms.

Turn to all the components of the Syrian people, all their intellectual trends and social classes, political parties, and cultural, economic, and social activities, and give them the opportunity to express their views, interests, and aspirations, and enable them to participate freely in the process of change.

Guarantee the freedom of individuals, groups, and national minorities to express themselves, and safeguard their role and cultural and linguistic rights, with the State respecting and caring for those rights, within the framework of the Constitution and under the law.

Find a just democratic solution to the Kurdish issue in Syria, in a manner that guarantees the complete equality of Syrian Kurdish citizens with the other citizens, with regard to nationality rights, culture, learning the national language, and the other constitutional, political, social, and legal rights on the basis of the unity of the Syrian land and people. Nationality and citizenship rights must be restored to those who have been deprived of them, and the file must be completely settled.

Commitment to the safety, security, and unity of the Syrian national [union] and addressing its problems through dialogue, and safeguard the unity of the homeland and the people in all circumstances, commitment to the liberation of the occupied territories and regaining the Golan Heights for the homeland, and enabling Syria to carry out an effective and positive Arab and regional role.

Abolish all forms of exclusion in public life, by suspending the emergency law; and abolish martial law and extraordinary courts, and all relevant laws, including Law 49 for the year 1980; release all political prisoners; [allow] the safe and honorable return of all those wanted and those who have been voluntarily or involuntarily exiled with legal guarantees; and ending all forms of political persecution, by settling grievances and turning a new leaf in the history of the country.

Strengthen the national army and maintain its professional spirit, and keep it outside the framework of political conflict and the democratic game, and confine its task to protecting the country's independence, safeguarding the constitutional system, and defending the homeland and the people.

Liberate popular organizations, federations, trade unions, and chambers of commerce, industry, and agriculture from the custodianship of the State and from party and security hegemony. Provide them with the conditions of free action as civil society organizations.

Launch public freedoms, organize political life through a modern party law, and organize the media and elections in accordance with modern laws that ensure liberty, justice, and equal opportunities for everyone.

Guarantee the right of political work to all components of the Syrian people in their various religious, national, and social affiliations.

Emphasize Syria's affiliation to the Arab Order, establish the widest relations of cooperation with the Arab Order, and strengthen strategic, political, and economic ties that lead the [Arab] nation to the path of unity. Correct the relationship with Lebanon, so that it will be based on liberty, equality, sovereignty, and the common interests of the two peoples and countries.

Observe all international treaties and conventions and the Universal Declaration on Human Rights, and seek within the framework of the United Nations and in cooperation with the international community to build a more just World Order, based on the principles of peace and mutual interest, warding off aggression, and the right of nations to resist occupation, and to oppose all forms of terrorism and violence directed against civilians.

The signatories to this declaration believe the process of change has begun, in view of its being a necessity that brooks no postponement because the country needs it. It is not directed against anyone, but requires everyone's efforts. Here we

Primary Documents

call on the Ba'athist citizens of our homeland and citizens from various political, cultural, religious, and confessional groups to participate with us and not to hesitate or be apprehensive, because the desired change is in everyone's interest and is feared only by those involved in crimes and corruption. The process of change can be organized as follows:

1. Opening the channels for a comprehensive and equitable national dialogue among all the components and social, political, and economic groups of the Syrian people in all areas and on the following premises:

The need for radical change in the country, and the rejection of all forms of cosmetic, partial, or circumspection reform.

Seek to stop the deterioration and the potential collapse and anarchy which could be brought upon the country by a mentality of fanaticism, revenge, extremism, and objection to democratic change.

Rejection of the change that is brought from abroad, while we are fully aware of the fact and the objectivity of the link between the internal and the external in the various political developments that are taking place in our contemporary world, without pushing the country toward isolation, adventure, and irresponsible stands, and anxiousness to safeguard the country's independence and territorial integrity.

2. Encourage initiatives for the return of society to politics, restore to the people their interest in public affairs, and activate civil society.
3. Form various committees, salons, forums, and bodies locally and throughout the country to organize the general cultural, social, political, and economic activity and to help it in playing an important role in advancing the national consciousness, giving vent to frustrations, and uniting the people behind the goals of change.
4. A comprehensive national accord on a common and independent program of the opposition forces, which charts the steps of the stage of transformation and the features of the democratic Syria of the future.
5. Pave the way for convening a national conference in which all the forces that aspire to change may participate, including those who accept that from among the regime, to establish a democratic national regime based on the accords mentioned in this declaration, and on the basis of a broad and democratic national coalition.
6. Call for the election of a Constituent Assembly that draws up a new Constitution for the country that foils adventurers and extremists, and that guarantees the separation of powers, safeguards the independence of the judiciary, and achieves national integration by consolidating the principle of citizenship.
7. Hold free and honest parliamentary elections that produce a fully legitimate national regime that governs the country in accordance with the Constitution and the laws that are in force, and on the basis of the view of the political majority and its program.

These are broad steps for the plan for democratic change, as we see it, which Syria needs, and to which its people aspire. It is open to the participation of all the national forces: political parties, civilian and civil bodies, and political, cultural, and professional figures. The plan accepts their commitments and contribution, and is open to review through the increase in the collectivity of political work and its effective societal forces.

We pledge to work to end the stage of despotism. We declare our readiness to offer the necessary sacrifices for that purpose, and to do all that is necessary to enable the process of democratic change to take off, and to build a modern Syria, a free homeland for all of its citizens, safeguard the freedom of its people, and protect national independence.

Signatories to the Declaration
Parties and Organizations:

Democratic National Grouping in Syria
Kurdish Democratic Alliance in Syria
Committees for the Revival of Civil Society
Kurdish Democratic Front in Syria
Future Party (Shaykh Nawwaf al-Bashir)

National Figures:

Riyad Sayf
Jawdat Sa'id
Dr Abd-al-Razzaq Id
Samir al-Nashar
Dr Fida Akram al-Hurani
Dr Adil Zakkar
Abd-al-Karim al-Dahhak
Haytham al-Malih
Nayif Qaysiyah

Source: Dr. Joshua Landis, Director: Center for Middle East Studies, University of Oklahoma, *SyriaComment*. http://joshualandis.oucreate.com/syriablog/2005/11 /damascus-declaration-in-english.htm. Accessed January 29, 2019.

---

5 Excerpts from the *United Nations Security Council Resolution 1973* (March 17, 2011)

Advocates of a "responsibility to protect" initially saw a resolution addressing the plight of civilians in Libya as an opportunity to practice this principle. The UN General Assembly had adopted this principle in 2005, but it took six months for the Security Council (UNSC) to similarly affirm it. After an initial protest in Benghazi on February 15, 2011, against Libyan leader Muammar al-Qaddafi, on February 17 the protests became widespread. On February 22, 2011, the Organization of Islamic Conference secretary-general Ihsanoglu condemned in the strongest terms the "excessive use of force against civilians" in Libya. On February 26, the UNSC adopted Resolution 1970, imposing an arms embargo and freezing regime assets. On March 7, 2011, the six-nation Gulf Cooperation Council released a statement backing a no-fly zone, followed by a resolution by the Arab League on March 12, 2011, calling on the UNSC to impose a no-fly zone over Libya and estab-lish safe areas, and on the international community to provide support and human-itarian assistance to the Libyan people. A large number of Arab organizations and

Primary Documents

prominent personalities issued an open letter, seeking to influence the delibera-tions of the UNSC members. On March 17, 2011, the UNSC adopted Resolution 1973 based on Chapter VII of the UN Charter. A U.S.-led coalition began air oper-ations on March 19, 2011, supplanted by the NATO Operation Unified Protector on March 31. The military operations quickly encountered criticism for going beyond the UN mandate. The disastrous Libyan civil war that followed has shaped inter-national responses to the Syrian civil war. While China and Russia permitted UNSCR 1973 by abstaining on the vote, they have vetoed resolutions on Syria.

Adopted by the Security Council at its 6498th meeting, on March 17, 2011
The Security Council,

- Recalling its resolution 1970 (2011) of 26 February 2011,
- Deploring the failure of the Libyan authorities to comply with resolution 1970 (2011),
- Expressing grave concern at the deteriorating situation, the escalation of violence, and the heavy civilian casualties,
- Reiterating the responsibility of the Libyan authorities to protect the Lib-yan population and reaffirming that parties to armed conflicts bear the primary responsibility to take all feasible steps to ensure the protection of civilians,
- Condemning the gross and systematic violation of human rights, includ-ing arbitrary detentions, enforced disappearances, torture and summary executions,
- Further condemning acts of violence and intimidation committed by the Libyan authorities against journalists, media professionals and associated personnel and urging these authorities to comply with their obligations under international humanitarian law as outlined in resolution 1738 (2006),
- Considering that the widespread and systematic attacks currently taking place in the Libyan Arab Jamahiriya against the civilian population may amount to crimes against humanity,
- Recalling paragraph 26 of resolution 1970 (2011) in which the Council expressed its readiness to consider taking additional appropriate mea-sures, as necessary, to facilitate and support the return of humanitarian agencies and make available humanitarian and related assistance in the Libyan Arab Jamahiriya,
- Expressing its determination to ensure the protection of civilians and civilian populated areas and the rapid and unimpeded passage of human-itarian assistance and the safety of humanitarian personnel,
- Recalling the condemnation by the League of Arab States, the African Union, and the Secretary General of the Organization of the Islamic Conference of the serious violations of human rights and international humanitarian law that have been and are being committed in the Libyan Arab Jamahiriya,
- Taking note of the final communiqué of the Organization of the Islamic Conference of 8 March 2011, and the communiqué of the Peace and

Security Council of the African Union of 10 March 2011 which established an ad hoc High Level Committee on Libya,

- Taking note also of the decision of the Council of the League of Arab States of 12 March 2011 to call for the imposition of a no-fly zone on Libyan military aviation, and to establish safe areas in places exposed to shelling as a precautionary measure that allows the protection of the Libyan people and foreign nationals residing in the Libyan Arab Jamahiriya,
- Taking note further of the Secretary-General's call on 16 March 2011 for an immediate cease-fire,
- Recalling its decision to refer the situation in the Libyan Arab Jamahiriya since 15 February 2011 to the Prosecutor of the International Criminal Court, and stressing that those responsible for or complicit in attacks targeting the civilian population, including aerial and naval attacks, must be held to account,
- Reiterating its concern at the plight of refugees and foreign workers forced to flee the violence in the Libyan Arab Jamahiriya, welcoming the response of neighboring States, in particular Tunisia and Egypt, to address the needs of those refugees and foreign workers, and calling on the international community to support those efforts,
- Deploring the continuing use of mercenaries by the Libyan authorities,
- Considering that the establishment of a ban on all flights in the airspace of the Libyan Arab Jamahiriya constitutes an important element for the protection of civilians as well as the safety of the delivery of humanitarian assistance and a decisive step for the cessation of hostilities in Libya,
- Expressing concern also for the safety of foreign nationals and their rights in the Libyan Arab Jamahiriya,
- Welcoming the appointment by the Secretary General of his Special Envoy to Libya, Mr. Abdel-Elah Mohamed Al-Khatib and supporting his efforts to find a sustainable and peaceful solution to the crisis in the Libyan Arab Jamahiriya,
- Reaffirming its strong commitment to the sovereignty, independence, territorial integrity and national unity of the Libyan Arab Jamahiriya,
- Determining that the situation in the Libyan Arab Jamahiriya continues to constitute a threat to international peace and security,

Acting under Chapter VII of the Charter of the United Nations,

1. Demands the immediate establishment of a cease-fire and a complete end to violence and all attacks against, and abuses of, civilians;
2. Stresses the need to intensify efforts to find a solution to the crisis which responds to the legitimate demands of the Libyan people and notes the decisions of the Secretary-General to send his Special Envoy to Libya and of the Peace and Security Council of the African Union to send its ad hoc High Level Committee to Libya with the aim of facilitating dialogue to lead to the political reforms necessary to find a peaceful and sustainable solution;

Primary Documents

3. Demands that the Libyan authorities comply with their obligations under international law, including international humanitarian law, human rights and refugee law and take all measures to protect civilians and meet their basic needs, and to ensure the rapid and unimpeded passage of humanitarian assistance;

Protection of civilians

4. Authorizes Member States that have notified the Secretary-General, acting nationally or through regional organizations or arrangements, and acting in cooperation with the Secretary-General, to take all necessary measures, notwithstanding paragraph 9 of resolution 1970 (2011), to protect civilians and civilian populated areas under threat of attack in the Libyan Arab Jamahiriya, including Benghazi, while excluding a foreign occupation force of any form on any part of Libyan territory, and requests the Member States concerned to inform the Secretary-General immediately of the measures they take pursuant to the authorization conferred by this paragraph which shall be immediately reported to the Security Council;

5. Recognizes the important role of the League of Arab States in matters relating to the maintenance of international peace and security in the region, and bearing in mind Chapter VIII of the Charter of the United Nations, requests the Member States of the League of Arab States to cooperate with other Member States in the implementation of paragraph 4;

No Fly Zone

6. Decides to establish a ban on all flights in the airspace of the Libyan Arab Jamahiriya in order to help protect civilians; [. . .]

Enforcement of the arms embargo

13. Decides that paragraph 11 of resolution 1970 (2011) shall be replaced by the following paragraph : "Calls upon all Member States, in particular States of the region, acting nationally or through regional organizations or arrangements, in order to ensure strict implementation of the arms embargo established by paragraphs 9 and 10 of resolution 1970 (2011), to inspect in their territory, including seaports and airports, and on the high seas, vessels and aircraft bound to or from the Libyan Arab Jamahiriya, if the State concerned has information that provides reasonable grounds to believe that the cargo contains items the supply, sale, transfer or export of which is prohibited by paragraphs 9 or 10 of resolution 1970 (2011) as modified by this resolution, including the provision of armed mercenary personnel, calls upon all flag States of such vessels and aircraft to cooperate with such inspections and authorizes Member States to use all measures commensurate to the specific circumstances to carry out such inspections";
[. . .]

16. Deplores the continuing flows of mercenaries into the Libyan Arab Jamahiriya and calls upon all Member States to comply strictly with their

342 Primary Documents

obligations under paragraph 9 of resolution 1970 (2011) to prevent the provision of armed mercenary personnel to the Libyan Arab Jamahiriya;

Ban on flights

17. Decides that all States shall deny permission to any aircraft registered in the Libyan Arab Jamahiriya or owned or operated by Libyan nationals or companies to take off from, land in or overfly their territory unless the particular flight has been approved in advance by the committee, or in the case of an emergency landing;

18. Decides that all States shall deny permission to any aircraft to take off from, land in or overfly their territory, if they have information that provides reasonable grounds to believe that the aircraft contains items the supply, sale, transfer, or export of which is prohibited by paragraphs 9 and 10 of resolution 1970 (2011) as modified by this resolution, including the provision of armed mercenary personnel, except in the case of an emergency landing;

Asset freeze

19. Decides that the asset freeze imposed by paragraph 17, 19, 20 and 21 of resolution 1970 (2011) shall apply to all funds, other financial assets and economic resources which are on their territories, which are owned or controlled, directly or indirectly, by the Libyan authorities, as designated by the Committee, or by individuals or entities acting on their behalf or at their direction. [. .]

Designations

22. Decides that the individuals listed in Annex I shall be subject to the travel restrictions imposed in paragraphs 15 and 16 of resolution 1970 (2011), and decides further that the individuals and entities listed in Annex II shall be subject to the asset freeze imposed in paragraphs 17, 19, 20 and 21 of resolution 1970 (2011);

23. Decides that the measures specified in paragraphs 15, 16, 17, 19, 20 and 21 of resolution 1970 (2011) shall apply also to individuals and entities determined by the Council or the Committee to have violated the provisions of resolution 1970 (2011), particularly paragraphs 9 and 10 thereof, or to have assisted others in doing so;

Panel of experts

24. Requests the Secretary-General to create for an initial period of one year, in consultation with the Committee, a group of up to eight experts ("Panel of Experts"), under the direction of the Committee to carry out the following tasks:

    (a)   Assist the Committee in carrying out its mandate as specified in paragraph 24 of resolution 1970 (2011) and this resolution;

    (b)   Gather, examine and analyze information from States, relevant United Nations bodies, regional organizations and other interested

Primary Documents
343

parties regarding the implementation of the measures decided in resolution 1970 (2011) and this resolution, in particular incidents of non-compliance;

(c) Make recommendations on actions the Council, or the Committee or State, may consider to improve implementation of the relevant measures;

(d) Provide to the Council an interim report on its work no later than 90 days after the Panel's appointment, and a final report to the Council no later than 30 days prior to the termination of its mandate with its findings and recommendations;

[...]

28. Reaffirms its intention to keep the actions of the Libyan authorities under continuous review and underlines its readiness to review at any time the measures imposed by this resolution and resolution 1970 (2011), including by strengthening, suspending or lifting those measures, as appropriate, based on compliance by the Libyan authorities with this resolution and resolution 1970 (2011).

29. Decides to remain actively seized of the matter.

Source: United Nations. S/RES/1973 (March 17, 2011). Available online at https://undocs.org/S/RES/1973(2011).

---

6   *The Al-Azhar Declaration in Support for the Arab Revolutions,* Nasr City, Cairo, Arab Republic of Egypt (October 31, 2011)

After the January 25, 2011, Egyptian Revolution, Sheikh Dr. Ahmed el-Tayyeb and the scholars of al-Azhar seized the opportunity to participate in the political debate concerning the future of Egypt and the Arab revolutions commonly referred to as the Arab Spring. This declaration represents the fruit of a series of consultations among the scholars of al-Azhar and Egyptian intellectuals representing different intellectual perspectives. Al-Azhar, as one of the first universities in the world, has exerted significant influence as a bastion of moderate Sunni Islam. This document is the second of four documents in which the scholars of Al-Azhar promoted their support for democratization based on the Islamic legal perspective, and wisdom in the context of the modern world—the first was issued on June 19, 2011.

Senior Al-Azhar scholars and the intellectuals participating with them:

Recognizing the necessities of the crucial historical stage faced by the people of the Arab nations in their legitimate struggle for freedom, justice and democracy and in pursuing their march of civilization; and

Inspired by the spirit of freedom in Islam and the Islamic rules on the legitimacy of authority and reform, and the achievement of the objectives and the supreme interests of the nation; and

344   **Primary Documents**

Consistent with the positions of Al-Azhar Al-Sharif, and the intellectual leaders in Egypt and the Arab world in supporting the liberation movements against brutal colonizers and tyrannical oppressors; and

Believing in the necessity to alert the nation to take up the causes of renaissance and progress, as well as to overcome historical adversities, and to establish citizens' rights to social justice on a solid foundation of the principles of Shari'a and its fundamental tenets, including the preservation of intellect, religion, soul, offspring, and property; and

Obstructing the path against the oppressive authorities that prevent the Arab and the Muslim community from entering the era of cultural luminescence and progress of knowledge, and from contributing in achieving economic prosperity and holistic development;

Considering all of the above, the group, which is representative of the spectrum of thought in Egyptian society, issued the Al-Azhar Document, organized several constructive dialogues regarding the achievements of the Arab revolutions for fruitful interaction and close collaboration between different movements and trends, and agreed on the set of principles derived from Islamic thought and the aspirations of the Arab nations;

Have concluded, under the auspices of Al-Azhar Al-Sharieef, on the need to respect the following principles according to this declaration:

First:

The religious and constitutional legitimacy of authority depends on the consent of people and their free choice, through a fair, transparent and democratic public ballot, as a modern alternative to the previous tradition of allegiance to Islamic good governance; and according to the evolution of governance systems and procedures in a modern and contemporary state; and in compliance with what has been established by the customary constitutional rules governing the distribution and definite separation of powers between the legislative, executive and judicial authorities. Based also on the mechanisms of checks and balances and accountability, by which the nation becomes the source of all legitimate powers, granter of legitimacy, and the withdrawal of it thereof;

The practice of many rulers, with aspirations to absolute power, is by clinging to the incorrect understanding of the Quranic verse: (O you who have believed, obey Allah and obey the Messenger (Prophet Muhammad) and those of you who are in authority) (Surah Al-Nisâ: 4/59), ignoring its clear and obvious contextual meaning in the preceding verse which states: (Verily, Allah commands you to render back the trusts to whom they are due; and when you judge between people, to judge with justice) (Surah Al-Nisâ: 4/58). This makes the violation of the conditions of good governance a valid ground for people to claim justice from their rulers, and to resist injustice and tyranny. It must be observed that those among our scholars who justified patience with tyrannical rulers, to ensure the well-being of the nation from chaos, have also allowed the ousting of the tyrannical oppressor, if the people have the ability to achieve this, and if there is no possibility of damage and harm to the nation and its communities.

Second:

When the voice of national popular opposition and peaceful protest arises, this is the inherent right of people to correct and guide their rulers when they do not respond to the call of their people by initiating required reform, and instead ignore legitimate demands, which call for freedom, justice and equity. Those patriotic protestors are not considered as committing illegitimate rebellion (*baghi*); the *baghi* offenders are those described by Islamic jurisprudence as having the power while isolating themselves from the nation, raising arms in the face of their dissenters, and spreading corruption on earth by force. On the other hand, peaceful national movements constitute the core of human rights in Islam, as confirmed by all international conventions. Furthermore, it is the people's duty to reform their society and correct their rulers. Responding to such demands is a duty of the rulers and those in power, without equivocation or obstinacy.

Third:

The confrontation of any peaceful patriotic protest with hostility, armed force, and bloodshed of peaceful civilians is considered a breach of the charter of governance between the nation and its rulers, which deprives the authority of its legitimacy and terminates its right to remain in power by mutual consent. If those in power persevere in their transgressions and tyranny into injustice, oppression and aggression, and recklessly shed the blood of innocent citizens to preserve their illegitimate survival, despite the will of the people, the authority becomes guilty of crimes that tarnish their very own legitimacy. It is therefore the oppressed people's right to strive to oust those tyrannical rulers and hold them responsible, and even modify the entire regime despite the pretexts made for stability or confronting disturbance and conspiracy. The infringement of the inviolability of the sacredness of human life is the decisive line between legitimacy of the government and its fall into wrongs and aggression. In these cases, the organised armies, in all our nations, should be committed to their constitutional duties to protect the homeland from external threats, and should not turn into an instrument of intimidation and oppression to citizens, or to shed their blood, since (If anyone killed a human being—unless it be [in punishment] for murder or for spreading corruption on earth—, it shall be as though he had killed all humankind; whereas, if anyone saves a life, it shall be as though he had saved the lives of all humankind) (Qur'an, Surah Al-Mâ'idah: 5/32).

Fourth:

The revolutionary, renovation, and reform forces ought to avoid entirely anything that could lead to bloodshed, and must safeguard themselves from external powers, regardless of their origins, pretexts, or justifications given for interference in the affairs of their countries and nations. Otherwise, they would be considered as committing *baghi,* betrayals to their nation and violating the legitimacy of their countries. In this case, it is the authorities' duty to lead them back to national unity, which is the primary religious duty and supreme obligation. The forces of the revolution and reform should unite in achieving their dream of justice and freedom. They should also avoid sectarian, ethnic, doctrinal, and religious conflicts, to preserve their national fabric and respect citizens' rights; and they should join forces to achieve a democratic transformation for the benefit of everyone, in a framework of national consensus and harmony aimed at building a future based on equality and justice. Furthermore, they must prevent the uprising to be exploited by sectarianism or denominationalism, or to provoke religious sensitivities. The revolutionaries and reformers should preserve the institutions of their countries and prevent squandering their wealth or conceding it to external actors. They should also avoid falling into the traps of disputes and rivalries, or reinforcing themselves by different powers that aim at exploiting and depleting their countries' resources.

Fifth:

Based on these Islamic and constitutional principles that illustrate the essence of civilized consciousness, the Al-Azhar scholars and intellectual and cultural leaders declare their full support of the will of the Arab people in reform and modernization, and in building societies based on freedom and justice that triumphed in Tunisia, Egypt and Libya, and for which the struggle continues in Syria and Yemen. They also condemn the brutal mechanisms of repression that tried to put a halt to the momentum. They call upon the Muslim and the Arab community to carry out decisive and effective initiatives to ensure its success with minimal losses, to affirm the absolute right of people in choosing their rulers and their duty to correct them in order to prevent tyranny, corruption and exploitation. The legitimacy of any authority is subject to the will of the people. The right of unarmed peaceful national resistance is guaranteed by the Islamic rule requiring 'the lifting of harm', in addition of being one of the fundamental human rights enshrined in all international conventions.

Sixth:

Al-Azhar scholars and the group of intellectuals participating with them urge the Arab and Islamic regimes to work voluntarily towards achieving political, social, and constitutional reform, and to begin the steps of transformation to democracy. The awakening of the oppressed people is inevitable and unavoidable. No ruler can now obscure from his people the light of freedom. It is a shame that the Arab region, along with some Islamic states, are still resting in the cycle of underdevelopment, oppression and tyranny, unlike other countries in the world, and attribute all of that unjustly and falsely to Islam and its culture, which is innocent of this malevolent allegation. Those countries should immediately and expeditiously endeavor to take full consideration of the reasons of scientific renaissance, technological progress of knowledge production, and invest their human and natural resources to serve their citizens and achieve prosperity for all mankind.

None of those sponsoring oppression and tyranny should believe that they are immune from the fate of the oppressors, or that they could mislead the people. This is the era of free communication and the explosion of knowledge, the supremacy of luminous religious and civilized principles, and the models of sacrifice and struggle which are witnessed in the Arab world; all of these made the awakening

Primary Documents

of people a glowing torch, from freedom a raising flag, and from the hope of the oppressed people a motivation leading them through their ongoing struggle to victory. And let those ignorant of the religion, those who are distorting the teachings of Islam, and the proponents of tyranny, injustice and oppression cease this improper absurdity. (And Allah is predominant over His affairs, but most of the people do not know) (Qur'an, Surah Yûsuf: 12/21)—Oh God, we ask you to grant us mercy that guides our hearts, embraces our unity and by which prevent us from temptations, Oh our God.

> *Note: Baghi* in the Arabic language and Islamic Shari'a means transgression or rebellion against the legitimate leader by the use of force. The crime of *baghi* includes, for example, the overthrow of the ruler by force and violence, and acts of destruction of public property [added by the translator].

> **Source:** Panepinto, Alice. *Islam, Law and Modernity,* translated by Adel Maged. Durham University (January 16, 2012). http://www.dur.ac.uk/resources/ilm/A1A zharDeclaration.pdf.

---

7   *United Nations Security Council Resolution 2118* (September 27, 2013)

This resolution, passed unanimously, represented a turning point in the conflict in Syria because it brought full international recognition to the Syrian government's use of chemical weapons against its own people. After a number of relatively small-scale incidents of chemical weapons usage, in the early morning hours of August 21, 2013, rocket attacks against 12 areas held by opposition forces distributed Sarin gas. On August 30, 2013, the U.S. State Department issued an official assessment, claiming significant evidence of Syrian government involvement. On September 14, the Syrian government acceded to the Chemical Weapons Convention (entered into force on October 14, 2013). The consensus decision of the Organization for the Prohibition of Chemical Weapons (OPCW) Executive Council, together with UNSC Resolution 2118, set out an ambitious program obligating Syria to cooperate fully in the elimination of its chemical-weapons program. This resolution provides international support for an agreement reached between the United States and Russia in which Russia agreed to accept and decommission Syria's chemical weapons capabilities. Initial reports seemed positive that negotiations had averted American military action. Syrian NGOs reported that the use of nerve agents had almost stopped, but the use of chlorine barrel bombs increased. By the summer of 2015, reports accused nonstate actors such as the Islamic State (Daesh) of using mustard gas and chlorine gas.

Adopted by the Security Council at its 7038th meeting, on 27 September 2013
The Security Council,

- Recalling the Statements of its President of 3 August 2011, 21 March 2012, 5 April 2012, and its resolutions 1540 (2004), 2042 (2012) and 2043 (2012),

- Reaffirming its strong commitment to the sovereignty, independence and territorial integrity of the Syrian Arab Republic,
- Reaffirming that the proliferation of chemical weapons, as well as their means of delivery, constitutes a threat to international peace and security,
- Recalling that the Syrian Arab Republic on 22 November 1968 acceded to the Protocol for the Prohibition of the Use in War of Asphyxiating, Poisonous or Other Gases and of Bacteriological Methods of Warfare, signed at Geneva on 17 June 1925,
- Noting that on 14 September 2013, the Syrian Arab Republic deposited with the Secretary-General its instrument of accession to the Convention on the Prohibition of the Development, Production, Stockpiling and Use of Chemical Weapons and on their Destruction (Convention) and declared that it shall comply with its stipulations and observe them faithfully and sincerely, applying the Convention provisionally pending its entry into force for the Syrian Arab Republic,
- Welcoming the establishment by the Secretary-General of the United Nations Mission to Investigate Allegations of the Use of Chemical Weapons in the Syrian Arab Republic (the Mission) pursuant to General Assembly resolution 42/37 C (1987) of 30 November 1987, and reaffirmed by resolution 620 (1988) of 26 August 1988, and expressing appreciation for the work of the Mission,
- Acknowledging the report of 16 September 2013 (S/2013/553) by the Mission, underscoring the need for the Mission to fulfil its mandate, and emphasizing that future credible allegations of chemical weapons use in the Syrian Arab Republic should be investigated,
- Deeply outraged by the use of chemical weapons on 21 August 2013 in Rif, Damascus, as concluded in the Mission's report, condemning the killing of civilians that resulted from it, affirming that the use of chemical weapons constitutes a serious violation of international law, and stressing that those responsible for any use of chemical weapons must be held accountable,
- Recalling the obligation under resolution 1540 (2004) that all States shall refrain from providing any form of support to non-State actors that attempt to develop, acquire, manufacture, possess, transport, transfer or use weapons of mass destruction, including chemical weapons, and their means of delivery,
- Welcoming the Framework for Elimination of Syrian Chemical Weapons dated 14 September 2013, in Geneva, between the Russian Federation and the United States of America (S/2013/565), with a view to ensuring the destruction of the Syrian Arab Republic's chemical weapons program in the soonest and safest manner, and expressing its commitment to the immediate international control over chemical weapons and their components in the Syrian Arab Republic,
- Welcoming the decision of the Executive Council of the Organization for the Prohibition of Chemical Weapons (OPCW) of 27 September 2013

establishing special procedures for the expeditious destruction of the Syrian Arab Republic's chemical weapons program and stringent verification thereof, and expressing its determination to ensure the destruction of the Syrian Arab Republic's chemical weapons program according to the timetable contained in the OPCW Executive Council decision of 27 September 2013,

- Stressing that the only solution to the current crisis in the Syrian Arab Republic is through an inclusive and Syrian-led political process based on the Geneva Communiqué of 30 June 2012, and emphasising the need to convene the international conference on Syria as soon as possible,
- Determining that the use of chemical weapons in the Syrian Arab Republic constitutes a threat to international peace and security,
- Underscoring that Member States are obligated under Article 25 of the Charter of the United Nations to accept and carry out the Council's decisions,

1. Determines that the use of chemical weapons anywhere constitutes a threat to international peace and security;
2. Condemns in the strongest terms any use of chemical weapons in the Syrian Arab Republic, in particular the attack on 21 August 2013, in violation of international law;
3. Endorses the decision of the OPCW Executive Council 27 September 2013, which contains special procedures for the expeditious destruction of the Syrian Arab Republic's chemical weapons program and stringent verification thereof and calls for its full implementation in the most expedient and safest manner;
4. Decides that the Syrian Arab Republic shall not use, develop, produce, otherwise acquire, stockpile or retain chemical weapons, or transfer, directly or indirectly, chemical weapons to other States or non-State actors;
5. Underscores that no party in Syria should use, develop, produce, acquire, stockpile, retain, or transfer chemical weapons;
6. Decides that the Syrian Arab Republic shall comply with all aspects of the decision of the OPCW Executive Council of 27 September 2013 (Annex I);
7. Decides that the Syrian Arab Republic shall cooperate fully with the OPCW and the United Nations, including by complying with their relevant recommendations, by accepting personnel designated by the OPCW, or the United Nations, by providing for and ensuring the security of activities undertaken by these personnel, by providing these personnel with immediate and unfettered access to, and the right to inspect, in discharging their functions, any and all sites, and by allowing immediate and unfettered access to individuals that the OPCW has grounds to believe important for the purpose of its mandate, and decides that all parties in Syria shall cooperate fully in this regard;
8. Decides to authorize an advance team of United Nations personnel to provide early assistance to OPCW activities in Syria, requests the

Director-General of the OPCW and the Secretary-General to closely cooperate in the implementation of the Executive Council decision of 27 September 2013 and this resolution, including through their operational activities on the ground, and further requests the Secretary-General, in consultation with the Director-General of the OPCW and, where appropriate, the Director-General of the World Health Organization, to submit to the Council within 10 days of the adoption of this resolution recommendations regarding the role of the United Nations in eliminating the Syrian Arab Republic's chemical weapons program;

9. Notes that the Syrian Arab Republic is a party to the Convention on the Privileges and Immunities of the United Nations, decides that OPCW-designated personnel undertaking activities provided for in this resolution, or the decision of the OPCW Executive Council of 27 September 2013 shall enjoy the privileges and immunities contained in the Verification Annex, Part II(B) of the Chemical Weapons Convention, and calls on the Syrian Arab Republic to conclude modalities agreements with the United Nations and the OPCW;

10. Encourages Member States to provide support, including personnel, technical expertise, information, equipment, and financial and other resources and assistance, in coordination with the Director-General of the OPCW and the Secretary-General, to enable the OPCW and the United Nations to implement the elimination of the Syrian Arab Republic's chemical weapons program, and decides to authorize Member States to acquire, control, transport, transfer and destroy chemical weapons identified by the Director-General of the OPCW, consistent with the objective of the Chemical Weapons Convention, to ensure the elimination of the Syrian Arab Republic's chemical weapons program in the soonest and safest manner;

11. Urges all Syrian parties and interested Member States with relevant capabilities to work closely together and with the OPCW and the United Nations to arrange for the security of the monitoring and destruction mission, recognizing the primary responsibility of the Syrian government in this regard;

12. Decides to review on a regular basis the implementation in the Syrian Arab Republic of the decision of the OPCW Executive Council of 27 September 2013 and this resolution, and requests the Director-General of the OPCW to report to the Security Council, through the Secretary-General, who shall include relevant information on United Nations activities related to the implementation of this resolution, within 30 days and every month thereafter, and requests further the Director-General of the OPCW and the Secretary-General to report in a coordinated manner, as needed, to the Security Council, non-compliance with this resolution or the OPCW Executive Council decision of 27 September 2013;

13. Reaffirms its readiness to consider promptly any reports of the OPCW under Article VIII of the Chemical Weapons Convention, which provides for the referral of cases of non-compliance to the United Nations Security Council;

Primary Documents 351

14. Decides that Member States shall inform immediately the Security Council of any violation of resolution 1540 (2004), including acquisition by non-State actors of chemical weapons, their means of delivery and related materials in order to take necessary measures therefore;
15. Expresses its strong conviction that those individuals responsible for the use of chemical weapons in the Syrian Arab Republic should be held accountable;
16. Endorses fully the Geneva Communiqué of 30 June 2012 (Annex II), which sets out a number of key steps beginning with the establishment of a transitional governing body exercising full executive powers, which could include members of the present Government and the opposition and other groups and shall be formed on the basis of mutual consent;
17. Calls for the convening, as soon as possible, of an international conference on Syria to implement the Geneva Communiqué, and calls upon all Syrian parties to engage seriously and constructively at the Geneva Conference on Syria, and underscores that they should be fully representative of the Syrian people and committed to the implementation of the Geneva Communiqué and to the achievement of stability and reconciliation;
18. Reaffirms that all Member States shall refrain from providing any form of support to non-State actors that attempt to develop, acquire, manufacture, possess, transport, transfer or use nuclear, chemical or biological weapons and their means of delivery, and calls upon all Member States, in particular Member States neighboring the Syrian Arab Republic, to report any violations of this paragraph to the Security Council immediately;
19. Demands that non-State actors not develop, acquire, manufacture, possess, transport, transfer, or use nuclear, chemical or biological weapons and their means of delivery, and calls upon all Member States, in particular Member States neighboring the Syrian Arab Republic, to report any actions inconsistent with this paragraph to the Security Council immediately;
20. Decides that all Member States shall prohibit the procurement of chemical weapons, related equipment, goods and technology or assistance from the Syrian Arab Republic by their nationals, or using their flagged vessels or aircraft, whether or not originating in the territory of the Syrian Arab Republic;
21. Decides, in the event of non-compliance with this resolution, including unauthorized transfer of chemical weapons, or any use of chemical weapons by anyone in the Syrian Arab Republic, to impose measures under Chapter VII of the United Nations Charter;
22. Decides to remain actively seized of the matter.

Source: United Nations. "Middle East." Security Council Resolution S/RES/2118, September 27, 2013. Available online at http://unscr.com/en/resolutions/2118.

352   **Primary Documents**

8   Excerpts from *The Peace and National Partnership Agreement* (September 21, 2014)

This agreement, between the Yemeni government of Abdu Rabbu Mansour Hadi and the Ansar Allah (the Houthis) after this militia took control of the capital, Sana'a, technically left Hadi's government still in charge but displaced the earlier agreement brokered by the Gulf Cooperation Council (GCC) in 2011. The Houthis complained that the 2011 GCC agreement, signed only by the two main political coalitions, excluded them and also the Southern Movement (Hiraak) from taking a part in government. This agreement is based on the National Dialogue, in which the Houthis did participate. This agreement forced a reorganization of the cabinet, allocating ministerial representation to the Houthis and Hiraak. However, the Houthis refused to withdraw their military forces, expanded south, and took the second-largest port Hodeida. Despite the provocations of both sides that voided this agreement, it established a set of objectives and principles for the subsequent UN-led negotiations of 2019.

Preamble:

Pursuant to the outcomes of the Comprehensive National Dialogue Conference, which have been agreed upon by all Yemeni constituencies and which laid the foundations for building a new, federal democratic Yemeni state based on the rule of law, equal citizenship, human rights and good governance; resolved to the unity, sovereignty, independence and territorial integrity of Yemen; committed to responding to the peoples' demand for peaceful change, economic, financial and administrative reforms, and to achieving economic welfare; dedicated to furthering the higher national interest through a spirit of partnership and consensus in diagnosis, solutions, and implementation; and committed to stabilizing the country and realizing a bright promising democratic future, the Parties, in the interest of national unity and building and promoting peace, commit to the following:

Article 1:

The President of the Republic shall engage in inclusive and transparent consultations with all of the constituencies represented in the National Dialogue Conference, immediately following the signing of this Agreement. The purpose of these consultations shall be to establish a competency-based government in a period not to exceed one (1) month. The current government shall remain responsible for the normal affairs until the formation of the new government. In establishing the new government, the principles of competence, integrity and national partnership shall be upheld, and broad participation of political constituencies shall be ensured.

Through this consultation process, constituencies shall be meaningfully engaged, and they shall be represented in the executive bodies at the central and governorate levels to ensure efficiency and national partnership.

Article 2:

Within three (3) days following the entry into force of this Agreement, the President of the Republic shall appoint political advisers from *Ansar Allah* and the

Primary Documents 353

Southern Peaceful Movement. The President of the Republic shall define the authorities and functions of his political advisers.

A new Prime Minister, who shall be a neutral and impartial national figure of competence and high integrity and who shall enjoy broad political support, shall be appointed. The President of the Republic shall issue a presidential decree charging the new Prime Minister to form a new government.

The political advisers to the President of the Republic shall develop criteria for candidates for posts in the new government. These criteria shall include: integrity, competency, requisite expertise in a field relevant to the ministerial portfolio, commitment to the protection of human rights and the rule of law, and impartiality in the conduct of state affairs.

The political advisers to the President of the Republic shall make recommendations to the President of the Republic and Prime Minister regarding the allocation of Cabinet seats to the political constituencies, ensuring representation of women and youth.

Within three (3) days following the announcement of the new Prime Minister, all constituencies shall nominate their candidates for the Cabinet to the President of the Republic and the Prime Minister. If any constituency fails to submit their nominees within an additional three (3) days after the initial three-day period, the President of the Republic and the new Prime Minister shall have the right to name candidates, as they see appropriate for the portfolios, provided that they meet the criteria listed above and that they reinforce the principle of national partnership.

The President of the Republic and the Prime Minister shall consult with a representative of each constituency of his political advisers in order to decide on any objections raised by the constituencies regarding whether candidates of other constituencies meet the criteria listed above within a period not to exceed three (3) days.

The President of the Republic shall, after consultations, select the Ministers of Defence, Finance, Foreign Affairs and Interior, provided that they meet the criteria listed above, and do not belong, or hold loyalty to any political party.

The Prime Minister shall, in consultation with the President of the Republic, select the Ministers for the remaining portfolios, provided they meet the criteria listed above.

The government shall, within thirty (30) days following the appointment of the Cabinet, develop a program that is consensual and based primarily on implementation of the Outcomes of the National Dialogue Conference. The program shall be submitted to the Parliament for a vote of confidence.

Within fifteen (15) days following the signing of this Agreement, the President shall issue a decree expanding the Shura Council according to the recommendations of the National Dialogue Conference, and in a manner that ensures national partnership.

Article 3:

Alleviating the burden of the people is a mutual responsibility and requires the collaborative efforts of all constituencies. To this end, the new government shall establish an economic committee of qualified experts and economists drawn from various political constituencies and relevant government ministries with expertise in the field of financial and economic regulation and management. The recommendations of the committee shall be binding on the government. The committee shall be formed within one (1) week after the formation of the government. The committee shall study the economic and fiscal situation in Yemen by reviewing the state budget and spending, and shall make recommendations on how the savings will be used to benefit people living in poverty, and previously marginalized areas.

The committee shall prepare an overall economic reform program that is time-bound, specific and clear, and that is primarily aimed at eradicating corruption in all sectors, addressing the imbalance in the public budget and rationalizing expenditures. The committee shall identify and report on the deficiencies caused by pervasive corruption and lack of adequate oversight, and shall propose solutions regarding the required comprehensive reforms for the oil and electricity sectors, together with the new government, in a manner that will achieve the demands and aspirations of the people.

. . .

Article 4:

[Provisions to reduce corruption and help people living in poverty].

Article 5:

The new government shall commit to the full implementation of the outcomes of the National Dialogue Conference relevant to countering corruption and shall provide the necessary resources in this regard.

Article 6:

The President of the Republic shall exercise his constitutional authorities to ensure fair representation of all constituencies in executive bodies at the central and governorate levels, as well as in oversight bodies, to ensure national partnership, competence, integrity and efficiency. Fair participation in judicial bodies shall be ensured according to the outcomes of the National Dialogue Conference.

A government operating under the principle of national partnership shall respect the high interests of Yemen in both domestic and foreign policies, and reflect the will of all of the people.

Article 7:

All constituencies shall participate in the preparations for the new biometric voter registry and the referendum on the constitution based on the new voter registry, and shall participate in the preparations and monitoring of elections according to the outcomes of the National Dialogue Conference.

Article 8:

The President of the Republic shall work closely with all constituencies in order to develop a consensus on a new constitution, through the mechanisms of the Constitution Drafting Commission and the National Body.

Article 9:

The membership of the National Body shall be revisited, within a period not to exceed fifteen (15) days to ensure fair representation of constituencies. The National Body shall prepare its rules of procedure through the committee established to undertake this task in accordance with the outcomes of the National Dialogue Conference.

Article 10:

The National Body, through its oversight of the Constitution Drafting Commission, shall, among other things, address the structure of the state in a manner that adheres to the outcomes of the National Dialogue Conference.

Article 11:

The government shall designate a committee with *Ansar Allah* to develop an expedited implementation matrix to execute the outcomes of the Sa'ada Working Group of the National Dialogue Conference. The Government shall designate a similar committee, in agreement with all constituencies, including the Peaceful Southern Movement, to develop an expedited implementation matrix to execute the outcomes of the Southern Issues Working Group of the National Dialogue Conference.

Article 12:

The outcomes of the Working Group on Building the Foundations for the Security and Military Institutions of the National Dialogue Conference shall be strictly implemented according to an agreed-upon timeline, with monitoring and follow-up by the National Body.

Article 13:

The military and security situation in and the issues related to Amran, Al Jawf, Mareb, Sana'a and any other governorate shall be dealt with in the Annex.

Article 14:

The political, public and media escalation shall end, and manifestations of the threat or use of force shall cease. This includes obliging State media and urging the private and partisan media to stop their inflammatory campaigns of a sectarian and regional nature.

Article 15:

[Stipulating the removal of militia camps in the vicinity of high security facilities, including Hezyaz, Al Sabaha and the airport, around the capital, Sana'a, as well as within the city limits, and dismantling unofficial checkpoints.]

Article 16:

The Parties commit to resolve any disputes regarding this Agreement through direct dialogue, within the framework of the outcomes of the Comprehensive National Dialogue Conference, and to continue negotiations through a joint committee established with the support of the United Nations. This joint committee shall be the appropriate forum to raise any concerns related to the interpretation and implementation of this Agreement.

Article 17:

The Parties request the Special Adviser to the Secretary-General on Yemen to continue United Nations support for the implementation of the measures agreed upon in this Agreement. In this regard, the Parties request the Special Adviser to continue to monitor any violations.

Signatures:

> **Source:** The Peace and National Partnership Agreement. September 21, 2014. Available online at https://peacemaker.un.org/yemen-national-partnership-2014.

---

9 *Marrakesh Declaration on the Rights of Religious Minorities in Predominantly Muslim Majority Communities,* **Marrakesh, Morocco (January 27, 2016)**

Over 300 Islamic scholars, politicians, and activists, as well as a small group of interfaith observers, gathered in Morocco in January 2016 to affirm the rights of minorities living in Muslim-majority contexts. They issued the Marrakesh Declaration *as a united response to the widespread persecution and violence against minorities, particularly by extremist groups in recent years that claim Islamic justification for their violence. The authority and reputation of the authors, as prominent personalities in the region, give it substantial legitimacy. They justified and substantiated this proclamation based on the seventh-century Charter of Medina and traditions of Islamic governance, which assert the value of mutual recognition of rights and responsibilities between groups in a multicultural society. As an elite vision of ideals and principles it can inspire a broader movement for social and legal change.*

In the Name of God, the All-Merciful, the All-Compassionate

Executive Summary

WHEREAS, conditions in various parts of the Muslim World have deteriorated dangerously due to the use of violence and armed struggle as a tool for settling conflicts and imposing one's point of view;

WHEREAS, this situation has also weakened the authority of legitimate governments and enabled criminal groups to issue edicts attributed to Islam, but which, in fact, alarmingly distort its fundamental principles and goals in ways that have seriously harmed the population as a whole;

WHEREAS, this year marks the 1,400th anniversary of the Charter of Medina, a constitutional contract between the Prophet Muhammad, God's peace and blessings be upon him, and the people of Medina, which guaranteed the religious liberty of all, regardless of faith;

WHEREAS, hundreds of Muslim scholars and intellectuals from over 120 countries, along with representatives of Islamic and international organizations, as well as leaders from diverse religious groups and nationalities, gathered in Marrakesh on this date to reaffirm the principles of the Charter of Medina at a major conference;

WHEREAS, this conference was held under the auspices of His Majesty, King Mohammed VI of Morocco, and organized jointly by the Ministry of Endowment and Islamic Affairs in the Kingdom of Morocco and the Forum for Promoting Peace in Muslim Societies based in the United Arab Emirates;

AND NOTING the gravity of this situation afflicting Muslims as well as peoples of other faiths throughout the world, and after thorough deliberation and discussion, the convened Muslim scholars and intellectuals:

DECLARE HEREBY our firm commitment to the principles articulated in the Charter of Medina, whose provisions contained a number of the principles of constitutional contractual citizenship, such as freedom of movement, property ownership, mutual solidarity and defense, as well as principles of justice and equality before the law; and that,

The objectives of the Charter of Medina provide a suitable framework for national constitutions in countries with Muslim majorities, and the United Nations Charter and related documents, such as the Universal Declaration of Human Rights, are in harmony with the Charter of Medina, including consideration for public order.

NOTING FURTHER that deep reflection upon the various crises afflicting humanity underscores the inevitable and urgent need for cooperation among all religious groups, we AFFIRM HEREBY that such cooperation must be based on a "Common Word," requiring that such cooperation must go beyond mutual tolerance and respect, to providing full protection for the rights and liberties to all religious groups in a civilized manner that eschews coercion, bias, and arrogance.

BASED ON ALL OF THE ABOVE, we hereby:

Call upon Muslim scholars and intellectuals around the world to develop a jurisprudence of the concept of "citizenship" which is inclusive of diverse groups. Such jurisprudence shall be rooted in Islamic tradition and principles and mindful of global changes.

Urge Muslim educational institutions and authorities to conduct a courageous review of educational curricula that addresses honestly and effectively any material that instigates aggression and extremism, leads to war and chaos, and results in the destruction of our shared societies;

Call upon politicians and decision makers to take the political and legal steps necessary to establish a constitutional contractual relationship among its citizens, and to support all formulations and initiatives that aim to fortify relations and understanding among the various religious groups in the Muslim World;

Call upon the educated, artistic, and creative members of our societies, as well as organizations of civil society, to establish a broad movement for the just treatment of religious minorities in Muslim countries and to raise awareness as to their rights, and to work together to ensure the success of these efforts.

Call upon the various religious groups bound by the same national fabric to address their mutual state of selective amnesia that blocks memories of centuries of joint and shared living on the same land; we call upon them to rebuild the past by reviving this tradition of conviviality, and restoring our shared trust that has been eroded by extremists using acts of terror and aggression;

Call upon representatives of the various religions, sects and denominations to confront all forms of religious bigotry, vilification, and denigration of what people hold sacred, as well as all speech that promote hatred and bigotry; AND FINALLY,

358   **Primary Documents**

AFFIRM that it is unconscionable to employ religion for the purpose of aggressing upon the rights of religious minorities in Muslim countries.

Source: The Ministry of Endowments and Islamic Affairs of the Kingdom of Morocco, and the Forum for Promoting Peace in Muslim Societies, based in the U.A.E. "Marrakesh Declaration." www.marrakeshdeclaration.org/.

Chronology

1948–1949
Israel's declaration of independence; Egypt, Transjordan, Syria, Iraq, Lebanon, and Saudi Arabia join the local Palestinian militias in attacking Israel.

October 29, 1956
Suez War: Israel, France, and Britain invade Egypt. U.S. and Soviet pressure forces them to withdraw.

September 26, 1962
North Yemen military coup sets up the Yemen Arab Republic; Egypt and Saudi Arabia intervene in the "Arab Cold War."

1960s–1970s
Dhofar Rebellion in Oman: Iranian troops and British officers enable the Omani Army to defeat a Marxist rebellion aided by South Yemen.

June 5–10, 1967
Six-Day War: Preemptive Israeli attack on Egypt, Jordan, and Syria. Fighting on the Egypt-Israel border continues until 1970.

June 8, 1967
Israeli planes and boats attack the USS *Liberty*, killing 34, wounding 174.

June 1969
A communist coup in South Yemen creates the People's Democratic Republic of Yemen.

September 1970
Jordan expels the Palestine Liberation Organization (PLO), which moves to Lebanon.

November 30, 1971
The shah of Iran seizes three islands from the United Arab Emirates.

October 6–25, 1973
Yom Kippur (Ramadan) War: coordinated attack by Egypt and Syria, later supported by Jordan and Iraq, against Israel.

September 17, 1978
The Camp David Accords: Egypt recognizes Israel, which withdraws from the Sinai.

April 1975–1990
Lebanese Civil War: PLO helps several Muslim militias; Israel helps the Maronite Phalange Party.

November 6, 1975
The Green March: King Hassan of Morocco orders hundreds of thousands of civilians to enter Spanish Sahara.

December 1975
Moroccan forces enter Spanish Sahara: start of the war for Western Sahara between Morocco and the Polisario Movement supported by Algeria.

May 1976
Maronite leader Suleiman Frangieh invites Syrian intervention to stop the Lebanese civil war, but this only extended and expanded it.

January 16, 1979
The shah of Iran leaves; revolution overthrows his government.

February 1, 1979
Ayatollah Ruhollah Khomeini returns to Iran and establishes the Islamic Republic of Iran.

July 16, 1979
Saddam Hussein takes over as president of Iraq and conducts a massive purge of the Ba'ath Party.

November 4, 1979
A large student mob occupies the American Embassy in Tehran, ultimately holding 52 people hostage for 444 days.

November 20, 1979
Juhayman Al-Otaybi occupies the Grand Mosque in Mecca and holds it for more than two weeks. Based on Iranian propaganda, Muslims blame the United States and burn the U.S. embassies in Pakistan and Libya.

March/April, 1980
The Berber Spring: Algerian security forces use violence against a developing Berber Cultural Movement in the Kabylie region.

September 22, 1980
Iraq invades Iran; war degrades into Iranian human wave attacks and Iraqi chemical warfare, missile attacks on cities.

June 7, 1981
Israeli planes bomb the Osiraq nuclear reactor under construction in Iraq.

June 6, 1982
Israeli invasion of Lebanon.

Chronology 361

September 1982
The Maronite Phalange Party massacres Palestinians in the Sabra and Shatila camps.

June 1985
Israel withdraws from most of Lebanon but still occupies a security zone on the border.

1987–1993
The First Intifada (Uprising) by Palestinians against Israel, concluded by the Oslo Accords establishing the Palestinian Authority.

May 17, 1987
An Iraqi F-1 Mirage attacks the missile frigate USS *Stark,* killing 37 sailors.

July 24, 1987
The United States decides to reflag Kuwaiti tankers and provides navy escorts in the Gulf to protect them from Iranian attacks. This leads to combined arms attacks on Iran's oil platforms and naval bases.

March 28, 1988
Saddam Hussein uses chemical weapons against the Kurds in Halabja, killing an estimated 5,000.

July 3, 1988
American missile cruiser USS *Vincennes* shoots down Iran Air Flight 655, killing all 290 civilians on board.

July 18, 1988
Iran agrees to a cease-fire, ending its eight-year war with Iraq.

October 1988
Black October riots in Algeria against economic conditions.

November 5, 1989
Taif Accords end Lebanese civil war and legitimize Syrian occupation.

May 1990
North and South Yemen unite under Ali Abdullah Saleh as president.

August 2, 1990
"Second Persian Gulf War": Iraqi invasion of Kuwait.

January 17, 1991
Operation Desert Storm: The U.S.-led coalition expels Iraq from Kuwait.

January 4, 1992
Military coup in Algeria begins the civil war.

March 1991
Shi'as and Kurds in Iraq rebel against Saddam Hussein, who recovers his forces and smashes both. Hundreds of thousands of Kurds flee to the mountains of Turkey.

April 15, 1991
The U.S.-led coalition establishes "no-fly" zones over northern and southern Iraq.

Chronology

October 1991
Madrid Conference on Middle East Peace.

September 13, 1993
Prime Minister Rabin and PLO leader Yasser Arafat sign the Oslo Accords in a Washington, DC, ceremony with U.S. president Bill Clinton.

May–July 1994
Yemeni Civil War; Northern Yemen defeats southern separatists.

October 1994
Jordan and Israel sign a peace treaty.

June 25, 1996
Khobar Towers bombing in Dhahran, Saudi Arabia, kills 17 servicemen.

1996
Kurdish civil war between the Kurdistan Democratic Party of Masoud Barzani and the Patriotic Union of Kurdistan of Jalal Talabani.

February 23, 1998
Osama bin Laden releases a declaration of war against all Americans.

April 15, 1999
Algerian military arranges the election of Abdelaziz Bouteflika, who promotes a Civil Concord Law providing amnesty.

May 2000
Israel withdraws from southern Lebanon.

September 2000
Second Intifada: Urban Palestinian attacks on Israeli settlements and targets, and Israeli invasions of Palestinian cities.

October 2000
Al-Qaeda suicide attack on the U.S. Navy destroyer USS *Cole* kills 17.

April/May 2001
In Algeria, extensive protests by Berbers in the Kabylie region against abusive behavior by security forces.

September 11, 2001
Al-Qaeda terrorists hijack four planes to attack American targets.

February 14, 2001
The National Action Charter of Bahrain approved in a referendum.

December 16, 2002
Hamad bin Isa Al Khalifa, the new ruler of Bahrain, proclaims a new constitution, making Bahrain a kingdom.

March 19, 2003
U.S.-led invasion of Iraq leads to protracted bloody insurgency, then sectarian civil war.

May 16, 2003
Fourteen suicide bombers strike six sites in Casablanca, Morocco, killing more than 40.

June 2003
The Quartet of the United States, Russia, the European Union, and the United Nations propose a Middle East Road Map for peace.

March 2, 2004
Suicide bombers attack Shi'a religious ceremonies in Karbala and Baghdad, killing 140.

June 2004–2010
"Sa'adah Insurgency": Rebellion by the Zaydi of northern Yemen against the government of Ali Saleh.

February 14, 2005
Assassination of Rafik Hariri sparks the March 2005 Cedar Revolution and propels Syria to remove its military forces from Lebanon.

September 2005
Israel withdraws all Jewish settlers and personnel from Gaza, while maintaining control over airspace and borders.

February 3, 2006
Twenty-three al-Qaeda leaders escape from prison in Yemen, help create Al-Qaeda in the Arabian Peninsula.

February 22, 2006
Bomb destroys the al-Askari Mosque, a Shi'a shrine in Samarra, leading to an expanding wave of sectarian war.

July 12, 2006–August 14, 2006
Israeli invasion of Lebanon.

September 11, 2006
Algerian Group for Salafist Preaching and Combat joins al-Qaeda.

January 2007
U.S. president Bush announces new Iraq "Surge" strategy.

April 2007
Three suicide bombers strike Casablanca, Morocco.

September 2007
Israel destroys nuclear reactor in Deir ez-Zor, Syria.

September 17, 2008
Al-Qaeda affiliate attacks U.S. embassy in Sana'a, killing 12.

December 27, 2008
Israel launches "Operation Cast Lead," invading Gaza.

June 2009
Green Movement in Iran: massive protests against election fraud.

May 2010
Israeli commandos board the ship *Mavi Marmara,* increasing conflict with Turkey.

August 2010
Last U.S. combat brigade leaves Iraq. Troop withdrawal is complete by December.

December 17, 2010
Self-immolation of Tarek el-Tayeb Mohamed Bouazizi sets off protests starting the Jasmine Revolution in Tunisia.

January 3, 2011
In Algeria, major protests over food prices and unemployment begin.

January 14, 2011
Tunisian president Zine al-Abidine Ben Ali flees to Saudi Arabia.

January 17, 2011
In Oman, initial Green March protests.

January 24, 2011
Yemen security forces arrest Tawakil Karman, starting a year of protests.

January 25, 2011
Tahrir Square Protests in Egypt begin.

February 11, 2011
Egyptian president Hosni Mubarak resigns after 18 days of revolution.

February 14, 2011
Both Sunni and Shi'a opposition groups occupy the Pearl Roundabout in Manama, Bahrain.

February 17, 2011
February 17th Revolution begins in Benghazi, Libya, and quickly spreads.

February 20, 2011
February 20 Revolution in Morocco begins an organized cycle of protests.

March 6, 2011
Saudi Arabia deploys massive security forces against Shi'a protests in the east.

March 15, 2011
Gulf Cooperation Council troops enter Bahrain to support the king's security forces in crushing the demonstrations.

March 18, 2011
In Yemen, government supporters kill 52 protesters, causing major military leaders to defect to the opposition.

March 18, 2011
Syrian government shoots five protesters in Dara'a, provoking the Syrian civil war.

Chronology

March 19, 2011
Operation Odyssey Dawn assault on Libya in support of the rebellion.

October 9, 2011
Egyptian Army forces kill peaceful Coptic Christian protesters at the Maspero television building.

November 23, 2011
Yemeni president Saleh hands over power to his deputy Abdu Rabbu Mansour Hadi.

May 25, 2012
Syrian government employs civilian militias to massacre civilians in the town of Houla.

June 24, 2012
Mohamed Morsi elected president of Egypt.

November 14–21, 2012
Israeli "Operation Pillar of Defense" military campaign in Gaza.

January 2013
Algerian special forces storm the In Amenas gas plant; Islamist al-Murabitoun kills dozens of foreign hostages in four-day siege.

May 27, 28, 2013
Turkey suppresses Gezi Park protesters with force.

July 3, 2013
Defense Minister Abdel Fattah el-Sisi deposes President Morsi in a military coup after the massive Tamarod protests.

August 14, 2013
The Egyptian military clearance operation at the Rabi'a al-Adawiya Mosque kills hundreds.

August 21, 2013
Syrian government launches large-scale chemical weapons attack on Ghouta.

June 10, 2014
The Islamic State (Daesh) captures Mosul.

July 8, 2014
The Israeli military launches Operation Protective Edge, a ground and air campaign against tunnels and missiles in Gaza.

October 2015
Beginning of the "Knife Intifada," a wave of shootings, stabbings, and car-ramming by Palestinians or Israeli Arabs against Jews.

February 2015
President Hadi flees house arrest under the Houthis: their attack on Aden triggers Saudi-led coalition war.

July 15, 2016
Attempted Turkish military coup against President Erdogan quickly suppressed with massive public support.

August 24, 2016–March 29, 2017
Operation Euphrates Shield: Turkish military invasion of Iraq and Syria.

November 26, 2016
The Iraqi parliament gives full legal status to the Popular Mobilization Forces as part of the Iraqi armed forces.

October 2016
Death of Mohsin Fikri triggers Al-Hoceima Rebellion in Morocco.

April 6, 2017
The United States attacks Al-Shayrat air base in Syria with 59 Tomahawk missiles in response to the April 4, 2017, Syrian use of chemical weapons against Khan Sheikhun.

May 2017
New wave of economic protests in Al-Hoceima, Morocco.

September 2017
Kurds support Kurdish Regional Government independence in a referendum. In response, Iraqi government forces conquer Kirkuk, impose punitive measures.

November 4, 2017
Lebanese prime minister Hariri announces his resignation during a state visit to Saudi Arabia, provoking outpouring of support. He rescinds his resignation on November 21.

December 2017
Demonstrations in Mashhad, Iran, over economic conditions quickly spread to smaller cities in most provinces.

April 7, 2018
Major chemical weapons attack on Douma, a suburb outside of Damascus, Syria. Human Rights Watch counts 85 chemical weapons attacks in Syria since 2013.

May 2018
Moqtada al-Sadr leads a diverse political bloc to win the most votes in the Iraqi parliament.

July 2018
Major protests occur in Basra, Iraq, over the lack of water, electricity, and jobs and against corruption. Protesters burn government buildings and the Iranian consulate.

February 22, 2019
Algerian president Bouteflika announces his intention to seek a fifth term in spite of his advanced age and poor health. Huge crowd protests.

April 2, 2019

In Algeria, the very large persistent peaceful protests persuade the military to force President Bouteflika to resign. Protests continue, demanding the arrest and trial of the most flagrantly corrupt members of the elite.

May 2019

Iraqi security forces protect Arabs burning more than 1,000 acres of Kurdish farmers' crops in the Kirkuk region.

Bibliography

Abraham, Paul. *The Maronites of Lebanon, the Staunch Catholics of the Near East.* Piscataway, NJ: Gorgias Press, 2011.

Al-Awadi, Hisham. *The Muslim Brothers in Pursuit of Legitimacy.* London: I. B. Taurus, 2014.

Almezaini, Khalid S., and Jean-Marc Rickli. *The Small Gulf States. Foreign and Security Policies before and after the Arab Spring.* New York: Routledge, 2017.

Al-Munajjed, Mona. *Women in Saudi Arabia Today.* London: Springer, 1997.

Al-Rasheed, Madawi. "Saudi Regime Resilience after the 2011 Arab Popular Uprisings." *Contemporary Arab Affairs* 9, no. 1 (2016): 13–26.

Al-Sharif, Manal. *Daring to Drive: The Young Saudi Woman Who Stood Up to a Kingdom of Men.* London: Simon & Schuster, 2017.

Arsan, Andrew. *Lebanon: A Country in Fragments.* London: Hurst and Co, 2018.

Ashrawi, Hanan. *This Side of Peace.* New York: Touchstone, 1996.

Baracsay, Daniel. *The Palestine Liberation Organization: Terrorism and the Prospects for Peace in the Holy Land.* Santa Barbara, CA: Praeger, 2011.

Barakat, Sultan. *"Qatari Mediation: Between Ambition and Achievement."* Analysis Paper No. 12. Doha: Brookings Doha Center, 2014.

Baser, Bahar, and Ahmet Erdi Öztürk. *Authoritarian Politics in Turkey: Elections, Resistance and the AKP.* London: I. B. Taurus, 2017.

Bassiouni, M. Cherif. *Chronicles of the Egyptian Revolution and Its Aftermath: 2011–2016.* New York: Cambridge University Press, 2017.

Bengio, Ofra, and Gabriel Ben-Dor, eds. *Minorities and the State in the Arab World.* Boulder, CO: Lynne Rienner, 1999.

Boulby, Marion. *The Muslim Brotherhood and the Kings of Jordan, 1945–1993.* Atlanta: Scholars Press, 1999.

Boulby, Marion, and Christie Kenneth. *Migration, Refugees and Human Security in the Mediterranean and MENA.* London: Palgrave Macmillan, 2018.

Brandt, Marieke. *Tribes and Politics in Yemen: A History of the Houthi Conflict.* London: Hurst & Company, 2017.

Burton, Fred, and Samuel Katz. *Under Fire: The Untold Story of the Attack in Benghazi.* New York: St. Martin's Press, 2013.

Cagaptay, Soner. *The New Sultan: Erdogan and the Crisis of Modern Turkey.* New York: I. B. Tauris, 2017.

Cavatorta, Francesco, and Fabio Merone, eds. *Salafism after the Arab Awakening: Contending with People's Power*. London: Hurst & Company, 2017.

Cederman, Lars-Erik, and Manuel Vogt. "Dynamics and Logic of Civil Wars." *Journal of Conflict Resolution* 61, no. 9 (2017): 1992–2016.

Cherribi, Sam. *Fridays of Rage: Al Jazeera, the Arab Spring and Political Islam*. New York: Oxford University Press, 2017.

Chivvis, Christopher S. *Toppling Qaddafi: Libya and the Limits of Liberal Intervention*. New York: Cambridge, 2014.

Ciment, James. *Algeria: The Fundamentalist Challenge*. New York: Facts on File, 1997.

Cockburn, Patrick. *Muqtada: Muqtada al-Sadr, the Shia Revival, and the Struggle for Iraq*. New York: Simon & Schuster, 2008.

Cole, Peter, and Brian McQuinn. *The Libyan Revolution and Its Aftermath*. New York: Oxford University Press, 2015.

Cook, David. *Understanding Jihad*. Berkeley: University of California Press, 2015.

Crystal, Jill. *Kuwait: The Transformation of an Oil State*. New York: Routledge, 2016.

Dabashi, Hamid. *Iran, The Green Movement and the USA: The Fox and the Paradox*. London: Zed Books, 2010.

Daher, Aurlie. *Hezbollah: Mobilization and Power*. New York: Oxford University Press, 2016.

David, Isabel, and Kumru F. Toktamis, eds. *Everywhere Taksim: Sowing the Seeds for a New Turkey at Gezi*. Amsterdam: Amsterdam University Press, 2015.

Demirtaş, Selahattin. "The Middle East, The Kurdish Peace Process in Turkey, and Radical Democracy." *Turkish Policy Quarterly* 13, no. 4 (Winter 2015): 27–33.

Elbadawi, Ibrahim, and Samir Makdisi, eds. *Democracy in the Arab World: Explaining the Deficit*. New York: Routledge, 2010.

Elling, Rasmus Christian. *Minorities in Iran: Nationalism and Ethnicity after Khomeini*. New York: Palgrave-MacMillan, 2013.

Evans, Martin, and John Phillips. *Algeria: Anger of the Dispossessed*. New Haven, CT: Yale University Press, 2007.

Fearon, James D., and David Laitin. "Ethnicity, Insurgency, and Civil War." *American Political Science Review* 97, no. 1 (February 2003): 75–90.

Gana, Nouri. *The Making of the Tunisian Revolution: Contexts, Architects, Prospects*. Edinburgh: Edinburgh University Press, 2013.

Gelvin, James. *The Arab Uprisings: What Everyone Needs to Know*. New York: Oxford University Press, 2012.

Ghubash, Hussein. *Oman: The Islamic Democratic Tradition*. New York: Routledge, 2006.

Gohnim, Wael. *Revolution 2.0: The Power of the People Is Greater Than the People in Power: A Memoir*. New York: Houghton Mifflin Harcourt Publishing Company, 2012.

Golkar, Saeid. *Captive Society: The Basij Militia and Social Control in Iran*. Washington, DC: Woodrow Wilson Center Press, 2015.

Bibliography

Guest, John S. *Survival among the Kurds: A History of the Yezidis.* New York: Routledge, 2015.

Gunter, Michael. *The Kurds: A Modern History.* Princeton, NJ: Markus Wiener Publishers, 2016.

Haider, Najam Iftikhar. *Shi'i Islam: An Introduction.* New York: Cambridge University Press, 2014.

Hale, Henry E. "Regime Change Cascades: What We Have Learned from the 1848 Revolutions to the 2011 Arab Uprisings." *Annual Review of Political Science* 16 (May 2013): 331–53.

Hashemi, Nader, and Danny Postel, eds. *The People Reloaded: The Green Movement and the Struggle for Iran's Future.* Brooklyn, NY: Melville House, 2010.

Hazran, Yusri. *The Druze Community and the Lebanese State: Between Confrontation and Reconciliation.* New York: Routledge, 2014.

Herb, Michael. "A Nation of Bureaucrats: Political Participation and Economic Diversification in Kuwait and the United Arab Emirates." *International Journal of Middle East Studies* 41, no. 3 (August 2009): 375–95.

Hill, Ginny. *Yemen Endures: Civil War, Saudi Adventurism and the Future of Arabia.* New York: Oxford University Press 2017.

Hoffman, Valerie J. *The Essentials of Ibadi Islam.* Syracuse, NY: Syracuse University Press, 2012.

Hoffmann, Andrea C. *Raif Badawi: The Voice of Freedom: My Husband, Our Story.* London: Little, Brown Book Group, 2016.

Hokayem, Emile, and Hebatalla Taha, eds. *Egypt after the Spring: Revolt and Reaction.* New York: Routledge, 2016.

Honwana, Alcinda. *Youth and Revolution in Tunisia.* London: Zed Books, 2013.

Ibrahim, Vivian. *The Copts of Egypt: The Challenges of Modernization and Identity.* New York: I. B. Tauris, 2011.

Jefferis, Jennifer. *Hamas: Terrorism, Governance, and Its Future in Middle East Politics.* Santa Barbara, CA: Praeger Security Studies, 2016.

Jenkins, Gareth H. "Post-Putsch Narratives and Turkey's Curious Coup." *Turkey Analyst,* July 22, 2016.

Joffé, George. *Insecurity in North Africa and the Mediterranean.* Rome, Italy: NATO Defense College, 2017.

Jones, Jeremy, and Nicholas Ridout. *A History of Modern Oman.* New York: Cambridge University Press, 2015.

Kamrava, Mehran, ed. *Beyond the Arab Spring: The Evolving Ruling Bargains in the Middle East.* New York: Oxford University Press, 2014.

Kechichian, Joseph A. *From Alliance to Union: Challenges Facing Gulf Cooperation Council States.* Brighton, UK: Sussex Academic Press, 2016.

Kelly, Sanja, and Julia Breslin, eds. *Women's Rights in the Middle East and North Africa: Progress Amid Resistance.* Lanham, MD: Rowman and Littlefield, 2010.

Khatib, Lina, and Ellen Lust, eds. *Taking It to the Streets: The Transformation of Arab Activism.* Baltimore: Johns Hopkins University Press, 2014.

King of Jordan, Abdullah II. *Our Last Best Chance: The Pursuit of Peace in Time of Peril.* New York: Penguin Books, 2012.

Köprülü, Nur. "Consolidated Monarchies in the Post–Arab Spring Era: The Case of Jordan." *Israel Affairs 20*, no. 3 (2014): 318–27.

Kuhn, Randall. "On the Role of Human Development in the Arab Spring." *Population and Development Review* 38, no. 4 (December 2012): 649–83.

Lackner, Helen, and Daniel Martin Varisco, eds. *Yemen and the Gulf States: The Making of a Crisis*. Berlin, Germany: Gerlach Press, 2018.

Lesch, David W. *Syria: The Fall of the House of Assad*. New Haven, CT: Yale University Press, 2013.

Le Suer, James D. *Between Terror and Democracy: Algeria since 1989*. New York: Zed Books, 2010.

Lister, Charles R. *The Syrian Jihad: Al-Qaeda, The Islamic State and the Evolution of an Insurgency*. New York: Oxford University Press, 2015.

Longva, Anh Nga, and Anne Sofie Roald, eds. *Religious Minorities in the Middle East: Domination, Self-Empowerment, Accommodation*. Boston: Brill, 2015.

Lori, Noora. "National Security and the Management of Migrant Labor: A Case Study of the United Arab Emirates." *Asian and Pacific Migration Journal* 20, no. 3–4 (2011): 315–37.

Maddy-Weitzman, Bruce. *The Berber Identity Movement and the Challenge to North African States*. Austin: University of Texas Press, 2011.

Malet, David. *Foreign Fighters: Transnational Identity in Civil Conflicts*. Oxford, UK: Oxford University Press, 2017.

Marr, Phebe, and Ibrahim Al-Marashi. *The Modern History of Iraq*, 4th ed. New York: Routledge, 2017.

Massicard, Elise. *The Alevis in Turkey and Europe: Identity and Managing Territorial Diversity*. London: Routledge, 2012.

Matthiesen, Toby. *Sectarian Gulf: Bahrain, Saudi Arabia, and the Arab Spring That Wasn't*. Stanford, CA: Stanford University Press, 2013.

McCarthy, Rory. *Inside Tunisia's Al-Nahda: Between Politics and Preaching*. New York: Cambridge University Press, 2018.

McDougall, James. *A History of Algeria*. Cambridge, UK: Cambridge University Press, 2017.

Milani, Abbas, and Larry Diamond, eds. *Politics and Culture in Contemporary Iran*. Boulder, CO: Lynne Rienner Publishers, 2015.

Mundy, Jacob. *Libya*. Cambridge, UK: UK Polity, 2018.

Naunihal, Singh. *Seizing Power: The Strategic Logic of Military Coups*. Baltimore: Johns Hopkins University Press, 2014.

Neumann, Ronald E. "Bahrain: A Very Complicated Little Island." *Middle East Policy* 20, no. 4 (Winter 2013): 45–58.

Nisan, Mordechai. *Minorities in the Middle East: A History of Struggle and Self-Expression*. London: McFarland & Company, 2015.

Osman, Tarek. *Islamism: What It Means for the Middle East and the World*. New Haven, CT: Yale University Press, 2016.

Ostovar, Afshon. *Vanguard of the Imam: Religion, Politics, and Iran's Revolutionary Guards*. New York: Oxford University Press, 2016.

Pack, Jason, ed. *The 2011 Libyan Uprising and the Struggle for the Post-Qadhafi Future*. New York: Palgrave Macmillan, 2013.

Bibliography

Parsons, Nigel Craig. *The Politics of the Palestinian Authority: From Oslo to Al-Aqsa*. London: Routledge, 2012.

Peters, Joel, and Rob Geist Pinfold, eds. *Understanding Israel: Political, Societal and Security Challenges*. New York: Routledge, 2019.

Peterson, J. E. *Yemen: The Search for a Modern State*. London: Routledge, 2017.

Robinson, Glenn E. "Palestinian Tribes, Clans and Notable Families." *Strategic Insights*. Monterey, CA: Naval Postgraduate School, 2009.

Rowe, Paul S., ed. *Routledge Handbook of Minorities in the Middle East*. New York: Routledge, 2019.

Ryan, Curtis R. *Jordan and the Arab Spring: Regime Survival and Politics Beyond the State*. New York: Columbia University Press, 2018.

Salamey, Imad. *The Government and Politics of Lebanon*. New York: Routledge, 2013.

Sassoon, Joseph. *Anatomy of Authoritarianism in the Arab Republics*. Cambridge, UK: Cambridge University Press, 2016.

Sater, James N. *Morocco: Challenges to Tradition and Modernity*. New York: Routledge, 2016.

Saykal, Amin, and Amitav Asharya, eds. *Democracy and Reform in the Middle East and Asia. Social Protest and Authoritarian Rule after the Arab Spring*. London: I. B. Tauris, 2014.

Shalaby, Marwa, and Valentine M. Moghadam, eds. *Empowering Women after the Arab Spring. Comparative Feminist Studies*. New York: Palgrave Macmillan, 2016.

Shane, Scott. *Objective Troy: A Terrorist, a President, and the Rise of the Drone*. New York: Tim Duggan Books, 2015.

Sheline, Annelle. *Royal Religious Authority: Morocco's "Commander of the Faithful."* Houston: Baker Institute for Public Policy, March 2019.

Sky, Emma. *The Unraveling: High Hopes and Missed Opportunities in Iraq*. New York: Public Affairs, 2015.

Smith, Charles D. *Palestine and the Arab Israeli Conflict: A History with Documents,* 9th ed. Boston: St. Martin's Press, 2016.

Sowers, Jeannie, and Chris Toesing, eds. *The Journey to Tahrir: Revolution, Protest, and Social Change in Egypt*. London: Verso, 2012.

Springborg, Robert. *Egypt*. Medford, MA: Polity, 2018.

Tadros, Samuel. "The Story of the Tunisian Revolution." Stanford, CA: The Hoover Institution, 2014.

Terrill, W. Andrew. *The Struggle for Yemen and the Challenge of Al-Qaeda in the Arabian Peninsula*. Carlisle, PA: Strategic Studies Institute, June 2013.

Tittensor, David. *The House of Service: The Gülen Movement and Islam's Third Way*. Oxford, UK: Oxford University Press, 2014.

Ulrichsen, Kristian Coates. *The United Arab Emirates. Power, Politics and Policymaking*. New York: Routledge, 2017.

Uskowi, Nader. *Temperature Rising: Iran's Revolutionary Guards and Wars in the Middle East*. Lanham, MD: Rowman and Littlefield Publishers, 2018.

Van Dam, Nikolaos. *Destroying a Nation: The Civil War in Syria*. New York: I. B. Tauris, 2017.

Wehrey, Frederic. *The Burning Shores: Inside the Battle for the New Libya*. New York: Farrar, Straus and Giroux, 2018.

Willis, Michael J. *Politics and Power in the Maghreb: Algeria, Tunisia and Morocco from Independence to the Arab Spring*. Oxford, UK: Oxford University Press, 2014.

Yassin-Kasab, Robin, and Leila Al-Shami. *Burning Country: Syrians in Revolution and War*. London: Pluto Press, 2016.

Zartman, I. William, ed. *Arab Spring: Negotiating in the Shadow of the Intifada*. Athens: University of Georgia Press, 2015.

About the Editor

Jonathan K. Zartman, PhD, is an associate professor in the Department of Research at Air Command and Staff College. As a Fulbright Fellow and a David L. Boren Fellow, he has taught in Tajikistan and Uzbekistan. He is author of "Negotiation, Exclusion and Durable Peace" in *International Negotiation* 13 (2008), and "Transition and Vulnerability Management in Uzbekistan" in *Journal of Central Asian Studies* 3, no. 2 (1999). Zartman earned his doctorate in international relations from the University of Denver Graduate School of International Studies in 2004.

Contributors

Benjamin V. Allison
Graduate Student
Department of History
Kent State University
Kent, Ohio

Dr. Bader Mousa Al-Saif
Assistant Professor
History Department
Kuwait University
Kuwait City, Kuwait

Dr. Philipp O. Amour
Associate Professor
Department of International Relations
Sakarya University
Sakarya, Turkey

Lieutenant Colonel Rebecca Antecki
Director, Political and Strategic Affairs Program
Department of Research
Air Command and Staff College
Maxwell Air Force Base, Alabama

Dr. Saphia Arezki
Associate Researcher
The Institute of Research and Study on the Arab and Muslim Worlds
Aix-Marseille University
Aix-en-Provence, France

Andrew Harrison Baker
Adjunct Instructor
History Department
Anderson University
Anderson, Indiana

Contributors

Dr. Lindsay J. Benstead
Associate Professor of Political Science
Mark O. Hatfield School of Government
Portland State University

Lieutenant Colonel Sean Nicholus Blas
Graduate Student
University of Utah
Salt Lake City, Utah

Dr. Carolina Bracco
Professor
Faculty of Social Sciences
University of Buenos Aires
Buenos Aires, Argentina

Dr. Sean Braniff
Assistant Professor
Department of International Security Studies
Air War College
Maxwell Air Force Base, Alabama

Dr. Gianfranco Bria
Post-Doc Fellow
University of Turin
Turin, Italy

Dan Campbell
PhD candidate
History Department
Auburn University
Auburn, Alabama

Luíza Gimenez Cerioli
Doctoral Researcher
Centre for Near and Middle East
University of Marburg
Marburg, Hessen, Germany

Dr. Autumn Cockrell-Abdullah
Lecturer of Anthropology
Department of History, Anthropology & Philosophy
University of North Georgia
Dahlonega, Georgia

Contributors

Dr. Isabel David
Assistant Professor
Orient Institute
Institute of Social and Political Sciences
University of Lisbon
Lisbon, Portugal

Dr. Emanuela Claudia Del Re
Professor of Political Sociology
Faculty of Communication Sciences
Uninettuno University
Rome, Italy

Dr. Robert C. DiPrizio
Associate Professor
Department of International Security
Air Command and Staff College
Maxwell Air Force Base, Alabama

Tom Dowling
Independent Scholar
Retired U.S. diplomat
Boyce, Virginia

Dr. Sabine Dreher
Contract Faculty
Department of International Studies
York University
Toronto, Ontario, Canada

Scott Edmondson
Assistant Professor
Air Force Culture and Language Center
Air University
Maxwell Air Force Base, Alabama

Amir Muhammad Esmaeili
Graduate Student
Faculty of Political Science and Islamic Studies
Imam Sadiq University
Tehran, Iran

Dusty Farned, JD
Instructor
Negotiation and Alternative Dispute Resolution
Air Force Negotiation Center
Maxwell Air Force Base, Alabama

Contributors

Dr. Valentina Fedele
Postdoctoral Fellow in History of Islamic Countries
Department of Cultures, Education and Society
University of Calabria
Arcavacata di Rende, Cosenza, Italy

Dr. Sarah Fischer
Assistant Professor
Criminal Justice
Marymount University
Arlington, Virginia

Dr. Kristin Hissong
Assistant Professor
Regional and Cultural Studies
Air Force Culture and Language Center
Maxwell Air Force Base, Alabama

Samanvya Singh Hooda
Research Assistant
Institute of Chinese Studies
New Delhi, India

Dr. Mir Zohair Husain
Professor
Department of Political Science
University of South Alabama
Mobile, Alabama

Dr. Sayed Hassan Akhlaq Hussaini
Research Fellow
Department of World Languages and Literatures
Boston University
Boston, Massachusetts

Dr. Kristin Kamøy
Adjunct Research Fellow
Asia Institute
Griffith University
Brisbane, Australia

Dr. Jeffrey Kaplan
Professor
School of Arts, Humanities, and Social Sciences
Habib University
Karachi, Pakistan

Contributors

Dr. Magdalena Karolak
Associate Professor
College of Humanities and Social Sciences
Zayed University
Dubai, U.A.E

Dr. Nur Köprülü
Associate Professor
Chair, Department of Political Science
Faculty of Economics & Administrative Sciences
Near East University
Nicosia, North Cyprus

Lieutenant Colonel Melvin R. Korsmo (PhD)
Director of Staff, Professor
School of Advanced Air & Space Studies
Maxwell Air Force Base, Alabama

Dr. Philip Leech-Ngo
Senior Fellow
Center on Governance
University of Ottawa
Ottawa, Ontario, Canada

Major David R. Leonard
Instructor
Department of Research
Air Command and Staff College
Maxwell Air Force Base, Alabama

Dr. Mark David Luce
4th Psychological Operations Group
U.S. Army Special Operations Command
1st Special Forces Command
Fayetteville, North Carolina

Dr. Fouad Gehad Marei
Research Associate
Max Weber Centre for Advanced Cultural and Social Studies
University of Erfurt
Erfurt, Germany

Dr. Ali A. Olomi
Assistant Professor of History
History Department

Penn State Abington
Abington, Pennsylvania

Dr. Muhammed Kursad Ozekin
Lecturer
Department of Political Science and International Relations
Usak University
Usak, Turkey

Taylan Paksoy
Graduate Assistant
Department of History
Graduate School of Economics and Social Sciences
Bilkent University
Ankara, Turkey

Dr. Melia Pfannenstiel
Assistant Professor
Department of Joint Warfighting
Air Command and Staff College
Maxwell Air Force Base, Alabama

Lieutenant Colonel Steven A. Quillman
Director of Staff
Department of Research
Air Command and Staff College
Maxwell Air Force Base, Alabama

Dr. Nicholas Michael Sambaluk
Assistant Professor
eSchool of Graduate Professional Military Education
Maxwell Air Force Base, Alabama

Dr. Alexander Shelby
Assistant Professor of History
Department of History
Indian River State College
Fort Pierce, Florida

Arhama Siddiqa
Research Fellow
Institute of Strategic Studies
Islamabad, Pakistan

Dr. Mohammad Dawood Sofi
Post-Doc Fellow
Department of International Relations

Ankara Yildirm Beyazit University
Ankara, Turkey

Dr. Paul J. Springer
Professor and Chair
Department of Research
Air Command and Staff College
Maxwell Air Force Base, Alabama

Dr. Samuel S. Stanton, Jr.
Chair and Professor of Political Science
Grove City College
Grove City, Pennsylvania

Dr. Ángela Suárez-Collado
Assistant Professor
Political Science and Public Administration Department
Salamanca University
Salamanca, Spain

Dr. James Tallon
Associate Professor
Department of History
Lewis University
Romeoville, Illinois

Dr. Kumru F. Toktamis
Associate Professor
Department of Social Science and Cultural Studies
Pratt Institute
Brooklyn, New York

Stephanie Marie Van Sant
Independent researcher
Montgomery, Alabama

Gowhar Quadir Wani
Senior Research Fellow
Department of Islamic Studies
Aligarh Muslim University
Aligarh, India

Alexander Weissenburger
Researcher
Austrian Academy of Sciences
Institute for Social Anthropology
Vienna, Austria

Major Andrew Zapf
Foreign Area Officer
United States Army
United States Africa Command
Stuttgart, Germany

Dr. Jonathan K. Zartman
Associate Professor
Department of Research
Air Command and Staff College
Maxwell Air Force Base, Alabama

Dr. Valentina Zecca
Research Fellow
Department of Culture, Education, and Society
University of Calabria
Rende, Cosenza, Italy

Index

Abbas, Mahmoud, **1**
 Fatah Party and, 93
 Fayyad, Salam, and, 93–94
 Hamas and, 116–117
 Intifadas (I, II, and Knife) and, 130–131
 Palestine and, 229–232
 Palestine Liberation Organization and,
  232–233
Abdullah II, King of Jordan, **2**
 Jordan, Hashemite Kingdom of, and,
  159–162
 Jordanian Protests (2011) and, 162–163
Academics for Peace in Turkey, **2–3**
 AKP-PKK Peace Talks (2005–2015)
  and, 7
Afghanistan, xx, xxi, 12, 16, 21, 24–27,
  38, 55, 56, 98, 133, 135, 142, 147,
  158,169, 249, 262, 268, 272, 314
Against Compulsory Hijab, **3–4**
 Iran, Islamic Republic of, and, 131–136
Ahmadinejad, Mahmoud, **4–5**
 Basij and, 52–53
 Green Movement (2009) and, 110–111
 Iran, Islamic Republic of, and, 131–136
 Islamic Revolutionary Guard Corps
  (IRGC) and, 141–143
 Khamenei, Ayatollah Sayyid Ali, and,
  167–168
 Rafsanjani, Ali Akbar Hashemi, and,
  252–253
Ahrar al-Sham Brigades, **6**
 Syrian Arab Republic and, 277–281
 Syrian Civil War and, 281–283
AKP-PKK Peace Talks (2005–2015) **7**
 Academics for Peace in Turkey and, 3
 Demirtaş, Selahattin and, 76–77
 Kurdistan Workers' Party (PKK) and,
  172–173

 Ocalan, Abdullah, and, 219
Al-Abadi, Haider, **7–8**
 Iraq, Republic of, and, 137–140
 Khamenei, Ayatollah Sayyid Ali, and,
  167–168
Al-Ahmar, Ali Muhsin **8–9**
 Saleh, Ali Abdullah, and, 264
 Yemen, Republic of, and, 310–313
 Yemen Uprising (2011), and, 316–317
Al-Assad, Bashar, **9–10**
 Ahrar al-Sham Brigades and, 6
 Free Syrian Army and, 100–101
 Ghouta Chemical Weapons Attack of
  2013 and, 108
 Ghouta Chemical Weapons Attack of
  2018 and, 109
 Hayat Tahrir al-Sham (HTS) and, 120
 Hezbollah and, 121–124
 Jumblatt, Walid, and, 163–164
 Syrian Arab Republic and, 277–281
 Syrian Civil War and, 281–283
Alawites (Nusayris), **10–11**
 Ba'athism and, 45–46
 Druze and, 80–81
 Ghouta Chemical Weapons Attack of
  2013 and, 108
 Minorities and, 198–200
 Syrian Arab Republic and, 277–281
 Syrian Civil War and, 281–283
Al-Awlaki, Anwar, **12–13**
Al-Azhar Declaration, **343–347**
Alevis, **13–14**
 Gezi Park Protests (2013) and, 104–105
 Minorities and, 198–200
Algeria, The People's Democratic
  Republic of, **14–18**
 Al-Qaeda Central and, 24–26
 Algerian Protests (2011), and, 18–20

Index

Algeria (*cont.*)
    Al-Qaeda in the Islamic Maghreb
        (AQIM) and, 27–28
    Armed Islamic Group (GIA) and, 38–39
    Army of Islamic Salvation (AIS) and,
        40–41
    Belmokhtar, Mokhtar, and, 56–57
    Berbers (Imazighen) and, 60
    Bouteflika, Abdelaziz, and, 63–64
    Foreign Fighters and, 98
    Ibadi Doctrine and, 129–130
    Islamic Salvation Front (FIS) and,
        143–144
    National Liberation Front (FLN) and,
        215–216
    Nezzar, Khaled, and, 217–218
    Rally for Culture and Democracy
        (RCD) and, 254
    Salah, Ahmed Gaid, 263–264
Algerian Protests (2011), **18–20**
    Algeria, The People's Democratic
        Republic of, and, 14–18
    Armed Islamic Group (GIA) and, 38–39
    Regime Change Cascades and,
        256–257
Al-Islah (Reform Party), **20–21**
    Hadi, Abdu Rabbu Mansour and, 115
    Saleh, Ali Abdullah, and, 264
Al Jazeera, **21–22**
    Arab Spring Movements (2011) and, 37
    Qatar and, 245–248
    Tunisia, Republic of, and, 289
Al-Maliki, Nouri, **22–23**
    Al-Abadi, Haider and, 7–8
    Al-Sadr, Muqtada and, 28–30
    Erdogan, Recep Tayyip, and, 90–91
    Iraq, Republic of, and, 137–140
    Khamenei, Ayatollah Sayyid Ali, and,
        167–168
    Popular Mobilization Forces (PMF)
        and, 239–241
    Sahwa (Sunni Tribal Awakening) and,
        261–262
Al Manar Television **23–24**
    Hezbollah and, 121–124
    Lebanese Republic and, 183–186
Al-Qaeda in the Arabian Peninsula
        (AQAP), **26–27**
    Al-Qaeda Central and, 24–26
    Al-Ahmar, Ali Muhsin and, 8–9
    Al-Awlaki, Anwar and, 12–13

Saudi Sahwa (Islamic Awakening) and,
        271–273
    Yemen, Republic of, and, 310–313
    Yemen Civil War (2015) and, 313–315
    Yemeni Socialist Party (YSP) and, 312
    Zaydi Doctrine and, 319
Al-Qaeda Central, **24–26**
    Ahrar al-Sham Brigades and, 6
    Al-Awlaki, Anwar and, 12–13
    Algeria, The People's Democratic
        Republic of, and, 14–18
    Al Jazeera and, 21–22
    Al-Qaeda in the Arabian Peninsula
        (AQAP) and, 26–27
    Al-Qaeda in the Islamic Maghreb
        (AQIM) and, 27–28
    Ansar Beit al Maqdis and, 34
    Belmokhtar, Mokhtar, and, 56–57
    Benghazi Attack and, 58–59
    Hayat Tahrir al-Sham (HTS) and, 120
    Islamic State (ISIS, ISIL, or *Daesh*) and,
        145–146
    Islamism and, 146–148
    Jihad and, 157–158
    Regime Change Cascades and, 256–257
    Sahwa (Sunni Tribal Awakening) and,
        261–262
Al-Qaeda in the Islamic Maghreb (AQIM),
        27–28
    Algeria, The People's Democratic
        Republic of, and, 14–18
    Al-Qaeda Central and, 24–26
    Ansar al-Sharia in Libya and, 33
    Armed Islamic Group (GIA) and,
        38–39
    Belmokhtar, Mokhtar and, 56–57
Al-Sadr, Muqtada, **28–30**
    Al-Abadi, Haider and, 7–8
    Iraq, Republic of, and, 137–140
    Popular Mobilization Forces (PMF)
        and, 239–241
    Quds Force and, 248–249
Al-Sharif, Manal, **30–31**
    Saudi Arabia, Kingdom of, and,
        266–270
    Social Media and, 275–277
    Women's Leadership in Protests and,
        307–308
Amman Message, The, **327–334**
    Abdullah II, King of Jordan and, 2
    Ibadi Doctrine and, 129

Jordan, Hashemite Kingdom of, and, 161
  Sectarianism and, 174
Ammar, Rachid, **31–32**
  Jasmine Revolution and, 155–157
Ansar al-Sharia in Libya, **33**
  Battle of Sirte in 2016 and, 54–55
  Libya, State of, and, 186–190
Ansar Beit al Maqdis, **34**
  Egypt, Arab Republic of, and, 84–87
April 6 Youth, **34–35**
  Egypt, Arab Republic of, and, 84–87
  Ghonim, Wael and, 107–108
  Social Media and, 275–277
  Tahrir Square Protests (2011) and, 285
  Women's Leadership in Protests and,
    307–308
Arab Nationalism, xx, **35–36**
  Ba'athism and, 45–46
  Druze and, 80–81
  Framing Model and, 98–99
  General People's Congress and, 104
  Ghannouchi, Rachid and, 106–107
  Iraq, Republic of, and, 137–140
  Jordan and, 159
  Patriotic Union of Kurdistan (PUK)
    and, 235–236
  Libya and, 189–190
Arab Peace Initiative **326–327**
  Hamas and, 116–117
  Israel and, 148–151
  Middle East Roadmap (2003) and,
    196–197
Arab Revolt (1916–1918), 35
Arab Spring Movements (2011), **36–38**
Armed Islamic Group (GIA), **38–39**
  Al-Qaeda in the Islamic Maghreb
    (AQIM) and, 27–28
  Belmokhtar, Mokhtar, **56–57**
  Islamic Salvation Front (FIS) and,
    143–144
Armenians, **39–40**
  Minorities and, 198–200
  Sectarianism and, 273–274
Army of Islamic Salvation (AIS), **40–41**
  Algeria, The People's Democratic
    Republic of, and, 14–18
Ashrawi, Hanan, **41–42**
  Fayyad, Salam, and, 93–93
Ataturk, Mustafa Kamal
  Alevis and, 13
  Kurds and, 173

Modernization and, 200
Turkey, Republic of, and, 295
Authoritarianism, xx, **42–43**
  Algeria, The People's Democratic
    Republic of, and, 14–18
  Arab Spring Movements (2011) and,
    36–38
  Bahrain, Kingdom of, and, 215
  Clientelism (Patrimonialism) and, 67–68
  Corruption and, 71–72
  Coup of 2016 and, 72–74
  Democracy Deficit and, 77–78
  Egypt, Republic of, and, 87
  Erdogan, Recep Tayyip, and, 91
  Ghonim, Wael and, 107–108
  Greed Model and, 109–110
  Grievance Model and, 112–113
  Hamas-Fatah Conflict and, 117
  Hizmet (Gulen) Movement and, 124
  Iran, Islamic Republic of, and, 133, 136
  Jasmine Revolution and, 155
  Jordanian Protests and, 162
  Justice and Development Party
    (Turkey), 165
  Kuwait, State of, and, 176
  Labor Migration: Receiving Countries
    and, 181
  Labor Migration: Sending Countries
    and, 182
  Military Coups and, 198
  Minorities and, 199
  Morocco, Kingdom of, and, 203–206
  Regime Change Cascades and,
    256–257
  Rentier State Politics and, 258
  Syrian Arab Republic and, 278
  Tunisia, Republic of, and, 289
  Damascus Declaration and, 334

Ba'athism **45–46**
  Alawites (Nusayris) and, 10–11
  Arab Nationalism and, 35–36
  Barzani, Masoud, and, 50–52
  Druze and, 80–81
  Iraq, Republic of, and, 137–140
  Patriotic Union of Kurdistan (PUK)
    and, 235–236
  Sectarianism and, 273
  Syrian Arab Republic and, 277–281
  The Damascus Declaration for
    Democratic Change and, 334, 337

Badawi, Raif, **46–47**
  Saudi Arabia, Kingdom of, and, 266–270
  Social Media and, 275–277
Bahrain, Kingdom of, **47–50**
  Al Jazeera and, 21–22
  Gulf Cooperation Council (GCC) and, 113–114
  Labor Migration: Receiving Countries and, 181–182
  National Action Charter and, 215
  Oman, Sultanate of, and, 219–224
  Pearl Roundabout Protests and, 236–238
  Qatar and, 245–248
  Quds Force and, 248–249
  Rajab, Nabeel, and, 253–254
  Saudi Arabian Protests (2011) and, 270–271
  Saudi Sahwa (Islamic Awakening) and, 271–273
  Shi'a and, 275
  United Arab Emirates (UAE) and, 301–303
Barzani, Masoud, **50–52**
  Iraq, Republic of, and, 137–140
  Kurdistan Regional Government (KRG) and, 170–171
  Kurds and, 173–175
  Patriotic Union of Kurdistan (PUK) and, 235–236
  Turkey, Republic of, and, 295–299
Basij, **52–53**
  Ahmadinejad, Mahmoud and, 5
  Economic Protests (2017–2018) and, 83–84
  Iran, Islamic Republic of, and, 131–136
  Islamic Revolutionary Guard Corps (IRGC) and, 141–143
  Khatami, Mohammad, and, 168–169
  Shabiha Militias and, 274
Battle of Sirte in 2011, **53–54**
  February 17th Revolution and, 94–95
  Libya, State of, and, 186–190
  Qaddafi, Muammar, and, 244
Battle of Sirte in 2016, **54–55**
  Libya Dawn Coalition and, 190–191
  Libya, State of, and, 186–190
  Libyan Civil War and, 191–192
Belhaj, Abdul Hakim, **55–56**
  February 17th Revolution and, 94–95
  Libya, State of, and, 186–190

Belmokhtar, Mokhtar, **56–57**
  Algeria, The People's Democratic Republic of, and, 14–18
  Al-Qaeda in the Islamic Maghreb (AQIM) and, 27–28
Ben Ali, Zine al-Abidine, **57–58**
  Ennahda Movement and, 89–90
  Ghannouchi, Rachid and, 106–107
  Jasmine Revolution and, 155–157
  Tunisia, Republic of, and, 289–293
  Tunisian General Labor Union and, 293–294
Benghazi Attack, **58–59**
  Ansar al-Sharia in Libya and, 33
  Libya, State of, and, 186–190
  Libyan Civil War and, 191–192
Benkirane, Abdelilah, **59–60**
  Justice and Development Party (Morocco) and, 164–165
  Morocco, Kingdom of, and, 203–206
Berbers (Imazighen), xxii, **60**
  Algeria, The People's Democratic Republic of, and, 14–18
  Bouteflika, Abdelaziz, and, 63–64
  Constitutional Drafting Assembly and, 69
  February 20 Movement and, 96
  Fikri, Mouhcine, and, 97
  Libya, State of, and, 186, 189
  Minorities and, 198–200
  Mohammed VI, King of Morocco, and, 202
  Morocco, Kingdom of, and, 203–206
  Rally for Culture and Democracy (RCD) and, 254
Black October Riots (1988), **60–61**
  Algeria, The People's Democratic Republic of, and, 14–18
  National Liberation Front (FLN) and, 215–216
  Nezzar, Khaled, and, 217–218
Black September, **61–62**
  Jordan, Hashemite Kingdom of, and, 159–162
Bouazizi, Tarek el-Tayeb Mohamed, xix; **62–63**
  Arab Spring Movements (2011) and, 37
  Ben Ali, Zine al-Abidine and, 57–58
  Fikri, Mouhcine, and, 97
  Jasmine Revolution and, 155–157
  Tunisia, Republic of, and, 289–293

Index

Bouteflika, Abdelaziz, **63–64**
  Algeria, The People's Democratic
    Republic of, and, 14–18
  Algerian Protests (2011), and, 18–20
  Al-Qaeda in the Islamic Maghreb
    (AQIM) and, 27–28
  Army of Islamic Salvation (AIS) and,
    40–41
  Islamic Salvation Front (FIS) and,
    143–144
  National Liberation Front (FLN) and,
    215–216
  Rally for Culture and Democracy
    (RCD) and, 254
  Salah, Ahmed Gaid, and, 263–264
Britain, xx, **7**

Cedar Revolution (2005), **65–66**
  Al-Assad, Bashar and, 9–10
  Druze and, 80–81
  Hariri, Saad, and, 119
  Hezbollah and, 121–124
  Jumblatt, Walid, and, 163–164
  Lebanese Republic and, 183–186
  Regime Change Cascades and, 256–257
Civil Wars, **66–67**
  Algerian Protests (2011), and, 18–20
  Arab Spring Movements (2011) and,
    36–38
  Clientelism (Patrimonialism) and, 67–68
  Foreign Fighters and, 98
  Framing Model and, 98–99
  Grievance Model and, 112–113
  Iraq, Republic of, and, 137–140
  Maronites and, 195–196
  Regime Change Cascades and, 256–257
  Syrian Civil War and, 281–283
Clientelism (Patrimonialism), **67–68**
  Authoritarianism and, 42–43
  Corruption and, 71–72
  Democracy Deficit and, 77–78
  Greed Model and, 109–110
  Iraq, Republic of, and, 137–140
  Jordan, Hashemite Kingdom of, and,
    159–162
  Kurdistan Regional Government (KRG)
    and, 170–171
  Mohammed VI, King of Morocco,
    201–202
  Oman Protests (2011) and, 224–226
  Oman, Sultanate of, and, 219–224

Patriotic Union of Kurdistan (PUK)
  and, 235–236
  Rentier State Politics, 258
  Wasta and, 306–307
Cold War, xx, 138, 278, 295, 296, 313
  Arab Cold War, xx
Constitutional Drafting Assembly, **68–70**
  Libya, State of, and, 186–190
Coptic Orthodox Church, **70–71**
  Ansar Beit al Maqdis and, 34
  Egypt, Arab Republic of, and, 84–87
  El-Sisi, Abdel Fattah Saeed Hussein
    Khalil, 88–89
  Minorities and, 198–200
  Tamarod Movement (2013) and,
    287–289
Corruption, xxi, **71–72**
  Al-Abadi, Haidar, and, 8
  Al-Ahmar, Ali Muhsin, and, 9
  Al-Assad, Bashar and, 9–10
  Alawites (Nusayris) and, 11
  Algeria and, 15
  Arab Spring Movements (2011) and,
    36–38
  Ashrawi, Hanan, and, 41–42
  Bahrain, Kingdom of, and, 49
  Barzani, Masoud, and, 50–52
  Ben Ali, Zine al-Abidine and, 57–58
  Black October Riots (1988) and, 60–61
  Bouazizi, Tarek el-Tayeb Mohamed,
    and, 62–63
  Clientelism (Patrimonialism) and, 67–68
  Coptic Orthodox Church and, 70–71
  Democracy Deficit and, 77–78
  Economic Protests (2017–2018) and, 81
  Egypt, Arab Republic of, and, 84–87
  Ergenekon Scandal and, 91–92
  Fikri, Mouhcine, and, 97
  Greed Model and, 109–110
  Grievance Model and, 112–113
  Hizmet (Gülen) Movement and,
    124–125
  Iran, Islamic Republic of, and, 131–136
  Jasmine Revolution and, 155–157
  Jordanian Protests (2011) and, 162–163
  Justice and Development Party
    (Morocco) and, 164–165
  Kurdistan Regional Government (KRG)
    and, 170–171
  Mohammed VI, King of Morocco, and,
    201–202

Index

Corruption (*cont.*)
Morocco, Kingdom of, and, 203–206
Mubarak, Muhammad Hosni, and, 207–208
Oman Protests (2011) and, 224–226
Patriotic Union of Kurdistan (PUK) and, 235–236
Popular Mobilization Forces (PMF) and, 239–241
Rafsanjani, Ali Akbar Hashemi, and, 252–253
Salah, Ahmed Gaid, 263–264
Tahrir Square Protests (2011) and, 285
Tunisia, Republic of, and, 289–293
Washington Consensus and, 305–306
Wasta and, 306–307
Coup of 2016, **72–74**
Erdogan, Recep Tayyip, and, 90–91
Turkey, Republic of, and, 295–299

Dahiya Doctrine, **75–76**
Damascus Declaration for Democratic National Change, **334–338**
Demirtaş, Selahattin, **76–77**
Democracy Deficit, **77–78**
Authoritarianism and, 42–43
Civil Wars and, 66–67
Corruption and, 71–72
Green Movement (2009) and, 110–111
Grievance Model and, 112–113
Hizmet (Gülen) Movement and, 124–125
Jasmine Revolution and, 155–157
Justice and Development Party (Turkey) and, 165–166
Military Coups and, 197–198
Rentier State Politics and, 258
Demographics (Youth Bulge) xviii. **78–79**
Labor Migration: Sending Countries and, 182–183
Development, **79–80**
Algeria, The People's Democratic Republic of, and, 15, 16
Arab Spring Movements (2011) and, 38
Barzani, Masoud, and, 51
Benghazi Attack and, 58
Corruption and, 71–72
Democracy Deficit and, 77–78
Fikri, Mouhcine, and, 97
Iranian Azerbaijanis and, 136
Iraq, Republic of, and, 139

Islamic Revolutionary Guard Corps (IRGC) and, 143
Kuwait, State of, and, 176
Labor Migration: Sending Countries and, 182
Military Coups and, 197
Modernization and, 200–201
Morocco, Kingdom of, and, 203, 204
Oman, Sultanate of, and, 219–224
Qaboos bin Said bin Taimur Al Said and, 243–244
Qatar and, 247
Salman, Mohammad bin, and, 265–266
Syrian Arab Republic and, 277
Tunisia and, 292
United Arab Emirates (UAE) and, 302
Washington Consensus and, 305–306
Druze, **80–81**
Al-Assad, Bashar and, 9–10
Alawites (Nusayris) and, 10–11
Cedar Revolution (2005) and, 65–66
Jumblatt, Walid, and, 163–164
Lebanese Republic and, 183–186
Maronites and, 195–196
Minorities and, 198–200
Syrian Arab Republic and, 277–281

Economic Protests (2017–2018), **83–84**
Iran, Islamic Republic of, and, 131–136
Egypt, Arab Republic of, **84–87**
Al Jazeera and, 21–22
Al-Qaeda Central and, 24–26
Ansar Beit al Maqdis and, 34
April 6 Youth and, 34–35
Armenians and, 39–40
Ba'athism and, 45–46
Coptic Orthodox Church and, 70–71
El-Sisi, Abdel Fattah Saeed Hussein Khalil, and, 88–89
Ghannouchi, Rachid and, 106–107
Ghonim, Wael and, 107–108
Israel and, 148–151
Labor Migration: Sending Countries and, 182–183
Military Coups and, 197–198
Minorities and, 198–200
Modernization and, 200–201
Morsi, Mohamed, and, 206–207
Mubarak, Muhammad Hosni, and, 207–208
Muslim Brotherhood and, 210–211

Index

Muslim Brotherhood in Jordan and, 211–212
Palestine and, 229–232
Palestinian Islamic Jihad, 234
Rabi'a al-Adawiya Massacre and, 251
Salafism and, 262–263
Saudi Sahwa (Islamic Awakening) and, 271–273
Tahrir Square Protests (2011) and, 285
Takfiri Doctrine and, 286
Tamarod Movement (2013) and, 287–289
El-Sisi, Abdel Fattah Saeed Hussein Khalil, **88–89**
April 6 Youth and, 34–35
Arab Nationalism and, 35–36
Egypt, Arab Republic of, and, 84–87
Morsi, Mohamed, and, 206–207
Mubarak, Muhammad Hosni, and, 207–208
Muslim Brotherhood and, 210–211
Rabi'a al-Adawiya Massacre and, 251
Tahrir Square Protests (2011) and, 285
Tamarod Movement (2013) and, 287–289
Ennahda Movement, **89–90**
Ghannouchi, Rachid and, 106–107
Tunisia, Republic of, and, 289–293
Erdogan, Recep Tayyip, **90–91**
Academics for Peace in Turkey and, 3
AKP-PKK Peace Talks (2005–2015) and, 7
Coup of 2016 and, 72–74
Demirtaş, Selahattin and, 76–77
Ergenekon Scandal and, 91–92
Gezi Park Protests (2013) and, 104–105
Hizmet (Gülen) Movement and, 124–125
Justice and Development Party (Turkey) and, 165–166
Turkey, Republic of, and, 295–299
Ergenekon Scandal, **91–92**
Turkey, Republic of, and, 295–299

Fatah Party, 1, **93**
Abbas, Mahmoud, and, 1
Black September and, 61–62
Fayyad, Salam, and, 93–93
Hamas and, 116–117
Hamas-Fatah Conflict and, 117–118
Intifadas (I, II, and Knife) and, 130–131

Mubarak, Muhammad Hosni, and, 207–208
Palestine and, 229–232
Palestine Liberation Organization and, 232–233
Palestinian Islamic Jihad and, 234
Fayyad, Salam, **93–94**
Hamas-Fatah Conflict and, 117–118
Palestine and, 229–232
February 17th Revolution, **94–95**
Arab Spring Movements (2011) and, 36–38
Battle of Sirte in 2011 and, 53–54
Constitutional Drafting Assembly and, 68–70
General National Congress and, 103
Libya, State of, and, 186–190
Libyan Civil War and, 191–192
National Transition Council, 216–217
Qaddafi, Muammar, and, 244
Regime Change Cascades and, 256–257
Social Media and, 275–277
Women's Leadership in Protests and, 307–308
February 20 Movement, **95–96**
Arab Spring Movements (2011) and, 36–38
Justice and Development Party (Morocco) and, 164–165
Mohammed VI, King of Morocco, and, 201–202
Morocco, Kingdom of, and, 203–206
Regime Change Cascades and, 256–257
Social Media and, 275–277
Fikri, Mouhcine, **97**
Mohammed VI, King of Morocco, and, 201–202
Morocco, Kingdom of, and, 203–206
Foreign Fighters, **98**
Demographics (Youth Bulge) and, 78–79
Iraq, Republic of, and, 137–140
Islamic State (ISIS, ISIL, or *Daesh*) and, 145–146
Quds Force and, 248–249
Refugees and, 254–256
France xx
Algeria and, 17, 144, 216
Al Jazeera and, 21
Ghannouchi, Rachid, in, 106
Hariri, Saad in, 119

392 Index

France (*cont.*)
 Hezbollah and, 121
 Libya and, 37
 Mujahedin-e Khalq (MEK) in, 209
 Refuge in, 46, 259
 Suez crisis and, 36, 85
 Syria and, 11, 277
 Tunisia and, 57, 63–64, 291
Framing Model, **98–99**
 Civil Wars and, 66–67
 Greed Model and, 109–110
 Grievance Model and, 112–113
 Jihad and, 157–158
 Social Media and, 275–277
Free Syrian Army, **100–101**
 Benghazi Attack and, 58–59
 Local Coordination Committees and,
  192–193
 Syrian Arab Republic and, 277–281
 Syrian Civil War and, 281–283

General National Congress, **103**
 Constitutional Drafting Assembly,
  68–70
 Haftar, Khalifa Belqasim and, 115–116
 Libya, State of, and, 186–190
 Libya Dawn Coalition and, 190–191
 Libyan Civil War and, 191–192
 National Transition Council and,
  216–217
General People's Congress, **104**
 Al-Islah (Reform Party) and, 20–21
 Hadi, Abdu Rabbu Mansour and, 115
 Saleh, Ali Abdullah, and, 264
 Yemen, Republic of, and, 310–313
Gezi Park Protests (2013), **104–105**
 Erdogan, Recep Tayyip, and, 90–91
 Regime Change Cascades and, 256–257
 Social Media and, 275–277
Ghannouchi, Rachid, **106–107**
 Ennahda Movement and, 89–90
 Tunisia, Republic of, and, 289–293
Ghonim, Wael, **107–108**
 Egypt, Arab Republic of, and, 84–87
 Tahrir Square Protests (2011) and, 285
Ghouta Chemical Weapons Attack of
  2013, **108**
 Al-Assad, Bashar and, 9–10
 Ghouta Chemical Weapons Attack of
  2018, and, 109
 Syrian Arab Republic and, 277–281

Syrian Civil War and, 281–283
Ghouta Chemical Weapons Attack of
  2018, **109**
 Ghouta Chemical Weapons Attack of
  2013 and, 108
 Syrian Arab Republic and, 277–281
 Syrian Civil War and, 281–283
Greed Model, **109–110**
 Civil Wars and, 66–67
 Framing Model and, 98–99
 Grievance Model and, 112–113
Green Movement (2009) xvi; **110–111**
 Ahmadinejad, Mahmoud and, 5
 Basij and, 52–53
 Economic Protests (2017–2018) and,
  83–84
 Iran, Islamic Republic of, and, 131–136
 Islamic Revolutionary Guard Corps
  (IRGC) and, 141–143
 Regime Change Cascades and, 256–257
 Social Media and, 275–277
Grievance Model, xxi, **112–113**
 Alawites (Nusayris) and, 11
 Algeria, The People's Democratic
  Republic of, and, 15
 Algerian Protests (2011) and, 18–20
 Ansar Beit al Maqdis and, 34
 Arab Spring Movements (2011) and, 38
 Authoritarianism and, 42–43
 Bahrain, Kingdom of, and, 50
 Ben Ali, Zine al-Abidine and, 57–58
 Bouazizi, Tarek el-Tayeb Mohamed,
  and, 62–63
 Civil Wars and, 66–67
 Clientelism (Patrimonialism) and, 67–68
 Corruption and, 71–72
 Demographics (Youth Bulge) and, 78–79
 Development and, 79–80
 Egypt, Arab Republic of, and, 84–87
 February 17th Revolution and, 94–95
 February 20 Movement and, 95–96
 Fikri, Mouhcine, and, 97
 Foreign Fighters and, 98
 Framing Model and, 98–99
 Ghonim, Wael and, 107–108
 Greed Model and, 109–110
 Iranian Azerbaijanis and, 136–137
 Jasmine Revolution and, 155–157
 Jordanian Protests (2011) and, 162–163
 Labor Migration: Receiving Countries
  and, 181–182

Military Coups and, 197–198
Oman Protests (2011) and, 224–226
Refugees and, 254–256
Sahwa (Sunni Tribal Awakening) and, 261–262
Tahrir Square Protests (2011) and, 285
Takrizards and, 286–287
Tamarod Movement (2013) and, 287–289
Tunisia, Republic of, and, 289–293
Washington Consensus and, 305–306
Gulf Cooperation Council (GCC), **113–114**
Bahrain, Kingdom of, and, 47–50
Benkirane, Abdelilah, and, 59–60
Kuwait, State of, and, 175–179
Labor Migration: Sending Countries and, 182–183
Oman, Sultanate of, and, 219–224
Pearl Roundabout Protests and, 236–238
Qatar and, 245–248
Saudi Arabian Protests (2011) and, 270–271
United Arab Emirates (UAE) and, 301–303
Yemen, Republic of, and, 310–313

Hadi, Abdu Rabbu Mansour, **115**
Al-Ahmar, Ali Muhsin and, 8–9
Al-Islah (Reform Party) and, 20–21
General People's Congress and, 104
Operation Decisive Storm and, 226–227
Saleh, Ali Abdullah, and, 264
Yemen, Republic of, and, 310–313
Yemen Civil War (2015) and, 313–315
Yemen Uprising (2011), and, 316–317
Haftar, Khalifa Belqasim, **115–116**
Benghazi Attack and, 58–59
Constitutional Drafting Assembly and, 68–70
General National Congress and, 103
Libya, State of, and, 186–190
Libya Dawn Coalition and, 190–191
Libyan Civil War and, 191–192
Saudi Arabia, Kingdom of, and, 266–270
Hamas, 1, **116–117**
Al-Assad, Bashar and, 9–10
Dahiya Doctrine and, 75–76
Fatah Party and, 93
Fayyad, Salam, and, 93–93
Hamas-Fatah Conflict and, 117–118
Hezbollah and, 121–124

Iran, Islamic Republic of, and, 131–136
Islamic Revolutionary Guard Corps (IRGC) and, 141–143
Israel and, 148–151
Jordan, Hashemite Kingdom of, and, 159–162
Middle East Roadmap (2003) and, 196–197
Mubarak, Muhammad Hosni, and, 207–208
Operation Cast Lead and, 226
Palestine and, 229–232
Palestinian Islamic Jihad and, 234
Quds Force and, 248–249
Hamas-Fatah Conflict, **117–118**
Fayyad, Salam, and, 93–93
Palestine and, 229–232
Hariri, Saad, **119**
Cedar Revolution (2005) and, 65–66
Hezbollah and, 121–124
Jumblatt, Walid, and, 163–164
Lebanese Republic and, 183–186
Hayat Tahrir al-Sham (HTS), **120**
Ahrar al-Sham Brigades, 6
Syrian Arab Republic and, 277–281
Syrian Civil War and, 281–283
Hezbollah, **121–124**
Al-Assad, Bashar and, 9–10
Al Manar Television and, 23–24
Al-Sadr, Muqtada and, 28–30
Cedar Revolution (2005) and, 65–66
Druze and, 80–81
Hamas and, 116–117
Hariri, Saad, and, 119
Iran, Islamic Republic of, and, 131–136
Islamic Revolutionary Guard Corps (IRGC) and, 141–143
Israel and, 148–151
Israeli Invasion of Lebanon (2006) and, 152–153
Jumblatt, Walid, and, 163–164
Lebanese Republic and, 183–186
Maronites and, 195–196
Nasrallah, Hassan Abdel Karim, and, 213–214
Popular Mobilization Forces (PMF) and, 239–241
Quds Force and, 248–249
Sectarianism and, 273–274
Shabiha Militias and, 274
Syrian Arab Republic and, 277–281

Index

Hizmet (Gülen) Movement, **124–125**
  AKP-PKK Peace Talks (2005–2015)
    and, 7
  Coup of 2016 and, 72–74
  Erdogan, Recep Tayyip, and, 90–91
  Ergenekon Scandal and, 91–92
  Turkey, Republic of, and, 295–299
Hussein, Saddam
  Invasion of Kuwait (1990), and, xx
  Al-Abadi, Haidar, and, 7
  Al-Maliki, Nouri, and, 22
  Al-Sadr, Moqtada, and, 28
  Arab Nationalism and, 36
  Ba'athism and, 45
  Bahrain, Kingdom of, 48
  Barzani, Masoud, and, 51, 52
  Iran, Islamic Republic of, and, 133, 134
  Iraq, Republic of, and, 138
  Islamic State (Daesh) and, 145
  Kurdistan Regional Government and,
    170
  Kurds and, 174
  labor Migration: Sending Countries
    and, 182
  Military Coups and, 198
  Minorities and, 199
  Mujahedin-e Khalq (MEK) and, 209
  Patriotic Union of Kurdistan (PUK)
    and, 236
  Popular Mobilization Forces (PMF)
    and, 240
  Turkey, Republic of, and, 296
Houla Massacre (2012), **126**
  Shabiha Militias and, 274
  Syrian Arab Republic and, 277–281
  Syrian Civil War and, 281–283
Houthis (Ansar Allah), **127**
  Al-Ahmar, Ali Muhsin and, 8–9
  Al-Islah (Reform Party) and, 20–21
  Al-Qaeda in the Arabian Peninsula
    (AQAP) and, 26–27
  General People's Congress and, 104
  Hadi, Abdu Rabbu Mansour and, 115
  Hezbollah and, 121–124
  Islamic Revolutionary Guard Corps
    (IRGC) and, 141–143
  Operation Decisive Storm and, 226–227
  Quds Force and, 248–249
  Saleh, Ali Abdullah, and, 264
  Yemen, Republic of, and, 310–313
  Yemen Civil War (2015) and, 313–315

  Yemen Uprising (2011), and, 316–317
  Zaydi Doctrine and, 319

Ibadi Doctrine, **129–130**
  Oman, Sultanate of, and, 219–224
  Qaboos bin Said bin Taimur Al Said
    and, 243–244
Ibn Taymiyya, Taqi al-Din Ahmad, xviii,
  158, 262, 286
Ideology, xx–xxi, 11, 16, 24
  Al Qaeda Central and, 24–25
  Arab Nationalism and, 35
  Armed Islamic Group and, 38–39
  Authoritarianism and, 42–43
  Amman Message and, 161
  Ba'athism and, 45–46
  Civil Wars and, 66–67
  Dhofar rebels and, 223
  Foreign Fighters and, 98
  Framing Model and, 98–99
  Hezbollah and, 121–122
  Houthis and, 127
  Iran and, 132–137, 238
  Islamic Salvation Front (FIS) and, 144
  Islamism and, 146–148, 314
  Kurdistan Workers' Party (PKK) and,
    172
  Nationalism and, 199
  Ocalan, Abdullah, and, 219
  Palestinian Islamic Jihad and, 234
  Popular Mobilization Forces and,
    239–240
  Qatar and, 246
  Regime Change Cascades and, 257
  Salafism and, 262, 268
  Saudi Arabia, Kingdom of, and
    268–269
  Saudi Sahwa (Islamic Awakening) and,
    272
  Syrian Arab Republic and, 278
  velayat-e faqih and, 122; 142
Intifadas (I, II, and Knife), **130–131**
  Ashrawi, Hanan, and, 41–42
  Fayyad, Salam, and, 93–93
  Hamas-Fatah Conflict and, 117–118
  Israel and, 148–151
  Middle East Roadmap (2003) and,
    196–197
  Palestine and, 229–232
  Palestine Liberation Organization and,
    232–233

Index

Iran, Islamic Republic of, **131–136**
Against Mandatory Hijab and, 3–4
Ahmadinejad, Mahmoud and, 4
Al-Abadi, Haider and, 7–8
Al-Sadr, Muqtada and, 28–30
Armenians and, 39–40
Barzani, Masoud, and, 50–52
Coup of 2016 and, 72–74
Economic Protests (2017–2018) and,
83–84
Green Movement (2009) and,
110–111
Gulf Cooperation Council (GCC) and,
113–114
Hamas and, 116–117
Iranian Azerbaijanis and, 136–137
Iraq, Republic of, and, 137–140
Islamic Revolutionary Guard Corps
(IRGC) and, 141–143
Israel and, 148–151
Khamenei, Ayatollah Sayyid Ali, and,
167–168
Khatami, Mohammad, and, 168–169
Khomeini, Ayatollah Sayyid Ruhollah
Mūsavi, and, 169–170
Kurdistan Regional Government (KRG)
and, 170–171
Kurdistan Workers' Party (PKK) and,
172–173
Kurds and, 173–175
Kuwait, State of, and, 175–179
Military Coups and, 197–198
Minorities and, 198–200
Modernization and, 200–201
Mujahedin-e Khalq (MEK) and,
208–210
Nasrallah, Hassan Abdel Karim, and,
213–214
Oman, Sultanate of, and, 219–224
Palestine and, 229–232
Palestinian Islamic Jihad and, 234
Political Decision-Making in Iran and,
238–239
Popular Mobilization Forces (PMF)
and, 239–241
Qaboos bin Said bin Taimur Al Said
and, 243–244
Qatar and, 245–248
Quds Force and, 248–249
Rafsanjani, Ali Akbar Hashemi, and,
252–253

Saudi Arabia, Kingdom of, and,
266–270
Sectarianism and, 273–274
Shi'a and, 275
Syrian Arab Republic and, 277–281
Turkey, Republic of, and, 295–299
United Arab Emirates (UAE) and,
301–303
Yazidi and, 309–310
Yemen, Republic of, and, 310–313
Iran, Islamic Revolution (1979) in, xx, 170
Ahmadinejad, Mahmoud, and, 4
Gulf Cooperation Council and, 113
Iran, Islamic Republic of, and, 133, 135
Islamism and, 147
Labor Migration: Receiving Countries
and, 181
Mujahedin-e Khalq (MEK) and, 209
Palestinian Islamic Jihad and, 234
Political Decision-Making in Iran
and, 238
Rafsanjani, Ali Akbar Hashemi, and, 252
Saudi Arabia, Kingdom of, and, 267
Syrian Arab Republic and, 278
United Arab Emirates, (UAE) and, 301
Iranian Azerbaijanis, **136–137**
Ahmadinejad, Mahmoud and, 4
Iran-Iraq War (1980–1988) xix, 133–134;
138
Iraq, Republic of, **137–140**
Al-Abadi, Haider and, 7–8
Al-Qaeda Central and, 24–26
Al-Sadr, Muqtada and, 28–30
Arab Nationalism and, 35–36
Armenians and, 39–40
Ba'athism and, 45–46
Barzani, Masoud, and, 50–52
Gulf Cooperation Council (GCC) and,
113–114
Iran, Islamic Republic of, and, 131–136
Islamic Revolutionary Guard Corps
(IRGC) and, 141–143
Islamic State (ISIS, ISIL, or *Daesh*) and,
145–146
Khamenei, Ayatollah Sayyid Ali, and,
167–168
Kurdistan Regional Government (KRG)
and, 170–171
Kurdistan Workers' Party (PKK) and,
172–173
Kurds and, 173–175

Index

Iraq (*cont.*)
  Kuwait, State of, and, 175–179
  Labor Migration: Receiving Countries
    and, 181–182
  Military Coups and, 197–198
  Mubarak, Muhammad Hosni, and,
    207–208
  Ocalan, Abdullah, and, 219
  Patriotic Union of Kurdistan (PUK)
    and, 235–236
  Popular Mobilization Forces (PMF)
    and, 239–241
  Quds Force and, 248–249
  Rafsanjani, Ali Akbar Hashemi, and,
    252–253
  Refugees and, 254–256
  Rouhani, Hassan Feridun, and, 258–259
  Sahwa (Sunni Tribal Awakening) and,
    261–262
  Sectarianism and, 273–274
  Shi'a and, 275
  Turkey, Republic of, and, 295–299
  Yazidi and, 309–310
Iron Dome, 122
Islamic Revolutionary Guard Corps
    (IRGC), **141–143**
  Ahmadinejad, Mahmoud and, 4
  Al-Sadr, Muqtada and, 28–30
  Basij and, 52–53
  Economic Protests (2017–2018) and,
    83–84
  Green Movement (2009) and, 110–111
  Iran, Islamic Republic of, and, 131–136
  Khamenei, Ayatollah Sayyid Ali, and,
    167–168
  Khatami, Mohammad, and, 168–169
  Khomeini, Ayatollah Sayyid Ruhollah
    Mūsavi, and, 169–170
  Military Coups and, 197–198
  Popular Mobilization Forces (PMF)
    and, 239–241
  Quds Force and, 248–249
  Rouhani, Hassan Feridun, and, 258–259
Islamic Salvation Front (FIS), **143–144**
  Algeria, The People's Democratic
    Republic of, and, 14–18
  Algerian Protests (2011), and, 18–20
  Al-Qaeda in the Islamic Maghreb
    (AQIM) and, 27–28
  Army of Islamic Salvation (AIS) and,
    40–41

Nezzar, Khaled, and, 217–218
Rally for Culture and Democracy
    (RCD) and, 254
Islamic State (ISIS, ISIL, or *Daesh*), xvi;
    145–146
  Ahrar al-Sham Brigades and, 6
  Al-Abadi, Haider and, 7–8
  Alawites (Nusayris) and, 10–11
  Al-Qaeda Central and, 24–26
  Ansar al-Sharia in Libya and, 33
  Ansar Beit al Maqdis and, 34
  Battle of Sirte in 2016 and, 54–55
  Foreign Fighters and, 98
  Hayat Tahrir al-Sham (HTS) and, 120
  Hezbollah and, 121–124
  Iran, Islamic Republic of, and, 131–136
  Iraq, Republic of, and, 137–140
  Islamism and, 146–148
  Jumblatt, Walid, and, 163–164
  Khamenei, Ayatollah Sayyid Ali, and,
    167–168
  Kurdistan Regional Government (KRG)
    and, 170–171
  Libya Dawn Coalition and, 190–191
  Libyan Civil War and, 191–192
  Minorities and, 198–200
  Patriotic Union of Kurdistan (PUK)
    and, 235–236
  Popular Mobilization Forces (PMF)
    and, 239–241
  Quds Force and, 248–249
  Sahwa (Sunni Tribal Awakening) and,
    261–262
  Syrian Arab Republic and, 277–281
  Syrian Civil War and, 281–283
  Turkey, Republic of, and, 295–299
  United Arab Emirates (UAE) and,
    301–303
  Yazidi and, 309–310
Islamism, **146–148**
  Alawites (Nusayris) and, 10–11
  Alevis and, 13–14
  Al-Qaeda Central and, 24–26
  Al-Qaeda in the Arabian Peninsula
    (AQAP) and, 26–27
  Al-Qaeda in the Islamic Maghreb
    (AQIM) and, 27–28
  Ansar al-Sharia in Libya and, 33
  Ansar Beit al Maqdis and, 34
  Arab Nationalism and, 35–36
  Armed Islamic Group (GIA) and, 38–39

Armenians and, 39–40
Belhaj, Abdul Hakim, and, 55–56
Belmokhtar, Mokhtar and, 56–57
Benghazi Attack and, 58–59
Benkirane, Abdelilah and, 59–60
Black October Riots (1988) and, 60–61
Black September and, 61–62
Coptic Orthodox Church and, 70–71
Egypt, Arab Republic of, and, 84–87
Ennahda Movement and, 89–90
Erdogan, Recep Tayyip, and, 90–91
Ergenekon Scandal and, 91–92
Foreign Fighters and, 98
Framing Model and, 98–99
Gezi Park Protests (2013) and, 104–105
Ghannouchi, Rachid and, 106–107
Hayat Tahrir al-Sham (HTS) and, 120
Hizmet (Gülen) Movement and,
    124–125
Iraq, Republic of, and, 137–140
Islamic Salvation Front (FIS) and,
    143–144
Islamic State (ISIS, ISIL, or *Daesh*) and,
    145–146
Jihad and, 157–158
Justice and Development Party (Turkey)
    and, 165–166
Khomeini, Ayatollah Sayyid Ruhollah
    Mūsavi, and, 169–170
Kuwait, State of, and, 175–179
Libyan Civil War and, 191–192
Minorities and, 198–200
Morocco, Kingdom of, and, 203–206
Muslim Brotherhood and, 210–211
Muslim Brotherhood in Jordan and,
    211–212
Palestine and, 229–232
Party of Authenticity and Modernity
    and, 235
Qaddafi, Muammar, and, 244
Salafism and, 262–263
Saudi Arabian Protests (2011) and,
    270–271
Saudi Sahwa (Islamic Awakening) and,
    271–273
Takfiri Doctrine and, 286
Tunisian National Dialogue Quartet
    and, 290
Turkey, Republic of, and, 295–299
Israel, **148–151**
    Al-Assad, Bashar and, 9–10

Al Manar Television and, 23–24
Ansar Beit al Maqdis and, 34
Ashrawi, Hanan, and, 41–42
Black September and, 61–62
Dahiya Doctrine and, 75–76
Druze and, 80–81
Erdogan, Recep Tayyip, and, 90–91
Fatah Party and, 93
Hamas-Fatah Conflict and, 117–118
Hezbollah and, 121–124
Intifadas (I, II, and Knife) and,
    130–131
Israeli Invasion of Lebanon (2006) and,
    152–153
Jordan, Hashemite Kingdom of, and,
    159–162
Lebanese Republic and, 183–186
Middle East Roadmap (2003) and,
    196–197
Minorities and, 198–200
Mubarak, Muhammad Hosni, and,
    207–208
Nasrallah, Hassan Abdel Karim, and,
    213–214
Operation Cast Lead and, 226
Palestine and, 229–232
Palestine Liberation Organization and,
    232–233
Palestinian Islamic Jihad, 234
Turkey, Republic of, and, 295–299
Israeli Invasion of Lebanon (2006),
    152–153
    Dahiya Doctrine and, 75–76
    Israel and, 148–151
Israeli-Palestinian Conflict, xx–xxi
    Camp David Peace talks and, 1
    Oslo Accords (1993) and, 1
    Middle East Roadmap (2003) and,
        196
    Palestine and, 231
    Palestinian Islamic Jihad and, 234

Jabhat al-Nusra (JAN), 6, 41, 120, 145,
    150, 269, 279, 282
    Tahrir al Sham (HTS), 120
Jasmine Revolution, **155–157**
    Al Jazeera and, 21–22
    Ammar, Rachid, and, 31–32
    Arab Spring Movements (2011) and,
        36–38
    Ben Ali, Zine al-Abidine and, 57–58

Index

Jasmine Revolution (*cont.*)
  Bouazizi, Tarek el-Tayeb Mohamed,
    and, 62–63
  Regime Change Cascades and, 256–257
  Social Media and, 275–277
  Takrizards and, 286–287
  Tunisia, Republic of, and, 289–293
  Tunisian General Labor Union and, 293
  Women's Leadership in Protests and,
    307–308
Jihad, **157–158**
  Al-Assad, Bashar and, 9–10
  Al-Qaeda Central and, 24–26
  Army of Islamic Salvation and, 41
  Belhaj, Abdul Hakim and, 55
  Hezbollah and, 122
  Islamic State (ISIS, ISIL, or *Daesh*) and,
    145–146
  Islamism and, 146–147
  Palestinian Islamic Jihad and, 234
  Salafism and, 262
  Saudi Arabia and, 266
  Takfiri Doctrine and, 286
  Salafism and, 262–263
  Saudi Arabia, Kingdom of, and,
    266–270
  Takfiri Doctrine and, 286
Jordan, Hashemite Kingdom of, **159–162**
  Abdullah II, King of Jordan and, 2
  Armenians and, 39–40
  Ba'athism and, 45–46
  Black September and, 61–62
  Israel and, 148–151
  Jordanian Protests (2011) and, 162–163
  Labor Migration: Sending Countries
    and, 182–183
  Minorities and, 198–200
  Muslim Brotherhood in Jordan and,
    211–212
  Refugees and, 254–256
Jordanian Protests (2011), **162–163**
  Arab Spring Movements (2011) and,
    36–38
  Jordan, Hashemite Kingdom of, and,
    159–162
  Muslim Brotherhood in Jordan and,
    211–212
  Regime Change Cascades and, 256–257
Jumblatt, Walid, **163–164**
  Cedar Revolution (2005) and, 65–66
  Hariri, Saad, and, 119

Lebanese Republic and, 183–186
Justice and Development Party (Morocco),
  164–165
  Benkirane, Abdelilah and, 59–60
  Morocco, Kingdom of, and, 203–206
Justice and Development Party (Turkey),
  165–166
  AKP-PKK Peace Talks (2005–2015)
    and, 7
  Alevis and, 13–14
  Coup of 2016 and, 72–74
  Demirtaş, Selahattin and, 76–77
  Erdogan, Recep Tayyip, and, 90–91
  Ergenekon Scandal and, 91–92
  Gezi Park Protests (2013) and, 104–105
  Hizmet (Gülen) Movement and,
    124–125
  Turkey, Republic of, and, 295–299

Khamenei, Ayatollah Sayyid Ali, **167–168**
  Ahmadinejad, Mahmoud, and, 4
  Economic Protests (2017–2018) and,
    83–84
  Iranian Azerbaijanis and, 136–137
  Iran, Islamic Republic of, and, 131–136
  Islamic Revolutionary Guard Corps
    (IRGC) and, 141–143
  Khomeini, Ayatollah Sayyid Ruhollah
    Mūsavi, and, 169–170
  Political Decision-Making in Iran and,
    238–239
  Rafsanjani, Ali Akbar Hashemi, and,
    252–253
  Rouhani, Hassan Feridun, and,
    258–259
Khatami, Mohammad, **168–169**
  Ahmadinejad, Mahmoud, and, 4
  Green Movement (2009) and, 110–111
  Iran, Islamic Republic of, and, 131–136
  Political Decision-Making in Iran and,
    238–239
  Rafsanjani, Ali Akbar Hashemi, and,
    252–253
  Rouhani, Hassan Feridun, and,
    258–259
Khomeini, Ayatollah Sayyid Ruhollah
  Mūsavi, **169–170**
  Ahmadinejad, Mahmoud and, 4
  Basij and, 52–53
  Iranian Azerbaijanis and, 136–137
  Iran, Islamic Republic of, and, 131–136

Khamenei, Ayatollah Sayyid Ali, and, 167–168
Mujahedin-e Khalq (MEK) and, 208–210
Political Decision-Making in Iran and, 238–239
Rafsanjani, Ali Akbar Hashemi, and, 252–253
Rouhani, Hassan Feridun, and, 258–259
Saudi Arabia, Kingdom of, and, 266–270
Sectarianism and, 273–274
Kurdistan Regional Government (KRG), **170–171**
Al-Abadi, Haider and, 7–8
Barzani, Masoud, and, 50–52
Erdogan, Recep Tayyip, and, 90–91
Iraq, Republic of, and, 137–140
Kurds and, 173–175
Patriotic Union of Kurdistan (PUK) and, 235–236
Turkey, Republic of, and, 295–299
Kurdistan Workers' Party (PKK), **172–173**
AKP-PKK Peace Talks (2005–2015) and, 7
Barzani, Masoud, and, 50–52
Demirtaş, Selahattin and, 76–77
Kurds and, 173–175
Ocalan, Abdullah, and, 219
Turkey, Republic of, and, 295–299
Kurds, **173–175**
Academics for Peace in Turkey and, 2
Alevis and, 13–14
Ba'athism and, 45–46
Barzani, Masoud, and, 50–52
Minorities and, 198–200
Ocalan, Abdullah, and, 219
Patriotic Union of Kurdistan (PUK) and, 235–236
Sahwa (Sunni Tribal Awakening) and, 261–262
Turkey, Republic of, and, 295–299
Yazidi and, 309–310
Kuwait, State of, **175–179**
Gulf Cooperation Council (GCC) and, 113–114
Iran, Islamic Republic of, and, 131–136
Oman, Sultanate of, and, 219–224
Qatar and, 245–248
Rafsanjani, Ali Akbar Hashemi, and, 252–253

Labor Migration: Receiving Countries, **181–182**
Kuwait, State of, and, 175–179
Qatar and, 245–248
Labor Migration: Sending Countries, **182–183**
Demographics (Youth Bulge) and, 78–79
Lebanese Republic, **183–186**
Al-Assad, Bashar, and, 9–10
Al Manar Television and, 23–24
Armenians and, 39–40
Ba'athism and, 45–46
Black September and, 61–62
Cedar Revolution (2005) and, 65–66
Dahiya Doctrine and, 75–76
Druze and, 80–81
Hariri, Saad, and, 119
Hezbollah and, 121–124
Iran, Islamic Republic of, and, 131–136
Israel and, 148–151
Israeli Invasion of Lebanon (2006) and, 152–153
Jumblatt, Walid, and, 163–164
Kurdistan Workers' Party (PKK) and, 172–173
Labor Migration: Receiving Countries and, 181–182
Labor Migration: Sending Countries and, 182–183
Maronites and, 195–196
Nakhla, Rami, and, 213
Nasrallah, Hassan Abdel Karim, and, 213–214
Ocalan, Abdullah, and, 219
Quds Force and, 248–249
Rafsanjani, Ali Akbar Hashemi, and, 252–253
Refugees and, 254–256
Shi'a and, 275
Libya, State of, **186–190**
Ansar al-Sharia in Libya and, 33
Battle of Sirte in 2011 and, 53–54
Battle of Sirte in 2016 and, 54–55
Belhaj, Abdul Hakim, and, 55–56
Benghazi Attack and, 58–59
Berbers (Imazighen) and, 60
Constitutional Drafting Assembly and, 68–70
General National Congress and, 103

400 Index

Libya, State of (*cont.*)
  Gulf Cooperation Council (GCC) and, 113–114
  Haftar, Khalifa Belqasim and, 115–116
  Ibadi Doctrine and, 129–130
  Labor Migration: Receiving Countries and, 181–182
  National Transition Council and, 216–217
  Qaddafi, Muammar, and, 244
  Refugees and, 254–256
  United Arab Emirates (UAE) and, 301–303
Libya Dawn Coalition, **190–191**
  Battle of Sirte in 2016 and, 54–55
  Belhaj, Abdul Hakim, and, 55–56
  Libya, State of, and, 186–190
  Libyan Civil War and, 191–192
Libyan Civil War, **191–192**
  Battle of Sirte in 2016 and, 54–55
  Belhaj, Abdul Hakim, and, 55–56
  Benghazi Attack and, 58–59
  Constitutional Drafting Assembly and, 68–70
  General National Congress and, 103
  Haftar, Khalifa Belqasim and, 115–116
  Libya, State of, and, 186–190
  Libya Dawn Coalition and, 190–191
  Women's Leadership in Protests and, 307–308
Local Coordination Committees, **192–193**
  Nakhla, Rami, and, 213
  Syrian Arab Republic and, 277–281
  Syrian Civil War and, 281–283

Maronites, **195–196**
  Al-Assad, Bashar and, 9–10
  Cedar Revolution (2005) and, 65–66
  Druze and, 80–81
  Hariri, Saad, and, 119
  Jumblatt, Walid, and, 163–164
  Lebanese Republic and, 183–186
  Minorities and, 198–200
Marrakesh Declaration, **356–358**
Middle East and North Africa (MENA) xix
  Democracy Deficit and, 77
  Demographics (Youth Bulge) and, 78
  Egypt and, 84
  Erdogan, Recep Tayyip, and, 90
  Foreign Fighters and, 98
  Ghonim, Wael, and, 107

Regime Change Cascades and, 257
Sectarianism and, 273
Social Media and, 275
Washington Consensus and, 303
Middle East Roadmap (2003), **196–197**
  Ashrawi, Hanan, and, 41–42
  Intifadas (I, II, and Knife) and, 130–131
  Israel and, 148–151
Military Coups, **197–198**
  Alawites (Nusayris) and, 10–11
  Algeria, The People's Democratic Republic of, and, 14–18
  Ammar, Rachid, and, 31–32
  Authoritarianism and, 42–43
  Ben Ali, Zine al-Abidine and, 57–58
  Civil Wars and, 66–67
  Coup of 2016 and, 72–74
  Greed Model and, 109–110
  Haftar, Khalifa Belqasim and, 115–116
  Hizmet (Gülen) Movement and, 124–125
  Iraq, Republic of, and, 137–140
  Morsi, Mohamed, and, 206–207
  Qaddafi, Muammar, and, 244
  Syrian Arab Republic and, 277–28
  Tamarod Movement (2013) and, 287–289
  Turkey, Republic of, and, 295–299
Minorities, **198–200**
  Alawites (Nusayris) and, 10–11
  Alevis and, 13–14
  Armenians and, 39–40
  Coptic Orthodox Church and, 70–71
  Demirtaş, Selahattin and, 76–77
  Druze and, 80–81
  Economic Protests (2017–2018) and, 83–84
  Grievance Model and, 112–113
  Iranian Azerbaijanis and, 136–137
  Jumblatt, Walid, and, 163–164
  Maronites and, 195–196
  Refugees and, 254–256
Modernization, **200–201**
  Al Jazeera and, 21–22
  Al-Sharif, Manal, and, 30–31
  Badawi, Raif, and, 46–47
  Demographics (Youth Bulge) and, 78–79
  Development and, 79–80
  Hizmet (Gülen) Movement and, 124–125
  Iran, Islamic Republic of, and, 131–136

Index

Khatami, Mohammad, and, 168–169
Khomeini, Ayatollah Sayyid Ruhollah
    Mūsavi, and, 169–170
Labor Migration: Sending Countries
    and, 182–183
Party of Authenticity and Modernity
    and, 235
Rafsanjani, Ali Akbar Hashemi, and,
    252–253
Salman, Mohammad bin, and, 265–266
Turkey, Republic of, and, 295–299
Washington Consensus and, 305–30
Mohammed VI, King of Morocco,
    201–202
Benkirane, Abdelilah and, 59–60
February 20 Movement and, 95–96
Morocco, Kingdom of, and, 203–206
Morocco, Kingdom of, **203–206**
Algeria, The People's Democratic
    Republic of, and, 14–18
Benkirane, Abdelilah and, 59–60
Berbers (Imazighen) and, 60
February 20 Movement and, 95–96
Fikri, Mouhcine, and 97
Justice and Development Party
    (Morocco) and, 164–165
Mohammed VI, King of Morocco, and,
    201–202
Party of Authenticity and Modernity
    and, 235
Morsi, Mohamed, **206–207**
April 6 Youth and, 34–35
Egypt, Arab Republic of, and, 84–87
Mubarak, Muhammad Hosni, and,
    207–208
Muslim Brotherhood and, 210–211
Rabi'a al-Adawiya Massacre and, 251
Tamarod Movement (2013) and, 287–289
Mubarak, Muhammad Hosni Sayyid,
    207–208
April 6 Youth and, 34–35
Egypt, Arab Republic of, and, 84–87
Ghonim, Wael and, 107–108
Morsi, Mohamed, and, 206–207
Tahrir Square Protests (2011) and, 285
Mujahedin-e Khalq (MEK), **208–21**
Iran, Islamic Republic of, and, 131–136
Khomeini, Ayatollah Sayyid Ruhollah
    Mūsavi, and, 169–17
Muslim Brotherhood, **210–211**
Al-Ahmar, Ali Muhsin and, 8–9

Al-Islah (Reform Party) and, 20–21
Al Jazeera and, 21–22
Egypt, Arab Republic of, and, 84–87
El-Sisi, Abdel Fattah Saeed Hussein
    Khalil, and, 88–89
Ennahda Movement and, 89–90
Erdogan, Recep Tayyip, and, 90–91
Ghannouchi, Rachid and, 106–107
Hamas and, 116–117
Morsi, Mohamed, and, 206–207
Muslim Brotherhood in Jordan and,
    211–212
Palestine and, 229–232
Palestinian Islamic Jihad and, 234
Qatar and, 245–248
Rabi'a al-Adawiya Massacre and, 251
Salafism and, 262–263
Saudi Sahwa (Islamic Awakening) and,
    271–273
Takfiri Doctrine and, 28
Tamarod Movement (2013) and,
    287–289
Muslim Brotherhood in Jordan, **211–212**
Jordan, Hashemite Kingdom of, and,
    159–162

Nakhla, Rami, **213**
Social Media and, 275–277
Syrian Arab Republic and, 277–281
Nasrallah, Hassan Abdel Karim, **213–214**
Al-Assad, Bashar and, 9–10
Hezbollah and, 121–124
Lebanese Republic and, 183–186
Maronites and, 195–196
Nasser, Gamal Abdel, xvii, xx
Arab Nationalism and, 36
Ba'athism and, 45
Egypt and, 85
Iraq and, 137
Muslim Brotherhood and, 219
National Action Charter, **215**
Bahrain, Kingdom of, and, 47–50
Pearl Roundabout Protests and, 236–238
Nationalism
Ahmadinejad, Mahmoud, and Persian, 4
Algerian, 14–15
Arab Nationalism, **35–36**, 80–81, 85
In Iran, 40
Authoritarianism and, 42
Ba'athism and, 46
Egyptian, 70

Index

Nationalism (*cont.*)
Kurdish, 76, 137, 172–4, 219, 296
Azerbaijani, 131–132
Islamism and, 147
Minorities and, 199
Modernization and, 200
Muslim Brotherhood and, 210
Salafism and, 262
National Liberation Front (FLN), **215–216**
Algeria, The People's Democratic
Republic of, and, 14–18
Algerian Protests (2011), and, 18–20
Bouteflika, Abdelaziz, and, 63–64
Islamic Salvation Front (FIS) and,
143–144
National Transition Council, **216–217**
Belhaj, Abdul Hakim, and, 55–56
Constitutional Drafting Assembly and,
68–70
February 17th Revolution and, 94–95
General National Congress and, 103
Libya, State of, and, 186–190
Libyan Civil War and, 191–192
Nezzar, Khaled, **217–218**
Algeria, The People's Democratic
Republic of, and, 14–18
Black October Riots (1988) and, 60–61
Salah, Ahmed Gaid, and, 263–264

Ocalan, Abdullah, **219**
AKP-PKK Peace Talks (2005–2015)
and, 7
Kurdistan Workers' Party (PKK) and,
172–173
Turkey, Republic of, and, 295–299
Oman, Sultanate of, **219–224**
Gulf Cooperation Council (GCC) and,
113–114
Ibadi Doctrine and, 129–130
Iran, Islamic Republic of, and, 131–136
Oman Protests (2011) and, 224–226
Qaboos bin Said bin Taimur Al Said
and, 243–244
United Arab Emirates (UAE) and,
301–303
Oman Protests (2011), **224–226**
Arab Spring Movements (2011) and,
36–38
Qaboos bin Said bin Taimur Al Said
and, 243–244
Regime Change Cascades and, 256–257

Operation Cast Lead, **226**
Israel and, 148–151
Turkey, Republic of, and, 295–299
Operation Decisive Storm, **226–227**
Al-Ahmar, Ali Muhsin and, 8–9
Al-Islah (Reform Party) and, 20–21
Gulf Cooperation Council (GCC) and,
113–114
Houthis (Ansar Allah) and, 127
Salman, Mohammad bin, and, 265–266
Saudi Arabia, Kingdom of, and, 266–270
Yemen, Republic of, and, 310–313
Yemen Civil War (2015) and, 313–315
Yemen Uprising (2011), and, 316–317
Ottoman Empire (1301–1922), xx, xxii
Abdullah II, King of Jordan and, 2
Alawites, (Nusayris) and, 11
Algeria, The People's Democratic
Republic of, and, 14
Arab Nationalism and, 35
Armenians and, 39–40
Iraq, Republic of, and, 137
Kurds and, 173
Kuwait, State of, 175
Libya, State of, and, 186
Maronites and, 195
Minorities and, 199
Syrian Arab Republic and, 277
Turkey, Republic of, and, 295
Yemen, Republic of, and, 310

Pahlavi, Reza Shah, 133, 167, 169, 200,
208, 267
Against Mandatory Hijab and, 3–4
Iranian Azerbaijanis and, 136–137
Palestine, **229–232**
Abbas, Mahmoud, and, 1
Al Manar Television and, 23–24
Palestinian National Authority and, 1,
41, 118, 233
Arab Nationalism and, 35–36
Armenians and, 39–40
Ashrawi, Hanan, and, 41–42
Dahiya Doctrine and, 75–76
Erdogan, Recep Tayyip, and, 90–91
Fatah Party and, 93
Fayyad, Salam, and, 93–93
Hamas-Fatah Conflict and, 117–118
Intifadas (I, II, and Knife) and, 130–131
Israel and, 148–151
Jordanian Protests (2011) and, 162–163

Index

403

Labor Migration: Sending Countries
and, 182–183
Middle East Roadmap (2003) and,
196–197
Operation Cast Lead and, 226
Palestine Liberation Organization and,
232–233
Palestinian Islamic Jihad and, 234
Refugees and, 254–256
Palestine Liberation Organization,
232–233
Black September and, 61–62
Fatah Party and, 93
Hamas and, 116–117
Hezbollah and, 121–124
Intifadas (I, II, and Knife) and, 130–131
Iran, Islamic Republic of, and, 131–136
Israel and, 148–151
Jordan, Hashemite Kingdom of, and,
159–162
Lebanese Republic and, 183–186
Middle East Roadmap (2003) and,
196–197
Palestine and, 229–232
Qaddafi, Muammar, and, 244
Palestinian Islamic Jihad, **234**
Hamas and, 116–117
Jihad and, 157–158
Palestine and, 229–232
Party of Authenticity and Modernity, **235**
Mohammed VI, King of Morocco and,
201–202
Morocco, Kingdom of, and, 203–206
Patriotic Union of Kurdistan (PUK),
235–236
Ahmadinejad, Mahmoud and, 4
Barzani, Masoud, and, 50–52
Iraq, Republic of, and, 137–140
Kurdistan Regional Government (KRG)
and, 170–171
Kurds and, 173–175
*Peace and National Partnership
Agreement,* **352–356**
Pearl Roundabout Protests, **236–238**
Arab Spring Movements (2011) and,
36–38
Bahrain, Kingdom of, and, 47–50
Rajab, Nabeel, and, 253–254
Regime Change Cascades and, 256–257
Women's Leadership in Protests and,
307–308

Persian language xvii, xxii, 84, 111,
132–133, 169
Political Decision-Making in Iran, **238–239**
Iran, Islamic Republic of, and, 131–136
Khatami, Mohammad, and, 168–169
Rouhani, Hassan Feridun, and, 258–259
Popular Mobilization Forces (PMF),
239–241
Iraq, Republic of, and, 137–140
Quds Force and, 248–249
Yazidi and, 309–310
Protest movements, xvii, xix, xxi, 37, 72,
96, 155, 198, 230, 244, 257, 276

Qaboos bin Said bin Taimur Al Said,
243–244
Oman Protests (2011) and, 224–226
Oman, Sultanate of, and, 219–224
Qaddafi, Muammar, **244**
Ansar al-Sharia in Libya and, 33
Battle of Sirte in 2011 and, 53–54
Belhaj, Abdul Hakim, and, 55–56
February 17th Revolution and, 94–95
Gulf Cooperation Council (GCC) and,
113–114
Haftar, Khalifa Belqasim and,
115–116
Libya, State of, and, 186–190
Libyan Civil War and, 191–192
National Transition Council and,
216–217
Qatar, **245–248**
Ahrar al-Sham Brigades, and 6
Al Jazeera and, 21–22
Belhaj, Abdul Hakim, and, 55–56
Egypt, Arab Republic of, and, 84–87
Erdogan, Recep Tayyip, and, 90–91
February 17th Revolution and, 94–95
Gulf Cooperation Council (GCC) and,
113–114
Hamas and, 116–117
Labor Migration: Receiving Countries
and, 181–182
Quds Force, **248–249**
Al-Sadr, Muqtada and, 28–30
Iran, Islamic Republic of, and, 131–136
Islamic Revolutionary Guard Corps
(IRGC) and, 141–143
Popular Mobilization Forces (PMF)
and, 239–241
Qutb, Sayid, xviii, 158, 286

Rabi'a al-Adawiya Massacre, **251**
  Egypt, Arab Republic of, and, 84–87
Rafsanjani, Ali Akbar Hashemi, **252–253**
  Ahmadinejad, Mahmoud and, 4
  Basij and, 52–53
  Green Movement (2009) and, 110–111
  Iran, Islamic Republic of, and, 131–136
  Khamenei, Ayatollah Sayyid Ali, and, 167–168
  Khatami, Mohammad, and, 168–169
  Quds Force and, 248–249
  Rouhani, Hassan Feridun, and, 258–259
Rajab, Nabeel, **253–254**
  Bahrain, Kingdom of, and, 47–50
  Pearl Roundabout Protests and, 236–238
Rally for Culture and Democracy (RCD), **254**
  Algeria, The People's Democratic Republic of, and, 14–18
Refugees, **254–256**
  Black September and, 61–62
  Foreign Fighters and, 98
  Hezbollah and, 121–124
  Jordanian Protests (2011) and, 162–163
  Yazidi and, 309–310
Regime Change Cascades, **256–257**
  Arab Spring Movements (2011) and, 36–38
  February 17th Revolution and, 94–95
  February 20 Movement and, 95–96
Rentier State Politics, **258**
  Algeria, The People's Democratic Republic of, and, 14–18
  Authoritarianism and, 42–43
  Black October Riots (1988) and, 60–61
  Democracy Deficit and, 77–78
  Greed Model and, 109–110
  Jordan, Hashemite Kingdom of, and, 159–162
  Kuwait, State of, and, 175–179
  Oman Protests (2011) and, 224–226
  Oman, Sultanate of, and, 219–224
  Saudi Arabian Protests (2011) and, 270–271
Rouhani, Hassan Feridun, **258–260**
  Economic Protests (2017–2018) and, 83–84
  Iran, Islamic Republic of, and, 131–136
  Islamic Revolutionary Guard Corps (IRGC) and, 141–143

Rafsanjani, Ali Akbar Hashemi, and, 252–253

Sahwa (Sunni Tribal Awakening), **261–262**
  Iraq, Republic of, and, 137–140
  Islamism and, 146–148
Said, Khaled, xix
  Ghonim, Wael, and, 107
Salafism, **262–263**
  Al-Ahmar, Ali Muhsin and, 8–9
  Al-Awlaki, Anwar and, 12–13
  Al-Qaeda in the Arabian Peninsula (AQAP) and, 26–27
  Badawi, Raif, and, 46–47
  Belmokhtar, Mokhtar, **56–57**
  Ennahda Movement and, 89–90
  Islamic State (ISIS, ISIL, or *Daesh*) and, 145–146
  Islamism and, 146–148
  Muslim Brotherhood and, 210–211
  Palestine and, 229–232
  Saudi Arabian Protests (2011) and, 270–271
  Saudi Sahwa (Islamic Awakening) and, 271–273
  Sectarianism and, 273–274
Salah, Ahmed Gaid, **263–264**
  Algeria, The People's Democratic Republic of, and, 14–18
  Bouteflika, Abdelaziz, and, 63–64
  Nezzar, Khaled, and, 217–218
Saleh, Ali Abdullah, **264**
  Al-Ahmar, Ali Muhsin and, 8–9
  Al-Islah (Reform Party) and, 20–21
  General People's Congress and, 104
  Hadi, Abdu Rabbu Mansour and, 115
  Houthis (Ansar Allah) and, 127
  Operation Decisive Storm and, 226–227
  Yemen, Republic of, and, 310–313
  Yemen Civil War (2015) and, 313–315
  Yemen Uprising (2011), and, 316–317
Salman, Mohammad bin, **265–266**
  Saudi Arabia, Kingdom of, and, 266–270
Saudi Arabia, Kingdom of, **266–270**
  Ahrar al-Sham Brigades, and 6
  Al-Ahmar, Ali Muhsin and, 8–9
  Al Jazeera and, 21–22
  Al-Qaeda Central and, 24–26
  Al-Qaeda in the Arabian Peninsula (AQAP) and, 26–27

Al-Sharif, Manal, and, 30–31
Saudi Sahwa (Islamic Awakening) and,
   271–272
Badawi, Raif, and, 46–47
Bahrain, Kingdom of, and, 47–50
Ben Ali, Zine al-Abidine and, 57–58
Egypt, Arab Republic of, and, 84–87
Erdogan, Recep Tayyip, and, 90–91
Gulf Cooperation Council (GCC) and,
   113–114
Hadi, Abdu Rabbu Mansour and, 115
Hariri, Saad, and, 119
Houthis (Ansar Allah) and, 127
Islamism and, 146–148
Labor Migration: Receiving Countries
   and, 181–182
Mubarak, Muhammad Hosni, and,
   207–208
Oman, Sultanate of, and, 219–224
Operation Decisive Storm and,
   226–227
Qatar and, 245–248
Rafsanjani, Ali Akbar Hashemi, and,
   252–253
Salafism and, 262–263
Salman, Mohammad bin, and, 265–266
Saudi Arabian Protests (2011) and,
   270–271
Saudi Sahwa (Islamic Awakening) and,
   271–273
Sectarianism and, 273–274
United Arab Emirates (UAE) and,
   301–303
Yemen, Republic of, and, 310–313
Yemen Civil War (2015) and, 313–315
Saudi Arabian Protests (2011), **270–271**
   Arab Spring Movements (2011) and,
      36–38
   Regime Change Cascades and, 256–257
   Saudi Arabia, Kingdom of, and,
      266–270
Saudi Sahwa (Islamic Awakening),
   271–273
   Al-Sharif, Manal, and, 30–31
   Saudi Arabia, Kingdom of, and,
      266–270
   Sectarianism and, 273–274
Sectarianism, **273–274**
   Alawites (Nusayris) and, 10–11
   Al-Sadr, Muqtada and, 28–30
   Bahrain, Kingdom of, and, 47–50

Ghouta Chemical Weapons Attack of
   2013 and, 108
Ghouta Chemical Weapons Attack of
   2018 and, 109
Grievance Model and, 112–113
Houla Massacre (2012) and, 126
Ibadi Doctrine and, 129–130
Iran, Islamic Republic of, and, 131–136
Islamic State (ISIS, ISIL, or *Daesh*) and,
   145–146
Khomeini, Ayatollah Sayyid Ruhollah
   Mūsavi, and, 169–170
Kuwait, State of, and, 175–179
Quds Force and, 248–249
Rajab, Nabeel, and, 253–254
Sahwa (Sunni Tribal Awakening) and,
   261–262
Saudi Arabian Protests (2011) and,
   270–271
Shabiha Militias and, 274
Syrian Arab Republic and, 277–281
Secularism
   Alawites and, 11
   Alevis and, 14
   Arab Nationalism and, 36
   Hizmet (Gulen) Movement and, 125
   Muslim Brotherhood and, 210
   Rally for Culture and Democracy
      (RCD) and, 254
   Tunisia, Republic of, and, 289
Shabiha Militias, **274**
   Houla Massacre (2012) and, 126
   Syrian Arab Republic and, 277–281
   Syrian Civil War and, 281–283
Shi'a, **275**
   Al-Abadi, Haider and, 7–8
   Alevis and, 13–14
   Al-Sadr, Muqtada and, 28–30
   Ba'athism and, 45–46
   Bahrain, Kingdom of, and, 47–50
   Ibadi Doctrine and, 129–130
   Lebanese Republic and, 183–186
   Minorities and, 198–200
   Nasrallah, Hassan Abdel Karim, and,
      213–214
   National Action Charter and, 215
   Pearl Roundabout Protests and,
      236–238
   Popular Mobilization Forces (PMF)
      and, 239–241
   Quds Force and, 248–249

406 Index

Shi'a (*cont.*)
  Sahwa (Sunni Tribal Awakening) and,
    261–262
  Saudi Arabia, Kingdom of, and, 266–270
  Saudi Arabian Protests (2011) and,
    270–271
  Sectarianism and, 273–274
  Zaydi Doctrine and, 319
Socialism
  Alawites and, 11
  Arab Nationalism and, 35–36
  Ba'athism and, 45
  Framing model and, 96
  Islamic revolution and, 169
  Islamism and, 147
  Jumblatt, Walid, and, 163
  Kuwait, State of, and, 176
  Libya and, 147
  Morocco, Kingdom of, and, 165, 203
  Mujahidin-e Khalq and, 170
  Nasser, Gamal Abdel, and, 85, 106
  National Liberation Front, and, 215–216
  Ocalan, Abdullah, and, 219
  Oman, Sultanate of, and, 220
  Qaddafi, Muammar, and, 244
  Rally for Culture and Democracy, and,
    254
  Syrian Arab Republic and, 277
  Tunisia and, 291–292
  Yemen Socialist Party and, 21, 26, 264,
    315–316
Social Media, **275–277**
  Against Compulsory Hijab and, 4
  Al Jazeera and, 21–22
  Al Manar Television and, 23–24
  Al-Sharif, Manal, and, 30–31
  April 6 Youth and, 34–35
  Arab Spring Movements (2011) and,
    36–38
  Bouazizi, Tarek el-Tayeb Mohamed,
    and, 62–63
  February 20 Movement and, 95–96
  Fikri, Mouhcine, and, 97
  Foreign Fighters and, 98
  Ghonim, Wael and, 107–108
  Green Movement (2009) and, 110–111
  Jasmine Revolution and, 155–157
  Nakhla, Rami, and, 213
  Pearl Roundabout Protests and, 236–238
  Regime Change Cascades and, 256–257
  Saudi Arabian Protests (2011) and,
    270–271

Takrizards and, 286–28
Tamarod Movement (2013) and,
  287–289
Tunisia, Republic of, and, 289–293
Suez Crisis (1956): 36, 45, 85
Syrian Arab Republic, **277–281**
  Ahrar al-Sham Brigades and, 6
  Al-Assad, Bashar and, 9–10
  Al-Qaeda Central and, 24–26
  Alawites (Nusayris) and, 10–11
  Arab Nationalism and, 35–36
  Armenians and, 39–40
  Ba'athism and, 45–46
  Cedar Revolution (2005) and, 65–66
  Druze and, 80–81
  Erdogan, Recep Tayyip, and, 90–91
  Free Syrian Army and, 100–101
  Ghannouchi, Rachid and, 106–107
  Hariri, Saad, and, 119
  Hayat Tahrir al-Sham (HTS) and, 120
  Hezbollah and, 121–124
  Houla Massacre (2012) and, 126
  Iran, Islamic Republic of, and, 131–136
  Iraq, Republic of, and, 137–140
  Islamic Revolutionary Guard Corps
    (IRGC) and, 141–143
  Israel and, 148–151
  Jordanian Protests (2011) and, 162–163
  Jumblatt, Walid, and, 163–164
  Khamenei, Ayatollah Sayyid Ali, and,
    167–168
  Kurdistan Workers' Party (PKK) and,
    172–173
  Labor Migration: Receiving Countries
    and, 181–182
  Labor Migration: Sending Countries
    and, 182–183
  Lebanese Republic and, 183–186
  Local Coordination Committees and,
    192–193
  Maronites and, 195–196
  Military Coups and, 197–198
  Minorities and, 198–200
  Nakhla, Rami, and, 213
  Nasrallah, Hassan Abdel Karim, and,
    213–214
  Ocalan, Abdullah, and, 219
  Palestinian Islamic Jihad and, 234
  Quds Force and, 248–249
  Refugees and, 254–256
  Sectarianism and, 273–274
  Shi'a and, 275

Index **407**

Yazidi and, 309–310
Syrian Civil War, **281–283**
  Al-Assad, Bashar and, 9–10
  Alawites (Nusayris) and, 10–11
  Arab Spring Movements (2011) and,
    36–38
  Army of Islamic Salvation (AIS) and,
    40–41
  Druze and, 80–81
  Foreign Fighters and, 98
  Free Syrian Army and, 100–101
  Ghouta Chemical Weapons Attack of
    2013 and, 108
  Ghouta Chemical Weapons Attack of
    2018 and, 109
  Houla Massacre (2012) and, 126
  Islamic State (ISIS, ISIL, or *Daesh*) and,
    145–146
  Kurds and, 173–175
  Local Coordination Committees and,
    192–193
  Nakhla, Rami, and, 213
  Regime Change Cascades and,
    256–257
  Saudi Sahwa (Islamic Awakening) and,
    271–273
  Shabiha Militias and, 274
  Social Media and, 275–277
  Syrian Arab Republic and, 277–281
  Turkey, Republic of, and, 295–299

Tahrir Square Protests (2011), **285**
  Al Jazeera and, 21–22
  April 6 Youth and, 34–35
  Arab Spring Movements (2011) and,
    36–38
  Coptic Orthodox Church and, 70–71
  Egypt, Arab Republic of, and, 84–87
  El-Sisi, Abdel Fattah Saeed Hussein
    Khalil, and, 88–89
  Ghonim, Wael and, 107–108
  Morsi, Mohamed, and, 206–207
  Mubarak, Muhammad Hosni, and,
    207–208
  Regime Change Cascades and,
    256–257
  Social Media and, 275–277
  Women's Leadership in Protests and,
    307–308
Taif Agreement, 184–185, **321–326**
  Nasrallah, Hassan Abdel Karim, and,
    213–214

Takfiri Doctrine, **286**
  Ibadi Doctrine and, 129–130
  Islamic State (ISIS, ISIL, or *Daesh*) and,
    145–146
Takrizards, **286–287**
  Jasmine Revolution and, 155–157
  Social Media and, 275–277
Tamarod Movement (2013), **287–289**
  Egypt, Arab Republic of, and, 84–87
  El-Sisi, Abdel Fattah, and, 88–89
  Morsi, Mohamed, and, 206–207
  Muslim Brotherhood and, 210–211
Tunisia, Republic of, **289–293**
  Ammar, Rachid, and, 31–32
  Ben Ali, Zine al-Abidine and, 57–58
  Berbers (Imazighen) and, 60
  Bouazizi, Tarek el-Tayeb Mohamed,
    and, 62–63
  Ennahda Movement and, 89–90
  Ghannouchi, Rachid and, 106–107
  Ibadi Doctrine and, 129–130
  Jasmine Revolution and, 155–157
  Military Coups and, 197–198
  Takrizards and, 286–287
  Tunisian General Labor Union and,
    293–294
  Tunisian National Dialogue Quartet
    and, 290
Tunisian General Labor Union, **293–294**
  Jasmine Revolution and, 155–157
  Tunisia, Republic of, and, 289–293
  Tunisian National Dialogue Quartet
    and, 290
Tunisian National Dialogue Quartet, **290**
  Tunisia, Republic of, and, 289–293
  Tunisian General Labor Union and,
    293–294
Turkey, Republic of, **295–299**
  Academics for Peace in Turkey and 2
  AKP-PKK Peace Talks (2005–2015)
    and, 7
  Alevis and, 13–14
  Al Jazeera and, 21–22
  Armenians and, 39–40
  Barzani, Masoud, and, 50–52
  Demirtaş, Selahattin and, 76–77
  Egypt, Arab Republic of, and,
    84–87
  Erdogan, Recep Tayyip, and, 90–91
  Ergenekon Scandal and, 91–92
  Gezi Park Protests (2013) and, 104–105
  Hamas and, 116–117

408   **Index**

Turkey, Republic of (*cont.*)
  Hizmet (Gülen) Movement and,
    124–125
  Islamic State (ISIS, ISIL, or *Daesh*) and,
    145–146
  Justice and Development Party (Turkey)
    and, 165–166
  Kurdistan Regional Government (KRG)
    and, 170–171
  Kurdistan Workers' Party (PKK) and,
    172–173
  Kurds and, 173–175
  Military Coups and, 197–198
  Minorities and, 198–200
  Modernization and, 200–201
  Ocalan, Abdullah, and, 219
  Operation Cast Lead and, 226
  Patriotic Union of Kurdistan (PUK)
    and, 235–236
  Refugees and, 254–256
  Yazidi and, 309–310

United Arab Emirates (UAE), **301–303**
  Egypt, Arab Republic of, and, 84–87
  Gulf Cooperation Council (GCC) and,
    113–114
  Hadi, Abdu Rabbu Mansour and, 115
  Labor Migration: Receiving Countries
    and, 181–182
  Oman, Sultanate of, and, 219–224
  Qatar and, 245–248
  Yemen Civil War (2015) and, 313–315
UN Security Council Resolution 598, 134,
  252
UN Security Council Resolution 688, 139
UN Security Council Resolution 1701, 152
*UN Security Council Resolution 1970,
  190, 338*
UN Security Council Resolution 1973,
  338–343, 190
UN Security Council Resolution 1559, 65,
  185
UN Security Council Resolutions 1701,
  152
UN Security Council Resolutions 1850;
  1860, 326
UN Security Council Resolution 2118,
  349–351
UN Security Council Resolution 2216, 310
United States
  Abdullah II, King of Jordan, and, 2

Al-Awlaki, Anwar, 12–13
Al-Qaeda Central and, 24–26

velayat-e faqih, 122, 142, 170

Washington Consensus, **305–306**
Wasta, **306–307**
  Clientelism (Patrimonialism) and,
    67–68
  Corruption and, 71–72
  Jordan, Hashemite Kingdom of, and,
    159–162
Women's Leadership in Protests, **307–308**
  Against Mandatory Hijab, 3–4
  Al-Sharif, Manal, and, 30–31
  Ashrawi, Hanan, and, 41–42
  Mujahedin-e Khalq (MEK) and,
    208–210
  Tunisia, Republic of, and, 289–293

Yazidi, **309–310**
  Minorities and, 198–200
Yemen, Republic of, **310–313**
  Al-Ahmar, Ali Muhsin and, 8–9
  Al-Awlaki, Anwar and, 12–13
  Al-Qaeda Central and, 24–26
  Al-Qaeda in the Arabian Peninsula
    (AQAP) and, 26–27
  General People's Congress and, 104
  Gulf Cooperation Council (GCC) and,
    113–114
  Hadi, Abdu Rabbu Mansour and, 115
  Houthis (Ansar Allah) and, 127
  Iran, Islamic Republic of, and, 131–136
  Islamic Revolutionary Guard Corps
    (IRGC) and, 141–143
  Jordanian Protests (2011) and, 162–163
  Labor Migration: Receiving Countries
    and, 181–182
  Labor Migration: Sending Countries
    and, 182–183
  Oman, Sultanate of, and, 219–224
  Operation Decisive Storm and, 226–227
  Qaboos bin Said bin Taimur Al Said
    and, 243–244
  Quds Force and, 248–249
  United Arab Emirates (UAE) and,
    301–303
  Women's Leadership in Protests and,
    307–308
  Yemen Civil War (2015) and, 313–315

Yemeni Socialist Party (YSP) and, 312
Yemen Uprising (2011), and, 316–317
Zaydi Doctrine and, 319
Yemen Civil War (2015), **313–315**
    Arab Spring Movements (2011) and,
      36–38
    Yemen, Republic of, and, 310–313
Yemeni Socialist Party (YSP), **312**
    Al-Islah (Reform Party) and, 20–21
    Al-Qaeda in the Arabian Peninsula
      (AQAP) and, 26–27
    Yemen, Republic of, and, 310–313
Yemen Uprising (2011), **316–317**
    Al-Islah (Reform Party) and, 20–21

Arab Spring Movements (2011) and,
    36–38
Houthis (Ansar Allah) and, 127
Regime Change Cascades and,
    256–257
Saleh, Ali Abdullah, and, 264
Social Media and, 275–277
Yemen, Republic of, and, 310–313
Yemen Civil War (2015) and, 313–315

Zaydi Doctrine, **319**
    Houthis (Ansar Allah) and, 127
    Shi'a and, 275
    Yemen, Republic of, and, 310–313

Milton Keynes UK
Ingram Content Group UK Ltd.
UKHW051649100724
445457UK00047B/1294